An Introduction to Computer Architecture Using VAX®

Machine
And Assembly
Language

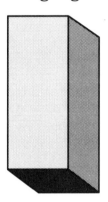

D1708018

An Introduction
to Computer
Architecture
Using
VAX®
Machine
And Assembly
Language

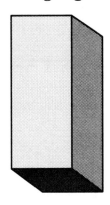

**Paul B.
Schechter**
University of Wisconsin-
Madison

**Edouard T.
Desautels**
University of Wisconsin-
Madison

wcb
Wm. C. Brown Publishers
Dubuque, Iowa

Fig. 19.1, p. 456 From *Micro-Electronics* by Millman, 1979, McGraw-Hill. *Fig. 19.2, p. 458* Repringed from George R. Stiblitz in *A History of Computing in the Twentieth Century,* edited by N. Metropolis, J. Howlett, and Gian-Carlo Rota, 1980, Academic Press. *Fig. 20.8, p. 477* Courtesy of Xerox Corporation. *Fig. 21.1* From *Communications of the ACM,* Vol. 4, No. 1, January 1961 cover, a publication of the Association for Computing Machinery. *Fig. 21.2, p. 486* "Pentagon pins its hopes on Ada; just ask any computer" by Richard Halloran, Nov. 30, 1980. Copyright Ⓒ 1980 by the New York Times Company. Reprinted by permission.

VAX ® is a registered trademark of Digital Equipment Corporation.

Copyright Ⓒ 1989 by Wm. C. Brown Publishers. All rights reserved

Library of Congress Catalog Card Number: 88-071990

ISBN 0-697-03060-1

No part of this publication may be reproduced, stored in a retrieval system, or transmitted, in any form or by any means, electronic, mechanical, photocopying, recording, or otherwise, without prior written permission of the publisher.

Printed in the United States of America

10 9 8 7 6 5 4 3 2 1

▪ Contents ▪

▪ Preface ▪

The title of this book is indicative of its goal: to teach introductory computer architecture by writing machine and assembly language programs. We believe that computer architecture is important for students of computer science and other disciplines because the explanations provided by its study are the first steps toward understanding that computers aren't magic. The reader of this book will, thus, be taking the first steps toward understanding how computers work.

Having stated that computers aren't magic and that the study of computer architecture will help students understand what they *really* are, we must also state that computer architecture doesn't explain *everything*. For example, computer architecture doesn't explain why ECL (emitter coupled logic) is faster than TTL (transistor-transistor logic), or why CMOS (complimentary metal-oxide-semiconductor) technology is currently favored over *n*MOS (*n*-channel metal-oxide-semiconductor) technology for microprocessor implementation. Nor does computer architecture explain how conductors conduct or how memories remember. We have tried, however, to provide the explanations available from the study of computer architecture in a complete manner, with few underlying assumptions. We assume, for example, no background beyond that provided by a one-semester course in a high-level algebraic programming language such as Pascal or FORTRAN.

What are the explanations that computer architecture provides? There is no universally accepted answer to this question, because there is no universally accepted definition of computer architecture. However, we are in general agreement with Myers,[1] who defines computer architecture as the "distribution of attributes across a boundary." The boundary, in this case, is between hardware and software, and the attributes are the functions performed by the computer. Computer architecture explains how computers work (at its own level, not that of Electrical Engineering or Physics) by explaining what is done by computer hardware and what is done by computer software. The study of a high-level programming language is not very illustrative of how a computer works because high-level languages are designed to hide exactly those details of a computer's design that we are interested in when we want to know how the computer works. We use machine and assembly language, rather, because they reveal exactly those details that high-level languages hide.

Why do we use the VAX for our introduction to computer architecture? First, we examine only one computer because we believe that it is easier to begin the study of computer architecture by studying one machine in detail. Once a particular machine's architecture is understood, students can easily examine other machines and understand their architectural features by comparing them with those of a machine they already understand. (This is analogous to the reason that students typically find it easier to learn a second programming language than a first one--regardless of which is first and which is second.) Second, the VAX is a relatively modern computer (designed in the mid-1970s), and so its machine language (and, therefore, its assembly language) is regular: there are few special cases, so students can learn general rules and apply them to new situations. Finally, VAXes are common in businesses and university computer science departments, and they are becoming ubiquitous.

The contents and organization of this book reflect our belief that assembly language is an excellent teaching tool for understanding computer architecture. We have, therefore, concentrated on the simple instructions and addressing modes in most of our examples throughout the book and have used the more complex ones only in particular chapters in which they are described and explained. For example, we discuss the VAX's extensive set of complex character string instructions in chapter 10, but in most of the rest of the book we use the more primitive instructions--ones that are less likely to encourage students to think of assembly language as "just another programming language" and

---

[1]Glenford, J. Myers, *Advances in Computer Architecture,* 2d ed. (New York: John Wiley & Sons, 1982).

that what computers do is magic, after all. Similarly, we confine discussion of index addressing mode (mode 4) primarily to a section of chapter 8. This is also the reason that, in our discussion of addressing modes, we stress that some combination of modes 5 and 6 can replace nearly any of the other modes, and the "exotic" addressing modes exist primarily for the convenience of computer programmers.

Although our bias is toward using machine and assembly language to illustrate computer architecture , we recognize that VAX assembly language *can* be used as a programming language. This book is also usable in courses whose goal is more the teaching of programming skills than architectural skills. For example, chapter 10 discusses character string instructions, chapter 14 explains how arrays are dealt with in assembly language, chapter 15 introduces macros and other tools of the assembler, and chapter 17 describes more complex macros, coroutines, threaded code, the implementation of several elementary data structures, and recursion in assembly language. In addition, there are two extensive case studies of the design and implementation of large programs--after chapters 10 and 17.

A course aimed primarily at introductory computer architecture would include chapters 1 through 9, and chapters 11, 12, 13, 16, 18, 19 and 21. A course aimed primarily at assembly language programming, on the other hand, would include chapters 1 through 10, and chapters 13, 14, 15, and 17. (Chapter 17, as its title indicates, is a collection of topics; it is intended that instructors may pick and choose among them.) With sufficient time, of course, there is information of interest (we hope) in all chapters. Our ideal course would use chapters 1 through 21, in order.

We are indebted to many people for this book's final contents. Several semesters' worth of students served as guinea pigs and detected numerous typographical errors, ambiguities, and less than perfectly clear questions. Milo Velimirovic and Brad Kjell read early versions of the first half of the manuscript and provided useful suggestions. The machine-language program-loading program that is available with this book (described in chapter 3) is more sophisticated than the one developed in the case study of chapter 10. This loader was written by George Bier to run on a VAX running UNIX; we modified it to run on VAXes running VMS.

A special note of appreciation is extended to Professors James M. Edmondson (Santa Barbara Community College); Kathryn T. Ernie (University of Wisconsin-River Falls), N. Gajendar (Grambling State University), James P. Ley (University of Wisconsin-Stout) and James McKim (Hartford Graduate Center) for their helpful reviews of the manuscript.

The Computing Context

Introduction

The goal of this book is to help its readers understand computing. Understanding computing involves learning something about both computer hardware and computer software, since they coexist and cooperate. In the process of discussing computing, we will see numerous programming examples written for a contemporary computer. There are many approaches that can be taken to learn more about computing; we believe that understanding **assembly language**--the lowest level symbolic language that computers use--leads to the fastest and firmest understanding of computing, for someone familiar with programming computers in a high-level language. In turn, an understanding of a computer's assembly language must be built on familiarity with its **machine language,** which is the sequence of numbers that a computer's hardware is designed to understand. We will work in machine language first, and then proceed to work in assembly language.

The experience of many students and teachers demonstrates that it is essential to write and execute low-level programs in order to understand and appreciate the concepts involved. To this end, we will suggest many exercises and will display and discuss transcripts of many actual computer runs.

The initial contact of most people with computers is often with a computer so cleverly disguised and integrated into the application that it is not even obvious that it is a computer. For instance, automated bank teller stations, many automobiles, and microwave ovens use computers, but ordinary users of those objects probably don't realize that.

The initial exposure of many people to computers *as computers* typically involves their using them to solve problems, usually by writing computer programs in some high-level language, such as BASIC, COBOL, FORTRAN, Pascal, or PL/I. These high-level languages are designed to hide the low-level details involved in actually getting the computing done, but it is just these low-level details that, in this book, we will examine. After learning about machine and assembly language, one can appreciate the marvelous intricacy of a computing system, including its potentials and limitations.

The Computing Context

We expect that you, the reader, will actually try many of the things discussed in this book by writing programs using the computer that you have access to. Without working with a computer, you will learn as much about computing as you would learn about cooking without going into a kitchen and trying things. However, since the actual hardware configurations (the make and model of the computer, the size of its main memory, the kind and amount of secondary memory such as magnetic disk and tape, the kind and number of input and output devices such as interactive video terminals, etc.) of different computers vary greatly, the support software (the operating system software, utility programs, special programs designed to help learning about computing, etc.) will also probably vary greatly. Since you are likely to be using only one kind of system while reading this book, it is worth describing the various configurations and support systems that you might encounter.

Software: Operating Systems and Other Programs

A single computer can support software packages with greatly different characteristics. One common way of categorizing the relationship between hardware and software is depicted in figure 1.1. We will often use the abbreviation CPU (for Central Processing Unit) to symbolize the computer hardware, and HLL (for High-Level Language) to represent languages such as BASIC, FORTRAN, Pascal, etc. The inverted triangle symbolizes the fact that the hardware alone is not very usable by most people. The operating system software transforms the hardware into a convenient system by providing a variety of functions. An operating system allows users to create programs, save them in files, retrieve them, and execute them. Similarly, collections of data can be prepared, stored, and then accessed by the programs that need them. The various services provided by an operating system include, but are not limited to, the following:

1.   An editor for creating and modifying program and data files
2.   Compilers for translating programs written in high-level languages into machine language programs for a specific computer
3.   A filing system to support the storing and retrieval of files (a file may contain data or a program)
4.   A librarian to manage files of subroutines
5.   Assemblers and loaders to allow the use of assembly and machine-language programs

Some of the kinds of operating systems you may encounter are discussed next, in terms of the richness of the hardware they support.

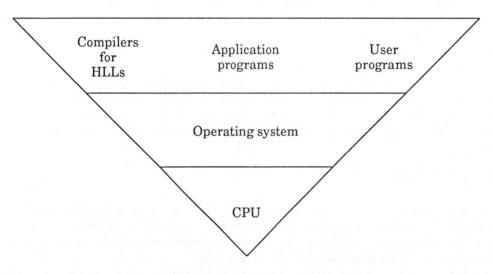

Figure 1.1 Hardware and software relationship

Hardware: Computers

A **computer** is a machine which processes information. This brief definition will be refined throughout the course of this book, until the details hidden by the words *machine, processing,* and *information* become very clear.

Using the above definition of a computer, one could say the telephone system and a photocopier are also computers: they both process information--the first by transmitting voices and other audio information, and the second by copying images. We will soon tighten our notion of processing to include more than mere *transmission* of information. In the meantime, it is worth noting that the telephone system and the more sophisticated photocopiers could not operate without computers.

Bare Machines and Single-User Systems

A **bare machine** is one that has almost no accessories (peripheral devices) attached to it, and almost no software. This may be what you get if you buy a Single-Board Computer (SBC)--a computer that fits on a single circuit board and has no devices connected to it. It is not unusual for a student (or employee) to be asked by a professor in the sciences (or an employer in industry) to "use this bare machine we just bought" to support some experiment (or industrial application). A bare machine is very hard to use to develop programs, and it is even harder to use to learn about computing.

A computer with an adequate number of peripheral devices is a step up from a bare machine. It is a step up because we can use it to develop software. A computer with a floppy disk (diskette) drive and either a video display terminal or a hard-copy keyboard-printer terminal constitutes a good system for learning. These are commonly marketed as personal computers; we will call them **single-user systems** (figure 1.2).

Multiuser Systems

Larger computers, and most VAXes (the computers that this book describes in detail), use an operating system that is designed to share the computer's resources among multiple users (figure 1.3). The most common operating systems for VAXes are VMS (Virtual Memory System), which was written

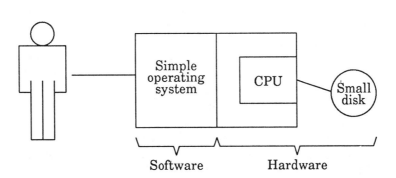

Figure 1.2 Single-user system

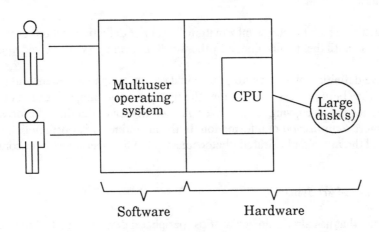

Figure 1.3 Multiuser system

by Digital Equipment Corporation (DEC), the manufacturer of the VAX, and UNIX, which was written by Bell Laboratories and also runs on many other computers.

Host and Target Computers

Single-user systems are used by only one person at a time, and often by only one person ever. In order to be affordable by one person, they must be relatively inexpensive; their cost is low because they provide only simple hardware and software. Multiuser systems, on the other hand, are designed to be used by many people, simultaneously and sequentially--each of whom can be expected to share the cost of the system. Therefore, a multiuser system is usually considerably more sophisticated than a single-user system, with respect to both hardware and software. Multiuser systems are capable of high performance, and they usually have convenient programming environments--but they must be shared among multiple users. Single-user systems, on the other hand, are dedicated to one user, but the level of service that they provide is usually lower than that of a multiuser system.

There is a particularly nice way of taking advantage of the best features of both a single-user system *and* a multiuser system, if it is impossible to provide each user with a private, single-user system that has the functionality of a multiuser system. This involves using a multiuser system for program development (which takes time because of the typing and debugging involved) and a single-user system for execution of the previously prepared program, when it is advantageous or necessary to do so. The transfer of programs can be accomplished either by using some removable storage medium common to both systems (e.g., a floppy disk), or by wire, if the systems are linked by a physical communication line. When using two systems in this way, the multiuser system is often called the **host** system, and the single-user system is called the **target** system (figure 1.4).

One should not take a narrow view of computing and assume that everyone uses the same kind of system. If we develop some sensitivity to the context in which computing takes place, we will realize that a technique which is appropriate for use on a small system may not be advisable for use on a larger system, or vice-versa.

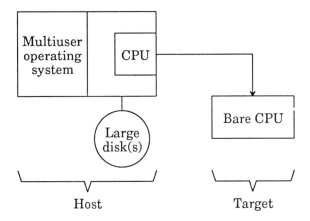

Figure 1.4 Host and target computers

Computing Machines: A Simple Calculator

We are all familiar with calculators of one kind or another. They are the simplest kinds of computing machines. Calculators are similar to computers in many ways, so it will be instructive to look more closely at a very simple calculator. Then we will add features to it until it becomes more like a computer. Let us begin by examining a simple four function calculator, as shown in figure 1.5.

The purpose of the keys is clear, since each is labeled. It is helpful to group the keys according to their functions:

Data Input Keys: (0, 1, . . ., 9)
Function Keys: (+, -, *, : , =)
Control Keys: (C, CE).

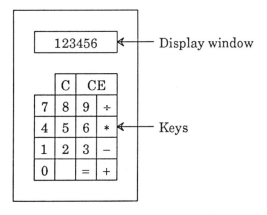

Figure 1.5 Simple four-function calculator

Control keys

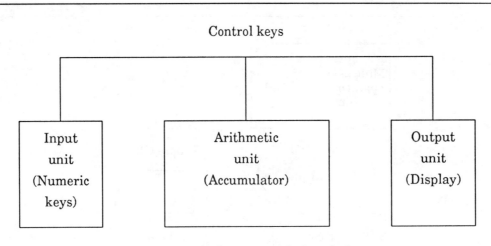

Figure 1.6 Abstract model of a calculator

(It is common to omit the " = " key when counting the functions a calculator supports.) The **display window** provides a way of verifying data entered and of examining results of a computation. We call this use **output.** The part of the calculator which performs the mathematical operations, the **arithmetic unit,** is hidden from view. Overall control of the calculator is provided by its human operator. The CE (Clear Entry) key allows one to immediately erase the number being entered if an error is made. The C (Clear) key also erases the current result (if any) being held within the arithmetic unit. As one uses the calculator, the intermediate result shown in the display window is also held within the arithmetic unit in a special place called the **accumulator register,** or simply the **accumulator.**

It is useful to picture the calculator in a more abstract way, as shown in figure 1.6. The accumulator register is in the arithmetic unit, the keys comprise the **input unit,** and the display window is the **output unit.** It is useful to describe the calculator in this abstract way because, as we will see, this description helps clarify the similarities--and differences--between a calculator and a computer.

We can explain what happens as the calculator is used by writing down a history, or **trace,** of the sequence of keystrokes, the visible effect on the display window, and the expected effect on the accumulator. Thus in adding the three numbers 123, 634 and 221, we would have the trace shown in figure 1.7. Since it is tedious to write down each digit on a separate line, we will shorten our traces by writing all the digits of the same number on a single line, as shown in figure 1.8. How might it be possible to write out, in advance, all of the keystrokes necessary to solve a particular problem, record these keystrokes in some way, then modify the calculator so that it could be driven by these prerecorded keystrokes? Without getting into any complicated electronics, consider the following:

1. The 17 keys of the keyboard are, in effect, push-button switches which are ordinarily in the open (up) position.
2. In the normal use of the calculator, only one of the 17 switches is closed at any one time.
3. Imagine 17 pairs of wires--one pair leading from each key to one of a bank of 17 sensors.
4. Imagine, also, a paper tape that is wide enough to accommodate up to 17 holes across its width (we can think of this as a 17-channel paper tape).

Keystroke	Display	Accumulator
1	1	?
2	12	?
3	123	?
+	123	123
6	6	123
3	63	123
4	634	123
+	757	757
2	2	757
2	22	757
1	221	757
=	978	978

Figure 1.7 Trace of all keystrokes

5.   Each sensor in the bank detects the presence or absence of a hole in one channel of the 17-channel paper tape. Detecting a hole in a channel of the paper tape is equivalent, in this enhanced calculator, to detecting the pushing of one of the keys in our previous calculator.

6.   As the tape is moved, it passes by the sensors one row at a time.

With such a 17-channel paper tape, we can automatically duplicate the activity of a human pressing any one of the 17 buttons of our simple calculator.

A punched tape that solves a particular problem can be described as a **program tape,** because the sequence of operations that solves a particular problem is called a **program.** Anyone with experience in computer programming using a high-level language will consider preparing these program tapes to be a very low level of programming. In fact, we can call it **machine-language programming.** The program tape for the addition problem described above is shown in figure 1.9. Each row of the program tape has one hole punched in it (indicated by an *X*), and can be regarded as an instruction to the calculator. Rows with no hole punched in them are used as leader and trailer tape; they surround the program itself. As the tape advances to the next row, a new instruction becomes available. This strangely modified calculator is not far removed from some computing machines in use in the 1950s. These kinds of machines execute programs that are *external* to the computer or

Keystrokes	Display	Accumulator
123	123	?
+	123	123
634	634	123
+	757	757
221	221	757
=	978	978

Figure 1.8 Tracing a Calculation

						Channel											Comments
0	1	2	3	4	5	6	7	8	9	+	–	*	÷	=	CE	C	
–	–	–	–	–	–	–	–	–	–	–	–	–	–	–	–	–	leader tape
–	–	–	–	–	–	–	–	–	–	–	–	–	–	–	–	–	leader tape
–	X	–	–	–	–	–	–	–	–	–	–	–	–	–	–	–	1
–	–	X	–	–	–	–	–	–	–	–	–	–	–	–	–	–	2
–	–	–	X	–	–	–	–	–	–	–	–	–	–	–	–	–	3
–	–	–	–	–	–	–	–	–	–	X	–	–	–	–	–	–	+
–	–	–	–	–	–	X	–	–	–	–	–	–	–	–	–	–	6
–	–	–	X	–	–	–	–	–	–	–	–	–	–	–	–	–	3
–	–	–	–	X	–	–	–	–	–	–	–	–	–	–	–	–	4
–	–	–	–	–	–	–	–	–	–	X	–	–	–	–	–	–	+
–	–	X	–	–	–	–	–	–	–	–	–	–	–	–	–	–	2
–	–	X	–	–	–	–	–	–	–	–	–	–	–	–	–	–	2
–	X	–	–	–	–	–	–	–	–	–	–	–	–	–	–	–	1
–	–	–	–	–	–	–	–	–	–	–	–	–	–	X	–	–	=
–	–	–	–	–	–	–	–	–	–	–	–	–	–	–	–	–	trailer tape
–	–	–	–	–	–	–	–	–	–	–	–	–	–	–	–	–	trailer tape
–	–	–	–	–	–	–	–	–	–	–	–	–	–	–	–	–	trailer tape

Figure 1.9 Program tape

calculator, and a program's instructions are brought in one at a time. Player pianos used this same idea: a player piano has as many channels on the piano roll (instead of a tape) as there are keys and pedals on the piano. This idea was probably invented by Joseph Jacquard who, in 1801, built a loom that was controlled by holes punched in paper tape.

We must now revise our (old) model of a calculator to reflect the automatic control mechanism provided by the addition of sensors and a program tape. This gives the calculator a **control unit,** which reduces the task of a human operator to that of merely mounting the correct program tape, entering necessary data at the appropriate time, and copying and reentering intermediate results as required. This revised model is shown in figure 1.10.

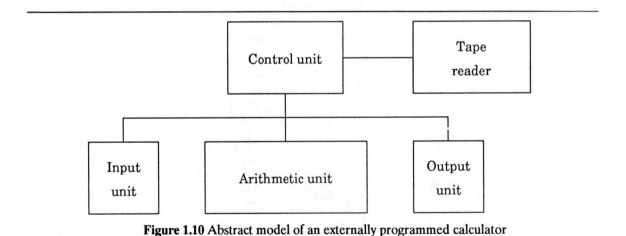

Figure 1.10 Abstract model of an externally programmed calculator

Programs written for this calculator will be of little interest after they have been used once. This is primarily due to the fact that the data items are embedded in the program itself; to solve the same kind of problem with new data items requires rewriting the program and preparing a new program tape. This is not an attractive proposition, and it severely limits the practicality of this kind of programming. Clearly, we need to find a better way of computing; we need some way of making the calculator more general-purpose, so that *reusable* program tapes can be prepared for it. One way of doing this is by adding two new keys to the calculator:

S   *Store* at some specified location *n*
R   *Recall* from some location *n*

In addition to adding these two keys, we also include a storage device capable of holding ten different numbers in ten locations referred to by some calculator manufacturers as **memories.** We will speak of them as "memory location 0, memory location 1, . . ., memory location 9." When the C key is depressed, all ten memory locations are **cleared**: each is set to hold the number 0. Whenever the store key, S, is depressed, the calculator expects one of the digit keys to be pressed next, to indicate in which of the ten memory locations the number currently being displayed should be stored. Storing a number in a memory location replaces the number previously stored at that location with the one being stored. Once a number has been stored in a memory location, it can be used over and over again simply by pushing the R key, followed by the single digit key which specifies the memory location from which to recall the value. Recalling a number from a memory location does not change the number in that memory location. It merely makes a copy of it and places that copy in the accumulator (and display).

Let us now write a program to calculate the surface area of a rectangular solid of height *H*, length *L*, and width *W* to run on the enhanced calculator we have just designed. The formula for the surface area of a rectangular solid is $2HW + 2LW + 2HL$. Suppose the dimensions of a box are 20 by 30 by 5 (*H, L, W*). Using the calculator without the storage unit, we would key in "2 * 20 * 5 =" to compute $2HW$, and we would have to record the result, 200, by hand. Then we would compute $2LW$ by keying in "C 2 * 30 * 5 =." We could compute $2HW + 2LW$ by keying in "+ 200 =;" we would record the result, 500. Finally, "C 2 * 20 * 30 =" provides $2HL$, to which we can add the intermediate result, 500. Notice that we cannot prepare a program tape to solve this problem because it requires recording intermediate results by hand.

Using a calculator with memory, on the other hand, the keystroke sequence to solve this problem could be:

20 S 0	(store the height, *H* (20), in location 0)
30 S 1	(store the length, *L* (30), in location 1)
5 S 2	(store the width, *W* (5), in location 2)
R 0	(recall *H*)
* R 1	(multiply times *L*, stored in location 1; we have *HL* now)
S 7	(store *HL* in location 7)
R 1	(get *L*, stored in location 1)
* R 2	(multiply times *W*, stored in location 2; we have *LW* now)
S 8	(store *LW* in location 8)
R 0	(get *H*, stored in location 0)
* R 2	(multiply times *W*, stored in location 2; we have *HW* now)
+ R 8	(add to what's stored in location 8; we have *LW* + *HW* now)
+ R 7	(add to *HL*, stored in location 7; we have *LW* + *HW* + *HL* now)
* 2	(multiply times 2, giving final result)

So, by having ten memory locations and a program tape with two extra channels to accommodate the two new keys R and S, we can write a program that performs the entire calculation without stopping to record or enter intermediate results.

An even greater advance is possible. We can prepare a program tape that deliberately leaves out the first three store operations. Then, whenever we need to calculate the surface area of a rectangular solid, we can store the dimensions in memory locations 0, 1, and 2, and use the program tape. By doing this, we avoid embedding the data in the program.

If we had many surface area calculations to perform, we could modify the control unit in two ways. First, we would design the control unit to cause the tape-reading mechanism to pause when it encounters a row of the program tape with all holes punched. This would allow a user to enter a number from the keyboard. Second, we would provide a GO button (on either the keyboard or the tape reader). When a user pushed the GO button, the reader would resume processing the program tape. After these modifications, a program which needed three numbers to perform a calculation could begin with the sequence Pause, S 0, Pause, S 1, Pause, S 2, assuming the program is written to expect to find these three operands in memory locations 0, 1, and 2 respectively. Furthermore, by splicing the end of the program tape to the beginning of the program tape, we would literally have **an infinite loop.** The program would keep on repeating itself as long as we kept entering new sets of three operands. If we expect to use such a loop, we should take care to either begin or end the program with a C command.

Bits

The program for adding three numbers is represented on the 17-channel tape we saw earlier in figure 1.9. Each row of the tape could be represented by a 17-digit number, as we can see in figure 1.11. In this figure, each *X* (hole) position has been replaced with the digit 1, and each "-" has been replaced with the digit 0. When the digits of a set of numbers can only have the two values 0 or 1,

Channel																	Comments
0	1	2	3	4	5	6	7	8	9	+	−	*	÷	=	CE	C	
0	0	0	0	0	0	0	0	0	0	0	0	0	0	0	0	0	leader tape
0	0	0	0	0	0	0	0	0	0	0	0	0	0	0	0	0	leader tape
0	1	0	0	0	0	0	0	0	0	0	0	0	0	0	0	0	1
0	0	1	0	0	0	0	0	0	0	0	0	0	0	0	0	0	2
0	0	0	1	0	0	0	0	0	0	0	0	0	0	0	0	0	3
0	0	0	0	0	0	0	0	0	0	1	0	0	0	0	0	0	+
0	0	0	0	0	0	1	0	0	0	0	0	0	0	0	0	0	6
0	0	0	1	0	0	0	0	0	0	0	0	0	0	0	0	0	3
0	0	0	0	1	0	0	0	0	0	0	0	0	0	0	0	0	4
0	0	0	0	0	0	0	0	0	0	1	0	0	0	0	0	0	+
0	0	1	0	0	0	0	0	0	0	0	0	0	0	0	0	0	2
0	0	1	0	0	0	0	0	0	0	0	0	0	0	0	0	0	2
0	1	0	0	0	0	0	0	0	0	0	0	0	0	0	0	0	1
0	0	0	0	0	0	0	0	0	0	0	0	0	0	1	0	0	=
0	0	0	0	0	0	0	0	0	0	0	0	0	0	0	0	0	trailer tape
0	0	0	0	0	0	0	0	0	0	0	0	0	0	0	0	0	trailer tape
0	0	0	0	0	0	0	0	0	0	0	0	0	0	0	0	0	trailer tape

Figure 1.11 Numeric equivalent of program tape

these numbers are called **binary** numbers; the digits comprising binary numbers are **binary digits**, which are commonly called by the contraction, **bits.** Thus, each row of our tape, which represents an instruction to the calculator, can also be thought of as a 17-bit number.

A 17-channel paper tape is very unwieldy. Can we get by with a narrower tape? In other words, can we manage with fewer channels, or equivalently, can we use fewer bits per row? Since each row has at most one bit **set** (we say a bit is **set** or **on** if its value is 1; we say it is **reset** or **off** if its value is 0), we might expect to do much better.

Binary Codes

Consider what can be done with a 1-channel tape. A row can have either a single 0 or a single 1. Rows of a 1-channel tape could be interpreted as meaning:

0 represents "push no key"
1 represents "push the only key"

A 2-channel tape would allow each row to specify one of four possible interpretations:

00 represents "push no keys"
01 represents "push key 1 of 3 keys"
10 represents "push key 2 of 3 keys"
11 represents "push key 3 of 3 keys"

Similarly, a 3-channel tape would allow support of a calculator with as many as seven keys. Each extra channel *doubles* the number of unique combinations of 1s and 0s that can be stored in a single row, so it doubles the distinct interpretations or meanings which can be associated with a row of bits. In the general case, if we have an n-channel tape (or an n-bit row), we can accommodate 2^n (2 raised to the power n, or $2 * 2 * 2 * \ldots * 2$ with n 2s) distinct cases. If we examine the table of selected powers of 2 in figure 1.12, we notice that a 4-channel tape suffices for a 15-key calculator,

n	2^n
1	2
2	4
3	8
4	16
5	32
6	64
7	128
8	256
10	1,024
.	.
.	.
.	.
16	65,536

Figure 1.12 Selected powers of 2

Key	Code
no key	00000
1	00001
2	00010
3	00011
4	00100
5	00101
6	00110
7	00111
8	01000
9	01001
0	01010
+	01011
−	01100
*	01101
÷	01110
=	01111
CE	10000
C	10001

Figure 1.13 A binary code table

Code	Comments
00000	leader
00001	1
00010	2
00011	3
01011	+
00110	6
00011	3
00100	4
01011	+
00010	2
00010	2
00001	1
01111	=
00000	trailer
00000	trailer

Figure 1.14 5-channel program tape

but that the narrowest tape we could use for a 17-key calculator would have 5 channels: 2^4 is 16, which is just too narrow for 17 keys; 2^5 is 32, which leaves 14 unused codes. Note that a 17-channel tape can handle a keyboard with 131,071 keys!

Base 2 is, of course, analogous to base 10. In the decimal number system, each digit can have one of ten possible values (0-9); in the binary system each digit can have one of only two possible values (0 or 1). Thus, while each additional binary digit *doubles* the possible values that a digit string can represent, each additional decimal digit increases the number of possible values tenfold. This is the reason that, in a decimal digit string, the digits represent, from right to left, the *ones* place, the *tens* place, the *hundreds* place, etc.: each successive digit position represents some number (between 0 and 9) of successive powers of 10. In binary, of course, successive digits represent the *ones* place, the *twos* place, the *fours* place, etc.: successive digit positions represent successive powers of 2.

Returning to our example, if we use a 5-channel tape, we must assign a 5-bit code to each key. The assignment of codes is arbitrary, but we must use it consistently. Let's assign the codes as shown in figure 1.13. The program tape for adding three numbers using the 5-channel tape and the codes from figure 1.13 is shown in figure 1.14. Of course the five sensors which read the holes on the the tape can no longer be connected directly to the keys on the keyboard. They must feed the bit values they sense through a piece of hardware called a **decoder.** When the decoder receives a string of 5 bits from the five sensors, it sends out the appropriate signal to the keys using exactly 1 of the 17 sets of lines to the keyboard. In effect, the decoder does a table-lookup using figure 1.13. The act of going from a compact binary code to the selection of a particular item associated with that code is called **decoding.** The original association of a particular item (a key) with a code word (a 5-bit binary string) is called **encoding.** Figure 1.15 is a symbolic representation of a calculator connected to a tape reader and a decoder for reading 5-channel paper tape.

Teletype (TTY)

Binary codes are used in many applications, not just those involving computers. One important use is in telecommunication, and one of the famous devices in the history of telecommunication is the ASR (Automatic Send and Receive) model 33 teleprinter terminal, often called the **TTY,** manufactured by the Teletype Corporation: over five hundred thousand have been built. The TTY's automatic send-and-receive ability derives from its use of punched paper tape. A person can prepare a message on

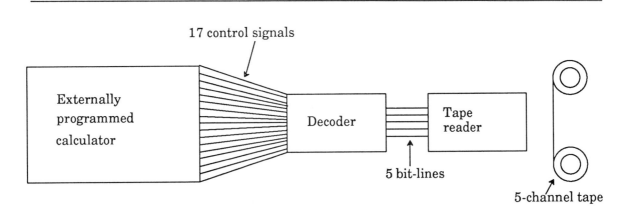

Figure 1.15 Calculator with decoder

the paper tape with the TTY disconnected from the communication network, or **off-line.** Then the paper tape can be read by the TTY **on-line,** which means that it will read the binary codes from the paper tape and broadcast them to all other TTYs connected to the network. A receiving TTY, if it is also on-line, can record the incoming message by using its paper tape punch. Such communication networks were used by many national weather services to report and record hourly weather observations.

The TTY is the precursor of the computer terminal, the teletypewriter, the CRT (Cathode Ray Tube) or VDT (Video Display Terminal), and other keyboard and display devices that we will discuss later. One thing they all have in common is their use of binary codes. In most computer systems, paper tape has been replaced by magnetic tape or disks, but the binary codes used with paper tape are the same ones used with the magnetic media.

The ASCII Code

The 7-bit binary code used on the ASR model 33 Teletype has been adopted as the American Standard Code for Information Interchange, or ASCII (pronounced "ask-kee"). The International Standards Organization (ISO) has also adopted it, and it is sometimes referred to as the ISO code.[1] Figure 1.16 lists the ASCII codes that are represented by all 128 possible combinations of 7 bits. The nonprinting codes, also called **control characters,** are shown as well as the codes that cause a character to be printed on a terminal or line-printer. Those characters marked with an asterisk (*) are *not* standard ISO characters. Their ASCII characters are shown, but in different countries, the same codes might cause different characters to be printed. This figure also shows the *restricted* ASCII character set, which includes only the uppercase letters. The use of standard codes on computers is not required by law; there are other binary codes in use in both computing and telecommunication.

Figure 1.17 shows how the 7 bits of an ASCII character are punched on an 8-channel paper tape. The eighth (leftmost) channel, bit 7, is unused (except for the **delete** code), so it is left unpunched. It can be used to accommodate a check bit; when it is so used, the check bit is often called a **parity** bit (see exercise 9 at the end of this chapter). Different parity schemes can be used, so it is possible to have two different bit patterns for the same ASCII character. For instance, see figure 1.18, which shows two different bit patterns for encoding the letter *A*. We will have more to say about binary numbers and codes in later chapters.

More Complex Machines: Programmable Calculators

Programmable calculators are now quite common. Of course, they are not programmed using the primitive paper tape mechanism we described earlier. Programmable calculators store their programs in an electronic storage unit which fits within the calculator. This storage unit, often called **program memory,** stores each program instruction as a number, and each such instruction is stored in a different memory location. Under normal circumstances, as the calculator's control unit reads an instruction from its program memory, it will expect to find the next instruction it needs in the next consecutive memory location, just as the paper tape reader expects to find instructions sequentially punched into the paper tape.

---

[1]The ISO code can differ from the ASCII code: some printing (i.e. graphic, as opposed to nongraphic) characters vary from country to country. Thus, the British monetary pound sign (£) is available as an ASCII character in those countries that need it, but some other character may be used in its place in other countries.

b_6	0	0	0	0	1	1	1	1
b_5	0	0	1	1	0	0	1	1
b_4	0	1	0	1	0	1	0	1
b_3—b_0								
0000	nul	dle	blank	0	@	P		p
0001	soh	dc1	!	1	A	Q	a	q
0010	stx	dc2	"	2	B	R	b	r
0011	etx	dc3	#	3	C	S	c	s
0100	eot	dc4	$	4	D	T	d	t
0101	enq	nak	%	5	E	U	e	u
0110	ack	syn	&	6	F	V	f	v
0111	bel	etb	'	7	G	W	g	w
1000	bs	can	(	8	H	X	h	x
1001	ht	em	)	9	I	Y	i	y
1010	lf	sub	*	:	J	Z	j	z
1011	vt	esc	+	;	K	[*	k	{*
1100	ff	fs	,	<	L	*	l	|*
1101	cr	gs	–	=	M	]*	m	}*
1110	so	rs	.	>	N	^*	n	~*
1111	si	us	/	?	O	_*	o	del
	Control characters‡		Printing characters					
	Restricted ASCII character set							

*These symbols are undefined in the ISO standard, and they vary according to national versions. The ones listed are those of the ASCII version of the ISO code.

‡Meanings of control characters for data transmission	
Layout characters	*Escape characters*
bs backspace *ht* horizontal tab *lf* line feed *vt* vertical tab *ff* form feed *cr* carriage return	*so* shift-out *si* shift-in *esc* escape
	Medium control characters
Ignore characters	*bel* ring bell *dc1-dc4* device control *em* end of medium
nul null character *can* cancel *sub* substitute *del* delete	*Communication control characters*
Separator characters	*soh* start of heading *stx* start of text *etx* end of text *eot* end of transmission
fs file separator *gs* group separator *rs* record separator *us* unit separator	*enq* enquiry *ack* acknowledgment *nak* negative acknowledgment *dle* data link escape *syn* synchronous idle *etb* end of transmission block

Figure 1.16 ASCII character set

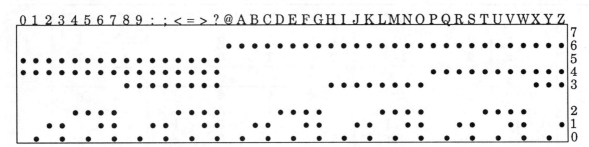

Figure 1.17 ASCII codes punched in paper tape

At this point we could enter into a detailed discussion of a particular programmable calculator. However, that is a sizable undertaking in its own right. Our primary objective is to understand computers, and we will fulfill this objective more rapidly by examining a simple hypothetical computer (in chapter 2), after which we will be ready to work with a real computer (beginning in chapter 3). First, however, let us briefly consider some other types of computers.

Analog and Hybrid Computers

This book is concerned solely with electronic digital computers. There are other kinds of computers, not necessarily digital, not necessarily electronic. Mechanical and hydraulic analog computers have been built. However, since almost all computers in use today are electronic and digital, the single word *computer* has come to be identified with that type of computer exclusively.

An analog computer uses a physical representation of the quantities that it manipulates. Physical quantities can be thought of as taking on continuous, smoothly changing attributes, such as temperature, length, loudness, etc. The quantities which a digital computer manipulates, on the other hand, are discrete: they change only by discrete increments. Furthermore, in an electronic digital computer, quantities bear no particular relationship to physical attributes. The qualifier **digital** emphasizes the characteristic of handling discrete numeric information (as with the ubiquitous digital-readout watch).

The slide rule is a simple example of an analog computer. It uses physical distances to represent the variables involved in a multiplication or division. An electronic analog computer uses electronic circuits to represent relationships between electrical quantities expressed as voltages (V), currents (I) and resistances (R). A simple electrical analog computer to perform division can be built based on Ohm's Law: $V = IR$. If we have a battery providing a constant voltage, V, and a potentiometer which allows us to vary the resistance, R, at will, we can connect these to an ammeter to display the resulting amperes as the current, I. Since $I = V/R$, this will perform division of the constant V by R.

Bit number:	7	6	5	4	3	2	1	0
A with parity bit 0:	0	1	0	0	0	0	0	1
A with parity bit 1:	1	1	0	0	0	0	0	1

Figure 1.18 Parity bit

To solve a problem with an analog computer, one must find a set of mathematical equations that represent a model for the problem and build an electronic circuit whose behavior reflects that predicted by the mathematical model. The circuit is usually realized by using a **patch board** to interconnect various parts of the analog computer.

A **hybrid** computer is one which combines the features of a digital computer with those of an analog computer. This makes the hybrid more useful, but also more expensive.

Analog computers and hybrid computers can solve certain classes of problems in **real time.** That is, once they are set up to solve a specific problem (this setup may take a significant amount of time), a change in an input variable elicits an immediate response from the computer. However analog computers and hybrid computers do not lend themselves to performing exact arithmetic, which is a necessity in business data processing, nor can they compute with the precision required for most scientific and engineering uses. They are not as general-purpose as are electronic digital computers, so neither are they as widely used; we will not discuss them further.

As an historical footnote, it is interesting to realize that, in the 1940s and early 1950s, the word *computer* referred to a person whose profession was the full-time operation of calculators. It was not unusual in those days for a large insurance company or a government agency to have hundreds of these human computers employed in large rooms, each working at a calculator. The word *computer* now refers to the computing hardware we see about us, and the previous occupation called *computer* has evolved into many different occupations, such as computer operator, data entry clerk, and computer programmer.

Summary

We have discussed computers in general terms, characterizing the richness of the hardware configurations (bare machine versus more fully configured computer systems). We have also pointed out some differences in the kinds of software computers can be endowed with (single-user versus multiuser operating systems). We will note some of the ramifications of these differences as we proceed.

The mechanics of computing with a simple calculator were introduced. We saw how calculator operations can themselves be represented as numbers (e.g., 17-bit or 5-bit commands). The process of automating the calculator led us to an understanding of the advantages of storing and retrieving numeric operands under program control. This made it possible to make the calculator's programs data-independent, and more useful (general-purpose) than they would otherwise have been.

In describing this transformation of the simple calculator, we introduced the use of binary numbers to encode data and commands. We briefly examined the popular ASCII character set; we will see more of it later. Finally, we touched upon the distinction between the most common kind of computers (electronic digital computers) and other kinds (analog and hybrid computers).

Exercises for Chapter 1

1. Rewrite the surface area program to use fewer memory locations. Use its trace as a model.
2. Write a program for the externally programmed calculator (with memory) that evaluates a polynomial of the form $a + bx + cx^2$ for selected values of x. (Hint: store the values of a, b, and c in memory locations.)
3. Most typewriters have keyboards which support the printing of approximately 90 symbols. How many bits would it take to encode 90 different symbols?

4.   The Baudot code used for international telegraphic service (TELEX) uses 5 bits. How can it encode a character set of about 60 symbols? (The technique is simple, and we will encounter it several other times in the course of our study.)

5.   Teletypes use a 7-bit code for domestic telegraph or TWX service. How large a character set can such a code support?

6.   The computer card we now call the **IBM card** originated in the late 1800s. It was designed by Herman Hollerith to record only numeric information for processing census data. Each card has 80 columns of 12 rows. The 12 rows are identified with the symbols +-0123456789, so in each column, at most one hole is punched to represent a sign or a decimal digit. We would say that the punched card uses a 12-bit code, the **Hollerith code.** How few rows could be used to represent these 12 symbols, if more than one hole is punched in each column? If you can examine a punched card, describe how non-numeric characters are encoded.

7.   A piano has 88 keys and three pedals. What is the shortest binary code length that can be used to encode musical compositions for the piano, if we assume that all notes have the same duration? Why is this so?

8.   Amateur radio operators use a code called the **Morse code.** It can be thought of as a binary code, but it is quite different from any we have seen. See the description of the Morse code in figure 11.8 (in the exercises for chapter 11) and contrast it with other binary codes.

9.   The **parity** of a group of bits is said to be odd if the group has an odd number of 1-bits; it is even if it has an even number of 1-bits. Using a check bit as an odd parity bit means setting the check bit so that the group it is part of comes to have odd parity. With this in mind:

   a.   Indicate the parity of (1) 1100, (2) 100010, (3) 011010.
   b.   Attach a check bit to the left of each of the above groups, forcing them to have odd parity.
   c.   Repeat (*b*), forcing even parity.
   d.   Write your initials in ASCII:

      (1)   with a 0 check bit.
      (2)   with an odd parity check bit.
      (3)   with an even parity check bit.

A Simple Hypothetical Computer

Introduction

In this chapter we will examine a hypothetical computer and we will write several machine-language programs for it. Conceptually, this hypothetical computer is similar to real computers, and our study of it will introduce us to most of the principles that we will encounter in our subsequent study of a real computer. However, the details of the hypothetical computer's operation are much simpler than those of most modern computers (the hypothetical computer resembles computers designed in the 1950s and early 1960s, in this respect). So, if we understand the principles behind the hypothetical computer's operation, it should be straightforward to generalize to the considerably more complex, real computer we will begin studying in chapter 3.

The Hypothetical Computer

A machine-language program is a series of instructions and data encoded as numbers, designed to be decoded by the hardware of a particular computer, to solve a specific problem or class of problems. Each of these instructions (numbers) must be stored in the computer's memory in order for it to be executed as part of the program. When the computer's control unit needs an instruction, it will *fetch* a copy of the desired instruction from memory and place it in a special location which is used to hold the current active instruction. That location is called the **Instruction Register** (IR). A **register** is similar to a memory location: both store numeric information. Some registers have special functions, as does the Instruction Register.

Programs can be stored in any part of the memory, but the control unit needs to know exactly where the next instruction is located in order to fetch it. The address of this memory location (recall that memory locations are numbered; the unique number for a location is its *address*) is kept in the control unit's **Program Counter** (PC). These registers, the PC and the IR, play a central role in the operation of the computer. We can paraphrase the role of the IR as reminding the control unit what is to be done now, while the PC points to a memory location containing the instruction which tells the control unit what to do next. The model for our simple hypothetical computer is shown in figure 2.1. This computer uses an accumulator register (AC) as did our calculator. Its arithmetic unit is more sophisticated than that of our calculator, and is called the **Arithmetic-Logic Unit,** or ALU. Although the model of this computer is similar to the model of our externally programmed calculator, the differences are important and they illustrate a fundamental property common to all modern digital computers: the program is stored *in the computer's memory.* From now on we will deal with **stored-program computers.**

The Instruction Fetch-Execute Cycle

The PC and IR are fundamentally involved in the computer's operation; this involvement is illustrated by the **instruction fetch-execute cycle.** This cycle is performed by the control unit, and it consists of the following steps:

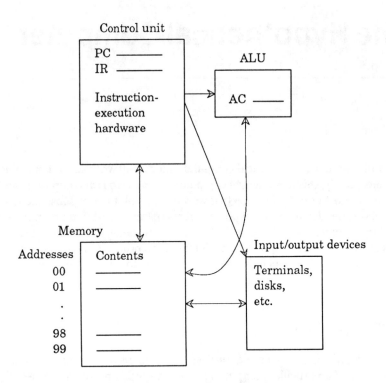

Figure 2.1 Model of a hypothetical computer

1. Send a signal to the memory system, requesting it to return a copy of the instruction whose address is in the PC.
2. Receive the new instruction from the memory system; place it in the IR.
3. Update the PC, so it contains the address of the new next instruction. This is a *new* next instruction because the *previous* next instruction has been placed in the IR and is now the *current* instruction.
4. Decode and execute the current instruction, which is in the IR. Go back to step 1, and repeat.

Machine-Language Instructions

The specific capabilities of a computer are determined by the complexity of its control unit and its ALU. Some of the capabilities of our hypothetical computer are described in figure 2.2. The notation (m) means *the contents* of the location whose two-digit address is m. The notation AC $\leftarrow (m)$ means the AC is loaded with a copy of the number that is stored in the memory location whose address is m. We use the notation (X) with an arrow pointing *away from* it to signify either that the computer will fetch a copy of a number from the memory location whose address is X, or that it will fetch a

Instruction	Code	Function	Comment
LAC	01	AC←(m)	load AC from memory location m
STO	02	m←(AC)	store AC in memory location m
ADD	03	AC←(AC) + (m)	add contents of m to AC; results in AC
SUB	04	AC←(AC) − (m)	subtract contents of m from AC; results in AC
MPY	05	AC←(AC) * (m)	multiply contents of m by AC; results in AC
HLT	00	halt	stop the control unit

Figure 2.2 Instruction subset for hypothetical computer

copy of the number from the register specified by X. Similarly, X ← (AC) is read as, "store a copy of the contents of the AC in the memory location whose address is X."

The hardware of the control unit is designed to decode and execute a variety of instructions. For our hypothetical computer, each instruction is four digits long and has two parts; a two-digit **opcode** (short for **op**eration **code**) followed by a two-digit memory address (symbolized by m in figure 2.2). These are called the **opcode field** and the **address field,** respectively.

The computer's accumulator register, AC, is similar to the one in the programmable calculator of chapter 1. An instruction instructs the control unit to perform an operation. The parts of an instruction are decoded by the control unit which, in turn, tells the ALU to take the number currently held in the AC and add it to, subtract it from, or multiply it by some other number--the one stored in the memory location indicated in the address field. Then the control unit places the results in the AC. The computer's AC, unlike that of the calculator, can obtain its second operand *only* from memory. The address field is necessary in each instruction; it is the method the programmer uses to tell the control unit where to find the second operand of an instruction.

With two-digit addresses, we can number the memory locations 00, 01, 02, . . ., 97, 98, 99. Each of these 100 memory locations is capable of storing a signed, four-digit, decimal number. This means that any memory location can store either a signed four-digit data item, or a four-digit instruction. How can the computer tell if an item in memory is a data item or an instruction? The computer has no way of telling them apart! It is only when a number is fetched from memory that its role becomes clear to the computer. If the number is directed to the IR, during the instruction-fetch phase of the instruction fetch-execute cycle, then it will be used as an instruction. If the number is sent to the ALU, then it will be used as a data item, not an instruction. The computer has no other way of distinguishing between the data item 0300, and the encoded instruction 0300, which means "ADD using the number at memory address 00."[1]

We are almost ready to construct a machine-language program, but first we must examine more carefully our instruction set (figure 2.2). Let us consider several individual instructions.

1. The number 0199 has just been copied into the IR, as illustrated in figure 2.3, steps 1 and 2. Each step in the execution of the LAC instruction is numbered. Dashed lines indicate use of an

[1]It is possible to build a computer in which this is not the case. Such a computer could have some memory locations reserved for storing programs, and other locations reserved for storing data. Most computers are not built this way.

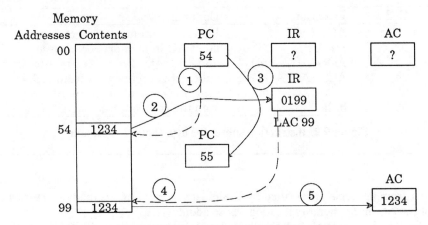

Figure 2.3 Executing an LAC instruction

address to *locate* an item in memory; solid lines indicate *copying* an item to or from memory. What happens next?

The IR contains 0199; the opcode is 01 (which is the encoding of the LAC instruction) and the memory address is 99. So the contents of memory location 99, symbolized (99), are copied into the AC (steps 4 and 5 of figure 2.3). The contents of location 99 will not be changed. If the number 0199 had been in memory location 54, then immediately after fetching the contents of location 54 and copying them into the IR, the control unit would update the PC (step 3). Prior to updating, the PC contained 54 (the address of the instruction about to be fetched); after updating, the PC contains 55--the address of the *next* instruction, which will be fetched from the *next* (consecutive) memory location. Updating the PC, for this computer, means adding 1 to it.

2.   The number 0234 has just been copied into the IR (see figure 2.4). After updating the PC (incrementing it by 1), the control unit divides the instruction into its opcode and address fields. The opcode is 02, which means "store the contents of the AC" in the indicated memory location; the address field contains 34, so the memory location is indicated by its address, 34. The contents of the AC do not change. Opcode 02, the STO operation (figure 2.2), is the only one in this computer which can change the contents of a memory location.

3.   If an ADD instruction, say 0350, is copied into the IR, then after updating the PC (again by 1), the control unit will decode the instruction into the opcode field (03, ADD) and address field (50). It will fetch a copy of the number found in location 50, add that number to the number found in the AC, and place the sum in the AC. The previous contents of the AC will be destroyed, but the number in memory will remain undisturbed. The execution of this ADD instruction is shown in figure 2.5.

Opcodes 04 and 05, for subtraction and multiplication, follow a similar pattern. For subtraction, the operand in memory is subtracted from the operand in the AC and not vice versa. As usual, the

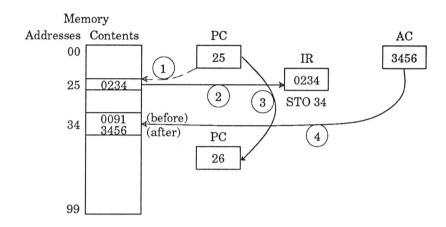

Figure 2.4 Executing an STO instruction

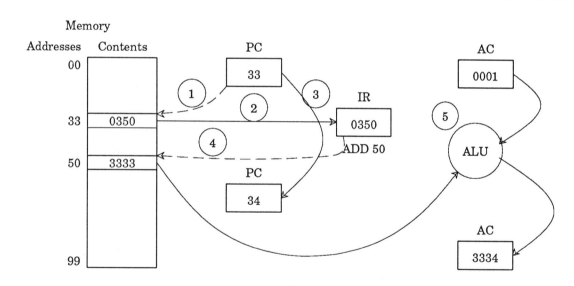

Figure 2.5 Executing an ADD instruction

Address	Contents	Comment
00	0123	item 1 to add
01	0634	item 2 to add
02	0221	item 3 tu add
	.	
	.	
	.	
10	0100	AC←(00)
11	0301	AC←(AC) + (01)
12	0302	AC←(AC) + (02)
13	0000	stop

Figure 2.6 A small machine-language program

new result is placed in the AC. In the case of a multiplication, we must restrict ourselves to using numbers whose product will fit in the AC; otherwise we will get an incorrect result.[2]

The First Machine-Language Program

We are now ready to write machine-language programs. Consider the simple problem of adding the three numbers 123, 634, and 221. If we were using a calculator, we would key the first two numbers followed by a "+," and then key the third number followed by "=."[3] With a computer, we must first place these numbers in memory, so we must find 3 unused memory locations for them. Since we are beginning our program, all 100 memory locations are free, and we can pick any 3 locations. We could pick 3 at random, but let us pick 3 consecutive locations, 00, 01, and 02.

Now we have the following situation in memory: locations 00-02 are used for the three operands. If we were using an externally programmed calculator, we would begin punching holes in successive rows of the paper tape to represent the instructions we want; the paper tape would become the program tape. With a stored-program computer, however, we store the program in the computer's memory, so we have another decision to make before writing the program: where will the program be placed? We can place it anywhere in memory, as long as it does not conflict with other uses of the memory locations. Since the only locations in use are 00, 01, and 02, let us begin placing the program's instructions at location 10. We now choose instructions to load the first number into the

---

[2]In general, the product of two *n* digit numbers is a 2*n* digit number. Since our memory can store only four-digit numbers, we allow only two-digit numbers (or, more accurately, four-digit numbers with at least two leading 0s) as operands for the multiply instruction.

[3]Although both the "+" and a comma (",") appear inside the quotes, we key only the "+," of course. The comma is inside rather than outside the quotes (as is the period, in the "=." at the end of the same sentence) because English usage (illogically) requires that it be there.

AC (01 00: 01 is the opcode for LAC; 00 is the address field), to add the second number using the AC for the running total (03 01), to add the third and last number into the AC (03 02), and (finally) to halt the computer (00 ??), since we have finished adding the three numbers and, therefore, finished our program. Figure 2.6 shows a picture of memory and its contents after we have placed these instructions and data in memory.

In order for the computer to execute the program shown in figure 2.6, we must place the numbers 123, 634, 221, and also the instructions 0100, 0301, 0302, 0000, in the two sections of memory beginning at 00 and 10, respectively. Note that the addresses, shown next to the data items and instructions in figure 2.6, are *not* stored in memory. These addresses are used to show us *where* a data item or instruction has been stored, but the address itself is *not* stored at that location. It is important to avoid confusing the address *of* an instruction (address 10 for instruction 0100, for example) with the address used *in* an instruction (the address 00 in the instruction 0100--which is stored in the location whose address is 10).[4]

Loading Programs into Memory

The process of placing a program in memory is called **program loading.** How can we load this program (and its data) into the memory? Every computer has some kind of a control panel or console. Some of these control panels have switches and keys which a person can use to halt the computer and key a starting address and a series of numbers to be stored in consecutive memory locations (with the first number going to the starting address location and following numbers going into consecutive memory locations). These numbers are either data items or instructions; exactly which is of no consequence to either the control panel or the memory.

When all the data items and instructions have been keyed into memory, it is possible to display the contents of an individual memory location on the control panel display. In this way we can verify that the program was properly loaded. Finally, to start program execution, we have to place the program's starting address into the PC. This is accomplished by using the control panel to key the starting address, then pushing a RUN switch. This places the just-keyed-address in the PC, after which the instruction fetch-execute cycle is initiated. A simplified computer control panel is shown in figure 2.7.

Some computer control panels have no displays, switches, or buttons to permit the kind of program loading we have just described. Those computers usually have, within their control units, some special feature which makes it possible to use a designated terminal, called the **console,** as if it were a control panel. When used in this special mode, various keys of the terminal's keyboard are temporarily given special meanings; a sample sequence of keystrokes for entering our program using this technique is shown in figure 2.8. When a terminal performs this function it is called a **control panel emulator.**

---

[4]This may be more clearly understood by considering the analogy that the use of the word *address* was designed to be. Memory location addresses are similar to house addresses: the number itself is more or less arbitrary; all that matters is that there be a *different* number for each house, and that there be some way of finding a house, if you know its address. (In computers, the memory control system is a piece of hardware that is built to take care of exactly this task: finding a location, given its address. We will not concern ourselves with that task in this book.) In addition, the contents of a house have nothing to do with what particular number constitutes that house's address.

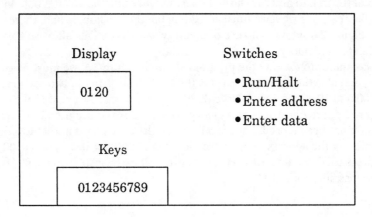

Figure 2.7 Simple control panel

```
@00/1111    0123
@01/0000    0634
@02/9999    0221
@10/1234    0100
@11/0000    0301
@12/4150    0302
@13/6140    0000
@10G
```

Figure 2.8 Console emulation trace

The italicized characters in figure 2.8 were typed by the computer. The "@" is a prompt to which we respond by typing an address. If we then type a "/" following an address, the computer responds by typing the current contents of the memory location with that address. If we type a number, it is stored in memory and replaces the number just displayed. In the last line of the trace, address 10 is followed by a *G*; this is a GO signal, with the preceding address used as the starting address. After we type the G, the console resumes being an ordinary terminal and the program just loaded is executed.

The IPL/Boot Switch

Some computers have a front panel switch labeled *IPL*, for Initial Program Load, or labeled *Boot*, for Bootstrap. If the computer is stopped (if its instruction fetch-execute cycle has been halted), then pushing an IPL or Boot switch forces a predetermined address into the PC, and the instruction fetch-execute cycle is resumed. The IPL/Boot address forced into the PC is the first address of a permanently recorded machine-language program. This program, when it is executed, issues an input instruction which copies another program into memory from some predefined location on a peripheral storage device (such as a disk). The IPL/Boot program then transfers control to the program it has just loaded, which may, in turn, load another program. By such a sequence of events, it is possible to load a user program (which is in machine-readable form on some device the computer can control) into memory and begin its execution.

As a general rule, in a computer system being used for routine data processing or general-purpose computing, the IPL/Boot switch is the only switch on the computer's front panel that the computer's operator uses. We, however, want to understand more about computers than how to use them; we have discussed program loading from a front panel because we want to know how we could run even without an IPL/Boot switch.

Program Execution

We load the program in figure 2.6 into memory at the specified locations, and we place the address of the first instruction (10) into the PC, using the control panel or the control panel emulator. This initiates execution of the program. We can follow its progress by hand-simulating the instruction fetch-execute cycle and recording significant events in the trace history, as shown in figure 2.9. The notation *memory[PC]* uses the analogy of memory as an *array* of locations (in Pascal, the "[ ]" notation is used for array indexing). This analogy will be further utilized in later chapters, when we discuss a real computer. In addition, the notation (=*n*) is used to indicate the contents of memory locations or the PC, or the results of an arithmetic operation; it is intended to provide a helpful reminder, and to allow you, the reader, to check your understanding of the fetch-execute cycle.

Since such a trace history is lengthy, we can abbreviate it into a trace table, showing the state of every significant item *immediately after* execution of the indicated instruction. A trace table for our program is shown in figure 2.10. This trace table presents a snapshot of the hypothetical computer at the end of each cycle of the instruction fetch-execute cycle. Therefore, the program counter has already been updated, and contains the address of the *next* instruction to be executed. Thus, in examining figure 2.10, we should not be confused by the fact that the value in the PC column is one more than the address of the instruction that is shown in the IR column.

A question mark in the table represents an item whose value is unknown or irrelevant. A dash means the previous value for this item was not affected by the execution of the instruction.The column headed *Opcode* shows the opcode extracted from the instruction which has just been executed, and if it involved using memory, the columns headed *Address* and *Operand* show the memory address of the instruction's operand, and the value left in memory after the instruction was completed.

If our control panel provides no way for us to display the contents of the AC, then we can't look at our program's result, since it is in the AC when the program halts. In this case, we can change the program to store the final AC value in memory, say at location 03 (which is not being used), and we can display the contents of location 03 when the program halts.

It is clear from our simple machine-language program, that it is much harder to add three numbers using a computer than using a calculator. Calculators are better for many kinds of problems. As we proceed, however, we will see problems at which computers excel.

Address	Contents
00	0123
01	0634
02	0221
.	
.	
.	
10	0100
11	0301
12	0302
13	0000

1. Fetch memory[PC (=10)]
2. IR←memory[10] (=0100)
3. PC←PC + 1 (=11)
4. Execute opcode 01 with address 00: AC←0123

1. Fetch memory[PC (=11)]
2. IR←memory[11] (=0301)
3. PC←PC + 1 (=12)
4. Execute opcode 03 with address 01: AC←(AC) + (01), or AC←0123 + 0634 (=757)

1. Fetch memory[PC (=12)]
2. IR←memory[12] (=0302)
3. PC←PC + 1 (=13)
4. Execute opcode 03 with address 02: AC←(AC) + (02), or AC←0757 + 0221 (=0978)

1. Fetch memory[PC (=13)]
2. IR←memory[13] (=0000)
3. PC←PC + 1 (=14)
4. Execute opcode 00 (address irrelevant): stop fetch-execute cycle

Figure 2.9 Trace of instruction fetch-execute cycles

PC	IR	Opcode	AC	Address	Operand	Comment
10	?	00	?	?	?	computer stopped
11	0100	01	0123	00	0123	load AC
12	0301	03	0757	01	0634	add
13	0302	03	0978	02	0221	add
14	0000	00	–	–	–	halt

Figure 2.10 Trace table, after execution

Reusing Instructions

The instruction subset we have used permits us to write only programs in which each instruction is used exactly once as the program flow proceeds from the first instruction to the next one and the next one until the last instruction is executed. These are called **straight-line** programs. If this were our only way of writing programs, we would need 100 instructions to add 100 numbers, 1,000 instructions to add 1,000 numbers, etc. We need a way of *reusing* instructions. With the externally programmed calculator of chapter 1, we spliced the end of the program tape to the beginning of the tape to form a program loop. With a stored-program computer, we can't easily splice the memory. Rather, we need a new kind of instruction--one that can transfer control from one part of the program to some other part of the program. Since control of the computer is governed by the instruction being executed, and the instruction being executed is determined by the number in the PC, we need instructions which can place a new value into the PC, thus causing the next instruction to be executed to be some instruction other than the one in the next, consecutive, location in memory.

A TRA *m* instruction places the two-digit address *m* in the PC. This is analogous to the GOTO statement of some high-level programming languages. Executing a TRA instruction *always* causes the two-digit address from its address field to be placed in the PC; for this reason it is often called an **unconditional transfer.**

There are times when we may wish to execute or not execute certain instruction sequences, depending upon the value of some program variable; this is similar to the IF statement of many high-level programming languages. This can be accomplished with **conditional transfer** instructions, which place their two-digit address fields in the PC only if the number in the AC meets some particular condition. Thus, TZE 75 will transfer control to the instruction sequence beginning at location 75, *if and only if* the contents of the AC are zero when the TZE is executed. If the AC contains any other number, the instruction following the TZE will be fetched as usual, and no transfer of control will occur. These new transfer instructions are summarized in figure 2.11.

Study these instructions carefully. Compare their actions with those of the instructions we saw earlier in figure 2.2. The notation $PC \leftarrow IR<0-1>$ means that the low-order two digits of the IR (we number digits from right to left, starting with 0) are copied into the PC. Another way of indicating this is $PC \leftarrow$ m. With this method, it is critical that we understand the difference between $\leftarrow$ m and $\leftarrow$ (m): $\leftarrow$ *m* means copy the two-digit number, *m,* into the specified target; $\leftarrow$ (*m*) means use the two-digit number *m* as an *address,* fetch a copy of the item in the location whose *address* is *m,* and place it in the specified target. Note that *m* $\leftarrow$ indicates a store into the memory location whose address is *m,* and not something as meaningless as "destroy the number *m,* replacing it by the specified number." Note also that the notation $PC \leftarrow$ m makes it clear that the program is transferring control to a different instruction (in a different location in memory), but does *not* make it clear how that instruction--in that location of memory--is found. On the other hand, the notation

Instruction	Opcode	Function	Comment
TRA	06	PC←IR<0-1>	unconditional transfer
TZE	07	if (AC) = 0 then PC←IR<0-1>	transfer if 0
TMI	08	if (AC) < 0 then PC←IR<0-1>	transfer if minus
TPL	09	if (AC) > 0 then PC←IR<0-1>	transfer if plus

Figure 2.11 Control-transfer instructions for hypothetical computer

$PC \leftarrow IR<0-1>$ makes it clear how the new contents of the PC are found (they are the low-order two digits of the IR), but it doesn't make it clear why those two digits are the address of an instruction.[5]

Let us examine a few machine-language programs using this expanded instruction set. The first example follows:

Address	Contents	Comment
50	0650	TRA 50

This is both the shortest and the longest program you can write for this hypothetical computer! It is very short because it has only one instruction. It is very long because it will run forever--until someone uses the control panel to stop the computer. As soon as the instruction is fetched from location 50, the PC is updated automatically so that it will hold the address of the next instruction; since the old contents of the PC were 50, the new contents of the PC are 51. But then execution of opcode 06 places the address 50 into the PC, and the control unit then continues to fetch and execute the same instruction again and again, forever and ever.

Let us consider a more useful example. A person is to be paid at a given rate for up to 40 hours per week, and at double that rate for all hours in excess of 40 per week. Let us store the hours worked (rounded up to whole hours) in location 50, and the hourly pay rate (in pennies) in location 51. Let the program calculate the regular pay, overtime pay, and the total pay, and store them in locations 60, 61, and 62, respectively. We can load the first instruction in location 70.

Address	Contents	Comment
50	--	hours
51	--	hourly pay rate
.		
.		
60	--	regular pay
61	--	overtime pay
62	--	total pay
.		
.		

We can sketch the program in the following pseudo-code:

```
If hours ≤ 40, overtime pay←0
     regular pay←hours * rate
     total pay←regular pay
     halt

If hours > 40, overtime pay←(hours – 40) * 2 * rate
     regular pay←40 * rate
     total pay←overtime pay + regular pay
     halt
```

---

[5]The reason, of course, is that we, as programmers, placed the address in the address field of the transfer instruction; that the control unit, after fetching the instruction from memory, placed it in the IR; and that, in the IR, the low-order two digits are the address field.

Address	Contents	Instruction	Comments
70	0150	LAC 50	put hours worked in AC
71	0469	SUB 69	subtract 40 from hours worked
72	09??	TPL ??	if result > 0, worked overtime
73	0168	LAC 68	if not, AC←0
74	0261	STO 61	and overtime←0
75	0150	LAC 50	put hours worked in AC
76	0551	MPY 51	multiply times rate (in 51)
77	0260	STO 60	regular pay←AC
78	0262	STO 62	total pay←AC
79	0000	HLT	stop computer
80	0551	MPY 51	extra hours * hourly rate
81	0567	MPY 67	AC * 2 (overtime = twice hourly rate)
82	0261	STO 61	overtime pay←AC
83	0169	LAC 69	put 40 in AC
84	0551	MPY 51	AC * hourly rate
85	0260	STO 60	regular pay←AC
86	0361	ADD 61	add overtime pay
87	0262	STO 62	total pay←AC
88	0000	HLT	stop computer
69	0040		40 hours at regular pay
68	0000		0, if no overtime
67	0002		double time for overtime
50			hours worked
51			hourly pay rate
60			regular pay
61			overtime pay
62			total pay

Figure 2.12 Pay program

It is likely that we will need the constant 40, so let us store it in location 69. If we need other constants as we write the program, we can store them in locations 68, 67, etc., as long as we don't "bump into" location 62! The entire program is shown in figure 2.12.

Notice that location 72 contains 09??: the address field is not filled in with a target address for the TPL instruction. This is because when we wrote the TPL, we did not yet know where in memory its target would be. Now that we have written the instructions that the TPL refers to, we can fill in the missing address, in place of the ??. Location 72 can now be changed to contain 0980.

When the program is loaded, the instructions will be copied into locations 70-89, the constants will be placed in locations 67-69, and the data for this particular execution of the program (hours and rate) will be placed in locations 50 and 51. There is no need to put anything in locations 60-62. These locations will be filled in by the program when it is executed.

Self-Modifying Programs

The program to add three numbers used one LAC and two ADD instructions. If we had to add n numbers, we would need a program with one LAC and $n - 1$ ADDs. It seems that the number of instructions in the program must be as big as the set of numbers to be added. Clearly, we would rather not have to write a 1-million-instruction program in order to add 1 million numbers. How can we harness the computer's power to significantly reduce the number of instructions we must write and load in memory? We are not suggesting that it is possible to add n numbers without *executing* $n - 1$ ADD instructions. However, there is a technique which can enormously reduce the number of instructions a programmer must write and load in memory--thus allowing programmers to be more productive. In addition, since this technique reduces the number of *instructions* in a program, more memory locations are available for data; thus, more numbers can be stored in memory, so more numbers can be added by the program.[6]

Consider the program to add three numbers. The instructions flowing through the IR are:

IR	Comment
0100	LAC 00
0301	ADD 01
0302	ADD 02
0000	HLT

These add the contents of locations 00, 01, and 02. If we had ten numbers to add, the following instruction would flow through the IR in the process of adding the ten numbers in locations 00-09.

IR	Comment
0100	LAC 00
0301	ADD 01
0302	ADD 02
0303	ADD 03
0304	ADD 04
0305	ADD 05
0306	ADD 06
0307	ADD 07
0308	ADD 08
0309	ADD 09
0000	HLT

The ADD instruction is repeated nine times; each instruction differs from its predecessor only in the address field, and that difference is always 1. If we could arrange for the program to have only a single ADD instruction (the "number" 0301), then after fetching and executing it the first time, the program could fetch the 0301 as a *data item*, add 1 to it, store it as a data item (0302) back in memory, and loop back to use it as an *instruction* (0302). We can keep repeating this process of treating an instruction as first an instruction, then a data item, and then an instruction again, until

---

[6]Recall that, so far, the entire program--instructions and data--must be stored in memory in order for a stored-program computer to execute it.

Address	Contents	Instruction	Comments

{These two instructions are for initialization}

| 84 | 0100 | LAC 00 | AC←first item, from loc. 0 |
| 85 | 0299 | STO 99 | initialize sum |

{This is the "add-modify instruction" loop}

86	0199	LAC 99	AC←sum
87	0301	ADD 01	THIS INSTRUCTION WILL CHANGE!
88	0299	STO 99	store sum
89	0187	LAC 87	put ADD in AC, to change it
90	0397	ADD 97	add 1 to instruction (change address)
91	0287	STO 87	replace old instruction with new

{Now, check counter to see if we're done yet}

92	0198	LAC 98	AC←counter
93	0497	SUB 97	decrement counter
94	0298	STO 98	replace (decremented) counter
95	0986	TPL 86	if counter > 0 then go to 86
96	0000	HLT	else (counter = 0): stop

{Variables and constants}

97	0001		constant 1, for modifying instruction
98	0009		counter, for loop control
99			location for sum

Figure 2.13 A self-modifying program

all the numbers to be added have been added. First, however, we have to worry about a few more details:

1. We must make sure that the program stops after the last data item has been processed.
2. We must avoid destroying the running total kept in the AC.

Consider a program to add ten numbers, shown in figure 2.13. Its execution can be sketched as follows:

	AC←(00)	get first data item
87:	AC←(AC)+(01)	add second data item
	87←(87)+1	modify ADD instruction
	98←(98)−1	decrement count: now 8 so continue
87:	AC←(AC)+(02)	add third data item
	87←(87)+1	modify ADD instruction
	98←(98)−1	decrement count: now 7 so continue

.
.
.

87:    $AC \leftarrow (AC)+(09)$ add tenth (last) data item
       $87 \leftarrow (87)+1$ modify ADD instruction
       $98 \leftarrow (98)-1$ decrement count: now 0 so stop

Notice that when the program begins, the count is 9 and the address in the ADD instruction at location 87 is 01. Each time we come back to execute that ADD instruction, the count is 1 less and the address field is 1 more; the sum of the two remains constant at 10. When the program ends, the count contains 0 and the address field contains 10. But since we don't execute the ADD instruction after its last modification, the last ADD we *executed* was ADD 09; this fits nicely with the program, in which we stored the last data item in the memory location whose address is 09. We have written a program that occupies 16 memory locations but that can process *any amount* of data, as long as the data can fit in memory. To add a different number of items with this program, we need only change the count in location 98 appropriately (count = number of data items - 1).

Let's examine the price we pay for this programming ease. Without the self-modification technique, a program to add n items requires the writing of n instructions; our self-modifying program requires the writing of only 13 instructions. However, now consider the number of instructions *executed*. The straight-line program, clearly, executes n instructions. With our self-modifying program, on the other hand, we have the overhead of changing the address field of the ADD instruction and counting how many times we have added. This program has a total of 13 instructions; 3 of them are executed once and the other 10 are executed $n - 1$ times; the total number of instructions executed is, thus, $10(n - 1) + 3$, which is $10n - 10 + 3$, which is $10n - 7$. Thus, while the self-modifying program is *short* in terms of memory requirements, it is *long* in terms of execution speed: it takes about ten times as long to execute as a straight-line program does!

Notice that it is possible to execute the self-modifying program a second time, with a new set of data, without reloading the program, providing that the ADD instruction in location 87 is reinitialized to 0301 (it has the value 0310 when the program halts after adding ten items).

A program that modifies itself is called **self-modifying code.** This illustrates one of the important ramifications of the stored-program computer: it can treat instructions as if they were data, and data as if they were instructions. In the next chapters, we will examine better ways of reusing instructions; we will see that it is possible to reuse instructions *without* actually changing the stored program! In fact, once we have learned these new techniques, we will generally look with suspicion on any program which changes itself.

So why do we study self-modifying programs? One of our major tasks in understanding how computers work will be to realize that in a computer's memory there is no difference between a number that is a data item and a number that represents an instruction. Early computer programmers took advantage of this fact and wrote programs that changed their own behavior by treating instructions like ordinary data, modifying them and then executing them. Modern computers provide safer ways of changing program behavior, without modifying the program in memory. If we understand the early techniques, we will be able to better understand and appreciate these safer ways, which eliminate the need to use self-modifying programming techniques.

Lest there be any misunderstanding, self-modifying programs should, in general, be avoided; we discuss them and write them for educational purposes only. Once we understand the capabilities of modern computers, we will not need to use the primitive technique of self-modifying code.

Consequences of Stored Programs

The very first electronic computers stored their programs *outside* of the computer's memory (they were *not*, therefore, stored-program computers). The idea of placing a computer's program in the computer's memory is generally attributed to John von Neumann. Why is it such an important idea? First, it makes it possible for a program to process itself as if it were ordinary data, as we saw when we discussed self-modifying programs. Though self-modification is no longer necessary or desirable, the ability to process a program as data makes it possible for programs such as compilers to "manufacture" other programs. In addition, programs can be stored in libraries, as data files.

The second consequence of storing programs in memory is that they may be executed much more rapidly. Consider having to use a computer which does not use stored programs. For instance, suppose such a computer reads each instruction from a paper tape. A slow tape reader reads 10 characters per second. For the sake of simplicity, let us assume that each instruction can be encoded as 1 paper tape character. Regardless of any other factors, this computer could not execute more than 10 instructions per second, simply because the tape reader would not let it read instructions into its IR any faster than that. A very fast paper tape reader might read 1,000 characters per second. A computer using this fast tape reader to fetch its instructions would still be unable to execute more than 1,000 instructions per second. In addition, it could achieve this rate only if it never branched or transferred control to a nonconsecutive instruction. If the program ever executed a backward transfer-of-control, the tape reader would have to be stopped, the tape motion reversed, and the appropriate tape frame found. This is an inherent characteristic of devices like paper tape readers. They support only *sequential access* in a reasonably efficient fashion.

The memory that stored-program computers store their programs in, on the other hand, is *random access* memory (RAM). (A better name for it would be *uniform access*.) Each memory location in a random access memory can be accessed in the same amount of time. There is no greater penalty for accessing a "faraway" instruction, forward or backward, than there is for accessing a "nearby" instruction. This is not the case with sequential access devices. Many modern computers are capable of fetching 1 million instructions per second from memory; some can go much faster.

Some years ago, almost all computers used ferromagnetic cores (**core**) for their random access memory. Memory designers now use RAM integrated circuit chips to build memories. When we discuss input-output devices in later chapters, we will see another kind of random access device in which access times are *not* uniform, despite the name!

Speed in Perspective

A person can walk briskly about 5 mph. Using an automobile can raise one's travel speed to 50 mph, more or less; this is an improvement by a factor of 10. By taking an airplane and flying at about 500 mph, one can gain another factor of 10 in speed, for a cumulative speedup of a factor of 100. A supersonic aircraft might provide for a speedup of another factor of 4. We see this below:

	MPH	Gain	Cumulative gain
Walk:	5	--	--
Auto:	50	*10	*10
Airplane:	500	*10	*100
Supersonic:	2,000	*4	*400

If we compute with a simple calculator, our calculating speed is limited by the speed of our keying. Perhaps we can key 2 operations per second, (disregarding the data keying). If we use an externally programmed calculator which reads instructions from a tape, say at the rate of 100 instructions per second, the calculation can proceed much more rapidly (once again, ignoring data input).

The first electronic computers (e.g., ENIAC) ran at approximately 1,000 instructions per second. The computers we will be examining in detail (VAXes) run at speeds from between 500,000 to over 10 million instructions per second. Some computers (e.g., Cray II) can perform up to 200 million computations per second. We can summarize the performance gains in computing as follows (IPS stands for Instructions Per Second):

	IPS	Gain	Cumulative gain
Calculator:	2	--	--
Early computer:	1,000	*500	*500
Modern computer:	1,000,000	*1,000	*500,000
High speed computer:	200,000,000	*200	*100,000,000

What does this mean? Suppose we calculated nonstop for 8 hours per day, 5 days a week, for 50 weeks (one working year). If we were using a calculator at the rate of 2 operations per second for 2,000 hours in that year, we would have performed 14.4 million operations. In principle an ordinary computer might get the same work done in as little as 14.4 seconds (2,000 hours divided by a speedup of 500,000). With a high-speed computer, it might take as little as 0.072 seconds.

Of course, these amazingly short times ignore many important aspects of using computers, such as data preparation time, program preparation time, program execution overhead time (i.e., time spent doing things that do not directly advance the computation, like modifying addresses). Nevertheless, an ordinary computer allows us to do in a few days or weeks what would otherwise have taken years. In fact, many of the things that were inconceivable in the 1940s we now do routinely--simply because of computer availability.

Summary

We have examined the concept of the stored-program computer, which gives rise to the need for special control-unit registers such as the Program Counter (PC) and the Instruction Register (IR). The execution of a machine-language program can be described in terms of an instruction fetch-execute cycle, which is repeated for each instruction that is executed.

The mechanics of loading a machine-language program into memory were discussed, as was the purpose of an Initial Program Load (IPL) switch.

An instruction set adequate for performing arithmetic operations that only permits us to write straight-line programs was examined. This makes computers impractical for handling either data dependent computations or large sets of data. This limitation is the motivation for conditional and unconditional transfer instructions. Using these, we can execute parts of a program both selectively and repeatedly. In addition, because of the computer's ability to modify its own program, a small program can process large amounts of memory-resident data.

The practicality of stored-program computers is enhanced by having the executing program and its data stored in a random access memory (RAM). The chapter concludes with a discussion of the dramatic performance improvements during the past 40 years of computing.

Exercises for Chapter 2

1. Rewrite the pay program shown in figure 2.12 so that it fits into one block of contiguous memory, beginning at location 0.

2. Improve the pay program so that it uses fewer instructions.

3. What is the largest pay rate that can be used with the pay program if you ignore overtime?

4. What do you think would happen if the pay program were incorrectly loaded so that the first instruction (at location 70) became 0170?

5. A Teletype paper tape reader can read 10 paper tape frames (a frame is a row of 8 bits) per second. A fast paper tape reader might read 500 characters per second (cps; the words *frame* and *character* are used interchangeably). If each 8-bit frame encodes one instruction for an externally programmed calculator, and the execution of each instruction is instantaneous, how many MIPS (millions of instructions per second) can an externally programmed calculator execute using a 500 cps tape reader?

6. The type of random access memory used in most computers can be accessed in times ranging from approximately 1 s (s = microsecond = 1/1,000,000 of a second) to 20 ns (ns = nanosecond = 1/1,000,000,000 second). Suppose that our hypothetical computer has a 1 s memory access time. That is, a request to fetch or store an instruction or data item takes 1 s. Further, suppose that instruction execution time is instantaneous (this is not an unreasonable first approximation). How many MIPS can this computer execute? Be careful to account for instruction fetch and operand store-or-fetch.

7. Why does the control unit update the PC by 1?

8. Write a program for the hypothetical computer which places 0s in (**clear**s) the 10 consecutive memory locations, 90-99.

9. How does the control unit distinguish between a number representing an instruction and one which represents data? Explain this clearly.

10. How does the ALU distinguish between a number representing an instruction and one which represents data? Explain this clearly.

11. Is it necessary for data to be placed in low memory and instructions in high memory? If so, why? If not, why not?

12. Rewrite the program in figure 2.6 so that all of it (instructions and data) fits into locations 20-26.

13. Rewrite the program in figure 2.6 so that all of it (instructions and data) fits into locations 50-56.

14. Compare the contents of memory for the programs in exercises 12 and 13. That is, compute (50) - (20), (51) - (21), etc. What has changed in memory? Account for each change.

15. Write the typing history generated in loading the program from exercise 12, using the technique shown in figure 2.8.

16. What is the difference between $d \leftarrow m$ and $d \leftarrow (m)$?

17. Write a program that uses a table of 20 locations, 50-69. The program should store each location's address in that location. Begin the instructions for the program at location 0.

18. Rewrite the program of figure 2.13 so that it tests for completion *before* the key addition.

19. Why would you want to test for completion *before* a computation in a loop rather than *after* it?

20. Suppose the TPL instruction began to malfunction (i.e., the control-unit hardware that interprets the TPL instruction began failing). Create an instruction sequence using the other instructions which could be used in place of the TPL.

21. Write a program to add ten numbers; then rewrite it so that it uses self-modification. If each instruction takes $1\,\mu$s to execute and each operand or instruction takes $1\,\mu$s to fetch or store, how long does each program take? How much faster (in terms of the ratio of their execution times) is the first program than the second one?

22. How much longer does it take to add n numbers using a self-modifying program than a non-self-modifying program? Express your result as a function of n.

23. If self-modifying programs are slower than their nonmodifying counterparts, why would you ever want to use self-modifying programs?

24. Compute the ratio of the program lengths (excluding data) for the two programs of exercise 21. How does this ratio compare to the ratio of their execution times?

25. Many of the sample programs use a HLT instruction and also use a constant with the value 0. Why shouldn't you use a single 0 for both purposes?

3

Machine-Language Programming for a Real Computer

Introduction

The real computer we will deal with in this book is the VAX (Virtual Address eXtension), manufactured by the Digital Equipment Corporation (DEC). What is it a virtual address extension of? It is an extension of its predecessor, the PDP-11, which is also manufactured by DEC. We have already learned enough to understand the *address* part of the name *VAX*; *extension* has the meaning of the ordinary English word. But what about *virtual*?

Virtual addressing is a method of dealing with memory addresses to make it appear to programmers that a computer has more memory than it actually does. The PDP-11 was limited to 65,536[1] memory locations. This may seem like a lot, and it was in the late 1960s, when the PDP-11 was designed and memory was very expensive. However, as memory became less expensive, computer programmers realized that it is more convenient *not* to worry about how much memory a program requires (recall that a stored-program computer must place both the program *and* the data in memory). Virtual addressing was created to remove from the programmer the problem of fitting a large program into a small memory; with virtual addressing, the operating system and the hardware combine to allow the programmer to pretend that the memory is nearly unlimited in size.

Although the VAX uses virtual addressing, we will not discuss it in any detail until later, when we understand more about the VAX. We do this in order to simplify our task of understanding the computer; in the mean time, we will assume that the VAX uses addresses for memory locations in exactly the same way that our programmable calculator and hypothetical computer did. This is a simplifying assumption, but it will not lead us far astray in our understanding of the VAX. For, although *programmers* use virtual addresses, the control unit communicates with the memory system with the same **real** (or, **physical**) addresses that we have already seen. What we ignore when we ignore virtual addressing is only the *translation* that must be done to turn a virtual address that a programmer uses into a physical address that the memory system uses.

The VAX is a *family* of computers, spanning a large range of performance and cost. Since it is a family, however, the machine language for *all* VAXes is identical. (The differences between different members of the family are in the hardware used to build them.) Since our goal is to understand the VAX at the level of its machine language, we will not be concerned with most of the details of its hardware that account for differences in performance of different models.

---

[1]Computer scientists use the symbol *K*, short for the prefix *kilo,* to denote one thousand. Thus, 65,536 is often written as *64K.* Why 64K and not 65K? Computer scientists use the binary number system (we had a brief introduction to it in chapter 1; we will see more of it soon) and 2^{10} (1,024), which is the power of 2 that is closest to 1,000 (see figure 1.13), is called 1K. Successive powers of 2 are 1, 2, 4, 8, 16, 32, 64, etc.; computer scientists call successive thousands, therefore, 1K, 2K, 4K, 8K, 16K, 32K, 64K, etc. So, 1K is not exactly 1,000 and 64K is not exactly 64,000; clearly, the inaccuracy is larger for larger numbers: 2K is 2,048; 64K is 65,536; 256K is 262,144.

At the time of writing, the VAX family includes the following models:

MicroVAX I, II, 2000, 3500, 3600
VAXstation II, 8000, 3200, 3500
VAX 11/725, 11/730, 11/750, 11/780, 11/782, 11/785
VAX 8600, 8650
VAX 8250, 8350, 8530, 8550, 8800, 8810 (8700), 8820, 8830, 8840, 8842, 8974, 8978

However, DEC is constantly introducing new models, so this list is likely to be out of date before you read it.

Our purpose in examining the VAX is not to understand only the VAX. Although details of the VAX design are different from those computers built by IBM or Unisys (formerly Sperry and Burroughs) or Intel, and are even different from those of other computer families built by DEC, the principles are basically the same. Once we are familiar with the details of any one computer, it is relatively easy to understand a second or a third different type of computer. So let us proceed with the VAX.

The performance and cost of VAXes extend from single-user table-top workstations such as the MicroVAX 2000, to multiuser systems capable of supporting 100 or more simultaneous users, such as the VAX 8978. The costs of different models range from less than $5,000 to more than $4,000,000. Well over 100,000 VAX systems have been manufactured; the features of the VAX are an excellent basis for an in-depth study of computing.

A Machine-Language Program

Let us examine a short machine-language program for the VAX, the program in figure 3.1. The bits are written in groups of 4 to make it easier for us to read them. This program illustrates several important properties of the VAX:

1.   Memory addresses are 32 bits long.
2.   Memory locations are 8 bits wide.
3.   Some instructions (add) take up several memory locations.
4.   Some instructions (halt) take up a single memory location.
5.   Each operand has an **operand specifier.**
6.   Opcodes are 8 bits long.
7.   Operand specifiers are 8 bits long.
8.   The VAX does everything in binary.

We will deal with points 1 through 7 in detail as soon as we have considered the last one: the VAX does everything in binary. This is true of the VAX, and of *all* other digital computers. So, let us learn more about binary numbers.

More About Binary

In our first encounter with binary, we used a set of binary digits to represent a particular keyboard action: if bit *i* in a 17-bit row is set, then push key *i* of a 17-key keyboard. Our next encounter with binary involved encoding and decoding; a 5-bit code can be used to represent any one of 32 distinct objects, actions, or events.

Address	Contents	Comment
0000 0000 0000 0000 0000 0010 0000 0000	1001 0000	*move* 1 byte
0000 0000 0000 0000 0000 0010 0000 0001	1001 1111	source operand specifier
0000 0000 0000 0000 0000 0010 0000 0010	0001 0111	address of source operand
0000 0000 0000 0000 0000 0010 0000 0011	0000 0010	
0000 0000 0000 0000 0000 0010 0000 0100	0000 0000	
0000 0000 0000 0000 0000 0010 0000 0101	0000 0000	
0000 0000 0000 0000 0000 0010 0000 0110	1001 1111	destination operand specifier
0000 0000 0000 0000 0000 0010 0000 0111	0001 1000	address of destination operand
0000 0000 0000 0000 0000 0010 0000 1000	0000 0010	
0000 0000 0000 0000 0000 0010 0000 1001	0000 0000	
0000 0000 0000 0000 0000 0010 0000 1010	0000 0000	
0000 0000 0000 0000 0000 0010 0000 1011	1000 0000	*add* 2 bytes
0000 0000 0000 0000 0000 0010 0000 1100	1001 1111	operand specifier for 1st operand
0000 0000 0000 0000 0000 0010 0000 1101	0001 1001	address of 1st operand
0000 0000 0000 0000 0000 0010 0000 1110	0000 0010	
0000 0000 0000 0000 0000 0010 0000 1111	0000 0000	
0000 0000 0000 0000 0000 0010 0001 0000	0000 0000	
0000 0000 0000 0000 0000 0010 0001 0001	1001 1111	operand specifier of 2nd operand
0000 0000 0000 0000 0000 0010 0001 0010	0001 1010	address of 2nd operand
0000 0000 0000 0000 0000 0010 0001 0011	0000 0010	
0000 0000 0000 0000 0000 0010 0001 0100	0000 0000	
0000 0000 0000 0000 0000 0010 0001 0101	0000 0000	
0000 0000 0000 0000 0000 0010 0001 0110	0000 0000	*halt*
0000 0000 0000 0000 0000 0010 0001 0111	0000 1100	source for *move* instruction
0000 0000 0000 0000 0000 0010 0001 1000	0000 0000	destination for *move* instruction
0000 0000 0000 0000 0000 0010 0001 1001	0000 0010	1st operand of *add* instruction
0000 0000 0000 0000 0000 0010 0001 1010	0010 1111	2nd operand of *add* instruction

Figure 3.1 A machine-language program for the VAX

We will now consider bits not as necessarily representing actions or objects, but as having *values,* and representing numbers. We can speak of the **binary number system** (base 2), just as we speak of the **decimal number system** (base 10).

In the decimal number system, ten distinct symbols are used to represent numbers; these are the decimal digits 0, 1, . . ., 8, 9. The relative position of a digit in a multidigit number gives that digit its value. Consider the number 234. It is really shorthand for "2 hundreds plus 3 tens plus 4 ones," or

$$2 * 100_{10} + 3 * 10_{10} + 4 * 1, \text{ or}$$
$$2 * 10^2 + 3 * 10^1 + 4 * 10^0$$

In a similar fashion, if we restrict the set of digits to the 2 bits (binary digits, remember?) 0 and 1, the binary number 11001 can be regarded as shorthand for:

$$1 * 10000_2 + 1 * 1000_2 + 0 * 100_2 + 0 * 10_2 + 1 * 1, \text{ or}$$
$$1 * 10^4 + 1 * 10^3 + 0 * 10^2 + 0 * 10^1 + 1 * 10^0$$

+	0	1
0	0	1
1	1	(1)0

Figure 3.2 Binary addition table

Note that, in the last line, the exponents are written in base ten (decimal), but the numbers that are being raised to those exponents are written in binary. That is, $1 * 10^4$ has the components 1 (binary) * 10 (binary) to the power 4 (decimal). If we wish to look at the binary number 11001's equivalent in the decimal system, then we simply have to evaluate

$$1 * 2^4 + 1 * 2^3 + 0 * 2^2 + 0 * 2^1 + 1 * 2^0$$

(since 10 binary is 2 decimal), and we get

$$16 + 8 + 0 + 0 + 1$$

which is 25.

For the immediate future, our major uses of binary will involve counting things (such as memory locations) and adding. Addition can be understood by examining the binary addition table in figure 3.2. This table shows us that there is only one case (of four possibilities) in which neither addend is 0: when we add 1 + 1, and get 0 with a **carry** of 1.

If we wish to add a pair of binary numbers, say 101 and 110, we proceed from right to left. First, we look up the sum of column 1 in the addition table; next, we look up the sum of column 2 in the addition table. Finally, we look up the sum for the third (and last) column. We then add the sums we have been writing down, again by looking them up in the addition table. Figure 3.3 shows this binary addition done in detail. We see, from figure 3.3, that the result of adding binary 101 and 110 is 1011; this is equivalent to adding decimal 5 and 6, giving a result of decimal 11. When adding 1 + 1 in binary, there is always a carry into the next position on the left.

Figure 3.4 shows another example of binary addition--one in which there are several instances of carry from one column to the next. This figure probably seems strange (as does figure 3.3, perhaps); it may suggest that binary addition is an odd beast indeed. However, we do binary addition in exactly the same way that we do decimal addition; the only difference is the addition table. So why do figures 3.3 and 3.4 seem strange? Because they illustrate each step in the addition process in detail, and most readers of this book will have been doing addition for 10 years or more, and so will not even be aware of all the steps (and all the table look-ups) involved. We emphasize this fact because, during the course of our examination of the VAX, things may often *seem* very different in binary only because we are doing them in binary, with which we are not yet familiar. In such situations it is often helpful to think back to our early years in school. We can (perhaps) remember that, before we became familiar with a particular operation in decimal, we had to take the same kinds of careful, deliberate (even plodding) steps that we are now taking until we become familiar with binary.

Counting is simple: it's just a special case of adding, namely, adding 1. Figure 3.5 shows the progression as we count by ones, from 0 to 1 to 10 (2 in binary) to 11 (3 in binary), and so on.

The binary number 10000000000, or 2^{10}, has the symbol K associated with it. Its value of $1,024_{10}$ is close to, but not identical with, the metric system's use of K for 1,000. Later on, when we refer

Column #:	3	2	1	
Addend 1:	1	0	1	
Addend 2:	1	1	0	
Result:				
a:			1	←adding column 1
b:		1		←adding column 2
c:	10			←adding column 3

Now, we add the numbers from lines a, b, and c:

Column #:	3	2	1	
Addend 1:	0	0	1	←from line a
Addend 2:	0	1	0	←from line b
Addend 3:	10	0	0	←from line c
Perform the addition:				
d:			1	←adding new column 1
e:		1		←adding new column 2
f:	10			←adding new column 3

We now simply rewrite these last three lines in a single line, getting 1 0 1 1

Figure 3.3 Performing a binary addition

to, for example, 4K of memory, the exact number we will mean is 4 times 1,024, or 4,096 (see note 1).

Hexadecimal Numbers

Having mastered binary counting and binary addition (we will look at other features of binary arithmetic later), we now emphasize that, although all (digital) *computers* use binary, *people* usually use a *shorthand* for binary. On the VAX, we will group bits together in sets of 4 (always proceeding from right to left) and replace each set of 4 bits with the corresponding **hexadecimal digit,** as shown in figure 3.6. Why do sets of *4* bits comprise one hexadecimal digit? Hexadecimal[2] is base 16; successive hexadecimal (**hex,** for short) digits represent successive powers of 16, just as successive *binary* digits represent successive powers of 2, and successive *decimal* digits represent successive powers of 10. A single binary digit can have one of 2 possible values: 0 or 1; a single decimal digit can have one of *10* possible values: 0, 1, . . ., 9; a single hexadecimal digit can have one of 16 possible values: 0, 1, . . ., F. So, in order to decide how many binary digits can be replaced with a single hexadecimal digit, we need to know how many bits it takes to represent one of 16 possible values. One bit can have one of 2 values; 2 bits, therefore, can have any one of 4 possible values (2 for the 1st bit, times 2 more for the 2nd bit); 3 bits can have any one of 8 possible values (2 times 2 times 2); 4 bits can have any one of 16 possible values (2 * 2 * 2 * 2), so a single hexadecimal digit replaces 4 bits--as shown in figure 3.6.

---

[2]Hexadecimal comes from the Greek words *hex* for 6 and *deca* for 10.

Column #:	3	2	1	
Addend 1:	1	0	1	
Addend 1:	0	1	1	
a:		1	0	←adding column 1
b:		1		←adding column 2
c:	1			←adding column 3

Now, we add the numbers from lines a, b, and c:

Column #:	3	2	1	
Addend 1:	0	1	0	←from line a
Addend 1:	0	1	0	←from line b
Addend 1:	1	0	0	←from line c

Now, perform the addition:

d:			0	←adding new column 1
e:		1	0	←adding new column 2
f:		1		←adding new column 3

We repeat the process one more time, adding the numbers from lines d, e, and f:

Column #:	3	2	1	
Addend 1:	0	0	0	←from line d
Addend 1:	1	0	0	←from line e
Addend 1:	1	0	0	←from line f

Perform the addition:

g:			0	←adding new column 1
h:		0		←adding new column 2
i:	10			←adding new column 3

We now simply rewrite these last three lines in a single line, getting 1 0 0 0

Figure 3.4 Another binary addition

Why are the hexadecimal digits 0, 1, . . ., 9, A, B, . . ., F? A single hexadecimal digit can represent any one of 16 possible values, so we need a way of specifying *which* value a particular hexadecimal digit represents. We can use the decimal digits (0-9) for the first 10 values, but then we still need 6 more! So, arbitrarily, the convention is to use the first 6 letters of the alphabet for the last 6 digits of the hexadecimal number system.

We can now rewrite the VAX machine-language program of figure 3.1 in a much more compact and readable form, as figure 3.7, by replacing each quartet of binary digits with a single hexadecimal digit.

The eleventh address in figure 3.7, and the ones following it, may seem wrong: shouldn't location 00000210 follow location 00000209? It should if we are counting in decimal, but we are counting in *hexadecimal*; the number after 9 is A, and the number after F is 10. In addition, if we understand successive digits in a number system as representing successive powers of the base of that system, then we realize that 10 hexadecimal is 16 decimal: $1 * 16^1 + 0 * 16^0$.

Binary	Decimal
0	0
1	1
10	2
11	3
100	4
101	5
110	6
111	7
1000	8
	. . .
1111	15
10000	16
10001	17
	. . .
1111111111	1023
10000000000	1024
	. . .

Figure 3.5 Counting in binary

Binary	Hexadecimal	Binary	Hexadecimal
0000	0	1000	8
0001	1	1001	9
0010	2	1010	A
0011	3	1011	B
0100	4	1100	C
0101	5	1101	D
0110	6	1110	E
0111	7	1111	F

Figure 3.6 Binary to hexadecimal conversion

A Model of the VAX

In order to make much sense of the previous machine-language program, and in order to write other programs, we need to see how the VAX is organized: we need a model. The first model we will use follows; as we learn more, the model will be refined to show more detail. The major components of a VAX are:

1.   A Control Unit
2.   An Arithmetic-Logic processing Unit (ALU)
3.   A Memory System
4.   Input-Output (I/O) devices

Address	Contents	Comment
00000200	90	*move* 1 byte
00000201	9F	operand specifier for source operand
00000202	17	address of source operand
00000203	02	
00000204	00	
00000205	00	
00000206	9F	operand specifier for destination operand
00000207	18	address of destination operand
00000208	02	
00000209	00	
0000020A	00	
0000020B	80	*add* 2 bytes
0000020C	9F	operand specifier for 1st operand
0000020D	19	address of 1st operand
0000020E	02	
0000020F	00	
00000210	00	
00000211	9F	operand specifier of 2nd operand
00000212	1A	address of 2nd operand
00000213	02	
00000214	00	
00000215	00	
00000216	00	*halt*
00000217	0C	source for *move* instruction
00000218	00	destination for *move* instruction
00000219	02	1st operand of *add* instruction
0000021A	2F	2nd operand of *add* instruction

Figure 3.7 Hexadecimal conversion of figure 3.1

Figure 3.8 illustrates how these components are interconnected by showing the control (dashed) lines which emanate from the Control Unit. (The status lines used by the Control Unit to find out what state each component is in at any time are included under control lines.) The solid lines represent the flow of data, which can be either instructions, addresses, or numeric operands, depending on how they are used. Each component will be discussed in turn; how they work together will occupy us for many more chapters. We will see this figure again, in later chapters; it will include more details, as our understanding of the VAX increases.

Control Unit

The **control unit** consists of the Program Counter (PC), which can hold a 32-bit address, and the Instruction Register (IR), capable of holding an instruction, as well as the hardware necessary to carry out (**execute**) each instruction. The VAX instructions we will discuss are between 8 and 128 bits long (others are even longer!); they can occupy, thus, between 1 and 16 consecutive 8-bit memory locations. We saw some 8 and some 88-bit instructions in the VAX machine-language program in figure 3.1.

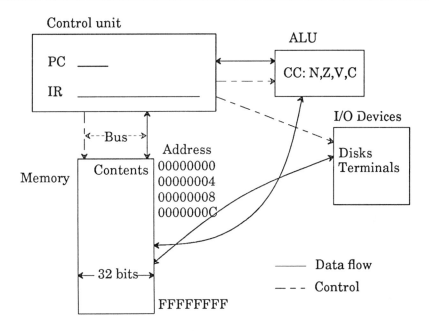

Figure 3.8 A model of the VAX

Arithmetic-Logic Unit

The **Arithmetic-Logic Unit** (ALU) consists of the hardware necessary to perform arithmetic, comparisons, and other operations. As data flow through the ALU, 4 bits called the **Condition Code** (CC) bits are used to store information about the latest result produced by the ALU. We will discuss 2 of those bits, the N (Negative) and Z (Zero) bits, now, and the other 2 (the C and V bits) later, after we have learned more about computer arithmetic. The Z bit is **set** $(Z = 1)$ if the result of the last calculation was 0, and it is **cleared** $(Z = 0)$ if the result was nonzero. Similarly, the N bit is set if the last result was negative and cleared if it was positive. In the VAX, a result is considered negative if its leftmost bit, (its **most significant bit,** or **msb**) is 1; otherwise it is considered positive. The CC bits are similar to Boolean variables in Pascal: their value (1 or 0) indicates whether it is true or false that the corresponding condition (the last result was 0, or the last result was negative) occurred. The ALU manages the CC; there is only one set of CC bits for the whole computer, not one set for each memory location!

Memory System

The VAX **memory system** is made up of consecutively numbered locations, each of which is capable of storing an 8-bit binary number; we will refer to such 8-bit-wide locations as **bytes.** VAX addresses are 32 bits wide; there are 2^{32} (4,294,967,296) unique combinations of 32 bits, so we should not be surprised to learn that the VAX's memory system can have 2^{32} bytes. The byte is the smallest addressable memory unit in the VAX. We can think of the VAX's memory system as an array of about 4 billion bytes. Since a byte is 8 bits wide, we can only store 8-bit numbers in a byte; the largest

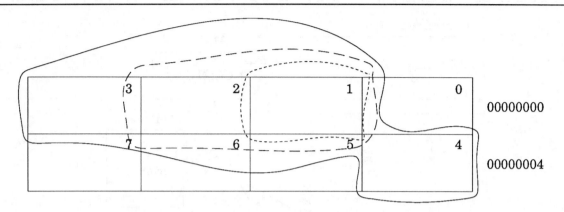

Figure 3.9 Byte-word-longword relationship in VAX's memory

8-bit number is 2^8-1 (it is 2^8-1 rather than 2^8 because we start counting at 0), or 255. What do we do if we wish to store a number larger than 255 in the VAX's memory?

The byte is the VAX's *smallest* addressable memory location, but it is not the VAX's *only* addressable memory unit. The VAX has addressable memory units of two other sizes: 16 bits and 32 bits. A 16-bit memory unit is called a **word,** and a 32-bit memory unit is called a **longword.**[3] Since consecutive bytes have addresses that differ by one and since each 16-bit unit (word) contains two 8-bit units (bytes), there are half as many words in the VAX's memory as there are bytes, and addresses of consecutive words differ by 2. Similarly, each 32-bit unit contains *four* 8-bit units, so there are four times as many bytes as there are longwords in the VAX's memory, and addresses of consecutive longwords differ by 4. Thus, we may use the VAX's memory system as an array of bytes with consecutive addresses, as an array of words with addresses differing by 2, or as an array of longwords, with addresses differing by 4.

If the VAX's memory may be used as an array of bytes *or* words *or* longwords, what are the differences between addresses of bytes, words and longwords? In short, there are none! *Any* address can be the address of a byte, a word, or a longword; the only difference between them is where the *next* byte, word, or longword would begin. For example, if 0 (or, 00000000_{16}) is the address of a byte in the VAX's memory, then the next available address, for either a byte, a word, or longword, is 1 (or 00000001; we will typically omit leading 0s, and write addresses in hexadecimal). If, however, 0 is the address of a *longword,* then (since a longword occupies 32 bits) that longword is stored in the same place that *4* bytes would be stored--the bytes with addresses 0, 1, 2, and 3--and the next available location (for either a byte, word, or longword) has address 4. Figure 3.9 shows this relationship between bytes, words, and longwords in the VAX's memory: the dotted line outlines the *byte* whose address is 00000001_{16}, the dashed line outlines the *word* whose address is 00000001_{16}, and the solid line outlines the *longword* whose address is 00000001_{16}.

Although the byte is the *smallest* addressable unit in the VAX's memory, we will find that the longword is, in one fundamental way, the *basic* addressable unit of the VAX. Namely, all addresses are 32 bits long, and a 32-bit address, of course, will not fit in either a byte or a word, but only in

---

[3]Some VAXes also have 64-bit addressable units called *quadwords* and 128-bit addressable units called *octawords.* This is one of the few cases in which not all members of the VAX family are identical.

3	2	1	0	00000000
7	6	5	4	00000004
B	A	9	8	00000008
F	E	D	C	0000000C
13	12	11	10	00000010
17	16	15	14	00000014
1B	1A	19	18	00000018
1F	1E	1D	1C	0000001C

Figure 3.10 VAX memory organization

a longword. It is important to understand that addresses of bytes, words, and longwords are *all* 32 bits long, and to understand why. Addresses must be 32 bits long because an address is exactly that: a way of telling one memory location from another. If there are 2^{32} memory locations, then it is *impossible* to give them all unique numbers (addresses) with fewer than 32 bits.

Figure 3.10 shows a picture of the VAX's memory as we will typically draw it: it is pictured as an array of longwords, with each byte being individually addressable. The right-most byte of a longword has the lowest address of the 4 bytes of that longword. The right-most byte also contains the lowest order 8 bits (numbered, from right to left, bits 0 through 7) of a 32-bit number (or the lowest order 2 hex digits of an 8-hexadecimal-digit number); we call it the **low-order** byte. The next byte, with the next highest address, contains the next 8 bits (bits 8 through 15); the third byte from the right contains bits 16 through 23, and the last byte (the **high-order** one) contains bits 24 through 31.

The memory system communicates with the CPU by sending addresses, data, and control signals along a series of wires called a **bus.** When the CPU requests the contents of a particular memory location from the memory system, it sends a **read request** to the memory system, and it sends the address of the particular location whose contents it is requesting. The memory system responds by sending the contents of that location to the CPU. When the CPU wishes to place a particular value in some location in memory, it sends a **write request** to the memory system, and then it sends the address of the location and the value to write. All of this communication occurs over the bus; on some VAXes, the bus is made up of *more than* 64 wires: 32 for addresses, 32 for data, and additional wires for the requests (**control**).

Input-Output Devices

Since the **Input and Output Devices** (I/O Devices) can't be understood until we know more about the VAX, we will defer detailed consideration of I/O until later. For the present, it is sufficient to realize that the control unit can cause bits to be transferred to the ALU or memory from any one of the various input devices, or from the ALU or memory to any one of the various output devices. Note that we are CPU-centered in describing a device as an input or output device: It is an **input** device if it provides information *to* the CPU; it is an **output** device if it accepts information *from* the CPU. We are using the acronym CPU (Central Processing Unit) to refer to the control unit and ALU as one item, or to the control unit and ALU and memory as one unit. As a general rule, I/O devices are not considered part of the CPU; in fact the common name given to I/O devices, **peripheral devices,** emphasizes their noncentral nature.

A Program Trace

Using the control panel, or a panel emulator, or some software developed specifically for loading machine-language programs, a program can be loaded into memory, a starting address can be placed in the PC, and a program's execution can be initiated.

The trace of the execution of the program shown in figure 3.7 (and, in binary, in figure 3.1) is shown in figure 3.11. If you have exclusive use of a VAX for a few minutes, you can load a program such as this into memory, and then cause it to be executed one instruction at a time. This manner of program execution is called **single-stepping.** The control unit pauses after executing each instruction, so you can examine what its effects were. Then you can cause the next instruction to be fetched and executed, and so on. It is obviously extremely time-consuming, and would normally be used only on a single-user system or if absolutely necessary, for debugging a program such as the operating system. It is of course very educational for us. The trace shown in figure 3.11 is an approximation to single-stepping; it actually provides *more* information than single-stepping a program would.

Before examining the trace in detail, we must explain what an **operand specifier** is. In the VAX, many instructions have one or more operands. For example, the add and move instructions both have two operands; the halt instruction, however, has no operands. In the VAX, there are many ways of locating operands, so each operand must have an **operand specifier.**[4] For now, we will specify operands in only one way, and so we will use only one operand specifier: $9F_{16}$. We can translate this operand specifier as, "the operand is specified by its address in memory, and its address immediately follows the operand specifier." So, although it will at first seem as if operand specifiers are unnecessary (because they are always the same--9F), we will soon see that there are many different ways of specifying operands, and that the operand specifier is critically necessary for the VAX's CPU to be able to find the correct operand(s) for each instruction. Now we are ready to examine the execution trace of our simple program as outlined in figure 3.11.

When we were working with the hypothetical computer that had an Accumulator (AC) register; the latest result was always held in the AC, so we tested the AC when we needed to know if the latest result was 0, negative, etc. In the VAX there is no AC register, but the state of the latest result produced by the ALU is reflected in the CC, so we can obtain information about it by testing the CC.

On the VAX, instructions are fetched into the IR one *unit* at a time; some units, such as opcodes and operand specifiers, are 1 byte, while others, such as addresses, are 4 bytes. Following each fetch into the IR, the control unit automatically updates the PC by adding the appropriate number to it--namely, the number of bytes just fetched--so that the PC is always either pointing to the next part of the current instruction, or pointing to the location immediately following the current instruction. Only fetches of *instructions,* from memory into the IR, cause the PC to be updated in this way. When *operands* (such as the number 0C, which was the first operand of the move instruction in figure 3.7) are fetched from memory, they are *not* placed in the IR, and so they have no effect on the PC.

---

[4]The branch instructions are exceptions to this rule. We will discuss them, and why they are exceptions, shortly.

PC	IR	Execution
200		Send for memory[PC(=200)]; request 1 byte because opcodes are 1 byte long. Update PC to 201 because requested 1 byte.
201	90	Place opcode in IR. It's a two-operand instruction, so it has two operands and two operand specifiers. Send for memory[PC(=201)] (for first operand specifier), requesting 1 byte (operand specifiers are 1 byte long); update PC to 202 (requested 1 byte).
202	90 9F	Operand specifier is 9F, sc operand's address follows. Send for memory[PC(=202)], request 4 bytes (addresses are 4 bytes long); update PC to 206 (because fetched 4 bytes).
206	90 9F 00000217	Get back 217, which is the *address* of the 1st operand. We need the *contents* of that address, so send for memory[00000217], requesting 1 byte (the opcode, 90, encodes move a *byte*). Don't update PC because it wasn't used.
206	90 9F 00000217	Get back memory[00000217], which is $0C_{16}$.
206	90 9F 00000217	Send for memory[PC(=206)]; request 1 byte for 2nd operand specifier of move instruction; update PC to 207 (fetched 1 byte).
207	90 9F 00000217 9F	Operand specifier is 9F: operand's address follows. Send for memory[PC(=207)], requesting 4 bytes (addresses are 4 bytes); update PC to 20B (207 + 4 = $20B_{16}$), since fetched 4 bytes.
20B	90 9F 00000217 9F 00000218	Get back 218, the *address* of the 2nd operand; move instruction does *not* require the contents of that address, so *execute* the instruction: send the address (00000218_{16}) to memory, with *write one byte* command, and send the byte to write ($0C_{16}$). Set CC: Z = 0, N = 0.

Execution of the move instruction is now completed.

Figure 3.11 Trace of a three-instruction program

Apart from the fact that the PC is updated by variable numbers, we see that the instruction fetch-execute cycles of the VAX and our hypothetical computer are similar. Following execution of the HALT instruction, both are left with the PC pointing to the next location after the halt. In the above example, when the HALT stops the CPU, the PC is left with the value 217, since the HALT was fetched from location 216.

PC	IR	Execution
20B		Send for memory[PC(=20B)]; request 1 byte (starting next instruction; opcodes are 1 byte). Update the PC to 20C.
20C	80	Place opcode in IR: two-operand instruction. Send for memory[PC(=20C)], requesting 1 byte (operand specifiers are 1 byte); update PC to 20D.
20D	80 9F	Get back 9F: 1st operand's address follows. Send for memory[PC(=20D)], request 4 bytes (for address); update PC to 211.
211	80 9F 00000219	Get back 219, the *address* of the 1st operand. We need the *contents* of that address, so send for memory[00000219]; ask for 1 byte (80 encodes add a *byte*). PC isn't updated because it wasn't used.
211	80 9F 00000219	Get back 02.
211	80 9F 00000219	Send for memory[PC(=211)]; request 1 byte for operand specifier of 2nd operand of add instruction. Update PC to 212.
212	80 9F 00000219 9F	Get back 9F: operand's address follows, so send for memory[PC(=212)], asking for 4 bytes (address). Update PC to 216.
216	80 9F 00000219 9F 0000021A	Get back 21A, the *address* of 2nd operand. For an add instruction, we need the *contents* of the 2nd operand's address also, so send for memory[0000021A], asking for 1 byte (80 encodes an add *byte* instruction). PC isn't updated.
216	80 9F 00000219 9F 0000021A	Get back 2F; send 2F and 02 to the ALU, telling it to add them. Get the result, 31_{16}, back from the ALU. Send address 0000021A to memory, along with command to write 1 byte, and send 31 to memory (the byte to write in location 21A). Set CC: Z = 0, N = 0.

Execution of the add instruction is now completed.

| 216 | | Send for memory[PC(=216)]; request 1 byte for next opcode. Update PC to 217. |
| 217 | 00 | Place opcode in IR and examine it: it has zero operands, so execute it: stop the instruction fetch-execute cycle. |

Execution of the program is complete.

Figure 3.11 *(cont.)*

Instruction	Mnemonic	Opcode	Action
Move byte	MOVB S, D	90	D←(S)
Move word	MOVW S, D	B0	D←(S)
Move longword	MOVL S, D	D0	D←(S)
Add byte	ADDB2 S, D	80	D←(S) + (D)
Add word	ADDW2 S, D	A0	D←(S) + (D)
Add longword	ADDL2 S, D	C0	D←(S) + (D)
Subtract byte	SUBB2 S, D	82	D←(D) − (S)
Subtract word	SUBW2 S, D	A2	D←(D) − (S)
Subtract longword	SUBL2 S, D	C2	D←(D) − (S)
Compare byte	CMPB S, D	91	(S) − (D) sets CC
Compare word	CMPW S, D	B1	(S) − (D) sets CC
Compare longword	CMPL S, D	D1	(S) − (D) sets CC
Branch if equal (to 0)	BEQL count	13	if Z = 1, PC←PC + count
Branch if positive	BGEQ count	18	if N = 0, PC←PC + count
Branch if negative	BLSS count	19	if N = 1, PC←PC + count
Jump	JMP D	17	PC←D
No operation	NOP	01	continue
Halt	HALT	00	stop

Figure 3.12 Instruction subset for the VAX

VAX Instruction Subset

The VAX has a large instruction set: opcodes are 1 byte long, so there can be 256 instructions;[5] the complete instruction set is summarized in appendixes 5 and 6. Because there are so many instructions, we will begin our study of the VAX with a manageable subset of them. We can learn many things, and write a surprisingly large number of programs, with the small subset of VAX instructions shown in figure 3.12.

The letters S and D stand for the address of the source operand and destination operand, respectively. Note that, although the instruction subset contains 18 different instructions, there are only 10 *conceptually* different ones. This is because the only difference between, for example, MOVB and MOVW is that the former copies an 8-bit quantity and the latter copies a 16-bit quantity. The same is clearly the case for the ADD(B,W,L)2, SUB(B,W,L)2 and CMP(B,W,L) instructions.

The ADD(B,W,L)2 and SUB(B,W,L)2 instructions are similar. Both assume that their two operands are in memory, and they cause the two operands to be fetched and processed by the ALU--which adds or subtracts them and updates the CC according to the result. Then they store the result in memory at the location from which the second operand (the D operand) was loaded. Thus, the second operand is called D because it is used as the *destination* for the result; it is, however, also used as the *source* for the second operand before it is used as the destination for the result. The execution

[5]Actually, some VAX instructions are 2 bytes long, so there are *more* than 256 (2^8) instructions. However, there are *fewer* than 65,536 (2^{16}) instructions. We will explain how it is possible for opcodes to be *either* 1 or 2 bytes long in a later chapter.

of an ADDB2 instruction is shown in the trace of figure 3.11; the opcode occupies location 20B, and the complete instruction is in locations 20B through 215_{16}.

The MOV(B,W,L) instructions are similar to the old LAC (load AC) instruction: they copy the source operand into the destination location and then update the CC. The difference between MOV(B,W,L) and LAC is that for the LAC instruction there is only one possible destination: the AC; for the MOV(B,W,L) instructions, however, the destination is specified explicitly, and so it can be *any* location in memory (even the same as the source!).

Since a number in the VAX's memory is considered negative if its most significant bit (msb) is 1, the setting of the N (negative) bit in the CC can be thought of as copying the msb of whatever number is being sent to the destination location, in the case of the MOV(B,W,L), ADD(B,W,L)2 or SUB(B,W,L)2 instructions. In the example of figure 3.7, executing the MOVB copies the contents of location 217 into location 218. The number copied is 0000 1100; its leftmost bit is 0, so this MOVB sets N = 0. If location 217 had contained the number 1000 1100, when the leftmost bit had been copied into the N bit, the N bit would have been 1.

Comparing two numbers can be performed by subtracting one from the other using a SUB(B,W,L)2 instruction and then using the appropriate branch instruction. However, the SUB(B,W,L)2 changes the destination operand. This can be avoided by using a CMP(B,W,L) (compare) instruction. It subtracts the destination operand from the source operand (exactly the *opposite* of the order in which SUB(B,W,L)2 treats its two operands!), but it does not store the results. The only effect the CMP(B,W,L) instruction has is to update the CC to reflect the value of the result. We will see, in chapter 7, that the rules for the setting of the CC bits are somewhat different for the CMP(B,W,L) instructions than they are for most other instructions.

The VAX has a large set of conditional branch instructions; we are examining a subset of them now. In order to use this subset, we must understand several things that are unusual about the branch instructions. First, the branch instruction may be thought of as a single-operand instruction, but its operand is *not* specified by the address of some location in memory; it is specified by a *count*, which is the number of bytes to skip (by adding that count to the PC) if the branch is taken. Second, since branch instructions can specify their operands in *only* this way, their operands do *not* need operand specifiers. The branch instructions are the *only* instructions whose operands are specified *without* operand specifiers. Third, the *count* field of the branch instruction is only 1 byte long, so a branch instruction can skip over a maximum of 256 bytes.[6]

What if we wish to skip over more bytes than a one byte count will permit? The JMP instruction specifies an address, and requires an operand specifier--just like all the other instructions in the subset of figure 3.12 (except the branches, of course). The jump can therefore place *any* address in the PC, and so we can combine a *branch on condition* with a JMP instruction and get an effect similar to that of the hypothetical computer's TMI, TPL, etc. We would have the target of the branch be a JMP instruction, and the target of the JMP be the next instruction we *really* wish to execute. This is generally not a good idea, however, because it makes understanding programs more difficult;[7] if we write well-structured programs, we can usually avoid having to branch any farther

---

[6]Actually, the branch instruction can skip over about 128 bytes in the forward direction, and 128 bytes in the backward direction. This is because the count can be either positive or negative. Since we have not yet discussed the details of the way the VAX represents negative numbers, we will use examples of branch instructions with *positive* counts only, which branch in the *forward* direction only. Positive counts cause forward branches because the PC normally gets *incremented* to go to the next instruction, which is in the memory location with the next larger address; incrementing it by a little extra will cause it to *skip* forward.

[7]Programs that make frequent use of techniques such as branching to a JMP instruction are disparagingly said to be "spaghetti code."

than a single byte count will permit. Branch and jump instructions do *not* affect the CC bits. The branch instructions examine the CC bits, but they *never* modify them.

It is often convenient to use the CMP(B,W,L) instructions in conjunction with the conditional branch instructions. For example, we may have two numbers in two locations, and wish to execute different sequences of instructions depending on whether or not the numbers are the same. If the locations are 00000201 and 00000202, we might write the following instruction sequence:

CMPB:	91
op. spec.:	9F
op. addr.:	00000201
op. spec.:	9F
op. addr.:	00000202
BEQL:	13
count:	??

The CMPB instruction subtracts the byte in location 202 from the byte in location 201, and sets the CC bits according to the result. If the two numbers are the same, then the result will be 0 ($X - X = 0$, of course) and the Z bit will be 1, and so the branch will be taken--skipping however many bytes were indicated in the *count* field of the branch instruction.

The NOP (no operation) instruction is unusual in having almost no effect; it occupies one byte and has no operands. It does cause the PC to increment in the normal way, however. We sometimes use a NOP to **patch** a machine language program that must be changed. A patch can nullify an instruction (by overwriting it with as many NOPs as necessary), and it is used to avoid the nuisance of having to rewrite the entire machine language program in order to remove a single instruction from it.

The HALT instruction is treated differently on different VAXes, depending on the operating system being used. On a single-user system, HALT causes the control unit to stop the instruction fetch-execute cycle. On a multiuser system, however, the CPU is shared among many users, and it is not considered polite to stop execution of your own program by stopping execution of all other programs as well. Therefore, on a multiuser system, HALT is a **privileged instruction**; if we place a HALT instruction in our program on such a system, the hardware will detect the fact that a nonprivileged user is trying to execute a privileged instruction, it will inform the operating system of this fact, and the operating system will abort our program. Our program will still terminate, of course, but not in a very graceful manner.

We can think of this simple instruction set as providing us with as many accumulators (ACs) as we need, since each memory location can be used as an accumulator. Computers which support **memory-to-memory** operations such as the MOV(B,W,L), ADD(B,W,L)2 and SUB(B,W,L)2 avoid the bottleneck which would otherwise be present if there were only a single accumulator. With our hypothetical computer, adding two numbers requires writing program sequences such as

```
LAC  S
ADD  D
STO  D
```

With the VAX, however, we can instead write

    ADDL2   S, D

Of course we still only have one condition code register; the CC changes after each instruction's execution (except for the branch and JMP instructions), so we can test only the results of the *last* instruction involving the ALU.

Sample Machine-Language Programs

We can now write some new programs. Counting is an important activity; we will often want to count the number of times a program segment has been executed in order to control looping. The machine language to cause something to be done four times is shown in figure 3.13; in this example, that *something* is *nothing,* because the body of the loop is NOP.

A Program Loading Program

The form of the program shown in figure 3.13 lends itself to loading by another program. If we stipulate a few simple rules of punctuation, it is reasonably easy (for someone else) to write a program which can read lines in the form of figure 3.13 from a disk file or keyboard input, process the data so that the *contents* field is loaded into memory in the location specified by the *address* field, and then initiate execution at the indicated entry point.

Address	Contents	Comment
00000200:	B0	;MOVW opcode
00000201:	9F	;op spec for src op of MOVW
00000202:	00000222	;address of src op
00000206:	9F	;op spec for dest op of MOVW
00000207:	00000220	;address of dest op
0000020B:	01	;NOP: do nothing
0000020C:	A2	;SUBW2 opcode
0000020D:	9F	;op spec for src op
0000020E:	00000224	;src address
00000212:	9F	;op spec for dest op
00000213:	00000220	;dest address
00000217:	13	;opcode for BEQL
00000218:	06	;count: skip 6 bytes
;Else, if result of subtract ≠ 0, go back and do NOP again.		
00000219:	17	;opcode for JMP
0000021A:	9F	;op spec for JMP
0000021B:	0000020B	;target of JMP
0000021F:	00	;HALT
00000220:	0000	;place for variable COUNT
00000222:	0004	;constant 4, as a word
00000224:	0001	;constant 1, for decrement
00000200		;entry point (starting address)

Figure 3.13 Machine-language program in loader-readable form

+3	+2	+1	+0	address
02	22	9F	B0*	00000200
20	9F	00	00	00000204
01*	00	00	02	00000208
02	24	9F	A2*	0000020C
20	9F	00	00	00000210
13*	00	00	02	00000214
0B	9F	17*	06	00000218
00*	00	00	02	0000021C
00	04	00	00	00000220
		00	01	00000224

Figure 3.14 Memory picture with program loaded

The rules of punctuation we have adopted are:

1. A hexadecimal address followed immediately by a colon (:) indicates that the numeric information following the colon should be loaded into memory at the specified address.
2. Addresses may be no smaller than 200_{16}, and no larger than 1200_{16}.
3. Several numbers may follow the colon; they must be hexadecimal numbers, and they must be separated by spaces. The numbers will be loaded into consecutive memory locations; the leftmost number will be loaded into the memory location specified by the address at the beginning of the line, the next number to the right will be loaded into the next available memory location, and so on. The next available memory location depends upon the size of the number loaded in the *previous* location: numbers that are two hexadecimal digits long will be loaded as bytes, 4-digit numbers will be loaded as words, and 8-digit numbers will be loaded as longwords.
4. A comment field may appear as the last item on a line by using a semicolon (;). A comment can go *anywhere* on a line, but it will always be *treated as* the last item on the line because the loader ignores everything that follows the comment character. A comment field has no effect on the loading process; blank lines are also ignored by the loader.
5. A line beginning with a hexadecimal number that is *not* immediately followed by a colon indicates the end of the program to be loaded. The specified number (the one *not* preceding a colon) will be used as the **entry point** for the program: it will be placed in the PC and execution will begin. Any lines which follow the entry point line will be ignored.
6. If two lines cause the same location to be loaded twice (by explicitly or implicitly referring to the same address), the more recent contents will overwrite the previous contents.

If you are using the loader available with this book, then you should be careful to use only addresses between 200 and 1200_{16}. The loader will inform you if it detects addresses outside of this range, it will change them (arbitrarily) to addresses inside this range, and your program will be very unlikely to work as you expect it to. If you have loaded the program shown in figure 3.13 in memory using the loader available with this book, then figure 3.14 is a picture of the VAX's memory, organized as an array of longwords with the low-order bytes on the right, showing the contents of each location. A location that contains an opcode has an asterisk (*) placed in it along with the opcode; this is just for our convenience--in memory, of course, there are only binary numbers

Address	Contents	Comment
200:	B0	;MOVW opcode
201:	9F	;op spec for src op of MOVW
202:	00000222	;address of src op
206:	9F	;op spec for dest op of MOVW
207:	00000220	;address of dest op
20B:	01	;NOP: do nothing
20C:	A2	;SUBW2 opcode
20D:	9F	;op spec for src op
20E:	00000224	;src address
212:	9F	;op spec for dest op
213:	00000220	;dest address
217:	13	;opcode for BEQL
218:	06	;count: skip 6 bytes

;Else, if result of subtract ≠ 0, go back and do NOP again.

219:	17	;opcode JMP
21A:	9F	;op spec for jump
21B:	0000020B	;target of JMP
21F:	00	;HALT
220:	0000	;place for variable COUNT
222:	0004	;constant 4
224:	0001	;constant 1, for decrementing
200		;entry point (starting address)

Figure 3.15 Machine-language program in loader-readable form

Address	Contents	Comment
200:	B0 9F 00000222 9F 00000220	;initialize count
20B:	01	;NOP: do nothing
2C:	A2 9F 00000224 9F 00000220	;decrement count
217:	13 06	;if count is 0, skip 6 bytes (JMP inst.)

;Else, if count ≠ 0, go back and do NOP again.

219:	17 9F 0000020B	;jump to NOP instruction
21f:	00	;HALT
222:	0004 0001	;data for count & decrement
200		;entry point (starting address)

Figure 3.16 Compact form of machine-language program

representing opcodes, operand specifiers, addresses, constants, and variables. Note that, if we did not know where the program began, it would be very difficult (in fact, impossible) to understand the program. For example, there is *no* difference between the *contents* of the byte whose address is 21E and those of the byte whose address is 21F, yet the latter will be treated as a HALT instruction and the former will be treated as the high-order 8 bits of an address (the target of the JMP instruction).

Figure 3.15 shows the same program that we saw in figure 3.13, except that leading (leftmost) 0s have been omitted for our convenience. The loading program detects the missing digits, and it fills in 0s to the left. This action is fairly common in many applications of computers; it is called a **zero-fill, right-adjusted** data transformation.

Figure 3.16 shows the same program, except that whole instructions, and constants loaded into consecutive memory locations, are written on a single line, with the parts separated by spaces. Note that, in figure 3.16, location 220 is not initialized at **program load time** (when the program is loaded into memory). Since the program stores the value that was in location 222 into location 220 (when the first instruction is executed) *before* it tries to use the value in location 220, there is no need to initialize this location at load time.[8]

Although the loading program will, in certain circumstances, fill in leading 0s, this feature must be used with care. The loader knows *nothing* about VAX machine language; for example, it does *not* know that the operand specifier 9F (in location 201) must be followed by an address, and that addresses are 4 bytes long. The loader is a substitute for a front panel; it provides us the convenience of using a conventional text editor rather than a front panel to compose our machine-language programs.

Figure 3.17 is a copy of a listing generated by the program-loading program that is available with this book. This listing could have been produced by any version of the program that we have seen in figures 3.13, 3.15, or 3.16. The first 4 lines of the listing contain information that we will explain later, when we know more about the VAX. The lines following those, up to the line that says "Execution begins; entry point is: 00000200," show the contents of memory just *after* the program was loaded, and just *before* execution was begun. This part of the listing is called a **memory dump.** After the initial memory dump is generated by the loading program, the execution of the program which it just loaded is initiated, using the entry point provided by the program as the starting address.

The second main part of the listing also has an initial 4 lines which we will temporarily ignore. Following those lines there is another memory dump, showing the contents of memory after the program has terminated. This second dump is often called a **post execution dump.** If we examine the post-execution dump carefully, we note that, bit-for-bit, nothing has changed since the program was loaded. This is not usually the case, but it is correct for this particular do-nothing program.

In examining the loading program's dump, we see that consecutive memory locations are printed, 16 (10_{16}) per line, in groups of four (as longwords), beginning with the address shown on the right, with higher addresses to the left. Thus the line

02249FA2 01000002 209F0000 02229FB0 : 00000200

may be read as,

---

[8]In some higher level languages, such as Pascal, all variables must be initialized while the program is running, at *run time*. In machine-language, however, we have two options; we can request that the loader initialize variable locations at load time, or we can write our programs to do it at run time.

```
Pre-execution memory dump:
PSL:   03C00000       PC:   0000148E
R0-R11, AP, FP, SP, PC:
0000020D 00001207 02229FB0 02249FA2 7FFE640C 7FFE64B4 00001207 00000008
00000003 00000000 00000226 7FFE33DC 7FF285CC 7FF28584 7FF28580 0000148E


02249FA2  01000002  209F0000  02229FB0  :  00000200
05000002  0B9F1706  13000002  209F0000  :  00000210

00000000  00000000  00000001  00040000  :  00000220
00000000  00000000  00000000  00000000  :  00000230


Execution begins; entry point is:   00000200

Post-execution memory dump:
PSL:   03C00000       PC:   0000156B
R0-R11, AP, FP, SP, PC:
00000200 00001207 02229FB0 02249FA2 7FFE640C 7FFE64B4 00001207 00000008
00000003 00000000 00000226 7FFE33DC 7FF285CC 7FF28584 7FF28580 0000156B


02249FA2  01000002  209F0000  02229FB0  :  00000200
05000002  0B9F1706  13000002  209F0000  :  00000210

00000000  00000000  00000001  00040000  :  00000220
00000000  00000000  00000000  00000000  :  00000230
```

Figure 3.17 Hexadecimal memory dumps for looping program

Address	Contents	Comment
;data		
200:	00000100 00000010 00000004	;values for 3 numbers to add
;instructions		
220:	D0 9F 00000200 9F 0000000C	;MOVL 1st number to sum
22B:	C0 9F 00000204 9F 0000000C	;ADDL2 2nd number to sum
236:	C0 9F 00000208 9F 0000000C	;ADDL2 3rd number to sum
241:	00	;HALT
220		;entry point

Figure 3.18 VAX program to add three numbers

location 200 contains B0 (first byte)
location 201 contains 9F (second byte)
location 202 contains 22 (third byte)
location 203 contains 02 (fourth byte)
location 204 contains 00 (fifth byte)
location 205 contains 00 (sixth byte)
location 206 contains 9F (seventh byte)

.
.
.

location 20F contains 02 (fifteenth byte)

Note that although the program dump prints the bytes in groups of four, as longwords, it is up to *us* to place the bytes in *meaningful* groupings. For example, we might read the dump as,

location 200 contains B0 (opcode)
location 201 contains 9F (operand specifier)
locations 202-205 contain 00000222 (address)

.
.
.

We now have a fairly convenient mechanism for writing VAX machine-language programs, which works together with the loading process. So let us proceed to rewrite some of the programs we wrote for our hypothetical computer.

The program to add three numbers can be rewritten for the VAX, and is shown in figure 3.18. This program adds three longwords, so the opcodes for longword instructions have been used, and longwords have been allocated and initialized as data. When we load and execute this program, the loader produces the pre- and post-execution dumps shown in figure 3.19. This program also shows that data may be stored above or below the instructions; where we put data is a matter of our convenience.[9]

We can generalize this program to add larger sets of numbers, using the self-modifying code technique discussed in the previous chapter. We must be careful about fetching the proper item to modify when generating a series of consecutive addresses. In the VAX, the address field is certainly *not* located in the first word of the instruction we wish to modify. Consider the program in figure 3.20. The data are loaded in locations 250, 251, 252, . . . ; the limit, which the program checks to tell whether it has added all the numbers, is determined by storing the address of the last data item, plus 1, in location 24C. Figure 3.21 shows the pre- and post-execution dumps for the looping addition program of figure 3.20. We can see that the sum, 16, is stored in location 248_{16}, and we can see that the only location in the program's instruction part that changed is the address in the longword whose address is $20D_{16}$. This address changed from 00000251_{16} to 00000253_{16}, just as it should have, because the program changed it twice, in order to add the 2 bytes at locations 251 and 252 to the one in location 248 (whose contents the program moved there from location 250). The address was 00000253 when the program terminated because we wrote the program to compare the address, after each time

---

[9]Some high-level languages (such as Pascal) insist that we write our programs so that data declarations come before instructions. This is a restriction imposed by the Pascal compiler; the VAX's hardware will work perfectly well regardless of where the data are with respect to the instructions.

```
Pre-execution memory dump:
PSL:  03C00000      PC:  0000148E
R0-R11, AP, FP, SP, PC:
0000020D 00001207 00000100 00000000 7FFE640C 7FFE64B4 00001207 00000008
00000003 00000000 00000242 7FFE33DC 7FF285CC 7FF28584 7FF28580 0000148E


00000000  00000004  00000010  00000100  :  00000200
00000000  00000000  00000000  00000000  :  00000210

0002049F  C0000002  0C9F0000  02009FD0  :  00000220
00020C9F  00000208  9FC00000  020C9F00  :  00000230

00000000  00000000  00000000  00000500  :  00000240
00000000  00000000  00000000  00000000  :  00000250


Execution begins; entry point is:  00000220

Post-execution memory dump:
PSL:  03C00000      PC:  0000156B
R0-R11, AP, FP, SP, PC:
00000220 00001207 00000100 00000000 7FFE640C 7FFE64B4 00001207 00000008
00000003 00000000 00000242 7FFE33DC 7FF285CC 7FF28584 7FF28580 0000156B


00000114  00000004  00000010  00000100  :  00000200
00000000  00000000  00000000  00000000  :  00000210

0002049F  C0000002  0C9F0000  02009FD0  :  00000220
00020C9F  00000208  9FC00000  020C9F00  :  00000230

00000000  00000000  00000000  00000500  :  00000240
00000000  00000000  00000000  00000000  :  00000250
```

Figure 3.19 Memory dumps for straight-line addition program

it changed it, with the address of the next location *after* the last data item--which is 00000253. Note that we store the constant 1, for changing the address in location $20D_{16}$, as a *longword,* and that we use the add *longword* instruction to modify the address. This is because *all* addresses are longwords, regardless of whether they are addresses of bytes, words or longwords.

When writing programs that use self-modification, we must be sure to account for *every* difference between the pre- and post-execution dumps. If we can't, then we don't understand how the program works. We should make it a habit to look for, and to account for, all changed items; if we do, we will find that our understanding of programming increases with each program we write.

We will shortly be learning about features of the VAX which make this address modification technique obsolete. We have demonstrated this primitive technique in order to illustrate the power of the simple idea that, in memory, both data and instructions are merely numbers; we can use a

Address	Contents	Comment
200:	90 9F 00000250 9F 00000248	;MOVB 1st item to sum
;this instruction is on several lines because part of it will change		
20B:	80	;ADDB2 opcode
20C:	9F	;op spec for 1st operand
20D:	00000251	;address of item to add
211:	9F 00000248	;address of sum, to add it to
;here, modify the source address in previous instruction		
216:	C0 9F 00000244 9F 0000020D	;modify src address of previous instruction
221:	D1 9F 0000020D 9F 0000024C	;compare new address to limit
22C:	13 06	;if equal: done, so skip over JMP and stop
;else, if not equal, then go back and add again		
22E:	17 9F 0000020B	;jump to ADDB2 instruction
234:	00	;HALT
244:	00000001	;constant, for changing address (of byte)
248:		;sum, uninitialized
24C:	00000253	;limit (last address + 1)
250:	01 10 05	;data to add
200		;entry point

Figure 3.20 A looping addition program

number as an instruction one time, and as data another time. It should also be clear, from the examples, that if a program happens to modify itself *by accident,* the hardware will continue to execute the program, despite the fact that it will be unlikely to make any sense whatsoever to the program's original writer. As a rule, we will avoid writing programs which modify themselves, because, when a program that is more than a few tens of bytes in length is not working, it is tedious to compare each byte in the pre-execution dump with each byte in the post-execution dump and, if it has changed, to try to figure out if the change was an intended one or an accidental one; it is more convenient to *know* that, if an instruction *ever* changes, then we have located an error in our program.

The listings of the post execution dumps shown in figures 3.17, 3.19, and 3.21 have actually been edited slightly. Each of the programs shown above used the HALT instruction to terminate, and as we have discussed, HALT is a privileged instruction on a multi-user computer. If we run the program shown in figure 3.17, for example, with the loader available with this book, then rather than terminating gracefully, with the message, "final memory dump:" (followed by the memory dump itself), our program will terminate with the message:

%SYSTEM-F-OPCDEC, opcode reserved to DIGITAL fault at PC=0000021F, PSL=03C00004

followed by several additional lines. Why will this happen? The operating system has detected that we, *un*privileged users, have tried to execute a privileged instruction, and so it has aborted our program. In the normal situation, the *loader* does more than just load our programs into memory--it also provides the pre- and post-execution memory dumps, and so, if our program terminates abnormally, the post-execution dump that the *loader* provides will *not* be executed. Rather, the

```
Pre-execution memory dump:
PSL:  03C00000        PC:  0000148E
R0-R11, AP, FP, SP, PC:
0000020D 00001207 02509F90 0002519F 7FFE640C 7FFE64B4 00001207 00000008
00000003 00000000 00000253 7FFE33DC 7FF285CC 7FF28584 7FF28580 0000148E


    0002519F   80000002   489F0000   02509F90   :   00000200
    00020D9F   00000244   9FC00000   02489F00   :   00000210

    9F170613   0000024C   9F000002   0D9FD100   :   00000220
    00000000   00000000   00000005   0000020B   :   00000230

    00000253   00000000   00000001   00000000   :   00000240
    00000000   00000000   00000000   00051001   :   00000250

    00000000   00000000   00000000   00000000   :   00000260


Execution begins; entry point is:   00000200

Post-execution memory dump:
PSL:  03C00000        PC:  0000156B
R0-R11, AP, FP, SP, PC:
00000200 00001207 02509F90 0002519F 7FFE640C 7FFE64B4 00001207 00000008
00000003 00000000 00000253 7FFE33DC 7FF285CC 7FF28584 7FF28580 0000156B


    0002539F   80000002   489F0000   02509F90   :   00000200
    00020D9F   00000244   9FC00000   02489F00   :   00000210

    9F170613   0000024C   9F000002   0D9FD100   :   00000220
    00000000   00000000   00000005   0000020B   :   00000230

    00000253   00000016   00000001   00000000   :   00000240
    00000000   00000000   00000000   00051001   :   00000250

    00000000   00000000   00000000   00000000   :   00000260
```

Figure 3.21 Memory dumps for looping addition program

operating system, in addition to aborting our program, provides us with some useful information: The contents of the PC when our program was aborted. If we examine figure 3.17, we will see that the HALT instruction was loaded into location 21F--and that was the value in the PC when our program was aborted. If, on the other hand, we don't use the HALT instruction to end our program but, rather, use the RSB (return from subroutine) instruction, then the loader will provide us with a post-execution dump, and we will not be told that we executed a reserved opcode.[10] The opcode for RSB is 05, so if we terminate our machine-language programs with 05 rather than 00, our post-execution memory dumps will look like the ones shown in figures 3.17, 3.19, and 3.21.

Common Errors

One of the most common errors is to attempt to execute a privileged instruction. Why is this so common? First, if we write self-modifying code and have an error in our program, we may easily modify some part of our program that we do not intend to. If we then try to execute a modified instruction, and we are lucky, it may be a privileged instruction; the control unit will inform the operating system, and the operating system will abort our program. Why is this the case if we are *lucky*? If we are *un*lucky, then our program will be changed to something that does not do what we want it to but still does *something*; the only way we will know that our program is not behaving correctly is by examining the contents of memory in the location specified as the contents of the PC, and looking at our program to see what we did wrong. This is unlucky because we will have no help in finding out *why* our program is behaving incorrectly. If, on the other hand, our incorrect program created and tried to execute a privileged instruction, we will be informed of this fact in a more timely (although blunt) manner.

Recall that the message from the operating system included both the contents of the PC and the contents of the PSL (Processor Status Longword). The processor status longword contains a variety of information about the status of the CPU (not surprisingly); its low-order 4 bits are the CC--N, Z, V, C, from high to low order. Thus, in the example above, the low-order hexadecimal digit of the PSL is 4, which is 0100 in binary and corresponds to the CC bit settings: N = 0, Z = 1, V = 0 and C = 0. We have already discussed the N and Z bits; we will not discuss the V and C bits until chapter 7. Figure 3.22 shows the PSL and the CC bits in it.

What if, in typing the program in figure 3.20, we typed 00100250 instead of 00000250 as the address of the source operand of the MOVB instruction loaded into locations 200 through 20A? When the control unit sends the number 00100250 to the memory system to fetch the contents of that location in order to execute the MOVB instruction, the operating system will notice that the address is too large to be a part of our program. Trying to access a memory location that is not part of our program generates a **memory access violation.**[11] In the example we are considering, the operating system would abort our program with the error message:

%SYSTEM-F-ACCVIO, access violation, reason mask = 01, virtual address = 00100250, PC = 00000200, PSL = 03C00000

If we examine the instruction beginning in the location indicated by the value in the PC, we will see that we have accidentally typed 00100250--which matches the virtual address (remember--VAX stands for Virtual Address eXtension) reported by the operating system as the cause of the access violation.

What if we forgot to provide a constant at load time? Suppose that, when typing the program in figure 3.20, we skipped the line with "244: 00000001." The loader initializes all memory locations from

---

[10]The RSB instruction, along with the special hardware support that the VAX provides for subroutines, will be discussed in detail in chapter 9.

[11]In most multiuser systems, the operating system maintains a variety of tables describing what memory locations have been allocated to what user's program. This is done, in part, to protect one user's program from being read, or written, by another user's program.

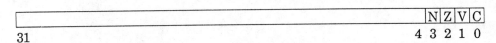

				N	Z	V	C
31 | | | | 4 | 3 | 2 | 1 | 0

Figure 3.22 Processor Status Longword (PSL), with CC bits

200 to 1200_{16} to 0 just before loading our program. Location 244 would contain the default value 0, so the address being modified would never change, and so our program would loop forever! If we were using a single-user system, we would soon notice that the program was taking a long time. If we were using a multiuser system, the operating system would likely enforce a time limit and terminate our program once that limit had been reached. If our system does not have a time limit, then our program will run until *we* terminate it.

Suppose that our program (in figure 3.20, once more) accidentally directed the loader to place 00000210_{16} into location $20D_{16}$. The program would proceed to add the items in locations 210, 211, . . . , 253! Suppose that we wrote the program so that, rather than modifying the address of the ADDB2 instruction's *source* operand, in location $20D_{16}$, it modified the address of the *destination* operand, in location 212_{16}. Our program would then add what is in location 251 (10) to each of the numbers in locations 248, 249, . . ., until it generated an address exceeding the limits of our program, and the operating system aborted our program with the access violation message.

There are many other ways that things can go wrong. Most of them can easily be avoided by careful checking *before* we run our programs. Logical errors are more difficult to find when they *don't* cause privileged instruction or access violation errors, because the hardware and software support is not very good at reading our minds and figuring out what we *meant* to do. Because machine-language programs involve such low-level, detailed understanding of the computer's workings, programs to solve very simple problems can be quite long. Since an error can be, literally, *anywhere* in a program, and since the encoding of instructions as numbers in machine-language programs is difficult for most humans to understand intuitively, machine-language programs are especially difficult to fix when they don't work. Just as we have found in writing programs in a high-level language, the more thought we put into designing a program, the less effort we'll have to put into fixing errors to make it run correctly.

Instruction Formats

The hypothetical computer we examined has an ADD instruction with only one explicitly specified operand; we have written this ADD symbolically as

   ADD S   ;AC ← (S) + (AC)

For the VAX, on the other hand, we have seen add instructions with *two* explicitly specified operands. We have symbolized these instructions as follows:

   ADD(B,W,L)2 S, D   ;D ← (S) + (D)

The VAX also has *three*-operand formats for some of its instructions (you may have wondered what

Instruction	Mnemonic	Opcode	Action
add byte 3 op	ADDB3 S_1, S_2, D	81	$D \leftarrow (S_1) + (S_2)$
add word 3 op	ADDW3 S_1, S_2, D	A1	$D \leftarrow (S_1) + (S_2)$
add longword 3 op	ADDL3 S_1, S_2, D	C1	$D \leftarrow (S_1) + (S_2)$
subtract byte 3 op	SUBB3 S_1, S_2, D	83	$D \leftarrow (S_2) - (S_1)$
subtract word 3 op	SUBW3 S_1, S_2, D	A3	$D \leftarrow (S_2) - (S_1)$
subtract longword 3 op	SUBL3 S_1, S_2, D	C3	$D \leftarrow (S_2) - (S_1)$

Figure 3.23 Three-operand instructions

the 2 meant in ADD(B,W,L)2 and SUB(B,W,L)2 instructions). Figure 3.23 shows the format, opcodes, and meanings of some of the three-operand instructions. The three-operand instructions do not change *either* of their source operands; they are designed to be used when we wish to add (or subtract) two numbers and place the result in a third location. The VAX's three-operand instructions *do not* add or subtract three numbers; they merely specify different locations for the second source operand and the result. They have three operands (and three operand specifiers), but they add and subtract only two numbers, just like the two-operand instructions.

Computers have been built (e.g., IBM 650) in which still *another* address field is used in most instructions. With this field, an ADD instruction becomes ADD S1, S2, D, NIA. The NIA field represents the "Next Instruction Address." A computer that uses this instruction format does not need a PC. Rather, each instruction explicitly specifies where its successor instruction is to come from. It's as if each instruction had a PC field built-in. This strange arrangement is a clever way of minimizing the delays introduced if you have to use a mechanical rotating storage device such as a magnetic disk or drum as your CPU's main memory. The time to fetch an item or an instruction from such a rotating memory varies according to the item's location relative to the location of the instruction currently being executed (such a memory is clearly not a RAM memory). For example, if an ADD instruction can fit into a single location on the drum, and the time to execute that instruction is just a little bit less than the time it takes for the drum to rotate past four locations, then the ideal place for the next instruction after the ADD instruction is *four* locations later: the drum will have just reached that location, and so the next instruction will be fetched into the IR with minimal delay. If, to continue the example, we place the next instruction in the location immediately after the ADD, then the control unit will have to wait for nearly one complete rotation of the drum to fetch that next instruction.

There are also computers which support arithmetic instructions with *no* explicitly specified operands. The general form of an ADD instruction for this type of computer is simply ADD; the locations of the operands and result are *implicit*. Any ADD of course needs two operands and a place to put its result. For an ADD with no explicitly specified operand, the operand values are understood to be found in a special set of locations called a **stack,** and the result of the ADD is understood to be placed in one of those special locations. The interpretation of the 0-operand ADD is: "add the numbers in the locations at the top of the stack and the next-to-top of the stack; remove those items from the stack, and place the result in the location at the top of the stack". This is illustrated in figure 3.24. You may be familiar with stacks if you have used Hewlett-Packard calculators. We will be discussing the implementation and use of stacks on the VAX in chapter 9.

We can summarize this discussion as follows: computers differ in the way they encode instructions and operands. Since all computers support arithmetic instructions such as ADD, we can

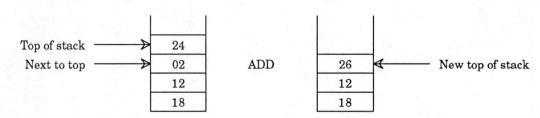

Figure 3.24 Stack before and after ADD

categorize computers according to the number of operands that must be explicitly specified for their arithmetic instructions. Some formats currently in use are:

Instruction format	Typical Computer
0-operand instruction	Hewlett-Packard 3000
1-operand instruction	UNIVAC 1100/80
2-operand instruction	VAX, IBM 4300 Series
3-operand instruction	VAX

What difference does it make if a computer uses one format rather than another? If everything else is the same, an instruction that must specify fewer operands is shorter than one that must specify more operands. The ADDB2 instruction, with both operands specified by address, requires 11 bytes: 1 for the opcode, 1 for each operand specifier, and 4 for each address. A comparable ADDB3 instruction requires 16 bytes: the same 11 bytes of the two-operand instruction, plus an additional 1 for the third operand specifier and an additional 4 for the third address. The operands' addresses take up four times as much memory as do the operand specifiers; if we could specify operands without storing their addresses in the instructions, we would reduce the length of instructions significantly.

We will soon see that we can do exactly that; as we have said, each operand requires an operand specifier because there are many ways to specify an operand. Some of those ways, we will see, allow us to write programs for the VAX that are nearly as short as those for computers using 0- or 1-operand instruction formats; the VAX has some sophisticated capabilities.

VAX Instruction Summary

We have been using VAX instructions that are either data-oriented or control-oriented. We classify them on this basis in figure 3.25. We have also discussed 0-, 1-, 2-, and 3-operand instructions; figure 3.26 shows the VAX instruction subset we have seen classified according to number of operands. As we proceed to examine the other VAX instructions, we will discover distinctions among the data-oriented instructions, and we will introduce more sophisticated instructions in all categories. The classes themselves will also be refined, as we shall see in chapter 10.

Data-oriented	Control-oriented
MOV(B,W,L)	JMP
ADD(B,W,L)[2,3]	BEQL
SUB(B,W,L)[2,3]	BGEQ
CMP(B,W,L)	BLSS
	NOP
	HALT

Figure 3.25 Classification of VAX instructions by function

Number of operands			
0	1	2	3
NOP	JMP	ADD(B,W,L)2	ADD(B,W,L)3
HALT	BEQL	SUB(B,W,L)2	SUB(B,W,L)3
	BLSS	CMP(B,W,L)	
	BGEQ	MOV(B,W,L)	

Figure 3.26 Classification of VAX instructions by number of operands

Summary

There are many members of the VAX family of computers. Like most computers, they all use binary representations for their instructions and data. Binary is awkward for people to deal with, so when binary is used by the computer, VAX software translates it into hexadecimal. Hexadecimal is easier for us to deal with, and it does not obscure the computer's design details as would be the case if we did everything in decimal.

The basic features of VAX organization follow. Its fundamental unit of information is the 32-bit longword, but 8- and 16-bit data items can be operated on as well. Consecutive bytes have addresses that differ by 1, consecutive words have addresses that differ by 2, and consecutive longwords have addresses that differ by 4. All memory addresses are 32 bits long. The VAX's ALU does not center around a single accumulator: every memory location can be used as an accumulator. A special location, the **Processor Status Longword** (PSL), reflects the status of the latest product of the ALU in its low-order four bits, the **Condition Code** (CC) bits. The two CC bits we have dealt with are the N (Negative) bit and the Z (Zero) bit.

Loading VAX machine-language programs c be facilitated by using a program-loading program. The machine-language programs are presented to the loading program in a form that is very much like that seen in a computer memory listing, or memory dump. A post-execution dump shows the state of a program's memory immediately after its execution terminates. When a program terminates because of an error (rather than by normal termination), the VMS operating system reports the value in the PC, which is the address of the instruction which triggered the error detected by the control unit.

Computers can be classified according to the number of addresses they use to explicitly specify operands of their arithmetic instructions. According to this classification, the VAX seems to use a 2-address and 3-address instruction format. We will soon see that it can also appear otherwise.

Exercises for Chapter 3

1. Some pairs of arithmetic bases are especially easy to convert between. This is one reason that we use hexadecimal (rather than decimal) for the VAX, when we don't want to use binary (which is the base that the computer uses). The following table contains some entries under the *binary* heading, and some under *hexadecimal.* Fill in the missing entries by converting from binary to hexadecimal, or from hexadecimal to binary.

binary	hexadecimal
0101010011001	
1000	
	1000
	6F
1111111	
	11111111
1001011	
10101010101010101010101010101	
	EFFEE
	EEFFE

2. Explain why K represents the number 1024 in the world of computers while it usually means exactly 1000 in the metric world.
3. What is the largest address you can write for the VAX? Write it in (a) binary; (b) decimal; (c) hexadecimal; (d) K-units.
4. Write the following binary numbers as decimal numbers:

    a. 11001
    b. 10101
    c. 10001
    d. 11111111

5. Perform the following binary additions:

    a. 11001   b.   10101   c.   11001
        10101   10001   10001

6. What bit pattern do all *even* binary numbers have in common?
7. If the BGEQ instruction began malfunctioning on your computer, how could you use the other instructions to create this instruction? Write one or more specific sequences of instructions.
8. Is the ADD family of instructions essential? If not, show how a program could replace any ADD instruction with a sequence of other, existing instructions.
9. Why is it useful to have both the SUB and the CMP families of instruction? If you had to sacrifice one, which would it be? Show exactly what you would use in its place.
10. You can convert decimal numbers into binary numbers by using the following algorithm: Given a number n, find the largest power of 2, pot, which is smaller than n. Then find the difference

between n and pot and call it n': n' prime <-- n pot. Record the number pot in binary; it will necessarily have only one 1 in it. Repeat the procedure beginning with n', which produces pot': n' <-- n' pot', etc. Stop when n'''. . .' is 0 (is this guaranteed to occur?). Finally, add pot, pot', . . ., to obtain the binary representation of the decimal number.

For example, given $n = 5$:

$5-2^4$: does not fit

$5-2^3$: does not fit

$5-2^2$: fits!

so:

$n' \leftarrow 5 - 4; n' = 1$, and $pot = 2^2 = 4 = 100_2$.

Repeat with $n' = 1$; find $pot' = 2^0 = 1$.

Then add $pot =$ 100
$+ pot' =$ 001
                101

Result: 101 binary = 5 decimal.

Using this algorithm, find the binary equivalents of the following decimal numbers:

a. 129   b. 55   c. 100   d. 512   e. 35

11. Part of the hexadecimal addition table is:

+	0	1	2	3	4	5	6	7	8	9	A	B	C	D	E	F
0	0	1	2	3	4	5	6	7	8	9	A	B	C	D	E	F
1	1	2	3	4	5	6	7	8	9	A	B	C	D	E	F	10
2	2	3	4	5	6	7	8	9	A	B	C	D	E	F	10	11
3	3	4	5	6	7	8	9	A	B	C	D	E	F	10	11	12
4	4	5	6	7	8	9	A	B	C	D	E	F	10	11	12	13
5	. . .															
.																
.																
.																
F	. . .															

a. Fill in the missing parts: complete all 256 entries in the table.

b. Using the addition algorithm described in the text, find the sums of the following hexadecimal numbers:

(1)   123   (2)   FF0   (3)   0FE   (4)   222
      321   123   FA6   EEE

12. What are the largest hexadecimal numbers representable in a VAX byte, word, and longword? What are their decima l equivalents? What are these numbers in K-units?

13. According to the behavior of the loading program we have been using, what would be in memory locations 200-208 after the following file had been processed by the loading program?

    0202: 1 2 3
    0200: 4 5
    0206: 6 7 10
    0200: 11 12
    0207: 13

14. If the VAX's control unit finds 0000001A following 9F in its IR, how does it know if the address refers to the *byte* at that location, the *word* beginning at that location, or the *longword* beginning at that location?

15. You can always expect memory locations to contain 0s until you change them: True or False? Explain your answer.

16. What is a post execution dump? What is it used for?

17. Write a VAX hexadecimal machine-language program which adds 4 longword data items stored in memory locations 250 through 25C; show a format of the program that would be acceptable by our program-loading program.

18. What would the loader do if you asked it to place the number 432_{16} in the location immediately following the opcode for the BLSS instruction? What would the control unit do?

19. How can a JMP instruction have an illegal destination address?

20. Can a conditional branch instruction ever *directly* cause a run-time error? Explain your answer. Can a conditional branch instruction ever *indirectly* cause a run-time error? Explain this answer, too.

21. How many bytes must the control unit read from and write to memory in order to fetch and execute a MOVB instruction using the 9F operand specifier? Explain your answer.

22. If you are running on a multiuser system, does your operating system impose an execution time limit on you? If so, what is its default setting, and how can you change it? If not, how do you terminate a program you suspect may be in an infinite loop?

23. Rewrite the pay program in figure 2.12 for the VAX, assuming the pay rate is 5. Why would such a program be inefficient for larger pay rates?

24. Compare the program you wrote in the preceding problem, with the program in figure 2.12. Assume that 1 hypothetical computer (HC) word is equivalent to 1 longword. Ignoring the data, are the programs of comparable length? How much difference does the 1-address instruction format of the HC make when compared with the 2-address instruction format of the VAX instruction subset you are working with?

25. Write a VAX machine-language program that uses self modifying code to move an array of consecutive words stored beginning at location 200 to location 300_{16}. Your program should move words until it encounters a word containing 0; you may move the word containing 0 or not, as you find convenient. Your program should not use a count to determine how many words to move. How will your program know when it has encountered a word of 0? Must it use a CMPW instruction?

    Run your program, and examine the pre- and post-execution dumps. Account for every difference between them, and explain, for each change, if it is a change of data or of an instruction.

26. The designers of the VAX software chose to represent all the binary numbers using hexadecimal. On the PDP-11, DEC's predecessor to the VAX, octal, or base 8, is used. In octal, the legal digits are 0-7; digits in successive positions represent successive powers of 8, and each octal digit can represent the same number of values as 3 bits. Thus, 40_{16}, which is $0100\ 0000_2$, would be 100_8. Similarly, $FFFF_{16}$, which is $1111\ 1111\ 1111\ 1111_2$, would be 177777_8.

Combine what you know about number systems in general with this brief description of base 8 in particular, and rewrite the first machine-language program of this chapter in octal.

27. The following table contains numbers in bases 2, 3, 8, 10, and 16, with only some entries filled in. Each row should contain the representations, in the various bases, of the *same* number. Complete the table. (Hint: In order to convert from base 3 to base 2, you may find it easier to convert from base 3 to base 10, and then from base 10 to base 2.)

binary	ternary	octal	decimal	hexadecimal
	2121			
11100011				
		7453		
				33E
1000				
	1000			
			9999	
			2048	
		1000		
			1000	
				1000

28. You are working in base 13; the legal digits are 0-9, !, @, and #. Convert the following numbers to decimal:

base 13	base 10
##@#	
9	
10	
100	
1000	
!#	
!5	
!!!	
393	
913	

29. If there are only 1/4 as many longwords as bytes in the VAX's memory, and only 1/2 as many words as bytes, then why aren't longword addresses 30 bits long, and word addresses 31 bits long?

30. What would happen if, in the program shown in figure 3.20, we accidentally replaced the $C0_{16}$ in location 216_{16} with 80_{16}? What *could* happen?

4

Assembly Language: A Better Way

Introduction

Programmers in the 1950s discovered that many of the low-level details and decisions involved in writing machine-language programs could be handled by a special computer program. In particular, writing out opcodes often involves repeated look-up in a table, and keeping track of addresses is tedious and error-prone. The program which does this for us, called an **assembler,** accepts as input a *symbolic* representation of a machine-language program, containing pseudo-English **mnemonics**[1] for opcodes, and referring to operands by *names* rather than addresses. This symbolic representation that a programmer writes is called an **assembly language program**; the version that the programmer provides to the assembler for processing is called the **source module.** The assembler translates its input, the source module, and produces a machine-language program called an **object module** as output. The object module is then processed by a linking and loading program, which is how the machine-language program is loaded into memory and executed. The transformation that an assembly language program undergoes when it is processed by an assembler is shown in figure 4.1

This process is similar to the one used in writing programs in high-level languages; the FORTRAN or Pascal compilers perform the function of the assembler and translate programs from a symbolic form (HLL) to an executable form (machine language). For the VAX, the assembler we will use is called **Macro.** A hand-written symbolic program can be made into an assembler-readable source module in any one of a variety of ways: by punching cards (using a keypunch), punching paper tape (using a teleprinter with a tape punch), or by typing on a CRT or other on-line terminal (using an interactive editor which stores the source module on a disk). This last method is becoming more and more common; as recently as the early 1980s, however, it was much less common than the others.

Let us look now at the flow of information in taking a program from its representation as a source module to a running machine-language program in memory, as shown in figure 4.2. This process may seem complicated, but it has a number of important benefits. First of all, we humans avoid the difficulty of writing machine-language programs. Second, when the assembler writes its output on a disk file, it can process a larger program than it would be able to if it placed the machine-language output directly in the computer's memory. The main memory of a computer

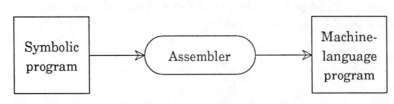

Figure 4.1 Assembling a source module

---

[1] *Mnemonic* means "memory assisting"; it comes from the Greek word *mnemon,* which means "memory."

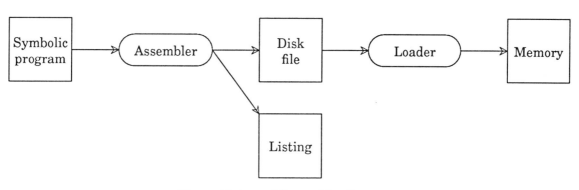

Figure 4.2 Assembling and loading a program

typically has fewer locations than does its disk memory, and memory size is what limits the size of a program. Finally, if we save the object module on a disk, we can rerun it later without reassembling it.

The simple loader we are considering here takes the assembler's output in a disk file, turns it into an executable program, places it into memory, and then transfers control to this copy in memory (by placing the address of its first instruction in the PC). We can achieve even greater advantages if we divide the processing that follows the assembler's work into one more step; we will discuss this step (called **linking**) later.

Macro Source Statements

Let us now focus on the VAX's assembler. What kind of input does it accept, what kind of output does it produce, and how can we use it intelligently? Macro processes input source modules consisting of a series of lines, each of which has the following format:

      <label:> <operation>   <operand list> <;comment>

The fields appearing inside the angle brackets "<" and ">", are *optional*: a line need not have a label, but if it has one, the label must be followed by a colon. In fact, *all* fields are optional; this suggests that a *blank* line might be acceptable input: it is. The fact that all fields are optional should not lead you to think that Macro accepts free format input: if an operation requires one or more operands, then they *must* follow the operation, (*on the same line,* as a rule); if a line has a label, the label *must* be the first field of that line, and it refers to that line *only*. If the operand list contains more than one operand, the operands *must* be separated by commas. Note that this is very different from modern high-level languages like Pascal, which are not particularly line-oriented. An assembler is not as complex a program as a Pascal compiler, however, so it is more restrictive in its input format requirements.

The comment field has no effect on the assembly process; any text to the right of a semicolon will only be echoed in the assembler listing. Statements containing nothing but comments can have the ";" in *any* position, including the leftmost. When preparing a source module, it is convenient to use the horizontal tab (usually associated with the key labeled *tab*) to separate the fields; this helps make a program readable.

	.ENTRY	label, 0
<label:>	.BLKB	count
<label:>	.BLKW	count
<label:>	.BLKL	count
<label:>	.BYTE	value
<label:>	.LONG	value
<label:>	.WORD	value
	.END	<label>

Figure 4.3 Some assembler directives

The operation field may contain either an instruction mnemonic such as MOV(B,W,L) or ADD(B,W,L)[2,3], or a new type of item which is used to direct the assembler in its work. This type of item is a **directive**; it is also sometimes called a **pseudo-op.**

Figure 4.3 is a list of some of the directives recognized by Macro. We can see that these directives begin with a period (.). This convention helps avoid confusion between instructions and directives, since no instruction mnemonics begin with a period; let us consider the directives in figure 4.3 in turn. All the directives in figure 4.3 use uppercase letters; uppercase is used in this example-- and in others--for purely historical reasons that date back to the time when punched cards (that encoded only the uppercase letters) and terminals with only uppercase letters were commonly used. Macro and the VMS operating system make no distinction between upper and lowercase, and every example would work exactly the same in lowercase as it does in uppercase.

.ENTRY

The .ENTRY directive is special: It should appear in *every* program we write. Macro searches for a line containing .ENTRY, associates with it the label specified as its first argument, and passes along its location to the loader, which uses it as the entry point. Thus, .ENTRY should be on the line before the first instruction we wish to have executed.[2]

The 0 which follows the label results in a word (16 bits) of 0 being allocated by the assembler. VAX subroutines begin with a 16-bit quantity (not necessarily 0), and our main program is treated as a subroutine by the operating system, so it, too, begins with a 16-bit quantity. This quantity (called a **register save mask**), and subroutines in general, are described in chapter 9.

Since VAX support software provides for independent assembly of subroutines and main programs, a convention has to be adopted to inform the support software as to which module is the main program (i.e., which module should be the first to be executed) when a complete program is constructed from a set of modules. When we write a main program in assembly language, we inform the support software that this source module is the main program by placing the line .ENTRY in that module. Only one module should have .ENTRY in it, and that module will be treated as the main program. Any module without .ENTRY will be assumed by the assembler to be called by some other module or modules, probably because it is written as a subroutine. We will discuss independent assembly, also, in chapter 9.

---

[2]This is similar to the use of the key word *begin* in Pascal.

.END

The .END directive should appear on the last line of an assembly language source program; it informs the assembler that this is the last line to be processed. If the module contains a main program (if it has an .ENTRY directive in it), then the .END directive should have an argument; that argument should be the same label as that specified for the .ENTRY directive.

.LONG, .WORD, and .BYTE

The .LONG, .WORD and .BYTE directives allow us to write decimal constants of varying sizes--a longword, a word, or a byte, respectively--and have them loaded into memory as part of our program. So, if we wish to use the constant 15 (decimal) as a byte, we can write

    .BYTE 15

If we wish to store 15 as a longword, we use the .LONG directive, with the same operand. Note that the default radix of the assembler is *decimal*; if we wish to specify a constant in hexadecimal, we must use the ^X prefix. So,

    .BYTE 15

will store the bit pattern 0000 1111 in a 1-byte memory location; however,

    .BYTE ^X15

will store the bit pattern 0001 0101 in a byte.

    Where in memory will these bit patterns be stored? Recall that when we wrote machine-language programs, we specified the location in which we wished each item to be stored by writing its address (followed by a colon) as the leftmost field of a line. How did we know what address to write in that field? We counted! Recall, also, that counting addresses was one of the most tedious and error-prone aspects of machine-language programming. In assembly language, *we* don't count, but the assembler does. The assembler, in the process of translating our assembly language programs into machine language, does exactly the same kinds of calculations that we did when we wrote machine-language directly: it starts allocating memory for our program at location 0, and knows, for example, that an opcode is 1 byte long, that an operand specifier is 1 byte long, that an address is 4 bytes long, etc. So, the assembler keeps track of how many bytes long a program is at any given time, and when it comes to a directive like .LONG 15, it places the bit pattern 0000 0000 0000 0000 0000 0000 0000 1111 into the next available memory location.

    If we wish to load values into several consecutive bytes (or words or longwords), we can either use several directives, each with a single operand, or we can use a single directive with an **operand list**. For example, if we wish to store the values 8, 5, and 11 (decimal) in consecutive bytes, we can write *either* :

    .BYTE   8
    .BYTE   5
    .BYTE   11

or we can write the single line:

    .BYTE   8, 5, 11

Symbolic Labels

Usually, we store values in memory in order to use them. In machine language, we use values in memory by specifying their addresses, and we know their addresses because we have counted them. One of the major advantages of assembly language over machine language, however, is that we no longer have to count addresses. Assembly language allows us to associate a **symbolic label** with a particular memory location, and when we wish to use the value stored in that location, we simply refer to it by its label.[3] For example, if we wish to use the number 12, we might write the following line in our assembly language program:

TWELVE: .BYTE 12

When a label appears as the leftmost item on a line, followed by a colon, we say that the label is being **defined.** Any use of the label TWELVE as an operand of an instruction will cause the assembler to generate machine language containing the *address* of the location in memory that has been assigned to it by the assembler. Each label we use must be defined somewhere in our program, and we can only provide one such definition. If TWELVE: were to appear more than once in the same program, Macro would have no way of knowing which address to substitute in the machine language it is generating, so it would complain that the label TWELVE has been redefined.

.BLKL, .BLKW, and .BLKB

The .BLKL, .BLKW, and .BLKB directives tell the assembler to reserve one or more longwords, words, or bytes of memory; how many is indicated in the *count* field that is the directive's operand. As usual, the operand is a decimal number; if we wish to reserve 10 longwords, we would write

.BLKL 10

We may wish to provide a label for a *block* of memory locations, so that our program can refer to it. For instance,

SUM: .BLKB 1

causes Macro to instruct the loader to allocate 1 byte of memory; any other reference to SUM in the program is understood by the assembler to mean the corresponding address. The assembler, in generating machine language, replaces the symbolic label SUM, which the memory system couldn't possibly understand, with a binary address, which the memory system can understand perfectly. If we reserve several locations with the .BLK(B,W,L) directive, the label associated with the directive will be the address of the *first* of these locations. If we wish to refer to the second longword, for example, of a series of ten that we allocated with the line,

BUNCH: .BLKL   10

we could use the symbolic label in a simple arithmetic expression. Macro will understand BUNCH+4 to mean, "calculate the address of BUNCH, add 4 to it, and place *that* address in the machine-language

---

[3]This is reminiscent of variable *names* in higher level programming languages, but--as we will soon see--is also different from them in some important details.

program that is being generated". Similarly, if we have allocated a series of bytes with the statement,

    STUFF: .BLKB   6

and we wish to refer to the byte just preceding the first one at location STUFF, we can use the expression STUFF-1.

It is important to note that .LONG, .WORD, and .BYTE reserve memory locations *and* ask the loader to initialize them--at load time--while .BLKL, .BLKW, and .BLKB reserve locations but do not initialize them.[4] We must also realize that if we *read* a value from a location that was allocated with a .BLK(B,W,L) directive, and our program has not yet assigned it a value, then we will read some unpredictable value--whatever happens to be the bit pattern stored in that memory location. Therefore, in assembly language (just as in higher level languages), we must be sure to initialize variables *before* we use them. Programs that do not initialize variables will compute with unknown values and will, therefore, have unpredictable results.

Operand Specifiers

We are almost ready to write an assembly language program. We know the general format of the lines the assembler can translate, we know that we will use labels rather than addresses to refer to operands, and we know that we will use mnemonics rather than binary (or hexadecimal) opcodes for instructions. However, what about operand specifiers? Just as we must tell the assembler that we want it to generate the opcode 90_{16} (or 1001 0000 binary) by typing the mnemonic MOVB in our assembly language program, so we must tell it to generate the operand specifier $9F_{16}$ (or 1001 1111 binary) by typing "@#" in front of each use of a symbolic label as an operand (see figure 4.4). Later, in chapter 6, we will learn about more of the VAX's **addressing modes,** and we will learn about some of the other operand specifiers and how they are written in both machine and assembly language.

Complete Source Programs

We can put all of these ideas to work by considering a program to add two numbers. Suppose the two numbers are 1 and 10 decimal. We can compose our program on a sheet having columns with the indicated headings. We can make up symbolic labels, say VAL1 and VAL2, for the two constants, use .BYTE directives, and place them at the beginning of the program. Then, we can use the .BLKB directive to reserve a byte for the result and give it the name SUM.

We begin the instruction part of the program with .ENTRY, use the MOVB and ADDB2 instructions to perform the arithmetic, and use the HALT instruction to terminate execution. The complete program is shown in figure 4.4.

When an opcode has two or more operands, the operands in the operand list must be separated by commas--as in the MOVB @#VAL1, @#SUM and ADDB2 @#VAL2, @#SUM instructions, and as when we provide more than one operand for a single .BYTE (for example) directive. All of the labels we used (VAL1, VAL2, SUM) are more or less arbitrary; they must obey some simple conventions, which

---

[4]Pascal, for example, allows only memory *allocation* at load time--similar to the .BLK(B, W, L) directives. In Pascal, all variable *initialization* must be done at run time.

Label	Operation	Operand(s)	Comment
VAL1:	.BYTE	1	;first data item
VAL2:	.BYTE	10	;second data item
SUM:	.BLKB	1	;1 byte for sum
;Execution begins here			
	.ENTRY	START, 0	;entry point
	MOVB	@#VAL1, @#SUM	;put 1st number in SUM, to add
	ADDB2	@#VAL2, @#SUM	;add 2nd number
	HALT		
	.END	START	

Figure 4.4 Assembly language source module

are similar to those of many high-level languages, and we should choose them to help us understand their role in our programs. The conventions that Macro expects for symbolic labels are:

1. Only letters, digits, underscore (-), period (.), and dollar ($) may be used in labels.
2. The first character may not be a digit.
3. Labels may be up to 31 characters long.

If we attempt to define or use a name with any other character in it (such as a space, a tab, punctuation, etc.), Macro will produce an error diagnostic. Since some of the VAX support software uses $ and "." in its labels, it is wise to avoid using these characters in the labels we define. We can even make up and use names such as MOVB, ADDB2, etc. Macro will not be confused, and will generate correct machine language using those labels. However, since our goal is to write *clear* programs, they should be used *only* as instruction mnemonics, in the operation field.[5]

Macro allows us to place data either before or after instructions. Thus, we could assign new names and also change the order of the lines in the last program, and rewrite the program of figure 4.4 as shown in figure 4.5. This program will produce the same results as the previous version, although instead of placing the sum in the third byte of the program (address 2, since we start with address 0), this program will store the sum in the *last* byte (the one labeled SUM).

Reading an Assembler Listing

As far as running a program is concerned, the most important output of the assembler is the machine-readable, machine-language object module. However, if requested, the assembler also produces another module as output; this module is only a byproduct of the assembler's job of creating an object module, but it is an extremely helpful byproduct, as far as human programmers are concerned. This output is the **assembly listing,** or printout. Consider the source module shown in figure 4.6 (the hand-coded machine-language equivalent of this assembly language program is shown in figure 3.7). The Macro listing of this program is reproduced in figure 4.7.

---

[5]This will avoid confusing mere mortals, such as fellow programmers.

Label	Operation	Operand(s)	Comment
	.ENTRY	START, 0	;entry point
	MOVB	@#FIRST, @#SUM	;put 1st number in SUM, to add
	ADDB2	@#SECOND, @#SUM	;add 2nd number
	HALT		
;Data for the program follow			
FIRST:	.BYTE	1	;first data item
SECOND:	.BYTE	10	;second data item
SUM:	.BLKB	1	;1 byte for sum
	.END	START	

Figure 4.5 Assembly language source module

Label	Operation	Operand(s)	Comments
	.TITLE	PROG4.1	
	.ENTRY	START, 0	;entry point
	MOVB	@#SRC, @#DST	;move byte
	ADDB2	@#VAL, @#SUM	;add bytes
	HALT		;stop
SRC:	.BYTE	12	;'s' of MOVB
DST:	.BYTE	0	;'d' of MOVB
VAL:	.BYTE	2	;'s' of ADD
SUM:	.BYTE	47	;'d' of ADD
	.END	START	

Figure 4.6 Assembly language source module

It is important to study this listing carefully, as much of our work from now on will involve understanding Macro listings. We notice that the text of the source module is reproduced in the listing; it always appears to the right of the information generated by Macro. The best way to examine the listing is from the middle, in both directions (not simultaneously!). If we begin in the middle, we see a column for line numbers, beginning with 1. These are consecutive decimal line numbers assigned by Macro as it reads lines of our source module; they have no effect on the assembling or executing of our program.

The next column to the left is the address column. As Macro processes each line of our source module, it anticipates having to allocate one or more memory locations to store the instruction or the data items it will encounter on that line. The address column shows what address Macro is assigning to the first item on that line. This field is also called the **location counter field**: Macro counts locations in memory which it has allocated in order to know which location is next to be allocated; the **location counter** thus tracks the assembler's generation of machine language at assemble-time. The field to the left of the address column shows what machine-language Macro has generated for the assembly language statement on that line.

```
PROG4.1             9-SEP-1987 14:13:37  VAX/VMS Macro V04-00        Page    1
                    9-SEP-1987 14:12:23  SYS$USER:[PB.CHAPTER4]P41.MAR;2   (1)


                            0000  1          .TITLE  PROG4.1
                      0000  0000  2          .ENTRY  START, 0        ;entry point
0000001A'9F 00000019'9F 90 0002  3          MOVB    @#SRC, @#DST    ;move byte
0000001C'9F 0000001B'9F 80 000D  4          ADDB2   @#VAL, @#SUM    ;add bytes
                        00 0018  5          HALT
                        0C 0019  6  SRC: .BYTE  12     ;'s' of MOVB
                        00 001A  7  DST: .BYTE  0      ;'d' of MOVB
                        02 001B  8  VAL: .BYTE  2      ;'s' of ADD
                        2F 001C  9  SUM: .BYTE  47     ;'d' of ADD
                           001D 10          .END START


PROG4.1             9-SEP-1987 14:13:37  VAX/VMS Macro V04-00        Page    2
Symbol table        9-SEP-1987 14:12:23  SYS$USER:[PB.CHAPTER4]P41.MAR;2   (1)

DST                 0000001A R      01
SRC                 00000019 R      01
START               00000000 RG     01
SUM                 0000001C R      01
VAL                 0000001B R      01

There were no errors, warnings or information messages.

MACRO/LIST P41
```

Figure 4.7 Assembler listing from source module

The first address is 0000, and the content of that location is a word containing 0; this is the register save mask that we described above in discussing the .ENTRY directive. The next address is 0002 (the 4 leading hexadecimal digits, which are all 0, have been omitted), because the word of 0000 occupies locations 0 and 1. The machine language that the assembler has generated is for the MOVB instruction, which occupies 11_{10} bytes: 1 for the opcode, 1 for each of the two operand specifiers, and 4 for each of the 2 addresses. Since the first memory location allocated has address 0000, and since the current instruction begins at address 0002 and requires 11 bytes, the address of the next available location is $000D_{16}$. So, when Macro reads the second line, it is ready to allocate location 000D for the opcode of the ADDB2 instruction. Since the ADDB2 instruction also takes up 11 bytes, when we get to line 4, the address field is 18 (hexadecimal!).

Macro always begins allocating memory locations starting with location 0, but our programs are always **relocated,** and loaded starting at address 200_{16}. We need not fear, however, that this will conflict with other users who may wish to run programs at the same time that we run ours, using the same locations that the assembler appears to have assigned to our program. This is because the

VMS loader (which is invoked when we type RUN followed by a program's name) ensures that our program is placed in some memory locations that are not being used by any other program.[6]

The rest of the listing shows the hexadecimal representation of the translation that Macro has made of our assembly language program in turning it into a machine-language program, which Macro then stores in the object module.

After the last line of our source program (which contains the .END directive, for which the assembler generates no machine language and allocates no memory), there is a **symbol table.** Each label we used in the program appears in this table, along with the address of the memory location assigned to it.

After Assembling, What Do We Do?

Macro produces an object module which contains the machine-language translation of the source module, information about the size of the machine-language translation and about where instructions should ultimately be loaded in memory, and additional information about any other object modules that may be referred to by the one currently being assembled. In order to understand more fully the process whereby a source module is transformed into a **load module** which can be loaded into memory and executed, we must understand two additional stages of processing, one of which *precedes* the assembler's translation of mnemonics into machine-language, and the other of which *follows* that translation. The first is called **macro expansion** and the second is called **linking**; we will discuss each of them in turn.

Macro Expansion

A macro is a series of assembly language statements which is given a name. It is a simple text-substitution process: whenever we wish to write a given set of assembly language statements, we simply write the macro's name instead. Of course, we (or, *someone*) must first **define** the macro; defining a macro is the process of making sure that its name is associated with a particular set of assembly language statements. Then, when we **invoke** the macro, the program which performs macro expansion (in this case, the assembler) recognizes that some particular name is a macro, looks up (in a table in which it maintains such information) the definition of the macro, and *substitutes* the definition for the name. Once all macros have been expanded, Macro begins translating the source module into machine language.

If our source module is in a file called PROGRAM1.MAR, and if we are using the VMS operating system and the software available with this book, then we assemble our file by typing

MACRO/LIST PROGRAM1.MAR[7]

---

[6]Recall that, in the beginning of chapter 3, we briefly discussed *virtual addresses.* The assembler, and all of the support software we use--which will be described shortly--provides us with virtual addresses. The operating system (VMS) changes them into real (or physical) addresses when our program is actually loaded into memory.

[7]Using the conventions of the VMS operating system, PROGRAM1 is the file name, and .MAR is the file type. In particular, MAR indicates that the file contains source statements to be processed by the Macro assembler.

Label	Opcode	Operand(s)	Comments
	.TITLE	PROG4.2	
	.SHOW	ME	
	.DISABLE	GLOBAL	
	.ENTRY	START, 0	;entry point
	MOVB	@#SRC, @#DST	;move byte
	ADDB2	@#VAL, @#SUM	;add bytes
	$EXIT_S		;stop program
SRC:	.BYTE	12	;'s' of MOVB
DST:	.BYTE	0	;'d' of MOVB
VAL:	.BYTE	2	;'s' of ADD
SUM:	.BYTE	47	;'d' of ADD
	.END	START	

Figure 4.8 Source module with macro

```
PROG4.2         9-SEP-1987 14:13:45   VAX/VMS Macro V04-00        Page    1
                9-SEP-1987 14:12:57   SYS$USER:[PB.CHAPTER4]P42.MAR;4    (1)

                            0000  1      .TITLE   PROG4.2
                            0000  2       .SHOW     ME
                            0000  3      .DISABLE GLOBAL
                     0000   0000  4      .ENTRY START, 0       ;entry point
00000022'9F 00000021'9F 90 0002  5        MOVB  @#SRC, @#DST ;move byte
00000024'9F 00000023'9F 80 000D  6        ADDB2 @#VAL, @#SUM ;add bytes
                            0018  7        $EXIT_S
                            0018            .GLOBL  SYS$EXIT
                     01 DD  0018            PUSHL  #1
       00000000'GF 01 FB    001A            CALLS  #1,G^SYS$EXIT
                            0021
                     0C     0021  8 SRC: .BYTE  12
                     00     0022  9 DST: .BYTE  0
                     02     0023 10 VAL: .BYTE  2
                     2F     0024 11 SUM: .BYTE  47
                            0025 12         .END START


PROG4.2         9-SEP-1987 14:13:45   VAX/VMS Macro V04-00        Page    2
Symbol table    9-SEP-1987 14:12:57   SYS$USER:[PB.CHAPTER4]P42.MAR;4    (1)

DST             00000022 R     01
SRC             00000021 R     01
START           00000000 RG    01
SUM             00000024 R     01
SYS$EXIT        ******** G     01
VAL             00000023 R     01
```

Figure 4.9 Assembler listing of source module with macro

This process produces two new files: PROGRAM1.LIS, which contains the assembler listing (if we had typed only MACRO PROGRAM1.MAR, then we would not get the .LIS file), and PROGRAM1.OBJ, which is the object module and contains the machine-language translation of the source module.

One macro that we will commonly use is $EXIT_S. Recall that in chapter 3 we learned that trying to execute the HALT instruction in a machine-language program on a multiuser system causes a privileged instruction fault. The same is true if we use HALT in an assembly language program: Macro translates the mnemonic HALT into the opcode 00 without complaining (because Macro has no way of knowing if we will execute this program on a single-user or a multiuser system), but when we run our program, the hardware and operating system cooperate to abort our program. If we wish to terminate our program gracefully, we can use the macro $EXIT_S, which expands into a **system service request** to the operating system, asking that our program be terminated normally.

Note that the program in figure 4.6 did not use the $EXIT_S macro; it would not, therefore, have terminated gracefully, although it assembled without error diagnostics. We wrote it this way because we had not yet discussed macro processing and macro expansion. Now we are ready to rewrite the program so that it will run correctly; the source module is shown in figure 4.8, and the assembler listing (from the .LIS file) is shown in figure 4.9. This program shows three new assembler directives: the .SHOW directive (with the argument ME), the .TITLE directive (with the argument PROG4.2) and the .DISABLE directive, with the argument GLOBAL. The .TITLE directive is a bookkeeping directive: it tells the assembler to consider the character string which is its argument as the title of the module it is assembling (attentive readers may have noticed that it was also used in the previous example). When we use macros, the assembler generally does not show us their expansion; if we include the line .SHOW ME (for macro expansion), then the .LIS file shows macro expansions. We will discuss .DISABLE GLOBAL, along with linking, below.

Linking

Observant readers may have noticed, in examining the .LIS file shown in figure 4.9, that the symbol table contains a symbol not defined in the source module: SYS$EXIT. Where did it come from? Expansion of the macro $EXIT_S generates a call to a subroutine named SYS$EXIT. There is a call to that subroutine, but no definition of the label; how can the assembler use a label that isn't defined?

The assembler generates a call to SYS$EXIT because that is the name of the subroutine that performs the system service of gracefully terminating a program: the assembly language statement in the listing that reads

CALLS #1, G^SYS$EXIT

is a subroutine call statement. However, a program with a subroutine call to subroutine SYS$EXIT cannot possibly run correctly if there is no such subroutine; it is the **linker**'s job to find the subroutine, if it exists. The linker takes source modules that have been assembled separately and *links* their respective object modules together to form a single load module. What are the separate object modules? In the example above, one module was produced by the assembler in translating the source module, PROGRAM1.MAR, which we just wrote. The other is an object module that contains a **library** of system services, one of which happens to be the subroutine SYS$EXIT, which we use more easily by invoking the macro $EXIT_S.

The linker, thus, has the job of **resolving external labels**: when a label has been used but not defined in a particular source module, the assembler makes a note of this in the object module. (This fact is also noted, for us, in the symbol table, where the notation G, following the symbol's address, indicates that it is a global, or external, label.) When the linker processes the object modules that it is linking, its primary task is to make sure that it finds a definition for each external label from each object module in exactly one other object module. If it does, then it can assign a **value** to that label; that value is the location counter value associated with that label, which is that label's virtual address. If it does not, then it will provide an error diagnostic complaining of an undefined label.

What about the .DISABLE GLOBAL directive? Macro, by default, assumes that any label not defined in the current program is an external label and will be resolved by the linker at link time. Thus, if we forget to define a label, Macro will not issue an error diagnostic. This is convenient for experienced assembly language programmers, but for beginners it is more useful to have the assembler tell us that we have forgotten to define a label that we used. If we do not intend to use external labels, then we can change the default that an undefined label is considered global by using the .DISABLE GLOBAL directive. (We can specify a label as external by using the .GLOBL directive, which will be discussed in chapter 9.)

How do we use the linker? The VMS linker is called LINK. If we type

LINK PROGRAM1.OBJ

the linker will link our program with the system services library.[8] The linker will produce a load module and call it PROGRAM1.EXE. We then invoke the operating system's loader and have our program executed by typing

RUN PROGRAM1.EXE

We don't need to type the full name of the file we wish to assemble, link, or run: in each case, we can omit the file extension. Thus, we can type

MACRO/LIST PROGRAM1
LINK PROGRAM1, and
RUN PROGRAM1

and the assembler will find PROGRAM1.MAR, the linker will find PROGRAM1.OBJ, and the loader will find PROGRAM1.EXE.

The process by which an assembly language program is transformed into a load module that can be executed on the VAX is shown in figure 4.10; it can be summarized as follows:

1.   Someone, perhaps a system administrator, has written a library of system services, including (in our case) $EXIT_S.
2.   We, ordinary programmers, write a program which makes use of some of these system services, and place it in file PROGRAM1.MAR.
3.   We assemble our program, by typing MACRO/LIST PROGRAM1. This begins a three-step process: first, the assembler expands any macros. Then, it generates machine language and creates an object module, which it places in a file called PROGRAM1.OBJ. Finally, Macro also produces a listing, which includes both the text of PROGRAM1.MAR and an ASCII representation of the machine language which it placed in PROGRAM1.OBJ. This listing is placed in a file called PROGRAM1.LIS
4.   After we have assembled our program, we must link it. We type LINK PROGRAM1 and the linker creates a load module called PROGRAM1.EXE.
5.   We execute our program by typing RUN PROGRAM1.

---

[8]We can, of course, also link several of our *own* object modules; we would do this by typing

LINK PROGRAM1.OBJ,PROGRAM2.OBJ,. . .

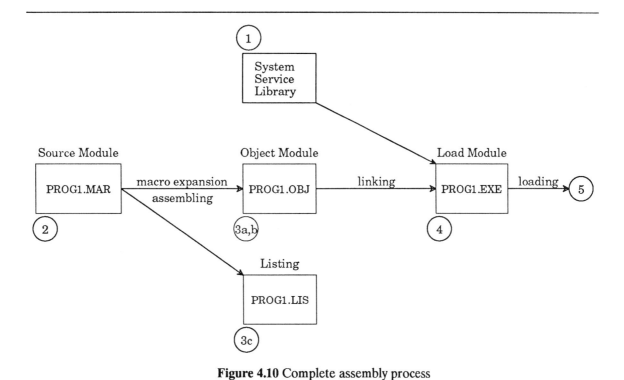

Figure 4.10 Complete assembly process

The information about our program's entry point also goes through a variety of steps between the time we use the .ENTRY directive and the time our program is loaded into memory to run. First, the assembler generates the label START (note this entry in the symbol tables in figures 4.7 and 4.9), and places information concerning its location relative to the beginning of the program in the object module. Then, the linker finds that information, and places it in the load module. Finally, when the operating system's loader loads a program into memory to execute it, it finds the entry point, places it in the PC, and the program begins execution.

Error Diagnostics

People are not perfect, nor are the programs they write; what happens if we write a program with errors in it? If the assembler detects an error, it informs us of this fact. However, the assembler is a relatively simple program, and it cannot detect errors as successfully as many compilers that we often use for higher level languages.

For example, consider the program in figure 4.11, which is the same as the one in figure 4.6, except that ADDB2 has been purposely misspelled as ADD2, and the definition of SRC has been purposely "forgotten." When the assembler processes the file, it tells us that it has found two errors, on lines 5 and 6. If we examine the assembler listing (PROGRAM1.LIS), we see that the assembler has produced helpful diagnostics under the appropriate line: under line 5, with the undefined label SRC, the assembler has told us that it found an undefined symbol. In addition, in the symbol table there is an entry for SRC, but the symbol table shows no value for it (just ********), and the entry is followed by a U, for undefined. Under line 6, the assembler has indicated an unrecognized statement; it has placed an exclamation mark ("!") under the ADD2 to indicate where it found the unrecognized

Label	Opcode	Operand(s)	Comments
	.TITLE	PROG4.3	
	.SHOW	ME	
	.DISABLE	GLOBAL	
	.ENTRY	START, 0	
	MOVB	@#SRC, @#DST	;move byte
	ADD2	@#VAL, @#SUM	;add bytes
	$EXIT_S		;stop program
DST:	.BYTE	0	;'d' of MOVB
VAL:	.BYTE	2	;'s' of ADD
SUM:	.BYTE	47	;'d' of ADD
	.END	START	

Figure 4.11 Source module with errors

statement, and it has generated no machine language corresponding to that line. Figure 4.12 shows the assembler listing (PROGRAM1.LIS), which includes the error diagnostics described.

System Services

Instead of using a special program-loading program to read a file containing a hand-coded machine-language program, as we did in chapter 3, we can now prepare a symbolic program, as shown in figures 4.6 and 4.8.

We can assemble it; after Macro produces an object module, we can have the linker produce a load module, and then we can run the program. However, since we are no longer using a special program-loading program to read, load and execute our machine-language program, we can't expect-- nor will we get--a post-execution dump of our program.

How do we get these useful, even essential, services? VMS provides a debugger, called DEBUG, for helping us track down run-time errors which cause our programs to terminate abnormally. In addition, there are several macros available with this book which provide output while our programs are running (these may be used to debug a program in much the way that Pascal **writeln** statements are used). One macro which is provided with this book is DUMP. DUMP and the use of DEBUG are briefly described below.

DEBUG

If we assemble our program by typing MACRO/LIST/DEBUG PROGRAM1, and link it by typing LINK/DEBUG PROGRAM1, then when we type RUN PROGRAM1, the debugger will be invoked automatically:

```
$ run p42

        VAX DEBUG Version V4.5-6

%DEBUG-I-INITIAL, language is MACRO, module set to 'PROG4.2'
DBG>
```

```
PROG4.3          9-SEP-1987 14:13:54    VAX/VMS Macro V04-00        Page   1
                 9-SEP-1987 14:13:24    SYS$USER:[PB.CHAPTER4]P43.MAR;2   (1)

                          0000    1          .TITLE     PROG4.3
                          0000    2          .SHOW      ME
                          0000    3          .DISABLE   GLOBAL
                  0000    0000    4          .ENTRY     START, 0
                    90    0002    5          MOVB    @#SRC, @#DST ;move byte
%MACRO-E-UNDEFSYM, Undefined symbol
00000016'9F 00000000'9F    0003
                          000D    6          ADD2    @#VAL, @#SUM ;add bytes
%MACRO-E-UNRECSTMT, Unrecognized statement  !
                          000D
                          000D    7          $EXIT_S                ;stop program
                          000D                 .GLOBL SYS$EXIT
                 01 DD    000D                 PUSHL  #1
    00000000'GF 01 FB     000F                 CALLS  #1,G^SYS$EXIT
                          0016
                    00    0016    8 DST:    .BYTE   0   ;'d' of MOVB
                    02    0017    9 VAL:    .BYTE   2   ;'s' of ADD
                    2F    0018   10 SUM:    .BYTE   47 ;'d' of ADD
                          0019   11          .END    START


PROG4.3          9-SEP-1987 14:13:54    VAX/VMS Macro V04-00        Page   2
Symbol table     9-SEP-1987 14:13:24    SYS$USER:[PB.CHAPTER4]P43.MAR;2   (1)

DST              00000016 R      01
SRC              ******* U 01
START            00000000 RG     01
SUM              00000018 R      01
SYS$EXIT         ******* G 01
VAL              00000017 R      01


There were 2 errors, 0 warnings and 0 information messages, on lines:
   5 (1)          6 (1)

MACRO/LIST P43
```

Figure 4.12 Assembler listing of source module with errors

The debugger's prompt is "DBG>", which indicates that the debugger is waiting for input from us. We can use the "e" command (for examine) to examine the contents of memory locations. DEBUG assumes that numbers are hexadecimal, and assumes that we wish to examine longwords unless we specify bytes with "e/byte", or words with "e/word". Our input to DEBUG is shown in lower case; this helps distinguish it from DEBUG's upper case output, but it could just as well have been upper case also (since VMS is not case sensitive). DEBUG also tells us that we have used the .TITLE directive to give this module the name PROG4.2.

So, let's examine some of the memory locations:

```
DBG> e/byte src
PROG4.2\SRC:      0C
DBG> e/byte dst
```

```
PROG4.2\DST:      00
DBG> e/byte val
PROG4.2\VAL:      02
DBG> e/byte sum
PROG4.2\SUM:      2F
DBG> e src
PROG4.2\SRC:      2F02000C
DBG>
```

There are no surprises here; the longword at SRC contains 2F02000C—which is the longword containing bytes SRC, DST, VAL and SUM.

We can also examine memory locations into which macro has loaded machine language instructions; if we type "e/inst", the debugger will *disassemble* our machine language program, and show us the assembly language statement that generated the machine language loaded in the location we wish to examine:

```
DBG> e/inst start+2
PROG4.2\START+2: MOVB      @#PROG4.2\SRC,@#PROG4.2\DST
DBG> e src-1f
PROG4.2\START+2: 02219F90
DBG> e start
PROG4.2\START:    entry mask ^M<>
DBG>
```

We see that the debugger correctly disassembled the first instruction, MOVB @#SRC, @#DST. This instruction begins at START+2 because location START contains the 1 word register save mask—as we see when we type "e start"—and the next free location is two more than that one. When we examine location SRC–1F, which is the same as START+2, as a longword (not particularly an instruction) we see that the first byte is 90_{16}, which is the opcode for the MOVB instruction. The next byte is 9F, which is the operand specifier, and the next two bytes—0221—are the low order two bytes of the address of SRC—00000221. Recall that, although in the .LIS file SRC is assigned address 00000021_{16}, it has been relocated by 200_{16}, so its address now appears as 00000221_{16}.

Now, we can execute the program by typing "go" to DEBUG, and then examine the data area to see what has changed:

```
DBG> go
%DEBUG-I-EXITSTATUS, is '%SYSTEM-S-NORMAL, normal successful completion'
DBG> e/byte src
PROG4.2\SRC:      0C
DBG> e/byte dst
PROG4.2\DST:      0C
DBG> e/byte val
PROG4.2\VAL:      02
DBG> e/byte sum
PROG4.2\SUM:      31
DBG> e src
PROG4.2\SRC:      31020C0C
DBG> exit
$
```

As we expect, neither SRC nor VAL has changed, but both DST and SUM have—and in just the way we expected. We exit from DEBUG by typing "exit" or "quit". A more thorough introduction to the use of DEBUG is provided in Appendix 7.

DUMP

We can always run assembly language programs with DEBUG. However, they execute much more slowly, and we may wish to have our program show us, in a more convenient way, the contents of some memory location or locations as it runs. The DUMP system service gives us this ability. DUMP is a macro, and it has two arguments: a starting address and a stopping address ($EXIT_S has no arguments). To invoke the DUMP macro, we simply type

    DUMP START, STOP

Then, at run time, we will see the familiar hexadecimal memory dump that we examined in chapter 3, which we have already learned how to read.

Other System Services

There are some more sophisticated system services available with this book; they are similar to **read** and **write** of Pascal, in that they provide us with more than hex memory dumps. These services will be discussed in later chapters, and are summarized in appendix 1. System services are often particular to each system; although all VAXes can execute *instructions* such as ADDB2 or MOVL, *not* all VAX systems have a service for providing programmers with a run-time memory dump that is called DUMP or used exactly the way the one described above is used. The VMS operating system provides a common set of system services, but many installations provide additional, tailor-made services. In addition, not all VAXes run the VMS operating system; another popular operating system for VAXes is UNIX, which provides services that look quite different from those provided by VMS. If you are working on a system that does not use the VMS operating system, and does not use the software package provided with this book, you will have to ask your instructor or a system administrator what services are provided, and how to use them.

If you are working on a bare machine, *none* of these services is available--you must provide your own. By the time you finish reading the next ten chapters, it sould be clear how you could do this.

Summary

The idea of a very low level symbolic language, called **assembly language,** has been introduced. Its purpose is to make it easier to write and to modify machine-languagelike programs; an assembler translates Englishlike mnemonics into machine-language opcodes and operand specifiers and associates symbolic labels with addresses. Almost every line of an assembly language program corresponds to a single machine-language instruction. Lines that do not represent instructions are commands to the assembler, called **directives.** Some of the most common directives are .BLKB, .BLKW, and .BLKL, which reserve uninitialized memory locations, and .BYTE, .WORD, and .LONG, which allow us to reserve and initialize memory locations.

The .ENTRY directive informs the assembler where we wish the entry point of our program to be, and the .END directive marks the end of our source module. The $EXIT_S macro provides us with a system service to terminate our program gracefully, without trying to execute a privileged instruction.

The assembler relieves us of having to assign or use numeric memory addresses. We can now use symbolic names instead of numeric addresses. Each name we make up and use must be defined once and only once, by appearing as the leftmost item of a source statement, immediately followed by a colon (:).

The assembly language program which we write is processed by a program called an **assembler**; the VAX's assembler is called *Macro*. The assembler produces two output files. One of these is the machine-language equivalent of the source module, the **object module,** which (after being further processed) will be loaded and executed, if we so request. The second output file is only produced if we request it, and contains the assembly listing. Among other things, it shows us what memory addresses the assembler has allocated for each instruction, data item, or space reservation request, and which address corresponds to each symbolic name.

Operating procedures for assembling, linking, and executing assembly language programs are discussed. Similar patterns of commands would be used with almost any operating system.

Since many users share a single VAX's memory without interfering with each other, it is clear that the addresses generated by the assembler are not real addresses: it is impossible to load more than one program into memory location 0 (which is where the assembler shows all program addresses beginning) at the same time. The operating system relocates our programs when they are loaded into memory: it finds a block of memory large enough for them and changes any addresses that must be changed to accommodate the new entry point.

Performing data input and data output as well as other operations can be accommodated by using the preprogrammed services provided by most operating systems. Predefined system services are often used by invoking **macros** which expand to sets of assembly language statements. The association of a macro name with a set of statements is the macro definition. When we wish to use a system service, we merely write the macro name associated with the desired macro definition. This use, called an **invocation,** results in the assembler replacing the 1-line invocation by the corresponding set of assembly language statements provided by the macro definition. We will learn to create our own macro definitions in chapters 15 and 17.

Exercises for Chapter 4

1. Familiarize yourself with the procedures for creating an assembly language source module in a machine-readable form. These procedures involve using an editor or some other means of creating a file and placing assembly language statements in it. Using an editor, create a file containing the program of figure 4.6. Then assemble it and obtain the listing generated by the assembler. If you do not find the same thing that is shown in the text, explain all differences.

2. Examine the listing you have just obtained from the assembler (exercise 1), and account for *every* byte of machine language. Explain exactly which part of each assembly language statement generated each byte of machine language (you may ignore the macro expansions of the system service requests your program used).

3. Take the listing you have just obtained and pretend you are the loader. Draw a picture of memory like the one in figure 3.10, and show what memory will look like after the program has been loaded. Assume that loading begins at address 0.

4. Familiarize yourself with the procedures for linking the machine-language output module of the assembler. Then try linking, loading, and executing the program that you wrote and assembled in exercise 1.

5. Pretend you are the assembler, and "hand assemble" the following assembly language program: translate each instruction into machine-language. Then show what memory will look like after it

has been loaded, beginning at address 0. Remember that the default radix of the assembler is decimal; show the picture of memory with all values in *hexadecimal*.

Label	Operation	Operand(s)	Comment
FIRST:	MOVL	@#NUM1, @#PLACE1	;move a long word
NEXT:	ADDB2	@#NUM2, @#NUM3	;add 2 bytes
THIRD:	SUBW3	@#NUM4, @#NUM5, @#PLACE2	;subtract words
DONE:	HALT		
PLACE1:	.BLKL	1	
PLACE2:	.BLKW	1	
NUM1:	.LONG	43	
NUM2:	.BYTE	12	
NUM3:	.BYTE	17	
NUM4:	.WORD	257	
NUM5:	.WORD	258	

6. In chapter 3 you made use of the loader to provide you with pre- and post-execution memory dumps. How did these memory dumps differ from the one provided by the system service DUMP? When should you use the DUMP system service in your assembly language programs?

7. Which one of these sequences correctly lists the order of transformations your assembly language source program undergoes from conception to execution?

    a. load, link, assemble, execute, print
    b. compile, load and go, expand macros, print
    c. assemble, translate, expand macros, link, run
    d. expand macros, assemble, link, load, run
    e. print, link, assemble, expand macros, load, run

8. Indicate whether each of the following events occurs at assemble time (A), at link time (L) or at run time (R).

    a. translation of ADDB2 to 80_{16}
    b. illegal instruction
    c. replacing labels defined in the current module with addresses
    d. replacing labels defined in another module with addresses
    e. execution of ADDB2 @#ARRAY, @#ARRAY+1
    f. calculation of value of labels ARRAY and ARRAY+1
    g. memory dump
    h. setting of CC bits
    i. macro expansion
    j. packaging of several object modules into a single load module

9. Rewrite the machine-language program for moving an array of words that you wrote as an exercise in chapter 3 in assembly language. Make judicious use of labels to solve the problem of modifying an address in an assembly language instruction.

■ 5 ■

More Hardware

Introduction

We have mentioned previously that the instruction subset we have been using presents the VAX as a very simple machine, but that this subset hides much of the VAX's complexity. We are now ready to begin expanding on the instruction subset and, in the process, to begin understanding more about the VAX's capabilities and sophistication.

Registers

The VAX instruction subset we have been using only supports memory-to-memory operations. These are very useful, but they are not very efficient when performing complex calculations. It is time-consuming to repeatedly fetch and store intermediate results of a computation from and to memory. When a computation produces many intermediate results, it is advantageous to have an accumulator register, and the designers of the VAX took this into account when they provided the VAX with not just 1, but several accumulators (12, to be exact).

The VAX accumulators are called **general purpose registers**. They are 32 bits wide, and they are numbered 0, 1, 2, 3, 4, 5, 6, 7, 8, 9, 10, and 11. The VAX has 4 other 32-bit registers, numbered 12, 13, 14, and 15; these *can* be used as general purpose registers, but they should *not* be unless we understand exactly what we are doing. For the meantime, we should use only registers 0 through 11.[1] In order to avoid confusing registers 0, 1, . . . , 11 with memory locations 0, 1, . . . , 11, the assembler recognizes a special notation when registers are being referred to. The assembler interprets the character R (or r), when followed by a number between 0 and 11, to mean that the specified register should be used. Without the R, the assembler would interpret the number as an ordinary memory address. Consider the following examples.

Previously, when we wanted to add some numbers, we could write a program segment such as:

```
MOVW  @#VAL1, @#SUM
ADDW2 @#VAL2, @#SUM
ADDW2 @#VAL3, @#SUM
```

Using register 0 as an accumulator, we can now write:

```
MOVW  @#VAL1, R0
ADDW2 @#VAL2, R0
ADDW2 @#VAL3, R0
MOVW  R0, @#SUM
```

---

[1]In Chapter 10 we will see that some of the more complicated of the VAX's instructions change R0 through R5. We will not use any such instructions until chapter 10, but experienced VAX assembly language programmers often use only R6 through R11.

94

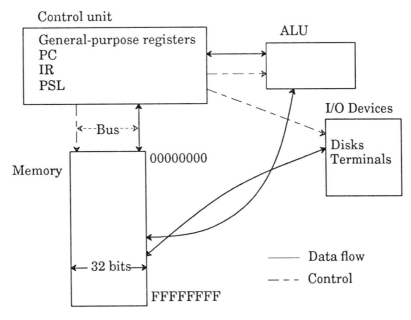

Figure 5.1 A model of the VAX

Is this an improvement? It certainly does not appear to be. Why bother using registers? First, registers are physically closer to the ALU, so obtaining a value from a register is faster than sending an address along the bus to the memory system and waiting for the value to be returned along the bus. Second, registers are usually constructed of higher speed components than the memory system's cells, so they can be accessed more rapidly than the regular memory system. (It is not unusual for registers to have an access time that is a factor of ten faster than memory access time.) These high-speed components are very expensive, so computers generally have far fewer registers than memory locations. On the VAX, we gain by using registers in another significant way. Instructions that use registers are shorter (they require fewer bytes) than the same instructions using memory locations! As a general rule, the shorter something is, the faster it can be fetched from memory, so we gain additional speed here. Figure 5.1 is an update of the model of the VAX that we saw in figure 3.8.

Consider a MOVW instruction. The MOVW @#VAL1, @#SUM uses 11 bytes. The MOVW @#VAL1, R0 uses only 7 bytes. Register-to-register operations are also allowed, and we see below that MOVW R0, R1 takes only 3 bytes! How is this possible? Consider, first, that, specifying 1 of 2^{32} addresses in memory requires 32 bits, and that specifying one of 2^4 registers requires 4 bits. Thus, it is clear that, if an operand is in a register, its "address"[2] should be shorter than if it is in the memory system. In order to more completely understand this issue, however, we must first look more closely at operand specifiers.

---

[2]We use "address" in quotes because normally the word "address" means a location in main memory; here we use it to mean, by analogy, "a way of finding something."

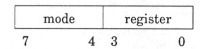

mode	register
7 4	3 0

Figure 5.2 Operand specifier, with mode and register fields

Operand Specifiers

Recall that we have already learned that every operand in a VAX instruction requires an operand specifier, and that an operand specifier is 8 bits long. An operand specifier is actually composed of two 4-bit fields: bits 4-7 (the high-order 4 bits) are the **mode field,** and bits 0-3 (the low order 4 bits) are the **register field.** Figure 5.2 shows this division of an operand specifier into two fields. The *mode* field, when decoded by the control unit, explains *how* an operand will be found; the *register* field tells *where*--with respect to which register. Thus, in the VAX, *every* operand will be found with respect to one or another of the 16 general-purpose registers.[3] So, in the case of MOVW @#VAL1, R0, the operand specifier for the first operand, VAL1, is 9F: mode 9, register F (this is hexadecimal, of course). We will not discuss what mode 9 is, or the use of register F_{16} (15_{10}), which is one of the registers we are avoiding for the time being, until later. The second operand, however, is in register 0. There is a particular mode (an **addressing mode**) that is used to tell the control unit that an operand is in a register: mode 5. So, the high-order 4 bits of the operand specifier of the second operand of the MOVW instruction are 5_{16}, or 0101 binary. The low-order 4 bits are the register field: since the operand is in register 0, the low order 4 bits are 0_{16}, or 0000 binary; the complete operand specifier is 50_{16}. If the instruction had been MOVW @#VAL1, R7, then the operand specifier for the second operand would be 57_{16}. Notice that we have no need for any kind of address to follow the operand specifier (as we *do* for 9F) because the register field of the operand specifier is 4 bits long--which happens to be exactly the right number of bits needed to uniquely identify one of the 16 general-purpose registers. So, when the control unit discovers a 5 in the mode field, it knows that the operand is in *some* register, because that's what mode 5 means; when it finds 0 in the register field, it knows that the operand is in register 0, and it has all the information necessary to fetch the operand.

When Can Registers Be Used?

As a general rule, whenever a memory address can be used to specify an operand, a register can also be used. So, for a MOVW instruction, any of the following combinations of operand specifiers is possible:

```
MOVW  X, Y          ;memory-to-memory: 11 bytes long
MOVW  X, R1         ;memory-to-register: 7 bytes long
MOVW  R2, Y         ;register-to-memory: 7 bytes long
MOVW  R0, R1        ;register-to-register: 3 bytes long
```

For 3-operand instructions as well, *any* combination of operands may be in registers and memory.

---

[3]This may sound strange: when we specify an operand by its address in memory, how is one of the general-purpose registers involved? We will soon see!

When we use memory locations, we can reserve them at load time by using the .BLK(B,W,L) directives and initialize them at run time by executing an instruction that places a result in a memory location, or we can request the loader to initialize them at load time, by using a .BYTE, .WORD, or .LONG directive. What directives can we use to reserve and initialize registers? None! There is no need to reserve or define registers, since the names R0-R11 are built-in. There is no directive which causes a register to be initialized when the program is loaded. The only way to place a value in a register is to write and execute an instruction that places the value there.

Careful use of registers can both speed up a program and reduce its memory requirements. Sloppy use of registers can make a program almost impossible to understand and debug!

In the execution of any instruction which uses the ALU (this includes the MOV(B,W,L) instructions), the CC will be updated to reflect the value of the result sent to the destination, regardless of whether that destination is a memory location or a register.

An Exception

If we were to place an *address* in a register, say in R1, we might be tempted to try executing

    JMP R1

if R1 contained the address of an instruction we wished to jump to. This particular form of addressing, however, cannot be used with the JMP instruction. If we try to use it in an assembly language program, the assembler will issue an error diagnostic complaining of an illegal addressing mode; if we try it in a machine-language program, the operating system will issue a **reserved addressing fault**. Why is this so? At first, this restriction seems to be an inconsistency in the VAX's ability to deal with operands: we can place the operand of a MOV(B,W,L) instruction in a register, so why can't we do the same with the operand of a JMP instruction? To answer this question, we must carefully consider the difference between an operand, and an operand's *address*.

In general, when we specify an operand for a VAX instruction, we specify a location (in memory or a register) where the operand can be found. In the case of the MOVW, we place the *operand* in the register; when we use addressing mode 5, we tell the control unit that the address of the operand is R5, so the control unit can fetch the operand from that register. With the JMP instruction, however, the case is somewhat different: when we specify the operand of the JMP instruction, we do *not* mean for the control unit to go to that location, fetch the contents of the location, and place the contents of the location in the PC. Rather, we mean for the control unit to place the location *specified in the instruction* in the PC.[4] So, if we were to write JMP R0, we would be saying to the control unit, "place *address* R0 into the PC"--something that is clearly impossible to do, because the PC can only contain the address of a memory location; it can't contain a register "name."

Registers, Bytes, and Words

Most VAX instructions allow us to deal with 8- and 16-bit data items as well as 32-bit ones; this is not a problem when operands are in memory because each *byte* has its own address. Registers, however, are *not* byte-addressable; a register name refers to a 32-bit location. So, what happens when we use a byte or a word instruction and specify that one of the operands is a register? For example,

---

[4]This distinction was emphasized in chapter 2, when we introduced the TRA instruction of our hypothetical computer.

what happens if we write ADDB2 R0, R1? Presumably, only one byte of each register will be added, but *which* byte?

This questions is resolved by decree of the designers of the VAX. They decided that a longword has the same address as the *lowest order* byte that is contained in it; they decided that, by analogy, when we refer to a register as the operand of a byte instruction, the byte referred to will be the *lowest* order byte of the register. Similarly, if we use a word instruction with a register operand, the control unit accesses the *low-order* word of the register. There are no simple instructions that allow us to directly access any byte other than the lowest order one, or any word other than the low-order one, of a register. We will see, however, that the VAX's instruction set is rich enough that, with a little ingenuity, we will have no difficulty manipulating any byte we wish, even in a register.

Renaming Things

It is sometimes convenient to use names other than built-in ones. In the case of constants, macro recognizes, for example, the digit string 255 as having the value of the number 255 ($2*10^2 + 5*101 + 5*10^0$). However, there is also a renaming feature that uses the equal sign, "=". For example, if we are writing a program that deals with the largest integer that can be stored in a particular memory location, we could write

```
MAXBYTE:  .BYTE 255
MAXWORD:  .WORD 65535
MAXLONG:  .LONG 4294967295
```

and then use those numbers as operands by referring to the assigned names. However, we can achieve a similar result *without reserving memory* by using the assemble-time equality operator; we could write:

```
MAXBYTE = 255
MAXWORD = 65535
MAXLONG = 4294967295
```

This latter alternative is similar to Pascal's **const**; it is an **assemble-time equality**: whenever the assembler encounters MAXBYTE in a program, after processing the assemble time equality, it will behave *exactly* as if it had encountered the *number* 255.[5] Soon (in chapter 6) we will see how to use this feature to help us write more understandable, modifiable programs.

SNAP System Service

In chapter 4, we discussed the use of the DUMP system service to provide us with a run-time hexadecimal memory dump and explained that there are other system services we may wish to use as well. Now that we know what the general-purpose registers are, we can explain the SNAP system service, which provides us with a **register snapshot,** at run time. SNAP shows us the contents of the general-purpose registers; its output consists of 4 lines. The third and fourth lines of output show the register contents, 8 registers per line: the third line shows, from left to right, R0 through R7, and the fourth line shows R8 through R15--also from left to right. Attentive users of the SNAP

---

[5]This is a text-substitution process very similar to that of macro definition and macro expansion.

macro will note that the PC seems to always contain exactly the same value as R15--because the PC *is* R15. Thus, the first line shows the contents of the PC only for convenience; it also shows the PSL, whose low-order 4 bits are the condition code bits. Soon, we will see why the designers of the VAX used R15 for the PC; we will see that it was a very clever decision.

Often, when we wish to debug a program (especially if we are working *without* a debugger like DEBUG), it is helpful to request a register snapshot while our program is running. If you are using the software package available with this book, then if you place the following line in your program, you will get a register snapshot at that point in your program's execution:

    SNAP

An example of the output produced by the SNAP system service follows:

```
PC:  00000279    PSL:  03C00000
R0-R11, AP, FP, SP PC:
00000000 FFFFFFFF FFFFFFFE FFFFFFFD FFFFFFFC FFFFFFFB FFFFFFFA FFFFFFF9
00000008 00000009 0000000A 0000000B 7FF285CC 7FF28584 7FF28580 00000279
```

ASCII Character Codes Revisited

In chapter 1, we saw that the 26 letters of the alphabet, the ten digits, and some punctuation can be represented using a 6-bit code, but if we add another bit we can represent a richer character set. The most widely used standard code is the 7-bit ASCII code; with a 7-bit code we can represent 128 items. We saw the ASCII code listed in binary, in figure 1.18; it is listed in decimal and hexadecimal in appendix 6.

It is common to attach an extra bit to each character code to provide some measure of error detection, particularly when transmitting codes over long distances. This extra bit, called a **check bit** or **parity bit,** has also been discussed in chapter 1 (see figure 1.16); it is usually positioned as the leftmost (high-order) bit. Even when no check bit is being used, an eighth bit (typically 0) is often added, so the 7-bit ASCII codes will usually be stored and transmitted as 8-bit quantities. One of the reasons that the VAX's memory is byte-addressable is that its designers recognized the importance of 7- and 8-bit codes and so have provided hardware support for a memory unit that can simply and efficiently deal with them.

Assembler Support for ASCII

We have already seen that VAX instructions can typically have operands that are longwords, words, or bytes. We programmers must remember only a single mnemonic, such as ADD or MOV, add the appropriate suffix--L, W, or B--and the assembler will generate the appropriate machine language. However, the assembler also provides us with assistance in using ASCII character codes: there are directives that are used particularly for dealing with ASCII codes.

The assembler as we already know it *could* be used to store ASCII codes in memory. If we assume that each code will occupy 1 byte, we could use the .BYTE directive. For example, if we wish to store the codes for "A" and "C" (perhaps to send them to a CRT which only accepts ASCII codes), we could type

    A: .BYTE ^X41   ; ASCII code for "A"
    C: .BYTE ^X43   ; ASCII code for "C"

We could also use a single .WORD directive, and type

     AC: .WORD ^X4341 ; "A" and "C"

but this is less clear than two separate .BYTE directives, for two reasons. First, it is less clear because using the .WORD directive implies that we are storing a word, but when we use it to store ASCII characters, we are really storing bytes. The second reason that it is less clear is that, in order to have the character representation for "A" precede that for "C" in the VAX's memory, we must write the 4-digit number in reverse order; if we use two .BYTE directives, there is no confusion concerning which comes first in memory.

    Although it is *possible* to use .BYTE directives to deal with ASCII character codes, it is tedious to do so. The people who wrote the assembler realized this, and built into Macro a table of ASCII codes as well as a table of the instruction mnemonics. Thus, if we wish to store "A" and "C" we can also make use of this knowledge of the assembler by using the .ASCII and .ASCIZ directives. If we use the line

     AC: .ASCII /AC/

the assembler will look up the ASCII codes for *every* character (including blank spaces, punctuation, etc.) between the delimiters (slashes, in this case), allocate 1 byte of memory for each one, and request the loader to place those values in memory when the program is loaded. The address of the ASCII code for "A" will, of course, be AC, the address of the ASCII code for "C" will be AC+1, etc. If we use the .ASCIZ directive, we get exactly the same thing as with the .ASCII directive, except the assembler adds a single byte *after* the last character inside the delimiters; that byte is 00_{16}, or 00000000_2, which is the NUL character. The following pairs of directives are equivalent in that they result in exactly the same values being placed in memory by the loader ("$\equiv$" means "is identical to"):

.ASCII /D/	$\equiv$	.BYTE ^X44
.ASCIZ /D/	$\equiv$	.BYTE ^X44, 0
.ASCIZ /0/	$\equiv$	.BYTE ^X30, 0
.ASCII /a?/	$\equiv$	.BYTE ^X61, ^X3F
.ASCIZ /a ?/	$\equiv$	.BYTE ^X61, ^X20, ^X3F, 0
.ASCIZ /abc/	$\equiv$	.ASCII /abc/<0>

    We may wish to store ASCII codes that have no visible print representation, such as a NUL character (code 00) or a line feed (LF, code 0A). Macro allows us to embed some special characters in an ASCII string by using the angle brackets, "<" and ">". For example, if we wish to store a sentence that ends with the carriage return and linefeed characters (so that after we print it the next thing printed will begin on another line--as with the **writeln** function of Pascal), we can use the following features of Macro:

    LF = ^X0A   ; line feed code (10 decimal)
    CR = ^X0D   ; carriage return code (13 decimal)
SENTENCE: .ASCIZ /This will put the cursor on the next line/<CR><LF>

If we wish to have the next line begin 2 lines later, we need only use *two* "<LF>"s:

    DOUBLE: .ASCIZ /This will skip an extra line./<LF><LF><CR>

If we wish to skip a line *before* printing the sentence, we can type the following:

NEW: .ASCIZ   <CR> <LF> /This will start on a new line./ <CR> <LF>

In each case, the nonprinting characters are placed *before* the 0 byte at the end of the ASCII character string.

Suppose we wish to have a "/" as part of an ASCII string; how would we request it? Clearly, since Macro accepts a variety of delimiters for ASCII strings, we need only choose another one-- perhaps "?"--and then we can write:

SLASH: .ASCIZ   ?This contains a / in the middle!?

In fact, macro accepts *any* character (other than "<") as a delimiter; it assumes that the very first printing character after the .ASCII or .ASCIZ directive is the delimiter, and the string continues until a matching character is found. Thus, the following are equivalent:

```
.ASCII    bThis will work just fine.b
.ASCII    "This will work just fine."
.ASCII    /This will work just fine./
.ASCII    ^This will work just fine.^
```

Although any delimiter allows all characters but itself in the string, it is common (and good) programming practice to limit ourselves to more obvious delimiters, such as the slash (/) and quotation marks (").

Single Operand Instructions

In chapter 2, we saw that addition, for example, is a binary operation that requires 2 operands (we can't add just one number), but that it is possible for an addition instruction to *explicitly* specify only a single operand. With the hypothetical computer, the second operand is *always* in the AC, so it needn't be explicitly specified in the instruction. We have seen that the VAX provides us with additional flexibility: it eliminates the bottleneck of a single accumulator, and allows the 2 operands of an addition instruction to be anywhere--in memory, or in a register. However, we pay a price for this additional flexibility: an instruction that explicitly specifies 2 operands is longer than one that explicitly specifies only one.

Some operations are performed so frequently that they warrant having special instructions to support them more efficiently. For example, *adding 1* is a common, special case of addition; it is frequently used for changing loop control variables. The VAX has several instructions that are special cases of more general operations. For each of them, one of the operands is explicitly specified but the other is implicit. The general format of these instructions is:

OPCODE D   ;use (D) as source, and place results in D

This section discusses some of the VAX's **single operand** instructions; we should realize that they are single-operand instructions in format, but not in operation--like the ADD instruction of the hypothetical computer. Figure 5.3 presents a summary of the opcodes and operations of the single-operand instructions discussed in this section.

Instruction	Mnemonic	Opcode	Action
Clear byte	CLRB D	94	D←0
Clear word	CLRW D	B4	D←0
Clear longword	CLRL D	D4	D←0
Increment byte	INCB D	96	D←(D) + 1
Increment word	INCW D	B6	D←(D) + 1
Increment longword	INCL D	D6	D←(D) + 1
Decrement byte	DECB D	97	D←(D) − 1
Decrement word	DECW D	B7	D←(D) − 1
Decrement longword	DECL D	D7	D←(D) − 1

Figure 5.3 Some single operand VAX instructions

The CLR(B,W,L) Instructions

Clearing a counter, setting a register to 0, and similar operations are performed frequently, so the designers of the VAX created a special instruction for them. The CLR(B,W,L) family of instructions is the first we will discuss of a class of instructions which *explicitly* specify only a single operand. The CLR instructions place 0 in their operands. Thus,

    CLRB @#DEST

has exactly the same effects on its operand as does

        MOVB   @#ZERO, @#DEST
          .
          .
          .
    ZERO: .BYTE   0

When used with a register, the CLRB instruction changes only the low order byte of the register, and the CLRW instruction changes only the low-order word of the register--as we would expect.

The INC(B,W,L) Instructions

Counting--adding 1--is also common enough that the VAX designers provided special instructions for doing it: the INC family of instructions. If we wish to count the number of times some event has occurred, we can use an INC instruction and write

    INCL @#COUNTER

rather than using the more general ADD instruction, as in

ADDL2 @#ONE, @#COUNTER

.

.

.

ONE: .LONG   1

If the result does not fit in 32 bits (or 8 or 16 bits, for the byte and word instructions) because we added 1 to $FFFFFFFF_{16}$ (or FF_{16}, or $FFFF_{16}$), the result will be 00000000 (or 00 or 0000). This problem is not particular to the INC(B,W,L) instructions; it will also occur with the ADD(B,W,L)[2,3] instructions. It is caused by the fundamental limitation of computer arithmetic, which is performed on operands of fixed size; it is similar to the behavior of a car's odometer when the car travels more than 99,999 (or, these days, 999,999) miles, and we will discuss it in detail in chapter 7.

The DEC(B,W,L) Instructions

Just as each member of the INC family of instructions adds 1 to its operand, so each member of the DEC family of instructions *subtracts* 1 from its operand. This makes it just as easy to count down as to count up. If we happen to decrement the most negative number (80000000_{16}; we will see why this is the most negative number soon, in chapter 7), we will suddenly get the most positive number ($7FFFFFFF_{16}$), much to our surprise. We will also discuss this apparently strange phenomenon in chapter 7.

Branch Instructions

The CC bits reflect the state of the most recent result, in so far as it is negative or 0 or some combination of these or their opposites. In chapter 3 we introduced a subset of the VAX's conditional branch instructions and described how to use them in machine-language; we have yet to explain how they are used in assembly language.

Offsets

Recall that the conditional branch instructions are the only VAX instructions that have operands but no operand specifiers. This is, of course, *not* because the control unit doesn't have to find the operands; rather, since the branch instructions provide only a single way of specifying their operands, the control unit doesn't need to be explicitly told which way the operand is being specified each time: it is specified in exactly the same way *every* time.

In chapter 3 we called the operand of the conditional branch instruction a *count*--of the number of bytes to be skipped if the branch is taken. Another, more general, way of describing this is as an **offset,** to be added to the PC in order to cause transfer of control. In assembly language, we write the mnemonic for the branch (e.g., BEQL, BLSS, etc.), followed by a symbolic label which we intend as the target of the branch instruction, and which appears in the label field of the instruction we wish to be executed if the branch is taken. When Macro encounters the mnemonic for the branch and the label for its target, it looks up (in its symbol table) the value of the label used as the target. It then calculates the *difference* between the value that will be in the PC when the branch instruction is being executed (which is the address *just after* the branch instruction, and which is maintained by the assembler in the **location counter,** as described in chapter 4) and the target address. This is the **offset** that Macro stores in the second byte of the branch instruction as its operand.

Thus, at run time, the control unit, in the process of executing the instruction fetch-execute cycle, fetches an opcode that happens to be that of a branch instruction. When the opcode is

Branch Condition	Mnemonic	Opcode	Action
Result=0	BEQL DEST	13	if Z=1, PC←PC+offset
Result≠0	BNEQ DEST	12	if Z=0, PC←PC+offset
Result≥0	BGEQ DEST	18	if N=0, PC←PC+offset
Result<0	BLSS DEST	19	if N=1, PC←PC+offset
Result>0	BGTR DEST	14	if N=0 *and* Z=0, PC←PC+offset
Result≤0	BLEQ DEST	15	if N=1 *or* Z=1, PC←PC+offset
Always (byte offset)	BRB DEST	11	PC←PC+offset
Always (word offset)	BRW DEST	31	PC←PC+offset

Figure 5.4 Branch instruction subset for the VAX

decoded, the control unit knows that it is a branch instruction and, therefore, has a 1-byte offset that must also be fetched. It fetches the offset (the PC was updated when the opcode was fetched, so it contains the offset's address) and updates the PC, and evaluates the branch condition: for example, it checks to see if the N bit is 1 if the opcode was 19_{16}, for BLSS. If the N bit is 1, then the offset is converted to a longword and added to the PC--which causes the transfer of control, since the next instruction fetched will be from the target address, if Macro has calculated the offset correctly. Offsets are discussed in greater detail in the next section, and an example is shown in figure 5.5.

Conditional and Unconditional Branches

In chapter 3 we described only some of the *conditional* branches. The VAX, however, also has two *un*conditional branches, which are *always* taken; they are similar to the JMP instruction, except that they are shorter because they specify offsets rather than addresses. There are two unconditional branches because one (BRB) specifies a byte offset just like the conditional branches, but the other (BRW) specifies a *word* offset; it can store 65536 (2^{16}) different offsets rather than only 256 (2^8). Figure 5.4 summarizes the usage of the branch instructions in assembly language. Notice that we do *not* write BEQL @#DEST, because the "@#" is the assembly language notation for an operand specifier, and branch instructions do *not* have operand specifiers. Figure 5.4 also introduces three new conditional branch instructions: branch if the result of the last operation is *not* equal to 0, branch if it is greater than 0, and branch if it is less than or equal to 0. The CC bit combinations that indicate whether these branches are taken or not are straightforward extensions of what we have seen before. Recall that the branch instructions and the JMP instruction do *not* change CC bit settings.

Consider the excerpt from an assembly printout in figure 5.5. The assembler equates the symbol ZERO with the address $0B_{16}$. The assembler knows that when BEQL ZERO at location 07 is being executed, the PC will have already been updated and will have the value 00000007 (address of instruction) + 2 (length of instruction), or 00000009. The distance from 09 to 0B hexadecimal is 2. Since the assembler has stored this distance as the offset for BEQL ZERO, the control unit can, at run time, reconstruct the desired address by fetching the offset (02), converting it to a longword (00000002), adding it to the PC contents (00000009), and getting the desired instruction address. A similar calculation is done for the BRB NO instruction on line 4 of the printout, whose offset (stored in location 0A) is 03.

This use of offsets is a form of **PC relative addressing.** The other type of addressing we have seen so far is often called **absolute addressing.** When we encode the absolute addresses of operands in

```
50 00000000'9F D0  0000  1        MOVL @#VAL1, R0
            02 13  0007  2        BEQL ZERO
                   0009  3        ;else, not zero
            03 11  0009  4        BRB NO
         51 50 D0  000B  5 ZERO:  MOVL R0, R1
               00  000E  6 NO:    HALT
```

Figure 5.5 Assembler printout with branches

the instructions, those addresses will clearly have to change if our program gets loaded into memory anywhere other than starting at location 0 (which almost always happens; we saw an example of this in chapter 4, when we examined, with the debugger, an address stored in our program, and found that it was relocated by 200_{16}. PC relative addressing, on the other hand, makes it possible to load a program into memory *without* changing any addresses--because the *addresses* are not stored in the program, only the offsets are. And no matter where our program gets loaded into memory, the distance between the PC when BEQL ZERO is being executed and the instruction with the label ZERO will *always* be 2 bytes. We will soon see that the VAX makes it possible to avoid using absolute addresses for operands of arithmetic instructions as well as branch instructions; one of the clever design features of the VAX permits us to use a similar but slightly different form of PC relative addressing for nearly all operands in our programs.

Branches and Registers

We have stated earlier that, in almost every case where we could use memory address within an instruction, we could substitute a register reference instead. However, from our previous discussion of offsets in branch instructions, we can see that branch instructions are special. Thus, just as we *cannot* write

BRB @#DEST

so we also *cannot* write

BRB R0

In both of these cases, the assembler will complain that we have used an illegal addressing mode. We reiterate that none of the branch instructions can have anything but a plain unadorned symbol in their address fields and that the symbol must be one with an offset that will fit into 8 bits. We will soon see addressing modes that provide us with great flexibility when using a JMP instruction.

Summary

The VAX provides a set of 16-general purpose registers, 12 of which can be used freely in place of memory locations, with instructions. No new instructions are needed to take advantage of these registers. The assembler recognizes a register reference is indicated when R is followed by a number between 0 and 11. Using registers can result in significantly shorter programs, which also have shorter execution times.

The importance of non-numeric applications has led to the support of operations on characters and character strings. The assembler facilitates the use of bytes to store ASCII character codes by supporting the the .ASCII and .ASCIZ directives.

In addition to making programs more compact and faster by providing registers, the VAX's designers also created single-operand instructions for some frequently used operations. These instructions have 2 operands, like their general case-counterparts, but they explicitly specify only 1-- the other is implicit. There are the CLR(B,W,L), INC(B,W,L) and DEC(B,W,L) families of instructions, which perform the functions of clearing, adding 1 to, and subtracting 1 from, their single specified operand.

The *un*conditional branch instructions, BRB and BRW, and some new conditional branch instructions BNEQ (branch if the last result 0), BGTR (branch if result>0) and BLEQ (branch if result ($\leq$0) were introduced. Conditional branch instructions examine the CC bits; *none* of the branch instructions change the CC bits. Branch instructions do *not* use operand specifiers, and they *cannot* use registers to specify their destinations; they can only use symbolic labels.

The assembler calculates an 8-bit offset, which is the distance in bytes between what the PC will contain when the branch is being executed and what it would have to contain if the instruction that is the target of the branch is to be executed. Branch instructions are only 2 bytes long (except for BRW), and they specify operands by using PC-relative offsets.

The VAX has other branch instructions and many ways of exploiting the registers we have just been introduced to. We are on the verge of an interesting exploration.

Exercises for Chapter 5

1. Rewrite the following statement as a VAX symbolic assembly language program (assume the operands are integers):

    if (A>C) and (C<D) then
        X := C+D
    else
        X := A-B

2. Rewrite the pay program of chapter 2 using registers to hold the regular, overtime and total pay figures. Assume the pay rate is not larger than ten.
3. Explain the fact that Macro produces an error message upon encountering BLAH = 12, after it has already processed the line

    BLAH: .BYTE 13

    Why does this cause a problem?

4. The concept of parity was defined in the text and exercises of chapter 1. ASCII codes often have a parity bit prefixed to them, which makes them 8-bit codes. Assume that the parity bit is chosen so that the 8-bit codes all have *odd* parity. Write down the "new" hex ASCII codes for the letters A, B and C.
5. Would any 1-bit error in sending or receiving the 7-bit ASCII codes ever be *un*detectable? Support your answer. If you were using 8-bit ASCII with odd parity, would the situation change? Explain.
6. What is the range (i.e., the maximum distance which a reference can encompass) of the BRB instruction? What is the range of the BRW instruction? What is the range of the JMP instruction?

7.   Encode, by hand, the message: "help me NOW!," using the hex ASCII codes, in a single .LONG statement.

8.   Interpret the following series of hexadecimal longwords as a single ASCII character string. Remember that the rightmost byte in a longword has the lowest address, and the leftmost byte has the highest address.

.LONG ^X20584156, ^X65737361, ^X796C626D, ^X6E616C20, ^X67617567, ^X73692065, ^X6E756620

Explain why this is a correct way to allocate memory for the message.

9.   Define each of the following items, and explain (briefly) why it is important.

   a.   PSL
   b.   PC
   c.   BNEQ
   d.   CC
   e.   branch offset
   f.   register
   g.   operand specifier
   h.   assembler listing

10.   How many bytes does each of the following generate?

   a.   .ASCII   "6 week exam"<CR><LF>
   b.   .ASCIZ   ?HELLO?
   c.   .ASCIZ   <LF><CR>:Hello, world:<LF><CR>
   d.   .ASCII   <^X0B>/"CS-304"/<LF><CR><0>

11.   If the line

   .ASCII "ABC"<0>

   were the first statement in your program, what would appear in the first 2 words of a hexadecimal memory dump, assuming the data were not modified?

▪ 6 ▪

Key Addressing Modes

Introduction

Recall that in chapter 3, we described a primitive technique for reusing instructions called **self-modifying code.** We explained that, with early computers, this was the only method available to programmers that allowed them to avoid using one ADD instruction, for example, for each and every pair of operands they wished to add. We also claimed that the VAX, as most modern computers, provides far superior techniques for reusing instructions. In this chapter, we will describe some of those techniques.

Deferred Addressing

So far, we have explained completely only **register mode,** mode 5, where the operand is in the register specified by the **register** field of the operand specifier. Most computers have an addressing mode called **register deferred,** or **register indirect,** in which not the operand, but the operand's *address* is in the register. When the control unit decodes an instruction with an operand specified in such a manner, it fetches a quantity from the appropriate register, but it then sends that quantity along the bus to the memory system as an *address,* and asks for the value stored in that location.

Mode 6

In the VAX, register mode deferred is mode 6; if an operand's address is in register 3, then the operand specifier for that operand would be 63_{16}. In assembly language, we indicate that the assembler should generate an operand specifier with 6 in the mode field by surrounding the register name with parentheses: (R n). Thus, if we wish to add the 2 longwords in registers 3 and 4 and store the results in register 5, we could write the following assembly language instruction:

   ADDL3 R3, R4, R5.

If, on the other hand, we wished to add 2 longwords *in memory,* but whose addresses were in registers 3 and 4, and store the results in the longword in memory whose address is in register 5, we would write

   ADDL3 (R3), (R4), (R5).

   Suppose that R3 contains 1000_{16}, R4 contains 1008_{16}, and R5 contains $100C_{16}$. Suppose, further, that memory location 1000 contains 16_{16}, that memory location 1008 contains 17_{16}, and that memory location 100C contains 44_{16}. We can summarize the contents of the relevant registers and memory locations as follows:

Location:	R3	R4	R5	1000	1008	100C
Initial Contents:	1000	1008	100C	16	17	44

Instruction	Mnemonic	Opcode	Action
Move address of byte	MOVAB S, D	9E	D←S
Move address of word	MOVAW S, D	3E	D←S
Move address of longword	MOVAL S, D	DE	D←S

Figure 6.1 Move address instructions

After execution of ADDL3 R3, R4, R5, the contents of R5 will be 2008_{16}. However, after execution of ADDL3 (R3), (R4), (R5), R5 will still contain $100C_{16}$, but location 100C will no longer contain 44: it will contain the sum of $16_{16} + 17_{16}$, which is $2D_{16}$. We can summarize the initial values, and the changes due to the execution of those two instructions, as follows:

Location:	R3	R4	R5	1000	1008	100C
Initial Contents:	1000	1008	100C	16	17	44
ADDL3 R3, R4, R5	–	–	2008	–	–	–
ADDL3 (R3), (R4), (R5)	–	–	–	–	–	2D

Move Address Instructions

It makes sense to use mode 6, of course, if an operand's address "happens" to be in a register. How can we arrange for an address to be in a register? In exactly the same way that we arrange for *anything* to be in a register: we *put* it there. One simple way to put operands in registers is with the MOV(B,W,L) instructions. When the operands we wish to put in registers are addresses, however, we use a different family of instructions: the MOVAB, MOVAW, MOVAL instructions. The mnemonics stand for "move address of (byte, word, longword)"; the use of these instructions is summarized in figure 6.1. Note that the notation "D ← S" in the Action column differs from the normal notation, "D ← (S)"; this indicates that it is not the *contents* of the source address that are placed in the destination, but the source address itself--which is what we expect with move address instructions.

Using Deferred Addressing

Let's see how mode 6, register deferred addressing mode, allows us to reuse instructions without writing self-modifying code. Consider the assembly language program fragment in figure 6.2. This program fragment demonstrates the MOVAL instruction, on line 6. It also shows how to alternate the use of mode 6--on line 7, to treat the value in R3 as the *address* of an operand--with mode 5--on line 8, to treat the value (which is an address) in R3 as an *operand* in order to change the address-- in order to reuse the CLRL instruction on line 7. Using the value in the register as, alternately, an operand's address and then an operand, is similar to our alternating use of the address field of machine-language instructions (of the hypothetical computer, in chapter 2, and of the VAX, in chapter 3) as an instruction and as an operand.

The comment for line 9 of figure 6.2 indicates that this is a dangerous loop--why? Because it won't terminate: after clearing the four longwords in array BUNCH, it will also clear the constant FOUR. Our program will then be adding 0 to R3 (in line 8), so the address in R3 won't change, and

```
1) BUNCH:      .BLKL 4                    ;4 longwords
2) FOUR:       .LONG 4                    ;constant, for changing addresses
3)                 .
4)                 .
5)                 .
6)             MOVAL @#BUNCH, R3          ;address of 1st longword to clear
7) CLEAR:      CLRL (R3)                  ;clear it
8)             ADDL2 @#FOUR, R3           ;now R3 has address of next longword
9)             JMP @#CLEAR                ;dangerous loop!
10)                .
11)                .
12)                .
```

Figure 6.2 Using deferred addressing

```
1) BUNCH:      .BLKL 4                    ;4 longwords
2) FOUR:       .LONG 4                    ;constant, for changing addresses
3) COUNT:      .BYTE 4                    ;loop control counter
4)                 .
5)                 .
6)                 .
7)             MOVAL @#BUNCH, R3          ;address of 1st longword to clear
8) CLEAR:      CLRL (R3)                  ;clear it
9)             DECB @#COUNT               ;decrement loop count
10)            BEQL CONTINUE              ;if done (count=0), continue
11)    ;else, change address, and clear another location
12)            ADDL2 @#FOUR, R3           ;now R3 has address of next longword
13)            JMP @#CLEAR                ;no-longer-dangerous loop
14) CONTINUE:      .
15)                .
16)                .
```

Figure 6.3 Deferred addressing and a loop count

it will continue to clear longword FOUR. We have sufficient programming skill to write a better program--one which counts the number of longwords to clear; this program is shown in figure 6.3.

Let's we assume that the program fragment of figure 6.3 is a complete program. If we remember that the .ENTRY directive generates a word of 0 for the register save mask, and if we assume that we stop our program with a HALT instruction at CONTINUE, then figure 6.4 shows the contents of memory after the machine language generated by the assembler for our assembly language program of figure 6.3 has been loaded into memory, and just before it is run. As in the past, we have placed an asterisk (*) in each memory location that contains an opcode; this is, of course, purely for illustrative purposes. Also, we have placed question marks in those locations whose contents are unknown at program load time. As usual, we should be able to account for every hex digit shown in this memory picture.

+3	+2	+1	+0	address
??	??	??	??	00000000
??	??	??	??	00000004
??	??	??	??	00000008
??	??	??	??	0000000C
00	00	00	04	00000010
DE*	00	00	04	00000014
00	00	00	9F	00000018
63	D4*	53	00	0000001C
00	14	9F	97*	00000020
0D	13*	00	00	00000024
00	10	9F	C0*	00000028
17*	53	00	00	0000002C
00	00	1E	9F	00000030
??	??	00*	00	00000034

Figure 6.4 Program of figure 6.3 in memory

Decoding Addressing Modes

The only difference between the second operand specifier of the ADDL2 instruction, 53 (in location 2E in figure 6.4), and the (only) operand specifier of the CLRL instruction, 63 (in location 1F), is the single hex digit in the mode field. Nevertheless, the control unit does completely different things when fetching the 2 operands. In the case of the CLRL instruction, the control unit knows that there is only 1 operand, because the CLR instructions are single-operand instructions. When it fetches the operand specifier, and sees that it is mode 6, it knows that the *address* of the operand is in a register; *which* register? Whichever one is specified in the register field--R3, in this case. It then fetches the value from R3, sends it to the memory system along with the *write* command, and sends the longword 00000000_{16} as the value to write at that address.

In the case of the ADDL2 instruction, on the other hand, no references are made to main memory for the second operand. The control unit fetches the opcode of the ADD instruction, decodes it, and knows that it must fetch 2 operands, and therefore 2 operand specifiers. After dealing with the first operand (as described in figure 3.11), the control unit fetches the operand specifier for the second operand, 53. It knows that mode 5 is register mode, which means that the operand is in the register specified in the register field. It fetches the value in R3, gets the 4 which it fetched from the memory location whose label is FOUR, which the assembler assigned address 00000010_{16} in figure 6.4, sends the two values to the ALU to be added, and stores the sum back in R3. Note that, with mode 6, it is not the register, but some location in memory, which changes; with mode 5, of course, the register contains the operand, and so the register changes (if the operand does).

Autoincrement Mode

With register deferred mode (mode 6), we use the contents of the register as the address of the operand. If we want to reuse an instruction, we use register mode (mode 5), with the register as the

```
 1) BUNCH:        .BLKL 4                    ;4 longwords
 2) COUNT:        .BYTE 4                    ;loop control counter
 3)                  .
 4)                  .
 5)                  .
 6)               MOVAL @#BUNCH, R3          ;address of 1st longword to clear
 7) CLEAR:        CLRL (R3)+                 ;clear it and generate next address
 8)               DECB @#COUNT               ;decrement loop count
 9)               BEQL CONTINUE              ;if done (count=0), continue
10)   ;else, clear next location
11)               JMP @#CLEAR                ;no-longer-dangerous loop
12) CONTINUE:        .
13)                  .
14)                  .
```

Figure 6.5 Autoincrement addressing mode

destination of an ADDL2 instruction, to change the contents of the register, and we then use register deferred mode again; even though neither the opcode nor the operand specifiers have changed, the instruction will operate on different operands. This is because mode 6 specifies that the operand's address is in a register; the register's contents have changed, so the instruction's operand has changed. The purpose of autoincrement mode (mode 8) is to enable programmers to combine the use of a register value as an address with automatic changing of the register value for its next use. This combination of use/change/reuse is, as the example in figure 6.3 suggests, especially common when sequentially accessing items stored in consecutive locations in memory (**arrays**).

Mode 8

Autoincrement mode is mode 8; if an operand's address is in register 3, and we would like the register to be *automatically* changed to contain the address of the next operand in memory, then we would use the operand specifier 83_{16}. In assembly language, we indicate that the assembler should generate an operand specifier with 8 in the mode field by surrounding the register name with parentheses, and following the closing parentheses with a +: (R n)+. Thus, we could rewrite the program fragment in figure 6.3 using autoincrement addressing, and avoid having to explicitly change the address in the register, as shown in figure 6.5. This program fragment is one instruction shorter than the one in figure 6.3: the ADDL2 on line 12 of figure 6.3 is no longer necessary because when the control unit finds 8 in the mode field, it understands that the register contains the address of the operand, and *after* the address is used to fetch the operand, the register contents are to be changed (so the register will contain the address of the next operand). Although a program we write using autoincrement is only one instruction shorter than one using register deferred mode, at *run* time the former might fetch and execute many fewer instructions than the latter because the address-changing instruction is usually in a loop (we wouldn't bother changing the address to reuse the instruction if it weren't in a loop). If the loop is executed 1000 times, then a program using autoincrement will execute 1000 fewer ADD instructions than one using register deferred.

Autoincrement with Bytes, Words, and Longwords

The purpose of autoincrement is to *automatically* change a register so that it contains the address of the next operand. How does the control unit know what the address of the next operand will be? If we are dealing with bytes, then the address of the next operand will be 1 more than the address of the current operand; if we are dealing with words, then the addresses will differ by 2, and if we are dealing with longwords the addresses will differ by 4--what does the control unit do? The control unit does exactly what we would like it to do: autoincrement with a byte instruction changes the register by 1, autoincrement with a word instruction changes the register by 2, and autoincrement with a longword instruction changes the register by 4. This means that the control unit does slightly different things, with the same operand specifier--depending on whether the opcode is for byte, word, or longword operands.

It is important to understand the difference between the **autoincrement** *addressing mode* and the **increment** *instruction*; inexperienced assembly language programmers often confuse the two. The increment instruction *always* adds 1 to its operand; that operand may be a byte, a word, or a longword, and may be specified with any of the operand specifiers we have seen (or any of the ones that we have not yet seen)--including autoincrement! The autoincrement addressing mode, on the other hand, is a way of specifying operands; it is designed to make our lives as programmers easier by changing the address in a register by an appropriate amount--1, 2, or 4, depending on the operand type.

It is also important to realize that, of the addressing modes we have seen so far, only autoincrement is guaranteed to change the value in the register. In addition, we might wonder just how the register changes if we refer to the same register with autoincrement addressing, more than once in the same instruction. For example, if we were to write

```
MOVAL  @#VALUE1, R0
ADDL2  (R0)+, (R0)+
```

what would get added to what? The designers of the VAX could have decided to do any one of several things in a case like this, but they chose to do the something that is consistent with the ordinary use of autoincrement: the register is changed *after* its contents are used as the address of the operand. So, after R0 is used for the address of the source operand, it is changed by 4 (because ADDL2 is a longword instruction). Then, after it is used for the address of the destination operand, it is changed by 4 again. But, then, one might wonder, does it get changed *three* times, since the destination address is used twice--once for the source of the second operand, and once for the destination of the result? Here, again, the VAX designers made their decision with consistency in mind: the 2-operand add instructions all use the *same address* for the second source operand and the destination operand, so the value in R0 is changed once after the first source operand is fetched, and once after the results are stored in the location from which the second source operand was fetched. The register is modified twice so that, in this case, its contents change by 8.

Autodecrement Addressing: Mode 7

The autodecrement addressing mode is very similar to the autoincrement addressing mode. In both cases the register contains the address of the operand, and in both cases the register's contents change. However, with autodecrement mode (mode 7), the register changes *before* it is used as the address of the operand (with autoincrement the change is *after* it is used as an address), and with autodecrement the register is *decremented*, while with autoincrement it is incremented. Autodecrement addressing may be used to deal with an array in reverse order--reverse order, that is, with respect to increasing addresses in memory. In other words, if we place the address of the next item after the last one in R7, and then access an array using autodecrement with R7, we will access, sequentially,

```
1) BUNCH:       .BLKL 4                    ;4 longwords
2) COUNT:       .BYTE 4                    ;loop control counter
3)                      .
4)                      .
5)                      .
6)              MOVAL @#COUNT, R3          ;address after BUNCH
7) CLEAR:       CLRL -(R3)                 ;generate next address; clear it
8)              DECB @#COUNT               ;decrement loop count
9)              BEQL CONTINUE              ;if done (count=0), continue
10)  ;else, clear next location
11)             JMP @#CLEAR                ;no-longer-dangerous loop
12) CONTINUE:          .
13)                    .
14)                    .
```

Figure 6.6 Autodecrement addressing mode

each item in the array, starting with the one with the largest address and ending (if we so write our program) with the one with the smallest address.

Autodecrement is mode 7; in assembly language, we use the register deferred notation, with a "-" to symbolize the decrementing: -(Rn). Notice that the placement of the "-" is designed to remind us of the fact that autodecrement is a *pre*decrement, just as the placement of the "+" for autoincrement is designed to remind us of the fact that it is a *post*increment. In addition, autodecrement is similar to autoincrement in that when we use it with byte instructions, the register changes by 1; when we use it with word instructions, the register changes by 2; and when we use it with longword instructions the register changes by 4. Figure 6.6 shows the program fragment for clearing 4 longwords, rewritten with autodecrement addressing.

Why is the increment of autoincrement done *after* the register is used, while the decrement of autodecrement is done *before*? Clearly, this is not an oversight; also, as long as we start out with the correct address, there is no particular advantage to either post or preincrementing or decrementing. However, we will soon see, in our discussion of stacks and the VAX, that the combination of predecrementing and postincrementing, is exactly the right combination for pushing items onto a stack and then popping them off. But before we discuss stacks, we must discuss more addressing modes, and several other topics as well.

Displacement Addressing

Deferred addressing is fine when we can place the address of some location in memory, and autoincrement is very convenient when we wish to step sequentially through successive locations in memory. But what addressing mode do we use if we wish to *randomly* access some array, for example, of data items? The VAX provides us with a new family of addressing modes (which are nearly identical to one another, we will soon see): modes A, C and E. These modes, the **displacement addressing modes,** allow us to specify a register and a *displacement*; the sum of the register contents and the displacement is the address of the operand. When an operand's address must be calculated, we often call the calculated address the **effective address.**

Displacements

Clearly, an operand specifier can specify only a mode and a register; where is the displacement? In the VAX, the displacement *immediately follows* the operand specifier. How big is the displacement? It can be either a byte, a word, or a longword--which is why there are *three* displacement modes. If we wish to store only a small displacement to add to the register contents, we use *byte* displacement, mode A. If we wish to store a medium-sized displacement, we use *word* displacement, mode C; if we wish to store a large displacement, we use longword displacement, mode E.

How do we specify displacement mode in assembly language? The assembler recognizes a syntax that is (conveniently) similar to that for register deferred addressing:

    ADDL2 DISP1(R0), DISP2(R3)

will add the longword whose address is R0+DISP1 to the longword whose address is R3+DISP2, and store the sum in the second location. If we wished, for example, to add the longword whose address was 12 more than the address in R0 to the longword whose address was 4 more than the address in R2, we would write the following:

    ADDL2 12(R0), 4(R2)

When we assemble our program, the assembler decides whether the displacements fit in bytes, words, or longwords, and generates the appropriate machine language. For the above example, the assembler would generate the following printout fragment:

    04 A2 0C A0 C0   0002 2   ADDL2   12(R0), 4(R2)

The machine-language portion of the printout is read, as usual, from right to left: the opcode C0 corresponds to the assembly language mnemonic ADDL2; the operand specifier A0 indicates byte displacement mode with register 0; the displacement is 0C in hexadecimal (which is 12_{10}); the second operand specifier, A2, indicates byte displacement on register 2, and the second displacement is 04, which is the same in decimal and hex. Note that, for both operands, the assembler has chosen byte displacement, and that in each case the displacement immediately follows the operand specifier. Note also that--as usual--we use base 10, but the assembler generates hexadecimal values for the displacements.

Using Displacement Modes

There are two different ways to use the displacement addressing modes. The first way, shown above, is to put the **base address** of a data structure such as an array into a register (with a MOVA(B,W,L) instruction, of course) and specify the displacement as some large or small number to be added to the base address. The second way works in exactly the same manner as the first, but we, as programmers, think about it differently. We will use the second way to rewrite the program of figure 6.3, in figure 6.7. The only difference between these two ways is that in the first method, we place the base address in the register and the displacement in the field that follows the operand specifier, while in the second method we place the base address in the displacement field and the displacement from that base address in the register. In this second case--when we use a symbolic label representing an address as the displacement--the assembler doesn't necessarily know how large the displacement must be. If, as in the previous example (ADDL2 12(R0), 4(R2)), the value of the displacement is known (because the symbols "12" and "4" have the built-in values 12 and 4), then the assembler uses the shortest displacement possible, as usual. If, however, the displacement is *not* known--as in figure 6.7, because the assembler doesn't know where in memory the program will

```
 1) BUNCH:        .BLKL 4              ;4 longwords
 2) FOUR:         .LONG 4              ;constant, for changing addresses
 3) COUNT:        .BYTE 4              ;loop control counter
 4)                   .
 5)                   .
 6)                   .
 7)               CLRL R3              ;start with R3=0
 8) CLEAR:        CLRL BUNCH(R3)       ;operand address: R3[=0]+BUNCH
 9)               DECB @#COUNT         ;decrement loop count
10)               BEQL CONTINUE        ;if done (count=0), continue
11)    ;else, change address, and clear another location
12)               ADDL2 @#FOUR, R3     ;R3 has offset for address of next longword
13)               JMP @#CLEAR          ;no-longer-dangerous loop
14) CONTINUE:         .
15)                   .
16)                   .
```

Figure 6.7 Using displacement addressing

finally be loaded, and so doesn't know the final value of the label BUNCH--then the assembler must make *some* assumption. It assumes that the displacement will fit into a word, and so uses word displacement--mode C. If this assumption is wrong, then the linker will produce an error diagnostic at link time. For cases in which the assembler doesn't know the value of the label before it must use it for a displacement, there are special operators we, programmers, can use to help the assembler. We can use B^DISP to indicate that DISP should be a byte, we can use W^DISP to indicate that DISP should be a word, and L^DISP to indicate that DISP should be a longword. Unless we write very large programs, word displacement will suffice; if we wish to be absolutely safe, however, we can always specify longword displacement with the "L^" operator.

Figure 6.8 shows the machine language that the assembler generates for the program of figure 6.7 (assuming that $EXIT_S generates the HALT instruction, and that figure 6.7 is the whole program) after it has been loaded into memory). In this case, as expected (since BUNCH is a symbolic label), the assembler used word displacement. As in the past, we have placed an asterisk (*) in each memory location that contains an opcode; this is, once more, only for illustrative purposes. The displacement addressing mode chosen by the assembler and loaded into location $1A_{16}$ is C3--word displacement on R3. The displacement in location $1B_{16}$ corresponds to the address assigned to BUNCH, which is 0000, since BUNCH is the first memory-allocating directive or instruction in this program; it will have to be changed, depending on exactly where in memory this program is loaded.

Calculating the Effective Address

It is important to understand, in the case of the displacement addressing modes as in other cases, what is done at assemble time and what is done at run time. Clearly, registers are initialized only at run time, so we need either a MOVA(B,W,L) instruction or a CLR(B,W,L) instruction in our program to initialize the register. The effective address is also calculated at run time--by the control unit. (A register's contents can't be added to a displacement at assemble time, because a register has no defined contents at assemble time.) The displacement, on the other hand, is calculated at assemble time; we must be sure that we understand exactly what the displacement is: it is one of a pair of addends (the other is a register's contents) whose sum is an address. It is *not* an address whose contents are to be added to a register, and it is not a number that will be added to a register to

+3	+2	+1	+0	address
??	??	??	??	00000000
??	??	??	??	00000004
??	??	??	??	00000008
??	??	??	??	0000000C
00	00	00	04	00000010
D4*	00	00	04	00000014
00	C3	D4*	53	00000018
14	9F	97*	00	0000001C
13*	00	00	00	00000020
10	9F	C0*	0D	00000024
53	00	00	00	00000028
00	19	9F	17*	0000002C
??	00*	00	00	00000030

Figure 6.8 Program of figure 6.7 in memory

calculate an *operand*. The contents of the register do *not* change when we use displacement modes: the sum of the register and displacement is stored in some location that is private to the control unit (we programmers have no access to it). We will encounter other private locations in the course of our examination of the VAX's architecture; one class of private locations which we will discuss in later chapters is the **privileged registers.**

So, let's review what the control unit does when it encounters an operand specifier that specifies displacement mode. It "knows" that the displacement immediately follows the operand specifier (as in locations 1A and 1B in figure 6.8), and it knows that when the operand specifier was fetched the PC was updated, and so the PC contains the address of the displacement. How long is the displacement? The mode field of the operand specifier answers this question: if it is mode A, then the displacement is a byte, so the control unit requests 1 byte from the memory system (that byte's address is memory[PC]). If it is mode C, then the displacement is 2 bytes long, and so the control unit asks for *2* bytes from address memory[PC], and if it is mode E the displacement is 4 bytes long, so the control unit asks for *4* bytes from address memory[PC]. When the control unit gets back the displacement, it adds it to the contents of the register specified in the **register** field of the operand specifier. This sum is the operand's address; it is sent along the bus to the memory system, which returns the operand itself.

Why So Many Variations?

The only addressing modes we really need are register mode and register deferred mode. From this pair, we can create the equivalent of displacement addressing, autoincrement addressing, and autodecrement addressing, albeit somewhat clumsily. For example, in Pascal, the record construct can be thought of as an array with unequal-sized elements; Pascal compilers often translate references to record fields into addresses using displacement addressing, where the beginning address of the record is the displacement, and the offset of the particular field is in the register: the sum of the register and the offset is the address of the record field. This *could* be done using only register and register deferred modes, but it is more easily done using the displacement mode.

We will demonstrate another case in which displacement mode is especially useful; this case involves a more sophisticated example of random access than either of the ones already described. Consider the following application: an automated teller machine (ATM) provides customers of a bank with 24-hour-per-day banking services from multiple locations. An ATM station may provide the following services:

1. deposit to savings   DTS
2. deposit to checking   DTC
3. withdrawal from savings   WFS
4. withdrawal from checking   WFC
5. transfer to savings   TTS
6. transfer to checking   TTC
7. loan payment   LP

The customer uses a special keyboard to select the desired service. Let us assume that pushing a digit key leads to the binary equivalent of that digit being placed in a 1-byte memory location called KEY. We can then write code to process requests as shown in figure 6.9. This exhaustive sequence of comparisons may be suitable for checking a short list of possibilities, but there is a better way when many cases must be distinguished. Consider the more sophisticated alternative in figure 6.10. The effective address (which is the sum of the contents of R6 and address TABLE) of the JMP instruction at NOTE selects the appropriate instruction from the series of JMP instructions beginning at TABLE. If someone picked 2, for a deposit to a checking account, the program would compute $[(2\text{-}1) * 2 * 2]$ + 2 (which is 6) in R6; then, TABLE(R6) would be, at run time, TABLE+6, the address of the instruction JMP @#DTC, which would (if we had written the entire program) deposit funds to the user's checking account. This construct is called a **jump table**; Pascal's **case statement** is often translated by a compiler into a jump table. We will soon learn about another VAX addressing mode which allows us to eliminate the JMPs in the table; this will make the technique even more useful. (The VAX also has instructions to implement a case statement directly.)

Recall that JMP Rn is illegal. However, the other addressing modes can all be used with JMP:

```
JMP DISPL(Rn)      ;displacement modes: PC←DISPL + (Rn)
JMP (Rn)           ;register deferred: PC←(Rn)
JMP (Rn)+          ;auto-increment:¹ PC←(Rn), then Rn←(Rn) + 1
```

In addition, nothing we have said about addressing modes changes the fact that the branch instructions can *never* use a register as part of their target address; branches have no operand specifier, and so the assembler will complain if we use anything other than a symbolic label as the target of a branch.

.LONG, .WORD, and .BYTE Revisited

We have, so far, concentrated on the use of the .LONG, .WORD, and .BYTE directives with only a single constant as an operand. In fact, these directives are much more general than that. Consider the following description:

<LABEL:> .LONG EXPR<,EXPR>*

---

[1] It is not clear why one would use autoincrement with a JMP instruction, but it is perfectly legal to do so.

```
                CMPB @#KEY, @#ONE          ;was a 1 pressed?
                BEQL DTS                   ;if so, deposit to savings
        ;else, check for some other key pressed
                CMPB @#KEY, @#TWO          ;was a 2 pressed?
                BEQL DTC                   ;if so, deposit to checking
        ;else, check for some other key
                        .
                        .
                        .
                CMPB @#KEY, @#SEVEN        ;was a 7 pressed?
                BEQL LP                    ;if so, loan payment
        ;else: ERROR!
                BRB ERROR
        DTS:            ;code for Deposit To Savings
        DTC:            ;code for Deposit To Checking
        LP:             ;code for Loan Payment
                        .
                        .
                        .
        ONE:            .BYTE 1
                        .
                        .
                        .
        SEVEN:          .BYTE 7
```

Figure 6.9 Exhaustive comparison technique

Recall that <...> means *optional.* The asterisk (*) in this case means "any number of occurrences of the preceding item (even none)." The symbol EXPR stands for *expression*; this can be any number representable in 32 bits. It may be symbolic (e.g., a user-defined label), and it may involve some limited arithmetic. Thus, if we define TABLE as a symbolic label, we may write, for example:

    .LONG TABLE, TABLE+8   ;2 addresses

If we have the line "TEN = ^X10" in our program, then we may write

    .LONG   3*TEN, TEN/2, TEN-4

and Macro will allocate 3 longwords and request that they be initialized at load time to 30_{16}, 8_{16} and C_{16}, respectively. Macro will perform the same kinds of simple arithmetic calculations for .BYTE and .WORD directives, except that valid operands must fit in 8 and 16 bits respectively.

The full set of rules for Macro expressions is lengthy and somewhat esoteric. Since our purpose is not to become experts in all the fine points of Macro, we won't discuss expressions much more; we have seen most of what we need already.

For each of the instructions listed below, assume that the initial contents of R1, R2, and memory locations 00001112 and 00002020 (in hexadecimal) are as follows:

R1:	00001112
R2:	00002020
00001112:	00054326
00002020:	00000123

Match each instruction below with the contents of R1 and R2 *after* the execution of that instruction. Ignore the results of preceding instructions.

Instruction		R1	R2
MOVB (R1)+, (R2)	a.	00001110	00002020
MOVW (R2)+, R1	b.	00001111	00002021
SUBW2 R1, R2	c.	00000123	00002022
MOVB R1, (R2)+	d.	00001113	00002017
MOVB (R1), R2	e.	00001113	00002020
ADDW2 #10, (R1)	f.	00001112	00002022
	g.	00001112	00002021
	h.	00001112	00000F0E
	i.	00001112	00002020
	j.	00001112	00002026

Figure 6.10 Jump table technique

The .ADDRESS Directive

In the preceding section, we saw an example of allocating a longword and initializing it to contain an address, using the .LONG directive. This will work perfectly well, but Macro has a special directive that makes such allocation clearer to programmers: the .ADDRESS directive. Thus, rather than writing

    ADDRS: .LONG TABLE, TABLE+8   ;2 addresses

we could write

    ADDRS: .ADDRESS TABLE, TABLE+8   ;2 addresses

These two statements generate the same machine language, but the latter makes our intentions clearer than does the former.

Copying

Copying things is a common occurrence. Suppose we wish to move a character string.[2] We could write the following code:

```
STRING1:    .ASCIZ "This is a test"     ;string to copy
STRING2:    .BLKB 50                    ;destination of copy
              .
              .

BEGIN:      MOVAB @#STRING1, R1         ;address of source in R1
            MOVAB @#STRING2, R2         ;address of dest in R2
LOOP:       MOVB (R1)+, (R2)+
            BNEQ LOOP
              .
              .
              .
```

The program begins at BEGIN and places the addresses of the source string STRING1 and the destination string STRING2 in registers 1 and 2, respectively. Then it does the following:

```
STRING2 ← (STRING1)              ;1st byte
STRING2 + 1 ← (STRING1 + 1)      ;2nd byte
  .
  .
  .
STRING2 + n ← (STRING1 + n)      ;last byte
```

Each MOVB updates the CC according to the value of the byte moved; the last byte of STRING1 is the 0 (NUL) generated by the assembler because of the .ASCIZ directive. When that 0 has been copied, the Z bit of the CC will be 1, so the BNEQ instruction, which is taken only if the Z bit is 0, will not be taken, and the loop will stop.

Why does the control unit change R1 and R2 by 1 and not by 2 or 4? Because when the autoincrement addressing mode is used with a byte instruction (which MOVB most certainly is), the control unit always modifies the registers by 1. This is exactly what we would want, of course, because addresses of consecutive bytes differ by 1, and we are using the MOVB instruction to copy consecutive bytes. Notice, also, that the Z bit (and other CC bits) are set according to the value of the byte moved. Although the autoincrement addressing mode changes R1 and R2, those changes *never* influence the CC bits.

If we were copying words, we would use a MOVW instruction, and the control unit would change the registers by 2; if we were copying longwords, we would use a MOVL instruction, and the control unit would change the registers by 4. In all cases, the registers change *after* the register has been used to find the address of the operand. Symbolically,

```
OPB (Rn)+     ;use address in Rn, then Rn←(Rn) + 1
OPW (Rn)+     ;use address in Rn, then Rn←(Rn) + 2
OPL (Rn)+     ;use address in Rn, then Rn←(Rn) + 4
```

---

[2]We won't really *move* it; we will duplicate it by copying it to a new area of memory.

Radix Control

Recall that the default radix of the assembler is decimal. Thus, if we were to write

    TEN: .BYTE 10

the assembler would allocate a byte and initialize it to $0A_{16}$. We have already seen that we can initialize a byte to 10_{16} by writing either one of the following:

    SIXTEEN: .BYTE 16, or
    SIXTEEN: .BYTE ^X10

Macro has operators for binary and octal radices, as well. The following four directives will all generate the same machine language:

    ONE: .BYTE 12   ;decimal, by default
    TWO: .BYTE ^X0C   ;hexadecimal
    THREE: .BYTE ^O14   ;octal (base 8)
    FOUR: .BYTE ^B1100   ;binary

Note that the octal operator is the uppercase letter "O," not the digit zero ("0").

Immediate Operands

It is a nuisance to have to make up names and set aside space for constants, addresses, and so forth; the VAX provides the **immediate operand** construction, which is another addressing mode, to help us avoid this nuisance. This addressing mode is used in assembly language by placing the character "#" in front of the desired symbol or constant. For example,

    OP #M, DEST

The number or symbol "M" will be used when OP is being executed, not as the *address* of the desired operand (which is the normal situation), but as the actual operand itself. Thus the name *immediate operand*: the operand is immediately available, as part of the instruction. This method of specifying operands only makes sense for the source operand of a 2 or 3-operand instruction. So we could write the following:

    ADDB2   #33, @#sum   ;SUM ← (SUM) + 33
    CMPW   @#ABC, #100   ;does (ABC) = 100?
    SUBL2   #60, R1   ;R1 ← (R1) − 60

This shortens, simplifies, and clarifies programs, and it may cause them to execute a little faster. In addition, we may wish to combine the assembler's renaming directive with immediate operands, much as we use Pascal's **const**: if we have the statement "MAX = 100" somewhere in our program *before* the instruction "CMPB R0, #MAX", then the instruction will be assembled *exactly* as the instruction "CMPB R0, #100". However, if we have used the assemble-time constant, our program will be clearer, and easier to change, than if we embed the *magic number*, 100, in our program.

Immediate ASCII Operands

The assembler also understands a special syntax for immediate ASCII character codes. Often, we wish to compare some character code with a special one: for example, we might write a program to read input from the keyboard until the user types the letter "q." If GETC is a system service that reads a typed character from the keyboard and places its ASCII code in the location specified by its argument,[3] then we could write the following program fragment:

        GETC R7   ;read a character
        CMPB R7, #^X71   ;check for "q"

However, it is tedious to look up the ASCII code for "q," and it is less than perfectly clear to have the hex number, 71, embedded in our program. The assembler understands the "^A" prefix, when preceding a delimited character, to mean that it is to supply the ASCII code for that character. Thus, we can replace "CMPB R7, #^X71" with "CMPB R7, #^A/q/"; the assembler will generate exactly the same machine language in either case. The delimited string that is the argument of the ^A operator can be up to 16 characters long, depending on the length of operand the opcode operates on.

Operand Specifier For Immediate Operands

The operand specifier generated by the assembler when it encounters a statement with "#constant" is 8F, and the constant itself immediately follows the operand specifier (this is similar to the operand specifier 9F, which is followed by the *address* of the operand rather than by the operand itself). The constant is as long as it needs to be for the opcode: for a byte instruction, the constant is 1 byte long; for a word instruction it is 2 bytes long, and for a longword instruction is 4 bytes long. The mode 8 used with immediate operands is the same mode 8, of course, that we have just learned is autoincrement mode; when used with register F (the PC!), however, interesting new possibilities arise. A careful reader of program listings may notice that in some cases immediate operands are *not* assembled using mode 8; we will discuss the use of mode 8--and some of the other addressing modes-- with the program counter in chapter 8.

Addressing Mode Summary

When writing data-oriented instructions, we can now choose among several addressing modes, in addition to using **absolute** addressing (with operand specifier 9F followed by the operand's address), which we have known about for some time. The addressing modes we have seen so far are summarized in figure 6.11.

The important points to remember about these addressing modes are:

1.   They can only be used freely with data oriented instructions such as MOV(B,W,L), ADD(B,W,L), CMP(B,W,L), INC(B,W,L), CLR(B,W,L), and so forth.
2.   The control-oriented JMP instruction cannot use register mode; it can, however, use register deferred, autoincrement, autodecrement, and the displacement modes.
3.   The control-oriented branch instructions cannot use any of these addressing modes; their operands can only be symbolic labels which the assembler can convert into a PC-relative offset.

---

[3]GETC, and the other *system service macros* described, are available with this book. Their use is described more thoroughly in Appendix 1.

Mode	Name	Format	Explanation
5	Register	Rn	Operand is in Rn.
6	Register deferred	(Rn)	Operand address is in Rn.
7	Autodecrement	–(Rn)	Rn ←Rn – dec *before* address is computed; *then* operand address is in Rn.[†]
8	Autoincrement	(Rn)+	Operand address is in Rn; Rn ← Rn + inc *after* operand is fetched.[‡]
A (C, E)	Byte (word, longword) displacement	X(Rn)	Operand address is X + Rn; X follows operand specifier.
8[PC]	Immediate	#X	Operand is X; X follows operand specifier.
9[PC]	Absolute	@#X	Operand address is X; X follows operand specifier.

[†]dec=1 for byte, 2 for word, 4 for longword instruction.

[‡]inc=1 for byte, 2 for word, 4 for longword instruction.

Figure 6.11 Basic addressing modes.

4. Of all the addressing modes we have seen, the only ones which *always* modify the register specified in the operand specifier are autoincrement and autodecrement. (Register mode *can* modify the register, but only if it is used to specify a *destination* operand.)

5. Immediate addressing only makes sense for the source operand(s) of 2- (or 3-) operand instructions, or for the CMP(B,W,L) instructions.

6. With the autoincrement addressing mode, the register is incremented by 1 (*after* it is used) for a byte instruction, by 2 for a word instruction, and by 4 for a longword instruction.

7. With the autodecrement addressing mode, the register is decremented by 1 (*before* it is used) for a byte instruction, by 2 for a word instruction, and by 4 for a longword instruction.

There are many other addressing modes for the VAX. We will describe the rest of the addressing modes in chapter 8, after we have had a chance to use the ones we have just introduced.

Exercises for Chapter 6

1. Each instruction uses the indicated initial values (i.e., the results of one instruction are *not* used by the next instruction). Fill in the contents of the requested locations (including the PC) *after* each instruction has been executed. Leave entries blank if no change occurs. Assume that symbolic label X has been assigned the value 1010_{16}.

Instruction	R1	R2	11100440	11100444	11100448	PC
Initial Values:	11100440	11100444	11200444	1120FFFF	0010FFFF	00001000
MOVL R1, R2						
MOVB R1, R2						
MOVB (R1), R2						
MOVW (R2)+, (R1)						
MOVL (R1), (R2)						
MOVL #66, R1						
MOVB R1, (R2)						
CLRW (R2)+						
CLRB (R2)+						
CLRL (R2)+						
CLRL 4(R2)						
CLRB 4(R2)						
JMP (R2)						
CMPB (R2)+, (R2)+						
ADDB3 #2, #2, (R1)						
INCW (R2)						
INCL (R2)						
INCB (R2)						
BRB X						

2. Write an assembly language program to take a string which ends in a 0 byte (NUL character) and create a new string with the same characters but without any spaces in it. Thus

.ASCIZ "TEST O NE TWO" becomes
.ASCIZ "TESTONETWO."

3. Each of the following may be acceptable or not to the assembler or to the CPU, depending on other parts of the program in which they are used. For each statement below, specify a circumstance under which it (or the code the assembler will generate for it) will *not* be acceptable. Use a reason only once. For example:

LOOP MOVB @#A, @#B   ;illegal label syntax: no colon

a. BRB   CONTINUE
b. JMP   R4
c. MOVW #3E99, R1
d. BRW   (R5)
e. JMP   (R5)
f. BEQL A+777
g. MOVB #44, #35
h. ADDB2 #443, R3

4.   Show the machine language the assembler generates for the following assembly language test:

```
                CONST = 64
                .ENTRY START, 0
BEGIN:          MOVB (R0), R0
                CLRB 44(R1)
                ADDL2 #CONST, (R0)+
                HALT
STORE:          .WORD 27
                .END START
```

5.   Write an assembly language program using ten or fewer instructions which, given a character string ending with a 0 byte, creates a new string with all the characters reversed. Thus, if the input string is

STRING: .ASCIZ "ABCDEFGHI"

the program will produce, as output, the same codes that the assembler would produce if you typed

REVERSE: .ASCIZ "IHGFEDCBA".

6.   Indicate if each of the following statements is true (T) or false (F):

a.   Uninitialized memory locations can be counted on to contain 0.
b.   An unconditional branch instruction should execute much faster than a jump instruction.
c.   In order to fetch and execute the instruction MOVL #100, R1, the control unit makes three references to memory.
d.   Some of the *conditional* branch instructions modify the CC bits.
e.   There is absolutely no difference between DECL R3 and SUBL2 #1, R3.

7.   When execution of the program shown below reaches the instruction at ABC, R1 contains a longword integer between 0 and 4, inclusive. Assume that labels L0, L1, L2, L3, and L4 are properly defined at various points in this program. Write no more than five instructions at location ABC that will cause control to be transferred to L0 if R1 contains 0, L1 if R1 contains 1, and so forth. Any needed items (but no instructions) may be inserted at the beginning of the program.

```
        .ENTRY  START, 0
            .
            .
            .
ABC:
            .
            .
            .
        $EXIT_S
```

8. Briefly explain what the following program segment does. Write down the final contents of AL, AL + 1, ..., AL + 4.

```
                    .ENTRY START, 0
                    MOVAB @#BUFFER, R1
                    MOVAB @#AL, R2
                    MOVL #30, R3
L1:                 CLRB (R2)+
                    DECL R3
                    BNEQ L1
L2:                 CMPB (R1), #10
                    BEQL FOUND
                    MOVB (R1)+, R3
                    SUBB2 @#A, R3
                    BLSS L2
                    INCB AL(R3)
                    BRB L2
FOUND:              DUMP AL, BUFFER
                    $EXIT_S
A:                  .ASCIZ "A"
AL:                 .BLKB 30
BUFFER:             .ASCIZ /THIS IS A TEST SEQUENCE/<^X0A><^X0D>
```

9. What does "MOVL #1, @#ABC" do? What does "MOVL @#ABC, #1" do?

10. For each of the instructions listed below, assume that the initial contents of R1, R2, and memory locations 00001112 and 00002020 (in hexadecimal) are as follows:

   R1: 00001112
   R2: 00002020
   00001112: 00054326
   00002020: 00000123

   Match each instruction below with the contents of R1 and R2, *after* the execution of that instruction. Ignore the results of preceding instructions.

Instruction		R1	R2
MOVB (R1)+, (R2)	a.	00001110	00002020
MOVW (R2)+, R1	b.	00001111	00002021
SUBW2 R1, R2	c.	00000123	00002022
MOVB R1, (R2)+	d.	00001113	00002017
MOVB (R1), R2	e.	00001113	00002020
ADDW2 #10, (R1)	f.	00001112	00002022
	g.	00001112	00002021
	h.	00001112	00000F0E
	i.	00001112	00002020
	j.	00001112	00002026

11. Write a program which counts the occurrences of the letter "m" in any string that ends with a 0 byte. The program should place the answer (the count) in R1. Be sure to add useful comments to your code.

12. Define each item and explain (briefly) why it is important.

   a. PSL
   b. PC-relative addressing
   c. effective address
   d. NUL character

13.   Briefly explain what the following program does. Assume that the macro PUTS is a request for a system service that displays all the ASCII characters from the address provided as its argument until it encounters a byte of 0. The code provided by the macro IOINIT must be executed before PUTS can be used.

```
                .ENTRY START, 0
                IOINIT
                MOVAB @#ABC, R2
OVER:           MOVAB @#STRING, R1
LOOP:           CMPB (R1), (R2)
                BEQL REPLACE
                ADDL2 #1, R1
                CMPB (R1), #10
                BNEQ LOOP
                ADDL2 #1, R2
                CMPB (R2), #10
                BNEQ OVER
REPLACE:        MOVB @#BLANK, (R1)
                MOVB @#BLANK, (R2)
PRINT:          PUTS ABC
                PUTS STRING
                $EXIT_S
ABC:            .ASCIZ /ANSWER/<^X0A><^X0D>
STRING:         .ASCIZ /QUESTION/<^X0A><^X0D>
BLANK:          .ASCII //
```

      If STRING2: .ASCIZ /LOOK OUT/<^X0A><^X0D> is substituted for the line beginning with STRING: and the program is run again, what changes?

14.   Outline how you might implement a program that loads VAX machine-language programs written according to the specifications provided in chapter 3.

15.   What is in registers 1 and 2 after the following pairs of instructions have been executed? Write your answers in hexadecimal.

      a)   MOVL   #^X12345678, R1
            MOVB   #0, R1
      b)   MOVW   #31245, R2
            MOVL   #100, R2
      c)   MOVL   #^X3E456, R1
            MOVW   #255, R1

16.   What would be left in registers 1 and 2 if, after the series of MOV instructions in the preceding problem, we had written

      a)   DECB   R1
      b)   CLRB   R2
      c)   INCB   R1

Computer Arithmetic

Introduction

The arithmetic capabilities of a computer are typically determined by its Arithmetic Logic Unit (ALU). The VAX supports both **integer** arithmetic and **floating-point** arithmetic (floating-point numbers are sometimes called **real numbers**). Integer arithmetic is supported for the operations provided by the ADD(B,W,L)[2,3], SUB(B,W,L)[2,3], INC(B,W,L), and other instructions. Hardware support for arithmetic with floating-point numbers is provided by a special floating-point ALU, or some other method, which will be described in chapter 13. In this chapter we will discuss most of the remaining details of integer arithmetic on the VAX. We will deal in particular with (1) representing signed numbers; (2) mapping the infinite number of integers into the finite number of possible representations in the VAX; and (3) what can go wrong, how to know, and what to do about it.

Unsigned Numbers

So far, we have barely mentioned negative numbers; we have merely said that, in the VAX, a negative number has its most significant bit set. In order to understand negative-number representations, however, we must examine more closely the kind of integers we have been using so far: **unsigned** integers. Unsigned integers range from 0 to the largest number representable in 8, 16, or 32 bits (depending on the type of instruction--byte, word or longword, respectively). Since these numbers are all larger than 0, we could call them *positive*. However, that would imply that there are also negative numbers, and when we use *all* the possible combinations of 8 (or 16, or 32) bits to represent numbers 0 and larger, there are *none* left for negative numbers.

Modular Arithmetic

In mathematics, unsigned numbers extend from 0 to ∞ ; given any number, we can always produce a larger number. In computers, however, numbers must be stored in memory locations; since memory locations have a finite number of bits, there is a finite number of possible combinations of those bits, and so there is a *largest* number that can be stored in a computer's memory. A number system with a finite number of numbers is a **modular** number system. Let us use 3-bit numbers for our examples: there are only 8 possible combinations of 3 bits, so there are only 8 different 3-bit numbers. This is a **modulo 8** number system; numbers that differ by 8 are indistinguishable from each other. It is often helpful to picture a modulo number system as taking a number *line* (stretching from 0 to some largest number) and connecting the ends--forming a number *circle*. This is shown in figure 7.1 for a modulo 8 system; 000 is the smallest number and 111 (7) is the largest.

Adding

With a number line, we can represent adding as moving to the right along the number line; with a number circle, we represent adding as moving clockwise around the number circle. We can see from figure 7.1 that the next number after 7 (111) is 0 (000); this is the same as saying that 8 ≡ 0,

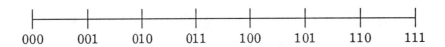

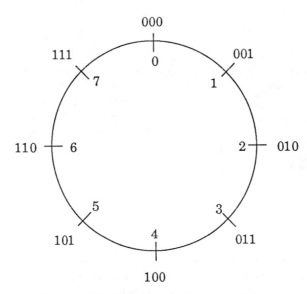

Figure 7.1 Number line and number circle

modulo 8. Note that 0 and 8 differ by 8 and so are indistinguishable, modulo 8; the same holds true for 1 and 9, 2 and 10, and so forth. Another way to think of this (perhaps strange, at first thought) phenomenon is to realize that, in a modulo 8 system, there are only 3 bits to represent numbers; if we try to represent a number that is too big for 3 bits, the most significant bit(s) "disappear."[1] So, *if* we had 4 bits, then adding 1 to 111 would produce the result 1000, which would be the unsigned representation of 8. However, since we only have 3 bits, the fourth bit cannot be stored, and so when we add 1 to 111 we get 000--the low-order 3 bits of the result. We will see that *all* the things that can go wrong with integer arithmetic go wrong because of the fact that computers use *fixed-length* numbers; it is impossible to map the infinite number of numbers in mathematics into the finite number of bit combinations available in a computer. When we examine different representations for *signed* numbers, one criterion for the quality of a representation is how easy it is to deal with these unavoidable mapping errors.

---

[1]Many cars have odometers that use a modulo 100,000 number system.

Bit pattern	Unsigned	Sign-magnitude
000	0	+0
001	1	+1
010	2	+2
011	3	+3
100	4	−0
101	5	−1
110	6	−2
111	7	−3

Figure 7.2 Sign-magnitude representation

Negative Numbers

The first decision we must make in designing a representation for negative numbers is how many negative numbers there will be.[2] A simple choice is to allocate one-half of the combinations for positive numbers, and the other half for negative numbers. Once we have decided that one-half of the bit combinations will represent positive numbers and the other one-half will represent negative numbers, we must decide *which* combinations will represent each. We will consider three choices; the first will probably be most familiar to us, because we use it in everyday life. We will discover, however, that it is a poor choice for high speed calculations. Of the other two choices we will consider, one is of primarily historical interest, while the other is commonly used in modern computers.

Sign-Magnitude Representation

We are all probably familiar with the **sign-magnitude** representation for signed numbers. Each sign-magnitude number has two parts: a *sign* part and a *magnitude* part. The sign part can have one of only two values: plus or minus; the magnitude part is an unsigned number, and it can have as many values as it has combinations of digits. Thus, if we wish to use the sign-magnitude representation for 3-bit binary numbers, we would use 1 bit for the sign (the high-order bit, typically) and the remaining 2 bits for the magnitude. Figure 7.2 shows the eight possible combinations of 3 bits, and the number that each combination represents if we are using unsigned numbers or if we are using the sign-magnitude representation. Note that, in the sign-magnitude system, 0 has two representations: one is positive and the other is negative. There is no obvious advantage to this fact, but it is a feature of the sign-magnitude number system--*every* number must have either a "+" or a "-" in front of it.

Some early computers (e.g., IBM models 7090 and 7094) had ALUs that processed numbers using the sign-magnitude representation, but modern computers use a different representation for signed numbers--primarily because this representation allows faster processing; let's see why. Consider addition of two binary sign-magnitude numbers; there are four possible combinations: (1) Both

---

[2]This is only an important decision for computers, because there is a fixed number of combinations of 32 bits (for example); if we allocate them all to positive numbers, there are none left for negative numbers, and we have an unsigned number system. For each bit-combination that we use to represent a negative number, there is one less combination available for the positive numbers.

(1):	010	(+2)	(2):	101	(−1)	(3):	011	(+3)	(4):	111	(−3)	
	+ 001	(+1)		+ 101	(−1)		+ 101	(−1)		+ 011	(+3)	
	011	(+3)		110	(−2)		010	(+2)		000	(0)	(desired result)
	011	(+3)		(1)010	(?)		(1)000	(?)		(1)010	(?)	(actual result)

Figure 7.3 Sign-magnitude addition

numbers are positive; (2) both are negative; (3) the larger magnitude is positive; and (4) the larger magnitude is negative. An example of each of these possibilities is shown in figure 7.3. We use 3-bit binary numbers for simplicity; it is straightforward to extend these examples to any number of bits. In this example, the row marked "desired result" shows the correct results in the sign-magnitude representation; the row marked "actual result" shows the results that are obtained when we apply the rules of the binary addition table (in figure 3.2). Clearly, the binary addition table does not produce the correct result for sign-magnitude arithmetic.

From example 1 we notice that when both numbers are positive, adding is simple--if we can decide what to do with the sign bit. Although it may be a strange thing to do, we can add the sign bits along with the magnitude part and still get the correct answer (since $0 + 0 = 0$).

From example 2 we see that when both numbers are negative, adding the sign bits with the magnitude will produce the right magnitude but the wrong sign. Also, we get an *extra* bit in the sign part ($1 + 1 = 10$)--however, since we have only 3 bits, we can't store the extra bit, and so ignore it. Combining the lessons of examples 1 and 2, we can decide that when both numbers are positive or both are negative, it is best to add the magnitude parts and *copy* the sign bit.

Examples 3 and 4 show us that what we do when we add numbers with opposite signs "in English", is not *adding* at all--we *subtract* them! In fact, the rule that we use is, "subtract the number with the smaller magnitude from the number with the larger magnitude". What about the sign? Again, examination of our "English" behavior shows us that the result gets the sign of the number with the larger magnitude.

From these examples, we can derive the following set of rules (such a set of rules is often called an **algorithm**) for sign-magnitude addition:

1.   Examine the sign bits of the addends.
2.   If the sign bits are identical, add the magnitudes; the result gets the sign of the addends.
3.   If the sign bits are different, compare the magnitudes. Subtract the smaller magnitude from the larger one; the result gets the sign of the addend with the larger magnitude.

Notice that something which we think of as very simple--adding two numbers--isn't really so simple for sign-magnitude numbers. If a computer is to use the sign-magnitude representation, then computer designers must build hardware to implement the above, relatively complex, addition algorithm. It would be preferable, of course, to build simpler addition hardware; we could do this if we could find a simpler addition algorithm. What would a simpler algorithm involve? First, adding 2 numbers should always mean *adding* them; second, it would be helpful *not* to have to treat the sign bit separately from all the other bits. Another way of thinking of this problem is realizing that it is easy to build a piece of hardware that implements the binary addition table (shown in figure 3.2); is there a representation for signed numbers in which addition is implemented by implementing that table?

We would not have asked this question, of course, if the answer were not yes; in fact, we will soon examine *two* such number systems. Before examining them, however, we must realize that we humans are, for better or for worse, committed to the sign-magnitude system. If we are to use

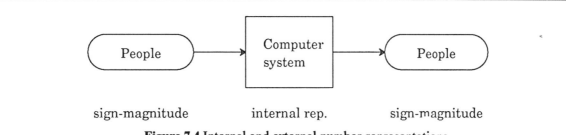

sign-magnitude   internal rep.   sign-magnitude

Figure 7.4 Internal and external number representations

computers that, for the sake of processing speed, use a different system, then we (or *someone*) will have to write programs that transform sign-magnitude numbers into the computer's representational system for processing, and then transform the numbers the computer has produced as results back into sign-magnitude for our use. We, as assembly language programmers, will often have the responsibility of writing such programs so that, to ordinary users, this process of transformation and retransformation, shown in figure 7.4, is transparent.

Two's Complement Representation

The most widely used representation for signed binary numbers in computers is the **twos complement** representation. If we are using an n-bit word in the twos complement system, then the number x and its negation X obey the following relationship:

$$x + X = 2^n.$$

Suppose, once more, that we are dealing with 3-bit words. If $x = 2$ (or, 010 in binary), what is X; or, how do we represent -2? Applying the definition: $n = 3$, so $2^n = 1000$; if $x + X = 1000$, then $X = 1000 - x$, or $X = 1000 - 010$, or $X = 110$. We can calculate *all* the two's complement negative numbers in the same way; figure 7.5 shows all combinations of 3 bits, and the value each represents as an unsigned number and as a twos complement number.

An examination of figure 7.5 shows that both the twos complement system and the sign-magnitude system divide the bit combinations so that one-half represent positive numbers and one-half represent negative numbers. We can also see from figure 7.5 that with the twos complement system--as with the sign-magnitude system--digit strings with their high-order bit set (1) represent

Bit pattern	Unsigned	Twos complement
000	0	0
001	1	+1
010	2	+2
011	3	+3
100	4	−4
101	5	−3
110	6	−2
111	7	−1

Figure 7.5 Two's complement representation

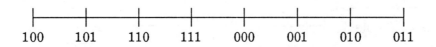

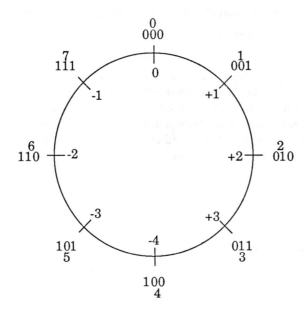

Figure 7.6 Number circle for two's complement numbers

negative numbers and those with their high-order bit cleared (0) represent positive numbers.[3] Each one of the negative twos complement numbers in figure 7.5, with the exception of 100, may be calculated from the definition--just as we calculated the twos complement representation of -2, above. The number 100 is an exception because it has no negation representable with 3 bits; or, its negation, if we apply the twos complement definition, is itself. So, how do we decide what number 100 represents? First, it must be a negative number, because its high-order bit is set. In addition, if we examine the number circle in figure 7.6, and follow the progression of the bit patterns and the numbers they represent, 100 comes after 101 and so should be one less than it; 101 is -3, and so 100 is -4. The binary digit adjacencies around the number circle are determined by the binary addition table: 011+001=100, so 011 is next to 100. The decimal numbers outside the circle are the values that each bit string represents as an unsigned number; the decimal numbers inside the number circle are the values that each bit string represents in the twos complement system.

From our discussion of modular arithmetic we know that 3+5= 8, which is 0, modulo 8. If we rewrite this as

---

[3]This implies that 0 is a positive number. Although we don't usually think of it as positive, it is appropriate to consider it a positive two's complement number.

    3+5=0, modulo 8,

it follows that

    5 = -3, modulo 8.

If we examine the relationship between the signed and unsigned numbers in figure 7.5, we see that this relationship always holds. For instance,

    unsigned 0   =   signed 0, modulo 8
    unsigned 1   =   signed 1, modulo 8
        .
        .
        .
    unsigned 4   =   signed -4, modulo 8
        .
        .
        .
    unsigned 7   =   signed -1, modulo 8

The number circle in figure 7.6 is a pictorial method of representing this relationship; the relationship holds for *any* binary word length, and for bases other than binary.

What do we learn from the table and number circle? There are several observations that we can make:

1.   In the case of *any* modular number system, if we add 1 to the largest number, we produce the smallest number. However, the largest and smallest numbers are different for the unsigned and twos complement numbers, and so this **discontinuity** (which can be thought of as the point at which the ends of the number line were joined to make the number circle) is in a different place for these two representations: between 111 and 000 for the unsigned numbers, and between 011 and 100 for the twos complement numbers. Note that there is *no* discontinuity between 111 (-1) and 000 (0) as twos complement numbers: if we add 1 to -1, we *expect* to get 0--which we do; note, similarly, that there is no discontinuity between 011 and 100 as unsigned numbers: if we add 1 to 3, we expect to get 4--which we do.

2.   The sum of the pair of bit patterns for representing a number and its negation always produces 1000, which is 0, modulo 8. This is not surprising, since we derived the negative numbers by applying the equation, $x + X = 2^n$, which is 1000 when $n = 3$.

3.   Although we can represent -4, we cannot represent +4, in a modulo 8 number system. This does *not*, however, mean that there are more negative numbers than positive ones, because 0 is considered a positive twos complement number. The fact that -0 +0 is an attraction of the twos complement system. Other numbers systems, such as the sign-magnitude system and the ones complement system (which we will examine shortly), have *two* representations for 0. This can be problematic if, for example, we wish to branch if the results of a computation are 0--we must check for both +0 and -0!

4.   We notice in the table that all of the numbers that we consider negative have a high-order bit of 1, and all the numbers we consider positive have their high-order bit of 0. So we can always determine if a number is positive or negative simply by examining its high-order bit, which is a **pseudo-sign bit**. We call a sign bit at all because it indicates the sign of the number; we call it a *pseudo*-sign bit because it is not a *true* sign bit: as we will soon see, the high-order bit is as much a part of a twos complement number's magnitude as is any other bit; it receives no special treatment for arithmetic.

(1):	010	(+2)	(2):	111	(−1)	(3):	011	(+3)	(4):	101	(−3)	
	+ 001	(+1)		+ 111	(−1)		+ 111	(−1)		+ 011	(+3)	
	011	(+3)		110	(−2)		010	(+2)		000	(0)	(desired result)
	011	(+3)		(1)110	(−2)		(1)010	(+2)		(1)000	(0)	(actual result)

Figure 7.7 Two's complement addition

5. Negating a twos complement number is very different from negating a sign-magnitude number. To negate an n-bit sign-magnitude number, we simply change its most significant bit. To negate an n-bit twos complement number, we subtract the number from 2^n.

6. The negative numbers closest to 0 have many 1s in their high-order bits; the negative numbers closest to -∞ have few 1s in their high-order bits. This is clearer when we look at numbers that are more than 3 bits long; for example, -1 as an 8-bit twos complement number is 11111111_2 (or, FF_{16}), and -128 is 10000000_2 (or 80_{16}). This may at first seem strange, but it shouldn't: 11111111 *looks* bigger than 10000000 (and it *is* bigger, if they are considered *un*signed numbers), and -1 *is* bigger than -128. It *seems* strange because, in English, we are often inconsistent in using the words "big" and "little" to compare negative numbers--we confuse the *absolute* value of a negative sign-magnitude number (which is the *magnitude* part) with the *signed* value, which is the whole number.

All of the above properties, described with respect to 3-bit numbers and a modulo $2^3 = 8$ number system, apply to the VAX, where we use 8-bit (byte), 16-bit (word) and 32-bit (longword) numbers, in modulo $2^8 = 256$, $2^{16} = 65,536$, and $2^{32} = 4,294,967,296$ number systems.

Our reason for examining representations of negative numbers *other* than sign-magnitude was that adding sign-magnitude numbers is very complicated: we must isolate the sign bits, compare the magnitude parts, and sometimes add and sometimes subtract. We claimed that there are representations that make adding easier, and we have implied that the twos complement system is one of those representations. Let's examine the same examples we saw in our study of the sign-magnitude system in figure 7.3. These examples of additions with (1) both numbers positive; (2) both numbers negative; and (3), (4) one positive and one negative, are rewritten in figure 7.7 as twos complement numbers.

Example (1) is straightforward, as it was in the sign-magnitude case; if we add the entire number, including the pseudo-sign bit, we get the correct result.

In example (2), when both numbers are negative, we find a very interesting result: the result seems to need 4 bits, and we only have 3; however, if we *ignore* the most significant bit, then we get the correct answer--as a 3-bit number! Note that we added, in this case as well as in the previous one, *the entire number*--including the most significant (pseudo-sign) bit.

In examples (3) and (4), we see, that we can *still* simply add the bits according to the binary addition table, and--if we *ignore* the extra bits, as we did in example (2)--we get the correct answers.

So, it seems that we have indeed found a representation for negative numbers in which we need only to implement the binary addition table to produce the correct result; does this mean that nothing can ever go wrong? Most certainly not! Recall that a computer has a fixed-size representation for numbers, but that mathematics places no such restrictions on numbers. If, for example, we try to add 011 and 011 (binary), we will get 110 (which is the bit pattern for -2), which is certainly *not* the correct answer, +6. This should not be surprising, because with 3-bit numbers (as figure 7.5 shows), positive numbers range from only 0 to +3, and negative numbers from -1 to -4; +6 is out of this range, of course. Neither should the *particular* wrong answer be surprising: recall, from

Bit pattern	Unsigned	Ones Complement
000	0	+0
001	1	+1
010	2	+2
011	3	+3
100	4	-3
101	5	-2
110	6	-1
111	7	-0

Figure 7.8 Ones complement representation

our discussion of modular arithmetic, that unsigned 6 = -2, modulo 8. We will soon discuss, in great detail, exactly what can go wrong, and what support the VAX provides for those occasions. First, however, we will discuss another representation for negative numbers.

Ones Complement Representation

The ones complement representation used to be common; it is rarely used for arithmetic on modern computers, but we will see that it is frequently used for other purposes. Using n-bit numbers, a number, x, and its ones complement negation, X, always obey the following relation:

$$x + X = 2^n - 1.$$

Using the laws of algebra, we can transform this into an equation to calculate the negative numbers in the ones complement system just as we transformed a similar equation for the twos complement system:

$$X = 2^n - 1 - x.$$

So, if we use 3-bit numbers as our examples, then 2^n is 1000, and $2^n - 1 = 111$. Then, 2 is 010, so -2 is 111-010 = 101. We can proceed for all of the combinations of 3 bits, and produce the table shown in figure 7.8. The observant reader will notice that we need not apply the equation (provided above) to calculate a number's ones complement: we may simply *invert* every bit. For example, +3 is 011 and -3 is 100, and so forth. Why is this the case? Consider the equation: it involves subtracting the bit pattern of some number from 2^n-1. Since 2^n is represented with a single 1 as the high-order bit, followed by n 0s, 2^n-1 will be simply a string of n 1s. If we subtract a 1 from a 1 we get a 0, and if we subtract a 0 from a 1 we get a 1--so when we subtract *any* binary number from a number that is all 1s, the result will have a 1 wherever the subtrahend (the number we subtract) has a 0, and a 0 wherever the subtrahend has a 1. Notice that the ones complement system is like the sign-magnitude system in that it has *two* representations for 0: 000, or +0, and 111, or -0.

Recall that ALU stands for arithmetic-*logic* unit; bit-wise complementing (*negating*, in the ones complement system) is an important logical function. Thus, although the VAX does not use the ones complement number system for *arithmetic* operations, we will see that for *logical* operations, in which each bit of a byte, word, or longword is more or less independent of its neighboring bits, the logical complement is of considerable interest.

Bit pattern	Unsigned	Sign-Magnitude	Twos Complement	Ones Complement
000	0	+0	0	+0
001	1	+1	+1	+1
010	2	+2	+2	+2
011	3	+3	+3	+3
100	4	−0	−4	−3
101	5	−1	−3	−2
110	6	−2	−2	−1
111	7	−3	−1	−0

Figure 7.9 Comparison of number representations

We will not discuss ones complement arithmetic in any detail--except to explain that it is *almost* like twos complement arithmetic. The difference is that whenever we cross 0 on the number circle (for example, by adding +3 to -2) we must add an additional 1 to the result. This is a direct consequence of the two representations of 0; if we did not add the extra 1, we would find, for example, that adding 1 to -0 would produce +0, which is clearly the wrong answer. This is sometimes called **end-around carry**; we can think of it as *adding* the "extra" 1 that, in the twos complement system (example 3 in figure 7.7) we ignored.

In summary, let us consider all of the different number systems we have examined, and compare them according to several features. Figure 7.9 shows all 8 combinations obtainable from 3-bit numbers, and the value each represents as an unsigned number, a sign-magnitude number, a twos complement number, and a ones complement number. What can we generalize from this table?

1. First, for all of the representations, the positive numbers are the same. So, we can always figure out what a positive twos complement number is by treating it as a sign-magnitude number, and summing successive powers of two.
2. We also see that the twos complement system is the only signed number system with a unique representation for 0; the others have both positive and negative representations for 0.
3. We notice that all positive numbers have a most significant bit of 0, and all negative numbers have a most significant bit of 1. However, the most significant bit is a true sign bit only for the sign-magnitude representation; for both ones and twos complement numbers, it is a pseudo-sign bit, and must be treated as part of the number for arithmetic.
4. All representations have four positive numbers and four negative numbers; in the twos complement system, the magnitude of the most negative number is larger than the magnitude of the most positive number, while in the ones complement and sign-magnitude systems these magnitudes are the same.
5. A number's negation in the sign-magnitude system can be computed by inverting its sign (most significant) bit. A number's ones complement (its negation, in the ones complement system) can be computed from the appropriate equation, or by inverting each of the number's bits. A number's twos complement can be computed from the appropriate equation, or by adding 1 to its ones complement. This fact is not magic: for a ones complement number, $X = 2^n - 1 - x$, and for a twos complement number, $X = 2^n - x$. Clearly, $2^n - x$ (the twos complement formula) $2^n - 1 - x + 1$ (the ones complement formula, plus 1).

Both Numbers Positive

001	001	001	010	010	011
001	010	011	010	011	011
010	011	100*	100*	101*	110*

Both Numbers Negative

111	111	111	111	110	110	110	101	101	100
111	110	101	100	110	101	100	101	100	100
(1)110	(1)101	(1)100	(1)011*	(1)100	(1)011*	(1)010*	(1)010*	(1)001*	(1)000*

One Number Positive and One Number Negative

001	001	001	001	010	010	010	010	011	011	011	011
111	110	101	100	111	110	101	100	111	110	101	100
(1)000	111	110	101	(1)001	(1)000	111	110	(1)010	(1)001	(1)000	111

* Incorrect result

Figure 7.10 Adding twos complement numbers

What Can Go Wrong In Two's Complement Arithmetic

Although the twos complement representation makes addition as simple as implementing the binary addition table, we have already seen that things can still go wrong. This is *not* due to some disadvantage of the twos complement representation, rather, it is a result of the fact that computers try to map the infinite number line into a finite number circle; *any* modular arithmetic system has a largest representable number (and a smallest representable number), and trying to add two numbers whose sum is larger than this largest number (or smaller than the smallest number) will clearly produce the wrong answer--just as, when a car has gone 99,999 miles, adding 1 to the odometer produces the wrong mileage. We will consider two questions now: (1) When will we get the wrong answer? and (2) How does the VAX tell us that the answer is wrong?

When Is the Answer Wrong?

Let's look at all possible pairs of 3-bit numbers we can add--in figure 7.10--and see when the answers are correct and when they are incorrect. Perhaps we will find that all the incorrect answers have something in common that will help us figure out how, if we were computer designers, we could provide hardware to help programmers know when a wrong answer has been generated. When we look at figure 7.10, we notice that in some cases, the answer will not fit in 3 bits--for example, when adding -1 (111 binary) and -2 (110 binary)--but that if we ignore the "extra" bit, the answer is correct. On the other hand, there are times when there is no "extra" bit, but the answer is *in*correct--for example, when adding +2 (010 binary) and +3 (011 binary). (There are also cases when a result with an extra bit is *in*correct, and--of course--cases when a result without an extra bit is correct.)

So, it is clearly *not* the case that a result's correctness is indicated by the presence or absence of an "extra" bit; is there some other feature that correct and incorrect results have in common? Rhetorical questions have obvious answers--there *is* such a feature, and it is the value of the result's most significant bit (msb). Careful examination of figure 7.10 shows us that, in *every* case where the result is incorrect, the two addends had the *same* msb (which we also call the pseudo-sign-bit), but the result has a different msb. It is not surprising that these are cases in which the result is wrong, because there are no two positive numbers that have a negative sum, and there are no two negative numbers that have a positive sum.

We can understand this strange behavior of computer arithmetic by examining the number circle in figure 7.6 once more. Recall that adding positive numbers can be pictured as moving in a clockwise direction around the number circle. If we add two positive numbers whose sum is "too big," then we cross over the discontinuity between +3 and -4, and the result is negative.[4] When we extend our word size from 3 bits to 4 bits, we increase the number of correct sums that we can represent, but wc don't eliminate the discontinuity--it "moves" to between +7 and -8, with 4 bit words. In fact, we can *never* eliminate the discontinuity in a modular number system; we must use a number line of infinite length rather than a number circle to do that. Infinite-length number lines may be used when we can represent an infinite number of numbers; no computers that are currently manufactured have this ability. We *can,* however, make the discontinuity arbitrarily far from 0--with 8-bit numbers, it is between +127 and -128; with 16-bit numbers it is between +32,767 and -32,768; with 32 bit numbers it is between +2,147,483,647 and -2,147,483,648; and so on.

Overflow

Let us formalize what we have learned from figure 7.10 by defining a function called **overflow.** This is a binary function, which means it can have two values: 0 or 1. We will define overflow for addition with the following pseudo-code:

> If (the msb's of two addends are the same) and (the msb of the result is different) then
> > **overflow = 1**
> Else
> > **overflow = 0**

Note that *overflow* sounds like an ordinary English word, but we are using it as a technical term; the ordinary English meaning is appropriate for reminding us "approximately" what the technical meaning is, but it is a mistake to think that, just because we understand the ordinary English meaning of overflow, we understand its technical meaning.

Clearly, if **overflow** is 1, then the answer is incorrect, and if overflow is 0, then the answer is correct. It just so happens that the designers of the VAX provided in the CPU an indication of the value of this overflow function; they called it the *V bit* of the condition code. Following each addition, the V bit will automatically be 1 when **overflow** as defined above is 1 (indicating *true,* or that it has occurred), and it will be 0 when **overflow** is 0 (indicating *false,* or that it has *not* occurred). We will consider subtraction, which is similar to addition but slightly different, shortly.

---

[4] If we add two negative numbers that are "too small," the same thing will happen, but in the opposite direction: adding negative numbers is pictured as moving in a counter-clockwise direction around the number circle. The same reasoning should convince us that if we add one positive and one negative number, we will always get the correct result.

```
              ADDL3 R0, R1, R2
              BVC OK
;else, ERROR!
              PUTS errormessage
      OK:     ;other instructions
                .
                .
                .
```

Figure 7.11 Sample use of BVC or BVS

BVS and BVC

What does the computer do when the V bit is set? Nothing at all--unless we tell it to! How do we tell it to? We use one of a pair of special conditional branch instructions: BVS--branch if the V bit is set--and BVC--branch if the V bit is clear. So, it is up to us, as assembly language programmers, to write programs that check the setting of the V bit after any arithmetic operation that we think might produce the wrong answer--which is to say, after *every* arithmetic operation. For example, we might write a program fragment such as the one shown in figure 7.11. (Alternatively, we could rewrite this fragment using BVS ERROR, rather than BVC OK, and allow the program to "fall through" to the other instructions if there is no error.)

Unsigned Arithmetic

So far, we have been concentrating on finding a representation for negative numbers that allows us to add using only the binary addition table. We have "discovered" the twos complement representation, we have seen that it meets this requirement, and we have seen what kinds of things can go wrong and how the VAX hardware assists us in knowing that something has gone wrong. But, what if we wish to use *unsigned* numbers--perhaps because we are computing with numbers that can never be negative--do we need to know anything special? At first we would think not, because the only purpose of the twos complement representation is to allow us to add negative numbers as if they were unsigned numbers (using only the binary addition table). On second thought, however, we may change our minds. For, although adding a signed number is the same as adding an unsigned number (since *each* is done by implementing the binary addition table), correct results and incorrect results may be different in the two cases, since particular bit patterns represent different numbers in the two cases.

Let's consider the case of adding 111_2 and 111_2. If we consider these bit patterns to represent twos complement numbers, then we are adding -1 and -1; the result should be -2, and there should be no error. If we look at figure 7.10, we see that this is, in fact, the case. However, what if we use these bit strings to represent *unsigned* numbers? In this case, we are adding 7 and 7. Clearly, the correct answer is 14, which is too big for 3 bits. Is there anything that all of the incorrect results have in common when we consider bit patterns as representing unsigned numbers?

Once again, the answer to this question is obvious. Let's look at all possible combinations of 3-bit addends again, this time considering them unsigned numbers, and let's see exactly what all incorrect results have in common and what all correct results have in common. Figure 7.12 shows all possible combinations of 3-bit addends. In the case of unsigned numbers we note, not surprisingly, that a change in the msb is irrelevant to the correctness of the result. Rather, we notice that every incorrect result is one in which an additional bit is generated, and every correct result is one in which there is no such additional bit.

001	001	001	001	001	001	001
001	010	011	100	101	110	111
010	011	100	101	110	111	(1000*

010	010	010	010	010	010	011
010	011	100	101	110	111	011
100	101	110	111	(1)000*	(1)001*	110

011	011	011	011	100	100	100
100	101	110	111	100	101	110
111	(1)000*	(1)001*	(1)010*	(1)000*	(1)001*	(1)010*

100	101	101	101	110	110	111
111	101	110	111	110	111	111
(1)011*	(1)010*	(1)011*	(1)100*	(1)100*	(1)101*	(1)110*

* Incorrect answer

Figure 7.12 Adding unsigned numbers

Carry

We can formalize what we have learned from figure 7.12 as we formalized what we learned from figure 7.10. In this case, however, we will define a binary function called **carry**. We will define **carry** for addition with the following pseudo-code:

    If (the carry out of the msb of a sum is 1) then
        carry = 1
    Else
        carry = 0

We have used *carry out* in the definition of **carry**, but the former is used in the ordinary English meaning of the word, while the latter is a technical term with the precise definition provided.

Clearly, if **carry** is 1, then a result is incorrect if we were adding two numbers (or, more accurately speaking, if we were adding two bit strings) that we consider representations of unsigned numbers. Conversely, if **carry** is 0, then the result is correct. In addition, just as the designers of the VAX provided a hardware indication of the value of the **overflow** function, so they have provided a hardware indication of the value of the **carry** function: it is called the *C bit* of the condition code. With each addition, the *C bit* will be 1 when **carry** as defined above is 1; it will be 0 when **carry** is 0.

BCS and BCC

The VAX does nothing special when it sets the C bit--just as it does nothing special when it sets the V bit--unless we tell it to. And just as there are conditional branches that check the setting of the V bit, so there are conditional branches that check the setting of the C bit: BCS and BCC, for "branch if the C bit is set" and "branch if the C bit is clear." Just as we must check the V bit in our programs, so we must check the C bit.

```
LOOP:       ADDL3 (R0), (R1), (R2)        ;add
            DECB @#COUNT                  ;decrement loop count
            BNEQ LOOP                     ;if not 0, add again
            BVS ERROR                     ;check for overflow
              .
              .
              .
```

Figure 7.13 Incorrect use of BVS

Why doesn't the hardware *automatically* do more than just set a bit in the condition code if a result we have just computed is in error? Surely we would never wish to continue computing with an incorrect result! The answer is that the computer doesn't know if the result we have just computed is in error or not! Consider figures 7.10 and 7.12: if we have executed an instruction to add the contents of two (3-bit) locations in memory, and those locations each contain the bit strings 111_2, then after the addition the V bit will be 0 and the C bit will be 1. Is the result correct or incorrect? Only we, the programmers, know! If we were adding signed numbers, then the result is correct; if we were adding unsigned numbers, then the result is incorrect. It is possible to produce all four combinations of C and V bit settings, and correct and incorrect results. For example, if we add 011_2 and 001_2, the V bit will be 1, and the C bit will be 0. If we were adding signed numbers, the result is wrong; but if we were adding unsigned numbers, the result is right. In addition, if we add 100_2 and 100_2, both the V and C bits will be 1, and the result is incorrect as both a signed and an unsigned number. Finally, if we add 001_2 and 101_2, both the V and C bits will be 0, and the result is correct as either a signed or an unsigned number.

Thus, the hardware updates (sets or clears) the V and C bits--just as it does the N and Z bits-- after each arithmetic instruction has been executed, according to the result just computed. It is up to us to do something with the information contained in the CC bits. Just as with the N and Z bits, so with the V and C bits, we may or may not care about them and therefore may or may not check them. If we are doing arithmetic on unsigned numbers, a result that produces an **overflow** value of 1 (as defined above) is not incorrect, so we need not check the V bit; similarly, if we are doing arithmetic on signed numbers, a result that produces a **carry** value of 1 is not incorrect and we need not check the C bit.

We have already seen in figure 7.11 an example of how to check for **overflow**; we can use the same strategy to check for **carry,** except that we must use either BCS or BCC. We must be careful, however, in use of these--and all other--conditional branches. For example, if we are adding numbers in a loop, we may wish to avoid the necessity of checking the V bit after *each* addition, and so may be tempted to write a program fragment such as the one in figure 7.13. However the V bit, even if it is set due to **overflow** resulting from execution of the ADDL3 instruction, will likely be cleared by the DECB instruction following the ADDL3 instruction. We must check for overflow as soon as it might occur--*before* the execution of another instruction which uses the ALU and which, therefore, sets or clears the CC bits.

In general, *all* arithmetic instructions update the CC bits. However, there are some exceptions. For example, it is impossible for a MOV(B,W,L) instruction to cause carry or overflow; what should happen to the C and V bits after a MOV(B,W,L) is executed? The designers of the VAX decided (sensibly) that the V bit should be set to 0, since overflow wasn't generated. Unfortunately, they also decided (for reasons that probably are related to PDP-11 compatibility) that the C bit should be unchanged. Appendix 3, which contains an alphabetical (by mnemonic) listing of all the VAX instructions, also summarizes the effect of each instruction on each bit of the condition code.

It is important to take this discussion of overflow and carry seriously. Once upon a time, one of the authors was asked to write a program for a large company--one of the largest in its field of business. Given historical data on the magnitude of numbers to be processed, he wrote a program, debugged it, tested it, and revised it (in assembly language, of course, since FORTRAN was still a curiosity back then, and COBOL had not yet been invented). The customer then tested the program and accepted it. About nine or ten months later, near the end of the year, there were screams of alarm: why were the year-to-date sales figures for December *lower* than those for November?

It turned out that no one associated with the company had ever expected the sales volume to be so large! So when the program specifications were drawn up almost a year earlier, the innocent programmer thought the word size sufficiently large (in light of the largest expected data), and so did not test for overflow. No person was hurt because of this error. Today, a programming oversight of this type in, for example, a hospital application, an airborne computer system, or a nuclear power plant control system, could have disastrous consequences. An incident regarding the shutting down of five power plants serving millions of people because of a computer programming error made years earlier is unfortunately not as rare as it should be. The moral of this story is: expect the specifications to be wrong. Check for every conceivable error. The error you don't check for is the one most likely to occur.

Subtraction

Subtraction, clearly, is related to addition: recall that, in the sign-magnitude system, we actually subtract in order to add, if the numbers we wish to add have different signs. In addition, consider the following identity:

$$a - b \equiv a + (-b)$$

In the VAX, as in most computers, subtracting is implemented as negating and adding. When we write an assembly language instruction such as SUBL3 S_1, S_2, D, we know that, symbolically, D <- (S_2)-(S_1). However, what the VAX actually does is add the twos complement of S_1 to S_2 and store the sum in D. (Perhaps the major reason that the ones complement system used to be popular is that negating a ones complement number--taking its ones complement--requires merely inverting each bit.)

Subtracting Signed Numbers

If we consider the examples in figure 7.14 as signed (twos complement) numbers, we see that examples (1) and (2) produce correct results (+3 - +1 = +2; and -2 - -1 = -1), but that example (3) produces an incorrect result (+2 - -3≠-3). It shouldn't surprise us that subtraction can produce incorrect results because subtraction is similar to addition: if we start with a positive number that is far from 0 and subtract from it a negative number that is far from 0, we will negate the negative number, and end up *adding* a positive number that is far from 0. The result will be a large *positive* number--one that is perhaps too large for the number of bits we have allocated for the result, as in example (3).

(1)	011	→	011	**(2)**	110	→	110	**(3)**	010	→	010	(minuend)
	−001	→	+111		−111	→	+001		−101	→	+011	(subtrahend)
			(1)010				111				101	

Figure 7.14 Subtracting by negating and adding

Does the VAX indicate an incorrect result from subtraction as well as from addition? Recall that we defined the binary function **overflow** with respect to addition--thereby implying that it is different for subtraction. It is, and the differences are directly derivable from the differences between addition and subtraction. Let us consider the rule for **overflow** with subtraction:

If (the subtrahend[5] and minuend have different msb's) and (the result has the msb of the subtrahend) then
      overflow = 1
Else
      overflow = 0

If we apply this rule to the examples in figure 7.14 we see that **overflow** is 1 for example (3), and it is 0 for examples (1) and (2). Why does this rule make sense, and how is it related to the rule for addition? According to the rule, **overflow** will always be 0 if the subtrahend and minuend have the same most significant bits; why is this the case? Consider the case of subtracting two positive numbers: clearly, they are both in the range -4 to +3 (in our 3-bit examples), because there are no 3-bit numbers outside this range. If we picture subtracting positive numbers as moving in a counterclockwise direction around the number circle of figure 7.6, then no matter how large a positive number we subtract from even the smallest positive number (0), we will never move far enough around the number circle to cross the discontinuity between the negative numbers and the positive ones. Alternatively, we can think of subtracting two positive numbers as adding one positive and one negative number; recall the rules for **overflow** with addition: adding numbers with different most significant bits can *never* produce an incorrect result.

So it is clear that **overflow** can occur only when subtracting numbers with different most significant bits; the rule states that if the result has the most significant bit of the *subtrahend,* then **overflow** is 1: why? In cases when **overflow** is 1, we start out subtracting two numbers with different most significant bits. The subtrahend is negated during subtraction, so its most significant bit changes to that of the minuend. Thus, we end up *adding* two numbers with the *same* most significant bit--that of the minuend. Thus, if the result has the most significant bit of the subtrahend, we have added two numbers with the same most significant bit and produced a result with a different most significant bit--which is the condition under which **overflow** = 1 for addition. Not surprisingly, the V bit of the VAX's condition code is set, during subtraction, according to the rule for **overflow** described above. We should check for incorrect results after subtracting signed numbers in the same way that we check for them after adding signed numbers: by using the BVS or BVC instructions.

Subtracting Unsigned Numbers

What happens when we subtract *un*signed numbers? The only way that something can go wrong is if we try to subtract a larger number from a smaller one; this *must* produce an incorrect result, because if we are considering bit patterns as representing unsigned numbers, we cannot represent negative numbers--and when subtracting a larger number from a smaller one, the correct result is always negative. Let us consider the examples in figure 7.14 as unsigned numbers.

First, although we may be confused by the idea of negating an unsigned number in order to subtract it (since, we may ask ourselves, "What is -1 in an *un*signed number system?"), careful consideration should lead us to the conclusion that all we are really doing is taking the twos complement of a bit pattern. Example (1) in figure 7.14 should convince us that subtracting unsigned

---

[5]The subtrahend is the S_1 operand, and the minuend is the S_2 operand in a VAX 3-operand subtract instruction. Or, the subtrahend is what we subtract; the minuend is what we subtract the subtrahend from. See figure 7.14.

numbers by negating the subtrahend and adding *does* produce the correct result, if we aren't trying to subtract a larger number from a smaller one.

Second, we notice a striking difference between adding and subtracting unsigned numbers: when the carry out of the msb of the result (of the addition!) is 1 the result is *correct* (example (1)), and when the carry out is 0, the result is *incorrect*. In fact, this is exactly the rule for the binary function **carry** with subtraction:

> If (the carry out from the msb of the addition is 0) then
> > **carry** = 1
> Else
> > **carry** = 0

It is important to understand that we compute the C bit according to the result of the *addition* that is actually performed, even though the total operation (negation and then addition) is equivalent to subtraction. After subtraction, not surprisingly, the C bit of the VAX's condition code is set according to the above rule. In fact, it is useful to consider the C bit as a *borrow* bit during subtraction: if the C bit is 1, then we need to borrow in order to subtract (a larger number from a smaller one). We will make use of this way of the thinking of the C bit shortly.

Given the above rules for **carry** and **overflow,** and knowing that the C and V bits of the condition code reflect the values of these two functions, we can write programs that may or may not produce correct results; but if we are careful, we can prevent any incorrect results that might be produced from going undetected.

Odds and Ends

We have nearly completed our examination of computer arithmetic. However, first we must consider a variety of details that we have been ignoring up to now, both in this chapter and in previous ones. These details are ramifications of the twos complement number system that the VAX uses, and of the fixed-length arithmetic that computers do.

Turning Short Numbers into Long Ones

The VAX allows us to add bytes, words, or longwords, but it does not allow us to add bytes to words or longwords, or words to longwords. What if we wish to do so? Clearly, it is possible to represent, for example, +3 in 3 bits, 8 bits, 16 bits, or 32 bits. In fact, it is quite simple to turn a 3-bit representation of 3 into an 8-bit one by adding 5 leading 0s, or an 8-bit representation into a 32-bit one by adding 24 leading 0s. However, what about -3? If we add 5 leading 0s to 101 (the 3-bit binary representation of -3), we get 00000101--which isn't -3 or any other negative number: it's +5! Let's return to the definition of twos complement numbers: for n bits, a number, x, and its negation, X, are related according to the rule,

$$X = 2^n - x.$$

So, for $x = 3$, if n is 3 then 2^n is 1000 and X is 101; if n is 4 then 2^n is 10000 and X is 1101; and if n is 8 then 2^n is 100000000 and X is 11111101.

In fact, turning a short twos complement number into a long one with the same value is accomplished by copying the most significant bit into each position to the left of it in the longer number. Thus, for positive numbers we copy leading 0s (since all positive numbers have a most significant bit of 0) and for negative numbers we copy leading 1s (since negative numbers have a most significant bit of 1). Copying the most significant bit of a number leftward is often called **sign**

Instruction	Mnemonic	Opcode	Action
Convert byte to longword	CVTBL S, D	98	D←(S), sign-extended
Convert byte to word	CVTBW S, D	99	D←(S), sign-extended
Convert word to longword	CVTWL S, D	32	D←(S), sign-extended
Move zero-extended byte to longword	MOVZBL S, D	9A	D←(S), zero-extended
Move zero-extended byte to word	MOVZBW S, D	9B	D←(S), zero-extended
Move zero-extended word to longword	MOVZWL S, D	3C	D←(S), zero-extended

Figure 7.15 Instructions for turning short numbers into long ones

extension; in the VAX, we can use the CONVERT family of instructions, some of which are described in figure 7.15, to sign-extend numbers. Thus, if we have an 8-bit representation of a signed number in the low-order byte of R0 and we wish to subtract it from a 32-bit signed number in R2, we would use the CVTBL instruction as follows:

```
CVTBL   R0, R1
SUBL2   R1, R2
```

For the CVT instructions described in figure 7.15, the setting of the N and Z bits of the CC is according to the result--as we expect. The C and V bits are cleared.[6]

What if we wish to turn short *un*signed numbers into long ones? We can't use the CVT instructions because unsigned numbers may have a leading 1 which should *not* be copied; short unsigned numbers are turned into long ones with *zero* extension. Figure 7.15 also summarizes some of the VAX's zero-extension instructions; if the 8-bit number in the low-order byte of R0 were unsigned rather than signed, we would turn it into a 32-bit unsigned number with the same value (and place it in R1) as follows:

```
MOVZBL   R0, R1
```

For the zero-extension instructions, the N and V bits are cleared, the C bit is unchanged, and the Z bit is set as usual.

Extended Range Arithmetic

The VAX has instructions for integer arithmetic operations on bytes, words, and longwords; what if we need to calculate with larger numbers? If we store a single number that is too large to fit in one location in more than one location--in two longwords, for example--we can perform arithmetic operations on each of the longwords separately, and then use the C bit to combine the results. Using this technique, we can create, and calculate with, arbitrarily long numbers.

Consider first some 3-bit examples. Suppose our computer does arithmetic only on 3-bit words, but we wish to add the numbers 12 and 17. We can't represent any twos complement number larger

---

[6]There are also instructions for converting longwords and words to bytes, and longwords to words. For these instructions, the V vit is set if the most significant bit of the source is different from that of the destination. This will occur if we try to convert, for example, -200 from a word to a byte.

Number	Representation	
	High-order	Low-order
1	000	001
−1	111	111
7	000	111
8	001	000
−8	111	000
12	001	100
−12	110	100
15	001	111
31	011	111
−31	100	001
−32	100	000

Figure 7.16 Some 2-word twos complement numbers

than 3 with 3 bits, but if we use a pair of 3-bit words for each number, it is as if our word size were 6 bits, and the range of 6-bit twos complement numbers is -32 to +31. So, we could store 12 and 17 in two pairs of 3-bit words: the high-order word for 12 would contain 001, and the low-order one would contain 100; the high-order word for 17 would contain 010, and the low-order one would contain 001. Figure 7.16 shows the twos complement representations of several other numbers in pairs of 3-bit words.

How would we add numbers that are stored in two memory locations? We all learned (many years ago, no doubt) that when there is no carry out of one digit position, adding a multidigit decimal number is exactly the same as adding a series of single-digit decimal numbers. If there is carry out, however, we must add the carry to the sum of the digits in the next position. Binary is the same as decimal in this respect (and most others, as well); we don't normally worry about carry from one position to the next, because the piece of hardware we call the ALU does it for us. However, the ALU propagates a carry from one position to the next only within a single memory location (or register); if we wish to add single numbers stored in multiple memory locations, we must take care of the carry out of the msb of the low-order location--which is the carry in to the lsb of the high-order location--ourselves.

How do we do that? With the C bit, of course! If, after we add the numbers in the two low order memory locations, the C bit is 1 (indicating carry out of the msb of the result, which would normally be an error), we add 1 to the number in one of the high-order memory locations, and then we add the numbers in the high-order locations. (Alternatively, we could add the high-order numbers first and then add 1 to their sum.) Consider the following program fragment, which will add the 64-bit value whose low-order 32 bits are in R0 and whose high-order 32 bits are in R1 to the 64-bit value whose low-order 32 bits are in R2 and high-order 32 bits are in R3, storing the low-order 32 bits of the result in R2 and the high-order 32 bits in R3:

```
              ADDL2 R0, R2        ;add low order parts
              BCC CONTINUE        ;if no carry: add high order parts
      ;else: add carry to high order parts first
              INCL R1             ;add carry
CONTINUE:     ADDL2 R1, R3        ;add high order parts
              BVS ERROR           ;check for overflow!
```

This will work just fine,[7] but the VAX has an instruction that provides us with a better way of doing it. The VAX has an instruction whose mnemonic is ADWC, which stands for *add with carry*. This instruction is a 2-operand instruction only, and it adds the first and second operands *and* the C bit, and stores the result in the location where the second operand was. So, we can re-write the above program fragment as follows:

```
ADDL2  R0, R2     ;add low-order parts
ADWC   R1, R3     ;add high-order parts (and carry)
BVS ERROR         ;check for overflow!
```

Note that it is perfectly safe to add the C bit to the high-order value, because if there was carry out then the C bit will be 1, which is exactly what we must add, and if there was *no* carry out then the C bit will be 0, which is always safe to add to anything.

What about subtraction? Can we use the C bit in the same way to subtract very large numbers? Recall that we described the C bit in subtraction as acting like a *borrow* bit: it is set when we would have had to borrow to get the correct answer. This sounds like just what we need, and it is. Subtraction requires slightly more care than addition, if we do it *without* the SBWC (subtract with carry) instruction, because we must subtract the borrowed 1 from the minuend rather than the subtrahend (addition is commutative so it doesn't matter which operand we add the carry to). But, with the SBWC instruction, we could subtract the 64-bit number in R0 and R1 from the one in R2 and R3 with the following three-instruction sequence:

```
SUBL2 R0, R2 ;subtract low-order parts
SBWC R1, R3 ;subtract high-order parts, and carry (borrow)
BVS ERROR   ;check for overflow!
```

It is intuitively clear, from the rules for setting the C bit in addition, that the program fragments for addition are correct. However, the setting of the C bit in subtraction is less intuitive, so let's consider an example using two pairs of 3-bit words, shown in figure 7.17. Suppose we wish to subtract 15 from 25; we would store 011_2 in the high-order word of the minuend and 001_2 in the low-order one (thus storing 011001, for 25), and we would store 001_2 in the high-order word of the subtrahend and 111_2 in the low-order one (storing 001111, for 15). When we subtract the low-order parts, we subtract 111 from 001; since subtraction is done by negating and adding, we take the twos complement of 111, which is 001, and add it to 001. The result is 010; what happens to the C bit? The rule for subtraction says that if there is *no* carry out of the msb, then **carry** = 1, so the C bit will be 1. We subtract this 1, representing a borrow, from the high-order part of the minuend, changing the 011 to 010. Then, subtracting 001 from 010 is performed by taking the twos complement of 001 and adding it to 010; the twos complement of 001 is 111, so we add 111 to 010, getting 1001. Since the carry out of the msb is 1, **carry** is 0 (for subtraction!), so the C bit is 0, indicating that the result is correct.

This technique can be extended to handle numbers of arbitrary length. After adding or subtracting each corresponding pair of lower order parts, we execute an ADWC or SBWC. Clearly, extended-range integer arithmetic takes longer than ordinary integer arithmetic. Adding a pair of long numbers, each of which is stored in n locations, thus takes much longer than adding n pairs of numbers, each of which is stored in a single location.

---

[7]Note that we use BCC CONTINUE rather than BVC CONTINUE. This is because we are interested only in whether or not we must propogate a carry from bit position 31 of R2 to bit position 0 of R3.

```
High-order    Low-order
      011      001
    –001      111
```

Subtract low-order parts first:

```
 001    →      001
–111    →    +001
               010
```

Carry out = 0, so C bit is 1.

Next, subtract C bit from high-order part of minuend:

```
 011    →      011
–001    →    +111
              1010
```

Finally, subtract high-order parts:

```
 010    →      010
–001    →    +111
              1001
```

Combined result:

```
High   Low
 011   001
–001   111
 001   010
```

Figure 7.17 Doubleword subtraction

The CMP Instructions Revisited

We have treated the CMP(B,W,L) family of instructions as if it were identical to the SUB(B,W,L)2 family, with the exception of which operand is subtracted from which and the fact that the CMP(B,W,L) instructions don't store a result. However, there is another difference, as well: the CMP(B,W,L) instructions set the condition-code bits somewhat differently from the SUB(B,W,L)2 instructions.

Recall that, for subtraction, the N bit is the same as the msb of the result, and the Z bit is set if the result is 0; otherwise it is 0. The V bit is set if the subtrahend and minuend have different msb's and the result has the msb of the subtrahend. The C bit is set if the carry out of the msb of the result (of the addition) is 0, and cleared if it is 1. The rules for the CMP(B,W,L) instructions are slightly different: the N bit is set if the S_1 operand is less than the S_2 operand when they are considered as *signed* numbers; the Z bit is set if the S_1 operand is equal to the S_2 operand; the V bit is always cleared; and the C bit is set if the S_1 operand is less than the S_2 operand when they are considered as *un*signed numbers.

Why are these rules specified in such different ways--and, are they really different? It is clear that the rule for setting the V bit is different for the CMP and SUB families of instructions; what about the others? It is simple to understand that the rule for the Z is the same for the two families of instructions: when equal operands are subtracted the result is 0; when a result is 0, the Z bit is 1. The rule for the C bit is also really the same (except for the case of comparing with 0, which we

a	b	XOR
0	0	0
0	1	1
1	0	1
1	1	0

Figure 7.18 Truth table for **exclusive or**

will discuss shortly): if the S_1 operand is less than the S_2 operand when they are considered as unsigned numbers, then when we try to subtract the S_2 operand from the S_1 operand we will need to borrow, and so the C bit will be set. What about the N bit? Its rule also seems, at first, to be equivalent: if the S_1 operand is less than the S_2 operand, and the S_2 operand is subtracted from the S_1 operand, then the result should be negative. Negative numbers on the VAX have msb's of 1, and if the msb of a result is 1, then the N bit should be set. However, there is one class of cases in which this is not true: those cases in which **overflow** (as defined for subtraction) is 1. For when **overflow** is 1, the result is too big for the number of bits available, and so the msb of the result is incorrect. Consider the 3-bit example of comparing 101 with 010 (-3 with +2): 101 - 010 is transformed into 101 + 110, which is 1011. If the CC were set according to the rules of subtraction, the N bit would be cleared; however, -3 is less than +2, and so, according to the rule for compare, the N bit will be set.

This rule for the setting of the N bit implies that the computer somehow "knows" that one operand is less than another one, independent of the result of subtracting one from the other: how is this possible? It is *not*, of course; rather, the hardware is actually computing a logical function called **exclusive or** (XOR for short) on the V bit (before it gets cleared) and the m.s.b. of the result, in order to set the N bit. What is **exclusive or**? It is a two-input function with a single output; the exclusive or of a and b is 1 if *either a* or *b* is 1, but *not* if both are 1 or if neither are 1. The truth table for the exclusive or of a and b is shown in figure 7.18. So, if *either* the V bit (before being cleared) *or* the msb of the result is 1, then the N bit is set; if both are 1 or if neither are 1 the N bit is cleared.

The C Bit and Subtracting 0

Although the rule for setting the C bit for subtraction says that the C bit is set if the carry out of the msb of the addition is 0, subtracting 0 is an exception. Why is this the case? Consider yet another 3-bit example: subtracting 000 from 010 is transformed into adding 000 (the twos complement of 000 is 000) to 010, with the result 010. If we obeyed the rule that the C bit is set if the carry out of the msb of the result is 0, then the C bit would be set--indicating that the answer is incorrect, or that we had to borrow in order to perform the subtraction. This is *not* the case, of course: we *never* have to borrow in order to subtract 0. So, subtracting 0 is a special case: whenever we subtract 0, the C bit is always cleared. This is true of both the SUB(B,W,L)[2,3] and CMP(B,W,L) families of instructions, as well as of the TST(B,W,L) family of instructions. The TST(B,W,L) are a family of single-operand instructions (their format is TST(B,W,L) D); they perform the same operation as comparing with 0 (CMP(B,W,L) D, #0). The C bit is always cleared (as is the V bit) after execution of a TST(B,W,L) instruction.

$$
\begin{array}{rclc}
010 & \rightarrow & 010 & \text{N: } 0 \\
-101 & \rightarrow & +011 & \text{Z: } 0 \\
\overline{} & & \overline{} & \text{V: } 0 \\
& & 101 & \text{C: } 1 \\
\end{array}
$$

Figure 7.19 Signed and unsigned comparisons

Conditional Branches Revisited

In chapters 3 and 5 we saw subsets of the VAX's conditional branch instructions, using only positive offsets. Now that wc understand computer arithmetic, we are ready for the complete set of conditional branches, we are ready to see how negative offsets are stored, and we will be able to understand the last part of the execution of a branch instruction when the branch is taken.

Unsigned Conditional Branches

In figure 5.4, we saw some of the conditional branches, and we argued that the mnemonics fit well with the CC bits that are tested. However, now that we realize that the very same bit pattern may be considered either an unsigned number or a signed number, we will see that the branches in figure 5.4 are useful only when we are working with what we consider *signed* numbers. For example, the BLSS (branch if less than) instruction will be taken if the N bit is 1; this makes sense if we are thinking of numbers as signed, because the N bit is set if the msb of a result is 1--which indicates a negative result when dealing with signed numbers. Let's consider the example of 010 and 101; if 010 is the S_1 operand and 101 the S_2 operand of a CMP instruction, then 101 will be subtracted from 010, which will end up as 011 being added to 010, and the result will be 101. This is shown in figure 7.19. The CC settings will be as follows: the N bit will be 0 (because 010 is $+2$ and 101 is -3 as signed numbers, and $+2$ is *not* less than -3; or, because the exclusive or of the msb of the result, 1, and the V bit before clearing, also 1, is 0), the Z bit will be 0, the V bit will (always) be 0, and the C bit will be 1. If we are thinking of these numbers as signed, then the BLSS instruction will be appropriate: it won't be taken because N = 0, and it *shouldn't* be taken, because $+2$ is *not* less than -3.

However, what if we are thinking of the bit patterns as *un*signed numbers--what branch can we use that *will* be taken as a result of this comparison, because 010 (2) *is* less than 101 (5) as unsigned numbers? The VAX has a set of conditional branch instructions that are used when we wish to compare bit patterns as unsigned numbers. The complete set of VAX conditional branches, and the conditions under which they are taken, is shown in figure 7.20. Note that the conditions for BGTR and BLEQ are different from those listed in figure 5.4, and appear to be wrong. However, the **or** in the expression "if (N **or** Z) = 0" is a *logical* **or** (not an "ordinary everyday English" **or**). **Logical or** is a logic function with two inputs and one output; its output is 1 if either one or both of its inputs is 1, and its output is 0 only if both inputs are 0. (This is an *inclusive* **or,** as distinct from the *exclusive* **or** we discussed above.) The truth table for inclusive **or** of *a* and *b,* usually called just OR, is shown in figure 7.21.

What do we gain from this new set of conditional branches? We gain the ability to write programs in a simpler manner. If we write the instructions,

Branch Condition	Mnemonic	Opcode	Action
Result=0	BEQL DEST	13	if Z=1, PC←PC+offset
Result≠0	BNEQ DEST	12	if Z=0, PC←PC+offset
Result≥0	BGEQ DEST	18	if N=0, PC←PC+offset
Result<0	BLSS DEST	19	if N=1, PC←PC+offset
Result>0	BGTR DEST	14	if (N **or** Z)=0, PC←PC+offset
Result≤0	BLEQ DEST	15	if (N **or** Z)=1, PC←PC+offset
Result=0 unsigned	BEQLU DEST	13	if Z=1, PC←PC+offset
Result≠0 unsigned	BNEQU DEST	12	if Z=0, PC←PC+offset
Result≥0 unsigned	BGEQU DEST	1E	if C=0, PC←PC+offset
Result<0 unsigned	BLSSU DEST	1F	if C=1, PC←PC+offset
Result>0 unsigned	BGTRU DEST	1A	if (C **or** Z)=0, PC←PC+offset
Result≤0 unsigned	BLEQU DEST	1B	if (C **or** Z)=1, PC←PC+offset

Figure 7.20 VAX conditional branch instructions

a	b	OR
0	0	0
0	1	1
1	0	1
1	1	1

Figure 7.21 Truth table for **inclusive or**

```
        CMPL R0, R1
        BLSS SMALLER
           .
           .
           .
SMALLER:   ;some code here
```

we would hope that control would transfer to label SMALLER if the value in R0 is smaller than the value in R1, when they are considered signed numbers. If we wish to consider them as *un*signed numbers, we could replace the BLSS with BCS. However, it is easier for us, as programmers, to replace BLSS with BLSS*U*. The VAX control unit will then make the comparison appropriate for unsigned numbers: rather than checking the N bit, it would check the C bit to see whether the branch should be taken.

Why does it follow that, if the C bit is 1, then the S_1 operand of a CMP instruction is smaller than the S_2 operand, as unsigned numbers? Consider the operation of the CMP(B,W,L) family of instructions: they compute $S_1 - S_2$. If S_1 is smaller than S_2 as unsigned numbers, then we will have to borrow in order to perform the subtraction (or, the result, if it were stored, would be incorrect), and so the C bit would be set. So, the designers of the VAX were correct in claiming that BCS and BLSSU are equivalent conditional branches (and that BCC and BGEQU are equivalent). We could make similar arguments for the BGTRU and BLEQU conditional branches, but we leave them to the reader, as an exercise.

What is a typical situation in which we would use the unsigned conditional branches? One common case is comparing ASCII character codes: we may design a program which accepts input from the keyboard. At some point in our program, the only legal input might be a number; if we wish to check for legal input (which is usually a good thing to do), we may, rather than checking the input against the ASCII character code for each of the 10 digits, simply check that the input is in the range 30_{16} to 39_{16}, inclusive. The following is a program fragment to perform this range check (GETC is a system service that is used to read a character from the keyboard; its use is described more completely in appendix 1.):

```
                .ENTRY START, 0
                IOINIT
                .
                .
                .
                GETC R7
                CMPB R7, #^A/0/   ;check lower bound
                BLSSU ERROR
;else, check upper bound
                CMPB R7, #^A/9/   ;check upper bound
                BGTRU ERROR
;else no error, so compute
                .
                .
                .
ERROR:          PUTS errormessage
```

Branch Offsets Revisited

The examples of conditional branches that we have seen so far have all been with positive offsets. This is *not* because we cannot specify a target of a conditional branch that is earlier in our program than the branch instruction, but rather because we did not yet know how negative numbers are stored. An assembly language program that is similar to a Pascal "for index : = 1 to 10" loop, is shown in figure 7.22. The assembler, of course, will translate this into machine language for us. The

```
                MOVL #10, R8     ;R8: terminating condition
                MOVL #1, R7      ;R7: loop count
LOOP:           CMPL R7, R8      ;check for done
                BGTR DONE
        ;else--continue
                ;loop body here
                INCL R7          ;increment loop count
                BRB LOOP
DONE:           ;end of loop
```

Figure 7.22 Assembly language "for loop"

```
58  0A  D0  0000  1          MOVL #10, R8    ;R8: terminating condition
57  01  D0  0003  2          MOVL #1, R7     ;R7: loop count
58  57  D1  0006  3   LOOP:   CMPL R7, R8     ;check for done
    04  14  0009  4          BGTR DONE
            000B  5       ;else--continue
            000B  6          ;loop body here
    57  D6  000B  7          INCL R7          ;increment loop count
    F7  11  000D  8          BRB LOOP
            000F  9   DONE:  ;end of loop
```

Figure 7.23 Assembler listing of "for loop"

listing generated by this program fragment is shown in figure 7.23. Note that there are two branches in this fragment, on lines 4 and 8 of the listing. The forward branch, on line 4, has an offset of 4, because the difference between $0000000B_{16}$ (the value held by the location counter when the branch offset was being computed) and $0000000F_{16}$ (the value of label DONE, which is the target of the branch) is 4. The backward branch, on line 8, has an offset of $F7_{16}$, or 11110111_2. Every number is the negation of its negation (really, it is!); the msb of 11110111 is 1, so we know that it is a negative number. If, therefore, we negate 11110111 (by taking its twos complement), we can see what (positive) number it is the negation of. The twos complement of 11110111 is 00001001, which is 9, so 11110111 (F7) is -9. And, the difference between the location counter when the branch offset is being computed ($0000000F_{16}$) and the value of label LOOP (00000006_{16}), which is the target of the branch, is -9. Observant readers may notice that the immediate operands 10 (line 1) and 1 (line 2) were not assembled using the 8F operand specifier. This will be explained shortly--in chapter 8.

Finally, now that we understand the twos complement number system and sign extension, we can complete our understanding of what happens in the control unit when a branch instruction is executed. We already know that the control unit fetches memory[PC], updates the PC, and places the branch opcode in the instruction register. Then, when the opcode is decoded, it fetches memory[PC] again (to get the branch offset), updates the PC again, and checks the low-order bits of the PSL (which contain the condition code bits) for the branch condition. If, for example, the branch was BLSSU, then if the C bit is set, the branch is taken--which is done by adding the offset to the PC. However, the offset is only 8 bits, and the PC contains a 32-bit address; so the offset must be sign extended to 32 bits before it can be added to the PC. For example, the offset for the BRB instruction, on line 8 of figure 7.23, is $F7_{16}$ (11110111_2); after it is sign extended it will be $FFFFFFF7_{16}$. Note that if zero extension rather than sign extension were done, the offset would be incorrect for backward branches; in the example above, -9 would be turned into +247, which is probably not what we meant when we wrote BRB LOOP.

Special Loop Control Branch Instructions

Figure 7.22 shows a program fragment that implements a higher level language "for loop"; it requires four instructions for loop control: a CMP to test the loop count against the termination value, a conditional branch (BGTR) on the condition that the loop count exceeds the termination value, an INC to increment the loop count, and an unconditional branch to the beginning of the loop. The VAX has two families of special branch instructions that provide the functions of these four separate instructions with a single instruction; one family is the general-purpose "add-compare-and-branch" instructions, and the other is the "add/subtract-1-and-branch" instructions. We will describe them in that order; they are summarized (using an abbreviated notation) in figure 7.24.

Instruction	Mnemonic	Op	Action
Add cmp branch byte	ACBB LIM,ADD,IND,D	9D	IND←IND+ADD; if IND≠LIM, PC←PC+offset
Add cmp branch word	ACBW LIM,ADD,IND,D	3D	IND←IND+ADD; if IND≠LIM, PC←PC+offset
Add cmp branch long	ACBL LIM,ADD,IND,D	F1	IND←IND+ADD; if IND≠LIM, PC←PC+offset
Add 1; branch on ≤	AOBLEQ LIM,IND,D	F3	IND←IND+1; if IND≤LIM, PC←PC+offset
Add 1; branch on <	AOBLSS LIM,IND,D	F2	IND←IND+1; if IND<LIM, PC←PC+offset
Sub 1; branch on ≥	SOBGEQ IND,D	F4	IND←IND−1; if IND≥0, PC←PC+offset
Sub 1; branch on >	SOBGTR IND,D	F5	IND←IND−1; if IND>0, PC←PC+offset

Figure 7.24 Loop-control instructions

The Add-Compare-and-Branch Instructions

The **add-compare-and-branch** instructions are 4-operand instructions; they specify a limit, an addend, an index, and a destination. The limit, addend, and index may be specified with nearly any one of the VAX's addressing modes; the destination is specified as a symbolic label for the target, and is assembled as a word offset, as with the BRW instruction. The difference between the ACBB, ACBW, and ACBL instructions is in the sizes of the limit, addend, and index: for ACBB they are each a byte, for ACBW they are each a word, and for ACBL they are each a longword. When the instruction is executed, the index is replaced by the sum of the addend and the index; if the new index is less than or equal to the limit (in the case of a positive addend), or if it is greater than or equal to the limit (in the case of a negative addend), the branch is taken.

The ACB(B,W,L) instructions are ideal for implementing a Pascal-type "for loop"; the program fragment of figure 7.22 has been rewritten using the ACBB instruction in figure 7.25. We see from figure 7.25 that the loop body is now only two instructions long: one instruction is the ACBB, and the other is the comment which would be replaced by some number of instructions in a real program. The assembler listing of this program fragment is shown in figure 7.26.

There should be no surprises for us in the listing: we have already seen register mode operand specifiers, and we have already seen negative branch offsets. The offset $FFFA_{16}$ which the assembler has calculated (in the leftmost field of line 5) is the number which must be added to the program counter when the ACBB instruction is being executed in order to produce the address of the target of the branch. The program listing shows us that LOOP has the value 9_{16}, and that DONE (whose address will be in the PC when the ACBB has been fetched and is being executed) has the value F_{16}. Simple arithmetic produces the offset: 9-15 = -6; is $FFFA_{16}$ -6? Sign extension works both ways: we can simplify our task by dropping the 8 leading 1s (represented by FF), and performing 8-bit rather

```
                   MOVB #10, R8         ;R8: limit
                   MOVB #1, R7          ;R7: addend
                   MOVB #1, R6          ;R6: index
        LOOP:      ;loop body here
                   ACBB R8, R7, R6, LOOP
        DONE:      ;end of loop
```

Figure 7.25 "For loop" using ACBB instruction

```
       58 0A 90  0000  1           MOVB  #10, R8    ;R8: limit
       57 01 90  0003  2           MOVB  #1, R7     ;R7: addend
       56 01 90  0006  3           MOVB  #1, R6     ;R6: index
                 0009  4    LOOP:  ;loop body here
FFFA 56 57 58 9D 0009  5           ACBB  R8, R7, R6, LOOP
                 000F  6    DONE:  ;end of loop
```

Figure 7.26 Listing with ACBB instruction

than 16-bit arithmetic. So, FA_{16} is 11111010_2; the twos complement of 11111010 is 00000110--which is +6. So, if the negation of FA_{16} is +6, then FA_{16} must be -6, which is exactly what we calculated the offset should be! As stated above, the limit, addend, and index operands can be specified with a variety of addressing modes, but there is an exception: the limit and addend can use immediate mode, but the index, which must change, cannot. If we use immediate mode for the limit and addend, we need only a single loop initialization instruction (to place the limit value in a register or somewhere else), and we can write ACBB #10, #1, R6, LOOP, for example.

We can also use the ACB(B,W,L) instructions to implement Pascal's "for index := 10 downto 1" statement, for example. In this case, the index would be 10, the limit would be 1, and the addend would be -1. The branch is taken if index$\leq$limit when the addend is positive, and if index$\geq$limit when the addend is negative.

The Add/Subtract-1-and-Branch Instructions

The **add/subtract-1-and-branch** instructions are special cases of the ACB(B,W,L) instructions. The addend is always +1 (for AOB) or -1 (for SOB); for the SOB instructions, the limit is either 0 (for SOBGEQ) or 1 (for SOBGTR). In addition, the limit (and the index, for the AOB instructions) is always a longword, and the destination is specified with a byte offset. We could replace the ACBB #10, #1, R6, LOOP in the above example with the instruction AOBLEQ #10, R6, LOOP. However, we must be careful: if we accidentally initialize R6 with a negative number (or if we initialize it with a byte or word instruction, which may amount to the same thing, since it will leave the high-order bits of the register unchanged), the loop may execute a very large number of times before R6 contains 11_{10}!

Just as we used an AOB instruction to replace the ACBB with a positive addend, so we can use an SOB instruction to replace an ACBB instruction with a negative addend. So, if we wish to write assembly language for the Pascal statement, "for index := 10 downto 1", we can use either ACBB #1, #-1, R6, LOOP, or the shorter, less general, SOBGTR R6, LOOP.

The loop control instructions provide an interesting analogy to the single-operand instructions we have seen: the INC(B,W,L), DEC(B,W,L), TST(B,W,L) and CLR(B,W,L) families of instructions. In the case of the single operand instructions, the VAX's designers created the INC instructions because adding 1 is a common operation. In the case of the loop-control instructions, they created the ACB instructions because adding, comparing, and branching is a common sequence of operations. In both cases, the special-purpose instructions are less general (by design) and perhaps more difficult to understand than the general purpose alternatives, but they are more efficient at run time. We have also seen this principle (and we will see it again, in chapter 8) in our discussion of complex addressing modes: we can do nearly everything with only modes 5 and 6; modes 7, 8 and A, C, and E are sometimes more convenient, but they can be constructed from combinations of modes 5 and 6.

Loop Instructions and the Condition-Code Bits

Although the loop-control instructions are similar to the conditional branch instructions in that they branch on some condition and specify the branch target as a PC-relative offset, they are different from the conditional branch instructions in that they *do* change CC bit settings. The ACB(B,W,L) instructions set the condition-code bits according the the value of the index operand: the N bit is set if the index is less than 0, the Z bit is set if the index is equal to 0, the V bit is set if the msb of the index changes, and the C bit is unchanged. The AOB and SOB instructions also set the CC bits according to the value of the index, in the same manner; the C bit is unchanged.

Which Branch Instruction Should We Use?

1.   If we are copying a value with a MOV(B,W,L) instruction, or comparing it to 0 with a TST(B,W,L) instruction, then the only branches which make sense are those which examine the N or Z bits.
2.   If we have just executed a CMP(B,W,L) instruction, then we must select the appropriate branch depending on whether we are treating the bit patterns as signed or unsigned numbers.
3.   If we have just executed an ADD(B,W,L)[2,3], SUB(B,W,L)[2,3], INC(B,W,L) or DEC(B,W,L) instruction, then we should check for **overflow** for signed arithmetic and **carry** for unsigned arithmetic, if they are at all likely. If we are doing extended-range integer arithmetic, then we can either test the C bit or use ADWC/SBWC following each ADD(B,W,L)2/SUB(B,W,L)2 instruction.
4.   If we are writing "for loops," "do loops," "while loops," "repeat until loops," and so forth, then we may either use the special loop-control and branch instructions, or we may construct our own out of the individual arithmetic, comparison, and conditional branch instructions.

Summary

The **sign magnitude representation** for signed numbers is used by humans, but it is rarely used by computers because it is not easily implemented in hardware: the sign bit must be treated separately from the magnitude part, magnitude parts must be compared, and addition is performed by sometimes adding and sometimes subtracting. The VAX uses the **twos complement representation** for signed numbers. With the twos complement representation, adding numbers (signed or unsigned) is performed according to the simple rules of the binary addition table. The twos complement system also has only one representation for 0, which makes checking for 0 as a sentinel value relatively simple. The twos complement system is closely related to another system used on some computers, the **ones complement representation**. Given a negative number, its ones complement representation, plus one, equals its twos complement representation. Taking the ones complement of a number is identical to logically complementing (inverting) each bit.

When adding numbers using the twos complement representation, it is not necessary to distinguish between various cases; unsigned numbers and positive and negative signed numbers are all treated the same--as strings of bits, to be added according to the binary addition table. The correct sum will be produced by the ALU, provided the result can be expressed as an 8-, 16-, or 32-bit number. When a result is too big (or too small) for the number of bits specified by the opcode, the ALU will set the the V bit to indicate **overflow** and/or the C bit to indicate **carry**. It is a programmer's responsibility to check for the possibility of an incorrect result by using BVC/BVS instructions for arithmetic on signed numbers, and by using the BCC/BCS instructions for arithmetic on unsigned numbers.

The C bit can also be used to perform extended-range integer arithmetic when each operand is stored in more than one location. The BCC/BCS instructions can be used to test for **carry** in extended range arithmetic, or we can use the ADWC/SBWC instructions, which add (or subtract) the carry bit to (or from) the location in which the next most significant part of the operand is stored.

In the twos complement system, a negative number always has its most significant bit set and a positive number always has its most significant bit cleared. Extending a signed number from a byte to a word or longword, or from a word to a longword, requires copying the most significant (pseudo-sign) bit into the high-order bits of the longer operand. This is done with the CVT(BW,BL,WL) instructions. Unsigned numbers are never less than 0, so extending an unsigned number from a byte to a word or longword, or from a word to a longword, requires copying 0s into the high-order bits of the longer operand. This is done with the MOVZ(BW,BL,WL) instructions.

When comparing signed numbers, the N bit provides important information about their relative magnitudes; therefore, the conditional branches that are designed to be used for signed comparison test various combinations of CC bits that include the N bit. When comparing unsigned numbers, the C bit provides this information, so conditional branches designed for use with unsigned comparisons test CC bit combinations that include the C bit. The CMP(B,W,L) family of instructions set the CC bits differently than the SUB(B,W,L)2 instructions; in particular, for the CMP instructions the V bit is always cleared, and the N bit is set according to the **exclusive or** of the result's most significant bit and the V bit before it is cleared.

The TST(B,W,L) family of instructions is similar to the INC(B,W,L), DEC(B,W,L) and CLR(B,W,L) families in that it replaces a general instruction that requires two explicitly specified operands with a special-case instruction that requires only one explicitly specified operand because the other one is implicit. With the TST family, the implicit operand is 0, and the instruction is a special case of the CMP instruction.

The VAX also provides some special cases of the conditional branch instructions that are designed particularly for loop control. The ACB(B,W,L) instructions are the most general and specify a limit, addend, and index for loop-control and a target that is branched to if the sum of the index and addend has not reached the limit. The AOB(LEQ,LSS) instructions have an implicit addend of $+1$, and the SOB(GEQ,GTR) instructions have an implicit addend of -1 and an implicit limit of 0 or 1. All of these loop-control instructions encode the branch target as a PC-relative offset; the ACB instructions have a word offset, and the AOB/SOB instructions have a byte offset.

Exercises for Chapter 7

1. The parity of a group of bits is said to be odd if it contains an odd number of 1 bits. Write a program which can find the parity of the low-order 3 bits of a byte, assuming the high order 5 bits are all 0.
2. Write a program to find the parity of the 3 *high*-order bits of a byte.
3. Many assemblers are written in assembly language. How can an assembler assemble itself? Outline a plausible scenario for constructing an assembler. (**Hint:** Consider the analogous problem of bootstrapping, discussed in chapter 2.)
4. Write each of the following numbers in binary:

    a. -49 as a 16-bit twos complement number
    b. the most negative 32-bit twos complement number
    c. the most positive 36-bit twos complement integer
    d. the logical complement of the hexadecimal number 17ACF953

5. When executing the BNEQ conditional branch, the CPU examines the Z bit, and when executing the BGEQ branch, it examines the N bit. However, we can replace every BRB X (where X is properly defined) with the pair of instructions, BNEQ X and BGEQ X, without changing the flow of control of the program in which they appear. Explain why this is the case.

6. The instruction ADDB2 R1, R2 could result in the CC having various bit patterns depending on the values in R1 and R2. For each CC bit pattern shown below, fill in a pair of values for R1 and R2 which would, after the execution of ADDL2 R1, R2, produce the specified setting of the condition code bits.

Condition Code Setting				Register Contents	
N	Z	V	C	R1	R2
0	0	0	0	_____	_____
0	1	1	1	_____	_____
1	0	0	1	_____	_____
0	0	1	0	_____	_____

7. Answer the following questions about the result produced by ADDL2 R0, R1, where the contents of R0 and R1 are $6443221A_{16}$ and $443ABB21_{16}$, respectively:

    a. Result?
    b. Under what conditions would this result be correct?
    c. Under what conditions would this result be incorrect?
    d. What would the settings of the condition-code bits be?

8. A hypothetical computer uses an 8-bit word. Answer the following about this machine, in binary.

    a. If an address is 1 word long, and the minimal addressable unit is the word, how many words can be addressed?
    b. If the computer uses the twos complement representation, what is the most positive number that can be represented in 1 word?
    c. What is the most negative twos complement number that can be represented in one word.

9. Convert the following 7-bit binary twos complement numbers to decimal sign magnitude numbers.

    a. 0010000
    b. 1000000
    c. 1111111

10. Show, in binary, a source operand for a MOVB instruction (if there is one) that will cause the following settings of the N and Z bits of the CC.

N	Z	MOVB source op
0	0	_____
0	1	_____
1	0	_____
1	1	_____

11. Assume that a memory reference is made each time an address is sent along the bus to memory, either with a request to read the contents of the location with that address, or with a request to write a value. (The value is sent along the bus, also, but consider a write request to be only a *single* memory reference, not one for the address and a second one for the data.) Assume, in

addition, that a memory reference takes .5 microseconds, but that execution of an instruction takes no time at all. Then, write the code to perform an extended-range integer addition from memory to memory, with each number stored in 3 longwords. Assume that the low-order longwords of the operands are in memory locations A and B, and the low-order longword of the result will be stored in memory location C. How much time does it take to perform the addition? Be sure to include the memory references to fetch both the instructions *and* their operands.

12. Show a case when INCB X and INCL X

    a.   produce the same result;
    b.   produce different results;
    c.   set the N bit (either instruction);
    d.   set the Z bit (either instruction);
    e.   set the V bit (either instruction);
    f.   set the C bit (either instruction).

13. Suppose you wish to report the setting of the four CC bits without changing them. Keeping in mind that even a MOV(B,W,L) may change the N and Z bits, show how you could copy the CC bits into memory, using only MOV(B,W,L) and the VAX conditional branch instructions. Show how you could restore the CC bits if they were changed in the process of recording their values. If this is impossible in the general case, explain why.

14. For each combination of N and Z bits shown, write one VAX instruction which sets the N and Z bits to the indicated values. Each one must use either A and/or B, which have been defined as follows:

    A: .WORD5
    B: .WORD4

N	Z	instruction
0	0	—————————
0	1	—————————
1	0	—————————

15. True or False?

    a.   INCW R2 and ADDW #2, R2 produce the same result.
    b.   Registers can be initialized at both run time and assemble time.
    c.   Every 2-operand instruction requires 3 bytes of memory.
    d.   The assembly language statements

       .BYTE 78, 79, 7A
       .ASCII /xyz/

       generate the same machine language when processed by the assembler.
    e.   If your program attempts to execute an illegal instruction, the operating system will always tell you what you did wrong.
    f.   Conditional branch instructions test the settings of the CC bits to decide whether or not to branch.
    g.   BRB (R3) is a useful way to transfer control to whatever address is in R3 at runtime.

h.   In the VAX, if you use the same instructions to add unsigned numbers that you use to add signed numbers, the result will be correct as an unsigned number but incorrect as a signed number.

16.   Consider the following hexadecimal numbers.

        1. FFFFFFFF   5. 6775
        2. 00000000   6. 42765
        3. 90354ACD   7. 236
        4. 80000000   8. 12345678

        a.   Suppose that they are VAX addresses: Which is smallest? Which is largest?
        b.   Suppose that they are VAX numbers: Which is the smallest signed number? Which is the largest signed number? Which is the smallest unsigned number? Which is the largest unsigned number?

17.   If you write a program that compares addresses in order to terminate a loop, should you use signed or unsigned branch instructions?

18.   Assume that when the following program gets to location CASES, R0 contains either 0, 4, 8, 12, or 16, and that labels ZERO, FOUR, EIGHT, TWELVE, and SIXTEEN are defined at various locations throughout the program. Write at most two instructions at location CASES that, when executed, would transfer control to one of locations ZERO, FOUR, EIGHT, TWELVE, or SIXTEEN, depending upon the value in R0. (**Hints:** You may add as much data at the beginning of the program as you like; you may wish to review the jump table example in chapter 6.)

        DATA: ;add data here
                     .
                     .
                     .
                  .ENTRY START, 0
                     .
                     .
                     .
        CASES: ;instruction(s) to branch to ZERO, FOUR, . . . , SIXTEEN here

19.   Prove the following statement: Given two numbers, S and D, if S < D, and if subtracting S from D causes the V bit to be set, then it must be true that S < 0 < D.

20.   Many different things can be seen in a memory dump. If you had no idea what some hexadecimal numbers were supposed to represent, name six different possibilities. Do not name data structures such as arrays, but more primitive objects--such as signed integers, for example.

21.   Consider the instruction sequence given below, where the "--" stands for a conditional branch instruction:

        MOVL   #^X945612A4, R1
        MOVL   #^XABCD1234, R2
        ADDL2   R1, R2
        --   LOOP

        a.   Show the values of the condition code bits after the ADDL2 R1, R2 is executed.
        b.   For each conditional branch instruction listed below, write a Y next to the ones that would be taken if they were substituted for "--," and write an N next to them if they would *not* be taken.

Branch	Y/N	Branch	Y/N	Branch	Y/N	Branch	Y/N
(1) BCS	——	(5) BCC	——	(9) BEQL	——	(13) BNEQ	——
(2) BGTR	——	(6) BGEQ	——	(10) BLSS	——	(14) BLEQ	——
(3) BVS	——	(7) BVC	——	(11) BEQLU	——	(15) BNEQU	——
(4) BGTRU	——	(8) BGEQU	——	(12) BLSSU	——	(16) BLEQU	——

22. Describe the similarities and the differences, if any, between the machine language generated by the following assembly language directives:

```
.BYTE   0, 0, 0
.ASCII  "000"
.BLKB   3
```

23. Assume R1 contains $FA1379AC_{16}$ and R2 contains 80000005_{16} and that R1 and R2 are reset to these values after execution of each of the following instructions. Fill in the spaces indicating the setting of the N and Z bits after each instruction is executed.

Instruction   N   Z

a. TSTL R1   _   _
b. CMPL R1, R2   _   _
c. SUBL2 R1, R2   _   _
d. MOVL R1, R2   _   _
e. ADDL2 R1, R2   _   _
f. BNEQ (R2)   _   _

24. Each of the following statements describes how one bit of the condition code (CC) is affected by arithmetic operations. Identify the condition-code bit described by each statement.

    a. Set if the msb of a result is 1, cleared if msb is 0, after ADD or SUB.
    b. Set during subtraction if there is a borrow into the msb; cleared otherwise.
    c. Set if two addends have the same msb and the result has a different msb
    d. Set if the result of an add is 0; cleared otherwise.
    e. If the addends are considered signed numbers, then if this bit is set, it indicates an error has occurred; if it is cleared, no error has occurred.
    f. Suppose operand A is subtracted from operand B. This bit is set only if A and B have different msb's and the result has the msb of A.
    g. Set if there is a carry out of the msb of a sum; cleared otherwise.
    h. If the operands of an ADD or SUB are considered to be unsigned, then if this bit is set, it indicates that the result is incorrect; if it is cleared, then the result is correct.

25. Write a program fragment that adds 2 128-bit integer operands, replaces the second operand with the result, and branches to a statement labeled ERROR if the result is invalid. Assume twos complement representations, and be sure to check for incorrect results *whenever* they might be produced.

26. In the following table, the leftmost column shows, in hexadecimal, a bit pattern in the VAX's memory. Fill in the remaining columns by writing, in decimal, the number that the hexadecimal number represents if it is interpreted as a twos complement number, a ones complement number, a sign-magnitude number, or an unsigned number. The first row is an example; these are 8-bit numbers. **Suggestion:** Convert the hexadecimal representation to binary and then convert from binary to the various decimal representations.

hexadecimal	twos complement	ones complement	sign-magnitude	unsigned
FE	− 2	− 1	− 126	254
(a) 7F				
(b) 77				
(c) 80				
(d) 81				
(e) 92				
(f) A3				
(g) B4				
(h) C5				
(i) FF				
(j) FD				
(k) FC				
(l) FB				
(m) F0				
(n) 70				
(o) 90				
(p) A0				

27. Perform the following subtractions using twos complement arithmetic as the VAX would do it. Show your work. If the result is negative, write it as a sign-magnitude hexadecimal number as well as a twos complement binary number. All numbers are hexadecimal; all operands are 8 bits.

$$
\begin{array}{cccccc}
14 & 14 & A0 & 10 & FF & 80 \\
-26 & -10 & -27 & -64 & -81 & -FF \\
\end{array}
$$

```
  00010100
 +11011010
  11101110     = −12
```

28. Perform the following binary additions; write the answer and indicate, in each case, the setting of the CC bits as a single hexadecimal digit, in the order NZVC (as seen in the PSL, in the SNAP output). Assume that you are doing 5-bit arithmetic.
    answer:

$$
\begin{array}{ccccccccc}
00001 & 10000 & 11110 & 11110 & 11111 & 10101 & 11111 & 01000 & 11001 \\
11111 & 10000 & 11101 & 11110 & 11111 & 01010 & 00000 & 11000 & 01101 \\
\end{array}
$$

answer:

CC(NZVC):

29. "Execute" each instruction, and indicate changes only to registers and memory. The initial contents of registers and memory are given; results do not accumulate, except when two instructions are in the same box. All numbers are hexadecimal, and your answers should also be; leading 0s have been omitted. Assume that the symbolic label X has been assigned the value 1010_{16}.

Instruction	R1	R2	100440	300448	30044C	PC
Initial Values:	100440	300448	200444	10FFFF	100001	1000
MOVB (R1), R2						
MOVL (R1), (R2)						
MOVB R1, (R2)						
CLRW (R1)+						
CLRL (R1)+						
CLRL 4(R2)						
CLRB 4(R2)						
CLRB −^X200008(R2)						
CLRW ^X20000C(R1)						
JMP (R2)						
SUBL2 (R2)+, (R1)+						
CMPW (R1)+, (R1)+						
CMPL (R2)+, (R2)+						
SUBB2 (R1)+, (R1)+						
ADDB2 (R2)+, (R2)+						
ADDW2 (R1)+, −1(R1)						
TSTB (R2)+						
INCB (R2)						
INCW (R2)						
INCL (R2)						
INCB (R2) INCB (R2)						
BRB X						

30. Given the following hexadecimal numbers:

1. 00000000   4. 80000000
2. FFFFFFFE   5. 70067777
3. 80345A6E   6. 042765EE

a. Which is the largest unsigned number?
b. Which is the largest signed number?
c. Which is the smallest unsigned number?
d. Which is the smallest signed number?
e. What is the sum of (3) and (4)?
f. What can you say (of relevance) about the result of (e)?

31. In the VAX, the conditional branches are taken or not, depending upon the results of the most recently executed arithmetic instruction. Different branches are different merely because they examine different combinations of condition code bits. In particular, the following table shows the branches and the conditions under which they are *taken*. In the table, (X or Y) means the **logical or** of X and Y.

Branch	Condition
BEQL	$Z = 1$
BNEQ	$Z = 0$
BLSS	$N = 1$
BGEQ	$N = 0$
BLEQ	(N **or** Z) $= 1$
BGTR	(N **or** Z) $= 0$
BLSSU	$C = 1$
BGEQU	$C = 0$
BLEQU	(C **or** Z) $= 1$
BGTRU	(C **or** Z) $= 0$

a.   For each of the ten conditional branches listed above, show values for R0 and R1 such that in the following program fragment the branch *will be* taken (example 1), and will *not* be taken (example 2). You will have, thus, 20 examples: 2 for each conditional branch. Use 3-bit arithmetic (i.e., assume that the registers are only 3 bits wide) for your examples. Also, indicate the setting of the condition-code bits (N, Z, V, C, in that order) for each example. The program fragment:

```
CMPL    R0,  R1
Bxxx        SOMEWHERE
```

b.   For each *pair* of signed-unsigned branches (e.g., BLSS-BLSSU), pick a *pair* of examples such that (1) the branch (in the above program fragment) will be taken by one *but not by the other,* and (2) the other way around. In other words, (1) choose a pair of 3-bit numbers such that, if one is in R0 and the other in R1, BLSS will be taken and BLSSU will not be, and then (2) choose another pair of numbers such that BLSSU will be taken and BLSS will not be. In this case, also, indicate the settings of the condition-code bits after each CMPL instruction has been executed.

c.   Repeat part(a) above, with the following program fragment:

```
ADDL3   R0,  R1,  R2
Bxxx        SOMEWHERE
```

Note that in the case of the unsigned branches, at least, you may have to work backward. It is *not* the case that there are fewer possible examples in this part than in part (*a*).

Branch	Condition
BEQL	$Z = 1$
BNEQ	$Z = 0$
BLSS	$N = 1$
BGEQ	$N = 0$
BLEQ	(N *or* Z) $= 1$
BGTR	(N *or* Z) $= 0$
BLSSU	$C = 1$
BGEQU	$C = 0$
BLEQU	(C *or* Z) $= 1$
BGTRU	(C *or* Z) $= 0$

▪ 8 ▪

The Rest of the Addressing Modes

Introduction

So far, we have thoroughly examined only some of the VAX's simple addressing modes: register mode, register mode deferred, autoincrement mode, autodecrement mode, and the displacement modes. We have been introduced to two other types of addressing--immediate and absolute--which use the PC, but which we do not yet completely understand. Immediate addressing uses mode 8 with the PC and absolute addressing uses mode 9 with the PC; we have already seen mode 8 in the general case, but not mode 9. In addition, we have not yet discussed the implications of using an addressing mode with the PC rather than one of the general-purpose registers: the PC is a general-purpose register in some senses, but clearly not in all senses.

Thus, we have seen 7 addressing modes so far: modes 5, 6, 7, 8, A, C and E; these addressing modes are summarized in figure 8.1, which is the same as figure 6.10. We have reproduced it here for review, and because we will, as usual, refer to what we already know in the course of explaining what we have not yet seen. Since the mode field of an operand specifier has 4 bits, we might guess that there are 16 addressing modes--and there are. We will see that 7 of the 9 modes that we have not yet seen are conceptually only 2, and we will also see that four of the addressing modes are used with the PC in special cases. In the remainder of this chapter we will examine the four different classes of addressing modes that we have not yet seen, and then we will see how some classes of addressing modes can be used with the PC to provide useful ways of specifying operands.

The Deferred Addressing Modes

Several of the addressing modes that we have not yet seen are straightforward extensions of ones that we *have* seen. The displacement modes and autoincrement mode have corresponding modes that involve an extra level of indirection: autoincrement deferred and displacement deferred. The model for both of these modes is the relationship between register mode (mode 5) and register mode deferred (mode 6): with register mode, the operand is in the register, and with register mode deferred the *address* of the operand is in the register. Autoincrement and autoincrement deferred have a similar relationship: with autoincrement mode, the operand's address is in the register (and the register is changed after the address in it is used), and with autoincrement mode deferred, the *address* of the operand's address is in the register (and the register is changed after the address in it is used). Displacement and displacement deferred also have that relationship: with displacement mode, the sum of the register contents and the displacement is the operand's address, and with displacement mode deferred the sum of the register contents and the displacement is the *address* of the operand's address. Let's consider these new addressing modes in more detail.

Autoincrement Deferred

Autoincrement mode deferred is mode 9 (yes, the same mode 9 we saw in 9F!). The assembler recognizes the syntax "@(Rn)+" (yes, the same "@" we saw in "@#"!) to indicate autoincrement deferred. With autoincrement mode, the register changes by 1, 2, or 4 depending on whether the

Mode	Name	Format	Explanation
5	Register	R*n*	Operand is in R*n*.
6	Register deferred	(R*n*)	Operand address is in R*n*.
7	Autodecrement	–(R*n*)	R*n* ←R*n* – dec *before* address is computed; *then* operand address is in R*n*.[†]
8	Autoincrement	(R*n*)+	Operand address is in R*n*; R*n* ← R*n* + inc *after* operand is fetched.[‡]
A (C, E)	Byte (word, longword) displacement	X(R*n*)	Operand address is X + R*n*; X follows operand specifier.
8[PC]	Immediate	#X	Operand is X; X follows operand specifier.
9[PC]	Absolute	@#X	Operand address is X; X follows operand specifier.

[†]dec=1 for byte, 2 for word, 4 for longword instruction.
[‡]inc=1 for byte, 2 for word, 4 for longword instruction.

Figure 8.1 Review of basic addressing modes

instruction's operands are bytes, words, or longwords. This is appropriate because if the operands are bytes, then the register contains the address of a byte, and the address of the next byte is 1 more than the address of the one whose address is in the register. The analogous explanation is made for words and longwords. With autoincrement deferred, however, the address in the register is not the address of an *operand;* it is the address of an *address* (of an operand). Since addresses are all longwords, the address of the next address is 4 more than that of the one whose address is in the register. Thus, with autoincrement deferred, the register *always* changes by 4, regardless of the operand size.

What is autoincrement deferred good for? Clearly, it steps through an array of addresses--but why would we ever have an array of addresses? Soon we will discuss subroutines, and we will see that it is often convenient to pass arguments to subroutines in **argument lists.** Since we will sometimes *not* wish to copy the arguments themselves (for example, if an argument is an array), we will, instead, pass the argument's address (as with, for example, **var** parameters in Pascal). In this case, an argument list may be an array of addresses. Figure 8.2 shows an example of the use of the autoincrement deferred addressing mode. It is, of course, possible to avoid using autoincrement deferred in this example (we could, for example, use a combination of register deferred and autoincrement modes)--and in any other example, as well--but the purpose of the example is to illustrate the use of the addressing mode rather than to describe a case in which its use is unavoidable. Figure 8.3 shows the assembler listing from this program, and figure 8.4 shows a picture of memory after the program has been loaded and just before it has been executed. In figures 8.3 and 8.4 we assume that $EXIT_S generates the halt instruction. Also (as usual), we have placed asterisks in the memory locations that contain opcodes, for clarity only.

There are several items of interest. First, examine figure 8.3 and note how the assembler treats the statement,

TABLE: .ADDRESS A, B, C, D

```
TABLE:     .ADDRESS A, B, C, D      ;address array
A:         .BYTE 1                  ;data
B:         .BYTE 2
C:         .WORD 3
D:         .WORD 4
           .ENTRY START, 0
           MOVAL @#TABLE, R0        ;R0 has address of address now
           ADDB2 @(R0)+, @(R0)+     ;add A to B
           SUBW2 @(R0)+, @(R0)+     ;sub C from D
           $EXIT_S
           .END START
```

Figure 8.2 Using autoincrement mode deferred

```
00000014'00000012'00000011'00000010'  0000  1 TABLE:  .ADDRESS A, B, C, D
                                 01    0010  2 A:      .BYTE   1
                                 02    0011  3 B:      .BYTE   2
                               0003    0012  4 C:      .WORD   3
                               0004    0014  5 D:      .WORD   4
                               0000    0016  6         .ENTRY START, 0
            50    00000000'9F   DE    0018  7         MOVAL @#TABLE, R0
                        90 90   80    001F  8         ADDB2 @(R0)+, @(R0)+
                        90 90   A2    0022  9         SUBW2 @(R0)+, @(R0)+
                                00    0025 10         HALT
                                      0026 11         .END START
```

Figure 8.3 Assembler listing with autoincrement deferred

+3	+2	+1	+0	address
00	00	00	10	00000000
00	00	00	11	00000004
00	00	00	12	00000008
00	00	00	14	0000000C
00	03	02	01	00000010
00	00	00	04	00000014
00	00	9F	DE*	00000018
80*	50	00	00	0000001C
90	A2	90	90	00000020
??	??	00*	90	00000024

Figure 8.4 Program using autoincrement deferred loaded in memory

There is only one way that the assembler could possibly treat it, and that is the way that it does: as a series of addresses. We have requested, with the .ADDRESS directive, that a series of longwords be reserved and initialized; they can't be initialized to the *contents* of the locations with addresses A, B, etc., because those contents are unknown until run time. They are initialized to addresses because the assembler deals with assemble-time values, not run-time values; at assemble time, the value of a label is the location counter value that was assigned to it, which we see in the address column of the listing. (At run time, of course, things are different: we place an address in an instruction or a register, and then the control unit, in the course of executing an instruction, does not add that *address*; it sends the address to the memory system and requests that the value stored in the memory location with that address be fetched, and then adds that *value*.) So, the first four longwords in the listing (and in the memory picture) are the addresses that correspond to A, B, etc.

Next, consider the operand specifiers of the two instructions ADDB2 and SUBW2; for both instructions, the operand specifiers are 90--does this mean the *operands* are the same? Of course not! All it means is that, for all 4 operands, the address of the address of each operand is in R0. Since R0 changes after each use, it contains a different address after each use, and if each of these different addresses is the address of a different address, then the 4 operands will be different operands.

Finally, let's consider what happens at run time, when this program is being executed. We already understand MOVAL instructions, so we can ignore the contents of memory locations 0 through $1E_{16}$. The ADDB2 opcode, 80_{16}, is in location 1F; what happens after it is fetched?

1. When the opcode is decoded, the control unit knows that it has 2 operands and, therefore, 2 operand specifiers. It fetches the first operand specifier from location 20, updating the PC to 21.

2. The operand specifier is 90; the control unit knows that mode 9 means that the register (which one? R0, as specified in the register field) doesn't contain an operand, but contains an address, so it sends the address in R0 to memory, asking for the longword stored in the location whose address is in R0 (which is 00000000_{16}).

3. The memory system sends back 00000010 (which is in the location whose address is 00000000), and the control unit knows that this is *still* not the operand, but this time it's the address of the operand, rather than the address of the operand's address.

4. The control unit sends 00000010 to memory, requesting a byte (because the opcode is a byte instruction); it updates R0 by 4 (because it contains the address of an address, and addresses are longwords), and gets back 01, which is the byte in location 00000010.

5. The control unit has the first operand, so now it sends the address in the PC to memory, asking for the second operand specifier, updates the PC to 22, and gets back 90 again.

The control unit executes the same series of steps to fetch the second operand that it did for the first one, with the result that it has both operands, and R0 contains 00000008. The operands are then sent to the ALU with the add command, the result is stored in location 00000011_{16} (which is the address of the second operand), and the control unit is ready to execute the SUBW2 instruction. This instruction is executed in the same way that the ADDB2 instruction was executed, except that its operands are words rather than bytes. Therefore, when the control unit finally gets the address of the operand, it sends that address to memory and asks for 2 bytes rather than 1. Note that R0 ends up with 00000010_{16}, which is 4 more than the address of the last address in the address array. The last incrementing of the register was unnecessary with regard to the program; however, it does no harm, and it is an unavoidable byproduct of using autoincrement deferred addressing.

```
TABLE:      .ADDRESS A, B, C, D         ;address array
A:          .BYTE 1                     ;data
B:          .BYTE 2
C:          .WORD 3
D:          .WORD 4
            .ENTRY START, 0
            MOVAL @#TABLE, R0           ;R0 has address of address now
            ADDB2 @0(R0), @4(R0)        ;add A to B
            SUBW2 @8(R0), @12(R0)       ;sub C from D
            $EXIT_S
            .END START
```

Figure 8.5 Using displacement mode deferred

Displacement Modes Deferred

The deferred displacement modes are modes B, D, and F--mode B is byte displacement mode deferred, mode D is word displacement mode deferred, and mode F is longword displacement mode deferred; in assembly language they are indicated by the same symbol we use for autoincrement mode deferred: @DISPL(R *n*). With the displacement modes deferred, as with the displacement modes, the assembler chooses between byte, word, and longword displacements depending on the value used by the programmer for the displacement. We can easily rewrite the program in figure 8.2 using displacement mode deferred; it is shown in figure 8.5. The assembler listing for this program is shown in figure 8.6. It is important to realize that the displacements are identical to those that would be used if we had written the program using displacement mode rather than displacement mode deferred. This is because in both cases the displacement is added to the register to calculate an address. The difference between displacement and displacement deferred, thus, is primarily at run time: when the control unit finds A, C, or E in the mode field, it knows that the sum of the register (specified in the register field, of course) and the displacement is the address of the *operand,* but when the control unit finds B, D, or F in the mode field it knows that the sum of the register and the displacement is the address of the operand's *address.* Note, also, that byte and word displacements must be sign-extended (not zero-extended) before they are added to the register contents to create a 32-bit address. Finally, with displacement mode deferred, as with displacement mode, the register contents do *not* change; the sum is calculated and stored in some memory location that is private to the control unit and not accessible to programmers.

Recall the example, in chapter 6, of an automated bank teller station, in which we used displacement mode to construct a **jump table** for handling the different keys a user might press. Recall, also, that we promised that a better way of handling such a jump table was forthcoming. Displacement mode deferred turns out to be just such a better way.

In the general case, a JMP must have an instruction in the location which its destination specifies. In other words, if we write JMP ABC, we expect some instruction in location ABC. Similarly, when we created our jump table by using displacement mode, we had to be sure that there was another JMP instruction in the location computed by adding the register contents and the displacement. Recall the program fragment from figure 6.10:

```
NOTE:   JMP TABLE(R6)
TABLE:  JMP DTS
        JMP DTC
          .
          .
          .
        JMP LP
DTS:    ;execute deposit to savings code
          .
          .
          .
```

With displacement mode deferred, we needn't make the target of a JMP instruction another JMP instruction; we can use a table of addresses as the target of the JMP instruction. Thus

```
        JMP @TABLE(R2) ;R2 has 0, 4, 8, . . .
          .
          .
          .
TABLE:  .ADDRESS DTS, DTC, LP, . . .
```

The addresses beginning at location TABLE form the *jump table*. For a value of 8 in R2, the sequence of addresses evaluated at run time is:

```
TABLE+(R2)  =    TABLE+8
(TABLE+8)   =    LP
PC          ←    LP
```

So, if R2 has 8, then JMP @TABLE(R2) has the same effect as JMP LP.

```
00000014'00000012'00000011'00000010'  0000   1 TABLE:  .ADDRESS A, B, C, D
                                  01   0010   2 A:      .BYTE   1
                                  02   0011   3 B:      .BYTE   2
                                0003   0012   4 C:      .WORD   3
                                0004   0014   5 D:      .WORD   4
                                0000   0016   6         .ENTRY START, 0
              50   00000000'9F    DE   0018   7         MOVAL @#TABLE, R0
                 04 B0   00 B0    80   001F   8         ADDB2 @0(R0), @4(R0)
                 0C B0   08 B0    A2   0024   9         SUBW2 @8(R0), @12(R0)
                                  00   0029  10         HALT
                                       002A  11         .END START
```

Figure 8.6 Assembler listing with displacement deferred

```
        ┌──┬──┬──────────────┐
        │ 0│ 0│   operand    │
        └──┴──┴──────────────┘
          7  6  5            0
```

Figure 8.7 Operand specifier for short literal modes

Short Literal Addressing

Addressing modes 0, 1, 2, and 3 are called **short literal** modes. Short literal addressing is a special case of immediate addressing; it is unique in that the operand specifier is the operand itself! How is it possible for the control unit to know when the operand specifier is the operand and when it is an ordinary operand specifier? Whenever the mode field of the operand specifier is 0, 1, 2, or 3, the operand specifier (all 8 bits of it) is an operand; whenever the mode field of the operand specifier is anything else, the operand specifier is an operand specifier. What operands can be specified using short literal addressing? Any operands between 0 and 63. Why this range? Because anything larger than 63 requires at least 7 bits ($63 = 2^6-1$; 2^n-1 is the largest number representable in n bits). If we store a number that requires more than 6 bits in the operand specifier, it would extend into the upper 2 bits of the mode field, and the mode would no longer be 0, 1, 2, or 3 (note that, as binary 4-bit numbers, 0, 1, 2, and 3 all have 2 high-order 0s). Figure 8.7 shows that the high-order 2 bits of the operand specifier are 0 for short literal addressing, and the low-order 6 bits are the operand. At run time, the low-order 6 bits are zero-extended to 8 bits for a byte instruction, to 16 bits for a word instruction, and to 32 bits for a longword instruction. How do we specify short literal addressing in assembly language? The same way that we specify ordinary immediate operands: we use "#operand"; the assembler checks to see if the operand is in the range appropriate for short literal.

The designers of the VAX chose *not* to allow short literal addressing for negative immediate operands. If they had allowed negative short literal operands, the range would have been -32 to +31, and the control unit would have had to *sign*-extend, rather than *zero*-extend, the 6-bit operand to the appropriate length. Figure 8.8 is an assembler listing of a program fragment that uses a variety of immediate operands; it shows how the assembler has chosen short literal when possible, and immediate mode otherwise. Note that short literal addressing can save as many as 4 bytes per operand. Soon, when we discuss the addressing modes that use the PC, we will see that short literal addressing can save as many as 4 bytes per operand, but as few as 1 byte per operand. Recall also that when we discussed loop-control instructions in chapter 7, we saw that some immediate operands were *not* assembled using the 8F operand specifier (in figures 7.23 and 7.26). We promised to explain what was happening, and we have: the assembler used short literal addressing for immediate operands 10 and 1.

```
          54 3F D0   0002   1     MOVL #63, R4
55 00000040 8F D0   0005   2     MOVL #64, R5
          56 01 D0   000C   3     MOVL #1, R6
57 FFFFFFFF 8F D0   000F   4     MOVL #-1, R7
```

Figure 8.8 Short literal and immediate addressing modes

```
                        ;first, displacement mode on R8; loop count in R9
                                CLRL R8                 ;array index
                                CLRL R9                 ;loop count
                LOOP1:          CLRL ARRAY1(R8)         ;clear
                                ADDL2 #4, R8            ;update index
                                AOBLSS #6, R9, LOOP1    ;do 6 times
                                .
                                .
                                .

                        ;now, index mode on R7, with base address in R6
                                MOVAL @#ARRAY2, R6      ;base address in R6
                                CLRL R7                 ;index in R7
                LOOP2:          CLRL (R6)[R7]           ;clear location
                                AOBLSS #6, R7, LOOP2    ;keep going 6 times
                                .
                                .
                                .
```

Figure 8.9 Comparing index and displacement addressing modes

Index Mode

Index mode is probably the most complex of the VAX's addressing modes; it is designed to make accessing arbitrary elements of arrays especially convenient for assembly language programmers. Index mode is mode 4; an operand specifier using index mode is always used in conjunction with another operand specifier--specifying any one of the addressing modes we have already seen, with the exceptions of register mode (5), any immediate mode (modes 0-3 or mode 8) or index mode. This second operand specifier is called the **base operand specifier;** it is used to determine a **base operand address,** just as if it were not being used in conjunction with index mode. The operand specified by index mode is called the **primary operand,** and its address is calculated by adding the base operand address to the product of the contents of the index register and the size of the primary operand. Or, if the index register is R n, we can express the formula for calculating the operand's address as follows:

$$\text{operand's address} = \text{base operand address} + [\text{size} * (\text{R } n)]$$

In assembly language, if we are using register n as an index register, we would specify index mode using square brackets: [R n]. In order to better understand index mode, let's compare index mode with displacement mode. If we wish to clear sequential longwords in an array using displacement mode, we could write code similar to that shown in the first part of figure 8.9. The second code fragment in this figure also clears an array of longwords, but it does so with index mode. Figure 8.10 shows the assembler listing of these program fragments.

The major difference between these two program fragments is that with index mode we place in the index register a number, n, which corresponds to the nth element of the array (we start counting, as we usually do in computers, with element 0). With displacement mode, on the other hand, we place in the register a number which corresponds to the offset, in bytes, from the beginning of the array of the nth element of the array. This may seem to be a trivial difference, but appearances can be misleading. Not only can we use the index register as the loop-control register for an (A,S)OB or ACB(B,W,L) instruction, but consider the case of random access to an array's elements. If we wish

```
                        0000   1  ;first, displacement mode on R8, with loop count in R9
               58 D4    0000   2          CLRL R8              ;array index
               59 D4    0002   3          CLRL R9              ;loop count
          0020'C8 D4    0004   4  LOOP1:  CLRL ARRAY1(R8)      ;clear
            58   04 C0  0008   5          ADDL2 #4, R8         ;update index
         F5 59   06 F2  000B   6          AOBLSS #6, R9, LOOP1 ;do 6 times
                        000F   7  ;now, index mode on R7, with base address in R6
56 0000003C'9F DE       000F   8          MOVAL @#ARRAY2, R6   ;base address
               57 D4    0016   9          CLRL R7              ;index
             6647 D4    0018  10  LOOP2:  CLRL (R6)[R7]        ;clear
         F9 57   06 F2  001B  11          AOBLSS #6, R7, LOOP2 ;do 6 times
                   00   001F  12          HALT
             0000003C   0020  13  ARRAY1: .BLKL 7
             00000058   003C  14  ARRAY2: .BLKL 7
                        0058  15          .END
```

Figure 8.10 Listing of index and displacement addressing modes

to write a program in which a user can examine the contents of an arbitrary element of an array, with index mode we need only write code to subtract 1 from the number supplied by the user (because, once more, computers start counting with 0, and people usually start counting with 1). With displacement mode, on the other hand, our program must take that element number, subtract 1, and multiply it by the size of the data item of which the array is composed. Clearly, it is far simpler to use index mode than displacement mode in that case. Notice, in figure 8.10, that the use of index mode on line 10 shows the *two* operand specifiers used when assembling the instruction, CLRL (R6)[R7]: first the one for index mode on register 7, 47, and then the base operand specifier, using register deferred on register 6, 66.

Perhaps (now that we have explained it) index mode no longer appears as complex as we warned that it would. However, there are several subtleties involved in using index mode. For example, what happens if we use 9F for the base operand specifier: where is the address of the operand stored? As we might expect, it immediately follows the base operand specifier, just as it does when we use it *without* index mode. If the symbolic label ARRAY has been assigned the value 00000007, then if we write the instruction CLRL @#ARRAY[R7], the assembler will produce the following machine language:

```
00000007'9F47 D4   0000   1   CLRL @#ARRAY1[R7]
```

If we use one of the displacement modes as the base operand specifier, similarly, the displacement will immediately follow the base operand specifier (just as it does in ordinary displacement mode), which will immediately follow the index mode operand specifier.

We have already mentioned that the base operand specifier cannot be immediate mode (or short literal), register mode, or index mode. In addition, the PC cannot be used as an index register, and if the base operand specifier uses an addressing mode that changes the register (autoincrement, autodecrement, or autoincrement deferred), then the same register cannot be the index register. These restrictions are sensible; it is a good test of our understanding to see if we can figure out why they have been made.

Mode	Name	Format	Explanation
0-3	Short literal	#X	Operand is operand specifier.
4	Index	BOS[Rn]	Base Operand Specifier specifies Base Operand Address. Operand address is BOA+[size*(Rn)].
5	Register	Rn	Operand is in Rn.
6	Register deferred	(Rn)	Operand address is in Rn.
7	Autodecrement	–(Rn)	Rn ←Rn –dec before address is computed; *then* operand address is in Rn.[†]
8	Autoincrement	(Rn)+	Operand address is in Rn; Rn ←Rn +inc *after* operand is fetched.[‡]
9	Autoincrement deferred	@(Rn)+	Address of operand address is in Rn; Rn ←Rn +4 *after* operand is fetched.
A (C, E)	Byte (word, longword) displacement	X(Rn)	Operand address is X+Rn; X follows operand specifier.
B (D, F)	Byte (word, longword) displacement deferred	@X(Rn)	Address of operand address is X+Rn; X follows operand specifier.

†dec=1 for byte, 2 for word, 4 for longword instruction.
‡inc=1 for byte, 2 for word, 4 for longword instruction.

Figure 8.11 General register addressing mode summary

Addressing Mode Summary

We have now seen all 16 of the VAX's addressing modes; we have only to examine the special case when some of them are used with the PC. First, however, let's summarize the general case of each addressing mode. Figure 8.11 lists the name, number, assembly language specification, and a brief description of each of the VAX's addressing modes. Figure 8.12 presents a more pictorial description of how the addressing modes work. When we understand the VAX's addressing modes, we understand a major feature of its architecture.

Program Counter Addressing

We have seen all 16 of the VAX's general register addressing modes, but we have not yet completed our examination of how VAX instructions can specify operands. This is because 4 classes of the general register addressing modes can be used with the PC to create special ways of specifying operands. It is important that we realize that these are not new addressing modes: the **mode** field in an operand specifier contains only 4 bits, and so there are only 16 addressing modes. However, one of the clever aspects of the VAX's design is that the PC is also a general-purpose register (register 15); therefore, if the hex digit F appears in the **register** field of an operand specifier, then the control

Mode	Instruction	Register Contents	Name

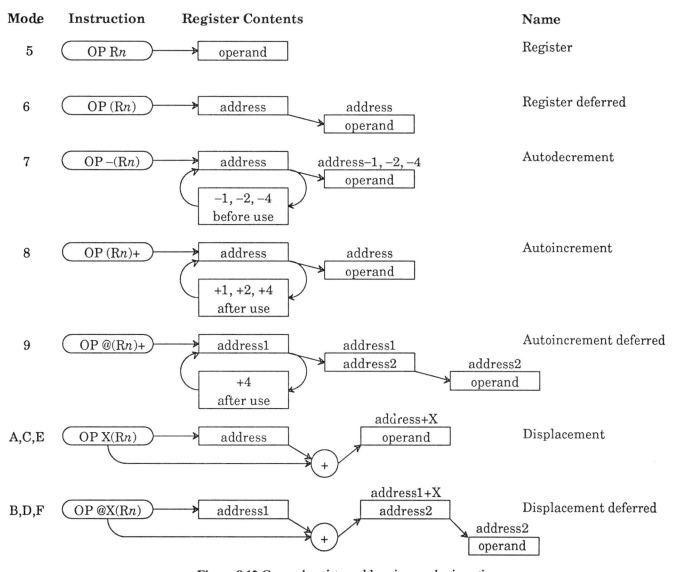

Figure 8.12 General register addressing modes in action

unit will try to do what it always does when it encounters an operand specifier--namely, whatever the mode indicates that it should do.

Before considering the particular addressing modes that make sense to use with the PC, let us consider, for purpose of illustration, one that does *not*: register mode. Suppose, for example, we write the following instruction in a program: ADDL3 PC, R6, R7. We can write perfectly reasonable machine language: C1 for ADDL3, 5F for PC, 56 for R6, and 57 for R7. What will happen at run time? Once more, something predictable, but perhaps not very reasonable: the contents of R15 (the PC) will be added to the contents of R6, and the result will be stored in R7. So, since the PC is a general-purpose register, the control unit is perfectly capable of performing the operation specified by mode 5, register F. (It is, of course, not very clear why anyone would ever wish to do such a thing!) If we change the order of operands in the above instruction, and write ADDL3 R6, R7, PC, we can still translate the statement into machine language, but at run time the effects will be less predictable: we will have created a transfer-of-control instruction by asking that some number be placed in the PC. Whatever the sum of the contents of R6 and R7 is, that is the address of the next instruction. In the remainder of this section, we will discuss the addressing modes that, when used with the PC, add useful capabilities to the VAX. Like register mode (discussed above), they are exactly the same addressing modes we have already discussed, used with the PC. Unlike register mode, however, they have clearly apparent advantages when used with the PC.

Relative Addressing

So far, when we have specified an operand by address, we have used the assembly language syntax OPC @#LABEL; we will discuss this type of addressing--absolute addressing--shortly. First, however, we will extend our understanding of PC-relative addressing--which we have seen only with conditional branches, so far--to the general case of *any* operand. We will see that using PC-relative offsets to specify an ordinary operand has the same advantages that using them to specify the target of a branch instruction has: first, if an offset is shorter than a longword, then it is shorter than an address, and second, the loader needn't change PC-relative offsets when a program is loaded into memory.

Relative addressing is indicated with the assembly language syntax OPC LABEL, with no "@#" preceding the label. The assembler translates this into displacement mode using (or, *relative to*) the PC. Recall that displacement mode means that the register contents plus a displacement is the address of the operand; how do we calculate such a displacement when the register is the PC? The same way we calculate a branch offset: we subtract the value the location counter has assigned to the label (that refers to the operand) from the value the location counter assigns to the location *following* the displacement (in the instruction). Consider the example in figure 8.13, which is a slight modification of the code shown in chapter 6 for copying a string of ASCII character codes. The upper portion of the figure is the assembly language program, and the lower portion is the corresponding assembler listing.

Notice that the assembler has used mode A, register F as the operand specifiers for the references to ARRAY1 and ARRAY2, on lines 4 and 5 of the listing. Notice, also, that the displacement for the reference to ARRAY1 (on line 4) is $E9_{16}$, and that for the reference to ARRAY2 (on line 5) is ED_{16}. Let's see how these displacements were calculated: if we examine the symbol table, we see that the assemble time values of ARRAY1 and ARRAY2 are 0 and 8, respectively. We know that when the displacement is added to the register (at run time), the displacement has already been fetched, and we know that the displacement is stored just after the operand specifier, so we know that the PC has been updated to just after the displacement when the register contents and displacement are added to create the effective address of the operand. The PC contains 17_{16} after the displacement for ARRAY1 has been fetched, so the displacement should, when added to 17, produce the sum 0_{16}--which is the address of ARRAY1. The displacement stored by the assembler is $E9_{16}$, or 11101001_2; and the PC contains 17_{16}, or 00010111_2. If we add, as the control unit will do at run time, we find that $11101001 + 00010111$ is, in fact, 0. Similarly, the displacement stored for the reference to ARRAY2 is ED_{16} (11101101_2) and the PC will contain address $1B_{16}$ (00011011_2) after this displacement has been fetched: $11101101 + 00011011 = 00001000_2$, which is 8_{16}. (Alternatively, we could calculate that E9 is -23_{10}, or -17_{16}, and clearly $+17 + -17 = 0$; we can perform a similar calculation for ED.) So, the assembler has calculated the displacements correctly; when the program is running, the operand specifier AF is fetched and decoded; it tells the control unit to fetch a byte displacement (and update the PC), sign-extend it to 32 bits, add it to register F (the PC, of course), and use the sum as the address of the operand--corresponding, as we have seen, to the addresss of the first bytes of ARRAY1 and ARRAY2.

In the example in figure 8.13, the assembler used byte displacement mode because the displacement was short enough to fit in a byte. What would have happended if ARRAY1 and ARRAY2

```
ARRAY1:      .ASCIZ "Testing"
ARRAY2:      .BLKB 10
             .ENTRY START, 0
             MOVAB ARRAY1, R0
             MOVAB ARRAY2, R1
LOOP:        MOVB (R0)+, (R1)+
             BNEQ LOOP
;else: done
             HALT
             .END START
```

```
00 67 6E 69 74 73 65 54   0000   1 ARRAY1: .ASCIZ "Testing"
               00000012   0008   2 ARRAY2: .BLKB 10
                   0000   0012   3          .ENTRY START, 0
            50 E9 AF 9E   0014   4          MOVAB ARRAY1, R0
            51 ED AF 9E   0018   5          MOVAB ARRAY2, R1
               81 80 90   001C   6 LOOP:    MOVB (R0)+, (R1)+
                  FB 12   001F   7          BNEQ LOOP
                          0021   8      ;else--done
                     00   0021   9          HALT
                          0022  10          .END START

Symbol table

ARRAY1              00000000 R     01
ARRAY2              00000008 R     01
LOOP                0000001C R     01
START               00000012 RG    01
```

Figure 8.13 Using relative addressing

were defined *after* the references to them (this is called a **forward reference**)? In this case, the assembler has no idea where that label will be defined. It has to choose *some* size for the displacement or it won't be able to continue assembling, because the location counter will have an indeterminate value. In such a case, the assembler will choose longword displacement--which is always safe, because a longword is sufficient to store the difference between *any* two memory locations. Figure 8.14 shows the assembler listing of the program in figure 8.13, with the data defined after, rather than before, the instructions. Since the assembler didn't know the values of ARRAY1 and ARRAY2 when it encountered references to them on lines 2 and 3, it allocated a longword for the displacements, knowing that if the displacement can fit in less than a longword, it is a simple matter to add leading 0s to make it a longword.

Although longword displacement makes our programs longer than byte or word displacement, there is a tradeoff: with byte or word displacement, the displacement (which can be either positive or negative) must be sign-extended at run time to 32 bits before it is added to the PC to form the effective address of the operand. It is not obvious whether it is faster to fetch a longword displacement which needs no sign extension, or to fetch a byte or word displacement which *does* need

```
                        0000  0000   1              .ENTRY START, 0
     50      00000016'EF    9E  0002   2              MOVAB ARRAY1, R0
     51      0000001E'EF    9E  0009   3              MOVAB ARRAY2, R1
                  81   80   90  0010   4  LOOP:       MOVB (R0)+, (R1)+
                       FB   12  0013   5              BNEQ LOOP
                                0015   6              ;else--done
                            00  0015   7              HALT
  00 67 6E 69 74 73 65 54      0016   8  ARRAY1:  .ASCIZ "Testing"
                    00000028   001E   9  ARRAY2:  .BLKB 10
                                0028  10              .END START
```

Figure 8.14 Relative addressing with forward references

sign extension; this is a subtle issue whose resolution depends upon hardware details that are beyond the scope of this book.

When the assembler uses byte or word displacement, programs using relative addressing are shorter than those using absolute addressing. However, even when the assembler must use longword displacements, relative addressing has an advantage over absolute addressing: relative "addresses" *never* need to be changed when a program is loaded into memory. This is so because the distance between the use of an operand and its definition is always the same, regardless of where a program is loaded. Now that we know about relative addressing, we should only use absolute addressing when we care particularly about the exact address that the assembler assigns to an operand. When would that ever be? So far, we have considered the VAX's memory as an array of bytes (or words, or longwords), each of which is identical to the other. We will soon see, however (in chapter 12), that this is not exactly true: there are some special locations in the VAX's memory, and there are times when we wish to refer to a particular one of them. In these cases, we will use absolute addressing.

Relative Deferred Addressing

The displacement modes, modes A, C, and E, have deferred counterparts, modes B, D, and F. These modes can also be used with the PC, to create **relative deferred** addressing, or **indirect** addressing. For relative addressing we would write ADDL3 A, B, C; at run time, the value stored in the memory location corresponding to label A will be added to the value in the location corresponding to label B, and the sum will be stored in the location corresponding to label C. (The *offsets* will be stored in our program at assemble time, and added to the PC to generate the addresses at run time, of course.) For relative deferred addressing we write ADDL3 @A, @B, @C; one extra level of deferral will be used for finding the operand. In other words, the location corresponding to label A won't contain the operand, but the operand's *address*--and similarly for labels B and C. With relative deferred addressing, as with relative addressing, the assembler calculates the offset from the PC to the label, and stores it immediately after the operand specifier, which is BF, DF, or FF. At run time, the offset will be added to the PC to calculate not the address of the operand, but the address of the operand's address--just like displacement mode deferred on any other register.

```
        ADDB3 #64, #127, R3        ;bytes
        ADDL3 #64, #127, R3        ;longwords
        ADDW3 #64, #256, R3        ;words


              53 7F 8F 40 8F 81    0002   1   ADDB3 #64, #127, R3    ;bytes
   53 0000007F 8F 00000040 8F C1   0008   2   ADDL3 #64, #127, R3    ;longwords
           53 0100 8F 0040 8F A1   0014   3   ADDW3 #64, #256, R3    ;words
```

Figure 8.15 Autoincrement and immediate operands

Immediate Operands

We have already used immediate operands, and have seen that they are assembled with mode 8 (autoincrement), using register F (the PC). What sense does this make? Autoincrement means that the operand's address is in the register, and that after the address is used, the register is changed by 1, 2, or 4, depending on whether it is a byte, word, or longword instruction. If we use autoincrement on the PC, it means that the address of the operand must be in the PC! But, doesn't the PC always contain the address of the next *instruction* (or instruction part)? How can the PC contain the address of an *operand*? It can contain the address of an operand if the assembler asks the loader to place the operand right after the operand specifier--because the PC will have been updated to contain the address of that location (as usual) at run time.

Consider the example in figure 8.15; the assembly language program is shown in the upper portion of the figure, and the assembler's listing in the lower portion. Note that, in each case (since we used operands too large for short literal mode), the assembler uses autoincrement on the PC (operand specifier 8F), and that the operand itself immediately follows the operand specifier. Note, also, that for longword instructions the immediate operands are longwords, for word instructions they are words, and for byte instructions they are bytes.

Absolute Addressing

Absolute addressing is the first addressing technique that we used, and we have continued to use it, along with other addressing modes, when first placing the address of an operand in memory, etc. We know that the operand specifier for absolute addressing is 9F: mode 9 (autoincrement deferred) on register F (the PC). Autoincrement deferred means that the register contains the address of the operand's address, and that after the register is used, it is incremented by 4 (always); let's see how this makes sense for absolute addressing. With absolute addressing, we store the operand's *address* as part of the instruction. When we use autoincrement mode on the PC, we are saying that the PC-- after it has been used to fetch the operand specifier and then updated--contains the address of the operand; in order to make this work, we must place the operand after the operand specifier. When we use auto-increment mode *deferred* on the PC, we are saying that the PC--after it has been used to fetch the operand specifier and then updated--contains the address of the operand's *address*; in order to make this work, we must place the operand's *address* after the operand specifier. Note that, with autoincrement deferred, the register is always incremented by 4; since we are placing an address after the operand specifier, this is exactly what we need (all addresses, of course, are 4 bytes long).

Mode	Name	Format	Explanation
8	Immediate	#X	Operand is X; X follows operand specifier.
9	Absolute	@#X	Operand address is X; X follows operand specifier.
A (C, E)	Relative	X	Operand address is X; X–PC follows operand specifier.
B (D, F)	Relative deferred	@X	Address of operand address is X; X–PC follows operand specifier.

Figure 8.16 Program counter addressing modes

Program Counter Addressing Summary

One of the reasons that the designers of the VAX (and of the PDP-11, before them) made the PC a general-purpose register (almost) just like any other general-purpose register, is that they realized that they could create new addressing modes by using the old ones with the PC. Thus, the VAX handles immediate operands without any additional addressing modes, and without any additional hardware. The only thing special about immediate operands is done by the assembler, which guarantees that the operand will immediately follow the operand specifier. Note that the assembler is a program, and that programs are usually easier to modify than hardware.

Figure 8.16 is a summary of the Program Counter addressing modes. There are no modes that we haven't already seen, in the general case--used with *any* general-purpose register. In figure 8.16, the description is particular to the use of each addressing mode with the PC, and assumes that an assembler or machine-language programmer has placed operands, addresses, or offsets, with the correct values, in the appropriate places.

Summary

We have completed our examination of the VAX's addressing modes. Autoincrement deferred (mode 9) and displacement deferred (modes B, D and F) are similar to autoincrement and displacement modes, except that for the latter, the register contents (or the sum of the register contents and displacement) are the address of the operand, while for the former, the register contents (or the sum of the register contents and displacement) are the address of the operand's *address*.

Short literal addressing (modes 0 through 3) is a special case of immediate addressing: if an immediate operand is between 0 and 63 (inclusive), the assembler uses one of the short literal modes. In the short literal modes, the high-order 2 bits of the **mode** field of the operand specifier are always 0, and the low-order 6 bits of the operand specifier (what would normally be the rest of the **mode** field and all of the **register** field) are used for the operand itself. At run time, the operand specifier (which is the operand) is zero-extended to the number of bits specified by the opcode for byte, word, or longword instructions.

Index mode is a complex addressing mode that makes array indexing especially easy for assembly language programmers. It is always used with a second operand specifier, which is used to compute a base address. The value in the index register is then multiplied by the size of the operand (in bytes) to calculate the offset from the address specified in the base operand specifier of the operand. This multiplication, addition, and base address calculation are all performed by the control unit automatically.

We also examined 4 addressing modes that can be used with the PC, register F. Modes A, C, and E are used with the PC to create **relative** addressing. In these cases, the assembler calculates the distance between the current instruction and the symbolic label referred to as the operand, and stores that distance as a PC-relative offset. At run time, the sum of the PC contents and the displacement is the operand's address; this is similar to the PC-relative offsets used with the branch instructions.

Modes B, D, and F are used with the PC to create **relative deferred** addressing. The assembler calculates the same PC-relative offset that it calculates for relative addressing, but at run time, the sum of the PC contents and the displacement is the address of the operand's address, rather than the operand's address.

We also saw that mode 8 can be used with the PC to create **immediate addressing.** In this case, the assembler must place the operand immediately after the operand specifier. Finally, we saw that mode 9 can be used with the PC to create **absolute addressing.** With absolute addressing, the operand's *address* must immediately follow the operand specifier.

One major advantage of the fact that the PC is one of the general-purpose registers is that (some) addressing modes can use the PC just as they would use any other register. However, because the PC is a special (general-purpose) register, these addressing modes have special effects. Using the PC with 4 existing addressing modes creates 4 new types of addressing, without adding the hardware that would be necessary to create 4 new addressing modes.

Exercises for Chapter 8

1.   Hand assemble the following assembly language statements, showing the machine language that would be generated by the assembler for each one.

  ADDL2 @(R0)+, @-4(R0)
  MOVW #63, R0
  ADDL3 (R8)[R4], -(R7), @12(R10)

2.   Assume that a memory reference is made each time an address is sent along the bus to memory, either with a request to read the contents of that address, or with a request to write a value. How many memory references are made in fetching *and* executing the following instructions? Explain each memory reference; consider how the VAX fetches parts of instructions.

  a.   CMPB #32, (R0)
  b.   CMPB #32, @(R1)+
  c.   CMPB #32, 4(R0)
  d.   CMPB #32, @4(R0)
  e.   CMPB #32, (R0)+

3.   After the opcode of the instruction MOVL 0(R0), (R1) has been fetched, the PC contains:

  a.   the next instruction to be executed
  b.   the address of the next instruction to be executed
  c.   the address of the source operand
  d.   the address of the destination operand
  e.   an offset
  f.   the address of an offset
  g.   an operand specifier

    h.   the address of an operand specifier
    i.   it cannot be determined from the given information
    j.   none of the above

4.   How many memory references are made in fetching and executing the instruction MOVB #7, (R0)+?

    a. 1   b. 2   c. 3   d. 4   e. 5

    Describe each reference.

5.   What is the value in R4 *after* executing the following two instructions:

    MOVL #^X1000, R4
    MOVB (R4)+, -(R4)

6.   True or false:

    a.   .BYTE 41, 42, 43 and .ASCII "ABC" are equivalent.
    b.   The loader initializes registers 0 through 11 to zero.
    c.   The $EXIT_S statement produces an instruction that is executed at run time.
    d.   Arithmetic overflow always clears the V bit.
    e.   Care must be taken to prevent conditional branch instructions from changing some of the condition-code bits.
    f.   The maximum distance between a BRB instruction and its destination is 300_{10} words.
    g.   The BGTRU instruction shouldn't be used following comparisons of signed numbers.
    h.   The only addressing modes that change the register contents are register, register deferred, and the displacement modes.

7. The initial contents of some registers and memory locations are provided in hexadecimal. Execute each instruction, and indicate *changes only* for the appropriate registers and memory locations. Write your answers in hexadecimal. Where relevant, choose the shortest addressing mode applicable (e.g., byte rather than word displacement). Symbolic label X has the value 100400_{16}, and label Y has the value 300408_{16}. *Results do not accumulate* except when two instructions are listed in the same box.

Instruction	R1	R2	R3	100400	100404	100408	300408	PC
Initial Values:	100400	300408	100404	100404	300408	10FFFF	100408	100000
MOVL @(R1)+, @(R3)+								
MOVB @(R1)+, @(R3)+								
MOVW @(R1)+, @(R3)+								
MOVL R1, @–^X200004(R2)								
INCB @(R2)+								
INCW @(R2)+								
INCL @(R2)+								
INCB @(R1)+ INCB @(R1)+								
INCW @(R1)+ INCW @(R1)+								
MOVB #32, @(R2)+								
ADDB3 #33, #44, (R1)								
ADDW3 #33, #44, (R1)								
ADDL3 #33, #44, (R1)								
JMP 100(R3)								
JMP @4(R1)								

8. Match each addressing mode syntax representation on the right, with its correct name on the left, and indicate how many memory references are needed to completely interpret this addressing mode (assume that the operand specifier has been fetched). Where relevant, specify which operand--and which instruction--you are using to compute the number of memory references.

Name	Syntax	Memory references
(a) Autoincrement	1. (R11)	_____
(b) Register	2. @10(R3)	_____
(c) Autodecrement	3. (R7)+	_____
(d) Autoincrement deferred	4. –10(R7)	_____
(e) Register deferred	5. R0	_____
(f) Displacement	6. @(R1)+	_____
(g) Displacement deferred	7. –(R7)	_____

9. On some computers, it is possible to execute instructions such as BLSS (R1). Why is this impossible on the VAX? How could you obtain the effect of executing such an instruction on the VAX?

10. Write a program using correct macro syntax that takes a string ending in a zero byte and replaces all the blanks in it with minus signs. Thus the text in .ASCIZ "A BB C" would become A-BB--C.

11. Show the code and addresses assigned by the assembler for the following symbolic program, assuming it starts with address 0:

```
LOOP:   MOVL A, R0
        BRB LOOP
A:      .LONG -1
```

12. Assume the following program is assembled and loaded beginning at memory location 0. Write down the contents (in hex) of memory locations A and B immediately before program execution and immediately after program execution.

```
ST: MOVL #14, @A
    HALT
A:  .ADDRESS B
B:  .ADDRESS A
```

13. How many memory references are made in fetching and executing CMPB ABC(R3), @X? Describe each reference.

14. The initial contents of some registers and memory locations are provided in hexadecimal. Execute each instruction, and indicate *changes only* for the appropriate registers and memory locations. Write your answers in hexadecimal. Where relevant, choose the shortest addressing mode applicable (e.g., byte rather than word displacement). The symbolic label X has the value 100400_{16}, and Y has the value 300408_{16}. Results do not accumulate.

Instruction	R1	R2	R3	100400	100404	100408	300408	PC
Initial Values:	100400	300408	100404	100404	300408	10FFFF	100408	100000
ADDL3 X, Y, R2								
ADDB3 @X, @Y, (R2)								
ADDB3 @X, @Y, @(R2)+								
ADDW3 X, Y, @Y								
ADDW2 @#X, @#Y								
ADDB3 #66, #77, (R1)								
ADDW3 #66, #77, (R1)								
ADDL3 #66, #77, (R1)								
JMP (R1)+								
JMP @(R1)+								
JMP X								
JMP @X								
JMP @#X								
BRW X								

15. True or false:

   a. Uninitialized memory locations may be assumed to contain 0.
   b. The instruction, MOVL #10, R1 requires two memory references for its fetch and execution.
   c. Some conditional branch instructions modify some CC bits.
   d. The JMP instruction *never* modifies the CC bits.
   e. The INCB instruction changes its operand by 1, the INCW instruction changes its operand by 2, and the INCL instruction changes its operand by 4.

16. Indicate the addressing mode or modes which can be used to make a register function as each of the following:

   a. an accumulator
   b. a pointer
   c. an index into a structure with equal size elements
   d. an index into a structure with unequal size elements

■ 9 ■

Subroutines and Stacks

Introduction: Necessity Is the Mother of Invention

The VAX's jump and conditional branch instructions allow us to include decision-making in our programs. When we add the rich set of addressing modes, we have the ability to re-use instructions in a productive way: a small program can process large amounts of data. Unfortunately, small programs turn into large programs almost spontaneously; problems seem to become more complex from one day to the next. Large programs are harder to design, write, test, document, improve, and maintain than are small programs; these difficulties seem to be disproportionate to the increase in size.

Much of the success of modern science and engineering is due to the systematic application of the maxim "Divide and conquer." Complex problems are analyzed and decomposed into sets of simpler subproblems. If the subproblems are still too complex to grasp easily, these in turn are decomposed. This process of successive problem analysis and decomposition can be illustrated with a structure called a **problem tree.** Computer scientists often view the world upside down, as in the case of the problem tree shown in figure 9.1.

In figure 9.1 a problem, represented by P, is decomposed into three subproblems P1, P2, and P3. P1 and P2 are, in turn, decomposed into subproblems P11 and P12, and P21 and P22. Note that some subproblems--like P3 in figure 9.1--may not require decomposition; the number of subdivisions at any level of a problem tree, therefore, may be as large or as small as necessary. Furthermore, there may be many levels in a problem tree. In figure 9.1, we have only three levels of subdivision (including the original problem); levels two and three have three and four subproblem modules, respectively. Note also that a problem tree is similar to the classical organizational chart that many companies display.

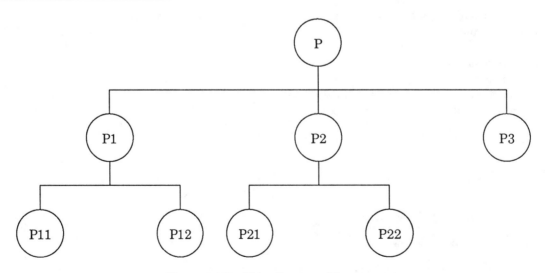

Figure 9.1 Problem decomposition as a tree

188

What is the connection between problem trees and computing? We can view a complete program as the **root** of a problem tree; we can then consider each module that the problem is decomposed into (these are often called the **nodes** of the tree) as a self-contained segment of instructions. Each of these modules solves one part of the problem that the complete program is being written to solve. Or, for the problem pictured in figure 9.1, we could say to ourselves, "Program P is very complex, but I could easily write it if I only had a piece of code (call it P1) to do do this, another piece of code (call it P2) to do that, and a third piece of code (call it P3) doing the rest." So, we write the main program, P, as a series of calls to subprograms P1, P2, and P3. Then, when we start writing subprogram module P1, we say to ourselves, "P1 is more complex than I thought, but I could easily write it if I only had a piece of code (call it P11) to do this, and another piece of code (call it P12) to do that." So we write P1 as a series of calls to subprogram modules P11 and P12 and continue with the same process, until the original, apparently difficult, problem P has been solved by writing a series of small, easy, subprograms--each of which solves only a small part of the original problem, but all of which together solve the complete problem. This process is often called **top-down** problem solving.

Higher level languages call subprograms **subroutines, procedures,** or **functions**; in the VAX, a distinction is made between subroutines and procedures. However, we will see that subroutines and procedures are conceptually more similar than they are different; we will use the term *subroutine* (for historical reasons) more often than the others, and will typically use it to refer to any one of the three types of subprograms. The fundamental similarity between subroutines, functions, and procedures is that each one is composed of a self-contained "piece of code" that has been packaged and is usable (and re-usable) by other programs or subroutines.

How is a subroutine different from a loop, which also allows re-use of instructions? They needn't be very different at all, except in the way that we think of them. We can think of a subroutine as taking a loop, giving it a name, and moving it somewhere else so that it doesn't intrude on our understanding of what our program is doing. Thus, we can think of a subroutine as a way of providing complex abilities that the hardware itself (via machine-language instructions) does not directly provide. When we solve a problem with subroutines, we can pretend that each subroutine is a single instruction that provides just that function that we wrote the subroutine to provide. Let us consider an example.

Suppose we had to multiply several numbers by ten in a program. Since we have not yet seen the multiply family of instructions, we might write code like this:

```
X:   MOVL A, R1        ;number to multiply
     MOVL R1, R2       ;save it
     ADDL2 R1, R1      ;*2
     ADDL2 R1, R1      ;*4
     ADDL2 R2, R1      ;*5
     ADDL2 R1, R1      ;*10
XX:  ;compute other things
Y:   MOVL Q, R1        ;number to multiply
     MOVL R1, R2       ;save it
     ADDL2 R1, R1      ;*2
     ADDL2 R1, R1      ;*4
     ADDL2 R2, R1      ;*5
     ADDL2 R1, R1      ;*10
YY:  ;continue computing
```

We could try to improve on this code; we could eliminate the duplication by writing only one code sequence:

```
MUL10:  MOVL R1, R2     ;save number
        ADDL2 R1, R1    ;*2
        ADDL2 R1, R1    ;*4
        ADDL2 R2, R1    ;*5
        ADDL2 R1, R1    ;*10
```

Then, the previous code sequences at X and Y could be shortened as follows:

```
X:   MOVL A, R1
     JMP MUL10
XX:  ;compute other things
Y:   MOVL Q, R1
     JMP MUL10
YY:  ;continue computing
```

Unfortunately, when we complete execution of the last ADDL2 instruction at MUL10, there is no way to return to the instruction labeled XX. Thus, the advantage of writing the multiply code only once and jumping to it will not be realized: the second number will never be multiplied, because control will not return to XX and so will not get to Y.

Clearly, in order to package a series of instructions (a piece of code) in a re-usable manner, we need not only to be able to jump *to* that series of instructions, but we also need a way to return *from* that series of instructions. In the above example, we need to be able to get back to XX and YY at the right times.

We could try to solve this problem in the following way:

```
X:   MOVL A, R1          ;number to multiply
     MOVAL XX, MULR      ;save return address
     JMP MULR+4          ;1st inst. after ret. addr.
XX:  ;compute other things
Y:   MOVL Q, R1          ;new number
     MOVAL YY, MULR      ;new return address
     JMP MULR+4          ;same 1st inst.
YY:  ;continue computing
;
MULR:   .BLKL 1          ;save return address
        MOVL R1, R2      ;save number
        ADDL2 R1, R1     ;*2
        ADDL2 R1, R1     ;*4
        ADDL2 R2, R1     ;*5
        ADDL2 R1, R1     ;*10
        JMP @MULR        ;return
```

The instructions from label MULR to the instruction JMP @MULR constitute a subroutine; using the subroutine, as at instruction sequences labeled X and Y, is called *calling* the subroutine. The first call of MULR (just before XX) places the address XX in location MULR. The subroutine returns control using deferred relative addressing: MULR is not the address to jump to, but it *contains* the address to jump to. Then the second call places return address YY in location MULR, and after the number is multiplied, the JMP @MULR places the address that was stored in location MULR in the PC thereby returning from the subroutine.

This subroutine return mechanism was used on most early computers; it is still used in some computers. However, it has its drawbacks;[1] the VAX provides better ways of calling and returning from subroutines. Before we examine them, however, we must understand one of the very powerful ideas that is used by most modern computers: the stack.

Stacks

A **stack** is a simple idea that has far-reaching consequences. A stack, for computer scientists, is a data structure (implemented, of course, from a series of memory locations) that obeys the Last In-First Out (LIFO) discipline. We don't often use stacks in everyday life--we usually think that fairness is better maintained with what computer scientists call a **queue,** which uses a First In-First Out (FIFO) discipline. (Consider the complex behavior required to get a good seat in a movie theater that used the LIFO rather than FIFO discipline!) But stacks *are* occasionally used for noncomputer applications: we may place items (bills, letters, messages, etc.) on top of others in an "in" basket on a desk. When we have a moment, we look at the thing on the top of the pile (stack) and take care of it. We then look at the next thing, which is now on top of the stack, and take care of *it.* If we proceed in an orderly fashion, we never reach into the middle of the stack. We always put things on top of the stack, and we always remove things from the top of the stack. We also often use stacks in cafeterias, where clean plates or trays are typically placed on top of a stack of other plates or trays, and where customers remove them from the top of the stack. Figure 9.2 shows several cases of putting things onto a stack and taking them off of it.

Stacks in Computers

Stacks were not common in computing in the early 1960s, except notably in Burroughs computers. In the 1970s, stacks became common in most minicomputers and micros; today, they are fairly common in large computers, as well.

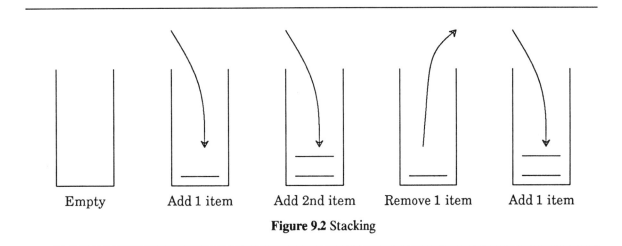

| Empty | Add 1 item | Add 2nd item | Remove 1 item | Add 1 item |

Figure 9.2 Stacking

---

[1]In particular, it does not support recursion. We will discuss recursion in chapter 17.

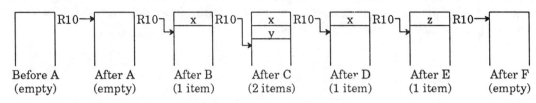

Before A   After A   After B   After C   After D   After E   After F

(empty)   (empty)   (1 item)   (2 items)   (1 item)   (1 item)   (empty)

Figure 9.3 History of personal stack

The VAX provides a pair of addressing modes that make it especially easy for programmers to create and manipulate stacks, without learning any new instructions. Suppose we wish to create a stack with a maximum capacity of 10 longwords. We must allocate memory for the stack (remember that a stack is simply an organized collection of memory locations), and we must keep track of where the top of the stack is (which is both where we put any new data item we wish to put on the stack, and where we find any data item we wish to remove from the stack). We can allocate any block of memory locations for our personal stack, and we can use one of the general-purpose registers to point to the top of the stack. If we use R10 as our **stack pointer,** we can write the following code to create and manipulate our stack:

```
BOTTOM:     .BLKL 9                 ;stack space
MAX:        .BLKL 1                 ;last longword of stack
;
A:          MOVAL BOTTOM, R10       ;initialize stack pointer
B:          MOVL X, (R10)+          ;push (X) onto stack
C:          MOVL Y, (R10)+          ;push (Y) onto stack
D:          ADDL2 -(R10), SUM       ;pop (Y) off stack, into SUM
E:          ADDL2 XXX, -4(R10)      ;TOS ← (XXX)+(TOS)
F:          MOVL -(R10), RES        ;pop stack into RES
```

If (X) is x, (Y) is y, and $x+$(XXX) is z, then our stack's behavior during the above instruction sequence is shown in figure 9.3. The abbreviation TOS stands for the current top-of-stack address; this address is always in our stack pointer (R10, in this example). In addition, we typically call putting an item onto a stack **push**ing it onto the stack, and we call removing an item from a stack **pop**ping it off the stack. Finally, the instruction at label E neither pushes an item on the stack nor pops one off; it simply changes the current top-of-stack item.

A stack is just a collection of memory locations; when we say that a stack is empty, or that one item was just popped off a stack, we clearly do not mean that the memory locations have somehow, magically, changed their contents. Memory locations retain their old values until new items are written to them; when we use a stack, we do so because we believe that the Last In-First Out discipline will be useful to us in programming. Therefore, using a stack implies deciding *not* to use anything other than what is accessible from the stack pointer--which is the (current) top of the stack.

If we ever push items onto our personal stack when the stack pointer contains an address larger than that of MAX, we should expect trouble: those items will be placed in memory locations with addresses MAX+4, MAX+8, etc.--these are *not* locations that we have reserved for our stack, so we will be over-writing other data (or instructions) in our program.

The System Stack and SP

We can now explain why we have avoided using R14. This register is reserved for use by the hardware and some support software as the system stack pointer; just as R15, the program counter, has a special name (PC), so R14, the system stack pointer also has a special name: SP. Certain instructions, such as the JSB and CALLS instructions, imply use of the PC even though they make no explicit reference to it. Similarly, certain instructions (including JSB and CALLS) will make use of the system stack pointer without explicit reference to it.

Normally, to use a stack, one must do the following:

1. Reserve a series of memory locations for the stack.
2. Designate some register to use as the stack pointer (recall that autoincrement and autodecrement work only with registers).
3. Initialize the stack pointer to point to the beginning of the stack.

We don't have to do any of this work if we wish to use the system stack. The operating system has already reserved memory locations, chosen a register, and initialized it to the beginning of the stack. Of course, if we are working on a bare machine (i.e., one without any operating system), we will be responsible for initializing R14. The symbol SP is predefined for Macro, so we needn't worry about the assembler understanding what we mean when we use it with any of the general register addressing modes. With VMS, the memory locations reserved for the system stack have large addresses--if we examine the value in R14 when we use the SNAP system service, we will see where the TOS was when the SNAP was executed.

If we plan to use the system stack initialized by the operating system, we must obey the ground rules. The ground rules governing use of the system stack are:

1. All pushes into the system stack are performed using auto*decrement* addressing mode.
2. All pops from the system stack are performed using auto*increment* addressing.

This is just the opposite of the example we looked at using our *personal* stack. This is because we created our personal stack to grow *down* in memory (toward higher addresses): we initialized our personal stack pointer to point to the memory location with the *smallest* address, and the address of each item we pushed onto our personal stack was *larger* than the address of any item already on the stack. (By convention, locations with smaller addresses are shown above locations with larger addresses.) The system stack, however, grows *up* in memory: the system stack pointer is initialized to point to the memory location with the *largest* address, and successive elements pushed onto the stack have smaller addresses. There is no reason to prefer stacks growing up over stacks growing down (or *vice versa*), but since the system grows its stack upward, life will be simpler if our future examples use stacks that grow upward.

We can rewrite the previous example taking advantage of the system stack, which has been initialized by the operating system. Note that when our program begins execution, we always assume that the system stack is empty.

```
A:          ;no need to initialize SP
B:     MOVL X, -(SP)        ;push (X) onto stack
C:     MOVL Y, -(SP)        ;push (Y) onto stack
D:     ADDL2 (SP)+, SUM     ;pop (Y) off stack
E:     ADDL2 XXX, (SP)      ;TOS ← (XXX)+(TOS)
F:     MOVL (SP)+, RES      ;pop stack into RES
```

Using the same notation we used before, we can illustrate the behavior of the system stack and stack pointer, as shown in figure 9.4. The stack pointer should always point to a valid top-of-stack item. If

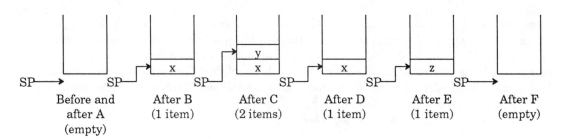

Figure 9.4 History of system stack

the stack is empty, then SP can't point to the first item in the stack, because there is none. Therefore, we show it pointing to the location just below the bottom (and top, in this case) of the stack.

Recycling Memory with Stacks

Why bother using stacks? Careful use of a stack can reduce a program's memory requirements. Suppose that we are in the middle of writing a lengthy program and all the registers are being used. We need three registers temporarily, to copy a group of bytes. We could write the following program fragment:

```
            MOVL R1, SAVER1          ;save registers
            MOVL R2, SAVER2
            MOVL R3, SAVER3
A:          MOVAB ARRAYA, R1         ;addresses in R1 and R2
            MOVAB ARRAYB, R2
            MOVL #50, R3             ;loop count in R3
LOOP:       MOVB (R1)+, (R2)+        ;move bytes
B:          SOBGTR R3, LOOP          ;do until done
            MOVL SAVER1, R1          ;restore registers
            MOVL SAVER2, R2
            MOVL SAVER3, R3
                .
                .
                .
SAVER1:     .BLKL 1                  ;space for registers
SAVER2:     .BLKL 1
SAVER3:     .BLKL 1
```

The locations SAVER1, SAVER2, and SAVER3 will be reserved at assemble time, and those 3 longwords will be allocated to our program for the entire duration of its execution--despite the fact that we use them for only a brief period of time.

The allocation of memory locations, when it is done at assemble time, is called **static memory allocation.** Memory that has been statically allocated remains reserved to our program for the duration of the program's execution.

We could avoid tying up these 3 longwords of memory by using the system stack instead. Consider the following:

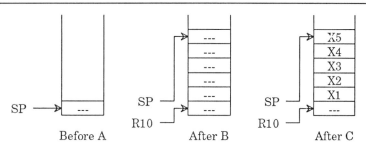

Figure 9.5 Borrowing space from the system stack

```
                MOVL R1, -(SP)          ;save registers
                MOVL R2, -(SP)
                MOVL R3, -(SP)
A:              MOVAB ARRAYA, R1        ;addresses in R1 and R2
                MOVAB ARRAYB, R2
                MOVL #50, R3            ;loop count in R3
LOOP:           MOVB (R1)+, (R2)+       ;move bytes
B:              SOBGTR R3, LOOP         ;do until done
                MOVL (SP)+, R3          ;restore registers
                MOVL (SP)+, R2
                MOVL (SP)+, R1
```

Since a stack obeys the LIFO discipline, the registers must be popped off the stack in an order that is exactly the reverse of the one in which they were pushed onto the stack: they were pushed on in the order R1, R2, R3, so they must be popped off R3, R2, R1. The last item in is always the first item out; if we made the mistake of popping them in the same order that we pushed them, we would *still* get the values in the order R3, R2, R1--only we would be putting the value that *was* in R3 in R1, and the value that *was* in R1 in R3 (R2 would be correct--completely fortuitously--in this example).

If we need a larger number of memory locations for a short period of time, we can borrow the space from the system stack. If we needed 5 longwords, for instance:

```
A:    MOVL SP, R10          ;save SP
B:    SUBL2 #20, SP         ;push 5 empty longwords on stack
      MOVL X1, -4(R10)      ;store item1
      MOVL X2, -8(R10)      ;store item2
      .
      .
C:    MOVL X5, -20(R10)     ;store item5
      .
      .
      .
```

The stack history for this code sequence is shown in figure 9.5. Our program and the system can continue to use the stack as if nothing unusual had happened. When our program no longer needs the space borrowed from the stack, *and* when the SP is pointing to the fifth longword (i.e., anything we pushed on the stack after borrowing the longwords has been popped off) we can release the space by,

Instruction	Mnemonic	Opcode	Action
Push longword	PUSHL S	DD	MOVL S, –(SP)
Push address byte	PUSHAB S	9F	MOVAB S, –(SP)
Push address word	PUSHAW S	3F	MOVAW S, –(SP)
Push address longword	PUSHAL S	DF	MOVAL S, –(SP)
Push registers	PUSHR MASK	BB	MOVL Rn, –(SP)
Pop registers	POPR MASK	BA	MOVL (SP)+, Rn

Figure 9.6 Push and pop instructions

in effect, popping off five longwords with the instruction ADDL2 #20, SP, which returns the stack to the configuration shown in the "Before 'A' " portion of figure 9.5.

In this example, R10 has not been changed since we copied SP to it, so we could also restore the SP with the instruction MOVL R10, SP. Note that adding something to the stack pointer will make any items above the new stack pointer inaccessible: although they will not yet have been over-written, subsequent pushes will store new items in those memory locations. If we change the SP by 20 prematurely, we will lose data that we still need!

Special Stack Instructions

Because use of the stack is so common, the VAX provides special instructions for pushing items onto and popping items off of the system stack. There is an instruction for pushing longwords on the stack--PUSHL SRC--but none for pushing bytes or words on the stack. In addition, there are instructions for pushing addresses of bytes, words, or longwords. These instructions are summarized in the first two parts of figure 9.6. Why are there no instructions for pushing bytes or words onto the stack? It *is* possible to push a byte onto the stack, and change SP by 1; however, one of the consequences of the VAX's memory system being "naturally" organized as an array of 32-bit quantities is that it is faster to store and retrieve operands from addresses that are divisible by 4. When we push only longwords onto the stack, we maintain **longword alignment** of the stack.

Since pushing and popping registers is so common in subroutines, the VAX also has special instructions for these actions. The PUSHR and POPR instructions specify their operands in an unusual manner: with a **mask**. The mask is a 16-bit quantity; each bit corresponds to one of the registers, from low to high order. Thus, if we wish to save R0, we would write PUSHR #^X1. If we wish to save R0, R1, R3, and R5, we would write PUSHR #^X2B; to restore the registers, we would write POPR #^X2B. Why is the mask 2B? $2B_{16}$ is 00101011 binary; reading from right to left, the bits corresponding to R0 and R1 are set, the bit corresponding to R2 is clear, the bit corresponding to R3 is set, the bit corresponding to R4 is clear, the bit corresponding to R5 is set, and the bits corresponding to all higher numbered registers are clear (there are eight leading 0s). It is easy to make mistakes when specifying the register save mask. Therefore, Macro also understands a special syntax for creating such masks: the "^M" operator. If we write

PUSHR #^M<R0, R1, R3, R5>,

Macro will generate the correct 16-bit mask, just as if we had used the hexadecimal immediate operand #^X2B.

In what order are the registers pushed? From high order to low order. Thus, writing PUSHR #^M<R1, R2, R6> is equivalent to writing

    PUSHL R6
    PUSHL R2
    PUSHL R1

In what order are they popped? From low order to high order--so writing POPR #^M<R1, R2, R6> is equivalent to writing

    MOVL (SP)+, R1
    MOVL (SP)+, R2
    MOVL (SP)+, R6

We may specify R15 (the PC) in the mask, but it will be neither pushed by the PUSHR instruction nor popped by the POPR instruction.

Subroutines and Stacks

The mechanism we have discussed for returning control from a subroutine to its caller is clumsy. It wastes space, because a longword must be statically allocated in each subroutine to store the return address. It wastes more space and time because, in order to call a subroutine, we must first save the return address--with an instruction like MOVAL RETURN, SUBR, if RETURN is the return address and SUBR is the subroutine. Finally, it does not support recursion (which will be discussed later). The VAX provides a better alternative, which makes use of the system stack.

The Subroutine Call and Return Instructions

The VAX allows us to eliminate this waste of time and memory by providing a family of instructions to support **subroutine linkage.** (Subroutine linkage is the mechanism which permits us to call a subroutine and then return to the appropriate return address--the instruction after the subroutine call.) The first of these instructions is JSB; JSB stands for Jump to Subroutine. Executing the instruction JSB SUB does the following:

1. The PC is pushed onto the system stack; since the PC is updated *before* the instruction is executed, it contains the address of the instruction following the JSB instruction, which is the return address of the subroutine.
2. The effective address of SUB (which is called the subroutine's **entry point,** and which may be specified with any addressing mode other than register, immediate, or short literal) is copied into the PC, thereby transferring control to the subroutine's entry point.

The VAX provides us with two shorter, more restricted versions of the JSB instruction: BSBB and BSBW. These are *branch* to subroutine instructions, with byte (BSBB) and word (BSBW) offsets. They have the same effect as the JSB instruction, except that they may specify the subroutine's entry point only with a symbolic label; as with any branch instruction, the assembler will calculate the PC-relative offset from the instruction to the subroutine's entry point, and store it in the byte (for BSBB) or word (for BSBW) following the opcode--with *no* operand specifier. Since BSBB and BSBW use PC-relative offsets (of 1 and 2 bytes, respectively), they may only be used when the calling point of the subroutine is near enough to the subroutine so that the distance between them is small enough to fit into 1 or 2 bytes. The JSB instruction, however, specifies its operand with a full address, the way the JMP instruction does.

The single instruction JSB SUB (or BSB(B,W) SUB) seems equivalent to the instruction sequence

```
MOVL PC, -(SP)
JMP SUB
```

It is, however, only *almost* equivalent: the PC value saved by the MOVL instruction is not quite the desired return address.

The other instruction needed for subroutine linkage is RSB--return from subroutine. The RSB instruction pops the stack into the PC. We can demonstrate how these instructions work by looking at a simple subroutine, one which multiplies its argument by 5.

```
MUL5:       MOVL R1, R2            ;save input parameter
            ADDL2 R1, R1          ;*2
            ADDL2 R1, R1          ;*4
            ADDL2 R2, R1          ;*5
            RSB                   ;return
;Main program starts here:
            .ENTRY START, 0
A1:         MOVL A, R1            ;MUL5 expects input in R1
A2:         JSB MUL5             ;call MUL5
A3:         ;compute other stuff
B1:         MOVL B, R1
B2:         JSB MUL5             ;call MUL5
B3:         ;continue computing
            $EXIT_S
            .END START
```

The program begins at A1; first, it places a value to be multiplied by 5 in R1 (with the MOVL instruction), then saves (with the JSB at A2) the address in the PC (which has been updated to A3) by copying it onto the system stack (with a push, automatically), and finally places the effective address MUL5 (found by adding the PC-relative offset, stored by the assembler, to the PC) in the PC. We now enter subroutine MUL5, and multiply the value in R1 by 5. When we execute the RSB, at the end of MUL5 the top of the stack will still hold the return address--A3. The RSB instruction causes it to be popped off the stack and copied into the PC; control is thus returned to location A3.

Similarly the JSB MUL5 at B2 will push the contents of the PC, address B3, onto the stack; this is the return address. After executing the subroutine's ADDL2 instructions, the RSB is executed. The stack is, once more, popped into the PC, but this time the value at the top of the stack is B3, which is the return address for the *second* call of MUL5.

What if R2, which MUL5 uses, had some value that was important to the calling program? Clearly, *after* MUL5 returns, the value in R2 will have been changed. We could discuss the issues concerning the responsibility of the user of a subroutine to be aware of which registers the subroutine changes, and to be sure not to place any value in one of the registers that will be needed after the subroutine is called. To be sure, we *should* know the **side effects** of a subroutine before we use it. However, it is generally accepted that a subroutine should have as few side effects as possible; if a subroutine's documentation specifies that it expects its input parameter in R1, and that it produces its result in R1, then it should not alter any other register. Is there some way we can use R2 in the subroutine, *without* destroying any value that a caller of the subroutine may wish to preserve?

Of course there is; we can rewrite MUL5 as follows:

```
MUL5:   MOVL R2, TEMP        ;save old value of R2
        ADDL2 R1, R1
        ;unchanged from above
        MOVL TEMP, R2        ;restore R2
        RSB
TEMP:   .BLKL 1
```

The calling of MUL5 is not changed; however, a careful reader may object that it is *unnecessary* (although not incorrect) to use location TEMP: why not use the stack to save values in registers?

```
MUL5:   MOVL R2, -(SP)       ;save R2
        MOVL R1, R2          ;save input parameter
        ADDL2 R1, R1         ;*2
        ADDL2 R1, R1         ;*4
        ADDL2 R2, R1         ;*5
        MOVL (SP)+, R2       ;restore R2
        RSB                  ;return
```

A *very* careful reader may ask, "Why use R2 at all?" Rewriting MUL5 once again:

```
MUL5:   MOVL R1, -(SP)       ;save input parameter
        ADDL2 R1, R1         ;*2
        ADDL2 R1, R1         ;*4
        ADDL2 (SP)+, R1      ;*5
        RSB                  ;return
```

We can use the same instruction to both add the saved input parameter and pop it off the stack. Keep in mind that when a subroutine uses the stack, it must restore the stack to its original configuration. If we saved a register on the system stack and forgot to pop it off, then when we executed the RSB instruction, the PC would get the old contents of some register, rather than the return address, copied into it!

Passing Parameters

We can use a subroutine as a mechanism to help us break large programs into small pieces, and we can also use a subroutine to provide a packaged function (these two uses are by no means mutually exclusive)--we write a subroutine to solve a problem once, and whenever we need to solve the same problem again, we dig out our trusty old subroutine and use it: it is convenient *not* to reinvent the wheel every time we wish to drive from one place to another, for example. Often, we use subroutines that we have not, ourselves, written. We can think of such a subroutine as a black box: it provides some specified function, but we have no idea *how* it provides that function, because we don't know what is inside the box. Many of us probably think of automobiles in this way; before reading this book, many of us probably thought of computers in this way, also.

A black box is given some inputs, called its **input parameters** or **input arguments.** The black box (subroutine) does something with its input parameters, and produces results called **output parameters** or **output arguments.** Figure 9.7 shows a subroutine as a black box. A subroutine is **transparent** (and,

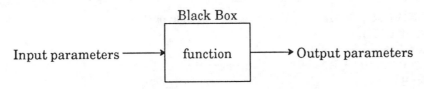

Figure 9.7 A subroutine as a black box

therefore, usable by *any* caller) to the extent that it avoids making reference to any instructions or data (except, of course, for its input and output parameters) outside of its own body.[2]

How do a subroutine and its caller communicate? How does the caller provide input parameters to the subroutine, and how does the subroutine return output parameters to the caller? These issues will be discussed in the next sections.

Passing Values as Parameters

In the MUL5 examples, we placed the *value* we wished to multiply by 5 in R1, and the subroutine placed that number, multiplied by 5, in R1--where the caller must know to look for it. Many of the mathematical functions provided in some high-level languages can be supported using this technique. For instance, a function MAX, which calculates the largest of its three inputs, can work nicely passing values as input parameters and returning a value as the result. In a high-level language, we might write something like **m = max(a, b, c)**, or **big := max(x, y, z)**. In VAX assembly language, we could write the first of these functions as follows:

```
            MOVL A, R1          ;input parameters in R1, R2, R3
            MOVL B, R2
            MOVL C, R3
            JSB MAX             ;find largest
            MOVL R1, M          ;largest in R1
            ;continue computing
;Subroutine MAX calculates the largest of 3 signed numbers
;in R1, R2 and R3, and returns it in R1
;
MAX:        CMPL R1, R2         ;find larger of R1 & R2
            BGEQ M1
    ;else, R2 > R1
            CMPL R2, R3         ;find larger of R2 & R3
            BGEQ M2
    ;else, R3 largest
M3:         MOVL R3, R1         ;R1 gets return value
            BRB RETURN          ;done
M1:         CMPL R1, R3         ;get here if R1 >= R2
            BLSS M3             ;R3 > R1 and R3 >= R2
    ;else, R1 is largest
```

---

[2]In higher level languages such as Pascal, a transparent procedure is one which uses no nonlocal variables.

```
        BRB RETURN          ;R1 already has largest
M2:     MOVL R2, R1         ;get here if R2 > R1 and R2 > R3
RETURN: RSB
```

The term **function** is often used to describe a subroutine which returns a single value, as in this example.

Passing Addresses as Parameters

It is not always practical to pass values as parameters. Suppose we want to write a subroutine which adds arrays. We don't want to have to copy the whole array in order to add it. How could we write a subroutine that adds all the elements in an array (of longwords), when that array's starting address is in R0, and its length (number of elements) is in R1? Consider the following example:

```
        .ENTRY START, 0
        MOVAL ARRAY, R0     ;array address passed in R0
        MOVL #50, R1        ;array size in R1
        JSB SUMIT           ;add all elements
        MOVL R2, TOTAL      ;sum returns in R2
        $EXIT_S
ARRAY:  .BLKL 50            ;array to add, 50 longwords
TOTAL:  .BLKL 1             ;place for sum
;
;Subroutine SUMIT adds each longword of the array whose starting
;address is in R0, and whose number of elements is in R1. It returns the sum in R2.
;
SUMIT:  CLRL R2             ;running sum here
LOOP:   ADDL2 (R0)+, R2     ;R0 has address of array
        SOBGTR R1, LOOP     ;number of elements in R1
        RSB
```

The distinction between arguments passed as values and those passed using their addresses is an important one; it is similar to the difference between ADDL3 R0, R1, R2 and ADDL3 (R0), (R1), (R2). If a caller wants a subroutine to perform some action in *its* memory locations rather than in the subroutine's memory locations, then the caller must provide the subroutine with the *addresses* of the arguments, not the values of the arguments. A classic example in high-level languages that is used to illustrate the difference between **pass by value** and **pass by address** (also called **pass by reference**) is the **switch(a, b)** subroutine, which will either interchange the values associated with names *a* and *b*, or it will not, depending on whether parameters *a* and *b* are passed by value or by address.

Parameter Passing with an Argument List

If we had a long list of arguments to pass to a subroutine, we might not want to pass each one (by reference *or* by value) in a register; we might make an **argument list.** Consider the following:

```
            .ENTRY START, 0
            MOVAL ARGLIST, R0        ;set up subroutine call
            JSB SUBR
            $EXIT_S
ARGLIST:    .ADDRESS ARG1, ARG2, ARG3, . . .
;
;Subroutine SUBR does such-and-such, using the so-and-so algorithm. It's input
;parameters are in an argument list (in some particular order, etc.), whose address
;is in R0.
;
SUBR:       MOVL R1, -(SP)           ;save registers
            MOVL R2, -(SP)
            MOVL (R0)+, R1           ;first arg. in R1
            MOVL (R0)+, R2           ;second arg.
            ;compute
            MOVL (SP)+, R2           ;restore registers
            MOVL (SP)+, R1
            RSB
            .END START
```

We could use more than one argument list, if that made our program clearer. The argument list(s) should go wherever the data for that part of our program are declared: for a main program, data typically go just before the .ENTRY directive, or just after the $EXIT_S macro; for subroutines, data typically go just after the RSB instruction (we will discuss subroutines that call other subroutines shortly).

Let us see what the array-summing subroutine looks like if we use an argument list to pass its parameters.

```
            SIZE = 50                ;for convenience
            .ENTRY START, 0
            MOVAL ARGLIST, R0
            JSB NEWSUM
            $EXIT_S
ARGLIST:    .ADDRESS ARRAY, SIZE, SUM
ARRAY:      .BLKL SIZE               ;SIZE longwords
SUM:        .BLKL 1                  ;for result
;Subroutine NEWSUM adds each longword of the array whose starting address is the
;first argument in the argument list, and whose number of elements is the second argument
;in the arglist. It returns the sum in the location whose address is the 3rd argument in
;the arglist. The argument list's address is in R0.
;
NEWSUM:     MOVL R1, -(SP)           ;save registers
            MOVL R2, -(SP)
            MOVL R3, -(SP)
            MOVL (R0)+, R1           ;array address
            MOVL (R0)+, R2           ;number of elements
            CLRL R3                  ;running sum
```

```
LOOP:       ADDL2 (R1)+, R3          ;add
            SOBGTR R2, LOOP
            MOVL R3, @(R0)+          ;return sum
            MOVL (SP)+, R3           ;restore registers
            MOVL (SP)+, R2
            MOVL (SP)+, R1
            RSB
            .END START
```

Notice that subroutine NEWSUM has returned the sum of the array to location SUM, *without ever referring to it by its symbolic label.* This is a major requirement for a re-usable subroutine (and for a well-written, modular, program, in general): it should *never* refer to any symbolic label that is not defined in its data section.

Why should we bother passing parameters via argument lists? Why can't we just use the labels ARRAY and SUM in the subroutine, just as we use them in the main program? By guaranteeing that a subroutine will change only its own local data and the arguments explicitly passed to it by its caller, we make our programs easier to understand and debug. Most modern high-level programming languages have **scope rules** that enforce these conventions. In assembly language, however, they are merely conventions; the assembler does not check that they are obeyed, and does not inform us if they are not. However, we ignore them at our own peril.

Passing Parameters on the Stack

We can also pass parameters to (and from) subroutines by placing them on the stack, rather than in registers or an argument list. Consider yet another version of the array summing program:

```
            SIZE = 50
            .ENTRY START, 0
            MOVAL ARRAY, -(SP)    ;array address
            MOVL #SIZE, -(SP)     ;number of elements
            JSB STACKSUM
RETADDR:    MOVL (SP)+, RESULT ;get sum from stack
            $EXIT_S
ARRAY:      .BLKL SIZE            ;array of longwords
RESULT:     .BLKL 1               ;where sum will go
;
;Subroutine STACKSUM adds each longword of an array. The number of elements and
;array address are on the stack, in that order. The sum gets returned on the stack, as
;well. This is a tricky way to pass parameters.
;
STACKSUM:   MOVL R0, -(SP)        ;save registers
            MOVL R1, -(SP)
P1:         MOVL R2, -(SP)
            MOVL 20(SP), R0       ;array address
            MOVL 16(SP), R1       ;number of elements
            CLRL R2               ;running sum
LOOP:       ADDL2 (R0)+, R2       ;add each element
            SOBGTR R1, LOOP
P2:         MOVL R2, 20(SP)       ;copy sum over array address
            MOVL (SP)+, R2        ;restore registers
            MOVL (SP)+, R1
```

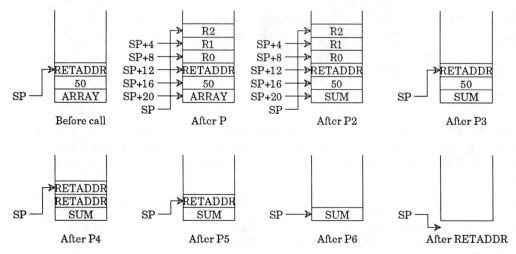

Figure 9.8 Passing parameters on the stack

```
P3:        MOVL (SP)+, R0
P4:        MOVL (SP), 4(SP)      ;copy return address over size
P5:        TSTL (SP)+            ;pop 2nd return address off stack
P6:        RSB                   ;return
           .END START
```

This is a difficult technique to use for passing parameters, primarily because it ignores the LIFO discipline of using a stack: we must put the parameters *under* the return address, but then access them *before* the RSB instruction uses the return address. It's easy to count wrong, and return to somewhere other than the correct return address. The stack history for the array summing subroutine with arguments passed on the stack is shown in figure 9.8.

Suggestions for Subroutine Design

A subroutine should be implemented as a black box. We have already discussed this idea, but now that we have seen some of the parameter passing techniques, we are in a better position to understand how to implement it. The *only* things that a subroutine should know about its caller are the input and output parameters. The very important consequence of this requirement is that, if a subroutine makes no reference to any of the symbolic labels used in the calling program, the subroutine can be written and assembled *independently* of the calling program.

The ability to assemble subroutines independently of their calling routines is a significant breakthrough in programming technology. Among other things, it means that it is possible to decompose a large application into many modules, and to design and implement each module simultaneously and independently--subject, of course, to appropriate coordination.

We can define the function of a subroutine, document it, test the code, fix the code, improve the code, and then store the object module in a **subroutine library.** Any program can use the subroutine library as a source of modules, for building-blocks, to solve the subproblems into which that program has been decomposed.

Internal versus External Subroutines

If we have a small problem, we may be able to solve it by writing a single source module. We may, of course, wish to use subroutines in this single module. These subroutines are called **internal** subroutines, because they are only used within the source module in which they are defined. Their names, and their very existence, are known to no other modules. The assembler does nothing special (beyond translating the mnemonics for JSB and RSB, which is not really very special) as a result of the fact that a module contains internal subroutines.

For example, we may wish to use a multiply-by-four subroutine because our program performs that action several different times. We are assuming this is a small program, so we will define and use the subroutine internally:

```
            MOVL X, R1          ;pass input parameter in R1
            JSB MUL4            ;multiply *4
            MOVL R1, PROD       ;return result in R1
            $EXIT_S
X:          .LONG 17
PROD:       .BLKL 1
;
;Subroutine MUL4 expects its input parameter in R1, and returns ;that number, *4, in
;R1. It's quite a simple subroutine.
;
MUL4:       ADDL2 R1, R1        ;*2
            ADDL2 R1, R1        ;*4
        RSB
```

Although there are many ways of placing the address of the instruction at label MUL4 in the PC, if we follow good programming practice, the only way control ever reaches that instruction is as a result of executing a JSB or BSB(B,W) instruction.

The .EXTERNAL Directive and Global Labels

If we are writing a large program, we may wish to write and assemble some subroutines independently of the main program; these are called **external** subroutines. In this case, we need to inform Macro to make special provisions to assure that all references to symbolic labels--even those to labels defined in another source module--can be resolved, eventually. There are two things about which we need to inform Macro: first, if we have used the .DISABLE GLOBAL directive (as described in chapter 4), then any reference we make to a symbolic label that is not defined in the current source module (but may be perfectly well defined in an external subroutine, in a different source module) will be flagged as an error. If, however, we inform Macro that that particular label is not defined in *this* source module because it is defined in *another* source module, then Macro will pass this information along to the linker, and the linker will search for a definition of the label in (exactly) one of the object modules it links (and complain if it doesn't find it), and complete the generation of machine language (by filling in an address or offset) at link time. We inform the assembler that a label is externally defined by using the .EXTERNAL directive.

The other half of the job of resolving external labels involves informing the assembler that a particular label will be referred to by another source module. Normally, the assembler maintains information concerning the location counter values corresponding to symbolic labels only while it is assembling a source module; if a particular module has labels that will be referred to by another module, then information concerning those labels will have to be saved until link time, when the linker will resolve those references. We indicate to Macro that a label will be referred to by another module (that it is a **global** label) by placing two colons after it, rather than the normal single colon.

For example, we could write the following main program:

```
                .DISABLE GLOBAL
                .EXTERNAL HELP, YEAR
                .ENTRY START, 0
                JSB HELP
                $EXIT_S
YR:             .ADDRESS YEAR
                .END START
```

There are two labels that are referred to, but not defined, in this source module: HELP and YEAR. Since we have declared them external, the assembler doesn't complain about not finding their definitions, and the linker knows to look for their definitions.

The required subroutine, HELP, might be written as follows:

```
YEAR::          .LONG 1988
HELP::          INCB DUMMY
                NOP                 ;helpless
                RSB
DUMMY:          .BYTE -3
                .END
```

The label DUMMY will be used only while assembling the module that the subroutine is in, but the labels HELP and YEAR will be saved by the assembler and passed on to the linker to enable resolving references to them made from other source modules. Except for the presence of the two colons following global labels, the *text* of an externally defined subroutine such as HELP is no different from that of an internal subroutine.

Since *no* subroutine should make references to symbolic labels defined in another module, we should be able to easily convert a well-written internal subroutine into an external subroutine should we desire to do so.

Linking Separately Assembled Subroutines

How do we link the separately assembled object modules into which we may have decomposed a problem? Suppose we have a subroutine called FIX that is assembled in its own source module called FIX.MAR. (The name of the source module is, of course, completely independent of the name of the subroutine--except that it helps us to remember what is in a file if we make the names similar.) The main program (whose source module, for example, is MAIN.MAR) would have in it the statements JSB FIX, and .EXTERNAL FIX; the symbolic label FIX in the source module FIX.MAR (FIX is the entry point of the subroutine) would have two colons after it. If we have assembled MAIN.MAR and FIX.MAR, the assembler will have created the object modules, MAIN.OBJ and FIX.OBJ. We link them by typing

    LINK MAIN,FIX

The linker resolves the reference to symbolic label FIX in module MAIN.OBJ, which the assembler could not, by looking at its offset from the beginning of FIX.OBJ and doing whatever calculation is necessary. (The necessary calculation depends on the addressing mode used in the FIX.MAR module; in this case, relative addressing is used, which is mode A, C, or E on the PC, and requires that the distance between the instruction using FIX and the definition of FIX be calculated.) When all unresolved labels have been resolved (including those provided in the library of system services, which is automatically linked with *every* object module we link), the load module is created as usual.

Link Map For External Subroutines

What if we have linked several object modules into a single main program, but our program doesn't work properly? We can, of course, use the debugger, just as we did in the case when our load module was created from only a single source module and object module. If, however, we use either the DUMP or SNAP system services, we may find that some addresses in them are no longer as helpful as they were. For the assembler assumes that each source module will be loaded beginning at address 0, and so all addresses in *each* .LIS file are relative to 0. How do we know, if an address in the PC or in our hexadecimal dump is larger than the last address in the main program, just which line of the assembler's listing corresponds to what we see from the SNAP or DUMP?

We need a **link map,** which tells us the addresses that the linker has assigned to the various modules. By default, the linker does *not* provide us with a link map, but if we type

LINK/MAP MAIN,FIX

then the linker will provide us with a link map, in a file called MAIN.MAP. The link map provides, in addition to other (for us less interesting) information, the starting and ending address of each module which we have linked, and the address of each global label we have defined.

Figure 9.9 shows a simple example of the .LIS files of two object modules, created from the source modules containing the main program and subroutine HELP that we saw above, that have been linked into a single load module called MAIN.EXE. The last part of this figure shows an edited version of the link map; it has been edited to show primarily the information of relevance to this discussion. Note, for example, that the symbol table for the main module lists the value (address) of label START as 0_{16}, and that the symbol table for the subroutine module lists the value of YEAR as 0 (since this is the first data item or instruction of the module), and the value of HELP as 04_{16}.

The link map, which is the third part of figure 9.9, shows only the global labels; START is shown with value 200_{16}, because the whole program has been relocated, as usual, to 200_{16}, and START is the first label in the main program. YEAR is shown with value 215_{16}: it corresponds to the first memory location in the subroutine, and since the main program occupies 15 bytes (from 200 to 214), as shown in the first part of the the link map, the next location would be 215, and that's where the subroutine gets loaded. Similarly, HELP has the value 219_{16}, which is 4 more than 215, since HELP is the 4th byte of the subroutine.

Transparency

When we use a subroutine, we have specific expectations and we don't want any surprises. A subroutine is surpriseless, or **transparent,** to a calling routine to the extent that is is invisible to that calling routine: it has no effects other than the production of results. If a subroutine is *not* completely transparent, then its documentation should specify all of its side effects. Unspecified side effects are similar to time bombs. Sooner or later they will cause trouble.

Subroutine Nesting

At the beginning of this chapter, we discussed problem decomposition as a process which can result in many levels of problems. If we think of the name P as representing the main program, and P1 and

Listing for Main Module, HELP:

```
                    0000  1         .DISABLE GLOBAL
                    0000  2         .EXTERNAL HELP, YEAR
          0000      0000  3         .ENTRY START, 0
00000000'EF 16      0002  4         JSB HELP
                    0008  5         $EXIT_S
         00000000'  0011  6 YR:     .ADDRESS YEAR
                    0015  7         .END START
```

Symbol table

```
HELP              *******   X    01
START             00000000 RG    01
SYS$EXIT          *******   G    01
YEAR              *******   X    01
YR                00000011 R     01
```

Listing for External Subroutine, HELPLESS:

```
   000007C3  0000  1 YEAR::   .LONG 1987
0000000C'EF 96 0004  2 HELP::   INCB DUMMY
          01  000A  3          NOP ;helpless
          05  000B  4          RSB
          FD  000C  5 DUMMY:   .BYTE -3
              000D  6          .END
```

Symbol table

```
DUMMY             0000000C R     01
HELP              00000004 RG    01
YEAR              00000000 RG    01
```

Link Map:

```
16-SEP-1987 16:23        VAX-11 Linker V04-00                Page    1
```

Psect Name	Module Name	Base	End	Length
	HELP	00000200	00000214	00000015
	HELPLESS	00000215	00000221	0000000D

Symbol	Value
HELP	00000219-R
START	00000200-R
YEAR	00000215-R

Figure 9.9 Listings and link map

P:		P1:		P2:	
	.		.		.
	.		.		.
A1:	JSB P1	B1:	JSB P11	C1:	JSB P21
	.		.		.
A2:	JSB P2	B2:	JSB P12	C2:	JSB P22
	.		.		.
	$EXIT_S		RSB		RSB

Figure 9.10 Problem decomposition with subroutines

P2 as subprograms called by P, then P11 and P12 would be subprograms called by P1, and P21 and P22 would be subprograms called by P2. This sequence is shown in figure 9.10; it could continue, in a similar manner, for an arbitrary number of subprograms. Schematically, we can depict the chronology of execution as shown in figure 9.11. The stack history of the calls to and returns from these subroutines is shown in figure 9.12.

Let us examine a simple example. We wish to write a program that reads numeric data from a file and adds the items. Suppose each entry in the file is a series of pairs of decimal digits. We have a library routine called GETS which reads a line of input from a file into a specified location. The program we write might look like the one shown in figure 9.13. We began by writing the main program. After reading an input line (with GETS), it seemed like a good idea to let a subroutine handle the details of processing the line. Later, while writing GETNUM, it seemed like a good idea to let some new subroutines (TENS, ONES) take care of even lower level details. Afterward, when reviewing our efforts, we may decide to eliminate subroutine ONES, and incorporate its one productive instruction where it is needed.

There is nothing wrong with admitting that a subroutine turned out to be unnecessary. It is not always clear before the fact how things will turn out. When we have a program to write, we should use the concept of problem decomposition (into subroutines) to sketch our solution. We should then test each subroutine, and fix it if necessary. When the program works correctly, we can try to improve it. There is little point to speeding up or otherwise improving a program that does not work.

Procedure Call Instructions

So far we have used only the JSB and BSB(B,W) instructions for subroutine calling, and the RSB instruction for returning from subroutines. These instructions provide adequate support for saving a return address on the stack when a subroutine is called, and then restoring it in order to return from the subroutine. If we wish to save registers, we must do it ourselves; if we wish to pass parameters, we must do that ourselves, also. In addition, a subroutine (or **procedure**) in many modern high-level languages provides a local environment (called a **scope**), with private variables that are accessible only to the subroutine. It is possible to build all of these features out of the primitives we have already seen, but the VAX provides a pair of procedure call instructions that make this especially easy for assembly language programmers. As we will see, these are among the more complex VAX instructions.

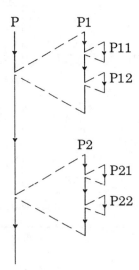

Figure 9.11 Execution chronology for nested subroutines

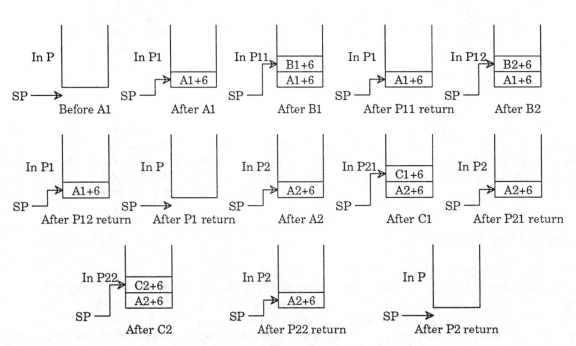

Figure 9.12 Stack history for nested subroutines

```
;Main program starts here
;
                .ENTRY START,0
                IOINIT
READ:           GETS BUFFER                     ;read a line
                MOVAL ARGLIST, R10
                JSB GETNUM                       ;process line
                TSTB EOF                         ;check end of file
                BNEQ DONE
;else, read another line of input
                BRB READ
DONE:           ;print output
                $EXIT_S
ARGLIST:        .ADDRESS BUFFER, EOF, SUM
BUFFER:         .BLKB 256                        ;enough for a line
EOF:            .BYTE 0                          ;false, at first
SUM:            .LONG 0                          ;place for sum
;
;Subroutine GETNUM converts ASCII coded 2-digit numbers into their binary representations.
;Its input parameters are in an arglist whose address is in R10: first, address of buffer to process;
;2nd, address of end-of-file flag, which gets 1 when input is exhausted--which is the case when a
;"q" is found (for quit).  The last arg is address of place to put the sum of this line of input.
;Each line of input is terminated by a NUL character.
;
GETNUM:         PUSHR #^M<R6, R7, R8, R9>        ;save registers
                MOVL (R10)+, R6                  ;address of digit string
                CLRL R9                          ;running sum
BEGIN:          TSTB (R6)                        ;check for end-of-line (NUL)
                BNEQ MORE                        ;if not end-of-line, continue
    ;else, must change R10, so sum goes in right place
                ADDL2 #4, R10
                BRB RETURN                       ;and done, for now
;not end-of-line; check for end-of-input
MORE:           CMPB (R6), #^A/q/                ;end of input: "q"
                BNEQ PROCESS                     ;if not end-of-input, continue
    ;else:  end of input
END:            INCB @(R10)+                     ;set end-of-input flag
                BRB RETURN
PROCESS:        CMPB (R6), #^A/,/                ;check for number separator
                BNEQ NEXT                        ;if not comma, continue
    ;else, consume comma and check again
                INCL R6                          ;consume
                BRB BEGIN                        ;go back to check for eoln or end-of-input
NEXT:           MOVZBL (R6)+, R7                 ;1st digit
                JSB TENS                         ;tens place digit
                MOVL R7, R8                       ;save 1st part of sum
                MOVZBL (R6)+, R7                 ;2nd digit
                JSB ONES                         ;ones place digit
                ADDL2 R7, R8                     ;add tens and ones digit to get number
                ADDL2 R8, R9                     ;add to running sum
                BRB BEGIN                        ;get another number
RETURN:         ADDL2 R9, @(R10)+                ;add sum to output arg.
                POPR #^M<R6, R7, R8, R9>         ;restore registers
                RSB
```

Figure 9.13 Example with nested subroutines

```
;
;Subroutine TENS converts an ASCII coded digit to its value as a tens digit in a string:
;It subtracts 30 (hex), and then uses a displacement table to, essentially, multiply it by 10.
;It expects a single ASCII coded digit as input, in R7, and returns the binary value, also in R7.
;Arguments are longwords.
;
TENS:          SUBL2 #^A/0/, R7                    ;convert from ASCII code to binary
               MOVZBL TENTABLE(R7), R7             ;change from bytes to longwords
               RSB
TENTABLE:      .BYTE 0, 10, 20, 30, 40
               .BYTE 50, 60, 70, 80, 90
;
;Subroutine ONES converts an ASCII coded digit to its value as a ones digit in a string:
;It just subtracts 30 (hex).  It gets its input in R7, and returns the binary digit in R7.
;Arguments are longwords.
;
ONES:          SUBL2 #^A/0/, r7
               RSB
               .END START
```

Figure 9.13 (*cont.*)

The CALLG instruction

One of the two VAX procedure call instructions is the CALLG instruction. The CALLG instruction has two arguments: the address of an argument list and the name of the procedure. By convention, an argument list is an array of longwords, the first one of which contains in its low-order byte the number of additional longwords in the argument list. The longwords in the argument list may be addresses or values (arguments may be passed by reference or by value). If we wish to call a procedure named PROC1, with three arguments, we could write the following code:

```
ARGLIST:       .LONG 3               ;3 arguments
               .LONG 457, 37, -12    ;arguments
               .ENTRY START, 0
               CALLG ARGLIST, PROC1
               $EXIT_S
```

If we wish to call PROC1 again, with different arguments, we may either use a different argument list, or replace the values in the argument list at run time.

The CALLS Instruction

The CALLS instruction is similar to the CALLG instruction, except that for the CALLS instruction, the argument list is on the stack, last argument first to first argument last. In addition, the first operand of the CALLS instruction is *not* the address of the argument list; it is the number of arguments pushed on the stack. Thus, to use the CALLS instruction for procedure PROC1, we could write the following code:

```
          .ENTRY START, 0
          PUSHL #-12              ;3rd argument
          PUSHL #37               ;2nd argument
          PUSHL #457              ;1st argument
          CALLS #3, PROC1
          $EXIT_S
```

For the CALLS instruction, the number of arguments is pushed onto the stack automatically, as part of executing the CALLS instruction.

Arguments and the Argument Pointer

We create argument lists for both CALLG and CALLS, but neither of the examples shows us placing the address of the list in a register for access in the procedure. How does the procedure find the argument list? Before transferring control to the called procedure, the control unit, as part of the execution of the CALLG or CALLS instruction, places the address of the beginning of the argument list--which is the address of the longword containing the number of arguments, and is either on the stack or elsewhere in memory--in the **argument pointer**, R12. (This is why we have advised against treating R12 as an ordinary general-purpose register.) Thus, in the procedure, we can access the arguments using displacement mode with R12; Macro also recognizes the name AP for R12 (which is the preferred name when we use it as the argument pointer), so we could write code as follows:

```
PROC1:    MOVL (AP), R5           ;number of args
          MOVL 4(AP), R6          ;1st argument
          MOVL 8(AP), R7          ;2nd argument
          MOVL 12(AP), R8         ;3rd argument
          ;procedure body
          RET
```

We access the arguments the same way, regardless of whether we call a procedure with the CALLG instruction or the CALLS instruction. Note that we return from a procedure called with CALLG or CALLS with the RET (RETURN) instruction; we will discuss this instruction shortly.

Saving Registers

We have already seen that it is possible to save registers with the PUSHR instruction and restore them with the POPR instruction. However, when we use the CALLG and CALLS instructions, there is no need for us to do this. When a procedure is called with the CALLG or CALLS instructions, the control unit expects that the very first word of the procedure will be a register save mask (just like the one we use for the PUSHR and POPR instructions); we can specify the register save mask using either the "^M" operator or an ordinary number as the argument for the .WORD directive. Before control is transferred to the instructions in the procedure, the registers specified by the mask are saved on the system stack. The register save mask is also saved on the stack, so that when the RET instruction is executed, the control unit will know how many registers were saved, will restore their old values, and will remove them from the stack before control is transferred back to the procedure's caller. Thus, procedure PROC1 would look something like this:

```
PROC1:    .WORD ^M<R6, R7, R8, R9>        ;save R6, R7, R8, R9
          ;procedure body
          RET
```

Condition handler				
SPA|S|0	Register mask	PSW	0
Saved AP				
Saved FP				
Saved PC				
Saved R0				
. . .				
Saved R11				

Figure 9.14 VAX call frame

Note that the preceding listing of PROC1 would not execute correctly because the control unit would have used the first 16 bits of the MOVL (AP), R5 instruction as a register save mask!

Recall that when we type .ENTRY START, 0, a 1-word register save mask of 0 is created, so that the first word of our programs in memory (and the first word shown in their .LIS files) is 0. This mask is created because the operating system treats user programs as procedures, which it calls and executes. The 0 in .ENTRY START, 0 specifies that the register save mask is 0 and not something else. This means that no registers will be saved--which is typically fine for the beginning of a main program.

The Call Frame

How does the control unit know which register values to restore and pop off the stack when it executes a RET instruction? By looking at the register save mask, which it has saved on the stack. How does the control unit find the register save mask? Just before control is transferred to the first *instruction* (1 word after the register save mask) of a procedure, register 13, the **frame pointer** (known as FP), is initialized with the address of the top of the stack. Since everything that is saved on the stack during execution of the CALLG or CALLS instruction is saved in a fixed position with respect to the frame pointer, the control unit knows where to find the proper values to restore to registers, the PC, and so forth when the RET instruction is executed. Figure 9.14 shows the organization of the VAX **call frame**; there are several fields that require explanation. The first longword, on the top of the new stack, contains a **condition handler,** which is the address of a routine that may be provided for dealing with exceptions (such as floating-point errors, which we will discuss in chapter 13), should they occur during execution of the procedure. The first 5 bits of the second longword are 0; they correspond to the low-order 5 bits of the PSL--the CC bits and the T bit (which we have not yet discussed)--which are not saved across procedure calls. Then, the rest of the PSL--containing information which we have also not yet discussed--is stored. The next field contains the register save mask that was defined by the programmer as the first word of the procedure body, followed by a single bit of 0 (this is bit number 28 of the second longword of the call frame). The next bit (S) is set if the procedure was called with the CALLS instruction and

	31 30 29 28 27	16 15	5 4	0
new FP, SP→	Condition handler			
	SPA 1 0 0 0 1 1 1 1 0 0 0 0 0 0	Saved PSW	0 0 0 0 0	
	Saved AP			
	Saved FP			
	Saved PC (return address)			
	R6			
	R7			
	R8			
	R9			
new AP→	3 (number of arguments)			
	457 (1st argument)			
	37 (2nd argument)			
	−12 (3rd argument)			
	Previous stack entries			
	.			
	.			
	.			

Figure 9.15 System stack after procedure call

cleared if the procedure was called with the CALLG instruction. Finally, the last 2 bits (SPA) indicate how many bytes must be pushed on the stack (subtracted from SP) for the stack to be longword aligned.

Figure 9.15 shows the stack just after procedure PROC1, which we have described in the preceding sections on the CALLG and CALLS instructions, was called. In this case, PROC1 was called with the CALLS instruction, so the arguments are on the stack (just below the call frame and pointed to by the AP), and the S bit in the call frame is set. Consideration of the above discussion and examination of these two figures should explain clearly why using R12 and R13 as ordinary general-purpose registers can be counter-productive and dangerous. Figure 9.16 is an update of the model of the VAX that we saw in figures 3.8 and 5.1; it includes some of the additional information we have learned in this chapter.

What Can Go Wrong?

Managing a stack introduces several interesting possibilities for getting into trouble. When we deal with arrays, we must beware of using an index that is out of the range of the array: if we have an array of 20 bytes, it is meaningless--and probably dangerous--to examine a byte with an offset of 30 from the starting address of the array, when sorting the array's elements. With a stack, we must also beware of acting as if the stack contains a different number of elements than it does. When we try to push more elements onto the stack than there is room for, we cause stack **overflow**; when we try to pop more elements off the stack than we have pushed onto it, we cause stack **underflow.**

Stack Overflow

A stack is created by imposing an arbitrary (from the memory system's point of view) organization on the memory. A stack's depth is, therefore, finite. When we create personal stacks, we must be careful

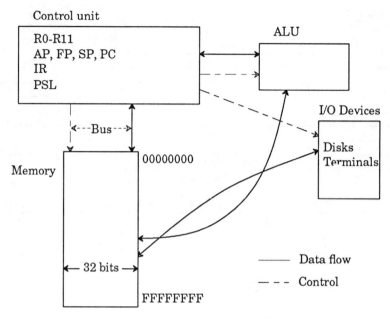

Figure 9.16 A model of the VAX

not to push too many elements on the stack; doing so will overwrite data items (or instructions) that are stored in memory locations adjacent to the stack. With the system stack, the VMS operating system will abort our program if we exceed the limit set for our stack. If we wish to enlarge the stack, we may do so by making an appropriate request to the operating system (see the VMS documentation for details). However, there is always *some* limit to the size of the stack; in the extreme, this limit is all of the memory that is left after our program has been loaded.

Stack Underflow

Stack underflow is the converse of the stack overflow problem. If we somehow lose track of how many things we have pushed onto a stack, we might begin popping off more than we pushed on. With a personal stack, we will simply pop meaningless data (from adjacent instructions or data items) into the destination of the pop. In addition, once we start pushing new items on the stack, we will overwrite these adjacent locations. With the system stack, the operating system detects that the address we are using is beyond the stack boundaries, and it aborts our program.

Summary

The ability to have a sequence of instructions used from various points in a program, to accomplish a specific function, is very important. We first saw that we can implement this idea with something called a *subprogram, subroutine, function,* or *procedure* without any new instructions. However, it is such an important idea that most computers provide special instructions to support subroutines efficiently. The VAX has the JSB and BSB(B,W) instructions for calling subroutines, and the RSB instruction for returning from them.

We also examined memory stacks. They support access on a LIFO (Last In, First Out) basis. Stacks make it easy to reallocate memory dynamically.

On the VAX, a register is specifically assigned to point to the top of an area of memory designated as the system stack. Register 14, or SP, is the system stack pointer. The SP should always contain the address of the current top of the system stack. On the VAX, a push onto the system stack is done with autodecrement mode on the stack pointer, and a pop off of the system stack is done with autoincrement mode on the stack pointer. Thus the system stack grows from high memory to low memory.

Subroutine linkage can be implemented easily on computers which support stacks. The JSB instruction saves its return address on the stack, and the RSB instruction pops the return address off of the stack (into the PC). Various ways of passing arguments to and from subroutines have been discussed, including the use of general-purpose registers and argument lists. We also described passing arguments on the system stack. This is a difficult method to implement because the subroutine must access the arguments from *under* the return address, which is at the top of the stack when the subroutine has been called. In all cases, we must know whether we are passing values or addresses.

The ability to assemble program modules independently increases the organizational advantages of using subroutines. When we indicate that a symbolic label is **global** (using two colons rather than one after it), the assembler understands that a label defined in the current module is to be kept available for reference in another module.

The VAX also has complex procedure call instructions, CALLG and CALLS, for calling procedures. These instructions allow us to save and restore registers automatically on the stack, to access arguments in an argument list whose address is in the argument pointer, AP, and to access local variables on the stack as displacements from the call frame pointer, FP. To return from a procedure called with the CALLG or CALLS instructions, we use the RET instruction, which restores registers and removes the entire call frame from the stack.

The use of stacks can lead to their misuse; stacks can overflow or underflow. The manner in which these problems manifest themselves depends on whether they occur with personal stacks or the system stack. With personal stacks, we destroy adjacent data or instructions, or pop meaningless values. With the system stack, different operating systems handle the problem in different ways.

Exercises for Chapter 9

1. Assume that the following program is loaded starting at location 0, with the stack pointer (SP) initially containing 7FFFFFFC. Draw a snapshot of the system stack after the execution of each instruction (assume that .ENTRY START, 0 generates no instruction):

```
                    .ENTRY START, 0
    1)              MOVL #1, –(SP)
    2)              MOVL #2, –(SP)
    3)              JSB SUB
    DONE:           $EXIT_S

    ;
    ;Subroutine SUB does something . . .
    ;

    4) SUB:         MOVL (SP)+, RETAD
    5)              MOVL (SP)+, JUNK1
    6)              MOVL (SP)+, JUNK2
    7)              MOVL RETAD, –(SP)
    8)              RSB
```

```
RETAD:          .BLKL 1
JUNK1:          .BLKL 1
JUNK2:          .BLKL 1
                .END START
TE
```

2.   Consider the following subroutine invocation:

```
MOVAL ARRAY1, -(SP)
MOVAL ARRAY2, -(SP)
MOVAL ARRAYSUM, -(SP)
JSB ARRAYADD
ADDL2 #12, SP
```

Labels ARRAY1 and ARRAY2 are the beginning addresses of two longword arrays with the same number of elements. The end of each is marked by a sentinel value of 0 (the number, not the ASCII code).

    a.   Write a subroutine ARRAYADD to sum corresponding elements of ARRAY1 and ARRAY2, and place the results into the corresponding location in array ARRAYSUM (which is a third array with the same number of elements as ARRAY1 and ARRAY2). Your subroutine must not have any side effects, and the only information your subroutine may have about the main program is that which is passed as arguments.

    b.   Show clearly how the stack is used.

3.   Write a subroutine which is passed the address of a character string in R0 and returns with the same string (in the same place) having all *contiguous* groups of the same character replaced by a single occurrence of that character. If the subroutine received the string OCCURRENNNNCE as its input, it would return the string OCURENCE. Assume that the string is terminated by a byte of 0 (the NUL character); also assume that the string is nonempty, so its first character is not 0. The subroutine can be written using 15 instructions.

4.   The SNAP system service provides a register snapshot, and the DUMP system service provides you with a hex memory dump. How could you examine the system stack at run time?

5.   Examine the following main program and subroutine:

```
DATA1:          .LONG 17
DATA2:          .LONG 20
ARGLIST:        .ADDRESS ARG1, ARG2
ARG1:           .BLKL 1
ARG2:           .BLKL 1
                .ENTRY START, 0
                MOVAL DATA1, ARG1
                MOVAL DATA2, ARG2
                MOVAL ARGLIST, R5
A→
                JSB FOO
B→
                $EXIT_S
;
;This is subroutine FOO ...
;
FOO:            MOVL (R5)+, FIRST
                MOVL (R5)+, SECOND
```

```
C→
                MOVL @FIRST, WHO
                MOVL @SECOND, @FIRST
D→
                MOVL WHO, @SECOND
                RSB
FIRST:          .BLKL 1
SECOND:         .BLKL 1
WHO:            .BLKL 1
                .END START
```

If this program is loaded beginning at address 0, what are the values of DATA1, DATA2, ARG1, ARG2, WHO, FIRST, R5, and SECOND at the points indicated by A, B, C, and D?

6. Write a subroutine that is given, in R0 and R1, the addresses of two strings of characters. Each string is terminated by a byte of 0 (the NUL character). The subroutine should return with the Z bit set if the two strings are equal and with the N bit set if the one whose address is in R0 alphabetically precedes the one whose address is in R1. Don't worry about saving registers. (What problems would there be if you wanted to save registers?)

7. Assume that the following program is loaded beginning at address 0:

```
D1:             .LONG D2
D2:             .LONG D1
ARGLIST:        .ADDRESS ARG1, ARG2
ARG1:           .BLKL 1
ARG2:           .BLKL 1
                .ENTRY START, 0
                MOVAL D1, ARG1
                MOVAL D2, ARG2
                MOVAL ARGLIST, R4
                JSB SUB1
B:              $EXIT_S
;
;This is subroutine SUB1 . . .
;
SUB1:           MOVL (R4)+, S11
                MOVL (R4)+, S12
A:              MOVL @S11, S13
                MOVL @S13, S12
                RSB
S11:            .BLKL 1
S12:            .BLKL 1
S13:            .BLKL 1
                .END START
```

What are the values, if known, stored in locations D1, D2, ARG1, ARG2, S11, S12, and S13 just *before* the instructions at labels A and B have been executed (use numeric or equivalent symbolic addresses)?

8.   Consider the following main program and subroutine outlines:

```
                .ENTRY START, 0
                PUSHL #13
CALL:           JSB A
                .

                .

                $EXIT_S
;
;Subroutine A
;
 A:             JSB B
                .

                .

                RSB
;
;Subroutine B
;
 B:             .

                .

 B1:            JSB C

                .

                RSB
;
;Subroutine C
;
 C:             .

                .

                RSB
                .END START
```

Assuming that no items have been pushed on the stack that are not shown in the bodies of the main program and subroutines A, B, and C (other than subroutine return addresses, of course), show the contents of the stack upon entering subroutine C.

More General-Purpose Instructions

Introduction

In this chapter, we will discuss several families of VAX instructions that we have not yet seen. Before doing so, however, we will consolidate what we already know about instruction families and types. There are two organizing concepts that are helpful for this consolidation: the first of these is the classification of instructions according to format; the second is their classification according to function.

Classification by Format

Classifying instructions by format means grouping together all instructions that *look* the same. The advantage of such a classification is that when we understand one instruction in a format class, we may be able to generalize our understanding to the other instructions in that class.

For some computers, classifying instructions by format means classifying them according to the format of their opcode. This classification scheme is of only marginal interest to us, because the VAX has only two opcode formats: 1-byte opcodes and 2-byte opcodes. An examination of Appendix 5 and 6 will show us that, when the opcode (bits 0 through 7 of the instruction) is between 00_{16} and FB_{16} (inclusive) it is a 1-byte opcode, and when it is between FC_{16} and FF_{16} (inclusive) it is a 2-byte opcode.

In chapter 3 we saw that it is also possible to classify instructions by format according to the number of operands the instructions require. VAX instructions have 0 to 6 operands; classification by format according to the number of operands is only occasionally useful. For example, there is a clear relationship between the ADD(B,W,L)2 instructions and the SUB(B,W,L)2 instructions, and these would both go in the 2-operand instruction class. However, there is no clear relationship between the BGTR (and all the other conditional branch instructions) and the CLR(B,W,L) instructions, but both are classified as single-operand instructions. Let us now consider the second classification scheme-- classification by function--and see if it is more useful than classification by format.

Classification by Function

A functional classification places instructions in groups according to the nature of the work they perform. This is perhaps the most useful classification to use when we are writing programs. It helps us answer the question, "Which arithmetic instruction should I use here?" An alphabetic listing of instruction mnemonics (such as that in Appendix 3) may be helpful when we forget what a particular instruction does, but it is clumsy to use when we know *what* we want to do, but don't know the "perfect" instruction(s) to use.

The VAX Architecture Reference Manual[1] (which describes each VAX instruction, among other things) divides the instruction set into 12 functional categories:

---

[1] T.E. Leonard, ed., *VAX Architecture Reference Manual.* (Bedford, Mass.: Digital Press, 1987).

Integer arithmetic and logical
Address
Variable-length bit-field
Control
Procedure call
Miscellaneous
Queue
Floating-point arithmetic
Character string
Cyclic redundancy check
Decimal string
Edit

We have already seen many of the integer arithmetic instructions, the address instructions, the procedure call instructions, and many of the control instructions. We will discuss the logical instructions, the variable-length bit-field instructions, and more of the integer arithmetic instructions in this chapter; we will discuss floating-point arithmetic instructions in chapter 13. Thus, we will discuss a large number of the VAX's instructions, but we will *not* discuss all of them. Our primary goal, in this book, is to gain an understanding of computer architecture by examining major elements of the VAX's organization; a discussion of the VAX's more complex and special-purpose instructions will not help us attain that goal.

Although we will discuss, in the remainder of this chapter, functional groups of instructions, grouping instructions by format is simpler when we are first learning about a computer. For example, if we had discussed functionally related instructions in chapter 3, we would have considered the 2- and 3-operand ADD instructions, the 2- and 3-operand MUL instructions (which we will see soon), and the single-operand INC instruction--simultaneously!

Logical Operations

The logical operations are in the same group as the integer arithmetic operations because such seemingly essential operations as addition and subtraction are actually derived from these more fundamental operations. Most computers have instructions for performing logical functions such as **and, or (inclusive or), not,** and **exclusive or.** We have already seen truth tables for the inclusive and exclusive **or** functions; in this section we will see that the VAX has instructions that implement these functions, as well as the **and** and **not** logical functions.

These functions are called *logical* operations because their operands can only have the logical values T or F (for True and False). We will equate T with 1 and F with 0. These are also called **Boolean** operations because George Boole discovered many useful relationships in this area over one hundred years ago.

Not: MCOM

The simplest logical operator is **not.** It has a single operand; this unary operator is often represented by placing a "~" or a "¬" in front of the operand, or by placing a horizontal line over it. Thus, given a logical variable, x (when we call x a logical variable, we mean that it can only assume two values: T or F, or 1 or 0), *not x* can be written as ~x, as ¬x, or as $\bar{x}$. We typically read $\bar{x}$ as x *bar*; it is equally correct to read it as *not x*. Given the logical variable, x, *not x* is defined by the following relationship:

¬$0 = 1$; ¬$1 = 0$.

x	not x
0	1
1	0

Figure 10.1 Truth table for **not**

It is always true that $(\neg x) \equiv x$. Another way to describe this logical function is by its **truth table** (we have seen truth tables in chapter 7); the truth table for the unary (single input) **not** function is shown in figure 10.1.

The VAX handles logical variables in groups of 8, 16 or 32 at a time. The logical operation **not** is implemented on the VAX as the MCOM(B,W,L) (move complemented) family of instructions. When one of the MCOM(B,W,L) S, D instructions is executed, each bit of the S operand is **not**-ed, or complemented (each 0 is replaced by a 1, and each 1 is replaced by a 0), and the result is stored in the location specified by the D operand. Recall from our discussion of the ones complement number system (in chapter 7) that the result produced by the MCOM(B,W,L) instructions is the ones complement of the S operand.

If we have written

X: .WORD ^X743A

then if we execute the instruction MCOMW X, Y, Y will contain $8BC5_{16}$. The N and Z bits of the CC are set according to the result; the V bit is cleared, and the C bit does not change.

And: BIT

The logical operator **and**, symbolized by an inverted v or by an ampersand (&), is a function with 2 operands. For two logical variables, x and y, we can define the **and** function from its truth table, shown in figure 10.2. The logical **and** of two variables is true (1) only if *each* of those variables is true (1). On the VAX, the instruction that implements the logical function **and** is the BIT(B,W,L) (bit test) family of instructions. These are 2-operand instructions; their format is BIT(B,W,L) S, D. A BIT instruction calculates the logical **and** of its S (source) and D (destination) operands, but doesn't change either of them. Like the CMP instructions, the BIT instructions' only result is to change the CC bits.

If, for example, we execute a BITB R0, R1 instruction, the logical **and** of the corresponding low-order 8 bits from R0 and R1 is calculated. If the *entire* result is 0 (if the logical **and** of each and every one of the corresponding pairs of bits is 0), then the CC's Z bit is set; otherwise it is cleared. If the logical **and** of the most significant pair of bits is 1, then the N bit is set; otherwise it is cleared. The V bit is always cleared, and the C bit is unchanged.

x	y	x and y
0	0	0
0	1	0
1	0	0
1	1	1

Figure 10.2 Truth table for **and**

x	y	x **or** y
0	0	0
0	1	1
1	0	1
1	1	1

Figure 10.3 Truth table for **inclusive or**

The typical way to use a BIT(B,W,L) instruction is to think of the first operand as a *mask*. For example, suppose we want to know if bit 5 of item Q is set; item Q contains the T/F answers for 8 questions. The mask ^X20 will select bit 5 (recall that, on the VAX, bits are numbered from right to left, beginning with 0). So, the instruction BITB #^X20, Q has the following effect: if Q contains, for example, $1A_{16}$, then the result of the BITB instruction (which is *not* stored anywhere) is 00_{16}; the Z bit is 1 and the N bit is 0. If Q contains 36_{16}, then the result of the BITB instruction is 20_{16}; the Z bit is 0, and the N bit is still 0.

We can also use the BIT instruction to examine several bits simultaneously. For example, to see if any of the 3 low-order bits of longword WIZ are set, we can write the following code:

```
        BITL #^X7, WIZ
        BNEQ SomeOn
;or:
        BITL #^X7, WIZ
        BEQL NoneOn
```

Or: BIS

We have already seen the truth table for logical (inclusive) **or,** in figure 7.21; it is reproduced in figure 10.3 for convenience. The logical **or** operation is represented by a lower case v, by a vertical bar, "|", or by a plus sign, "+". It is a function with two inputs, as shown in figure 10.3; the logical **or** of two variables is true if either variable is true, or if both are true. Figure 10.4 shows an everyday use of the **or** function.

The logical **or** function is provided by the VAX BIS(B,W,L)[2,3] (bit set) family of instructions. These are 2- or 3-operand instructions; in the former case, their format is BIS(B,W,L)2 S, D, and in the latter case their format is BIS(B,W,L)3 S_1, S_2, D. In both cases, the first operand (S or S_1) is thought of as a mask; the bit-wise logical **or** of the mask and the second operand (D or S_2) is calculated, and the result is stored in the location specified by the D operand.

The BIS instructions, as their mnemonic suggests, are used to *set* a certain combination of bits in the destination operand. Thus, the instruction BISB2 #^X81, A will set both the most and least significant bits of A. Note that these bits will be set *regardless* of their former value: this is because the **or** of 1 and 0 is 1, and the **or** of 1 and 1 is also 1. Note also that, for the same reason, any bits that are not 1 in the mask will remain unchanged in the destination. The N and Z bits of the CC are updated according to the result, as expected; the V bit is cleared, and the C bit is unchanged.

Reprinted by permission of NEA, Inc.

Figure 10.4 A very, very inclusive **or**

Bit Clear: BIC

The BIC(B,W,L)[2,3] (bit clear) instructions combine the **not** function with the **and** function: the destination operand is replaced by the bit-wise logical **and** of the ones complement of the first operand (S, or S_1) and the second operand (D, or S_2). If we think of the first operand as a mask (again), then for each bit of the mask that is *set,* the corresponding bit of the destination will be *cleared.*

For example, suppose we want to clear every other hexadecimal digit in longword WOW; we can write BICL2 #^X0F0F0F0F, WOW. If WOW contains 12345678_{16} before the instruction is executed, the instruction will compute **not** $0F0F0F0F_{16}$ **and** 12345678_{16}; this is equivalent to $F0F0F0F0_{16}$ **and** 12345678_{16}, which is 10305070_{16}. The N and Z bits are set according to the result; the V bit is cleared, and the C bit is unchanged.

Exclusive Or: XOR

We also discussed **exclusive or** in chapter 7; we saw its truth table in figure 7.18, and we have reproduced it in figure 10.5 for convenience. **Exclusive or** is a logical function with two inputs; we

x	y	x **xor** y
0	0	0
0	1	1
1	0	1
1	1	0

Figure 10.5 Truth table for **exclusive or**

typically represent it as **xor,** as a V with a line through it ($\forall$), as "not equal" ($\neq$), or as a plus inside a circle ($\oplus$). If two logical variables, x and y, are unequal, then x **xor** y is True; if they are equal (both 1 or both 0), then x **xor** y is False. Clearly, x **xor** x is always False.

The VAX implements the **exclusive or** logical function with the XOR(B,W,L)[2,3] family of instructions. Once more, the first operand (S or S_1) is considered a mask, and the bit-wise **exclusive or** of the mask and the second operand (D or S_2) is calculated; the result is stored in the location specified by the destination operand. Consider an example of the use of the XOR instruction: suppose we are machine-grading a True/False test. With the XOR instruction, we can compare responses to 32 questions at a time: SA is the location in which 32 student answers--represented as a series of 1s and 0s, corresponding to T and F--are stored, and the correct answers are similarly stored in R6. If we execute the instruction XORL3 SA, R6, R7, then R7 will contain a 1 for each question where the student and the grader have different answers. We can count the 1s in R7 to see how many answers are wrong (we will see a way to count 1s shortly). For example, suppose that R6 contains $03AF9786_{16}$ and SA contains $13EF9806_{16}$. If we convert these to binary, it is clear which answers are wrong, and what the result of the XOR instruction will be:

```
R6   00000011101011111001011110000110
SA   00010011111011111001100000000110
R7   00010000010000000000111110000000
```

In hex, the result is 10400F80; there are 7 incorrect answers.

If we rewrite the **xor** truth table as a **look-up table,** as shown in figure 10.6, we notice a striking similarity between the **xor** function and the binary addition table, reproduced from figure 3.2 as figure 10.7. The only difference between them is the **carry** for the sum of 1 and 1, in the addition table. We will see, when we discuss computer hardware, that computers often use the **xor** function to build the hardware that performs binary addition. The difference between the **xor** truth table and the binary addition table, however, must be taken into account.

xor	0	1
0	0	1
1	1	0

Figure 10.6 Look-up table for **exclusive or**

+	0	1
0	0	1
1	1	(1)0

Figure 10.7 Binary addition table

The Rotate Instruction

The rotate instruction rotates the bits of a longword to the left or right, in a circular fashion, a specified number of times. It may seem strange to consider this a logical operation, but the rotate instruction treats neighboring bits independently of each other: bits are treated as independent logical values. We will soon see another rotate-*like* instruction that treats the bits in its operand as part of a signed binary number; the two instructions have very different effects.

The instruction ROTL COUNT, S, D rotates the S operand COUNT bits, and places the result in the location specified by the D operand. The COUNT operand is only one byte long, but the S and D operands are longwords; if the count is positive the operand is rotated to the left, if the count is negative the operand is rotated to the right, and if the count is 0, the D operand is replaced by the S operand.

What does it mean to rotate a number in a circular fashion? With a COUNT of 1, the ROTL instruction moves each bit one place to the left; what happens to bit 31 (the leftmost bit), which cannot be moved to its left? Bit 31 is rotated into the bit 0 position, as bit 0 is rotated into the bit 1 position, bit 1 into the bit 2 position, and so on. Similarly, with a negative count, bit 0 (the rightmost bit)--which cannot be moved to its right--is rotated into bit 31 (the leftmost bit). So, rotating a longword to the right or the left 32 times is the same as rotating it 0 times: each bit returns to its original position. Figure 10.8 shows schematically what occurs when the ROTL instruction is executed.

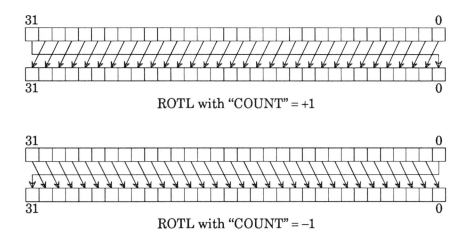

Figure 10.8 Operation of the ROTL instruction

Instruction	Mnemonic	Opcode	Action
Move complemented	MCOM(B,W,L) S, D	92, B2, D2	D←¬S
Bit test	BIT(B,W,L) S, D	93, B3, D3	S and D sets CC
Bit set, 2-operand	BIS(B,W,L)2 S, D	88, A8, C8	D←S or D
Bit set, 3-operand	BIS(B,W,L)3 S_1, S_2, D	89, A9, C9	D←S_1 or S_2
Bit clear, 2-operand	BIC(B,W,L)2 S, D	8A, AA, CA	D←¬S and D
Bit clear, 3-operand	BIC(B,W,L)3 S_1, S_2, D	8B, AB, CB	D←¬S_1 and S_2
Exclusive or, 2-operand	XOR(B,W,L)2 S, D	8C, AC, CC	D←S xor D
Exclusive or, 3-operand	XOR(B,W,L)3 S_1, S_2, D	8D, AD, CD	D←S_1 xor S_2
Rotate longword	ROTL COUNT, S, D	9C	D←S rotated COUNT times

Figure 10.9 Logical instruction summary

For example, if we begin with R7 containing 12345678_{16}, and execute ROTL #4, R7, R8, then 12345678_{16} will be rotated 4 bits to the left, and the result, 23456781_{16}, will be stored in R8. We can also use the ROTL instruction to count the number of 1s in a longword; this allows us to use the XOR instruction for machine grading a True/False test, as suggested above. Consider the following code fragment:

```
        MOVL CORRECT, R6        ;answer key
        CLRB WRONG              ;start with 0 wrong
        XORL3 R6, SA, R7        ;R7 has wrong answers now
        BEQL DONE              ;none wrong
;else, count number of 1s in R7: rotate, and check msb (N bit)
        MOVL #32, R2           ;loop control: 32 times
NEXT:   ROTL #1, R7, R7        ;rotate R7 once left
        BGEQ OK                ;N bit clear: msb = 0
;else, N bit set: incorrect answer
        INCB WRONG             ;another error
OK:     SOBGTR R2, NEXT
```

After we execute this fragment, WRONG will contain the number of incorrect answers found in SA.

Logical Operation Summary

The VAX instructions that implement logical operations all deal with operands in a bit-wise manner: every bit in a byte, for example, is independent of every other bit. Figure 10.9 summarizes the operation of the instructions that we have discussed in this section.

Variable-Length Bit-Field Instructions

The VAX has instructions for extracting, inserting, or comparing bit strings, from 1 to 32 bits long. The variable-length bit-field instructions are related to the logical instructions because both are appropriate when a longword is used as a collection of 32 binary values (such as True/False) rather than a single integer value. We might use bit-field instructions if we were writing a routine to

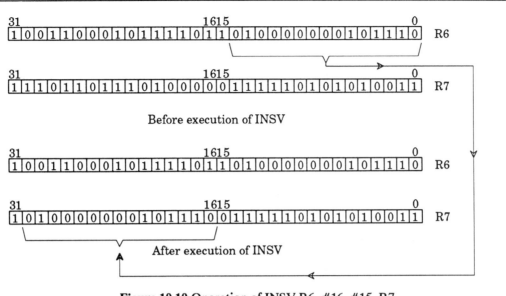

Figure 10.10 Operation of INSV R6, #16, #15, R7

maintain a **memory map,** indicating which portions of memory are currently allocated and which locations are still available; multiuser operating systems typically have such memory maps. If memory is always allocated in **blocks** (of, for example, 512 bytes), then we can think of memory as an array of *blocks* (rather than bytes, words, or longwords), and create another array of *bits.* Bit 0 of the bit array would correspond to block 0 of memory, bit 1 would correspond to block 1, and bit n to block n. If bit 1 were set, it would indicate that block 1 is in use; if it were clear, it would indicate that block 1 is available. We could use bit-field instructions to find free blocks of memory, to set a bit when the corresponding block is no longer free because the loader has just loaded a program into it, and to clear a bit when the block is no longer needed (because, for example, the program that was using it has executed the $EXIT_S system call, indicating that it has completed).

A bit string is specified by 3 operands: the base address of the string, the position of the first bit of the string relative to the base address, and the number of bits in the string. The bit-field instructions typically have a fourth operand specifying the destination of the bit string specified with the other 3 operands.

The Extract-Field Instructions

There are two instructions for extracting bit strings; one--EXTV--*sign*-extends the bit string into the destination; the other--EXTZV--*zero*-extends the bit string into the destination. The format of these instructions is EXT(Z)V POS, SIZE, BASE, D. In both cases, SIZE bits are extracted, beginning with bit number POS, from address BASE; the bit string is either sign-extended or zero-extended, and placed into the longword specified by D. For example, if we wish to extract bit 0 from R4 and zero-extend it into R5, we would execute the instruction EXTZV #0, #1, R4, R5. If we wish to extract bits numbered 12 through 17 from R8 and sign-extend them into R9, we would execute the instruction EXTV #12, #6, R8, R9. We discussed sign extension and zero extension in Chapter 7; we use the former to extract a *signed* number, and the latter an *unsigned* number that we have stored as a bit string.

The Compare-Field Instructions

There are also two instructions for comparing bit fields: one compares the *sign*-extended bit string with the instruction's fourth operand (CMPV), and the other compares the *zero*-extended bit string with the fourth operand (CMPZV). As with the other CMP instructions, these change only the CC bit settings, in the expected manner: if the bit string (zero-extended or sign-extended, depending on the instruction) is less than the fourth operand as signed numbers, the N bit is set; if the bit string is less than the fourth operand as unsigned numbers then the C bit is set; if the bit string and the fourth operand are equal then the Z bit is set; the V bit is always cleared. The format of these instructions is CMP(Z)V POS, SIZE, BASE, S; the fourth operand is called S, for source, because it does not change.

The Insert Field Instruction

The VAX also has an instruction for inserting a specified number of low-order bits from a longword into an arbitrary bit string. Its format is INSV S, POS, SIZE, BASE; the SIZE low-order bits from the location specified by S (these are bits numbered 0 through SIZE-1) are inserted into the SIZE bit positions starting with bit number POS in the longword at address BASE. Thus, to insert the low-order 15 bits from R6 into the high-order word of R7, we would execute the instruction INSV R6, #16, #15, R7. Figure 10.10 is a schematic representation of the operation of this instruction.

The Find-First-Bit Instructions

The remaining variable-length bit-field instructions are used for finding the first bit set (FFS), or the first bit clear (FFC), in a specified bit string. The format of these instructions is FF(SC) POS, SIZE, BASE, FINDPOS. The first 3 operands of these instructions specify a bit string in the manner of the other bit-field instructions. If a bit is found set (or clear, depending on the instruction), then the Z bit of the CC is 0, and the position where the bit was found is returned in the longword that is the instructions's fourth operand. If no bit is found set (for the FFS instruction) or clear (for the FFC instruction), the Z bit is set, and the fourth operand contains the number of the bit *after* the last bit of the field. For example, if we execute the instruction FFS #0, #32, R1, R2, the following table indicates the results of the instruction, for different values of R1 (all values are hexadecimal):

R1	R2	Z bit
0	32	1
1	0	0
2	1	0
8	3	0
9	0	0
80	7	0

Instruction	Mnemonic	Opcode	Action
Extract field, sign-extend	EXTV POS, SIZE, BASE, D	EE	see text
Extract field, zero-extend	EXTZV POS, SIZE, BASE, D	EF	see text
Compare field, sign-extend	CMPV POS, SIZE, BASE, S	EC	see text
Compare field, zero-extend	CMPZV POS, SIZE, BASE, S	ED	see text
Insert field	INSV S, POS, SIZE, BASE	F0	see text
Find first bit set	FFS POS, SIZE, BASE, FINDPOS	EA	see text
Find first bit clear	FFC POS, SIZE, BASE, FINDPOS	EB	see text

Figure 10.11 Variable-length bit-field instruction summary

Summary of Variable-Length Bit-Field Instructions

Figure 10.11 is a summary of the variable-length bit-field instructions. The POS operand always specifies a longword, as do the S operand (for the CMP(Z)V and INSV instructions) and the D operand (for the EXT(Z)V instructions). The SIZE operand always specifies a byte; this operand can be no larger than 32. If the bit field is in a register, and the SIZE operand is not 0, then the POS operand must be no greater than 31; if the field is *not* in a register, the POS operand is not constrained. This is so because in memory, which has contiguous addresses, a POS value of 32 is equivalent to a POS value of 0 with a BASE value of the address of the next longword (thus, EXTV #0, #1, BASE+4, R4 and EXTV #32, #1, BASE, R4 are equivalent); registers, however, are not contiguous in this manner.

Multiplication and Division

The VAX has both general-purpose multiplication and division instructions, and a special instruction that multiplies or divides a number by any power of 2. These instructions treat their operands as signed numbers, and produce results that are correct (if possible) as signed numbers. Recall that this is different from the VAX's instructions for addition and subtraction, which--because of the twos complement number representation--produce the correct result (if possible) for both signed *and* unsigned operands. We will briefly describe these instructions in the following sections.

Arithmetic Shift: ASHL

The format of the arithmetic shift instruction is ASHL COUNT, S, D. This appears to be similar to the rotate instruction, ROTL: both instructions have 3 operands: the first is a 1-byte count, the second is a source operand that is to be shifted COUNT bits, and the third specifies the destination location in which the result is to be stored. Further, the source operand of both instructions is shifted to the left if COUNT is positive, and to the right if COUNT is negative. However, ROTL is a logical instruction, while ASHL is an arithmetic instruction; what difference does this make? The rotate instruction rotates bits in a circular manner: every bit is independent of every other bit (we have seen how to use the instruction to count the number of 1s in a longword). The arithmetic shift instruction, on the other hand, is used to multiply and divide signed numbers by powers of 2; the source is treated as a single (32-bit) integer rather than 32 (1-bit) logical values.

Why would we use the ASHL instruction? When we multiply a decimal number by a power of 10, we can perform *longhand* multiplication, or we can shift each digit in the number to the left once for each power of 10 we multiply it by, and add a trailing zero each time we shift the number. Thus, 100 is 10^2, so when we multiply 16 times 100, we add 2 trailing 0s, and 16 * 100 = 1600. Similarly, when we divide a decimal number by a power of 10, we can perform the general case division, or we can shift each digit to the right once for each power of 10 we divide it by (if the low-order digits are not 0s, we must either save them--as the remainder--or be satisfied with an approximate answer). In binary, of course, the same relationship holds: multiplying a binary number by a power of 2 may be done by shifting the number to the left, and dividing it by a power of 2 may be done by shifting the number to the right.

When we use the ASHL instruction with a positive count, each bit is shifted to the left COUNT times, and the low-order COUNT bits are filled with 0s; this is equivalent to multiplying the source by 2 for each bit position shifted: 10_2 shifted left once is 100_2, and 2 * 2 = 4. What happens to the *high*-order bits when we use ASHL with a *negative* count, and shift each bit to the right? Bit 31 of the source operand (the pseudo-sign bit) is copied into the high-order COUNT places of the destination; this assures that the source and destination operands will be either both positive or both negative--as they should be.

How are the CC bits set for the ASHL instruction? The N and Z bits are set as expected; the V bit is set if the msb of the source operand differs from that of the destination operand (because we shifted a negative number to the left "too many" times), and the C bit is always cleared. If COUNT is larger than 32, the destination operand is 0; if COUNT is less than -32, all bits of the destination operand are copies of the msb of the source operand. Because of these special cases, the result of the ASHL instruction is not always correct: for example, $-1 \div 2 = -1$, and $80000000_{16} * 2 = 0$!

Multiplication In General

Some computers have no multiply or divide instructions; these operations are constructed out of a series of shifts and adds, or shifts and subtracts. For example, to multiply the number X by 5, a user of such a computer might write the following code sequence:

```
MOVL X, R6
ASHL #2, R6, R7      ;R7 ← R6 * 4
ADDL2 R6, R7         ;R7 ← R6 * 5
```

These three instructions might actually execute as fast as, or faster than, a multiply instruction on the VAX (or any other computer with similar instructions). However, for more complex cases, a general-purpose multiply instruction is often faster, and certainly easier to program correctly, than a combination of shifts and additions or subtractions.

The MUL Instructions

The VAX has a family of multiply instructions that is similar to its families of other arithmetic instructions: the operands can be bytes, words, or longwords, and there are 2- and 3-operand versions. For the 2-operand multiply instructions, the format is MUL(B,W,L)2 S, D; for the 3-operand multiply instructions, the format is MUL(B,W,L)3 S_1, S_2, D. As usual, in the 2-operand case the result (the product of the S and D operands) is stored in the location specified by the D operand, and in the 3-operand case the product of the S_1 and S_2 operands is stored in the location specified by the D operand.

Multiplication is different from other arithmetic operations in that the product of two n-bit numbers is typically a $2n$-bit number; this is the case for decimal and binary multiplication, as well as multiplication in any other base. If, then, a MULB3 instruction computes the product of 2 bytes, how can it store a 16-bit result in the destination, if the destination is also only 1 byte long? Clearly it can't; the designers of the VAX decided that only the low-order 8 bits of the result of the MULB[2,3] instructions--and only the low-order 16 bits of the result of the MULW[2,3] instructions, and only the low-order 32 bits of the result of the MULL[2,3] instructions--are stored in the destination operand location. If the result has more significant bits than can be stored, then the full result will *not* be equal to the sign extension of the low half of the result, and the V bit will be set.

The EMUL Instruction

If we expect that the product of two 32-bit operands will not fit in 32 bits, then we can use the EMUL--extended multiply--instruction. The format of the extended multiply instruction is EMUL S_1, S_2, A, D; the product of the 32-bit S_1 and S_2 operands is computed, the 32-bit A operand is added to this product, and the result is stored in the location specified by the D operand. If we do not wish to add anything to the product, we can specify 0 as the A operand.

The result of the EMUL instruction is 64 bits; where, exactly, does this result go? We have already seen that a particular address can be the address of a byte, of a word, or of a longword; in each case, the address is of the *low*-order byte, and the context (the type of instruction) makes it clear what size location the address refers to. In the case of the EMUL instruction, the destination operand specifies a **quadword**[2]--8 consecutive bytes. So, just as the address of a longword is the same as the address of its low-order byte, so the address of a quadword is the address of its low-order byte. What about specifying a destination operand using register mode--for example, EMUL R4, R4, #0, R6? In this case, both R6 *and* R7 will change; the low-order 32 bits of the result will be in R6, and the high-order 32 bits will be in R7.

Division in General

Division, like multiplication, need not be implemented in hardware: if we are writing programs on a computer that doesn't have a divide instruction, we can create such an instruction from others. In particular, as multiplication is, essentially, repeated addition, so division is repeated subtraction. In the general case, however, it is even more difficult to write the correct sequence of instructions to implement division than it is to implement multiplication, so many computers, including the VAX, have divide instructions.

The DIV Instructions

If we think back to our first introduction to division (probably in third or fourth grade), we may recall that when we divide, we divide a **dividend** by a **divisor,** to produce a **quotient** and a **remainder;** this is *integer* division. Thus, dividing 137 (the dividend) by 10 (the divisor) produces a quotient of 13 and a remainder of 7. Many of us habitually use calculators that represent the result of a division as a real number (with an integer part and a fraction part, separated by a decimal point). The VAX division instructions that we are about to discuss perform *integer* division, and operate in a manner similar to that which we learned many years ago, and which we probably still do when we divide "by hand."

The VAX has 2- and 3-operand divide instructions, that deal with bytes, words, or longwords. The format of the 2-operand instructions is DIV(B,W,L)2 S, D, and the format of the 3-operand instructions is DIV(B,W,L)3 S_1, S_2, D. For the 2-operand instructions, the D operand (the dividend) is

---

[2]Some models of the VAX provide a quadword counterpart for nearly every byte, word, and longword instruction.

divided by the S operand (the divisor), and the D operand is replaced by the quotient. For the 3-operand instructions, the S_2 operand (the dividend) is divided by the S_1 operand (the divisor), and the quotient is stored in the location specified by the D operand. For both the formats, the remainder, if any, is lost.

Division may be thought of as *backward* multiplication: if we divide an integer dividend by an integer divisor, the quotient will be smaller than the dividend (unless the divisor is 1, in which case the dividend and quotient will be the same). Therefore, the only things that can go wrong with division are caused by dividing by 0, and dividing the most negative number by -1. If the divisor is 0, the quotient is infinite; on the VAX, the quotient of a 2-operand instruction with a divisor of 0 is unchanged, and the quotient of a 3-operand instruction with a divisor of 0 is replaced by the dividend. If we divide the most negative number by -1, the quotient will be the same as the dividend, because--in the twos complement number system--the negation of the most negative number is itself. This is the wrong answer (for example, -128 ÷ -1 = +128, *not* -128), so the V bit will be set. The V bit is also set when the divisor is 0; the C bit is always cleared after a DIV(B,W,L)[2,3] instruction, and the N and Z bits are set according to the value of the quotient.

The EDIV Instruction

As there is an extended multiply instruction, so there is also an extended divide instruction--EDIV. The format of the EDIV instruction is EDIV S_1, S_2, Q, R: the S_2 operand is divided by the S_1 operand; the quotient is stored in the location specified by the Q operand, and the remainder is stored in the location specified by the R operand. The S_1, Q and R operands are all longwords; the S_2 operand is a quadword. The sign of the remainder is the same as the sign of the dividend (the S_2 operand).

The EDIV instruction can be used to divide a divisor that is too big for 32 bits (just as the EMUL instruction can be used to produce a product that is too big for 32 bits). If the divisor is larger than 32 bits, then if the dividend is "too small," the quotient won't fit in 32 bits; we will get an incorrect answer, and the V bit will be set.

EDIV is also used when we wish to save the remainder as well as the quotient of a division; we would use the remainder generated by EDIV to implement Pascal's **mod** function. We will see a use of the EDIV instruction to save the remainder in the next section, when we discuss processing ASCII coded numeric data.

Summary of Multiply and Divide Instructions

Figure 10.12 summarizes the VAX's shift, multiply, and divide instructions; the CC bit settings are summarized in Appendix 3, and additional details of the operation of these instructions are in the *Vax Architecture Reference Manual*. It is important to remember that these instructions *always* treat their operands as signed numbers.

Processing ASCII Coded Numeric Data

Numeric information is usually transmitted to a computer using one character code (such as the ASCII code) to represent each digit. For example, the decimal number 123 would be encoded as the series of bytes 31_{16}, 32_{16}, 33_{16}. If we use an ASCII terminal and type the following line (and then press the *return* key)

123 + 304

Instruction	Mnemonic	Opcode	Action
Arithmetic shift long	ASHL C, S, D	78	$D \leftarrow S$ shifted C bits
Multiply, 2-operand	MUL(B,W,L)2 S, D	84, A4, C4	$D \leftarrow S * D$
Multiply, 3-operand	MUL(B,W,L)3 S_1, S_2, D	85, A5, C5	$D \leftarrow S_1 * S_2$
Extended multiply	EMUL S_1, S_2, A, D	7A	$D \leftarrow (S_1 * S_2) + A$
Divide, 2-operand	DIV(B,W,L)2 S, D	86, A6, C6	$D \leftarrow D \div S$
Divide, 3-operand	DIV(B,W,L)3 S_1, S_2, D	87, A7, C7	$D \leftarrow S_2 \div S_1$
Extended divide	EDIV S_1, S_2, Q, R	7B	$Q \leftarrow S_2 \div S_1$; $R \leftarrow S_2$ mod S_1

Figure 10.12 Shift, multiply, and divide instruction summary

then the string of bytes (in hex) that is generated by the terminal and sent to the computer is:

31 32 33 20 2B 20 33 30 34 0D

On some systems the ASCII code for the *return* key ($0D_{16}$) is replaced, by the system software, with the ASCII code for *line feed* ($0A_{16}$); this is not the case with VMS, and it is not important for the present example. But if we were writing a program to read input from the keyboard, we would probably have our program scan the input for the *carriage return* character, to know when we had found the end of an input line; it would be necessary to know which character to look for.

How can we process such input from a terminal? We want to add two numbers; how do we do it? If we had the binary numbers 1111011 (123) and 100110000 (304) in memory, then we could simply execute an ADDW[2,3] or ADDL[2,3] instruction, specifying those numbers as the operands. However, when the input comes from a terminal, we have the binary representation of the above ASCII codes for the decimal digits and other characters in memory: 00110001 (31), 00110010 (32), 00110011 (33), 00100000 (20), 00101011 (2B), 00100000 (20), 00110011 (33), 00110000 (30), 00110100 (34), and 00001101 (0D). There are two methods for processing such ASCII coded numeric information. One involves converting each ASCII character string into the binary integer that the string represents, and the other involves adding the ASCII representations of the decimal digits themselves. We will examine the first method first; we will see that the multiply instructions are particularly useful for converting ASCII coded decimal character strings into binary integers, and that the EDIV instruction is useful for the reverse conversion.

Conversion from ASCII Coded Decimal Digits to Binary Integers

If our program reads its input and stores it in a series of bytes in memory, it can then examine the string of bytes, convert the two digit strings (separated by codes for space, "+", and space, which are 20, 2B and 20) into the binary numbers they represent, and then add them and store the sum.

The process of converting a string of ASCII codes for digits into the number that the digit string represents is straightforward when we realize two facts. First, the ASCII code for each digit is 30_{16} more than the number the digit represents. Thus, the ASCII code for the character "0" is 30_{16}, the ASCII code for the character "1" is 31_{16}, and so on. Second, the digits in a digit string have different *weights*. For example, the leftmost 2 and the rightmost 2 in 222_{10} represent very different values: the former represents 200 ($2 * 10^2$), while the latter represents 2 ($2 * 10^0$).[3] Keeping these two facts in mind, we can create the following algorithm for converting a string of ASCII coded digits into the number they represent:

1. Subtract 30_{16} from the ASCII code; call this the *running sum*. The running sum now contains the binary number that this ASCII code represents.
2. If there are no more ASCII digit codes, then we are done, and the running sum contains the binary number that the ASCII digit string represents.
3. If there is another ASCII digit code, multiply the running sum by 10_{10}, subtract 30_{16} from the next ASCII digit code, and add that number to the running sum. Go to step 2.

Let's apply the above algorithm to the example we have been using and convert the ASCII codes for the character string "123" into the number 123. We will have stored the three bytes, 31_{16}, 32_{16} and 33_{16}; if we stored them in the order in which they were received (which is the order in which they were typed and sent), then 31 is stored in the first byte, 32 in the second, and 33 in the third:

Step	Operation	Running Sum
1	31 - 30 = 1	1
2	more digits? yes	1
3	1 * 10 = 10; 32 - 30 = 2	10 + 2 = 12
2	more digits? yes	12
3	12 * 10 = 120; 33 - 30 = 3	120 + 3 = 123
2	more digits? no: done	123

We can use the same algorithm to convert the ASCII codes for 304 (33_{16}, 30_{16}, 34_{16}) into the integer 304, and then it is straightforward to add the two integers and store the sum, 427. If we had encountered the ASCII code for "-" ($2D_{16}$) rather than that for "+", we would have converted the two numbers in exactly the same way, but we would *subtract* them rather than *add* them after the conversion.

Conversion from Binary Integers to ASCII Coded Decimal Digits

The algorithm above for converting a string of ASCII character codes for digits into the integer they represent is only part of the work. Once we have converted the digit string into an integer, we can process it as necessary. However, we typically want to *see* the results of the processing that we do; in order to see those results, we often display them on a terminal's screen, or send them to the line printer. In either case, we will have to convert the integer(s) that we have computed into a string of ASCII character codes (for decimal digits, unless we want the output to be in hex, or some other base). This conversion process is the reverse of the one for converting an ASCII coded digit string into an integer; it will use repeated division, where the previous one used repeated multiplication.

The algorithm for converting a binary integer into a string of ASCII coded decimal digits is as follows:

1. Divide the integer by 10_{10} (since we are converting to base 10).
2. The remainder is the next rightmost digit of the string; add 30_{16} to it to convert it to an ASCII coded digit.

---

[3]This, of course, is because, in any base, successive positions in a digit string represent successive powers of that base.

3.   If the quotient is 0, the conversion process is complete; if the quotient is *not* 0, let the integer to be converted be the quotient, and go to step 1.

Continuing our example, we have converted the digit strings "123" and "304" into the integers they represent, and we have added them, producing the result 427--which is 110101011_2, or $1AB_{16}$. To convert it to a string of ASCII coded decimal digits, we perform the following steps:

Step	Number	Operation	Digit String
1	427	$427 \div 10^1 = 42$ R 7	?
2	427	7 + 30 = 37	37
3	427	set number = 42	37
1	42	$42 \div 10^1 = 4$ R 2	37
2	42	2 + 30 = 32	32 37
3	42	set number = 4	32 37
1	4	$4 \div 10^1 = 0$ R 4	32 37
2	4	4 + 30 = 34	34 32 37
3	4	quotient = 0; done	34 32 37

Now, all we need to do is transform the above algorithms into code (as subroutines, perhaps), and we will be able to compute with data provided as a sequence of ASCII character codes, and produce output that can be displayed on a terminal or lineprinter. There is a tradeoff, however: if we plan to do only a little computing with some data--for example, if we are only going to add one number to another one--then the work of converting from ASCII codes to binary integers, and then converting integers back into strings of ASCII codes, is too time-consuming. In such a case, we can use the technique we will examine next. If, on the other hand, we expect to do a considerable amount of computing with a number, then the conversion is worthwhile. This tradeoff is due to the fact that converting from ASCII codes to integers, and then back to ASCII codes, requires considerable effort, but adding binary integers is very simple. On the other hand, we can avoid the work of conversion, but adding strings of ASCII codes is more time-consuming than adding binary integers.

ASCII Coded Decimal Arithmetic

How can we add two numbers without first converting them to binary? The answer to this question requires a return to first principles. How do we, when we don't have the aid of a calculator, add *big* numbers? We process them one digit pair at a time--just as we first did binary addition, in chapter 3.

Using the example we have already seen, let's try adding the ASCII character codes for 123 and 304 (we will also have to compensate for the extra 30 from adding *two* character codes):

100s place	10s place	1s place	Number
31	32	33	123
+ 33	+ 30	+ 34	+ 304
64	62	67	427
− 30	− 30	− 30	
34	32	37	

The reason to add the ASCII codes directly is to save the time of converting *from* ASCII codes to integers and then, right away, back from integers into ASCII codes. Adding the codes themselves make sense when we realize that there is a direct relationship between the ASCII code and the number it represents--namely, the code is 30_{16} greater than the number. However, when we add two ASCII codes, we are adding this 30_{16} *twice*: the sum is no longer an ASCII code for a digit. But, as the above example illustrates, the sum of two ASCII codes is only 30_{16} more than an ASCII code-- and not just *any* ASCII code, but the ASCII code that represents the sum of the two numbers whose ASCII codes we just added. So, we add the codes, subtract 30_{16} from the sum, and we have the ASCII code for the sum.

However, things may not always turn out so simply. Consider adding 345 and 507:

100s place	10s place	1s place	Number
33	34	35	345
+ 35	+ 30	+ 37	+ 507
68	64	6C	852
− 30	− 30	− 30	
38	34	3C	

The numbers 38_{16}, 34_{16} and $3C_{16}$ are the ASCII codes for "8", "4" and "<"; what number does the string "84<" represent? None, of course; what has gone wrong is that the sum of 5 and 7 generated a carry into the next digit position: we need to check for carry and "fix things up" when it occurs.

So, if we wish to write a program to perform arithmetic on ASCII coded decimal digits, we must modify our procedure slightly. After adding the two ASCII codes and subtracting 30_{16}, we must check to see if the result is larger than the ASCII code for 9, which is 39_{16}. If it is, then we subtract the number A_{16} (which is 10_{10}) from that ASCII code, and we add 1 to the sum of the next (from right to left) pair of ASCII codes. Thus, in the example above, we would first add the ASCII codes for the low-order digits: 35 + 37 = 6C. Then we would subtract 30: 6C - 30 = 3C. We would notice that 3C > 39, so, we would subtract 10: 3C - A = 32, and then add 1 to the tens place number (so the next addition will be 35 + 30). The hundreds place digit doesn't change, and we end up with the ASCII codes 38, 35, and 32; these are the codes for "8", "5", and "2", and 852 is the correct answer.

There might, of course, be more than one carry in an addition: work out the details for adding 567 + 894, for example. However, if we check for a result greater than the ASCII code for 9, we can handle carry from the tens to the hundreds place just as we handle carry from the ones to the tens place.

Notice that this process is slower than the execution of an ADDL2 (or ADDL3) instruction; notice also that we can process numbers of arbitrary length--as we can using the ADWC instruction in extended range integer arithmetic. Also, an *n*-digit number takes longer to add than a number with *n*-1 digits. In some data processing applications (for example, payroll preparation), the numeric information is rarely used more than a few times. Some computers, including the VAX, have special hardware--and corresponding instructions--for dealing with numbers represented by ASCII coded decimal digit strings. We will discuss these instructions for the VAX in the next section.

String Instructions

So far, most of the VAX instructions we have seen deal with bytes, words, and longwords. We have seen that typical data items stored in those memory locations have been integers or ASCII character codes. The VAX also has a large set of complex instructions that deal with **strings** of bytes. These strings typically (but not always) store ASCII character codes; they can be divided into strings that

7	43	0	
2	B	STRING
3	1	STRING+1
3	2	STRING+2
3	3	STRING+3
3	4	STRING+4
3	5	STRING+5

+12345

7	43	0	
2	D	STRING
3	1	STRING+1
3	2	STRING+2
3	3	STRING+3
3	4	STRING+4
3	5	STRING+5

−12345

Figure 10.13 Leading separate numeric string representation

represent numbers in particular, and strings that store arbitrary characters. In the following sections,we will discuss the VAX instructions that deal with strings representing numbers, and then those that deal with general character strings.

Decimal String Instructions

In the VAX, a character string that represents a sign-magnitude decimal number is called a **decimal string.** The VAX has instructions for dealing with two types of decimal strings: **numeric strings** and **packed decimal** strings. In a **numeric string,** the ASCII code for each decimal digit occupies 1 byte. When the sign of the number precedes the first digit, the string is called a **leading separate** numeric string; when the sign is superimposed on the last digit, it is called a **trailing** numeric string. In a **packed decimal** string, *two* decimal digits are *packed* into a single byte; obviously, digits in a packed decimal string are not represented by their ASCII codes.

Leading Separate Numeric Strings

When a leading separate string represents a positive number, the first (low-address) byte of the string contains $2B_{16}$ (which is the ASCII code for "+"); when it represents a negative number, the first byte contains $2D_{16}$ (which is the ASCII code for "-"). A leading separate numeric string is specified by the address of its first (low-address) byte--which contains the code for the sign--and by its length in digits. The length of a leading separate numeric string can be from 0 to 31 digits; the value of a string with length "0" is 0. Since the length specifies the number of digits, a leading separate numeric string of length L occupies $L + 1$ contiguous bytes. The highest address byte contains the least significant digit; the lowest address byte (after the sign) contains the most significant digit. Figure 10.13 shows the representation of the numbers -12345 and +12345, in the leading separate numeric string format.

Trailing Numeric Strings

A trailing numeric string is also specified by the address of its first byte and its length, and its length can also be from 0 to 31 digits (the value of a trailing numeric string with length 0 is also 0). With a trailing numeric string, however, the first byte doesn't contain the sign--it contains the ASCII

With a trailing numeric string, however, the first byte doesn't contain the sign--it contains the ASCII

	Zoned		Overpunch	
Digit	+	−	+	−
0	30	70	7B	7D
1	31	71	41	4A
2	32	72	42	4B
3	33	73	43	4C
4	34	74	44	4D
5	35	75	45	4E
6	36	76	46	4F
7	37	77	47	50
8	38	78	48	51
9	39	79	49	52

Figure 10.14 Combined sign and last digit for trailing numeric strings

code of the most significant digit. Also, because the sign of a trailing numeric string is *superimposed* on the ASCII code for its least significant digit (which is stored in the high-address byte), a trailing numeric string's length in digits is the same as its length in bytes.

The VAX recognizes two ways in which the sign of a trailing numeric string can be superimposed on the last digit: **zoned** and **overpunch**. The last digit of a positive *zoned* trailing numeric string is simply the ASCII code for the digit--it is the same as if it were a digit *without* a superimposed sign. The last digit of a negative *zoned* trailing string is the ASCII code for the digit, with 40_{16} added to it. The last digit of a positive *overpunch* trailing numeric string is the ASCII code for the digit with 10_{16} added to it; the last digit of a negative overpunch trailing numeric string is the ASCII code for that digit with 19_{16} added to it. Zero is an exception: a combined "+" and 0 is represented as $7B_{16}$, and a combined "-" and 0 is represented as $7D_{16}$. Figure 10.14 shows the value of the last byte (combined sign and digit) for zoned and overpunch trailing numeric strings. Figure 10.15 shows the representation of -12345 and +12345 in both the zoned and the overpunch trailing numeric formats.

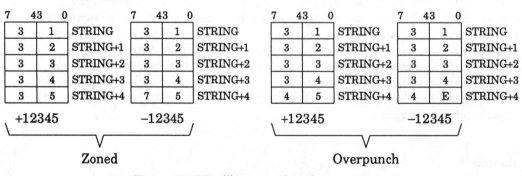

Figure 10.15 Trailing numeric string representation

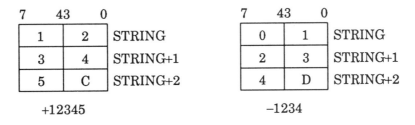

Figure 10.16 Packed decimal string representation

Packed Decimal Strings

ASCII codes aren't stored in packed decimal strings; rather, the binary representations of the decimal digits of the number are placed in successive 4-bit **nibbles**. A packed decimal string is specified by the address of its first (low-address) byte and its length, as the number of digits (not counting the sign) in the string. The number of digits can range from 0 through 31; the value of a 0-length string is 0. Digits are stored 2 per byte; the more significant digit of each pair goes in the high-order nibble (bits 4-7) and the less significant digit goes in the low order nibble (bits 0-3). The sign of the number is stored in the low-order nibble (bits 0-3) of the last byte of the string; the "sign" for a positive number is C_{16}, and that for a negative number is D_{16}. Since the sign must go in the low-order nibble of the last byte of the string, a string with an even number of digits has 0 placed in the high-order nibble of the first byte. A number represented in the packed decimal string format is often called a **binary coded decimal** (BCD) number: each decimal digit is separately encoded as a 4-bit binary number. Figure 10.16 shows the numbers +12345 and -1234 represented as packed decimal strings; this example is slightly different from the preceding ones, in order to illustrate the 0 that is added to a string with an even number of digits.

Packed Decimal Arithmetic Instructions

The VAX has no instructions for doing arithmetic on numeric strings; it has instructions for arithmetic *only* on packed decimal strings. This might seem strange, because if input is read from an (ASCII) I/O device, and output is sent to such a device, then we would prefer to do arithmetic on ASCII coded strings rather than BCD strings. However, the VAX has CVT instructions for converting from numeric strings to packed decimal strings and from packed decimal strings back to numeric strings, so this limitation is not unduly inconvenient.

The VAX has instructions for addition, subtraction, multiplication and division, as well as for moving (copying) and comparing packed decimal strings. The add and subtract instructions have both 4- and 6-operand variants; these are equivalent to the integer arithmetic 2- and 3-operand instructions, because both the address and length of each string must be explicitly specified.[4] All of the packed decimal arithmetic instructions change some registers: either R0 through R3 (in the case of the 4-operand instructions), or R0 through R5 (for the 6-operand instructions). The even numbered

---

[4]For integers, there are different opcodes for adding bytes, words, and longwords. Thus, the length of the integer must still be specified, but it is specified as an opcode rather than an operand.

registers contain 0, and the odd numbered registers contain the addresses of the bytes containing the most significant digits of the first, second, and third (if relevant) strings. This is convenient when we execute several consecutive instructions using the same numeric string; however, we must be careful not to forget to save important values that are in those registers when we execute a packed decimal string instruction. Figure 10.17 is a summary of some of the packed decimal instructions; additional detail on their operation is available in the *Vax Architecture Reference Manual*.

Two Examples

Let's look at two examples of using the decimal string instructions. First, figure 10.18 is a source program that defines two leading separate numeric strings at assemble time, converts them to packed decimal strings, adds them, and converts the result back to a leading separate numeric string. Without much additional difficulty, we could read the leading separate numeric strings from the keyboard, at run time (using a system service such as GETC), and print the sum (after converting it from packed decimal to leading separate numeric) string on the screen (with a system service such as PUTC). Note that the LENGTH operand is the same for all strings in figure 10.18, even though the packed decimal strings are 3 bytes long and the leading separate numeric strings are 6 bytes long; this is because LENGTH represents the number of *digits,* not bytes, in a string. This makes programming easier because we need not count bytes; we must remember, however, to specify LENGTH as a digit count rather than a byte count.

Before the program runs, only STRING1 and STRING2 are initialized. After it completes, however, all three packed decimal strings have values, as does STRING3. A register snapshot and hexadecimal memory dump after the program has executed looks as follows (STRING1 was assigned address 200):

```
PSL:  03C00000     PC:  00000287
R0-R11, AP, FP, SP, PC:
00000000 00000218 00000000 0000020C 00000000 00000218 7FFED78A 7FFED78A
7FFED052 7FFED25A 7FFEDDD4 7FFE33DC 7FF285CC 7FF28584 7FF28580 00000287


3230382B  30393837  362B3534  3332312B  :  00000200
0A2B1100  005C2380  0C89675C  34123533  :  00000210

75707475  6F247379  73000002  27010E00  :  00000220
```

The CVTSP instructions placed the packed decimal representation of STRING1 in locations 212_{16} through 214_{16}, and the packed decimal representation of STRING2 in locations 215_{16} through 217_{16}. The ADDP6 instruction placed the packed decimal sum in locations 218_{16} through $21A_{16}$, and the CVTPS instruction converted the sum from a packed decimal string to a leading separate numeric string and placed it in locations $20C_{16}$ through 211_{16}. The last nibble of each packed decimal string contains C_{16}, and the first byte of each leading separate numeric string contains $2B_{16}$, because all numbers are positive. Registers R0 and R2 contain 0 because the CVTPS instruction has that side effect. Similarly, side effects of the CVTPS instruction dictate that R1 contains the address of the byte containing the most significant digit of the source string (218_{16}), and that R3 contains the address of the sign byte of the destination string ($20C_{16}$). Side effects of the ADDP6 instruction caused R4 to contain 0, and R5 to contain the address of the byte containing the most significant digit of the sum (218_{16}).

Mnemonic	Action	Operands
ADDP4	Add string SADDR of length SLEN to string DADDR of length DLEN; place sum in string DADDR.	SLEN, SADDR, DLEN, DADDR
ADDP6	Add S_1 string of length S_1LEN to S_2 string of length S_2LEN; place sum in string DADDR of length DLEN.	S_1LEN, S_1ADDR, S_2LEN, S_2ADDR, DLEN, DADDR
ASHP	Shift string S, of length SLEN, COUNT decimal digits. For right shift (COUNT negative), add ROUND, then shift. Place result in string D of length DLEN.	COUNT, SLEN, S, ROUND, DLEN, D
CMPP3	Compare S_1 and S_2 strings, of length LEN; update CC.	LEN, S_1ADDR, S_2ADDR
CMPP4	Compare S_1 string of length S_1LEN with S_2 string of length S_2LEN; update CC.	S_1LEN, S_1ADDR, S_2LEN, S_2ADDR
CVTLP	Convert longword to packed decimal string.	S, DLEN, DADDR
CVTPL	Convert packed decimal string to longword.	SLEN, SADDR, D
CVTPS	Convert packed decimal string to leading separate numeric string.	SLEN, SADDR, DLEN, DADDR
CVTPT	Convert packed decimal string to trailing numeric string; TABLE specifies the sign representation.	SLEN, SADDR, TABLE, DLEN, DADDR
CVTSP	Convert leading separate numeric string to packed decimal string.	SLEN, SADDR, DLEN, DADDR
CVTTP	Convert trailing numeric string to packed decimal string; TABLE specifies the sign representation.	SLEN, SADDR, TABLE, DLEN, DADDR
DIVP	Divide string S_2 (length S_2LEN) by string S_1 (length S_1LEN). Place quotient in string DADDR (length DLEN); remainder is lost.	S_1LEN, S_1ADDR, S_2LEN, S_2ADDR, DLEN, DADDR
MOVP	Move packed decimal string S to D, both with length LEN.	LEN, S, D
MULP	Multiply string S_1ADDR times string S_2ADDR. Place product in string DADDR.	S_1LEN, S_1ADDR, S_2LEN, S_2ADDR, DLEN, DADDR
SUBP4	Same as ADDP4, but subtract S from D.	SLEN, SADDR, DLEN, DADDR
SUBP6	Same as ADDP6, but subtract S_1 from S_2.	S_1LEN, S_1ADDR, S_2LEN, S_2ADDR, DLEN, DADDR

Figure 10.17 Summary of packed decimal string instructions

```
STRING1:    .ASCII "+12345"          ;addend1
STRING2:    .ASCII "+67890"          ;addend2
STRING3:    .BLKB 6                  ;place for result
PACK1:      .BLKB 3                  ;converted addend1
PACK2:      .BLKB 3                  ;converted addend2
PACK3:      .BLKB 3                  ;packed sum
;Define assemble time constant for LENGTH: number of digits (not bytes) in string!
            LENGTH = STRING2–STRING1–1
            .ENTRY START, 0
;First, convert leading separate strings to packed decimal
            CVTSP #LENGTH, STRING1, #LENGTH, PACK1
            CVTSP #LENGTH, STRING2, #LENGTH, PACK2
;Now, add packed decimal strings
            ADDP6 #LENGTH, PACK1, #LENGTH, PACK2, #LENGTH, PACK3
;Finally, convert packed decimal sum to leading separate format
            CVTPS #LENGTH, PACK3, #LENGTH, STRING3
            $EXIT_S
```

Figure 10.18 Adding numeric strings

The second example illustrates the use of the ASHP instruction to scale a packed decimal number. We have seen that the ASHL instruction multiplies or divides a number represented as a binary integer by a power of 2; the ASHP instruction similarly multiplies or divides a number represented as a packed decimal string, by a power of 10. Suppose we wish to have a binary number that represents prices in cents; suppose, further, that we wish to perform calculations in binary and express the result in dollars. We can use the CVTLP instruction to convert from a binary (longword) integer to a packed decimal representation and then use the ASHP instruction to divide the cent value by 100. Since we wish to round the result, we specify the ROUND operand as 5, which is added to the source operand before it is shifted (each time). The sum, rounded, is then placed in the location specified by the destination operands. (Specifying the ROUND operand as 0 causes truncation rather than rounding.)

Figure 10.19 illustrates conversion from binary to packed decimal and then division of the packed decimal string by 100 by shifting it 2 digits to the right. The length of each string, as usual, is specified by its digit count, not by its byte count. A hexadecimal dump and register snapshot after this program has run looks like this (ICENTS was loaded at address 200):

```
PSL:   03C00000      PC:   0000026F
R0-R11, AP, FP, SP, PC:
00000000 00000204 00000000 0000020C 7FFE640C 7FFE64B4 7FFED78A 7FFED78A
7FFED052 7FFED25A 7FFEDDD4 7FFE33DC 7FF285CC 7FF28584 7FF28580 0000026F


8C563402  0000009C  78563402  0165EC15  :  00000200
79730000  021E010E  000A2B11  00000000  :  00000210
```

String PCENTS occupies the bytes with addresses 204 through 208 (note that the high order nibble of the first byte contains 0, because there is an even number of digits in the string). String DOLLARS is 2 digits--and 1 byte--shorter than string PCENTS. DOLLARS occupies bytes $20Z_{16}$ through $20F_{16}$,

```
ICENTS:      .LONG 23456789        ;integer cent value
PCENTS:      .BLKB 8               ;packed decimal cent value
DOLLARS:     .BLKB 6               ;packed decimal dollars
             CLENGTH = 8
             DLENGTH = 6
             .ENTRY START, 0
             CVTLP ICENTS, #CLENGTH, PCENTS
             ASHP #–2, #CLENGTH, PCENTS, #5, #DLENGTH, DOLLARS
             $EXIT_S
             .END START
```

Figure 10.19 Dollars and cents

and its last digit (not counting the sign) is 8 because 789 was rounded to 8. Registers R0 and R2 contain 0 because of the ASHP instruction; R1 contains 204 and R3 contains $20C_{16}$ because those are the addresses of the bytes with the most significant digits of the source and destination strings, respectively.

Character String Instructions

The leading separate and trailing numeric strings are similar to but less general than the **character string** instructions. A character string is a sequence of 0 to 65,535 contiguous bytes, each of which typically contains the ASCII code for a character. It is specified by 2 operands: its length in bytes and the address of its first (low-address) byte. The VAX has instructions for moving (copying) and comparing character strings, and for locating a particular character or characters within a character string. Character string instructions change the values in registers R0 through R1, R0 through R3, or R0 through R5, depending on the action of the instruction. We discuss these instructions in more detail below.

Copying Character Strings

The VAX has two instructions for copying character strings; one copies strings of equal length; the other copies strings of unequal length. The instruction for copying equal-length strings specifies a single length (in bytes) and the address of the source and destination strings; its format is MOVC3 LEN, S, D: the LEN bytes beginning at address S are copied into the LEN locations beginning with address D. The instruction for copying unequal-length strings specifies a length as well as an address for each string; its format is MOVC5 SLEN, SADDR, FILLC, DLEN, DADDR: SLEN bytes are copied from SADDR, and the first DLEN of them are placed in locations beginning at DADDR. If SLEN is less than DLEN, the high-address bytes of the destination string are filled with the **fill character,** FILLC.

In chapter 6, we copied a character string by placing the addresses of the source and destination strings in registers and using autoincrement addressing (mode 8) with the MOVB instruction. We can now rewrite that example, using the MOVC3 instruction:

```
STRING1:          .ASCIZ "This is a test"              ;string to copy
STRING2:          .BLKB 50                             ;destination of copy
;
   ;copy STRING1 to STRING2
COPY:             MOVC3 #STRING2-STRING1, STRING1, STRING2
                  .
                  .
```

If we wish to place the same value in a block of memory, we can use the MOVC5 instruction, with a source string length of 0. For example, to zero the 256 bytes beginning at address BLOCK, we could write MOVC5 #0, (R0), #0, #256, BLOCK. We need not initialize R0 with a valid address: the length of the source string is 0, so the address in R0 is never used.

The MOVC3 instruction clears registers R0, R2, R4, and R5; R1 contains the address of the next byte after the source string, and R3 contains the address of the next byte after the destination string. The MOVC5 has the same side effects that MOVC3 has on R2 through R5; R0, however, contains the number of unmoved bytes in the source string (which is non-zero only when the source string is longer than the destination string), and R1 contains the address of the byte after the last byte in the source string that was moved. The MOVC3 instruction clears the N, V, and C bits of the condition code and sets the Z bit; the MOVC5 instruction also clears the V bit, but it sets the Z bit if the lengths of the two strings are equal, it sets the N bit if the source string's length is less than that of the destination string as *signed* numbers, and it sets the C bit if the source string's length is less than that of the destination string as *un*signed numbers.

Comparing Character Strings

The VAX has a pair of instructions for comparing character strings that are similar to the instructions for copying character strings. One instruction compares equal-length strings: its format is CMPC3 LEN, S_1, S_2. Each byte in S_1 is compared with the corresponding byte in S_2, until a difference is found, or until the end of the strings is reached. If an unequal byte is found, the N bit is set if the byte in S_1 is less than that in S_2 as signed numbers, and the C bit is set if the S_1 byte is less than the S_2 byte as unsigned numbers. If the last byte of the two strings is the same, the Z bit is set; the V bit is always cleared. The CMPC3 instruction changes the values of R0 through R3, as follows:

1. R0 contains the number of bytes remaining in S_1, including the byte that terminated the instruction. Thus, R0 contains 0 only if the strings are equal.
2. R1 contains the address of the byte in S_1 that terminated the instruction, and R3 contains the address of the byte in S_2 that terminated the instruction. If the strings are equal, then R1 contains the address of the byte after S_1, and R3 contains the address of the byte after S_2.
3. R2 is cleared.

The second instruction compares strings of unequal length. Its format is CMPC5 S_1LEN, S_1ADDR, FILLC, S_2LEN, S_2ADDR. The two strings are compared byte for byte; if one string is shorter than the other, the extra bytes of the longer are compared with the fill character FILLC. The comparison terminates when a pair of unequal bytes is found, or until all pairs of bytes have been compared. The condition codes are set--as in the CMPC3 instruction--according to the results of the last pair of bytes compared. Registers R0 through R3 are also changed, as follows:

1. When the instruction terminates, R0 contains the number of bytes remaining in S_1, including the byte that terminated the comparison, and R2 contains the number of bytes remaining in S_2, including the byte that terminated the comparison. Thus, R0 contains 0 only if the two strings

are the same length and equal, or if the end of S_1 was reached before the comparison terminated; R2 contains 0 only if the two strings are the same length, or if the end of S_2 was reached before the comparison terminated.

2.   R1 contains the address of the last byte compared in S_1, and R3 contains the address of the last byte compared in S_2. If the end of S_1 was reached before the comparison terminated, then R1 contains the address of the byte after S_1. If the end of S_2 was reached before the comparison terminated, then R3 contains the address of the byte after S_2.

Matching within Character Strings

The VAX has three instructions that are useful for matching individual characters, or character substrings, within character strings. The *match characters* instruction has the format MATCHC OBJLEN, OBJADDR, SLEN, SADDR; it searches source string SADDR, of length SLEN, for a substring that matches the object string OBJADDR, of length OBJLEN. If a substring match is made, the Z bit is set; otherwise, it is cleared. After this instruction completes, R0 through R3 are changed:

1.   R0 contains 0 if a match occurred; it contains the number of bytes in the object string if a match did not occur.
2.   R1 contains the address of the next byte after the object string if a match occurred or the address of the object string if a match did not occur.
3.   R2 contains the number of bytes remaining in the source string if a match occurred or 0 if a match did not occur.
4.   R3 contains the address of the next byte after the last byte matched, if a match occurred or the address of the byte after the source string, if a match did not occur.

The other two instructions in this group are for locating or skipping a particular character in a string. The *locate character* instruction has the format LOCC CHAR, LEN, ADDR. The string with address ADDR is searched until character CHAR is located or until the end of the string. If the character is located, R0 contains the number of bytes remaining in the string (including the located byte), R1 contains the address of the byte located, and the Z bit is cleared. If the character is not located, R0 is cleared, R1 contains the address of the byte after the end of the string, and the Z bit is set. The *skip character* instruction is the reverse of LOCC. Its format is SKPC CHAR, LEN, ADDR. The character CHAR is compared with successive bytes in the string with address ADDR and length LEN until all bytes have been compared or until a *non*matching character is found in the string. If a nonmatching character is found, R0 contains the number of bytes remaining in the string (including the nonmatching one), R1 contains the address of the nonmatching byte, and the Z bit is cleared. If no nonmatching character is found, R0 is cleared, R1 contains the address of the byte after the end of the string, and the Z bit is set.

Table Look-Up Operations on Character Strings

The VAX has four character string instructions that use successive bytes in a string as indices into a table of 256 values; the contents of each entry in the table determine the action taken for each byte. The *move translated characters* instruction has the format MOVTC SLEN, SADDR, FILLC, TABLE, DLEN, DADDR. Each byte in SADDR is used to index into array TABLE; the entry in the array thereby selected is placed in the location in DADDR that corresponds to the location from which the index was found in SADDR. If the destination string is longer than the source string, then its high-address bytes are filled with the fill character, FILLC; if the source string is longer than the destination string, then its high-address bytes are not translated and moved. The MOVTC instruction is reminiscent of the MOVC5 instruction: with the MOVC5 instruction, each byte is moved; with the MOVTC instruction, each byte is *translated* and then moved.

After the MOVTC instruction, the V bit is cleared, the N bit is set if SLEN is less than DLEN as signed numbers, the Z bit is set if they are equal, and the C bit is set if SLEN is less than DLEN as unsigned numbers. The MOVTC instruction changes R0 through R5 as follows:

1.   R0 contains the number of untranslated (and unmoved) bytes in the source string after the instruction completes. Thus, R0 contains 0 unless the source string is longer than the destination string.
2.   R1 contains the address of the byte after the last byte in SADDR that was translated and moved.
3.   R2 and R4 both contain 0.
4.   R3 contains the address of the translation table.
5.   R5 contains the address of the byte after the end of DADDR.

The MOVTC instruction can be used to convert uppercase to lowercase letters (or vice versa), or ASCII codes to some other type of codes, or ASCII coded digits to the integers they represent, and so forth.

The format of the *move translated until character* instruction is MOVTUC SLEN, SADDR, ESCAPE, TABLE, DLEN, DADDR. Each byte in the source string SADDR is translated--by using it as an index into array TABLE--and placed into the corresponding location in the destination string DADDR. Translation continues until the end of either string, or until a character equal to the escape character ESCAPE (specified by the programmer) is found in the source string. If the instruction terminates because the escape character is found, the V bit is set; otherwise, it is cleared. The N, Z, and C bits are set according to the comparison of SLEN and DLEN, as in the MOVTC instruction. The MOVTUC instruction also changes R0 through R5:

1.   R0 contains the number of bytes remaining in the source string, including the escape character. Thus, R0 contains 0 only if no escape character was found in the source string.
2.   R1 contains the address of the escape character or of the end of DADDR. If there was no escape, and SADDR ended before DADDR, then R1 contains the address of the byte after the end of SADDR.
3.   R2 contains 0.
4.   R3 contains the address of the table.
5.   R4 contains the number of bytes remaining in DADDR.
6.   R5 contains the address of the byte in DADDR that would have had the escape character moved into it or that would have received the next translated character if SADDR had not been exhausted. If SADDR is not exhausted and there was no escape character, then R5 contains the address of the byte after the end of DADDR.

The final two character string instructions use a table of values in combination with a mask to select the presence or absence of particular patterns. They are, in this respect, similar to some of the logical instructions that we discussed earlier in this chapter. The format of the *scan characters* instruction is SCANC LEN, ADDR, TABLE, MASK, and the format of the *span characters* instruction is SPANC LEN, ADDR, TABLE, MASK. The SCANC instruction is similar to the LOCC instruction, except that SCANC terminates when a character meeting some criterion with respect to the mask is found (recall that LOCC terminates when an identical character is found). SPANC is similar to SKPC, except that SPANC terminates when a character *not* meeting some criterion with respect to the mask is found. For both instructions, successive bytes of string ADDR are used to index array TABLE, and the logical **and** of the entry from the array and the MASK operand is computed. The SPANC instruction continues until the result of the **and** is 0--in which case the Z bit is cleared--or until all bytes of the string have been used; the SCANC instruction continues until the result of the **and** is

Mnemonic	Action	Operands
CMPC3	Compare S_1 and S_2 strings, of length LEN; update CC.	LEN, S_1ADDR, S_2ADDR
CMPC5	Compare S_1 string of length S_1LEN with S_2 string of length S_2LEN; update CC. If one string is longer, compare its high-address bytes with character FILLC.	S_1LEN, S_1ADDR, FILLC, S_2LEN, S_2ADDR
MATCHC	Search string SRC for substring OBJ. If a matching substring is found, Z bit is set.	OBJLEN, OBJ, SRCLEN, SRC
MOVC3	Move character string S to D; both have length LEN.	LEN, S, D
MOVC5	Move character string S with length SLEN to D with length DLEN. If D is longer than S, its high-address bytes are filled with the fill character, FILLC.	SLEN, S, FILLC, DLEN, D
MOVTC	Use each byte of string S as an index into array TABLE. Place the element found in TABLE in the corresponding location in string D. If D is longer than S, its high-address bytes are filled with the fill character, FILLC.	SLEN, S, FILLC, TABLE, DLEN, D
MOVTUC	Use each byte of string S as an index into array TABLE. Place the element found in TABLE in the corresponding location in string D. Continue until a character matching the escape character, ESCAPE, is found in the array, or until the end of string S.	SLEN, S, ESCAPE, TABLE, DLEN, D
SCANC	Use each byte of string S as an index into array TABLE. Compute the logical **and** of the array element and the mask, MASK. Continue until the result of the **and** is nonzero, or until the end of the string.	LEN, S, TABLE, MASK
SKIPC	Compare each byte of string S with character CHAR. Continue comparing until a nonmatching character is found, or until the end of the string. If a nonmatching character is found, the Z bit is cleared.	CHAR, LEN, S
SPANC	Use each byte of string S as an index into array TABLE. Compute the logical **and** of the array element and the mask MASK. Continue until the result of the **and** is 0, or until the end of the string.	LEN, S, TABLE, MASK

Figure 10.20 Summary of character string instructions

1--in which case the Z bit is cleared--or until the end of the string is reached. For both instructions, the N, V, and C bits are cleared. Also, registers R0 through R3 are changed by these instructions:

1.   R0 contains the number of bytes remaining in the string, including the byte that terminated the instruction.
2.   R1 contains the address of the byte that terminated the instruction. If the instruction terminated because the end of the string was reached, R1 contains the address of the byte after the string.
3.   R2 is cleared.
4.   R3 contains the address of the table.

Because an 8-bit mask is used with these instructions, each byte in the string can be checked for the presence of eight attributes. With the SCANC instruction, we can search for bytes possessing all of the attributes specified by the mask, and with the SPANC instruction we can skip over any bytes not possessing all of the attributes specified by the mask. We might search for such attributes as ASCII codes for digits, letters, punctuation, and so forth.

Figure 10.20 is a summary of the VAX's character string instructions.

Summary

We have seen two ways of classifying instructions: by format and by function. Classification by format is more useful for novices, but classification by function is often of more interest to experienced programmers.

We have also discussed several families of the VAX's instructions. The logical instructions treat bytes, words, and longwords as collections of single bits, or Boolean values. The VAX has instructions that implement the **not** function, the **and** function, the **or** function, the **exclusive or** function, and a combination of the **and** and **not** functions. There is also an instruction for shifting groups of bits to the right or left.

The variable-length bit-field instructions specify an arbitrary bit string with an arbitrary length. These instructions do not implement logical functions, but they allow us to group together arbitrary collections of bits. They are useful for dealing with operands that don't fit conveniently into a byte, a word, or a longword.

The VAX also has a large collection of instructions for multiplication and division. The arithmetic shift instructions multiply or divide by powers of 2; the general multiply and divide instructions can multiply or divide by other numbers.

We examined the processes involved in converting an ASCII coded decimal number into the binary number represented by the ASCII digit string and converting back from a binary number to a string of ASCII coded decimal digits. It is possible to process numeric data without converting from ASCII character codes to integers; it is desirable to avoid the cost of conversion if the data will not be used for very many computations.

We discussed the VAX's instructions for dealing with **numeric strings** and **packed decimal** strings, which can contain as many as 31 decimal digits. The VAX has arithmetic instructions for packed decimal strings only (these perform BCD arithmetic), but there are instructions for converting from the different numeric strings (and longword integers) to packed decimal strings, and *vice versa*.

The VAX also has instructions for dealing with general character strings. General character strings contain from 0 to 65,535 characters; they can be moved, compared, translated, and searched in several ways.

In all, the VAX has a large number of instructions. Different families of instructions are designed to be used for different applications.

Exercises for Chapter 10

1. If R10 contains 12345678_{16}, show the contents of R11 (in hexadecimal) after the following ROTL instructions have been executed. The first one is done, as an example.

Instruction	R11 contents
ROTL #1, R10, R11	2468ACF0
ROTL #-1, R10, R11	
ROTL #4, R10, R11	
ROTL #-4, R10, R11	
ROTL #11, R10, R11	
ROTL #-5, R10, R11	
ROTL #20, R10, R11	
ROTL #-12, R0, R11	

2. If R9 contains $AAAAAAAA_{16}$, R10 contains 55555555_{16} and R11 contains 0, show the (hexadecimal) contents of R11 after each of the following instructions has been executed. Results do not accumulate, except when two instructions are in the same box.

Instruction	R11 contents
BICB3 R9, R10, R11	
BICL3 R9, R10, R11	
BISL3 R9, R10, R11	
XORW3 R9, R10, R11	
ROTL #1, R9, R9 XORW3 R9, R10, R11	
MCOMB R10, R11	

3. True or False; explain your answers:

    a. The MULL3 instruction can never produce a result that is too large to fit in the destination location.
    b. The EMUL instruction can never produce a result that is too large to fit in the destination location.
    c. The remainder computed by the EDIV instruction is never negative.
    d. Conversion from ASCII coded decimal digit strings to binary numbers is preferable when the amount of computing to be done on the numbers is minimal.
    e. Executing the RSB instruction to return from a subroutine does not change the CC bits.

4. Use the logical and/or the bit-field instructions introduced in this chapter (as well as instructions from earlier chapters, if necessary) to write a subroutine that computes the parity of an eight-bit byte.

5. Consider the following code:

```
1)              MOVL A, R1
2)              MOVL B, R2
3)              MOVAL C, R3
;
4)              CMPL R1, R2
5)              BLEQ Z
6)              MOVL R2, -(SP)
```

```
7)                      MOVL R1, R2
8)                      MOVL (SP)+, R1
;
9)            Z:        TSTL R1
10)                     BEQL Y
;
11)                     BITL ONE, R1
12)                     BEQL X
;
13)                     ADDL2 R2, (R3)
14)           X:        ASHL #1, R2, R2
;
15)                     ASHL #-1, R1, R1
16)                     BRB Z
;
17)           Y:        $EXIT_S
;
18)           A:        .LONG 10
19)           B:        .LONG 20
20)           C:        .LONG 0
21)           ONE:      .LONG 1
```

The following questions refer to the previous code.

a.   What does the above code do? How does it do it?

b.   If lines 4 through 8 were removed, would the program run faster if the value in R2 were larger than that in R1, or would it run faster if the value in R1 were larger than that in R2?

c.   What would happen if either R1 or R2 (but not both) contained a value less than 0?

d.   If A contains 1, what is the largest value of B that will *not* produce overflow?

e.   What is the (hexadecimal) value of C, if A contains 56_{10} and B contains 2?

f.   It is possible to rewrite the above program, using *no* logical instructions or ASHL instructions. Outline two ways to do it, one of which will be much slower and the other much faster than the above program.

Be sure to state clearly all assumptions that you make in answering these questions.

6.   Using the algorithm described in the text, write a subroutine that has as its input parameter the address of an array of ASCII codes representing a decimal (sign-magnitude) number and that produces as its output parameter the 32-bit twos complement binary number represented by the ASCII digit string. You must decide how to deal with decimal digit strings whose binary representation is too large for 32 bits.

7.   Using the algorithm described in the text, write a subroutine that has as its input parameter a 32-bit binary number and that returns as its output parameter an array of ASCII character codes representing the decimal value of that binary number. Be sure that you handle positive and negative numbers correctly; consider how to handle the most negative number representable in 32 bits.

8.   Write a main program that calls both of the subroutines you wrote in the previous two exercises. Write your main program so that it calls the first subroutine with an ASCII coded digit string and then calls the second one with the binary number that the first one returned to it. Then have your main program print the ASCII string returned by the second program.

   If you didn't already do so, place the two subroutines that your main program will call in separate files, and the main program in a third file. Use the facilities for separate assembly to create three object modules (one for the first subroutine, one for the second one, and one for the main program); link the object modules, run the program, and request a link map of the load module created by the linker. (Review the appropriate section of chapter 9 if you don't remember how to link separately assembled object modules.)

9. Write a subroutine that takes the 32-bit longword passed to it in R0 and places the ASCII character codes for its *hexadecimal* representation in an array of 8 bytes whose starting address is passed to the subroutine in R1. The ASCII character code for the lowest order hex digit should be in the highest address byte, and that for the highest order hex digit should be in the lowest address byte.

This subroutine is similar to the one you wrote for exercise 7, but since you are converting from binary to hexadecimal, you can use some shortcuts that you can't use when converting from binary to decimal. Because of these shortcuts, you should be able to write this subroutine using fewer than 20 lines of data and instructions; if you use the EXTZV instruction and index mode (mode 4), you should be able to write it using fewer than 10 lines.

10. There is no *single* CVT instruction that can replace the subroutines that convert numeric strings to longword integers and longword integers to numeric strings, but it is possible to perform the transformation using only CVT instructions. List the instructions in the correct order you would use to convert numeric strings (leading separate or trailing) into longword integers and then from longword integers to leading separate or trailing numeric strings.

11. Write a program that takes a character string as input, and produces a character string containing only the uppercase letters found in its input string. Try writing the program using *no* character string instructions, and then try writing it using character string instructions. (Hint: you may wish to use MOVTC and SKPC.) Compare the number of instructions in the two programs, and then consider the data required for each program. Which program would you rather write? Why?

12. Write a program that converts the lowercase letters in a character string into uppercase ones but does not change the uppercase letters, the digits, the punctuation, or any other characters. Write this program using the MOVTC instruction. After you have created the *translation table* required by the MOVTC instruction, how difficult would it be to rewrite the program to use the MOVB instruction with displacement addressing?

Case Study for Chapter 10

In discussing machine-language programming for the VAX (in chapter 3), we used a machine-language program loading program. This program processed lines such as:

```
00000200: 17
00000201: 9F
00000202: 00000200

00000200
```

The *processing* involved means taking the ASCII character codes representing the machine language (hexadecimal numbers), converting them to binary numbers (that are *not* ASCII codes), and loading them into memory. For the above example, location 00000200_{16} gets 00010111_2 loaded into it, location 0000201_{16} gets 10011111_2, and so forth. The loading program stops loading when it encounters a number on a line not immediately followed by a colon, and it uses that number as the program's entry point. After loading the above program the loader could use the DUMP system service to provide a pre-execution memory dump. The loader could then execute the instruction JSB @#00000200 in order to run the program--since 00000200_{16} is specified as the program's entry point. Then, if the program terminates with the RSB instruction, control will return to the loader, which can provide a post-execution memory dump. Let us try to write such a machine-language program-loading program in assembly language. As we proceed, we will use some of the system services described in the text and in Appendix 1.

First, let's outline what needs to be done in a few lines of English. We can then refine our outline (over and over again), until we have a series of well-commented assembly language statements that perform the desired processing. This is sometimes called *the method of successive refinement.* In order to keep things simple, we will not worry about some of the fancier features of the chapter 3 loader, such as processing comments, ignoring blanks or blank lines, handling blank-separated numbers on the same line, and so on; we can add these later, if we so desire. So, let's write an outline:

```
Repeat until entry point line is found:
    read a line;
        if no line is available, exit with a message.
    process the line;
End of Repeat block.
Entry-point line found:
    provide pre-execution memory dump;
    copy entry point address into PC;
    provide post-execution memory dump;
```

We could proceed with the top-down method for writing this program, but first we will digress into some bottom-up design. In top-down design we deal with a series of abstractions; in bottom-up design we try to implement a specific abstraction on a real computer.

One major concern, as we look at the loading problem from the bottom up, is that we must convert a hexadecimal number string, presented to us as an ASCII character string, into its binary, numeric, equivalent. How can we do this? Consider the statement,

```
A: .ASCIZ /304/
```

If we are given a NUL-terminated (because of the .ASCIZ directive) string of numeric ASCII character codes for the digits 0 through 9, we can generate the string's numeric equivalent as follows:

```
        MOVAL A, R0             ;use R0 as a string pointer
        CLRL R1                 ;create the number in R1
LOOP:   MOVB (R0)+, R2          ;get next character
        BEQL DONE               ;if 0, done
;else, not 0, so keep creating the number
        SUBB2 #^A/0/, R2        ;subtract ASCII code offset
;binary rep. of hex digit in R2; there are more digits--in particular, the one in R2.
;The one in R0 is a higher order digit, so shift it left
        ASHL #4, R1, R1         ;shift over 4 bits, to 16s place
        ADDL2 R2, R1            ;add 1s place number
        BRB LOOP                ;do it again, until done
```

Given the hexadecimal digits 3, 0, and 4, what we are doing is equivalent to evaluating the arithmetic expression,

$$3*16^2 + 0*16^1 + 4*16^0,$$

which is the value of the hexadecimal number 304. The "*16" is performed by the ASHL instruction, which shifts the number in R1 four bits to the left.

This works fine for digits between 0 and 9, because the ASCII code for each of these numbers is 30_{16} larger than the number that the code represents. (Note that we have avoided using *magic numbers* in our program by subtracting the number that is the ASCII code for 0.) However, A, B, . . . , F (and a, b, . . . , f) are also hexadecimal digits; the above code will not deal correctly with them. In order to convert *any* hexadecimal digit string into the binary number that it represents, we must modify the above code; we can make those modifications as follows:

```
              MOVAL A, R0            ;use R0 as a string pointer
              CLRL R1               ;create the number in R1
LOOP:         MOVB (R0)+, R2        ;get next character
              BEQL DONE             ;if 0, done
;else, not 0, so check for what kind of subtraction to do
              CMPB R2, #^A/0/       ;check for digit
              BLSSU NOTHEX          ;smaller than 0: not hex digit
;else, check for range 0-9
              CMPB R2, #^A/9/
              BLEQU NUMBER          ;number from 0 to 9: subtract 30
;else, check for A-F, or a-f
              CMPB R2, #^A/A/
              BLSSU NOTHEX          ;9 < number < A: not hex
;else, number > A; check for < F
              CMPB R2, #^A/F/
              BLEQU CAPS            ;it's in range A-F
;else, check for range a-f
              CMPB R2, #^A/a/
              BLSSU NOTHEX          ;F < number < a: not hex
;else, check for range a-f
              CMPB R2, #^A/f/
              BLEQU LOWERS          ;it's in range a-f
;else, not legal digit
              BRB NOTHEX
NUMBER:       SUBB2 #^A/0/, R2      ;change 0-9 to binary
              BRB SHIFT
;
;To change an uppercase hex digit ("A"-"F") to binary: subtract 55_16,
;because A represents 10_10 and ASCII code for "A" is 65_10.
;
CAPS:         SUBB2 #55, R2         ;change "A"-"F" to binary
              BRB SHIFT             ;get other digits
;
;To change a lowercase hex digit ("a"-"f") to binary: subtract 87_10,
;because "a" represents 10_10, and ASCII code for "a" is 97_10.
;
LOWERS:       SUBB2 #87, R2         ;ASCII code for "a": 97
;
;Now, we have binary representation of hex digit in R2; there are more
;digits--in particular, the one in R2.  The one in R1 is a higher order
;digit, so shift it left
;
```

```
                ASHL #4, R1, R1              ;shift over 4 bits, to 16s place
                ADDL2 R2, R1                 ;add 1s place number
                BRB LOOP                     ;do it again, until done
    NOTHEX:                                  ;set error flag
```

Now that we can convert ASCII coded hexadecimal digit strings to the binary numbers those strings represent, we can resume our top-down development. Let's refine what we mean by *process a line*:

```
    Echo the line;
    Scan it for a number;
            if no colon is found:
                    set Entry Point flag;
                    stop processing;
            if a colon is found:
                    use number as the load address ADDR;
                    scan remainder of line for next number;
                    store number in location with Address ADDR (or, ADDR + 1, ADDR + 2, ADDR + 3);
                    keep track of highest and lowest addresses;
```

We can now consider what memory our program will need, what constants it may need, *etc.,* as we begin writing some of the higher level code:

```
    MEMORY:     .BLKB ^X1000                 ;memory for machine-language program
                .ENTRY START, 0              ;entry point
                IOINIT
                PUTS STARTMESS               ;print starting message
    REPEAT:     TSTB EPFLAG                  ;entry point reached?
                BEQL DUMMY                   ;if not, continue
    ;else, process entry point
                BRW YES
    DUMMY:      GETS LINE                    ;read another line
    ;process the line
                PUTS LINE                    ;first, echo the line
                MOVAB LINE, R0               ;R0 has address of 1st byte
                JSB SCAN                     ;call scan
                TSTB ERFLAG                  ;errors?
                BEQL DUMMY2                  ;dummy branch because of range
    ;else, quit
                BRW QUIT
    DUMMY2:     BRW REPEAT                   ;get another line
    ;
    YES:        PUTS EPMESS                  ;print entry point message
                PUTS PREDUMPMESS             ;print dump message
                DUMP @LOW, @HIGH             ;and, dump memory
                JSB @EP                      ;start user's program
                PUTS DUMPMESS2               ;post-execution memory dump
                DUMP @LOW, @HIGH             ;memory dump
                BRB DONE                     ;exit
    QUIT:       PUTS QUITMESS                ;print illegal char message
    DONE:       $EXIT_S                      ;and done
    ;
```

;These are data for the main program (and a few flags)
;
```
EP:        .LONG ^X200              ;entry point address (default: 200)
EPFLAG: .BYTE 0                     ;flag for when find entry point
ERFLAG:.BYTE 0                      ;error flag
HIGH:      .ADDRESS ^X200           ;initialize high to low address
LOW:       .ADDRESS ^X1200          ;initialize low to high address
ADDR:      .BLKL 1
;
QUITMESS:
           .ASCIZ /Illegal character; loading terminated/<CR><LF>
STARTMESS:
           .ASCIZ /Loader Working/<CR><LF>
PREDUMPMESS:
           .ASCIZ /Pre-execution memory dump follows:/<CR><LF>
POSTDUMPMESS:
           .ASCIZ /Post-execution memory dump follows:/<CR><LF>
EPMESS: .ASCII /Entry point:/
EPSTRING:
           .BLKB 8                  ;to store entry point
           .ASCIZ //<CR><LF>        ;to terminate printing
LINE:      .BLKB 82                 ;one screen's worth of bytes
           .END START
```

We still have to take care of some *administrative* details (such as setting HIGH and LOW), but first, let's try to write subroutine SCAN. Recall how natural it was to convert a line containing ASCII digits into a number by calling a subroutine; we will use this technique again. An outline of SCAN is:

Given a character string with its address in R0:
     call FINDNO, which processes hex digits, creating a 32 bit number in R1, leaving the first
          non-hex character in R2;
     is R3 (*found a number* flag) 0? If so, ignore line and repeat.
     if not, does R2 contain a colon?
          if yes:
               save R1 as ADDR;
               if ADDR < LOW, set new LOW;
               if ADDR > HIGH, set new HIGH
               call FINDNO
               is R2 ok?
                    if not, bad line, so terminate.
                    if so, store data from R1 in memory, at location ADDR; increment ADDR.
          if no (R2 doesn't contain a colon):
               check for errors;
               if none, set Entry Point flag

This outline can be translated into the following code:

```
SCAN:    CLRB ERFLAG            ;assume line is ok to start with
         JSB FINDNO             ;get first number
         TSTB R3                ;is the line empty?
         BNEQ SCANA             ;if not, continue
;else, return (ignore line)
         BRB RETURN
SCANA:   CMPB R2, #^A/:/        ;first nondigit character is in R2
         BNEQ SCANNO            ;wasn't a colon
;else, was a colon, so this is address must load into
         MOVL R1, ADDR          ;save address, for loading into
;and now get next number, to load into ADDR
         JSB FINDNO             ;get next number
         TSTB R3                ;number?
         BNEQ SCANB             ;yes, so continue
;else, no number, so ignore
         BRB RETURN             ;return
SCANB:   CMPB R2, #CR           ;is 1st nondigit a carriage return?
         BNEQ SCANC             ;if not, error!
;else, load number into address ADDR
         MOVL R1, @ADDR         ;store number in memory
         JSB HILOW              ;update high and/or low address
         ADDL2 R4, ADDR         ;adjust load address for next number
         BRB RETURN             ;and done
;if not a colon or carriage return: error!
SCANC:   INCB ERFLAG            ;set error flag
         BRB RETURN
;if number not followed by colon: entry point
SCANNO:CMPB R2, #CR
         BEQL SCANOK
;else, invalid char: error!
         INCB ERFLAG
         BRB RETURN
SCANOK:MOVL R1, EP              ;entry point
         INCB EPFLAG            ;set flag for finding entry point
RETURN:RSB                      ;and return
```

Subroutine SCAN calls two other subroutines: FINDNO and HILOW. The former is by far the more complex of the two; we have already written most of it, and will complete it as soon as we write the very simple HILOW subroutine:

```
HILOW:   CMPL ADDR, LOW         ;new low address?
         BGEQU HILOWA           ;if not, continue
         MOVL ADDR, LOW         ;else, new low address
HILOWA:CMPL ADDR, HIGH          ;new high address?
         BLEQU HILOWDONE        ;if not, done
         MOVL ADDR, HIGH        ;else, new high
HILOWDONE:
         RSB
HIGH:    .LONG ^X200            ;initialize high very low
LOW:     .LONG ^X1200           ;initialize low very high
```

Now we can finish writing FINDNO. FINDNO converts 2-, 4-, and 8-character ASCII digit strings into the binary numbers they represent. It expects R0 to have the address of the ASCII string, and it returns the number in R1. R2 points to the first nondigit character, and R4 contains the length of the number (in bytes), so that the loading address (ADDR) can be changed by the appropriate amount. We can write FINDNO as follows:

```
FINDNO:     CLRL R1                  ;R1 will return the number
            CLRL R3                  ;R3 is number was found flag
            CLRL R4                  ;R4 will return the length of the number
FNDNXT:     MOVB (R0)+, R2           ;get next ASCII code
            CMPB R2, #^A/0/          ;check for digit
            BLSSU FNEND              ;smaller than 0: not a number
;else, check for range 0-9
            CMPB R2, #^A/9/
            BLEQU NUMBER             ;number between 0 to 9
;else, check for A-F, or a-f
            CMPB R2, #^A/A/
            BLSSU FNEND              ;9 < char < A: not a number
            CMPB R2, #^A/F/
            BLEQU CAPS               ;else, in range A-F
            CMPB R2, #^A/a/
            BLSSU FNEND              ;F < char < a: not a number
            CMPB R2, #^A/f/
            BLEQU LOWERS             ;else, in range a-f
;else, not a number: done
            BRB FNEND
NUMBER:     SUBB2 #^A/0/, R2         ;change to binary
            BRB SHIFT
CAPS:       SUBB2 #55, R2            ;ASCII code for "A": 65
            BRB SHIFT
LOWERS:     SUBB2 #87, R2            ;ASCII code for "a": 97
SHIFT:      ASHL #4, R1, R1          ;shift R1, for adding R2
            ADDL2 R2, R1            ;add low order digit
            INCL R3                  ;indicate that we found a digit
            INCL R4                  ;number of digits in number
            BRB FNDNXT              ;do until done
FNEND:      ASHL #-2, R4, R4         ;1/2 as many bytes as digits
            RSB                      ;done
```

We have now written the major pieces of the program-loading program. We can collect them, insert some additional definitions and directives, and end up with a working program, as follows:

```
            LF = ^X0A                ;ASCII code for line feed
            CR = ^X0D                ;ASCII code for carriage return
FORCE:      .BLKB ^X200              ;forces MEMORY to address 200, hex
MEMORY:     .BLKB ^X1000             ;memory for program to be loaded
;
            .LIBRARY /[PB]IOMAC.MLB/ ;I/O macro library
;
            .ENTRY START, 0          ;entry point
            IOINIT                   ;initialize I/O channels
            PUTS STARTMESS           ;print starting message
```

```
REPEAT:     TSTB EPFLAG              ;entry point reached?
            BEQL DUMMY               ;if not continue
;else, process entry point
            BRW YES
DUMMY:      GETS LINE                ;read another line
;now, process the line
            PUTS LINE                ;first, echo the line
            MOVAL LINE, R0           ;R0 has address of 1st byte
            JSB SCAN
            TSTB ERFLAG              ;errors?
            BEQL DUMMY2              ;dummy branch, for range
;else, quit
            BRW QUIT
DUMMY2:     BRW REPEAT               ;get another line
;
YES:        PUTS PREDUMPMESS         ;print dump message
            DUMP @LOW, @HIGH         ;and dump memory
            JSB @EP                  ;start user's program
            PUTS EPMESS              ;print entry point message
            PUTS POSTDUMPMESS        ;print dump message
            DUMP @LOW, @HIGH         ;provide memory dump
            BRB DONE                 ;and quit
QUIT:       PUTS QUITMESS            ;print illegal char message
            DONE: $EXIT_S            ;and done
;
EP:         .LONG 0                  ;for entry point address
EPFLAG:     .BYTE 0                  ;flag for if found entry point
ERFLAG:     .BYTE 0                  ;error flag
HIGH:       .ADDRESS ^X200           ;initialize high to low address
LOW:        .ADDRESS ^X1200          ;initialize low to high address
ADDR:       .BLKL 1
;
QUITMESS:
            .ASCIZ /Illegal character; loading terminated/<CR><LF>
STARTMESS:
            .ASCIZ /Loader Working/<CR><LF>
PREDUMPMESS:
            .ASCIZ /Pre-execution memory dump follows:/<CR><LF>
POSTDUMPMESS:
            .ASCIZ /Post-execution memory dump follows:/<CR><LF>
EPMESS:     .ASCII /Entry point: /
            .BLKB 8                  ;for ASCII codes for entry point
            .ASCIZ //<CR><LF>        ;to terminate printing
LINE:       .BLKB 82                 ;one screen's worth of bytes
;
```

;This is subroutine SCAN. It expects R0 to have the address of a string of
;ASCII codes to search for numbers. If it finds a number followed by a
;colon followed by a number, it loads the second number into the address
;indicated by the first. If it finds just a number (not followed by a
;colon), it considers that number the entry point.
;

```
SCAN:       CLRB ERFLAG              ;assume line is ok, to start with
            JSB FINDNO               ;get first number
            TSTB R3                  ;is the line empty?
            BNEQ SCANA               ;if not, continue
;else, return (ignore line)
            BRB RETURN
SCANA:      CMPB R2, #^A/:/          ;first non digit character is in R2
            BNEQ SCANNO              ;wasn't a colon
;else, was a colon, so this is address must load into
            MOVL R1, ADDR            ;save address, for loading into
;and now get next number, to load into ADDR
            JSB FINDNO               ;get next number
            TSTB R3                  ;number?
            BNEQ SCANB               ;yes, so continue
;else, no number, so ignore
            BRB RETURN               ;return
SCANB:      CMPB R2, #CR             ;is 1st non-digit a carriage return?
            BNEQ SCANC               ;if not, error!
;else, load number into address ADDR
            MOVL R1, @ADDR           ;store number in memory
            JSB HILOW                ;update highest and/or lowest address
            ADDL2 R4, ADDR           ;adjust load address for next number
            BRB RETURN               ;and done
;if not a colon or carriage return: error!
SCANC:      INCB ERFLAG              ;set error flag
            BRB RETURN
;if number not followed by colon: entry point
SCANNO:     CMPB R2, #CR
            BEQL SCANOK
;else, invalid char: error!
            INCB ERFLAG
            BRB RETURN
SCANOK:     MOVL R1, EP              ;entry point
            INCB EPFLAG              ;set flag for finding entry point
RETURN:     RSB                      ;and return
;
;This is subroutine HILOW, which checks to see if the address (just placed)
;in ADDR is either larger than HIGH, or smaller than LOW. If it's one or the
;other, then HIGH or LOW is changed; if it isn't, then nothing happens.
;
HILOW:      CMPL ADDR, LOW           ;new address smaller than LOW
            BGEQU HILOWA             ;if not, check vs. HIGH
;else, adjust LOW
            MOVL ADDR, LOW           ;new LOW
HILOWA:     CMPL ADDR, HIGH          ;check if bigger than HIGH
            BLEQU HILOWB             ;if not, done
;else, adjust HIGH
            MOVL ADDR, HIGH          ;new HIGH
HILOWB:     RSB
;
```

```
;This is subroutine FINDNO; it converts ASCII coded hex digit strings
;into their binary equivalents. The address of the digit string is in
;R0; the converted number is returned in R1, the length of the number
;in digits is returned in R4, and whether any number at all was found is
;returned by a non-zero value in R3. The subroutine works by subtracting the
;appropriate offset from the ASCII code (for digits, lowercase "a"-"f", or
;uppercase "A"-"F"), shifting the previous digit, and adding the present one to
;it.
;
FINDNO:     CLRL R1                    ;R1 will return the number
            CLRL R3                    ;R3 is number was found flag
            CLRL R4                    ;R4 will return the length of the number
FNDNXT:     MOVB (R0)+, R2             ;get next ASCII code
            CMPB R2, #^A/0/            ;check for digit
            BLSSU FNEND                ;smaller than 0: not a number
;else, check for range 0-9
            CMPB R2, #^A/9/
            BLEQU NUMBER               ;number between 0 to 9
;else, check for A-F, or a-f
            CMPB R2, #^A/A/
            BLSSU FNEND                ;9 < char < A: not a number
            CMPB R2, #^A/F/
            BLEQU CAPS                 ;else, in range A-F
            CMPB R2, #^A/a/
            BLSSU FNEND                ;F < char < a: not a number
            CMPB R2, #^A/f/
            BLEQU LOWERS               ;else, in range a-f
;else, not a number: done
            BRB FNEND
NUMBER:     SUBB2 #^A/0/, R2           ;change to binary
            BRB SHIFT
CAPS:       SUBB2 #55, R2              ;ASCII code for A: 65
            BRB SHIFT
LOWERS:     SUBB2 #87, R2             ;ASCII code for a: 97
SHIFT:      ASHL #4, R1, R1           ;shift R1, for adding R2
            ADDL2 R2, R1              ;add low order digit
            INCL R3                   ;indicate that we found a digit
            INCL R4                   ;number of digits in number
            BRB FNDNXT               ;do until done
FNEND:      ASHL #-2, R4, R4         ;1/2 as many bytes as digits
            RSB                      ;done
            .END START
```

The above loader will work correctly (providing the system services are available), but it is less sophisticated than the loader available with this book (and whose output is discussed in chapter 3). The simple implementation we have produced in this case study can be enhanced in many ways. Some of the features which might be added are:

1. Handle more than one number per line, with a blank, tab, or comma separating numbers. The loader available with this book accepts a blank or a tab as a separator.
2. Handle blank lines--perhaps by ignoring them.
3. Handle comments by ignoring anything following a semicolon.

4. Check for more than eight hex digits in a number.
5. Warn a user if a memory location is loaded twice.
6. Check that only addresses in the range from 200_{16} to 1200_{16} are used.
7. Handle instruction *mnemonics*: Instead of typing

200: 80 9F 00000220 9F 00000221

(assuming the loader already handles more than one number per line), we could type

200: ADDL2 00000220 00000221

8. Have the loader assign addresses if they are not specified in the program. (But be careful to specify data by addresses, since they will be referenced by addresses.)
9. For each branch instruction, specify the target of the branch as an address, and have the loader calculate the correct offset. Some special syntax might help; for example,

200: 11 > 300

would inform the loader to calculate the offset from 202 (the address *after* the offset) to 300, and store that offset after the opcode.
10. Have the loader *interpret* symbolic labels. By now, the loader is turning into an assembler: it will assemble, load, and execute symbolic programs.
11. Have the loader understand calls to a library of predefined system services. At this point, the loader is also providing some features of a linker.

What about the *predefined* system services? How are they defined, and by whom? We can't answer those questions yet, but by the end of chapter 12 we will know how to write system services for a bare machine. It is much easier to write system services that will be used with a sophisticated operating system like VMS--however, if we wish to do so, we will have to consult the VMS documentation. We will see that the operating system makes writing system services easier, but that it does so by hiding many interesting details of the VAX's architecture.

11

Keyboards, Codes and Terminals

Introduction

We have yet to discuss how the VAX performs input or output operations. Before we do so, it will be helpful to examine the details of the devices that people typically use to communicate with a computer. These devices have evolved rapidly in the last ten years; we will briefly examine some of the simpler ones.

Punched Cards and Paper Tape

Some computing facilities use punched cards as the preferred medium for preparing machine-readable input. We described the standard punched card in an exercise for chapter 1; we saw that it has the capacity for 80 character codes of 12 bits each. As a general rule, keypunched data are **verified** by being fed through a machine that resembles a keypunch; this machine is called a **verifier.** The original data are rekeyed, and each new keystroke is compared with that had already been punched in the card. If this process is successful, only valid data reach the computer.

A different approach is used when preparing data on paper tape. If an error is discovered when the tape is being typed and punched, the tape can be backed up and the erroneous frame can be overpunched with the DEL (delete) code. This is why the DEL code is $3F_{16}$: *any code can be* transformed into DEL. A program which expects to process data from a paper tape must expect to read (and discard) the DEL character. As we will soon see, the situation is even more interesting with CRTs.

Glass Teletypes

We briefly discussed the model 33 Teletype in chapter 1. Well before interactive computing existed, teletype-like devices--**teletypewriters**--were used for nonvoice communication by the military and common carriers (e.g. Western Union Telegrams). They were also used as (primitive) *automatic* typewriters, because of their ability to generate and replay paper tape.

When interactive (timeshared) computer systems became feasible in the mid 1960s, the least expensive device with which a user could interact with a computer system was the model 33 Teletype (TTY). As a result, many Teletypes were pressed into service as computer terminals. Non-timesharing computers also used the Teletype as their interactive device of choice, especially for the then new breed of **minicomputers.**

Other manufacturers, sensitive to the growing market for teletypewriters and the limitations of the TTY, built new products which emulated the TTY in an **upward compatible** fashion: they could do everything a TTY could, and more. The term **glass teletype** refers to a terminal which does little more than emulate a TTY. Such TTYs are usually the least expensive terminals available.

The TTY operates at 10 characters per second (**cps**), which is very slow for a computer that can execute thousands or millions of instructions per second. The TTY is an electro-mechanical device: it tends to be noisy, it needs oiling and cleaning, and it consumes paper and ribbons. Subsequently, manufacturers eliminated the paper and ribbons and substituted a CRT display. The only major mechanical component of such a terminal is often the fan, for internal cooling. Many modern

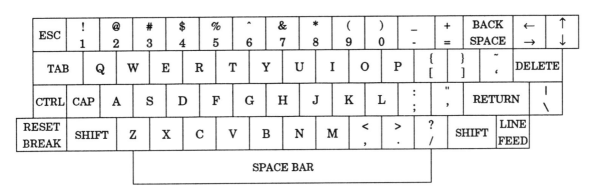

Figure 11.1 A typical keyboard

terminals provide switch selectable speeds from a 10 cps to 1,920 or even 3,840 cps. Terminals emulate the TTY so that they can be substituted for one (they even emulate the TTY Bell signal), but they provide other features in addition to a range of speeds. The TTY only has a 72 character line; most terminals accommodate an 80 character line, some even more. The TTY does not support lowercase letters--which is one reason that many assemblers, and compilers for early high-level languages such as FORTRAN, are biased toward uppercase letters. Most terminals support both upper-*and* lowercase letters (since both are included in the ASCII character set). What about keyboards?

Keyboards

Except for the QWERTY arrangement of the letters of the alphabet, there is little standardization of the terminal's keyboard. The location of punctuation characters, control keys, and so forth varies from one brand to another. One manufacturer may have several different keyboard layouts, even for the same model of terminal. The keyboard for a typical terminal is shown in figure 11.1. In most cases, pressing a key results in transmission of the corresponding ASCII character code. Some of the keys transmit no code, but have a local significance which may affect future code transmission. The keys which cause an ASCII code to be transmitted when depressed are referred to as **encoded** keys.

When we use the ASCII character set, the **shift** key does not transmit a code (if we are using a Baudot code or an IBM PTTC code it does). Any other character key which is pressed while *shift* is pressed (or while it is locked, if we have a **shift-lock** key) will transmit the code corresponding to the alternate marking on the key, or an uppercase letter code, as appropriate. Even nonprinting keys, such as *backspace, return, line feed,* and *tab* transmit an ASCII character code.

The CTRL and Break Keys

Perhaps the most misunderstood keys are the CTRL and *break* keys. The CTRL key is the *Control* key; it is very much like a shift key: any transmitting key that is pressed while CTRL is held down is assigned an alternate meaning. (On some keyboards, the alternate meaning is shown on the keycaps.) For example, CTRL-H generates a *backspace* code, CTRL-G sends a *bell* code which rings the terminal's bell (once per transmission), and CTRL-I sends a *Tab* (HT). These codes are sent regardless of whether these alternate meanings are shown on the keycaps, because they are so

```
 _____
/                                \
|   ABC                          |
|           DEF                  |
|   ZYZ                          |
|                                |
|                                |
|   123                          |
|                                |
|                                |
|                                |
_____/
```

Figure 11.2 Display image on CRT screen

defined by the ASCII character code set. Pushing and releasing the CTRL key has no effect unless some other key is pressed at the same time.

The *break* key is the only one which sends a code that is not part of the ASCII character set! One of the uses of the *break* key is to allow us to *break in* in the middle of a communication. A receiver of a long message may wish to signal the sender of the message to cease transmitting. If the receiver, R, and the sender, S, share a minimal communication line (one pair of wires) it is not possible to reliably send an ASCII code from R to S (requesting, for example, that S cease sending) while S is sending ASCII codes to R. If R and S try to send simultaneously, both parties will get garbled messages. The *break* key provides a solution to this dilemma by forcing all bits (each of which is a high or low voltage level), and all inter-bit gaps, to the same voltage level, for at least one character's transmission time (on a 10 cps terminal, this would be .1 seconds). Thus, the *break* signal will override any in-progress transmission; break-detection circuitry is used to recognize the *break* signal. Both parties in a communication hookup (TTY to TTY, or TTY to CPU) can easily generate or detect a *break* signal. If we receive one, we interpret it, by convention, as a request to cease sending until further notice, or to revert to some previously agreed-upon protocol.

Terminal Displays

Many names are used for computer terminals which display information on a glass screen; some of them are VDU and VDT for Video Display Unit or Terminal, and CRT for Cathode Ray Tube. Such display terminals are manufactured in hundreds of different models with dozens of different attributes. We will describe a typical CRT.

Our CRT can display 24 lines of 80 characters; this is a maximum of 1,920 characters/page (24 * 80 = 1,920). The word *page* is often used to refer to the amount of information that can be displayed at one time on the screen. The information we see on a CRT's screen is being regenerated at the rate of 60 times per second--much like a television image. Without regeneration, the image would rapidly fade and disappear. In order to regenerate a page, a CRT needs a display memory capable of storing (at least) one page of information (1920 bytes). It was this need for memory that kept the cost of CRTs high as recently as the early 1970s.

The relationship between the display memory and the display image is worth looking into. Suppose our CRT screen were displaying the image shown in figure 11.2. This particular screen image may have been caused by a variety of different keystroke sequences (or by no keystrokes at all, if it was generated by received character codes). The keystroke sequence

A,B,C,RET,LF,HT,D,E,F,RET,Z,Y,Z,RET,LF,LF,1,2,3

could have produced the image in figure 11.2. The eight spaces in front of the DEF could have been produced by either a single *horizontal tab* character (as in the keystroke sequence listed above), or by eight spaces, or by two *horizontal tab*s and eight *backspaces,* etc. The keystroke sequence

A,B,C,RET,HT,D,E,F,...

may cause the display memory to store the earlier string, if the CRT hardware interprets the *return* key as a request to send a *return* code ($0D_{16}$), followed (automatically) by a *line feed* code ($0A_{16}$).

An ASCII code that is sent from the keyboard is not necessarily stored in the CRT's display memory. For example, when we log on to an interactive system, our terminal does not usually display our password as we type it. If our terminal is operating in **full duplex** mode (which we will discuss shortly), an ASCII code must be sent to the CPU (from the keyboard) and then sent back to the CRT in order for it to be stored in the CRT's display memory and displayed on the screen. So, the first of the keystroke sequences shown above would be stored in the display memory only if the operating system (which handles I/O) echoes every character it receives.

When we type a *backspace* we may "see" a character disappear, or we may see the cursor back up. However, what we see on the display is not necessarily what is transmitted to the CPU. The operating system must understand that some particular ASCII code means "erase the last character." With some operating systems, the *backspace* character is user selectable; it is not necessarily the same as the *backspace* key (if any) on a terminal. Thus, the behavior of a CRT depends in part on the software running on the CPU it is attached to. In addition, the characteristics of different CRTs often vary greatly.

What happens when the display memory is full? As a general rule, the oldest information is at the top of the screen; when a new line is received, all lines are moved up one line position, and the bottom line is used for the incoming text. This action is called **scrolling.** Some terminals have several pages of display memory; these usually have forward and backward scroll **function keys,** allowing users to browse.

Hard-Copy Terminals

The TTY is an early example of a hard-copy terminal. It was limited to uppercase letters with lines of 72 characters and a speed of 110 baud (10 cps). Many modern hard-copy terminals have selectable speeds in the 10-30 cps range, or as high as 120 cps. Line lengths of 80, 120 or 132 characters are common, and the full ASCII character set (including lowercase) is supported.

Form control is part of the ASCII code set, primarily for the benefit of hard-copy terminal users. The ability to force a continuous-form, fan-folded paper source of 2,500 sheets to begin printing a new page at the precise *top-of-form* is important for hard-copy terminals.

Some terminals interpret the *horizontal tab* code as a signal to skip to the next *tab stop* position (analogous to a typewriter); tab stops may be fixed at every eighth character position, or they may be set by the user. Other terminals ignore the tab code; still others replace it with a single blank.

Modern operating systems accept a description of each terminal's characteristics, and then cooperate with their peripheral hardware. If such a system is told that a CRT has a hardware tab feature, it will send tab codes to that CRT. If the operating system is told that a CRT does *not* have this feature, it can simulate hardware tabs by sending an appropriate number of blanks in place of the tab code it would otherwise have sent. In this case, tabs will have to be replaced by different numbers of blanks, depending on how many nonblank characters precede the tab.

The term **soft-copy** is sometimes used to describe CRTs, to emphasize the contrast with **hard-copy** (paper-using) terminals. In addition, there are soft-copy CRTs with built-in hard-copy printers; on these, we only print what we want to save.

Most hard-copy interactive terminals print each character as it is received; these are **character-printers.** There are also **line-printers,** which print a whole line at a time. Few interactive hard-copy terminals use this technique because it is expensive; it is usually used only for high-speed printing-- in the range of several thousand cps.

Intelligent Terminals

TTYs and glass TTYs are **dumb** terminals. The other kind, **smart** terminals, usually have a built-in microprocessor (or two). Not all terminals with a built-in microprocessor are smart. CRT designers sometimes find it is cheaper to build a dumb terminal by using a microprocessor than by not using one (some microprocessors retail for less than $10.00, and cost much less when purchased in quantity), but these terminals do not provide the additional features that they could easily provide. (This is analogous to the PDP-11 Model 20--the first model of the VAX's predecessor--which was first shipped with an integrated circuit containing hardware for 16 registers, because that was the cheapest way to provide the registers. Since the PDP-11 can "address" only 8 general-purpose registers, every buyer of a PDP-11/20 paid for 16 registers, but could use only 8 of them.) A smart terminal offers a variety of special services. The variety is enormous and bewildering; we will mention just a few.

Programmable Cursor Control

Every CRT has a cursor, which is a symbol that indicates where the next printing character received by the CRT will be displayed. When a character is received, the cursor moves one character position to the right so the new character can be displayed. When the cursor would otherwise pass beyond the end of the line, it instead goes to the beginning of the next line; if necessary, all preceding lines are scrolled up one line. Programmable cursor control allows the distant CPU to send codes to the CRT so that the cursor may be placed at an arbitrary spot on the screen, within the limits of the display's resolution. Often a simple coordinate system is used: the character string

DC4, x (in binary), y (in binary)

would place the cursor at line x in character position y. The DC-n is the ASCII Device Control code. Other CRTs use an **escape sequence** rather than a DC-n sequence. In these cases, *esc* (an ASCII code) is interpreted as a generalized shiftlike code. It *does* transmit an ASCII code, but the receiver presumably treats the immediately following characters in a special way.

Local Editing

If local editing is supported, an *insert line* function key may be available. In this case, after we move the cursor (using special cursor-control keys) to the desired line, if we press the *insert line* key, the terminal squeezes a blank line after the current line (the one on which the cursor is currently positioned)--or before the current line. We may then type a new line's worth of characters in this space. Several other editing functions would normally accompany the insert-line function. In the general case, we use local editing with the terminal in **local mode** (when it is *not* transmitting characters to the CPU). When we have a "perfect" screenful of input, we place the cursor in the *home* position (top left corner of screen); we press the *block transmission* key, our CRT is placed in **remote mode (on-line)**, and the whole screenful of characters is transmitted as a single **block**.

Data-processing-oriented systems often operate in this one-screen-at-a-time manner--as opposed to the one-character-at-a-time method we described earlier. Bank teller systems (used by the clerks, not the customers) and airline reservation systems often use the screen-at-a-time method of interacting with the CPU.

Software Selectable Terminal Characteristics

Some terminals have no switches (for things like speed selection and tab setting): the switches have been replaced by software. These terminals have the same (or more) functional capability that terminals with switches have, but the mechanical switches are gone. To change the characteristics of such a terminal, we enter a special **terminal configuration mode** by pushing a special key or a special sequence of keys. We then select the desired speed, parity, behavior on hitting *return,* etc. from a built-in menu or menues. Replacing hardware by software is not unique to terminals: remember the front panel emulators we discussed when considering machine language program loading programs (in chapter 2)? That was another case of using software to replace hardware.

Parity Selection

Most terminals have a switch-selectable parity option. If it is set to **odd parity,** then an eighth bit will be placed in the high-order position of each byte (whose low-order 7 bits are an ASCII code). The value of this **parity bit** will be such that such that there is an *odd* number of 1 bits in the byte. If **even parity** is selected, the eighth bit's value will guarantee that there is an *even* number of 1s in the byte. A third choice is **zero parity,** which always places a 0 in the high-order bit (this serves no useful function, of course). When set to even or odd parity, a terminal generates the correct parity bit for each outgoing character. In addition, it checks each incoming character for correct parity. If it receives a byte with an odd number of 1s when using even parity, or a byte with an even number of 1s when using odd parity, it should have a way of informing the user that a transmission error (*parity error*) has occurred.

Using Personal Computers with a VAX

It is possible to interact with a VAX without using any of the kinds of terminals we have just described. More and more people who use VAXes do so by using **personal computers** instead of ordinary (smart *or* dumb) terminals. What difference does this make, for someone who writes programs for a VAX? Under most circumstances, it makes almost no difference. Since personal computers such as the IBM PC or the Apple Macintosh are computers in their own right, how can using them as communicating terminals connected to a VAX make very little difference to the program being used on the VAX?

First, a personal computer is not designed specifically for the purpose of being used as a communicating terminal. In order to use a personal computer as a terminal, it has to be equipped with communication hardware (such as an asynchronous port) and communication software. Since DEC, the manufacturer of the VAX, has been supplying communicating terminals such as the VT-100 and the VT-220 for years, it is clear that VAX operating systems know how to respond to codes they receive from these terminals. So, a user of a personal computer would do well to use software that imitates a terminal such as the VT-100 or VT-220 (among others). Imitating a communicating terminal is called **emulating** it. There are software packages available for personal computers which emulate a number of widely-used terminals.

So, when we consider the actual programming of the VAX (or any other computer), the fact that we are using a personal computer as the communicating terminal will have no consequences--if the emulation program has successfully fulfilled its design objectives and causes the personal computer to appear to the VAX as a VT-100, VT-220, or other *simple* terminal.

Connecting Terminals to Computers

There are many ways to connect a terminal to a computer. We will describe two of the most commonly used ones in the following sections.

Half-Duplex Communication

The two-wire communication link that we mentioned above (as the simplest link between a CPU and a terminal) allows reversible one-way communication; this is called a **half-duplex** communication circuit. In other words, one of the two parties sharing the link may send while the other listens, or vice versa. If the two parties transmit simultaneously, both messages will be garbled. This requires a certain discipline on the part of the users, similar to that used on *walkie-talkies* or (more recently) on CB radios. The word *over* is used to indicate that one party has finished sending for the moment, and is listening for messages from the other party.

When we communicate with a computer in half-duplex mode, each character we transmit is echoed on our CRT display by *our* CRT hardware. One purpose of the Full-Duplex/Half-Duplex switch on most CRTs is to cause the CRT to perform **local echo.** With a half-duplex line, we cannot afford the luxury of having the CPU echo each character; that would reduce the line's communication capacity by more than half.

Full-Duplex Communication

An interactive terminal incorporates two distinct communication functions: sending and receiving. Noninteractive terminals also exist: a printer is often a receive-only (RO) device, and it typically has no keyboard. A sensor in an environmental monitoring system, which sends an ASCII coded message when the temperature that it measures exceeds a particular level, is an example of a send-only (SO) device. By definition, an interactive terminal is a send-receive (SR) device. A Model 33 Teletype equipped with a paper tape reader is called an ASR (Automatic SR) device because its reading of a prepositioned paper tape can be started and stopped by another, remotely located, TTY.

If we have an interactive terminal, we may want to receive independently of any sending which we do; sending and receiving are logically distinct, so why not make them electrically distinct, as well? In order to separate sending from receiving, we need more than a two-wire link. One-way communication needs at least one pair of wires (see next section), so it stands to reason that simultaneous two-way communication needs at least two pairs of wires. A simultaneous two-way communication link is called a **full-duplex** communication circuit. Cost was a sufficient reason to use half-duplex communication when the transcontinental telegraph lines were being installed: the cost of doubling the amount of wire to support full duplex communication was too high. In addition, we don't usually think of sending a telegram as an interactive process.

With a CRT connected to a full-duplex line, in full-duplex mode, the codes we send are usually not displayed unless the receiving CPU echoes them (by sending them back to the display). This shows us what the CPU has received and gives us the opportunity to see transmission errors. Let's

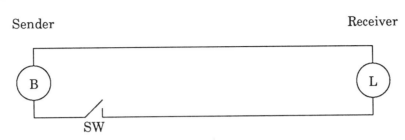

Figure 11.3 Simplex communication link

briefly discuss how half- and full-duplex links can be implemented; many of the apparent mysteries in computing hardware and software are the result of a poor understanding of how bits are transmitted.

Suppose we want a one-way communication link from our house to a friend's house. How can we build something simple, reliable and inexpensive (without involving sophisticated electronics)? Let B be a battery (maybe a six-volt lantern battery), let L be a six-volt light bulb (or a bell or buzzer), and let SW be a switch. With two wires, we can connect the sender, S, and receiver, R, as shown in figure 11.3. Such a one-way communication system is called a **simplex** circuit. By closing the switch (SW), the sender can alert the receiver (R). With a little training, S can send Morse code to R, which is only one step removed from sending bits. This is called a **digital communication circuit.** We will examine how a typical computer communication circuit behaves shortly.

What if we want to allow R and S to exchange roles, so that R can also send to S? One solution is to duplicate the simplex system; in the second circuit, we reverse the placement of L and SW, as shown in figure 11.4. Now, we don't have a *single* sender and a *single* receiver; we have Site 1 and Site 2, and each can be either sender *or* receiver. In fact, Site 1 can send to Site 2 at the same time that Site 2 is sending to Site 1. This is the essence of a full-duplex communication circuit. However, a thinking person on a tight budget might ask, "Do I really need simultaneous two-way communication? Could we not agree to take turns sending and receiving?" If the answer to the

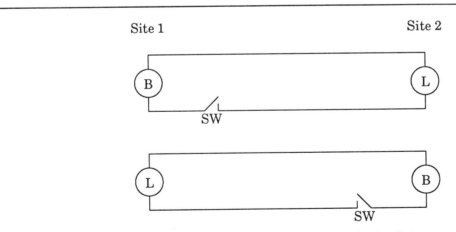

Figure 11.4 Full-duplex communication link

Figure 11.5 Half-duplex communication link

second question is yes, then it is possible to get along with just two wires, as shown in figure 11.5. Site 1 can send to Site 2; and the light at Site 1 echoes what is being sent to Site 2 (this is **local echo**). Site 2 can also send to Site 1, and Site 2 also gets a local echo while sending. If Site 1 and Site 2 try to send simultaneously, both messages will be garbled. This simple circuit depicts a two-wire half-duplex communication circuit. When we build such a circuit, we might use wire which comes as a **twisted pair,** because such wire has higher immunity to electrical *noise* than does telephone wire. So, in talking about CRTs which are *hardwired* (directly and permanently connected) to a CPU, we often hear about some number of twisted pairs being used.

Binary Transmission Codes

The practical code for the simple systems shown in figures 11.3, 11.4 and 11.5 is the International Morse Code, which represents each character by a combination of short and long light flashes (or buzzer signals, etc.). By convention, we use a dot (.) and a dash (-) to represent the two digits of this strange-looking binary code. (The Morse Code is listed in one of the exercises at the end of this chapter.) Many people are familiar with SOS, the international distress signal (vocalized as "Mayday"); it is written as "· · · - - - · · ·" in Morse Code. Morse Code is practical for nonvoice, people-to-people communication. We can even buy computer hardware for transmitting and receiving Morse Code. In Morse Code, time intervals are critical: a dot is a signal of specified duration, a dash must last a specified number of times longer than a dot, the dot and dash separation interval is specified, and the interval between character codes is a specified duration. How does this compare with conventions for transmission of ASCII character codes?

The technique used to transmit ASCII codes is also used with other binary character codes (EBCDIC, etc.), but we will use only ASCII codes in our examples. A standard technique for transmitting bits is to associate with each 1 bit a **mark** signal corresponding to a voltage level in a particular range, say -5 to -15 volts. A 0 bit is then represented as a signal corresponding to a positive voltage level, say in the range +5 to +15 volts; a 0 is traditionally called a **space** (as distinct from a **mark**). The voltage levels for a 0 or a 1 must be held constant for a specified period of time (a **bit time**), and the bit-separation time is also specified. When the bits of a byte have been transmitted, the time before sending the first bit of the next character must exceed a specified duration. If we understand how bits are transmitted in a simplex system, we can understand full- and half-duplex systems by analogy.

How does the receiver, R, on a simplex circuit know when a byte is being sent by the sender, S? Every ASCII code is preceded by a single mark bit. The receiving hardware at R monitors the communication line, looking for what may be a **mark** voltage level. If we were manually simulating the R hardware algorithm, we would be doing the following:

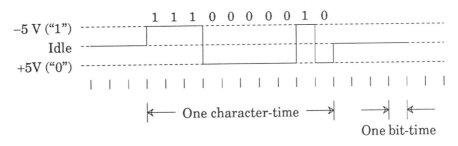

Figure 11.6 Sending an ASCII A

1.   Are we seeing a voltage level which represents a 1?
         If not, go back to step 1 (keep looking).
         If maybe, keep looking for a few milliseconds:
                  If the level is still in the right range, go to step 2.
                  If the level fluctuates, consider it noise and go to step 1.
2.   When the (presumed) initial mark bit ends, begin timing:
         Expect a new bit every 10 ms, and begin counting the bits.
         When a full character's worth of bits has been collected, present the byte to R's
                  processing unit.
         Go to step 1.

Let's see how the ASCII code for A would be transmitted: the ASCII code is 41_{16}, or $100\ 0001_2$. If
we add an odd parity bit, the code is 1100 0001; when we add **framing bits,** we get 1 1100 0001 0.
The framing bits are comprised of a preceding space bit (the **start** bit) and a following mark bit (the
stop bit). Actually, an ASR TTY uses *2* stop bits; more modern devices--those communicating at rates
of 300 bits per second and above--use only a single stop bit. The communication hardware converts
this bit stream, beginning with the **start** bit, into voltage levels, as shown in figure 11.6.

    The general case of transmitting a character is shown in figure 11.7. The ASCII code bits are
preceded by the **start** bit; then the code is sent, from low-order to high-order bits, followed by the
parity bit, followed by the **stop** bit. The framing bits are transparent to the user; our program never
sees them, and we never create them. The communication hardware puts them in at the transmitting
site, and strips them off at the receiving site. These start and stop bits make it possible for R and S
to communicate without a **common clock.** R and S each need a clock, of course, because timing
determines when the sender sends the next bit, and when the receiver looks for the next bit.

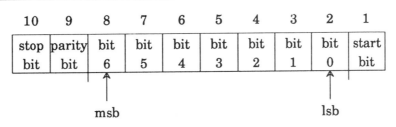

Figure 11.7 Bit-transmission sequence

However, the clocks of R and S need not be synchronized as long as they each measure time intervals with sufficient accuracy. Clock synchronization usually requires a common clock and special wiring to share its signals; this is expensive. When we communicate *without* clock synchronization we have a *self-clocking* system; such a system supports **asynchronous** communication.

If the framing bits are transparent to computer users, why do we mention them? We mention them because it would otherwise be unclear why a 110 baud (**baud** designates bits per second) transmitter can send only 10 characters per second, if each character is composed of a 7-bit ASCII code with a single parity bit. If there were only 8 bits per character, then 10 characters per second would add up to 80 baud, not 110. Clearly, the framing bits account for the missing 30 bits per second. At 110 baud there are 3 framing bits per character: 1 start bit and 2 stop bits. Thus each ASCII code requires that 8 + 3 = 11 bits be transmitted. At 10 cps, this comes out to 110 baud. At higher baud rates--300 baud and above--only 2 framing bits are used: 1 start bit and 1 stop bit. So a 300 baud ASCII terminal can send or receive:

$$\frac{300}{(2+8)=10} = 30 \text{ cps}$$

Similarly, at 9600 baud, 960 characters can be transmitted in one second.

Framing bits are added and removed by the communication hardware. Our programs never see these bits, even though they influence the data communication rate. Our programs might or might not see a nonzero parity bit; it depends on the communication software being used. Some software makes parity handling transparent to user programs, so we always see the parity bit with the value 0. Other software sends the whole byte, including the parity bit, on to our programs.

The voltage level conventions, framing bit conventions, etc. that we have described are those used by a common serial data communication standard--RS-232C.

Baud and Bits per Second

The term **baud,** in honor of Emil Baudot, is used for transmission rates in both the computing business and the telecommunication business. The latter group used it first, and we should understand that their definition is slightly different from that commonly used in computing. In telecommunication, **baud** is the number of signal events per second. A **signal event** could be a light flash (which is identical to a bit), or it could be a flag used in ship-to-ship communication. Since a flag can have more than two positions (up, down, left, right, top-right quadrant, etc.), the bit rate in the latter case may be considerably higher than the baud rate. Whenever a signal event can convey more than 1 bit of information, baud and BPS (bits per second) are not equivalent. In computing, baud rate is usually equivalent to BPS; we will discuss an important exception when we discuss telecommunication.

We have dealt with **serial communication** in this section; the communication is *serial* when we transmit bytes (or anything else) 1 bit at a time. Clearly, we can transmit many more bits per unit time if we transmit several of them at once. This involves using **parallel communication**; if we want to send *n* bits at a time, we need *n* pairs of wires. We will discuss parallel transmission in a later chapter.

One word of caution before we finally discuss how the VAX performs I/O operations (in the next chapter): many problems encountered in learning about I/O are caused by a misunderstanding of what the I/O device itself is capable of doing--what switches it has, what their various settings mean, and so on. If we understand the material in this chapter, we will be in a better position to understand the material in the next chapter and to deal with the problems that we encounter when we write programs that perform input and output operations, I/O.

Summary

Character-oriented devices play an important role in computing. Most of the interactive devices we work with are character-oriented. Punched cards, paper tape, and many printers and other devices are character-oriented, as well. Of the character-oriented devices, the CRT has become the most common. We have briefly examined the characteristics of a composite CRT. The importance of distinguishing between the **encoded** keys and the **unencoded** keys (*shift, control,* etc.) has been stressed.

We have discussed simple communication schemes that link CRTs and other devices to each other and to computers. We examined **simplex, half-duplex** and **full-duplex** communication. The roles of the parity bit and the framing bits and their relationship to the common measure of transmission speed, **baud,** have been defined.

A clear understanding of what devices can or cannot do and how they are linked to a computer is a prerequisite for understanding our next topic: computer input and output.

Exercises for Chapter 11

1. If you have access to a CRT, perform the following experiment. Put the CRT in local (off-line or not-remote) mode. Type CTRL-G: what happens? How long (how many characters) can a line be? How many lines can be displayed? What does the CRT do in response to:

   a. CTRL-G
   b. CTRL-H
   c. CTRL-I
   d. CTRL-J
   e. CTRL-K
   f. CTRL-M

   Does your CRT have any keys that, without simultaneously pressing the CTRL key, perform the functions listed above? After this experiment, put your CRT back on-line.

2. If you are using a hard-copy interactive terminal, put it in local mode and see how it responds to the ASCII forms-control characters such as vertical tab, horizontal tab, form feed, line feed, carriage return, and bell. Does a carriage return also cause a line feed? What is the line length and printing speed?

3. Test the operating system you are using in the following ways:

   a. What program do you execute to have the operating system tell you what information it has about your terminal's characteristics?
   b. What program do you execute to inform the operating system that you have, for example, changed the switch settings on your terminal from 2400 baud to 4800 baud, or from full-duplex to half-duplex?
   c. Use the command from (a) to see what the system knows about your terminal. Use the command from (b) to temporarily change

      (1.) your duplex mode
      (2.) your "erase" character

   d. What happens if you tell the operating system that your terminal is in half-duplex mode, but the switch is in the full-duplex position? Why does this happen?
   e. What happens if you tell the operating system that your terminal is in full-duplex, but the switch is in the half-duplex position? Why?

A	·-	B	-···	C	-·-·	D	-··	E	·
F	··-·	G	--·	H	····	I	··	J	·---
K	-·-	L	·-··	M	--	N	-·	O	---
P	·--·	Q	--·-	R	·-·	S	···	T	-
U	··-	V	···-	W	·--	X	-··-	Y	-·--
Z	--··								
1	·----	2	··---	3	···--	4	····-	5	·····
6	-····	7	--···	8	---··	9	----·	0	-----
.	·-·-·-	?	··--··	:	---···	;	-·-·-·	-	-···-

/   -··-·   End-of-message   ·-·-·

Figure 11.8 International Morse Code

4. Write a program that translates from Morse Code to ASCII codes and from the corresponding ASCII subset back to Morse. Write the program using a table with an entry for each of the Morse codes; represent each Morse code as a pair of bytes: a bit count, followed by the code itself. Use 0 for "." and 1 for " -". (The bit count is useful because not all letters have the same number of "bits": for example, "E" is ".", and ":" is "- - - · · ·".) The Morse Code is shown in figure 11.8.

5. Write another Morse-to-ASCII translator, but do not use a bit-count field. Instead, use a single 16-bit word for each Morse character.

6. Using either of the techniques from the previous two exercises, generalize your program so that it accepts or generates all printing ASCII characters. Clearly describe the mechanism you use for mapping a rich character set into a poor one, and vice versa.

7. Since the first IBM 360, IBM main frame computer systems have used the 8-bit EBCDIC code. Find a reference which shows the EBCDIC code; compare it to ASCII. Answer the following questions, for each code set:

   a. How many printing characters are supported?
   b. How many nonprinting characters are supported?
   c. Which printing characters are unique to each set?
   d. Does either code support some unique function?
   e. Are the codes for alphabetic characters contiguous--are there intervening nonalphabetic codes?
   f. Are the codes for alphabetic characters in lexicographic order?

8. Outline a program which could perform ASCII-EBCDIC conversion. Is any part especially tricky? If so, which part?

9. Suppose you are sending visual messages from ship to ship, using flags. You have a red and a green flag (one in each hand). Assume that each flag operates independently, that the legal flag positions are up, down, left, right, hidden, and that it takes two seconds to move a flag from one setting to the next.

   a. What is the baud rate?
   b. What is the information transmission rate?

10. If a CRT has a 24-line by 80-character display, how long does it take to fill the screen when operating at

   a. 300 baud
   b. 1200 baud
   c. 9600 baud
   d. 19,200 baud
   e. 38,400 baud

11. If you are using a CRT:

   a. What is its baud rate?
   b. How fast can the screen fill at that baud rate?
   c. Is there any variance in the speed with which the screen fills? If so, why?

12. What is the parity of each of the following?

   a. 132 octal
   b. 101 binary
   c. 1011 binary
   d. 101 decimal
   e. AB hexadecimal

■ 12 ■

Character-Oriented Input and Output

Introduction

The input and output operations used by assembly language programmers on multiuser systems are not very different from those used by high-level language programmers. The software available with this book provides system services to read characters (GETC) or lines (GETS) and to print characters (PUTC) or lines (PUTS); Pascal provides similar input and output functions. In high-level languages a great deal of support software (the run-time I/O library) is provided so that I/O *appears* easy. When we work on a bare machine, this support software is not available, and I/O seems much more complicated. The problem is not that I/O is complicated; the problem is that, when we work on a bare machine, *we* must do *all* of the work--including that required for I/O.

One of the reasons that I/O seems complicated is that we often confuse two related but distinct phenomena:

1. Transforming numbers from their internal (binary) representation to their external (ASCII coded decimal, perhaps) representation, or vice versa;
2. Getting bits *to* the computer (for input), and getting them *from* the computer (for output).

If we treat the data representation transformations as the separate problem that they are, I/O seems simpler. I/O is simpler, but it is not trivial; we will discover that understanding I/O on the VAX involves additions to the picture that we currently have of both the instruction fetch-execute cycle and the VAX's memory system. We will begin our discussion of I/O on the VAX with an examination of the hardware involved in connecting a terminal and a CPU.

CRT-CPU Interconnect Hardware

A layperson's view of a CRT-CPU link is shown in figure 12.1. A layperson typically thinks of this link as one along which data are transmitted from the terminal to the CPU and from the CPU to the terminal.

This view is correct as far as it goes, but it doesn't go very far; we are interested in more detail. A more detailed view is shown in figure 12.2. A CRT is usually connected to a computer by connecting a **serial interface controller** to the CPU. This piece of hardware is called an *interface* because it connects two different pieces of hardware: the CPU and the CRT. It is called a *controller* because it controls the CRT. It is called *serial* because the terminal is a serial device: it sends bits to the CPU one at a time. This serial interface controller is often called just a *controller,* an *interface, or a serial interface,* for short. The interface uses two or more wires to transfer the serial *input* of characters from the CRT to the CPU, and two or more other wires to transfer the serial *output* from the CPU to the CRT.

The wires connecting the keyboard to the CPU receive information from the keyboard, and so are *receive* wires from the CPU's perspective. However, the same wires *send* information from the keyboard to the CPU, and so are *transmit* wires, from the keyboard's perspective. Similarly, the CPU *transmits* information to the CRT on the wires connecting the CPU to the display, while the display *receives* information from the CPU along those wires. These considerations might suggest that it is unclear whether a given pair of wires is used for transmitting or for receiving; this is true,

Figure 12.1 Layperson's view of an I/O link

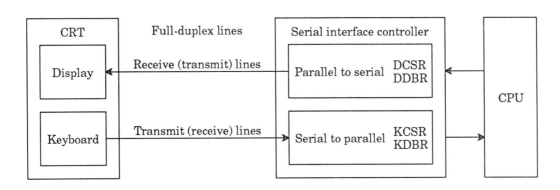

Figure 12.2 Assembly language programmer's view of an I/O link

philosophically, but we adopt conventions: our world is CPU-centered, so *output* means output *from* the CPU, and *input* means input *to* the CPU.

The four wires described above are the minimum required for full-duplex communication. There are cases when more wires are desirable; some of these situations will be discussed in the chapter on telecommunication.

Data Buffer Registers (DBR); Control and Status Registers (CSR)

For full-duplex communication, we need only two pairs of wires connecting the serial interface controller with the CRT. However, we need more than two pairs of wires to connect the controller with the CPU, because the CPU transfers 1 *byte* at a time to, and receives 1 byte at a time from, the controller. One of the functions of the serial interface controller is to accept information from the CPU 1 byte at a time, and transmit it to the CRT 1 *bit* at a time. For input, similarly, the controller receives information 1 bit at a time from the terminal, and (after collecting 8 bits) presents it to the CPU 1 byte at a time. The CPU does **byte parallel** transmission and reception; the CRT does **bit serial** transmission and reception.

The serial interface hardware provides two kinds of registers for use by the CPU and terminal: Data Buffer Registers (DBR), and Control and Status Registers (CSR). The DBR for a CRT controller typically has a 1 byte capacity; when the CPU wishes to have the CRT display a character, it places the character's 7- or 8-bit code in the DBR. On the other hand, when the CPU expects to receive a character code from the CRT, it "looks for" it in the DBR. How can we use the DBR for transmitting characters both to and from the CPU?

A CRT that is connected to a CPU in full-duplex mode permits simultaneous sending from the CRT to the CPU and from the CPU to the CRT; therefore, there must be a DBR for *each* of these functions. Since the CPU does not necessarily know when the CRT completes transmission of a byte, and since the CRT does not necessarily know when the CPU completes transmission of a byte, (in other words, the CPU and CRT operate **asynchronously**) each of these functions also requires a Control and Status Register. We will call the DBR that receives bits from a keyboard the *Keyboard* DBR (KDBR); the CSR associated with such a device will be called the KCSR. Similarly, we will call the DBR that receives bits from the CPU for transmission to a display device the *Display* DBR (DDBR), and the CSR associated with such a device the DCSR. Occasionally, we will not need to distinguish between sending to the CPU and sending to the terminal; in those cases, we will use CSR and DBR.

Let's examine the sequence of events that occurs when a user types a key on a terminal:

1. The ASCII code for the character whose "picture" is on the cap of the key that was pressed is sent (by the terminal's hardware), 1 bit at a time, along the pair of wires connecting the keyboard with the serial interface controller.
2. The interface collects the bits, accumulates a byte's worth of information, and places the byte in the KDBR.
3. The CPU gets the byte from the KDBR.

The situation is analogous for transmission of a byte from the CPU to the CRT; it will be discussed in more detail shortly.

The CRT and the CPU must (usually) use the same character codes if useful interaction is to take place. This does not mean that we cannot connect an EBCDIC terminal to the CPU with one interface, and an ASCII terminal with a separate but identical interface; the code conversion can be handled by software (if you don't remember the MOVTUC instruction, review its action, described in chapter 10). In addition, the CRT and the interface it is connected to must be operating at the same baud rate. For hard-wired terminals (terminals permanently connected to a particular CPU), this is not a problem, as the speed selection switches on the CRT and its interface can be set to match and left that way. For nonhard-wired terminals, (*e.g.,* those using telephone dialup lines), however, baud rate detection must be done so that the interface can set its baud rate to match that of the dialup terminal. We will discuss speed detection along with telecommunication, in chapter 20. Note that a CRT's *send* baud rate and its *receive* baud rate need not be the same; this is a freedom allowed by a full-duplex line.

Input and Output Instructions

One approach to implementing I/O functions in hardware is to provide a special set of instructions for I/O. This approach assumes that all I/O devices are specified to the CPU by a device number. To have a CRT, for example, display the letter *A,* we need to use an instruction that sends a byte containing the ASCII code for *A* to the CRT's controller. A computer that uses this approach might execute a hypothetical instruction such as ODB R1, D7. This would mean "transmit an *output* data byte from R1 (in the CPU) to device 7's DBR." Once a byte gets to an output device's data buffer register, the device's controller assumes responsibility for having the bits sent (one at a time, if it is a serial device) to the device itself. The data transfer from the CPU's register to the device's DDBR occurs at the instruction execution rate of the CPU; it is, essentially, a register-to-register copy, and on most VAXes would take much less than 1 microsecond.

For input, a computer using I/O instructions might execute the instruction IDB R2, D6, which would input a data byte from device 6's KDBR and copy it to R2. What if device 6 had not completed transmitting the byte to its controller's KDBR when the CPU executed the IDB instruction? Similarly, what if the CPU executed an ODB instruction to device 7, before device 7's interface had completed transmitting the previous byte to the display? Both of these situations would result in garbled transmission; how can we avoid that?

The problem we have just described is called **data overrun.** It results in corrupted data, or data loss. We can usually avoid it by using the device's CSR to check the device's status. If the device is still busy transmitting a byte, and we (the CPU) want to send the next byte, then we either wait until it becomes nonbusy (i.e. *ready* for more work), or we do something else for a while, and then come back and check again. The DCSR has a **done/ready bit** which is automatically set (by the serial interface controller, not our program) when the CPU executes an instruction that loads the device's data buffer register with a new byte to be output (i.e., sent to the device). The device's interface controller clears the done/ready bit in the DCSR when it is *done* transmitting: when the last framing bit is sent along the wires to the device. The DDBR now contains *old* data--data which have already been sent to the device and can be harmlessly over-written by the next byte placed by the CPU in the device's DDBR.

The KCSR also has a done/ready bit. When a device's serial interface controller finishes collecting the bits sent (one at a time) from the device, and places the assembled byte in the device's KDBR, it sets the done/ready status bit in that device's CSR, indicating that it is *ready* for the CPU to read the byte. When the CPU executes an instruction that reads the byte in the device's KDBR, the interface controller clears the done/ready bit in the device's CSR.

A beginner's attempt to use the hypothetical I/O instructions ODB and IDB could result in the following code segment:

```
          MOVAB HELPMSG, R1
NEXT:     MOVB (R1)+, R2
          BEQL DONE
          ODB R2, D6              ;not a VAX instruction
          BRB NEXT
DONE:     .
          .
          .
HELPMSG:  .ASCIZ "HELP!"<^X0D><^X0A>
```

This code fragment is intended to send the the message "HELP!", as if ODB were a VAX instruction. Unfortunately, the message received will be garbled. As soon as the first framing bit for the "H" is on its way to device 6, the CPU will over-write the partially transmitted bits for "H" with the code for "E", and so on--because the CPU can execute the ODB instruction much faster than the serial interface controller can send bits to the device. The problem can be eliminated by modifying our program as follows:

```
          MOVAB HELPMSG, R1
NEXT:     ISW R3, D6             ;check input status (hypothetical instruction)
          BLSS NEXT             ;if current byte not yet sent, check again
          MOVB (R1)+, R2        ;if sent, can send next byte
          BEQL DONE
          ODB R2, D6            ;hypothetical instruction
          BRB NEXT
DONE:     .
          .
          .
HELPMSG:  .ASCIZ "HELP!"<^X0D><^X0A>
```

The ISW instruction (a hypothetical one) is used to copy the DCSR for device 6 into register 3. If the done/ready bit is the most significant bit of the DCSR, and if this bit is *set* while bit-serial transmission (of bits from the device to the DDBR) is in progress, then the two instruction loop

```
NEXT:     ISW R3, 6              ;check input status (hypothetical instruction)
          BLSS NEXT              ;if current byte hasn't been sent, check again
```

can be used to synchronize the CPU's high instruction execution speed with the device's much slower transmission speed. This loop is called a **busy-wait loop.** It is a *wait* loop because the CPU is branching back to the same instruction, *waiting* for the device's serial interface controller to clear the done/ready bit. It is called a *busy*-wait loop because the CPU is *busy* (waiting). The CPU does nothing productive while it is executing the loop. If we took the busy-wait loop out of context, it would seem puzzling: it would look like an infinite loop, because neither of the two instructions in the loop changes anything--it is up to the device's controller to change the done/ready bit, so that, eventually, when we execute the ISW instruction, the high-order bit of the device's CSR is 0, and so the BLSS will *not* be taken.

Many computers use instructions similar to ISW, ODB, and IDB to perform I/O. On the other hand, many computers have no special I/O instructions of any kind; the VAX is one of the latter. Fortunately, we have not been wasting our time considering the approach that uses I/O instructions. Everything we have seen has a counterpart on the VAX.

I/O without I/O Instructions

If we expect to attach several (or, many) I/O devices to a computer, it seems reasonable to assign an identification number to each one. Device identification numbers serve the same purpose for I/O devices that memory addresses serve for memory locations: they specify which of a number of possible things we wish to use. The designers of the VAX (and the designers of the PDP-11, before them) realized that, if they could *really* treat device numbers as addresses, they would not have to create special I/O instructions. Rather, ordinary instructions, most of which can specify a destination in memory (or a general-purpose register), could specify a *device address* in order to perform I/O. If, however, an instruction doesn't specify that it is an I/O instruction, how will I/O actually occur? Why won't a byte that our program wishes to send to a CRT just be placed in some memory location, never to see the light of day?

Up to now, we have dealt with the VAX's memory as an array of homogeneous, identical, locations. However, if we are going to use memory addresses instead of device identification numbers, and if we are not going to have special I/O *instructions,* then we will have to have special I/O *addresses*--which is just what the VAX has. So, the VAX *partitions* its memory system into two parts: program addresses and I/O device register addresses. Where are these parts? The answer is system-dependent and involves a review of the VAX's **virtual memory.**

Recall that (in chapter 3) we briefly discussed the fact that the addresses that our program uses are *not* necessarily the addresses that are sent along the bus to the memory system. Our program generates **virtual addresses,** as if the VAX actually had 4,294,967,296 (2^{32}) bytes of memory. Many computer purchasers cannot afford that much memory (the largest VAX system currently available can have a maximum of "only" 268,435,456 bytes of physical memory); what do they do? The virtual addresses generated by our program are translated by hardware in the CPU (called the **Memory Management Unit,** or MMU) into **physical addresses**--addresses that correspond to memory locations actually present in the memory system. In the VAX, the operating system and the hardware cooperate to keep track of where in physical memory our program happens to be loaded and to translate the virtual addresses which our program generates into the appropriate physical addresses. This topic is usually discussed in depth in operating system courses; we needn't concern ourselves with its details, for now.

So, for a given VAX system, the I/O device registers are assigned addresses that are *larger* than the address of any physical memory location installed in that VAX system. Thus, connecting an I/O device to a VAX involves plugging its controller into the CPU, running wires (however many may be

```
                  DCSR = ^X????????          ;address of display CSR
                  DDBR = DCSR+2              ;address of display DBR
                  MOVAB HELPMSG, R1
SEND:             TSTB @#DCSR               ;check busy bit in CSR
                  BGEQ SEND                 ;check again if busy (busy-wait loop)
;else, device not busy, so OK to send it another byte
                  MOVB (R1)+, @#DDBR        ;send the byte
                  BNEQ SEND                 ;send bytes until done
                     .
                     .
                     .
HELPMSG:          .ASCIZ "HELP!"<^X0D><^X0A>
```

Figure 12.3 Output code

necessary) between the device and its controller, and assigning addresses for the device's DBR(s) and CSR(s) by setting the appropriate switches. A device will usually have more than one address, because a device will usually have at least one DBR and one CSR; a terminal, recall, is both an input device (the keyboard) and an output device (the display); each device requires both a DBR and a CSR, so a terminal's I/O registers are assigned four addresses. This approach to I/O has been adopted by many minicomputers and microcomputers; it is called **memory-mapped** I/O.

As a rule, device buffer registers are assigned word addresses even if they only support byte data. In the VAX, some CSRs are 16 bits wide and others are 32 bits wide; the size of a device's CSR(s) and DBR(s) is dependent upon the characteristics of the device. A receive-only device would be assigned two addresses--for its CSR and DBR--as would a send-only device. Device registers are usually contiguous, so a terminal would be assigned four consecutive (word) addresses.

We can now write a *real* VAX program, shown in figure 12.3, which performs a useful I/O function. This code segment will display the message "HELP!" on the CRT whose CSR and DBR have been assigned the specified addresses. Note that it is appropriate to use absolute addressing (@#DDBR) when referring to device registers. Normally, we don't care where our program is loaded into memory; we only care that when we use a symbolic label, the control unit finds the value that we have stored in the corresponding location, *wherever* it is. With device CSRs and DBRs, however, we care very much about *exactly* the address that we specify; if we use the wrong address, we will try to send a byte to a different terminal, or perhaps to some location in the middle of our program. We use absolute addressing because we must insist on a particular address.

The assumption of the program fragment in figure 12.3 is that bit 7 of the device's CSR indicates the device's done/ready status. As long as the most significant bit of the low byte of the CSR is 0, our program will continue to execute the BGEQ instruction--it will be in the busy-wait loop. When the device's serial interface controller completes transmitting the last bit from the device's DBR along the wires to the display, the controller will set bit 7 of the CSR, so the BGEQ will *not* be taken, and the program will place another data byte in the DBR, for transmission to the device. Placing a byte in the device's DBR has the side effect of clearing the done/ready bit in the device's CSR.

It is important that we understand that the code in figure 12.3 (and other examples of code for I/O) would work correctly only if it were executed by a privileged user. I/O devices (such as line printers) are often shared by many users; the operating system and hardware cooperate to prevent ignorant (or malicious) users from using these shared resources inappropriately by ensuring that only a privileged (trusted and knowledgeable) user can directly access their registers. Thus, ordinary users must use **system service requests**--such as PUTC, GETC, etc.--for I/O.

```
                    KCSR = 0x????????            ;input CSR
                    KDBR = KCSR+2                ;input DBR
                    DCSR = KDBR+2                ;output CSR
                    DDBR = DCSR+2                ;output DBR
                    .ENTRY START, 0
        ;first, check if keyboard has sent a character
        INPUT:      TSTB @#KCSR                  ;check if input waiting
                    BGEQ INPUT                   ;if not, check again
        ;else, check if display is ready for output
        OUTPUT:     TSTB @#DCSR                  ;is display busy?
                    BGEQ OUTPUT                  ;if so, check again
        ;else, echo typed character on display
                    MOVB @#KDBR, @#DDBR          ;output device ← input
                    BRB INPUT                    ;keep echoing
```

Figure 12.4 I/O echo code

Let us now examine a code segment that performs both input *and* output, shown in figure 12.4. This is the kind of test program we might use when trying to determine if a CRT, its interface, the CPU, or a cable is responsible for a communication failure.

It is important to understand who does what, and when, to either a device's DBR or CSR, in order understand how I/O works. For input, the following events occur:

1. The user presses a key on the CRT's keyboard.
2. The ASCII code for the letter on the cap of the key that was pressed is sent, bit-serially, along the pair of wires connecting the CRT to its serial interface controller.
3. The serial interface controller receives the bits one at a time from the device; it assembles the byte in the correct order (low-order bits in the low-order bit positions and high-order bits in the high-order bit positions), and places the byte in the KDBR.
4. The done/ready bit, bit 7, in the KCSR is set when the byte is placed in the KDBR.
5. The next instruction that uses the address of the KDBR as its source operand (such as MOVB @#KDBR, R0) clears bit 7 of the KCSR.

For output, the following sequence of events occurs:

1. When an instruction uses the address of the display's DBR as its destination operand (such as MOVB R0, @#DDBR), the device's controller clears bit 7 of the DCSR.
2. The device's serial interface controller shifts the bits out the the DDBR one at a time, and sends them along the wires (bit-serially) to the CRT.
3. The interface controller sets the done/ready bit, bit 7, in the DCSR when the last bit has been sent to the display device.

How does use of the DDBR address as a destination operand (or of the KDBR as a source operand) clear bit 7 in the appropriate CSR? Clearing this bit can't be under control of the CPU, because with memory-mapped I/O, the CPU doesn't even know that the destination (or source) is anything other than an ordinary memory location. The setting and clearing of bit 7 is another function of the device's controller. All device register addresses are larger than any ordinary memory location addresses, so the memory system controller ignores CSR or DBR addresses that are sent along the bus. However, when the device's controller is connected to the CPU, its register addresses

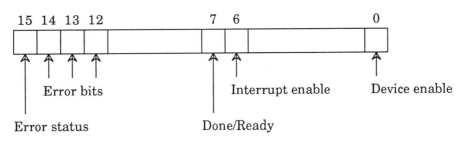

Figure 12.5 Typical CSR

are chosen, and set (usually with a series of switches) appropriately. Thus, the controller also monitors addresses that are sent on the bus, and when it sees an address for one of *its* registers, it either provides the data that are in the KDBR (if it sees the KDBR address accompanied by a *read* request) or loads the data into the DDBR (if it sees the DDBR address accompanied by a *write* request).

One might wonder why it is necessary to have *two* busy-wait loops in the echo program in figure 12.4. This clearly is necessary when the send and receive baud rates are different--as is often the case in data processing systems. A 300 baud keyboard input rate, and a 1200 baud display output rate, is not an unusual combination; if the sender goes faster than the receiver, or vice versa, one of them has to wait for the other.

What if the send and receive data rates are identical, however? Recall that in an asynchronous communication link, the sender and the receiver do not have a common clock. So, slight variations in the data rate could occur, and they could result in data overrun. It is wiser to be safe than sorry, so we use two busy-wait loops rather than one. What if, somehow, data overrun (or some other error) occurs? Let us take a closer look at the CSR to see how a device's interface reports "bad" data to us.

Control and Status Bits

The CSR has two functions. We have already seen one of these functions--the *status* function--which is provided by the done/ready bit. The done/ready bit indicates the status of a device by showing when a byte sent by an input device has been shifted into its DBR, or by showing when all bits of a byte have been shifted out of the DBR and sent to an output device. The other function of the CSR is related to the CPU's *control* of I/O devices. Simple devices (such as terminals) cannot do very many different things, so the control function provided by the CSR is minimal. More sophisticated devices (some of which we will examine later) can perform so many different operations (any one of which must be specified by the CPU) that they need more than a single CSR: there are not enough bits in one CSR to adequately specify which function the device is to perform at any particular time.

The CSR for a typical simple device is organized as shown in figure 12.5. Bit 15, the **error status** bit, is the logical **or** of bits 12, 13, and 14, which report specific error situations. A typical meaning for the error bits in the CSR of a serial interface controller is shown in figure 12.6.

The CSR is unusual in that some bits are **read-only** and others are **write-only.** Bit 7 (the done/ready bit) in a CSR is a read-only bit: no program ever sets or clears it; it is set and cleared by the serial interface controller as a side effect of placing a byte in the DBR. If we write a program that has the instruction CLRB @#DCSR, it will have no effect on bit 7.

Error Bit	Meaning
12	Parity error on received character
13	Framing error; no *stop* bit
14	Data overrun
15	Error status

Figure 12.6 Error status bits

Bit 0 of a TTY's CSR is an example of a write-only bit. If we try to examine this bit, even immediately after we have set it, we will always see it with the value 0. Trying to read bit 0 clears it. When we execute INCW @#KCSR, we will always *set* it: the INCW instruction first *reads* its operand from memory, then adds 1 to it, and then *writes* it back to memory; the act of reading the value of the CSR clears bit 0, and then adding 1 to it sets this bit. Historically, bit 0 was used to signal an ASR TTY: when the bit is set, the ASR TTY's paper tape reader will read one more character, and then stop.

It is unfortunate that some bits in CSRs are read-only or write-only. When we can't directly manipulate every bit of a computer's memory and registers, it is difficult to simulate the computer's operations that *do* manipulate those bits. It is often desirable to simulate an operation in order to develop or debug software.

Overlapped I/O and Processing

It is tricky and time-consuming to synchronize input with output, or input with processing, or processing with output, with busy-wait loops. The time spent executing a busy-wait loop can usually be devoted to more useful computing.

Consider an application which processes one data item per line. Suppose that lines are read at the rate of 100 lines per minute, and that each data item is processed by the CPU in 50 msec. Suppose, further, that one line of output is printed for each data item processed, by a line printer that prints 60 lines per minute.

A simple, straightforward, way to program this application would be:

Type line 1, process line 1's data, print output;
Type line 2, process line 2's data, print output;

     .
     .
     .

Type line *n*, process line *n*'s data, print output.

If R is the time it takes for the CPU to read one line, if P is the time to process the data on the line (the compute time), and if O is the time to print the result, then the total time to process n lines is:

$$(R_1 + P_1 + O_1) + (R_2 + P_2 + O_2) + \ldots + (R_n + P_n + O_n)$$

or, since $R_1 \equiv R_2 \equiv \cdots \equiv R_n$, since $P_1 \equiv P_2 \equiv \cdots \equiv P_n$, and since $O_1 \equiv O_2 \equiv \cdots \equiv O_n$, the time to process n lines is

$$n(R + P + O).$$

t_0	t_1	t_2	t_3	t_4	t_5	t_6
Read 1	Read 2	Read 3	Read 4	Read 5		
	Process 1	Process 2	Process 3	Process 4	Process 5	
		Output 1	Output 2	Output 3	Output 4	Output 5

Figure 12.7 Overlapped processing and I/O

Suppose we had 10,000 lines to process; R is 60 msec, P is 50 msec and O is 100 msec, so the total time is 10,000*(60 + 50 + 100) = 10,000*(.210 sec) = 2,100 seconds = 35 minutes.

What if we had a computer that could process data from the second line of input while the output from the first line was being printed, and while the third line of input was being read? Figure 12.7 shows a time line of such a computer's activities as the above application is processed, for 5 data items. Time proceeds from left to right in figure 12.7; the computer performs the activity shown in one column at each point in time. Since the read, process, and output times are, respectively, 60, 50 and 100 msec each, each time slice in figure 12.7 will have to be 100 msec. So, during the time slice when data from line n_m are processed, results from line n_{m-1} are printed, and data from line n_{m+1} are read. This whole operation takes 100 msec, so processing 10,000 lines will take 10,000 * 100 msec, or 1000 seconds, which is just under 17 minutes--about one half the time required *without* overlapped processing and I/O.

How is it possible to overlap I/O and processing? The technique is analogous to *management by exception*; according to this technique, a manager manages the people involved by saying, "don't bother me unless something important happens." The manager is analogous to the CPU, and the people managed are the I/O devices. Thus, for several different I/O devices, the CPU might instruct them as follows:

1. The CPU instructs a card reader to read a card, and to let the CPU know when the card has been read.
2. The CPU instructs a printer to print a line, and to let the CPU know when the line has been printed.
3. The CPU instructs a CRT to display a character, and to let the CPU know when it is ready to display another.
4. The CPU instructs a CRT to let the CPU know when a character is waiting in the KDBR to be read.

Of course, in all cases, the CPU actually instructs the device's *interface controller* to do the reading, printing, displaying, and transmitting.

Note that this is a new way of knowing when I/O has completed. Instead of, for example, having the CPU execute a busy-wait loop until a user has pressed a key and the terminal's controller has received its character code and placed it in the KDBR, the CPU can do other things while it waits. What other things can the CPU do while it waits? Anything it wants to. Of course a CPU never *wants* to do anything in particular other than execute the instruction fetch-execute cycle. But, rather than execute a busy-wait loop until the line printer (from the above example) has printed output from the current line, the CPU can execute instructions to process data from the next line. Similarly, rather than wait (perhaps indefinitely) for a user to press a key on a keyboard, the CPU can initialize the device's CSR appropriately (which is how the CPU *instructs* a device to inform it when something interesting has happened), and then it can process input that it has already received.

The mechanism that supports this process of an I/O device informing the CPU that "something important has happened" is called *interrupting* the CPU. When the CPU does whatever is appropriate to deal with the device that has interrupted it, it **handles** the interrupt. In the next section, we will discuss **interrupt handling** on the VAX.

Interrupt Handling

The CPU instructs a device that it has permission to **interrupt** the CPU by setting the **interrupt enable bit** in the device's (interface controller's) CSR, which is typically bit 6. Each device has its own CSR; although we often say that a *device* is enabled for interrupts, we actually mean that the device's *controller* is enabled for interrupts.

The device's controller is a piece of hardware that is built so that it will not interrupt the CPU unless something important happens. Usually, the important event is the normal completion of an output operation initiated by the CPU, or the availability of input requested by the CPU. Occasionally, the important event will be reporting that the expected I/O activity did *not* complete normally; it may have completed with an error (such as a parity error), or it may have aborted in mid-operation (for example, the card reader may have jammed, or the printer may have run out of paper).

Processing an Interrupt

Suppose that we have set the interrupt enable bit (bit 6) in the CSR for keyboard input from a CRT. When and if a key is pressed on that CRT's keyboard--if the CRT is not in local mode, if the communication line to the CRT's serial interface controller is in working order, if the key generated a code to be transmitted, and so on--then, when the interface controller receives all the bits of a character code transmitted from the CRT, it will request an interrupt. That is, the interface will signal the CPU that the device needs service.

If the CPU *honors* the interrupt request, the CPU will save what it needs to remember in order to resume whatever it is currently doing (which is what is being interrupted), and it will then fetch the address of the piece of code that, when executed, will service the device. This piece of code is the device's **interrupt handler.** What must be saved in order to resume execution at a later time (after the interrupt has been handled)? No less than what is saved when calling a subroutine, certainly. The PC contains the address of the next instruction to execute, so that must be saved. In addition, the PSL is saved, in part because the CC bits will probably change when executing the interrupt handler, so they must be restored to their prior values after the interrupt has been handled, and before the CPU resumes whatever was interrupted.[1] So, when the CPU honors an interrupt request, it pushes the PC and PSL onto the stack. The control unit then fetches a longword associated with the interrupting device, which is the address of the device's interrupt handler, and places it in the PC. Changing the PC is similar to executing a JMP instruction: control is transferred to the interrupt handler whose address was placed in the PC.

The System Control Block (SCB)

We have already explained that, when an interrupt request is honored, the control unit fetches a longword associated with the interrupting device. How is that association made? Each interrupting

---

[1] The property which ensures that execution of an interrupt handler will not introduce errors in the task which is interrupted is called *transparency;* we discussed transparency in the design of subroutines, in chapter 9.

device has a unique interrupt handler, because each device, when it interrupts the CPU, has unique requirements. How does the CPU find the address of the interrupt handler?

The VAX has a data structure called the System Control Block (SCB); it is an array of longwords, each of which contains the address of an interrupt handler. The base address of the SCB is stored in a privileged register, the System Control Block Base register (SCBB). (A privileged register is not accessible to users the way the general-purpose registers are; we will discuss privileged registers in more detail shortly, in the section on software interrupts.) Recall that, when an I/O device is connected to the VAX, its interface controller must be connected, and it must be assigned addresses for its DBR(s) and CSR(s). If the device is to request interrupts from the CPU, then the device must also be assigned an address in the SCB; this location will contain the address of the device's interrupt handler. The address assigned to the device in the SCB is its **interrupt vector**.

Interrupt Handling Hardware

The VAX hardware assumes that when a device's interrupt request is granted, the device's interrupt vector has already been initialized so that it contains the address of the device's interrupt handler, which will be placed in the PC. What does it mean to say "the CPU has interrupt handling hardware?" We must refine our understanding of the instruction fetch-execute cycle to answer this question. The instruction fetch-execute cycle, which we first saw in chapter 2, is implemented in the VAX as follows:

1. IR ← memory[PC].
2. PC ← PC + 1 (or some other appropriate increment).
3. Continue steps 1 and 2 until the opcode, operand specifiers, displacements and operands (if necessary) have been fetched.
4. Execute the instruction in the IR.
5. Go back to step 1, and repeat.

The purpose of interrupt handling hardware is to *avoid* having to execute the instructions that ask "Is this device done?" or "Is that device still busy?" So, interrupt handling hardware automatically keeps asking these questions for us, more often than we could imagine asking them ourselves. The control unit is modified, to take advantage of interrupt handling hardware, and the instruction fetch-execute cycle is now as follows:

0. Are any interrupts requested? If so, go to step 6; if not, continue.
1. IR ← memory[PC].
2. PC ← PC + 1 (or some other appropriate increment).
3. Continue steps 1 and 2 until the opcode, operand specifiers, displacements, and operands (if necessary) have been fetched.
4. Execute the instruction in the IR.
5. Go back to step 0 and repeat.
6. Is the interrupt request at a high enough priority?
    If so, push PSL and PC on the stack, PC ← (IV), go to step 1.
    If not, ignore request; go to step 1.

IV is the device's Interrupt Vector address, which is one of the locations in the System Control Block. Clearly, if there are several devices capable of interrupting the CPU, the hardware must find the appropriate IV address; this is done automatically by the hardware in much the same way that a device's CSR and DBR are found.

Interrupt Handlers: REI

When the CPU honors an interrupt request, it in effect jumps to a subroutine, which is the interrupt handler; the destination address of the handler is provided by the interrupt vector. The PC is saved as the return address, and the PSL is saved in order to maintain transparency.

When the interrupt has been handled by the interrupt handler, ending the handler with an RSB instruction would not do quite enough to restore the CPU to the condition that it was in before it was interrupted. The instruction REI (Return from Exception or Interrupt) is used to exit from an interrupt handler. It pops the stack into the PC and pops it again, restoring the PSL.

Clearly, an interrupt handler is not transparent if it fails to save and restore what it uses. In particular, each interrupt handler is responsible for saving and restoring any registers it uses.

Polling and Vectored Interrupts

Some computers funnel all interrupt requests through one special memory location. In this case, the hardware is informed only that *some* device has requested an interrupt; the CPU must then execute instructions to **poll** each device, in order to find out which one has requested service. Part of the polling software might include a data structure like a jump table (described in Chapter 8), which contains the location of each device's interrupt handler.

In the VAX, polling is unnecessary; the purpose of interrupt vectors is to eliminate polling, which is time-consuming. Rather, the CPU **vectors** ("goes in this direction") directly to the interrupt handler uniquely associated with the interrupting device. Response to interrupts is thus faster with vectored interrupts than with polling.

Interrupt Priorities

What if several devices request interrupts at the same instant? ("The same instant" typically means "within a few microseconds of each other.") This is not as farfetched as we might think; when many devices are active on one system, simultaneous interrupt requests are likely to occur. How are these conflicts resolved?

Most people have priorities. We would probably interrupt reading the day's mail if there were a knock on the door. We are likely to interrupt talking with whoever knocked on the door if the telephone were to ring. After dealing with the telephone call, we would presumably continue talking to the person at the door (perhaps subject to another telephone call interruption). Finally, after the person at the door has left (or been otherwise dealt with), we would finish reading the mail, and return to what we left when we heard (or saw) the mail carrier. If we get too much mail, or too many visitors, or too many telephone calls, we may never get anything else done; when this happens to computers, it is known as **interrupt overload.** It means that either we have set our priorities incorrectly, or we take too long to handle an interrupt, or that we need help (a secretary, or another CPU).

Single-Level Hardware Priority

Some simpler computers have a one-level priority scheme, according to which a device's interrupt priority is determined by its physical proximity to the CPU. A device's priority is determined by its position on the interrupt-request line, to which every device capable of generating an interrupt is connected. The closer to the CPU the device's connection on that line is, the higher its priority is in the event of a conflict due to simultaneous interrupt requests. Consider figure 12.8. The interrupt-request logic (IRL) is a piece of hardware that determines which of the devices simultaneously

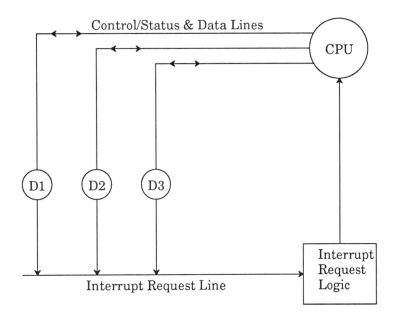

Figure 12.8 Single-level interrupt priority system

requesting interrupt service (by sending a signal along the interrupt-request line) will have its request passed through to the CPU. With the interrupt priorities shown in this system, a request from device D3 will override a simultaneous request from devices D2 and D1, and one from D2 overrides one from D1 (if D3 has no simultaneous request).

What happens if the lowest priority device, D1, has its request for an interrupt overridden by a simultaneous request from D2 or D3? In a well-designed system (which is properly programmed), device D1's interrupt request will be considered **pending**; it will be honored after all higher priority interrupt requests have been honored. If this takes too long, the reason for D1's original interrupt request may be superseded by more recent activity at D1. Suppose, for example, that D1 is a CRT; the CPU is very busy when we type an *A,* and so it doesn't respond immediately to D1's interrupt request because it is still taking care of D2's or D3's requests. If D1 is a full-duplex CRT (on a full-duplex line, connected to a full-duplex interface), we feel free to type ahead and strike the next key (*B,* perhaps). It is conceivable that the code for *B* will over-write the code for *A*--which is in D1's Data Buffer Register, waiting for the CPU to honor its interrupt request by fetching it. In this case, the interrupt request to process *A* is never honored. When the CPU eventually honors the interrupt request from the device, it is D1's *second* request, and *second* character code, that the CPU is seeing; the first request and first code are lost. In this case, D1's interface controller will notice that the KDBR has received *two* character codes from the device, but that the CPU has executed only a single MOVB @#KDBR, R6; therefore, the controller will report a data overrun error in the device's CSR.

If interrupts are lost too often, the whole computer system is in trouble and needs to be fixed; this often indicates a system on which the workload has grown beyond projections made when the system was designed and implemented.

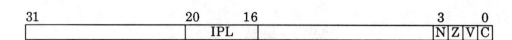

Figure 12.9 PSL with interrupt priority level bits

Multilevel Priorities

The VAX's interrupt priority scheme is more complex (and more flexible) than the single-level scheme discussed above. The VAX has 32 Interrupt Priority Levels (IPLs); in the PSL, bits 16 through 20 indicate the current IPL of the CPU. When we speak of the CPU's IPL, we mean the IPL of the program that is currently running; all user programs run at IPL 0. Figure 12.9 shows the PSL, with the CC bits and the IPL bits marked.

Hardware Interrupt Priority Levels

Each device, when its controller is assigned addresses for DBR(s) and CSR(s) and an interrupt vector, is also assigned an interrupt priority level. All hardware devices have IPLs between 10_{16} and 17_{16}; IPLs from 18 to $1F_{16}$ are used for urgent conditions, such as power failure. Higher numbers correspond to higher priorities; the highest priority is, thus, 1F. If a device with a higher IPL than the current processor IPL requests an interrupt, that request will be honored immediately; if a device with an IPL lower than or the same as the current processor IPL requests an interrupt, that request will be deferred until the current processor IPL is lower than that of the request. Since all user programs run at IPL 0, and since the lowest device IPL is 10_{16}, *any* device requesting an interrupt while a user program is running will have its request honored immediately.

Recall that the PSL is saved (in addition to the PC) when an interrupt request is honored, and it is restored by the REI instruction executed by the interrupt handler when it has completed. When a lower priority program is interrupted by a higher priority request, the interrupter's handler is given the IPL of the requester. So, a lower priority program is interrupted, a higher priority program (the interrupt handler) executes, and then when interrupt handler restores the saved PSL, the priority is lowered from the IPL of the handler back to the IPL of the interrupted program. Figure 12.10 is a schematic representation of the 16 hardware interrupt priority lines and their connection to Interrupt Request Logic (IRL), which passes along the highest priority request to the CPU.

Software Interrupt Priority Levels

Interrupt priority levels 0 through $0F_{16}$ are software priority levels: all hardware devices (CRTs, disks, etc.) interrupt at higher priority than 0F. These software priority levels are provided for user programs (level 0), and for operating system routines (such as the SNAP and DUMP routines we have been using). Thus, if a particular operating system routine always executes at IPL 2, then another, more important, operating system routine can execute at IPL 3 in order to assure that it is never interrupted by a lower priority system routine (or a user program).

We have already seen how hardware devices request interrupts: they have controllers, which are pieces of hardware, that are connected to the CPU's Interrupt Request Logic. When a device's controller requests an interrupt, the IRL passes that request (if it is the highest priority request at the moment) to the CPU; if the CPU's priority is lower than that of the interrupt request, then the request is honored: the current PSL and PC are pushed onto the stack, the PC is loaded with the

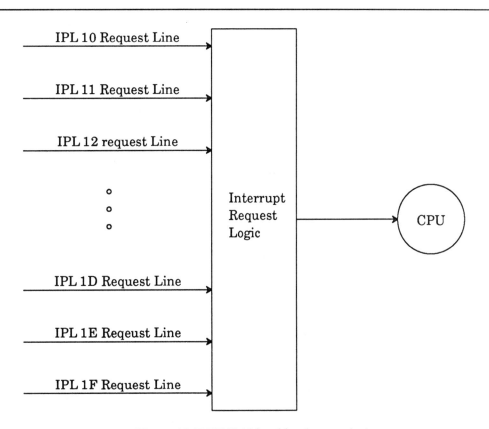

Figure 12.10 VAX 16 level hardware priority

value in the requester's interrupt vector, and the interrupt handler is executed. How does a *program* (an operating system routine, for example) request an interrupt? If a software interrupt request is honored, how is the appropriate interrupt vector found? These questions are answered next.

For each of the 15 software levels that can request interrupts (IPL 01 through $0F_{16}$), there is a single interrupt vector in the System Control Block. When an operating system routine requests an interrupt at, for example, IPL 3, the CPU, if it honors the request, finds the interrupt handler's address in the interrupt vector for IPL 3 in the SCB. Thus, only a single operating system routine can run at each of the software IPLs, because there is only a single interrupt vector corresponding to each of the software IPLs.[2] This is not a serious shortcoming, because many operating system routines run at IPL 0; despite their low priority, these routines are not interruptible by user programs, because user programs also run at IPL 0, and requests for interrupts are only honored if they are made at a *higher* IPL than the CPU's current IPL.

So, every operating system routine that will ever request an interrupt must be assigned an interrupt vector in the SCB; *how* are these software interrupts requested? There is a special version

---

[2]This is not strictly true. It is possible for the interrupt handler at a particular software IPL to be written to keep track of several requests for different operating system routines. This is a complex issue that is beyond the scope of the present discussion; the interested reader is referred to the *Vax Architecture Reference Manual*.

Offset	Exception or Interrupt
04	machine check
08	kernel stack not valid
0C	power failure
10	reserved or privileged instruction
18	reserved operand
1C	reserved addressing mode
20	access-control violation
24	translation not valid
30	compatibility
34	arithmetic
40-4C	CHM(K,E,S,U) instructions
50-60	bus or memory error
84	software level 1
88	software level 2
8C	software level 3
90-BC	software levels 4-F
C0	interval timer
F8	console terminal receive
FC	console terminal transmit
100-13C	device level 14, devices 0-15
140-17C	device level 15, devices 0-15
180-1BC	device level 16, devices 0-15
1C0-1FC	device level 17, devices 0-15
200-3FC	device vectors
400-5FC	device vectors

Figure 12.11 VAX System Control Block

of the MOV instruction, called MTPR, for Move To Processor Register. The source operand of the MTPR instruction is a longword that may be specified using any legal addressing mode; the destination operand is a longword which specifies the number of a **privileged register.** To request a software interrupt, we execute the MTPR instruction and specify, in the low order 4 bits of the source operand, the IPL of the handler we wish to execute. The destination is the Software Interrupt Request Register (SIRR), which is privileged register 14_{16}.

The System Control Block Revisited

The SCB is an important data structure, because it contains interrupt vectors for the hardware devices and software routines that can request interrupts on a VAX. Let's look more closely at it, in order to better understand some of the issues involved; some of the vectors contained in the SCB are shown in figure 12.11. The following points are relevant to what we have recently discussed, or what we will shortly discuss:

1. Vectors with offsets from 4 through $4C_{16}$ contain addresses of handlers of **exceptions** rather than interrupts. Exceptions and interrupts are very similar, except that an exception is caused by the execution of the current instruction, while an interrupt is caused by an event that may be independent of the current instruction. We have already discussed interrupts requested by I/O device completion; when ordinary users try to execute the HALT instruction, a privileged instruction *exception* is generated. It is the exception handler for this exception, whose vector is 10_{16}, that aborts our program and provides us with a listing of the contents of the PC (and a stack trace).
2. There is a vector in the SCB (offset $0C_{16}$) for power failure; dealing with power failure is a very high priority event, so its handler runs at IPL $1E_{16}$.
3. The vector whose offset is 34 contains the address of the handler for arithmetic exceptions. Some of these are discussed in chapter 13.
4. The interrupt vectors for software interrupts at IPLs 01 through 0F have offsets 84_{16} through BC_{16} in the SCB.
5. The interval timer (which may be thought of as a clock, which *ticks* once every *interval*) is assigned vector C0, with IPL 16_{16} or 18_{16}; we will examine an interrupt handler for a simpler clock in the next section.
6. Recall that a VAX has a terminal called the **console,** which is used for special things like starting the bootstrap program (which begins execution of the operating system). The console, like other terminals, is both a send device (keyboard) and a receive device (display). Each device may interrupt the CPU, so each has an interrupt vector: the interrupt vectors for the console are at offsets $F8_{16}$ and FC_{16} in the SCB.
7. Most I/O devices (because of PDP-11 compatibility) are assigned IPLs 14_{16} through 17_{16}. At each IPL there are 16 vectors, so 16 devices may be assigned IPL 15, for example.
8. Vectors with offsets 200_{16} through $5FC_{16}$ are assigned IPLs and associated with devices according to the needs of each particular installation.

A Brief Review

Before we examine two relatively simple interrupt handlers, let us briefly review what we have learned about interrupts and I/O. Figure 12.12 is the model of the VAX we have seen in figures 3.8., 5.1 and 9.16, with some of the information we have learned in this chapter added to it. In the following summary, we will pay special attention to *who* does *what, when*.

Connecting Devices

When a device is connected to a VAX, its CSR(s) and DBR(s) are assigned addresses in the memory's *I/O space*. If, as is usually the case, the device is to perform I/O with interrupts (rather than with busy-wait loops), then it is also assigned an interrupt vector and an interrupt priority level (IPL). At some time after a device is connected, but before it requests an interrupt, the interrupt enable bit in its CSR is set. This is usually done when the operating system is loaded into memory, at bootstrap time.

Writing Interrupt Handlers

A system programmer usually writes a device's interrupt handler. An interrupt handler deals with the physical characteristics of a device; since different I/O devices perform different operations, their interrupt handlers also differ. For example, a line-printer prints a line at a time, while a character-printer (such as a dot-matrix printer or a typical hard-copy terminal) prints a character at a time.

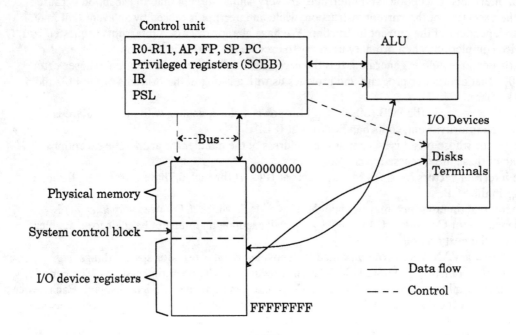

Figure 12.12 A model of the VAX

Thus, the interrupt handler for a line-printer must send the line-printer a line to print, while the interrupt handler for a character-printer need only send it a character to print. In the next section we will examine interrupt handlers for a clock and a keyboard, and we will see how greatly they differ.

At some time after a device's interrupt handler has been loaded, but *before* the device requests an interrupt, its interrupt vector must be initialized (in the SCB) to contain the address of the interrupt handler. This initialization is commonly done at bootstrap time.

Performing I/O Operations

When a user presses a key on a keyboard, for example, the CRT's hardware sends the ASCII character code (if it is an ASCII terminal), along with the framing bits and parity bit, bit-serially, to its serial interface controller. The controller receives the bits one at a time, strips the framing bits, and checks the parity; it places the data bits in the KDBR. If the parity is incorrect, it sets the appropriate error bit(s) in the KCSR, and sets the done/ready bit; if the parity is correct, the controller just sets the done/ready bit. Then, if the interrupt enable bit in the device's CSR is set, the controller requests an interrupt.

The interrupt request logic (IRL), which is part of the CPU, knows the IPL and interrupt vector of each device connected to it; when a device's controller requests an interrupt, the IRL checks the current IPL of the CPU (in bits 16-20 of the PSL), and if the requester's IPL is higher than the current IPL, the IRL causes an interrupt. The interrupt request is honored when the CPU saves the PC and PSL on the stack and the IRL provides the interrupt vector of the requester. The contents of the interrupt vector (the address of the device's interrupt handler) are placed in the PC, the

```
CLOCK:      INCL TIME+4      ;low-order longword
            BCC DONE         ;no carry: done
;else, increment high-order longword
            INCL TIME        ;low-order will be 0
DONE:       REI              ;pop stack to PSL and PC
TIME:       .LONG 0, 0       ;start with no ticks
```

Figure 12.13 Interrupt handler for a 60 Hz clock

interrupt handler is executed, and when the handler exits (by executing the REI instruction), the stack is popped twice, to restore the PC and PSL.

If the interrupt handler is well written (i.e., if it is transparent), then the interrupted program never knows that it has been interrupted; if it runs more than once, it produces exactly the same results in those cases when it *is* interrupted as in those cases when it is *not* interrupted. We (as users) might know if a program of ours is interrupted *many* times, because it would take longer to complete than when it is interrupted only a few times, or not at all. One reason that everything seems *so slow* on a heavily loaded multiuser system is that our programs are usually interrupted many times before they complete.

Example Interrupt Handlers

The ordinary computer user never sees, let alone writes, an interrupt handler. However, as students of computer architecture, we are not interested in limiting our knowledge to that of the ordinary computer user. Therefore, we will conclude our discussion of interrupts and I/O by examining some simple interrupt handlers, for some simple devices.

Hypothetical Clock Interrupt Handler

The first interrupt handler we will examine is for a clock that *ticks* 60 times per second (or, 60 Hertz, abbreviated *Hz*). There may be no such clock on a VAX; VAXes have a much more sophisticated **interval timer,** whose use is described in the *VAX Architecture Reference Manual.* We will consider this hypothetical device (which usually exists on PDP-11s and other computers that are less complex than the VAX) because it is simple and because its interrupt handler is simple.

If bit 6 in the CSR of the 60 Hz clock is set, then it will request an interrupt every time it ticks--every 60th of a second. The program in figure 12.13 is a simple interrupt handler for this clock. The handler counts clock ticks, and stores the count in a pair of longwords. Each time the clock ticks, the handler increments the low-order longword, COUNT+4. When the value in COUNT+4 reaches $FFFFFFFF_{16}$, the next time it is incremented it will generate a carry out of the msb of COUNT+4, so the C bit be will be set. When this happens, the handler increments the high-order longword, COUNT. In order for this interrupt handler to be executed, of course, the clock's interrupt vector must be initialized to address CLOCK, its interrupt enable bit must be set, and its IPL must be greater than the IPL of the program running when it requests an interrupt.

No check is made, in the interrupt handler, for carry out from the msb of COUNT; the count will, therefore, return to 0 once every approximately 9,749,040,289 years (there are approximately 2^{64} 60^{th}s of a second in 9,749,040,289 years).

```
                    KCSR = ^X????????          ;Keyboard CSR; for ease of reference
                    KDBR = KCSR+2              ;Keyboard DBR; for ease of reference
                    CR = ^X0D                 ;carriage return character
;
;Here's the start of the handler code proper.
;
CRTHANDLER:         TSTW @#KCSR               ;check error bit
                    BLSS ERROR                ;error bit was set: see what happened
        ;else, no problems, so get byte
                    MOVB @#KDBR, @BUFPTR
                    CMPB @BUFPTR, #CR         ;is it carriage return?
                    BEQL ENDLINE              ;if so, process end-of-line
        ;else, continue processing
                    CMPB @BUFPTR, #^A/!/      ;is it "!", the erase character?
                    BEQL ERASE                ;if so, "erase" last character
        ;else, increment buffer pointer
                    INCL BUFPTR               ;ready for next character
                    BRB DONE                  ;done, until next interrupt
ENDLINE:            INCB LINE                 ;set end-of-line flag
                    BRB DONE                  ;done; someone better process this line now
;
ERASE:              DECL BUFPTR               ;erase last character: decrement buffer pointer
                    BRB DONE                  ;done, until next interrupt
ERROR: ;code to deal with error conditions
DONE:               REI                       ;return:  pop stack into PC and PSL
;Here are data for the handler
BUFFER:             .BLKB 256                 ;line buffer
BUFPTR:             .ADDRESS BUFFER           ;pointer into BUFFER
LINE:               .BYTE 0                   ;end-of-line flag
```

Figure 12.14 Simple input interrupt handler

CRT Keyboard Interrupt Handler

A CRT is more complex than a simple 60 Hz clock; let us see what is required to handle an interrupt from a CRT's keyboard. A CRT keyboard interrupt handler is shown in figure 12.14. This handler places incoming characters in consecutive byte locations starting at location BUFFER; it sets flag LINE when it encounters the ASCII carriage return character code, $0D_{16}$. It is up to *someone else* (a user, perhaps) to check if the LINE flag is set. If LINE were set, the user would reset the flag, and would also reset the pointer to the input buffer (BUFPTR), after processing the line of text.

Note that the interrupt handler does not test the KCSR to see if the data are in the KDBR. The fact that the interrupt handler is being executed *guarantees* that the keyboard's controller has received a complete byte from the keyboard (or that it won't receive one because an error has occurred). Thus, if a device is enabled to interrupt, its controller requests an interrupt at the same time that it sets the done/ready bit in the CSR. By using interrupts, however, we avoid using busy-wait loops to check the CSR to see if the device has transmitted (or received) a byte yet, and thereby allow the CPU to do productive work until it is interrupted.

A more sophisticated handler than the one shown would echo the input, and check that a user does not accidentally back up too far by typing too many "!"s. It is clear from this example, however, how an operating system can implement and change the "erase the last character" function. It is probably preferable to use register deferred (mode 6) rather than relative deferred addressing when dealing with the buffer pointer. If we place the address of the buffer in a register, however, we must be sure to maintain transparency by saving (and then restoring) the registers that we use.

Summary

It is easier to understand I/O if we distinguish the *transfer* of data from the *transformation* of data which often precedes and follows the data transfer. On character-oriented devices, data are typically transferred one byte at a time. Many computers have special instructions for I/O; the VAX has none. Ordinary VAX instructions refer to I/O devices rather than "ordinary" memory locations when they use addresses that are larger than the largest address of the particular system's physical memory. These are addresses of devices' control and status registers (CSRs) and data buffer registers (DBRs).

Since I/O devices usually transfer data much more slowly than the CPU executes instructions, the CPU must check to see if a device is *done* transmitting the last data item, or is *ready* with a new data item, before trying to send or receive the next data item. One way to synchronize the CPU with I/O devices is with a **busy-wait loop**: the CPU waits for the device. Another way to synchronize the CPU with I/O devices is with **interrupts**: the CPU performs other work until a device interrupts it because it has received another byte, or can send another one.

A device's busy or ready status is determined by examining a bit in its CSR--usually bit 7. An error associated with an I/O activity is also reflected in the device's CSR--usually bit 15. A device is only permitted to interrupt the CPU if its interrupt enable bit is set; this is usually bit 6 of the device's CSR. Devices that are more complex than a CRT may have control registers that are separate from their status registers.

Adding interrupt capability to a CPU involves a number of things. The instruction fetch-execute cycle must be modified to check for interrupt requests after each instruction is executed. Each I/O device controller must have an interrupt request line into the interrupt request logic, which passes the highest priority request on to the CPU. Each device must be assigned a memory location--an **interrupt vector**--in the System Control Block. The interrupt vector contains the address of the device's **interrupt handler,** which is the program that is executed to service the device when its interrupt request is honored. When the CPU honors an interrupt request, it saves the current PC and PSL values on the stack. A device's interrupt handler terminates with the REI instruction, which pops the stack into the PC and PSL.

The VAX has 16 software **interrupt priority levels** and 16 hardware priority levels. The IPLs, thus, range from 0 to $1F_{16}$; higher numbers indicate higher priority. All user programs, and many operating system routines execute at IPL 0. Most I/O devices are assigned IPLs of 14_{16} to 17_{16}; urgent events (such as power failure) interrupt with priority 18_{16} to $1F_{16}$. In the PSL, there are 5 bits (bits 16 through 20) which contain the IPL of the program currently executing. An interrupt request will be honored only if its priority exceeds the priority currently in the PSL.

A device's interrupt handler runs at the IPL at which the device requests interrupts; thus, *any* hardware device will interrupt any user program, or any operating system routine that is executing as a result of a software interrupt. Software interrupts have interrupt vectors associated with their IPLs; a software interrupt is requested by executing the MTPR instruction, with the software interrupt request register (SIRR) as the destination operand.

We will deal with the ideas we have discussed in this chapter again, when we examine high-speed, non-character-oriented, I/O.

Exercises for Chapter 12

1. The following code segments beginning at CLOCK and OUTPUT are interrupt handlers for a clock and an output device such as a CRT display. The code segment after the .ENTRY directive is a main program.

    a. How should the symbols which are not otherwise defined be defined?
    b. What does each interrupt handler do?
    c. How do the two interrupt handlers interact--what does the whole program do?

    The clock control and status register is CCSR, and its interrupt vector is CIV; the output device's control and status register is OCSR, and its interrupt vector is OIV.

    ```
    CLOCK:      INCL R1
                CMPL #59, R1
                BGTR RETURN
                CLRL R1
                INCB MBOX
                MOVW #^X40, @#OCSR
    RETURN:     REI

    OUTPUT:     CMPB #^X3A, MBOX
                BNEQ NOWORK
                MOVB  #^X2F, MBOX
    NOWORK:     MOVB MBOX, @#OUTBUF
                CLRW @#OCSR
                REI

                .ENTRY START, 0
                CLRL R1
                MOVAL OUTPUT, @#OIV
                MOVAL CLOCK, @#CIV
                MOVW #^X40, @#CCSR
    X:          BRB X
    MBOX:       .BYTE 57
                .END START
    ```

2. a. Describe two ways of selectively blocking interrupts.
    b. What kinds of interrupts should not be blocked?
    c. What are the advantages of vectored interrupts?
3. a. Why are interrupts used for I/O, particularly?
    b. Can an interrupt handler call subroutines? Explain why or why not.
4. Since interrupt handlers are very much like subroutines, and since requesting an interrupt is very much like calling a subroutine, why is it necessary to use REI rather than RSB or RET to return from an interrupt handler?

Floating Point Numbers and Floating Point Arithmetic

Introduction

People who write compilers for high-level languages (or assemblers for low-level languages) or who write operating systems are often content with the arithmetic facilities we have been using. Integer arithmetic is sufficient for most system-programming purposes. However, system programmers are not the majority of users that computers are designed for.

Commercial data processing applications manage nicely with a combination of integer arithmetic and hardware-supported ASCII coded decimal arithmetic and/or **binary coded decimal** (BCD, or **packed decimal,** on the VAX) arithmetic. Is there a need to represent numbers in any other ways, and to provide special hardware and/or software to support these representations? Consider figure 13.1; it shows the range of numbers we encounter in the world of physics. It is not entirely coincidental that we chose physics for this example. Many of the computer characteristics we are about to see are the direct result of requirements to support work of physicists. Very little of the research and development in the area of nuclear weapons and nuclear energy would have been possible without this support. This is an important reminder of the fact that any tool can be used for purposes that some may argue are antisocial. One should not necessarily blame the tool: advances in nuclear medicine (such as CAT and NMR imaging systems) are also directly traceable to what we are about to discuss.

If the smallest number in figure 13.1 is 10^{-10} cm and the largest is 10^{25} cm, there is a range of 10^{35} from the smallest to the largest numbers dealt with by physicists. A general-purpose computer, thus, to be useful for scientists and engineers, must support high-speed arithmetic with operands of 35 decimal digits! This is not practical: using 4 bits per decimal digit, we would need 140 bits for 35 decimal digit numbers. What if we use a "word" capable of holding *binary* numbers as large as 10^{35}? This would be a slight improvement, since we would need only about 120 bits to represent 10^{35}: $10^{3^{12}} \approx 10^{35}$, $2^{10} \approx 10^3$, so $2^{10^{12}} \approx 10^{35}$, and $2^{10^{12}} \equiv 2^{120}$. So we have reduced our word length to 120 bits--only about 4 times as long as a VAX longword; this is still impractical, because hardware to support high-speed arithmetic with 120-bit operands is expensive.

The solution to this problem is based on acceptance of the fact that few (if any) of the numbers that scientists deal with are known with absolute accuracy. If we are willing to work with approximations, we can greatly extend the range of 32-bit numbers. We will not, of course, *magically* provide more than 2^{32} unique 32-bit numbers. Rather, we will make a compromise between accuracy and range: with integers, the range of 32-bit numbers is 0 to 4,294,967,296 (as unsigned numbers), and we can represent *every single integer* in this range. If we decide, for example, that we are willing to represent only every *other* integer, we can double the range of 32-bit numbers, to 0 to 8,589,934,592. This doubling of the range by halving the precision doesn't even give us a full 10 decimal digits of range (recall that physicists need 35), but it illustrates the technique we will use: if we want to increase the range of 32-bit numbers from 9 to 35 decimal digits, we will have to give up the ability to represent every number in the range.

What kind of representation do we use? We adapt **scientific notation** (used by scientists for centuries); this way, we can represent both very large numbers and very small ones using a word size such as 32 bits. Note that this is also what most calculator manufacturers have done: a calculator that displays only ten decimal digits provides an enormous range ($10^{\pm 99}$ is common).

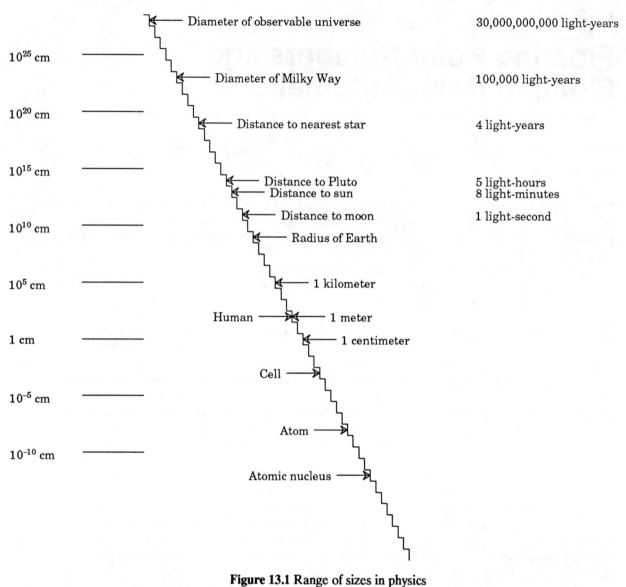

Figure 13.1 Range of sizes in physics

Scientific notation has the general form:

$$\pm d_1.d_2 d_3 \ldots d_m * 10^{\pm n}$$

where $d_1, d_2, \ldots, d_m$ are decimal digits, and n is a decimal exponent. A scientist would not normally write "100 moles," or "3000 grams"; neither would a chemistry student. They would write "$1.00 * 10^2$ moles," or "$3.000 * 10^3$ grams." The zeroes following the decimal point, in both cases, express the confidence of the measurements. If we say 1.00, we mean that the result is between 0.995 and 1.004; the implications of 1.00 are different from those of either 1.0 or 1.0000. For numbers smaller than one, we use negative exponents: we would write the fraction 13/1000th of a kilogram as $1.3 * 10^{-2}$ kilogram ($10^{-2} \equiv 1/10^2 \equiv 1/100 \equiv .01$). If the exponent, n, is limited to 2 digits (as on many calculators), the largest number that can be expressed (or computed) with 10 digits is 9.9999999 * 10^{99} (about 10^{100}), and the smallest number is 0.0000001 * 10^{-99} (about 10^{-107}). If we want to use a number with too many digits (say 1.234567892) on a 10-digit calculator, we have to compromise. We can only use an approximation of that number. We have to introduce an unavoidable error. The simple approach is to **truncate** the extra digits from the end. In this case, we would get 1.2345678.

A better approach involves **rounding.** Rounding means examining the tail we are about to chop off. If it is of the form 5 . . . or larger, a 1 is added to the last digit of the new tail. Otherwise, the tail is truncated as before. If we round in our previous example, then dropping the tail 92 from 1.234567892 would require adding 1 to the last digit of the new tail (8), so the number would be 1.2345679. If the number had been 1.234567843, then the 8 would not have been changed: rounding and truncating would both produce 1.2345678. Rounding rounds numbers away from 0; truncation brings numbers closer to 0. The purpose of rounding is to reduce the error in the approximation we are forced to use.

Floating-Point Numbers

The representation that computers use for scientific notation numbers is called the **floating-point** representation. One of the major issues in designing a floating-point representation is deciding how many bits to allocate to the exponent and how many to allocate to the number part; allocating more bits to the exponent increases the range of numbers representable, but decreases their accuracy. Designing a floating-point representation has three major goals:

1. To maximize the **range** of numbers that can be represented with a fixed number of bits.
2. To minimize the **loss of accuracy** that inevitably occurs when, as in floating-point numbers, only some of the bits are used for the number part of the number.
3. To provide a **unique representation** for each floating-point number.

In order to better understand these goals, let's consider some examples of 5 decimal digit scientific notation numbers; these examples will generalize directly to binary. If we allocate all 5 digits to the number, we have none left for the exponent; the range of numbers we can represent is 0 to 99999, and there is no loss of accuracy because *every* number in that range is representable. If, at the other extreme, we allocate 1 digit to the number part and 4 digits to the exponent, then the range is greatly expanded--to 0 to 9 * 10^{9999}; the largest number we can represent is now about 10,000 decimal digits long. However, no matter what the range is, there are still only 10^5 combinations of 5 decimal digits; if the range has been increased, then accuracy must suffer. In other words, although the distance between the smallest and largest numbers has been increased, there are now many numbers between them that we cannot represent. For example, 200 would be written as 2 * 10^2, and 201 would *also* be written as 2 * 10^2. This may seem like only a slight loss of accuracy, but there is *no* number between 200 and 300 that can be accurately represented; we may be tempted to change our minds about the slightness of this loss of accuracy. If we allocate 3 digits to the exponent and 2 digits to the number, we decrease the range to "only" about 1,000 decimal digits, but we simultaneously increase the accuracy of the representation: we still cannot represent 201, but we *can* represent 210, 220, 230, etc.--as 2.1 * 10^2, 2.2 * 10^2, etc.

The above discussion explains the relationship between the first two goals of a floating-point number representation: maximizing the range of numbers representable while minimizing the loss of accuracy. These goals are mutually exclusive because the major way to maximize the range is to allocate more bits to the exponent, but more bits for the exponent means fewer bits for the number part, which causes decreased accuracy. What about the third goal, that of a unique representation? Consider that if we allocate 3 digits of our 5-digit numbers to the exponent and 2 digits to the number part, then 210 can be written as *either* .21 * 10^1, *or* 2.1 * 10^2, *or* .21 * 10^3. Humans are good at noticing that these all represent the same number, but computers would need additional hardware to notice this fact. In addition, if we have three different representations for each number, then we have used up three (rather than only one) of the 10^5 combinations that there are of 5 decimal digits. So, it is desirable to represent floating-point numbers in such a way that each number has only one representation. Let's see how the VAX designers attained all three goals.

The first step toward attaining these goals is to view a floating-point number as composed of two parts: a **signed exponent** and a **signed fraction.** The fraction part is what we have called the *number* part above; we now call it a fraction because we assume that a binary point appears immediately to its left. Thus, it will always be true that the magnitude (i.e. the unsigned value, designated by using a pair of bars) of the fraction is less than 1: |fraction| < 1. Given an exponent e and a fraction f, the value represented by the pair (e, f) is $f * 2^e$, if the exponent's radix is 2. The exponent radix is 2 for the VAX and many other computers, but some designers decided to use a radix of 16 (notably, the IBM 360 series--since 1964--continuing with the 370 and its successors).

If we allocate a sufficient number of bits to the exponent so that e can have large positive or negative values, we satisfy the range goal. If we choose enough bits for our floating-point number that--after we use up some for the exponent--there are enough left for the fraction to have a sufficient number of significant digits, we satisfy the goal of maintaining accuracy. Finally, if we reduce the number of leading 0s to none, we satisfy the goal of a unique representation for each number. Thus, $.0034 * 10^0$ must be **normalized** (put in a standard, or *normal,* form) by writing it as $.34 * 10^{-2}$; $5600 * 10^0$ is normalized to $.56 * 10^4$. Note that 000.123 *is* normalized: the leading 0s have no significance whatsoever, and writing a number this way has no scientific meaning. (It is sometimes used for printing checks, in order to reduce the likelihood that someone will be able to alter the number.)

The definition for **normalization** of a VAX floating-point number follows: a floating point number (e, f), with radix r, is normalized if

$$1/r \le f < 1,$$

for all f except 0. This means that with a radix of 2 ($r = 2$), a normalized fraction always has its leading bit set, except for the fraction with the value 0. Let's see why this is the case. Consider the number 2, which is $10.0_2 * 2^0$. This is *not* normalized, because 10.0 is *not* < 1; if we move the binary point one place to the left, we have $1.00 * 2^1$, but this is *still* not normalized, because 1.00 is also not < 1 (although it *is* = 1). If we move the binary point one more place to the left, we get $.100 * 2^2$, and this *is* normalized, because .100 < 1, and $.100 \ge 1/2$ (1/2 is $1 * 2^{-1}$ which is .1).

What would happen if we kept moving the binary point to the left? Our fraction would continue to satisfy the right side of the inequality--namely, .100 < 1, and .0100 < 1, and .00100 < 1, etc. However, it would no longer satisfy the left side of the inequality: .0100 is *not* $\ge$ .1, and .00100 is *not* $\ge$ .1, etc. Thus, the right side of the inequality assures that the binary point will be to the left of the first 1, and the left side of the inequality assures that there will be no leading 0s. Together, the inequality assures that there is a unique floating-point representation for each number.

As a practical matter, rather than storing the signed exponent as a twos complement number, it is stored as a **biased exponent.** The twos complement representation of the exponent has a constant **bias** added to it; this transforms the signed exponent into an *unsigned,* biased exponent. So we now speak of floating-point numbers as consisting of

(biased exponent, signed normalized fraction).

The biased exponent is sometimes called the **characteristic,** and the fraction is often called the **mantissa.** Since positive numbers are larger than negative numbers, it is convenient to store the fraction's sign, *sf,* where (pseudo) sign bits are usually kept in a computer number. So, now a VAX floating-point number has *three* fields:

(sf, biased exponent, normalized fraction).

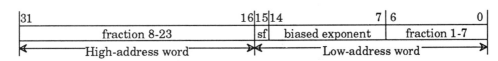

Figure 13.2 F_format floating-point representation

Floating-point numbers are sometimes called **real numbers,** in part because common high level languages such as FORTRAN and Pascal use the term *real* for them. A real number used in a computer is usually only an approximation of what a mathematician calls a real number.

VAX Floating-Point Number Representation

The VAX has four different types of floating-point number representations; one uses 32 bits (F_format), two use 64 bits (D_format and G_format), and the fourth (H_format) uses 128 (!) bits. The only difference between the different floating-point formats is in the number of bits allocated to the exponent and the fraction. They all have the same general format: a sign-magnitude representation of the fraction and a biased exponent. The most significant bit of the first (low address) *word* contains the sign of the fraction; this is followed by the exponent, which is followed by the fraction. Since the different floating-point formats are so similar conceptually, we will discuss the F_format in detail (it is shorter and therefore simpler to deal with); we will only briefly describe the other formats. Figure 13.2 shows the organization of the VAX's F_format floating-point numbers. Eight bits are allocated to the exponent, 23 bits are allocated to the fraction's magnitude, and a single bit represents the fraction's sign.

The distribution of bits appears strange because the fraction is divided into two parts: bits 0 through 6 contain the most significant 7 bits of the fraction, and bits 16 through 31 contain the least significant 16 bits of the fraction. Why did the designers of the VAX make this choice? For compatibility with the PDP-11, upon which the VAX is based (and of which the VAX is a Virtual Address eXtension). The *natural* width of the PDP-11's memory is 16 bits, so a 32-bit floating-point number occupies 2 16-bit words in the PDP-11. If we consider the VAX F_format floating-point number as a pair of words rather than a single longword--as shown in figure 13.3--we see that the first (low-address) word contains the sign of the fraction, the biased exponent, and the high order 7 bits of the fraction, and the second (high-address) word contains the low-order 16 bits of the fraction. We will, from now on, often refer to a F_format floating-point number as a pair of words, rather than as a single longword.

The exponent is an 8-bit field, and it is biased by 80_{16}. In other words, the stored exponent is the true exponent plus 80_{16}. So, when the biased exponent is between 00 and $7F_{16}$, the true exponent is between -128 and -1; when the biased exponent is between 81 and FF_{16}, the true exponent is between +1 and +127.

Although the fraction field is stored in two parts, all 23 bits are a single sign-magnitude number. The sign for the whole fraction is stored in bit 15 of the first word. The *stored* fraction contains 23 bits (7+16), but the fraction has 24 bits of accuracy; how is this possible? The rules of normalization for VAX floating-point number fractions guarantee that the leading bit is always set (except when representing the number 0, which we will discuss shortly). There is no reason to use up a bit--which can be either 1 or 0--to store a value which is always 1. So, the designers of the VAX floating-point representation decided that the most significant bit of the fraction, which is always 1, is not stored! With this **hidden** bit, we get 24 bits of accuracy (or, **precision**) out of only 23 bits in memory.

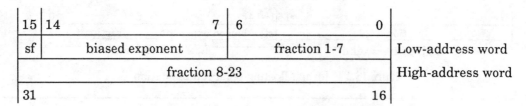

Figure 13.3 F_format floating-point number as two words

Let us consider a few examples of VAX F_format floating-point numbers to put together what we have seen. Zero is a special case: since every fraction hides the most significant 1, a true fraction of 1/2 ($.1_2$) is stored as 23 bits of 0--this, of course, is indistinguishable from 0. So, whenever the biased exponent is 0 and the sign of the fraction is 0 (i.e., whenever bits 7 through 15 of the low-address word are 0), the number is taken to represent 0--regardless of the value of the fraction.

Now let's consider 1: $1.0 * 2^0$ is *not* normalized, because it is *not* < 1. If we move the binary point one place to the left, however, we get $.1 * 2^1$, and this satisfies both sides of the normalization inequality: $1/2 \leq .1 < 1$. So, we have the following situation:

true exponent:	1	true fraction	10000000000000000000000
biased exponent:	81	stored fraction	00000000000000000000000
sign of fraction:	0		

Or:

```
   15 14           7 6           0
    0  1 0 0 0 0 0 0 1 0 0 0 0 0 0 0   low-address word
    0  0 0 0 0 0 0 0 0 0 0 0 0 0 0 0   high-address word
   31                          16
```

In hexadecimal, the low address word contains 4080 and the high address word contains 0000.

What about 2? In binary, this is $10.0 * 2^0$, which is not, of course, normalized. We move the binary point two places to the left, and we get $.100 * 2^2$; this has the same fraction as 1, but the exponent is different:

true exponent:	2	true fraction	10000000000000000000000
biased exponent:	82	stored fraction	00000000000000000000000
sign of fraction:	0		

Or:

```
   15 14           7 6           0
    0  1 0 0 0 0 0 1 0 0 0 0 0 0 0 0   low-address word
    0  0 0 0 0 0 0 0 0 0 0 0 0 0 0 0   high-address word
   31                          16
```

In hexadecimal, then, the low-address word contains 4100 and the high-address word (still) contains 0000.

What about numbers smaller than 1--how are they handled? Consider .125, which is 1/8, which is $1/2^3$, which is $0 * 2^{-1} + 0 * 2^{-2} + 1 * 2^{-3}$, which is $.001 * 2^0$. This is not normalized; if we move the binary point two places to the right, we get $.1 * 2^{-2}$, which has the following representation as an F_format floating point number:

true exponent:	-2	true fraction	10000000000000000000000
biased exponent:	7E	stored fraction	00000000000000000000000
sign of fraction:	0		

Or:

15	14						7	6						0	
0	0	1	1	1	1	1	1	0	0	0	0	0	0	0	low-address word
0	0	0	0	0	0	0	0	0	0	0	0	0	0	0	high-address word
31													16		

In hexadecimal, the low-address word contains 3F00 and the high-address word contains 0000.

Let's try a number that is *not* an even power of two: 10_{10}. In binary, this is $1010 * 2^0$, which is not, of course, normalized. Moving the binary point four places to the left, we get $.1010 * 2^4$, and the following F_format floating-point representation:

true exponent:	4	true fraction	10100000000000000000000
biased exponent:	84	stored fraction	01000000000000000000000
sign of fraction:	0		

Or:

15	14						7	6						0	
0	1	0	0	0	0	1	0	0	0	1	0	0	0	0	low-address word
0	0	0	0	0	0	0	0	0	0	0	0	0	0	0	high-address word
31													16		

In hexadecimal, the low-address word contains 4220 and the high-address word contains 0000.

What about a negative number, such as -10? Clearly, the only difference between -10 and +10 will be the sign bit, bit 15 of the low-address word:

true exponent:	4	true fraction	10100000000000000000000
biased exponent:	84	stored fraction	01000000000000000000000
sign of fraction:	1		

Or:

15	14						7	6						0	
1	1	0	0	0	0	1	0	0	0	1	0	0	0	0	low-address word
0	0	0	0	0	0	0	0	0	0	0	0	0	0	0	high-address word
31													16		

So, in hexadecimal, the low-address word for -10 is C220 (that for +10 is 4220), and the high-address word is still 0000.

Finally, what about a *mixed* number, with both an integer and a fraction part? Consider 19.03125. It is easiest to deal with mixed numbers by converting the two parts to binary separately: 19_{10} is 10011_2, and .03125 is 1/32, which is $1/2^5$, which is 2^{-5}, which is $.00001_2$. So, 19.03125_{10} is $10011.00001 * 2^0$; we normalize it by moving the binary point five places to the left, and end up with $.1001100001 * 2^5$:

true exponent:	5	true fraction	100110000100000000000000
biased exponent:	85	stored fraction	00110000100000000000000
sign of fraction:	0		

Or:

```
 15|14              7|6              0|
 | 0| 1 0 0 0 0 1 0 1| 0 0 1 1 0 0 0| low-address word
 | 0 1 0 0 0 0 0 0 0 0 0 0 0 0 0 0| high-address word
 |31                            16|
```

In hexadecimal, the low-address word contains 4298, and the high-address word contains 4000. If we were representing -19.03125, the only difference would be the sign bit of the fraction (bit 15 in the low-address word), so the low-address word, in hexadecimal, would be C298, and the high-address word would (still) be 4000.

Floating-Point Arithmetic

Now that we have seen the VAX F_format floating-point number representation, we can write an algorithm to add (or subtract) pairs of floating-point numbers. We call this kind of arithmetic **floating-point arithmetic,** for obvious reasons. If we start with two normalized floating-point operands, we should produce a normalized result, as well. What are the steps involved in doing floating-point arithmetic, or addition, in particular?

We will, as usual, use a simpler format to illustrate the steps required to perform floating-point arithmetic. These examples will, also as usual, extend readily to the VAX's F_format (and D_, G_ and H_format, as well) floating-point representations. We will use decimal numbers with 2-digit fractions and 1-digit signed exponents, with a radix of 10. So 10 is normalized to $.1 * 10^2$; 1 is normalized to $.1 * 10^1$, 12.5 is normalized (and rounded) to $.13 * 10^2$, etc. If we were to add 12.5 and 1.0 as normalized floating-point numbers, we would process $.13 * 10^2 + .10 * 10^1$. Addition requires that we **align** the decimal points, by adjusting the exponent of 1 of the 2 operands. A little reflection shows that it is better to scale the operand with the smaller exponent. So we pick $.10 * 10^1$, shift the decimal point to the left, and increase the exponent by 1 for each shift. We stop shifting and increasing when the exponents match, so $.10 * 10^1$ becomes $.01 * 10^2$. Now we can perform the addition: we add the fraction parts:

$$
\begin{array}{r}
.13 * 10^2 \\
+ .01 * 10^2 \\
\hline
.14 * 10^2
\end{array}
$$

Since the result is in normal form (i.e., it is already normalized), the operation is complete. What if we wish to add $.95 * 10^1 + .60 * 10^1$? The result, $1.55 * 10^1$, is *not* normalized; when we normalize it, we get $.16 * 10^2$ (with a loss of precision).

What if we add 120 and 2 as floating-point numbers? Aligning exponents, 120 turns into $.12 * 10^3$, and 2 turns into $.002 * 10^3$. The sum is $.122 * 10^3$, which is already normalized. However, it must be truncated (or rounded), because the representation we are using only allows two decimal digits for the fraction. As a result, we find that $.12 * 10^3 + x = .12^3$, with $x \neq 0$! This violates a fundamental law of mathematics: only the number 0 is supposed to have the property that, when it is added to a number, the sum is the same as that number. This violation of a mathematical law is an unavoidable consequence of using fixed-length numbers. If we add a large number to a small nonzero number, the result may be identical to the larger number we started with. In such a case, the operands are said to have been **incommensurate.**

This problem also appears when we add a series of floating-point numbers. Given three floating-point numbers (a, b, c), the law of associativity tells us that the sum of $(a + b) + c$ should be the same as the sum of $a + (b + c)$. However, it is easy to find triplets of floating-point numbers that violate this law. We can minimize the likelihood that we will get an incorrect result by sorting the numbers from smallest to largest, and then adding them in that order, smaller operands first.

Floating-point addition is, clearly, more complex than integer addition. If we were to write a subroutine to add two floating-point numbers, the subroutine would implement something like the following algorithm:

1. Extract the fractions and biased exponents of the two numbers; restore the hidden 1 to the fraction. Place the fractions and exponents in registers, perhaps.
2. Compare the exponents. If they are different, adjust the smaller to the larger by adding a leading 0 to its fraction for each number by which the exponents differ. When the fractions have been aligned, examine the sign of each fraction; if it is 1, negate the fraction (take its twos complement).
3. Add the fractions (check for errors).
4. If the sum is negative, negate it and place a 1 in the most significant bit of the low-address word of the result; if the sum is positive, place a 0 in the msb of the low-address word of the result.
5. Renormalize the fraction of the sum, if necessary, adjusting its exponent by 1 for each shift (to the right or left) of the fraction.
6. Place the exponent in bits 7 through 14 of the low-address word of the result.
7. Remove the hidden bit from the fraction; place the high-order 7 bits of the fraction in bits 0 through 6 of the low-address word of the result, and place the low-order 16 bits of the fraction in bits 0 through 15 of the high-address word of the result.

Floating-point subtraction is similar to floating-point addition, but floating-point multiplication and division turn out to be a little simpler. To multiply the floating-point representations for 12 and 3 ($.12 * 10^2$ and $.30 * 10^1$) we simply multiply the fraction parts ($.12 * .30 = .0360$) and add the exponents (the 2 from 10^2 and the 1 from 10^1 lead to the 3 in 10^3). The result, $.036 * 10^3$, then must be normalized to $.36 * 10^2$.

To divide 12 by 3 ($.12 * 10^2 \div .30 * 10^1$), we divide the fraction parts ($.12 \div .30 = .4$) and subtract the exponents (the 1 of 10^1 from the 2 of 10^2 produce a 1, for 10^1); the result, $.30 * 10^1$, is already normalized. The VAX also has instructions specifically for adding, subtracting, multiplying, and dividing floating-point numbers; these will be discussed shortly.

Comparing Floating-Point Numbers

The VAX provides a complete set of CMP instructions to compare the various floating-point representations: CMPF, CMPD, CMPG, and CMPH. However, the floating-point format used by the VAX allows us to use the same comparison scheme for comparing floating-point numbers that we use when comparing signed integers. How is this so? We compare the floating-point numbers one word at a time: first, we compare the low-address words, which contain the sign of the fraction, the biased exponent, and the most significant 7 bits of the fraction. If they are the same, then we compare the high-address words. Since the fraction is a sign-magnitude number, the low-order 16 bits (in the high-address words) are *un*signed numbers, and so their comparison should be followed by branches appropriate for unsigned numbers.

Let's consider this issue in more detail: given two floating-point numbers, A and B, if they have different most significant bits, then the one whose msb is 0 is larger than the one whose msb is 1 (a negative number, no matter how big, is smaller than a positive number, no matter how small). If the two numbers have the same sign (assume, first, that both numbers are positive), then the number with the larger (biased) exponent is the larger number (since the fractions are normalized). If the biased exponents are also the same, then the number with the larger fraction is the larger number. Since the bit fields in the VAX representation of floating-point numbers are arranged in the above order, all of these considerations are consistent with the way the CMP instruction works when comparing integers.

If the two floating-point numbers we wish to compare are both negative (i.e., if each has an msb of 1), we must be careful, because we are dealing with a sign-magnitude representation. However--as with sign-magnitude numbers in general (see chapter 7)--if we change the sign bits of both operands, we can proceed with the comparison as if both numbers were positive and then take the original signs into account after the comparison by *reversing* the outcome of the comparison and using *opposite* conditional branches: -4 is *smaller* than -3, but +4 is *larger* than +3.

What Can Go Wrong?

Many things can go wrong when we work with floating-point numbers. Every floating-point addition, subtraction, multiplication or division is capable of producing either **floating-point overflow** or **floating-point underflow**. **Floating-point overflow** occurs when a floating-point instruction, after normalization, produces an exponent that is larger than the largest one representable in the format used by the instruction. **Floating-point underflow,** similarly, occurs when an instruction produces an exponent that is smaller than the smallest one representable in that format.

Consider the following examples of overflow and underflow, using our simple decimal format for floating-point numbers. If we multiply $.90 * 10^5$ by $.80 * 10^5$, we get $.7200 * 10^{10}$. Since we have allocated only a single decimal digit for the exponent, the exponent of the result, 10, is too large-- this is a case of floating-point overflow. Consider another example: $.25 * 10^9$ added to $.80 * 10^9$ produces $1.05 * 10^9$; when normalized, we get $.11 * 10^{10}$. In this case, floating-point overflow occurred not during the arithmetic operation, but during the process of normalizing the result.

What about floating point underflow? Consider adding two very small numbers, as in the following example:

$$
\begin{array}{r}
-.12 * 10^{-9} \\
+\underline{.13} * 10^{-9} \\
.01 * 10^{-9}
\end{array}
$$

The result, $.01 * 10^{-9}$, when normalized, produces $.1 * 10^{-10}$; our representation cannot store an exponent smaller than -9, so floating-point underflow has occurred.

One of the subtle problems in dealing with floating-point numbers is related to an earlier observation: it is possible for two nonzero floating-point numbers, a and b, to satisfy the equality $a + b = a$. In effect, the number b is too small to have any effect when added to a. This problem can show up as follows: we are looking for a floating-point number, x, which satisfies some relation such as $f(x) = 0$. The function $f(x)$ might be a polynomial, such as $f(x) = 3.5x^2 + 2x - 5$, and we may be trying to find the roots of this quadratic expression. In a high-level language, we could write something like

    if $(f(x)$ 0) then
        try again

However, if x and $f(x)$ are floating-point numbers, then since we are working with computers (which do not perfectly implement mathematics), the appropriate way to write this expression is

    if $(f(x)$ is not small enough) then
        try again

We must define what *small enough* means. It depends not only on the specifics of the floating-point number representation our computer uses, but also on the problem we are trying to solve. If we make *small enough* too small, our program might iterate forever, looking for the *right x* and never finding it. Writing quality software for dealing with floating-point numbers is difficult; naive first attempts may succeed in some situations and fail in many other ones--as the report in figure 13.4 demonstrates.

Other VAX Floating-Point Representations

For some applications, a 24-bit fraction is not adequate. In those cases, the VAX supports three other floating-point formats, with 52, 55, and 112 bits allocated to the fraction (but, which, because of the hidden first bit, actually represent fractions of 53, 56, and 113 bits). In this section, we will briefly describe these formats. The D_format floating-point number representation gets its name from the fact that it is twice as long as the F_format, and is therefore often called **double precision.** In fact, however, it has *more* than twice the precision of the F_format. A D_format floating-point number occupies 4 consecutive words in memory; its first word is identical to the first word of the F_format: it contains the sign of the fraction, an 8-bit biased exponent, and the most significant 7 bits of the fraction. The next 3 words contain bits 8 through 23 of the fraction, bits 24 through 39 of the fraction, and bits 40 through 55 of the fraction, respectively. Since D_format and F_format use the same normalization rule, the D_format also has a hidden first bit; thus, although they store only 55 bits of fraction, D_format floating-point numbers have 56 bits of precision. Figure 13.5 shows the D_format floating-point representation as a series of 4 words.

The VAX's G_format floating-point representation is similar to the D_format in that both are 64 bits long, but it is different with respect to the allocation of bits to the exponent and fraction: G_format floating-point numbers have 11 bits for the biased exponent, so the range of numbers representable with G_format is greater than that of D_format. However, since more bits are used for the exponent, fewer are available for the fraction: G_format floating-point numbers have slightly less precision than do D_format. G_format numbers, like F_format and D_format numbers, store the sign of the fraction in bit 15 of the lowest address word; the next 11 bits (bits 14 through 4) are used for the exponent, which is biased by 400_{16}. The low-order 4 bits of the lowest address word contain the most significant 4 bits of the fraction (the leading 1, as usual, is hidden and not stored), the next lowest address word contains the next most significant 16 bits of the fraction, and so on, for the next 2 words. The G_format floating-point representation is shown in figure 13.6.

The Computing Center at Purdue University has made the IMSL Library available to its users since 1973 on a CDC 6500 system. The Center has published a series of articles illustrating library features and promoting usage.

The following reprint* illustrates characteristics of ZQADR from the Zeros and Extrema Chapter of the library. ZQADR finds the roots of a quadratic equation having real coefficients. The article has been modified slightly for editorial purposes.

"The object of this article is to illustrate, by way of an example, the quality which has been built into the IMSL Library. We do this by writing a subroutine to solve a rather simple problem, using the algorithm many people would use, and then by comparing the results we obtain with those of the corresponding IMSL routine.

"The problem we choose is to find the roots of a quadratic equation: given real numbers a, b, and c, find x such that $ax^2 + bx + c = 0$. For simplicity, we assume that a, b, and c are such that the solution is also real. The two roots of a quadratic equation may be found by the well-known 'Quadratic Formula,'

$$x = \frac{-b \pm \sqrt{b^2 - 4ac}}{2a},$$

where one root is obtained by using the "+" of the "±", and the other is obtained with the "−". The assumption that the roots are real means that $b^2 - 4ac \geq 0$. We can solve this problem with the following straight forward subroutine:

```
SUBROUTINE QUAD
(A,B,C,X1,X2)
D = SQRT (B*B−4.0*A*C)
X1 = 0.5*(−B+D)/A
X2 = 0.5*(−B−D)/A
RETURN
END
```

"When we use this subroutine to solve the rather difficult quadratic $x^2 + 10^7x + 1 = 0$ we obtain

$$X1 = -8.940696716309 \cdot 10^{-8},$$
$$X2 = -1.000000000000 \cdot 10^7.$$

This is not the correct solution, however. The corresponding IMSL routine ZQADR does compute the correct solution which is

$$X1 = -1.000000000000 \cdot 10^{-7},$$
$$X2 = -1.000000000000 \cdot 10^7$$

to the number of digits shown.

"Where did QUAD go wrong? The second statement computes D slightly less than 10^7. Then the third statement forms the difference between D and B, losing almost all significance in the process. ZQADR is more careful than QUAD and thus is able to retain full significance.

"Now we touch briefly on several additional problems with QUAD. The first deals with problem scaling. If the quadratic equation above is multiplied by a constant, the solution is not changed mathematically, but it is changed computationally. For example, the quadratic

$$10^{200}x^2 + 10^{207}x + 10^{200} = 0$$

results in a MODE 2 (use of infinite operand) error because 10^{400} cannot be represented by the computer. Similarly, the quadratic

$$10^{-200}x^2 + 10^{-193}x + 10^{-200} = 0$$

yields the solution

$$X1 = X2 = -5.000000000000 \cdot 10^6$$

because 10^{-400} cannot be represented by the computer and is treated as zero. However, ZQADR still computes the same, correct solution.

"Finally, consider QUAD's actions if the coefficient of x^2 in the quadratic is zero. In this case QUAD returns an infinite value for one root and an indefinite value for the other. ZQADR returns the mathematically correct value $-c/b$ for one root and infinity for the other.

"What is the point of this article if you never solve difficult quadratic equations? The point is that if it is hard to solve a simple problem and take all of the various problem areas into consideration, why attempt a really difficult problem yourself when robust state-of-the-art routines are already available? In other words, before writing a routine to solve a particular problem, check the IMSL Library first—you might save yourself a lot of time and trouble."

*NEWSLETTER, Purdue University Computing Center, Vol. X, No. 5, West Lafayette, IN, p. 9–10.

Figure 13.4 Good and bad floating-point software

15	14 ... 7	6 ... 0	
sf	biased exponent	fraction 1-7	Low-address word
fraction 8-23			Low-address word + 2
fraction 24-39			Low-address word + 4
fraction 40-55			Low-address word + 6

Figure 13.5 D_format floating-point number

15	14 ... 4	3 ... 0	
sf	biased exponent	fraction 1-4	Low-address word
fraction 5-20			Low-address word + 2
fraction 21-36			Low-address word + 4
fraction 37-52			Low-address word + 6

Figure 13.6 G_format floating-point number

15	14 ... 0	
sf	biased exponent	Low-address word
fraction 1-16		Low-address word + 2
fraction 17-32		Low-address word + 4
fraction 33-48		Low-address word + 6
fraction 49-64		Low-address word + 8
fraction 65-80		Low-address word + A
fraction 81-96		Low-address word + C
fraction 97-112		Low-address word + E

Figure 13.7 H_format floating-point number

The VAX's H_format floating-point numbers are 128 bits long. Bit 15 of the lowest address word is used for the sign of the fraction, and bits 14 through 0 are used for the exponent, which is biased by 4000_{16}. The most significant 16 bits of the fraction (less the usual hidden first 1) are stored in the second lowest address word, the next 16 bits in the next lowest address word, and so on, until all 8 words are filed with all 112 bits of fraction. The H_format floating point number representation is shown in figure 13.7.

Why does the VAX have so many floating-point number representations? Clearly, with different numbers of bits and/or with different allocations of the same number of bits to the fraction and exponent, it is possible to represent different ranges of numbers with different degrees of precision. The VAX provides a complete set of floating-point arithmetic instructions (which we will describe

Format	Length	Range		Precision
F_format	32 bits	$\approx .29 * 10^{-38}$ to	$1.7 * 10^{38}$	≈ 7 decimal digits
D_format	64 bits	$\approx .29 * 10^{-38}$ to	$1.7 * 10^{38}$	≈ 16 decimal digits
G_format	64 bits	$\approx .56 * 10^{-308}$ to	$.9 * 10^{308}$	≈ 15 decimal digits
H_format	128 bits	$\approx .84 * 10^{-4932}$ to	$.59 * 10^{4932}$	≈ 33 decimal digits

Figure 13.8 Comparison of floating-point formats

shortly) for each format, so it is just as easy for us to write programs that use H_format numbers as it is to write programs using F_format numbers. H_format numbers provide an expanded range and increased precision, but they do so at a price: increased memory requirements, and slower execution time. The H_format floating-point numbers occupy 4 longwords, while F_format numbers occupy only a single longword. In addition, fetching 128 bits from memory takes longer than fetching 32 bits, and adding (or subtracting, multiplying or dividing) 128-bit operands either requires more expensive hardware than does processing 32-bit operands, or it takes longer on the same hardware (when we use an algorithm similar to the one we used for extended-range integer arithmetic--described in chapter 7).

So, which floating-point format should we use? As a rule, the shortest one that meets our expected range and/or precision requirements. Figure 13.8 lists the length, range, and precision of the VAX's four floating-point formats.

Converting Fractions

We discussed how the external representation of integers could be converted into binary numbers some time ago--in a program example in chapter 9. What if we wish to read input (from a keyboard, for example) that represents real numbers rather than integers? In both cases, of course, our program will be dealing with strings of ASCII character codes, but the process of converting an ASCII coded string into an integer is considerably simpler than the process of converting such a string into a floating-point number.

Recall that in the example in chapter 9, we converted character codes into integers by first replacing each ASCII code by its integer equivalent (we subtracted 30_{16}), and then (proceeding from right to left) by multiplying each binary digit by a successive power of 10. Finally, we added the products, producing the desired result. For example, given the 3-digit string 234, we process the bytes containing ASCII codes 32_{16}, 33_{16} and 34_{16}. We subtract the ASCII code *offset*, which is 30_{16}, and convert these into 2, 3, and 4. Then we compute $2 * 10^2 + 3 * 10^1 + 4 * 10^0$. We usually calculate in decimal, but the computer, of course, calculates in binary; the result is 11101010_2, or EA_{16}. How does this relate to converting ASCII character strings that represent decimal integers *and* fractions into floating point number representations?

The process of converting a decimal fraction in its external representation into a binary fraction, is basically the reverse of the process of converting whole numbers into binary. Instead of using repeated multiplication, we use repeated division. Let us examine a simple case first: the digit string .5. We interpret .5 as $5 * 10^{-1}$, which is $5/10^1$, which we "instinctively" reduce to $1/2^1$, which is $1 * 2^{-1}$, or .1, binary. Recall that a binary fraction of the form $.b_1b_2b_3b_4$ represents the number $b_1 * 2^{-1} + b_2 * 2^{-2} + b_3 * 2^{-3} + b_4 * 2^{-4}$. This is exactly analogous to the decimal fraction, $.d_1d_2d_3d_4$, which represents the number $d_1 * 10^{-1} + d_2 * 10^{-2} + d_3 * 10^{-3} + d_4 * 10^{-4}$.

A program r.ading the 2 character string .5 will see the bytes $2E_{16}$ and 35_{16}. The program can easily count how many (ASCII coded) decimal digits appear to the right of the decimal point ($2E_{16}$); in this simple example there is only 1. We convert all the fraction digits as if they represented an integer; in this case, we get the value 5. We *double* the number and get 10_{10}, and divide by 10. The quotient is the first bit of the fraction, and we repeat the process of doubling and dividing the remainder by 10, until we get a remainder of 0. In this case, we divide 10 by 10 and get a quotient, q_1, of 1 and a remainder of 0; since the remainder is 0, we are done. In the general case, we perform several divisions, and get several quotients: $q_1, q_2, q_3, \ldots, q_n$. The fraction, in this general case, is $.q_1 q_2 q_3 \ldots q_n$. In this case, there is only one quotient, 1, so the fraction is .1. (This algorithm works whether we do the arithmetic in decimal, binary, hexadecimal, or any other base. For our examples, we do the arithmetic in decimal; the computer, of course, does arithmetic in binary.)

Let us consider a second example: .25. This fraction is 25/100; we double 25 and get 50 and divide by 100. The quotient, q_1, is 0, and the remainder is 50. We repeat the process: double 50 to get 100, divide by 100, and get a quotient, q_2 of 1 and a remainder of 0. We stop because the remainder is 0 and the binary fraction is $.q_1 q_2$, or .01. This makes sense, for we started with .25, which is 1/4, and got .01, which is $0 * 2^{-1} + 1 * 2^{-2}$ or $0/2^1 + 1/2^2$, which is $1/2^2$, which is 1/4.

It is always possible that the process will not terminate--that we will *never* get a remainder of 0. Just as 1/3 (.1 in base 3) has no finite representation as a decimal fraction, so 1/10 (.1 in base 10) may not have a finite representation in other bases. Fractions with non-terminating representations are called **repeating fractions**; when we encounter one, we stop doubling and dividing when we have generated *enough* fraction bits.

If we wish to convert numbers with both an integer part *and* a fraction part (i.e., **mixed numbers**), what do we do after converting the fraction? When we have generated the desired binary fraction, we convert the integer part, write it *next to* the fraction part (by shifting one or the other the appropriate number of bits), normalize the whole number, adjust the biased exponent, discard the most significant bit of the fraction (which must be 1, since the fraction is normalized), place the sign bit in the most significant bit of the lowest address word of the floating-point number, and we have *created* the floating-point representation of an ASCII coded decimal real number.

Software and Hardware Support for Floating-Point Numbers

The VAX has four floating-point number formats; both the assembler and the control unit deal with them in ways that are analogous to the ways that they deal with integers. The assembler helps us allocate and initialize memory locations by converting decimal real numbers to one of the VAX's binary floating-point number representations, and the control unit can perform a variety of arithmetic operations on floating-point numbers. In the following sections, we discuss some of the VAX's software and hardware support for floating-point numbers.

Floating-Point Directives

The assembler, Macro, has four directives for allocating memory locations and initializing them with floating-point numbers; not surprisingly, one directive corresponds to each of the four floating-point representations. These directives are:

```
.F_FLOATING     ;F_FORMAT
.D_FLOATING     ;D_FORMAT
.G_FLOATING     ;G_FORMAT
.H_FLOATING     ;H_FORMAT
```

Instruction	Mnemonic	Opcode	Action
Add F_floating, 2 operand	ADDF2 S, D	40	$D \leftarrow (S) + (D)$
Add F_floating, 3 operand	ADDF3 S_1, S_2, D	41	$D \leftarrow (S_1) + (S_2)$
Add D_floating, 2 operand	ADDD2 S, D	60	$D \leftarrow (S) + (D)$
Add D_floating, 3 operand	ADDD3 S_1, S_2, D	61	$D \leftarrow (S_1) + (S_2)$
Add G_floating, 2 operand	ADDG2 S, D	40FD	$D \leftarrow (S) + (D)$
Add G_floating, 3 operand	ADDG3 S_1, S_2, D	41FD	$D \leftarrow (S_1) + (S_2)$
Add H_floating, 2 operand	ADDH2 S, D	60FD	$D \leftarrow (S) + (D)$
Add H_floating, 3 operand	ADDH3 S_1, S_2, D	61FD	$D \leftarrow (S_1) + (S_2)$
Clear F_floating	CLRF D	D4	$D \leftarrow 0$
Clear D_floating	CLRD D	7C	$D \leftarrow 0$
Clear G_floating	CLRG D	7C	$D \leftarrow 0$
Clear H_floating	CLRH D	7CFD	$D \leftarrow 0$
Compare F_floating	CMPF S_1, S_2	51	$(S_1) - (S_2)$ sets CC
Compare D_floating	CMPD S_1, S_2	71	$(S_1) - (S_2)$ sets CC
Compare G_floating	CMPG S_1, S_2	51FD	$(S_1) - (S_2)$ sets CC
Compare H_floating	CMPH S_1, S_2	71FD	$(S_1) - (S_2)$ sets CC
Convert			see figure 13.11
Divide F_floating, 2 operand	DIVF2 S, D	46	$D \leftarrow (D) \div (S)$
Divide F_floating, 3 operand	DIVF3 S_1, S_2, D	47	$D \leftarrow (S_2) \div (S_1)$
Divide D_floating, 2 operand	DIVD2 S, D	66	$D \leftarrow (D) \div (S)$
Divide F_floating, 3 operand	DIVD3 S_1, S_2, D	67	$D \leftarrow (S_2) \div (S_1)$
Divide G_floating, 2 operand	DIVG2 S, D	46FD	$D \leftarrow (D) \div (S)$
Divide F_floating, 3 operand	DIVG3 S_1, S_2, D	47FD	$D \leftarrow (S_2) \div (S_1)$
Divide H_floating, 2 operand	DIVH2 S, D	66FD	$D \leftarrow (D) \div (S)$
Divide H_floating, 3 operand	DIVH3 S_1, S_2, D	67FD	$D \leftarrow (S_2) \div (S_1)$
Extended multiply and integerize			see text
Move negated F_floating	MNEGF S, D	52	$D \leftarrow -S$

Figure 13.9 VAX floating-point instructions

They are similar to the .BYTE, .WORD and .LONG directives, in that several constants may appear in the operand field. Each one of them will be transformed into the format of the floating-point representation, and stored in 1, 2 or 4 consecutive longwords. How do we specify operands for these directives? In approximately the same way that we specify operands for the directives that initialize integers, but with some extra complexity. The assembler recognizes floating-point formats similar to those recognized by a compiler for a high-level language such as FORTRAN or Pascal. Thus

.F_FLOATING -1.0E0, -1E0, -10.E-1, -100E-2, -1, -1.0, -0.1E1

will produce the same floating-point representation seven times. Each will occupy 1 longword (2 consecutive words); the low-address word of each will contain $C080_{16}$, and the high-address word of each will contain 0000.

Move negated D_floating	MNEGD S, D	72	D←−S
Move negated G_floating	MNEGG S, D	52FD	D←−S
Move negated H_floating	MNEGH S, D	72FD	D←−S
Move F_floating	MOVF S, D	50	D←S
Move D_floating	MOVD S, D	70	D←S
Move G_floating	MOVG S, D	50FD	D←S
Move H_floating	MOVH S, D	70FD	D←S
Multiply F_floating, 2 operand	MULF2 S, D	44	D←(S)*(D)
Multiply F_floating, 3 operand	MULF3 S_1, S_2, D	45	D←(S_1)*(S_2)
Multiply D_floating, 2 operand	MULD2 S, D	64	D←(S)*(D)
Multiply D_floating, 3 operand	MULD3 S_1, S_2, D	65	D←(S_1)*(S_2)
Multiply G_floating, 2 operand	MULG2 S, D	44FD	D←(S)*(D)
Multiply G_floating, 3 operand	MULG3 S_1, S_2, D	45FD	D←(S_1)*(S_2)
Multiply H_floating, 2 operand	MULH2 S, D	64FD	D←(S)*(D)
Multiply H_floating, 3 operand	MULH3 S_1, S_2, D	65FD	D←(S_1)*(S_2)
Polynomial evaluation			see text
Subtract F_floating, 2 operand	SUBF2 S, D	42	D←(D)−(S)
Subtract F_floating, 3 operand	SUBF3 S_1, S_2, D	43	D←(S_2)−(S_1)
Subtract D_floating, 2 operand	SUBD2 S, D	62	D←(D)−(S)
Subtract D_floating, 3 operand	SUBD3 S_1, S_2, D	63	D←(S_2)−(S_1)
Subtract G_floating, 2 operand	SUBG2 S, D	42FD	D←(D)−(S)
Subtract G_floating, 3 operand	SUBG3 S_1, S_2, D	43FD	D←(S_2)−(S_1)
Subtract H_floating, 2 operand	SUBH2 S, D	62FD	D←(D)−(S)
Subtract H_floating, 3 operand	SUBH3 S_1, S_2, D	63FD	D←(S_2)−(S_1)
Test F_floating	TSTF S	53	S−0 sets CC
Test D_floating	TSTD S	73	S−0 sets CC
Test G_floating	TSTG S	53FD	S−0 sets CC
Test H_floating	TSTH S	73FD	S−0 sets CC

Figure 13.9 *Continued*

Floating-Point Numbers and Registers

What happens if we try to put a 64-bit floating-point number in a register--where does it go? There is no obvious answer, because the registers are 32 bits wide, and it is impossible to place a 64-bit operand in a 32 bit location. However, the designers of the VAX chose the solution of least surprise: if we execute an instruction such as MOVD BIGNUM, R0 (and have defined BIGNUM with the .D_FLOATING directive), then the low-address (most significant) 32 bits--those stored in locations BIGNUM and BIGNUM+2--will go in R0, and the high-address (least significant) 32 bits--those stored in BIGNUM+4 and BIGNUM+6--will go in R1.

Floating-Point Instructions

The assembler supports floating-point arithmetic by converting decimal numbers into their corresponding floating-point formats; the control unit executes a large number of instructions with floating-point operands. Figure 13.9 summarizes these floating-point instructions. Many of them are similar to integer instructions, and require little explanation; others are more complex, and we will describe their operation and purpose.

The CVT Instructions

In chapter 7, we discussed a subset of the CVT family of instructions when we explained turning short numbers into long ones. We saw that there are CVT instructions for converting from bytes to words, from bytes to longwords, and from words to longwords. In chapter 10, we discussed another subset of the CVT family of instructions; these instructions were used for converting between integers and packed decimal strings, and between packed decimal strings and numeric (ASCII coded) strings of different formats. The VAX also has a large number of CVT instructions for converting integers to floating-point numbers, floating-point numbers to integers, and floating-point numbers of one format to floating-point numbers of another format. When converting floating-point numbers to integers, we can choose CVT instructions that truncate or ones that round. For all of the CVT instructions, the N bit is set if the destination operand is less than 0 and the Z bit is set if it is equal to 0; the V bit is set if integer overflow occurs (this can only happen when converting to a byte, word, or longword), and the C bit is always cleared.

Figure 13.10 is a summary of the CVT instructions. We can see from this figure, that there are (surprisingly) no instructions for converting from D_format to G_format, or from G_format to D_format floating-point numbers. In order to perform this conversion, we must first convert from G_format or D_format to H_format (this avoids loss of precision), and then to either D_format or G_format.

The POLY Instructions

The VAX also has a family of instructions, the POLY(F,D,G,H) instructions, that evaluate polynomials of the general format,

$$a_0 x^0 + a_1 x^1 + a_2 x^2 + a_3 x^3 + \cdots + a_{n-1} x^{n-1} + a_n x^n.$$

When one of the POLY instructions is used to evaluate a polynomial in this format, it refers to the coefficients of the polynomial as $a_0 \ldots a_n$, to the degree of the polynomial as n, and to the argument of the polynomial as x.

The general format of the POLY family of instructions is POLY(F,D,G,H) ARG, DEGREE, TABLE. The ARG operand is the argument; it is an F_format, D_format, G_format, or H_format floating-point number, as specified by the instruction. The DEGREE operand is 1 word long, specified as an unsigned integer. The TABLE operand is the starting address of a table of coefficients, listed as floating-point operands of the same type as the argument; the highest order coefficient is in the lowest address, and decreasing-order coefficients are stored at increasing addresses.

The result of the POLYF instruction is stored as an F_format floating-point number in R0; the POLYD and POLYG instructions place the high-order 32 bits of their D_format or G_format result in R0 and the low-order 32 bits in R1; and the POLYH instruction places the high-order 32 bits of its H_format result in R0, the next 32 bits in R1, the next 32 bits in R2, and the low-order 32 bits in R3. This is exactly the same order in which an ordinary instruction, with a register as a destination, places floating-point operands in registers. The POLYF instruction also changes R1 through R3, the POLYD and POLYG instructions also change R2 through R5, and the POLYH instruction also changes R4 and R5; figure 13.11 shows the changed registers after execution of the POLY(F,D,G,H) instructions.

Instruction	Mnemonic	Opcode	Action
Convert byte to F_floating	CVTBF S, D	4C	D←convert(S)
Convert word to F_floating	CVTWF S, D	4D	D←convert(S)
Convert long to F_floating	CVTLF S, D	4E	D←convert(S)
Convert byte to D_floating	CVTBD S, D	6C	D←convert(S)
Convert word to D_floating	CVTWD S, D	6D	D←convert(S)
Convert long to D_floating	CVTLD S, D	6E	D←convert(S)
Convert byte to G_floating	CVTBG S, D	4CFD	D←convert(S)
Convert word to G_floating	CVTWG S, D	4DFD	D←convert(S)
Convert long to G_floating	CVTLG S, D	4EFD	D←convert(S)
Convert byte to H_floating	CVTBH S, D	6CFD	D←convert(S)
Convert word to H_floating	CVTWH S, D	6DFD	D←convert(S)
Convert long to H_floating	CVTLH S, D	6EFD	D←convert(S)
Convert F_floating to byte	CVTFB S, D	48	D←convert(S)
Convert F_floating to word	CVTFW S, D	49	D←convert(S)
Convert F_floating to long	CVTFL S, D	4A	D←convert(S)
Convert rounded F_floating to long	CVTRFL S, D	4B	D←convert(S)
Convert D_floating to byte	CVTDB S, D	68	D←convert(S)
Convert D_floating to word	CVTDW S, D	69	D←convert(S)
Convert D_floating to long	CVTDL S, D	6A	D←convert(S)
Convert rounded D_floating to long	CVTRDL S, D	6B	D←convert(S)
Convert G_floating to byte	CVTGB S, D	48FD	D←convert(S)
Convert G_floating to word	CVTGW S, D	49FD	D←convert(S)
Convert G_floating to long	CVTGL S, D	4AFD	D←convert(S)
Convert rounded G_floating to long	CVTRGL S, D	4BFD	D←convert(S)
Convert H_floating to byte	CVTHB S, D	68FD	D←convert(S)
Convert H_floating to word	CVTHW S, D	69FD	D←convert(S)
Convert H_floating to long	CVTHL S, D	6AFD	D←convert(S)
Convert rounded H_floating to long	CVTRHL S, d	6BFD	D←convert(S)
Convert F_floating to D_floating	CVTFD S, D	56	D←convert(S)
Convert F_floating to G_floating	CVTFG S, D	99FD	D←convert(S)
Convert F_floating to H_floating	CVTFH S, D	98FD	D←convert(S)
Convert D_floating to F_floating	CVTDF S, D	76	D←convert(S)
Convert D_floating to H_floating	CVTDH S, D	32FD	D←convert(S)
Convert G_floating to F_floating	CVTGF S, D	33Fd	D←convert(S)
Convert G_floating to H_floating	CVTGH S, D	56FD	D←convert(S)
Convert H_floating to F_floating	CVTHF S, D	F6FD	D←convert(S)
Convert H_floating to D_floating	CVTHD S, D	F7FD	D←convert(S)
Convert H_floating to G_floating	CVTHG S, D	76FD	D←convert(S)

Figure 13.10 The CVT instructions

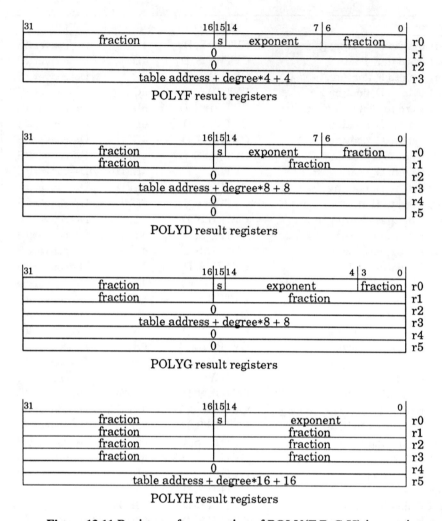

Figure 13.11 Registers after execution of POLY(F,D,G,H) instructions

Let us consider a simple example, in order to understand better the operation of the POLY(F,D,G,H) family of instructions. Suppose that we wish to evaluate the following polynomial:

$$y = 3x^4 + 2x^3 - .1x^2 + 7x - 19.86,$$

for $x = 2.448$. If we use F_format floating-point numbers, we would create the following data structures, and execute the following instruction:

```
ARGUMENT:     .F_FLOATING 2.448                        ;value to solve x for
DEGREE:       .WORD 4                                  ;degree of polynomial
TABLE:        .F_FLOATING 3.0, 2.0, –.1, 7.0, –19.86   ;coefficients
              .
              .
              .

              POLYF ARGUMENT, DEGREE, TABLE
              .
              .
              .
```

After execution, R0 will contain the F_format floating-point value of x (C1274405$_{16}$), R1 and R2 will contain 0, and R3 will contain the address of the byte after the last entry in the coefficient table.

The EMOD Instructions

The EMOD(F,D,G,H) instructions perform extended floating-point multiplication (similar to the EMUL and EDIV instructions discussed in chapter 10), and then they *integerize* the result. The format of these instructions is EMOD S$_1$, S$_1$EXT, S$_2$, INT, FRACT. The S$_1$EXT operand is an *extension* of the S$_1$ operand, which is a floating-point number of the type corresponding to the instruction. It provides an additional, low-order, 8 bits for the fraction of the EMODF and EMODD instructions, an additional 11 bits for the fraction of the EMODG instruction, and an additional 15 bits for the fraction of the EMODH instruction. The combined S$_1$ and S$_1$EXT operands are multiplied by the S$_2$ operand, and the product is computed as a 32-bit fraction (for EMODF), a 64-bit fraction (for EMODD and EMODG) or a 128-bit fraction (EMODH). The product is then considered the sum of a 32-bit integer part (which is stored in the INT operand) and a 32-bit (EMODF), 64-bit (EMODD and EMODG) or 128-bit (EMODH) fraction part, which is stored in the FRACT operand. The S$_1$EXT operand is 1 byte long for EMODF and EMODD, and it is 2 bytes long for EMODG and EMODH. These instructions are typically used for added precision when computing trigonometric functions such as *sine* and *cosine*.

Executing Floating-Point Instructions

Now we know that the VAX has a versatile floating-point instruction set--but how is floating-point arithmetic actually done? There is a continuum of possibilities; which one is used on any particular computer system depends upon what kind of price/performance tradeoff the person who purchased the system was willing to make. The least expensive--and slowest--method of implementing floating-point instructions is in software. In this case, rather than actually having the control unit execute the ADDF3 instruction (for example), we simply call a subroutine that performs each of the steps necessary for adding a pair of F_format floating-point numbers. At the other extreme, many VAX's are available with a special floating-point ALU (often called a **floating-point accelerator,** or a **floating-point coprocessor**), which is expensive, special purpose hardware, designed expressly for executing floating-point instructions quickly.

Which technique any particular computer uses is largely a matter of what options the manufacturer provides, and how much money the purchaser is willing to spend. Regardless of which technique is used, the same steps must be performed to execute a floating-point instruction--with special hardware they can be performed very quickly, and without special hardware they are performed rather slowly. Since this book is not a hardware book, we are satisfied with an understanding of what those steps are; we will not concern ourselves with the design of the hardware that actually executes them.

Floating-Point Exceptions

If certain types of incorrect results occur during the execution of floating-point instructions, an **exception** occurs. An exception is like an interrupt: the PC and PSL are saved on the stack, and control is transferred to an **exception handler.** There are six floating-point exceptions; they are mutually exclusive, so the exception handler for all floating-point exceptions has the same vector in the System Control Block: 34_{16}. The exceptions are distinguished from each other by a type code, which is pushed on the stack as a longword above the saved PC and PSL.

When the result of a floating-point operation is nonzero and its exponent is too *small* for the representation being used, a **floating-point underflow** exception occurs. When a result's exponent is too *large* for the representation being used, a **floating-point overflow** exception occurs. When the divisor of a DIV(F,D,G,H)[2,3] instruction is 0, a **floating-point divide by zero** exception occurs.

Each floating-point exception can be one of two types: a **trap** or a **fault.** A **trap** is an exception that occurs *after* an instruction has been executed and has produced incorrect results; in the case of a trap, appropriate condition-code bits are set, the PC and PSL are saved, and execution is typically continued by the operating system. The saved PC points to the instruction *after* the one that caused the exception.

The second type of floating-point exception is a **fault.** A **fault** occurs *during* an instruction's execution; the control unit does *not* complete execution of the instruction, and it leaves the registers and memory in a consistent state. Thus, if the fault condition is removed, the instruction can be restarted and it will produce correct results when it completes. In the case of a fault, leaving the registers and memory in a consistent state includes *not* changing the destination and *not* changing the CC bits (in fact, the CC bits are unpredictable after a fault). The fault condition is removed by the exception handler (whose address is in location 34_{16} of the System Control Block). In the case of a fault, the saved PC points to the instruction that caused the exception, so when the handler completes (and the saved PC and PSL are restored), execution continues with the instruction that originally caused the fault.

What actually happens when a floating-point exception occurs? We must distinguish between a floating-point underflow trap and a floating-point underflow fault, a floating-point overflow trap and a floating-point overflow fault, and a floating-point divide by zero trap and a floating-point divide by zero fault.

1. In the case of a floating-point overflow trap, the sign of the result's fraction is 1 and the exponent and fraction are all 0. This is a **reserved operand**; any subsequent floating-point instruction that tries to use it will cause a **reserved operand fault.** In the saved PSL, the N and V bits are set, and the Z and C bits are cleared.
2. In the case of a floating-point overflow fault, the destination is unaffected, and the CC bits in the saved PSL are unpredictable.
3. For a floating-point underflow trap, the result stored is 0; the N, V, and C bits are cleared, and the Z bit is set.
4. For a floating-point underflow fault, the destination is unchanged, and the CC bits are unpredictable.
5. For a divide by zero trap, the reserved operand (described above) is stored in the destination; the N and V bits are set, and the Z and C bits are cleared.
6. For a divide by zero fault, the quotient is unchanged, and the CC bits are unpredictable.

Floating-point underflow is somewhat different from floating-point overflow and floating-point divide by zero, because it can be enabled or disabled. Bit 6 of the PSL is the **floating-point underflow enable** (FU) bit. If FU is 0, no exception will occur when floating-point underflow occurs; if FU is 1, then the exceptions, as described above, will occur. Figure 13.12 shows the PSL, including the CC bits, the FU bit and the Interrupt Priority Level (IPL) bits. Figure 13.12 also shows the **decimal overflow enable** (DV) bit which, when set, allows a trap to occur when a decimal string

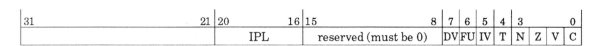

31	21	20	16	15	8	7	6	5	4	3	0
		IPL		reserved (must be 0)		DV	FU	IV	T	N	Z	V	C

Figure 13.12 PSL, including FU, DV and IV bits

instruction produces a result that is too large for its destination. This figure also shows the **integer overflow enable** (IV) bit which, when set, causes a trap when an integer instruction sets the V bit.

Floating-point exceptions cannot be lightly dismissed. Some years ago, a renowned research institution went through a transition from an older brand X computer to a newer, more powerful, brand Y computer. Users began moving their FORTRAN programs from computer X to computer Y. The computing center began getting complaints that "machine Y is messing up our output listings" because it was reporting floating-point overflow errors. Since the programs in question had been running satisfactorily on machine X for many years, it was clearly *not* the programs that were at fault: it had to be a problem with the new machine Y. The management yielded to pressure from irate users, the floating-point exception enable bit was cleared, and the customers went away happy. After all, they were getting the answers they expected.

What was the *real* problem with computers X and Y? Brand X used a 64-bit word with a very large exponent field, but brand Y used a "more efficient" representation of 32 or 36 bits--with a correspondingly smaller exponent field. Obviously, some operations not leading to floating-point overflow on machine X could, and *would,* lead to overflow on machine Y.

Who is to blame in this incident? It seems clear to the authors that the computer center management, presumably aware of the significance of floating-point overflow, should not have cleared the enable bit. Any results computed after even a single floating-point overflow are meaningless. Neither should the researchers be let off the hook, however. Their failure to look into why their time-tested programs were suddenly misbehaving is inexcusable. Pity the unsuspecting users who began using system Y only after the floating-point exception bit had been cleared. They may never know why their results were so good--or so bad!

Megaflops

For many organizations, a computer's floating-point capabilities are of primary concern when selecting a new computer. Thus, we must expand our earlier list of the goals of a floating-point representation:

1. Range
2. Precision
3. Speed

The speed, or the rate at which floating-point operations can be executed, is crucial in many problems in science and engineering. It is important enough that there is a term used specifically for its measurement: a **megaflop** (or **mflop**) is a million floating-point operations per second. We measure a computer's *typical* performance in **mips,** or millions of (typical) instructions per second; a *typical* instruction is an integer addition or comparison. Floating-point arithmetic usually takes considerably longer than integer arithmetic, so when choosing a computer that will be used extensively for floating-point arithmetic, its megaflop rating is crucial. The VAX family of computers provides mflop ratings from less than 1 to more than 10 mflops; with the addition of special hardware (such as that provided by Floating Point Systems), the limit can be extended to over 100 mflops.

Summary

We have discussed the need to represent a greater range of numbers than is possible with integers and to do so with as little loss of accuracy as possible. VAX **floating-point numbers** use the techniques of scientific notation to attain these goals. **Normalization** of fractions maximizes the number of significant bits that constitute a floating-point number.

There are four formats for VAX floating-point numbers. An F_format floating-point number is 32 bits long; it has an 8-bit biased exponent, and a 24-bit sign-magnitude fraction. D_format and G_format floating-point numbers are both 64 bits long; a D_format number has an 8-bit biased exponent and a 56-bit sign-magnitude fraction, while a G_format number has an 11-bit biased exponent and a 53-bit sign-magnitude fraction. Finally, an H_format floating-point number is 128 bits long; it has a 15-bit biased exponent and a 113-bit sign-magnitude fraction. For all formats, normalization guarantees that the fraction has a leading 1; this bit is not stored, so there is room for one more bit--increasing precision by 1 bit.

The VAX has a complete set of instructions for doing floating-point arithmetic. The algorithms for doing floating-point arithmetic in software were discussed, with the warning that it is difficult to do correctly. Macro also has a set of directives for allocating and initializing floating-point data.

Any arithmetic operation on floating-point numbers can cause floating-point overflow or floating-point underflow. If one of these occurs, it triggers a special interrupt, called a **floating-point exception.**

Exercises for Chapter 13

1.   For the following decimal numbers, write the corresponding F_format VAX floating-point numbers in hexadecimal.

a. -1/2
b. 36.75
c. -127
d. .1

2.   For the following F_format floating-point numbers, identify the one which is:

a. most positive (largest)
b. most negative (smallest)
c. closest to 0
d. would produce floating-point overflow on multiplication (a *pair* of numbers).

The floating-point numbers are shown as they would appear in a hex memory dump.

1. 0000C580
2. 00004580
3. D70A4223
4. 00005080
5. 0000D080
6. 76997F16
7. 000041A0

3.   What are the three fields of a floating-point number used for? Give two reasons why the VAX only deals with normalized floating-point numbers.

4. In the VAX's memory, there are only strings of bits; the same bit-string can represent an opcode, operand specifier, address, ASCII character code, integer, or floating-point number. In the following table, the left-most column shows, in hex, a bit-string in the VAX's memory. For each row, fill in the decimal (sign-magnitude) value of the bit-string if it is interpreted as a twos complement number, a sign-magnitude number, or the low-address word of an F_format floating-point number. The first row has been done as an example.

Hex	Twos complement	Sign-magnitude	Floating-point
4080	16512	16512	1
4271			
3F80			
C288			
42FF			
437F			
BF80			
3E00			
C3C8			
C680			
5080			
D080			
D200			
4A80			

5. What are the largest positive numbers (within a factor of ten) in each of the following categories which can be processed by a VAX? Write your answers in decimal.

    a. unsigned integer
    b. signed integer
    c. F_format floating-point number
    d. D_format floating-point number
    e. signed 64-bit integer

6. Suppose you added a new floating-point format to the VAX, one in which the radix of the exponent is 16 rather than 2. Compare the the range and precision of numbers using this new format with those of numbers using the current VAX format.

7. Write the code to compare two F_format floating-point numbers, using CMP(B,W,L) instructions. Write it as a subroutine and document the algorithm and parameter-passing techniques you use.

8. Write the code to compare two D_format floating-point numbers using the CMP(B,W,L) instructions.

9. Convert the fraction $.1_{10}$ into binary, accurate to 10 bits. Is this a repeating fraction?

10. Describe an algorithm to convert binary fractions into decimal fractions.

11. When two floating-point numbers are to be added, their binary points must be aligned (by shifting and adjusting the exponent of one of them). Why is it preferable to scale the number with the smaller exponent rather than the one with the larger exponent?

▪ 14 ▪

Arrays

___

Introduction

We have been using one dimensional arrays since chapter 3, when we described the VAX's memory system as an array of bytes, words or longwords. In addition, we have seen that the directive

ARRAYA: .WORD 2, 4, -7

may be considered a request to the assembler to allocate a one-dimensional array of 3 words; each word is initialized at program load time to contain a signed integer. When we write

ARRAYB: .BYTE 255, 136, 17, 223

we are allocating and initializing a one-dimensional array of 4 bytes, each of which contains an unsigned number.If we write

ARRAYC: .ASCIZ   "THIS IS A TEST"

we are also allocating and initializing an array of bytes, but we indicate its length--or rather its *end*--by marking it with a sentinel value (a byte containing 0), rather than by specifying a count of the number of elements in the array. We also saw in chapter 13 that we can allocate and initialize arrays of floating point numbers:

ARRAYD: .F_FLOATING -1, -10E-1, 19.03125, 1, -1E-2

is an array of five F_format floating point numbers.

What can we generalize from the above examples, and from what we know about arrays from programming in high-level languages such as Pascal or FORTRAN? Arrays have three distinguishing features:

1.   The number of dimensions of an array is determined when the array is *declared*.
2.   The number of elements in each dimension is determined when the array is *declared*.
3.   Each array element is of the same type.

We often call the last property **homogeneity** (as with homogenized milk). This property makes arrays easy to work with: given an element's subscripts, it is straightforward to find that element (which is done, of course, by calculating its address). There are no surprises, because the size of the array is known, the number of elements in each dimension is known, and each element occupies the same amount of space.

Arrays are frequently used data structures in computer science; the process of finding an element of an array is straightforward, but it is not trivial. In this chapter, we will see what work must be done to calculate an array element's address, given its subscripts.

One-Dimensional Arrays

In the course of our discussion of the VAX, we have already dealt with one-dimensional arrays in considerable detail; what must we add? We have not considered the issue of the origin of an array's indexing. Two common varieties are 0-origin and 1-origin indexing; in our assembly language programming, we have used 0-origin indexing implicitly. However, in everyday life, we usually start counting with 1, not with 0. In addition, some higher level languages (such as FORTRAN) use 1-origin indexing exclusively, others (such as C) use 0-origin indexing exclusively, and still others (such as Pascal) allow user defined origin indexing. So, let's clarify the terms, and let's see what effects different origin indexing has on our goal of calculating an array element's address, given its subscripts.

Let ARRAYA be an array of five longwords. In FORTRAN, for example, the five elements would be referred to with the notation

    ARRAYA(1), ARRAYA(2), ARRAYA(3), ARRAYA(4), ARRAYA(5).

In C, we would refer to those elements with the notation

    arraya[0], arraya[1], arraya[2], arraya[3], arraya[4].

In Pascal, we define the origin of the indexing when we declare the array; the elements of a 5-element array could be referred to as

    arraya[123], arraya[124], arraya[125], arraya[126], arraya[127]

or, perhaps, as

    arraya[-2], arraya[-1], arraya[0], arraya[1], arraya[2].

In assembly language, we could define the array with the .BLKL directive:

    ARRAYA: .BLKL 5

the array's 5 elements have addresses ARRAYA+0, ARRAYA+4, ARRAYA+8, ARRAYA+12, ARRAYA+16. With a 0-origin array, the first item is referred to as ARRAYA[0]; if we wish to access the ith item of a 0-origin array, we can write the following code:

```
MOVL I, R5
ASHL #2, R5, R5        ;longword occupies 4 bytes
MOVL ARRAYA(R5), R6
```

This works because ARRAYA[i] refers to the ith+1 item of the 0-origin array, ARRAYA; the first item has offset 0 from the starting address of the array, the second item has offset 1 (* 4, for a longword array), etc.

With a 1-origin array, things are slightly more complicated: the first item of 1-origin array of longwords, ARRAYB, is referred to as ARRAYB[1], but its address is ARRAYB+0. To place item ARRAYB[j] into R7, we can write the following code:

```
MOVL J, R5
DECL R5                ;ith item has offset i-1
ASHL #2, R5, R5        ;4 bytes per longword
MOVL ARRAYB(R5), R7
```

If we use index mode (mode 4) addressing rather than displacement mode addressing, the ALU performs the multiplication (that we did above by shifting two places to the left, with the ASHL instruction) for us, but *we* must still know if we are dealing with a 0-origin or a 1-origin array. The difference between 0-origin and 1-origin arrays is not difficult to understand, but we must know which we are dealing with in order to correctly translate from a high-level programming language reference to an array element by its subscript to the correct address of that element in the computer's memory. With this background, we are ready to look into the more interesting problem of mapping a two-dimensional array, or an *n*-dimensional array, into a computer's one-dimensional memory.

Two-Dimensional Arrays

Before we discuss *n*-dimensional arrays, let us examine a two-dimensional array. Suppose we create a 2-by-2 array of bytes, called ARRAYC. Using 1-origin indexing, each element has the subscripts indicated in the following table:

Rows	Columns 1	2
1	1,1	1,2
2	2,1	2,2

How can we store the 4 elements of this array in memory in order to maximize the ease of computing the address of each element? There are two possibilities: by row or by column. When we store an array's elements by row, we store all elements in the first row, then all elements in the second row. In our 2-by-2 example, address ARRAYC is where the element specified as ARRAYC[1,1] is stored. Then, element ARRAYC[1,2] is stored at address ARRAYC+1 (completing the first row), element ARRAYC[2,1] is stored at address ARRAYC+2, and element ARRAYC[2,2] is stored at address ARRAYC+3--completing the second row and the whole of this 2-by-2 array.

Alternatively, we can store this array by column: all elements in the first column are stored in memory, then all elements in the second column and so forth. If we store our 2-by-2 array by column, ARRAYC[1,1] is stored at address ARRAYC, ARRAYC[2,1] is stored at address ARRAYC+1 (completing the first column), ARRAYC[1,2] is stored at address ARRAYC+2, and ARRAYC[2,2] is stored at address ARRAYC+3--completing the second column and the whole array.

The choice of storing by row *versus* storing by column seems trivial, but different high-level languages have not made the same choice. For example, the designers of FORTRAN, in the mid-1950s, decided to store two dimensional arrays by column; this is called **column major** ordering. A few years later, the designers of ALGOL (and those of other, more modern, high-level languages such as C and Pascal) ignored FORTRAN's precedent and decided to store arrays by rows, using **row major** ordering. As a consequence, if we wish to transfer array data between a FORTRAN program and a Pascal program, for example, the linear ordering of the multidimensional arrays used by our FORTRAN program is incompatible with that used by our Pascal program. We must either transform the data from one linear representation to the other or modify one of the programs. Neither approach is desirable: both take time and introduce one more possibility for error.

The designers of FORTRAN probably decided to use column major ordering of arrays because the applications they were aware of (written in assembly language and machine language) used this ordering. The ALGOL choice of row major ordering can be defended on the basis of a universal practice: **lexicographic** ordering. Does A[2,1] come before or after A[1,2]? The lexicographer (the person who writes dictionaries) says that A[1,2] comes first, because 1 comes before 2. Since row major ordering is consistent with the way we file everything else, the ALGOL argument concludes, why make array ordering an exception?

	Columns		
Rows	1	2	3
1	1,1	1,2	1,3
2	2,1	2,2	2,3

Figure 14.1 Two by three array

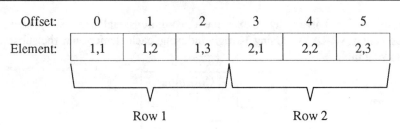

Figure 14.2 Mapping subscripts into offsets

Consider the 2-by-3 array (with 2 rows and 3 columns) shown in figure 14.1. The 1-origin subscripts for each array element position are shown in the position that the element would occupy. When we map this array into a computer's one-dimensional memory using lexicographic (row major) ordering, we see what is shown in figure 14.2. The relationship between the subscript pairs i, j, and their offsets from the beginning of the array is:

$$\text{offset} = (i\text{-}1)*3 + (j\text{-}1)$$

The rows are labeled in figure 14.2 to make this relationship clearer. We can easily generalize this formula to compute the offset of an element in *any* two-dimensional array:

$$\text{offset} = (\text{row subscript-1}) * \text{number of columns} + (\text{column subscript-1})$$

Of course, we must remember to adjust the calculated offset for the size of each element: if our array is one of bytes, then the offset is correct as calculated; if it is an array of words, we must double the offset, and if it is an array of longwords, we must multiply it by 4. As we saw in earlier examples, multiplying by 4 may be performed easily on the VAX by using the ASHL instruction with a count of 2, or by placing the offset in a register and using index mode (mode 4).

Consider a final example with a two-dimensional array: we wish to access element [4,3] in a 7-by-5, 1-origin array of words (ARRAYD) stored in row major order. We must find the fourth row, and the third element in that row. The first row occupies the first 10 memory locations (5 words, 2 bytes per word), with elements stored at offsets 0, 2, 4, 6, and 8 from address ARRAYD. The second row occupies the next 10 locations (with elements stored at offsets 10 through 18 from ARRAYD), and the third row's elements occupy the 10 locations with offsets 20 through 28 from ARRAYD. The fourth row begins at ARRAYD+30; the first element in the fourth row is stored there, the second element at ARRAYD+32, and the third element--the one we are interested in--is at ARRAYD+34. Let's apply the formula derived above: the offset is the row subscript minus 1 (4-1 = 3) times the number of columns

(5), plus the column subscript minus 1 (3-1 = 2). So, 3*5 = 15; 15+2 = 17; since each element is a word, we double the offset: 17*2 = 34, and this is what we calculated the long way.

N-Dimensional Arrays

As we go from two-dimensional arrays to three, four, and n-dimensional arrays, the mapping of the multiple array dimensions into the single memory dimension generalizes as follows. Given a 1-origin array, A, of dimension n, it has n subscripts, $i_1, i_2, \ldots, i_n$. Each subscript, i_j, ranges from 1 to s_j; in other words, $1 \leq i_j \leq s_j$, for $j = 1, 2, \ldots, n$. Then, we can calculate the offset of element $A(i_1, i_2, \ldots, i_{(n-1)}, i_n)$, using the following formula:

$$
\begin{aligned}
\text{offset} \quad = \quad & (i_1 - 1)*s_2*s_3* \cdots *s_{n-1}*s_n \\
+ \quad & (i_2 - 1)*s_3*s_4* \cdots *s_n \\
+ \quad & \cdots \\
+ \quad & (i_{n-1} - 1)*s_n \\
+ \quad & (i_n - 1)
\end{aligned}
$$

We can illustrate this with a 2-by-4-by-3 array of bytes, ARRAYF. The relevant parameters are:

dimensionality, n (number of subscripts): 3
number of rows, s_1: 2
number of columns, s_2: 4
number of layers, s_3: 3
total size of ARRAYF, in bytes: 2 * 4 * 3 = 24

In Pascal, we could declare this array as follows:

var arrayf : array[1..2,1..4,1..3] of char;

The base address, ARRAYF, is the First Element Address (FEA);if we wish to translate the Pascal reference to element ARRAYF[i,j,k] into the address of the item, we would calculate as follows:

$$
\begin{aligned}
\text{FEA} + \quad & (i\text{-}1) * s_2 * s_3 \\
+ \quad & (j\text{-}1) * s_3 \\
+ \quad & (k\text{-}1)
\end{aligned}
$$

This is equivalent to

$$
\begin{aligned}
\text{ARRAYF} + \quad & (i\text{-}1) * 4 * 3 \\
+ \quad & (j\text{-}1) * 3 \\
+ \quad & (k\text{-}1)
\end{aligned}
$$

This, in turn, is equivalent to

$$
\text{ARRAYF} + (i\text{-}1) * 12 + (j\text{-}1) * 3 + (k\text{-}1)
$$

We can picture array ARRAYF as shown in figure 14.3. We can think of this three-dimensional array as having three *layers*; each layer contains 2 rows, and each row has 4 elements. The lexicographical order of the elements of this array is shown in figure 14.4; clearly, the left-front-bottom corner element, referred to as "arrayf [1,1,1]" in Pascal, maps into address ARRAYF + 0 + 0 + 0, which is address ARRAYF. As we step through the array in lexicographical order, the third subscript varies

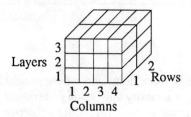

Figure 14.3 Three-dimensional array

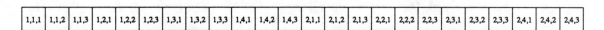

Figure 14.4 Lexicographical order of elements in a three-dimensional array

most rapidly, the second subscript changes once for every complete cycle of the third subscript, and the first subscript changes once for every complete cycle of the second *and* third subscripts together. This is reminiscent of the observation that, when counting, the high-order digits of a number change more slowly than do the low-order digits.

We can add an important refinement to the array offset formula presented above: we can generalize it for handling arrays with elements that are larger than 1 byte. If we let w be the element-addressing increment, then the formula for an element's offset becomes:

$$
\begin{aligned}
\text{offset} \quad = \quad & w*(i_1-1)*s_2*s_3*\cdots*s_{n-1}*s_n \\
+ \quad & w*(i_2-1)*s_3*s_4*\cdots*s_n \\
+ \quad & \cdots \\
+ \quad & w*(i_{n-1}-1)*s_n \\
+ \quad & w*(i_n-1)
\end{aligned}
$$

Some values of w are:

$$
\begin{aligned}
w = \quad & 1 \text{ for bytes} \\
& 2 \text{ for words} \\
& 4 \text{ for longwords}
\end{aligned}
$$

Writing Code to Compute Array Displacements

There are three basic methods for converting a subscript reference into the appropriate offset (or displacement) for the desired array element. They are:

1. In-line code
2. Dope vector
3. Hybrid

```
MOVL I, R1              ;subscript I
DECL R1                 ;change to 0-origin
ASHL #2, R1, R1         ;(I–1)*4 = (I–1)*NCOL
MOVL J, R2              ;subscript J
DECL R2                 ;0-origin, again
ADDL2 R2, R1            ;(I–1)*NCOL + (J–1)
ASHL #2, R1, R1         ;longwords: offset * 4
ADDL2 A(R1), SUM
```

Figure 14.5 In-Line Array Reference Code

We will discuss each of these methods in turn, below.

In-Line Code

In-line code is what we usually write when we want something done here and now. We simply write all the instructions needed where they are needed. If we are trying to compute

ADD item A[i, j] to SUM

we write, in-line, the instructions needed to fetch item A[i, j]. For a 3-by-4 array (A) of integers (longwords), if we store the "i" subscript in the memory location with label I and the "j" subscript in the memory location with label J, we can write the code shown in figure 14.5. Note that we use seven instructions to generate the necessary array offset. We can reduce the instruction count to six by using index mode: we would replace the last two instructions in figure 14.5 with ADDL2 A[R1], SUM.

Dope Vectors

Using a **dope vector** to access array elements implies that we use a subroutine call for each array reference, and provide the subroutine with a description of the relevant array parameters and its subscripts. This description of an array is traditionally called its dope vector ("dope" is slang for "information"). There is no standard format for a dope vector, but the following information is helpful:

Array base address
Array size (not essential, but useful)
Array element type (byte, word, longword, etc.)
Number of subscripts
Range for each subscript
Addresses or values for current subscripts

Given this information, we can arrange to place it in a dope vector (i.e., in a table). Thus a 2-by-3 array of words, beginning at location ABC, could have the following dope vector:

```
DOPEVECABC:    .ADDRESS ABC    ;array's base address
               .LONG 6         ;size: 2 * 3
               .LONG 2         ;element size: 2 bytes/word
               .LONG 2         ;2 subscripts
               .LONG 2         ;subscript 1 range from 1 to 2
               .LONG 3         ;subscript 2 range from 1 to 3
               .ADDRESS I, J   ;current subscript at addresses I and J
```

A 3-by-2-by-4 array of bytes starting at Q might have the following dope vector:

```
DOPEVECQ:      .ADDRESS Q
               .LONG 24, 1, 3, 3, 2, 4
               .ADDRESS I1, I2, I3
```

We could, for this example (and for the previous one), use a single .LONG directive, rather than the combination of .LONG and .ADDRESS directives.

A subroutine to interpret such a **descriptor block** (which is what a dope vector is) might have the following invocation:

```
MOVAL DOPEVECABC, R0
JSB SUBSCRIPT
MOVL ABC(R1), X
     .
     .
     .
MOVAL DOPEVECQ, R0
JSB SUBSCRIPT
MOVL Q(R1), Y
     .
     .
     .
```

Subroutine SUBSCRIPT expects R0 to contain the address of the dope vector of the array for which it is to calculate an offset, and it returns that offset in R1. It could return the array element's *address* in R1 (rather than its *offset* from the array's base address), in which case, the caller would, after SUBSCRIPT has returned, execute MOVL (R0), X, or MOVL (R0), Y.

A Hybrid Approach

The hybrid approach is appropriate for special situations when the array dimensionality is relatively small and high speed array referencing is important. Suppose we have an n-by-3 array of bytes with base address X, and we are using variables I and J as 1-origin subscripts. Fast access can be provided by using in-line code and a table of addresses. Consider the following example:

```
MOVL J, R1            ;column number
ASHL #2, R1, R1       ;multiply * 4
MOVL COLS-4(R1), R1   ;column address
ADDL2 I, R1           ;add row number
MOVB -1(R1), R0       ;1-origin, so subtract 1
```

```
COLS:      .ADDRESS COL1, COL2, COL3
X:
COL1:      .BYTE 1, 2, 3, . . . , N          ;note 2 labels here
COL2:      .BYTE . . .
COL3:      .BYTE . . .
```

What is going on here? First, we multiply the column number by 4, and we then use that number--less 4--as an index into the array of column addresses (less 4 because--as usual, for a 1-origin array--the first element has offset 0 from the beginning of the array of column addresses). Once we have the address of the column, we need only add to it the offset of the correct row, to calculate the offset of the element. We add the row number to the column address, and then subtract one because this is a 1-origin array.

Note that this provides high-speed access to the elements of X, but with the additional overhead of storing an array of column addresses. This is another example of the time versus space tradeoff that we often make in computer science. It is probably not practical to access an array with n columns this way if n is a very large number.

The INDEX Instruction

Now that we have seen how to calculate the address of an array's elements the hard way, we can mention a special purpose VAX instruction that is designed to make such calculations easier for us as programmers. The format of this instruction is INDEX SUBSCRIPT, LOW, HIGH, SIZE, INDEXIN, INDEXOUT; the CPU calculates (INDEXIN + SUBSCRIPT) * SIZE, and stores the result in INDEXOUT. Operands LOW and HIGH are used to check for subscript out-of-range errors: if SUBSCRIPT is less than LOW or greater than HIGH (as signed numbers), then a subscript-range trap occurs (this is a type of arithmetic trap, so its vector is 34_{16} in the System Control Block). The INDEX instruction is designed to be used primarily by high-level language compilers (not by assembly language programmers), so we will not discuss it further; it is described in more detail in the *Vax Architecture Reference Manual*.

Random and Sequential Array Access

An array is a data structure that is sometimes accessed *randomly* and sometimes sequentially. The preceding discussion of calculating array element offsets is relevant only for random element access. When we access an array's elements sequentially, the appropriate technique is one we have seen since chapter 6: autoincrement or autodecrement addressing modes. This technique takes advantage of the fact that we know that an array's elements are stored in consecutive locations in memory, no matter how many dimensions the array has, and no matter how many items in each dimension. If we use the address calculation techniques we have described above when sequentially accessing an array's elements, we will pay a high price in run time overhead: our program may run more than ten times more slowly.

Consider the example of clearing a 10-by-10 array. If we use sequential access, we can clear the array with a loop containing only two instructions (CLRL and SOBGEQ), for a total of 200 instructions. (We can also use the MOVC5 instruction with a 0 source operand length and NUL as the fill character, for a total of only 1--albeit long and complex--instruction.) If we use in-line code to calculate each array element's offset, we need about 10 instructions per array reference, and so about 1000 instructions to clear the array; this is about 5 times slower than sequential access. If we use a dope vector, we execute about 20 to 30 instructions per array reference, for a total of 2,000 to 3,000 instructions executed, which is 10 to 15 times slower than sequential access. The speed degradation increases quickly as the dimensionality of the array increases.

If a dope vector is so much slower than in-line code, why would anyone ever use a dope vector? It allows us to defer some decisions until run time--at which time we can bind both the array's size and its location. This may sound strange to programmers whose primary experience is with Pascal or FORTRAN, but modern programming languages such as Ada[1] permit run-time determination of an array's size. Run-time storage allocation (dynamic storage allocation) increases program flexibility, and permits more efficient use of memory. These advantages sometimes justify the increased time cost involved.

What Can Go Wrong?

Subscripts might be out of bounds. For a 2-by-3 array using subscripts I and J, we expect that

$$1 \leq I \leq 2, \text{ and } 1 \leq J \leq 3.$$

If it happens that one of I or J is not in the correct range, the offset might still be between 0 and 5, which seems fine, but of course is wrong. On some computers, the hardware maintains an **offset limit** register, which detects a computed offset that generates an address beyond the end of the array. This is a useful feature, but it is not a substitute for checking that each subscript is in its correct range. If we use the VAX's INDEX instruction, it will perform the check for us.

If the subscripts are not out of bounds, then the offset cannot be wrong. The only way to guarantee that a subscript is in the correct range is to check it each time an array reference occurs. Sometimes--when, for example, we reference an array with subscripts that are assemble-time constants, such as A[3,7]--a compiler or assembler can check that the subscripts are in bounds. In the general case, however, subscripts may be computed at run time, and so they must be checked at run time. It is often time-consuming to check each subscript, but we must balance this cost against that of accessing the wrong element because we have used an erroneous subscript.[2] If we use dope vectors, it is straightforward to incorporate run-time subscript checking as part of the subroutine that *interprets* the dope vector.

What else can go wrong? The wrong *step size* might be used. Addresses of consecutive elements in an array of bytes differ by 1, those of an array of words differ by 2, and so forth. We are less likely to make an error concerning the correct element size when we use a dope vector than when we use in-line code, because with a dope vector the step size is stored in a single place (the dope vector); with in-line code, on the other hand, we must use the correct step size many times--once for each array access. Clearly, if we insist on using in-line code for array referencing, we would be wise to create a set of macros or make other use of assemble-time constants, to help us.

Special Arrays

A two-dimensional array is also called a **matrix**. An n-by-n array is also called a **square matrix**. When a square matrix can be folded in half over the diagonal entries [1,1], [2,2], ..., [n, n] without loss of information, the matrix is said to be **symmetric**. Most mileage tables found on maps are symmetric in this way. When most of the values in a matrix are 0, the matrix is said to be **sparse**. This

---

[1]Ada is a registered trademark of the U.S. Government, Ada Joint Program Office.

[2]Some people don't believe in checking subscripts, because they think the cost is too high. This is tantamount to saying, "I don't mind getting the wrong answer, so long as I get it quickly."

in this way. When most of the values in a matrix are 0, the matrix is said to be **sparse**. This terminology is used in many other disciplines (e.g., statistics, economics); computers are also widely used in these fields.

Summary

Arrays are an important tool in computing. We have seen that an n-dimensional array must be mapped into a computer's single-dimensional memory. The two principal ways of storing two-dimensional arrays are by row (**row major**) or by column (**column major**). Although it makes no difference which we use, we must know how an array is stored in order to calculate the offset from its base address of any particular element. Array offsets can be calculated by using in-line code, or by using subroutine calls to interpret a dope vector. Sometimes, we can attain higher execution speed by using a hybrid method, which involves storing and using an array of row or column addresses.

Exercises for Chapter 14

1.   Write a segment of code to place the value of the array element from row I and column J of a 3-row-by-4-column array of bytes in R0. Then indicate the changes in the code necessary to:

   a.   use it with a 3-by-4 array of words (or longwords)   instead of bytes
   b.   use it with a 5-by-8 array of bytes

   If you used index mode, would it be easier to change your code than if you didn't?

2.   What is the general formula for accessing element X[i, j, k] of a 3-by-4-by-5 array of integers (assume an integer is 4 bytes long)?
3.   What advantage does a dope vector have over in-line code? What advantage does in-line code have over a dope vector?
4.   Write the code required to fetch item [i, j] of a 32-row-by-16-column array of longword items, stored by row (i.e., item [1,1] is followed by item [1,2] etc.).
5.   Write a program which takes a 3-by-4 array that is stored in row major order and stores it in column major order.
6.   Write a subroutine that uses in-line code to place an arbitrary element of a two-dimensional array of bytes in R0.
7.   Determine the overhead involved in using an array:

   a.   How many instructions must be executed to calculate the sum of all of the elements in a 100-by-100 array of longword integers? You may use sequential access for each dimension, but do not "pretend" that it is a one-dimensional array.
   b.   How many instructions must be executed to sum the elements of a one-dimensional array with the same number of elements as the two dimensional array above?
   c.   What is the ratio of the instruction counts from (a) and (b), above? What is the ratio of instructions *written* (not executed) from parts (a) and (b)?

■ 15 ■

The Assembler Revisited

Introduction

An assembler is not an especially complex program. However, Macro does more than just translate instruction mnemonics and symbolic representations for the addressing modes, resolve internal labels, and understand the few directives we have seen. After all, the VAX *Macro Reference Manual* has more than 300 pages. What are we missing? Not much, really; we will describe much of what concerns us here.

Why doesn't *everything* concern us? The purpose of this book is *not* to teach every aspect of assembly language programming; it is the opinion of the authors (and most other computer scientists) that high-level languages provide a much more efficient, productive way to write programs. Rather, we believe that assembly language is worth studying primarily because it makes explicit the architectural details of a computer that high-level languages (purposely) hide. Since we are not interested in using assembly language as our primary programming language, we will not describe all of the features of the assembler that are designed to make assembly language programming *look like* high-level language programming.

Housekeeping Directives

VAX Macro is a descendent of the PDP-11's MACRO-11, which was written when serious computer professionals still regarded high-level languages as toys. Truly important programs (people then thought) would always be written in assembly language, because (they thought) no high-level language compiler could generate machine language code as compact or run-time efficient, or both, as could an experienced assembly language programmer. That view of high-level languages may have been justified ten or more years ago, but it can no longer be defended now (which is not to say that there are no poor high-level language compilers in use).

As a consequence of this early view of an assembler, Macro has facilities that are appropriate for writing large programs, involving several programmers. Since our purpose of illustrating the VAX's architectural features is better served by writing small (one-person) programs, we have not missed the features we are about to see.

Documentation Support

Properly documenting one's programs is necessary, and one should use those software tools that assist in this regard. It is not an issue central to understanding computing, although it helps understand people who compute, and it helps with sound management of computer-based services. The following directives can make programs easier to understand, maintain, and enhance.

.TITLE

The .TITLE directive has two arguments: a **module name,** which is an identifier (with no white space) and can be up to 31 characters long, and a **comment string,** which can be up to 40 characters long. The arguments of the .TITLE directive appear in the header line that is at the top of each page of a multipage listing. In addition, the module name will be assigned to the object module created by Macro; it will be listed in a link map and will be recognized by the debugger. If there is no .TITLE directive, Macro assigns the default module name .MAIN. to the object module. An example of the .TITLE directive is:

    .TITLE   PROG3   Bubble sort algorithm

.SUBTITLE

An additional level of descriptive information may be included by also using the .SUBTITLE directive. Its operand field (up to 40 characters long) appears as the second line of each page of a multipage listing, until it is changed by a subsequent .SUBTITLE directive. When we use the .SUBTITLE directive, the assembler produces a table of contents, and lists the pages and line numbers in the source program that correspond to the places where the directive is used.The table of contents precedes the listing, in the .LIS file.

.PAGE

When paper was inexpensive, the .PAGE directive was used to request page ejects, to visually separate different parts of the program listing; it can still be used, if we wish to act as if paper were inexpensive.

.IDENT

Some problems can't be readily solved by writing just one module. Even if they could be, it is unwise to write lengthy modules (some people claim that a single module should fit on a single sheet of paper). In any case, we frequently wind up with many modules to solve one problem. The linker and the assembler can help us keep track of things; the .IDENT directive has a single argument, which is a delimited ASCII character string of up to 31 characters. It is an identification of the module *in addition* to that provided by the .TITLE directive. The statement

    .IDENT /4-12/

might be used to indicate that this is version 4, edition 12 of the module whose title is provided by the .TITLE directive. The character string "4-12" will be included in the information available in the object module, and it will be listed in a link map.

.ENABLE, .DISABLE

The pair of directives

    .ENABLE argument list, and
    .DISABLE argument list

control a set of seven assemble-time functions. For instance, if we place the line

    .ENABLE GLOBAL

in our program, the assembler assumes that any symbolic label referenced but not defined in the current module--even if it is *not* declared with the .EXTERNAL directive, is defined in another module. If we type

    .DISABLE GLOBAL

(as we saw in chapter 4), then any referenced label that is neither defined nor declared with the .EXTERNAL directive will be flagged by Macro as an undefined label. The *Macro Reference Manual* lists the other arguments for the .ENABLE/.DISABLE directives.

.SHOW, .NOSHOW

The .SHOW directive, and its companion .NOSHOW, allow us to control five assemble-time listing features. We have already seen one of them, ME (for Macro Expansions), in chapter 4. The others are listed and described in the *Macro Reference Manual*.

Conditional Assembly

This is perhaps the most misunderstood aspect of working with assembly language, but the basic idea is simple; failure to understand it is symptomatic of a lack of knowledge of the interaction between hardware and software.

When Do Things Happen: At Assemble Time or at Run Time?

If we saw the following statements in a program,

    MOVL #5, R1
    ADDL2 R1, R1

we might shake our heads, saying, "Why not write MOVL #10, R1?" When we can either compute something (such as 2*5, here) at assemble time or compute it at run time, we should only choose to do it at run time if doing it at assemble time doesn't provide sufficient flexibility for our application.
    If, on the other hand, we saw

    SILLY: MOVL 2*X, R1
           .

           .
    X: .BLKL 1

we would, hopefully, realize that the presumed intent to multiply the contents of location X by 2 at assemble time is ludicrous--because when we use the .BLKL directive, we are implying that the contents of X won't be available until *run* time, and the assembler can only perform *assemble*-time arithmetic. (In fact, the assembler will do arithmetic on the *address* X, which is probably not what we want, but which is the only *assemble*-time value available for X.)

Computing literature refers to **binding time** as the time at which a particular symbol is assigned a particular value. When we defer the binding time, we usually add flexibility, at the expense of performance: a simple example that we have seen since chapter 3 is the choice of initializing variables at run time or at assemble time (really, at run time or at load time). When we initialize variables at assemble time, we don't have to execute *any* instructions to do so at run time; the loader must do a little extra work, but it must load our program anyway, and can initialize variables with little or no extra time cost:

```
X:    .LONG 100      ;bind now (assemble/load time)
Y:    .BLKL 1        ;bind at run time
```

The preceding discussion of binding time, except for the case of initializing variables, may seem abstract. Let us look at a more specific application, which involves debugging an assembly language program.

Debugging Statements

The SNAP debugging tool was described in chapter 5. If we place it in the opcode field of a line, our program will include instructions which, if executed, print the contents of the 16 registers and the PSL. When we believe a program has passed all tests and is ready to be used by others, we can remove all the SNAP debugging statements we were using. However, since something may turn up after the program is distributed, we may prefer to leave the SNAP statements in place but *disable* them by surrounding each SNAP with the following code:

```
      TSTB DEBUG
      BEQL S1
      SNAP
S1:   ;continue
```

The distributed version of the program is assembled with DEBUG defined as follows:

```
DEBUG: .BYTE 0 ;skip debug code
```

When we are still testing the program, we can assemble it either with the statement,

```
DEBUG: .BYTE 1
```

or we can execute the instruction (at run time),

```
MOVB #1, DEBUG
```

In any case, all the SNAP, TSTB, and BEQL instructions are assembled and loaded as part of the distributed program, and the program must execute all of the TSTB/BEQL instruction pairs, even when DEBUG is 0. The alternative--maintaining two source files, one with and one without the debug statements--is even less appealing: inconsistencies inevitably creep in; corrections made to the version with the debugging code may not be made to the other version (due to human error), or they may be made incorrectly. Even if consistency is maintained, storage costs are doubled; there must be a better way.

Conditional Assembly Blocks

Consider having a single source module for the preceding application. If we only have one source module, presumably it will contain the debugging code. If we can use *assemble*-time conditional *assembly* directives (rather than *run*-time conditional *execution* instructions), we can decide, at assemble time, whether the assembler should generate debugging code or *no* debugging code.

.IF and .ENDC

The .IF and .ENDC are conditional assembly directives, and they must always be used as a pair. The .IF directive introduces a **conditional assembly block**; the .ENDC terminates the block. The general form of this pair of directives is:

> **.IF** *condition argument(s)*
> conditional block
> **.ENDC**

The conditional block is a set of one or more Macro statements (even including nested .IFs and .ENDCs, but not including .END). The meaning is, *IF* the assemble time condition *condition* (with an optional argument or arguments *argument(s)*) is met, then the conditional assembly block is assembled, just as if it had been written in our program without the .IF. If *condition* is *not* met, then the statements are ignored, as if they had not been written.

What kinds of conditions can determine conditional assembly? Perhaps the simplest one is EQUAL, which tests if its argument is equal to 0. For example,

> .IF EQUAL SW1
> SNAP
> .ENDC

If, at assemble time, SW1 has the value 0, then the condition is said to be **satisfied,** and so the conditional assembly block *is* assembled. If the condition is *not* satisfied, then the conditional assembly block is *not* assembled: it will occupy no space in the object module and will incur no run-time overhead.

We must be sure to understand what we mean when we say "SW1 has the value 0"; since the test is being done at assemble time, it is the *assemble*-time value of SW1 that is being checked. What if SW1 is defined with the statement,

> SW1: .BYTE 0

Does SW1 have the value 0 at assemble time? It might, but it probably doesn't! The assemble-time value of SW1 is the location counter value assigned to the symbolic label. This *could* be 0, if SW1 were the very first thing in our program, but *whatever* its assemble-time value is, it would be unchanged by the operand of the .BYTE directive.

So, how do we change SW1's assemble time value? With the assemble-time constant operator, "=":

> SW1 = 0   ;assemble debugging code
> or
> SW1 = 1   ;any nonzero value: debugging code not assembled

Examine carefully two ways of getting *the same result*:

	A		**B**
1.	SW1 = 0	DEBUG:	.BYTE 1
	.		.
	.		.
	.		.
2.	.IF EQUAL SW1		TSTB DEBUG
3.	SNAP		BEQL S1
4.	.ENDC		SNAP
	;continue	S1:	;continue

In column A, lines 1, 2, and 4 generate no code, and so no run time overhead. In column B, each of lines 1, 2, 3, and 4 lead to code being generated or storage being allocated, with commensurate overhead at run time.

We must clarify one more (related) item: at run time, a TST(B,W,L) instruction examines the CC bits, but when the assembler evaluates assemble-time conditions, the CC bits are not involved in any way visible to us. In the course of assembling our program, Macro examines the specified condition and the arguments provided, and concludes "the condition is satisfied (or not)."

Additional .IF Conditions

Other conditions that may be used with the .IF conditional assembly directive are shown in figure 15.1. These conditions may involve an assemble-time arithmetic expression: we could write,

    .IF NOT_EQUAL ABC+SW7
    BLAH   ;assemble some code
    .ENDC

and if both the symbols ABC and SW7 have assemble time values of 0 (or if they have opposite signed values) then the condition will not be satisfied, and BLAH will be skipped by the assembler. There are several additional conditions for the .IF directive; they are described in the *Macro Reference Manual*.

Life would be simpler if all assemble-time variables were colored red, and the *usual* variables that our program manipulates at run time were colored green; then we would be less likely to confuse them. Some high-level languages have compile-time variables analogous to the assemble-time variables we have been discussing. These may be required to have a special character prefix (e.g.,"%" in PL/1), so we don't confuse them with *ordinary* variables. In other words, the idea of assemble time as distinct from run time variables can also be supported by high-level programming languages. It is one vehicle for managing immediate and deferred bindings.

Test	Meaning
EQUAL/NOT_EQUAL	Arg =/≠ 0
GREATER/LESS_EQUAL	Arg >/≤ 0
LESS_THAN/GREATER_EQUAL	Arg </≥ 0

Figure 15.1 Condition tests for conditional assembly

Reusing Labels

It is often a nuisance to make up a symbolic label for something that has no particular significance.
For example, consider the "for loop" example we saw in chapter 7 (figure 7.22):

```
                MOVL #10, R8       ;R8: terminating condition
                MOVL #1, R7        ;R7: loop count
LOOP:           CMPL R7, R8        ;check for done
                BGTR DONE
        ;else--continue
                ;loop body here
                INCL R7            ;increment loop count
                BRB LOOP
DONE:           ;end of loop
```

Both labels in this loop--LOOP and DONE--have no particular meaning. In fact, we would be tempted
to use them for *every* loop, except that the assembler won't let us. What we would like is some kind
of label that the assembler *will* let us reuse. Macro provides such a label type: **local labels,** which
have the form *nn*$, where *nn* is any number between 1 and 65535 (although it is recommended that
we use only labels in the range of 1$ to 29999$).

We can use local labels exactly as we would use symbolic labels, and we can use the same labels
over again, with no complaint from the assembler. Consider the following program skeleton:

```
1$:     MOVL X, Y             ;(a)
        ;intervening code
        BEQL 1$               ;(b)
        ;more intervening code
        BLSS 1$               ;(c)

        ;still more code
1$:     ADDL2 A,B             ;(d)
        ;code here, too
        BEQL 1$               ;(e)
        ;the program continues . . .
```

We see here two definitions for the label 1$ and three uses of it. What sense does this make?

The assembler maintains a **local label block** within which local labels must be uniquely defined.
However, across local label blocks, the same local label may be reused, with no confusion. A new
local label block is implicitly begun (and the previous one is implicitly ended) whenever the assembler
encounters the definition of a *symbolic* label. Alternatively, local label blocks may include several
symbolic label definitions if we use the .ENABLE LOCAL_BLOCK directive to explicitly begin a local
label block, and the .DISABLE LOCAL_BLOCK directive to explicitly end a local label block. Thus, in
the example above, if there is a symbolic label defined between points (c) and (d), then references
to 1$ at (b) and (c) are to the definition at (a), and the reference at (e) is to the definition at (d).
If no symbolic label is defined between points (c) and (d), and if no .ENABLE or .DISABLE
LOCAL_BLOCK directive is there, then 1$ will be multiply-defined, and Macro will produce an error
diagnostic complaining about this mistake.

So now, instead of writing:

```
NEXT:    TSTW @#KCSR
         BGEQ NEXT
```

we can write

    3$:   TSTW @#KCSR
          BGEQ 3$

Or, in our "for loop" example, we can replace LOOP with (for example) 10$, and DONE with 20$. Although it is conventional to use local labels in numeric (ascending) order, we needn't do so. Local labels are not placed in the assembler's symbol table, and so they are not available to the debugger (unless we assemble our program with the .ENABLE DEBUG directive). A word of caution is in order, however: local labels have no *meaning*--that is exactly why they exist--and so we should be sure to use them only in situations where we have no need for *symbolic* labels.

Using the Location Counter

Recall that in chapter 4 we discussed the assembler's maintenance of the **location counter.** The location counter contains the value, relative to the beginning of the program, of the memory location that will be used by the next item in our program that uses memory. What can *we* do with the location counter? Its name is "." (yes, period or dot); so, we can write lines such as:

    CMPL A, B
    BEQL .+3
    BGTRU XYZ

instead of

        CMPL A, B
        BEQL SKIP
        BGTRU XYZ
    SKIP: ;continue

When assembling, the value of "." is always the current value of the location counter. Thus, in an interrupt handler we might write

    TSTW @#KCSR
    BGTR .-7

instead of

    LOOP: TSTW @#KCSR
          BGTR LOOP

Similarly, the two statements

    A: .LONG . , .   ;dot comma dot
    A: .LONG A, A+4

are equivalent.

If we wish, we can explicitly increment the location counter by using the assemble-time equality operator:

    . = . + 10

will increase the location counter by 10, just as would the statement

    .BLKB 10

We have avoided using "." in our programs for several reasons. First, "." is already used as part of assembler directives (such as .LONG). More seriously, however, the risk of miscounting the offset in a statement such as ". + offset" is too great, and very likely to introduce future problems. One of the explicit purposes for writing an assembler was to remove from us (programmers) the tedium and danger of dealing directly with addresses (as we must when we write machine-language programs). Usually, explicit use of the location counter should be considered a step in the wrong direction. We can almost always use local labels if symbolic labels are inappropriate; we may thereby avoid explicit reference to the location counter.

Simple Macros

We have been using the assemble-time equality operator, "=", for some time. It allows us to write a short (or long) name in place of some other name, number, or expression. We can write the following:

              K = 1024
              SIZE = 100
                   .
                   .
                   .
              MOVL #K, R1
                   .
                   .
                   .
    ABC: .BLKB SIZE

We have also discussed (in chapter 4) **macros,** which are a text substitution feature of our assembler. We shall see that macros are a generalization of the assemble-time equality operator.

A macro is a body of text to which we assign a name. When we use that name (when we **invoke** the macro), the body of text we previously associated with that name--its **replacement text**--is substituted for the name; this happens at assemble time. The last point is worth emphasizing: *all of this happens at assemble time.* Macros are often confused with subroutines, but there should be no confusion if we understand the distinction between run time and assemble time. A macro causes the substitution of a replacement text for a name; it is done by the assembler, before the assembler generates machine language for our program. (The replacement text may or may not lead to the generation of any instructions or directives that get loaded into memory and "exist" at run time.) A subroutine, however, is a series of instructions that have been put somewhere. The subroutine's entry point is jumped to, and its last instruction is returned from, at run time; at assemble time, a subroutine is just another series of assembly language statements for which the assembler must generate machine language.

Macro Definitions

Defining a macro includes assigning it a name. When we define a macro, we use the the pair of directives .MACRO and .ENDM. If we wanted to define a macro to help us write the code to save registers 1 and 2 on the system stack, we could write:

```
.MACRO SAVE12    ;name:  SAVE12
MOVL R1, -(SP)       ;two lines of text
MOVL R2, -(SP)
.ENDM SAVE12
```

Then, we can invoke this macro at any point *after* its definition simply by writing its name in the opcode field, as if it were an ordinary instruction. The assembler, upon encountering the name SAVE12 used as an opcode, will look in the table of macro names it has been collecting; it will find the name SAVE12 in its macro name table, and will replace that name with its replacement text. If we invoke a macro that we have forgotten to define, the assembler will issue a diagnostic regarding an undefined opcode.

Processing Macros

When a .MACRO statement is encountered, the assembler places the name of the macro in its Macro Name Table (MNT). The macro's replacement text--that is, the text between the .MACRO and its matching .ENDM, which is substituted for the macro's name during macro expansion--is stored in such a manner that, upon encountering the macro's name, its replacement text can be found. (We are purposely vague on this point, as there is a variety of methods for storing macro names and associated replacement texts).

When the assembler is processing a symbol in the opcode field of a statement, it searches for a definition in the following order:

1.   The Macro Name Table, which contains previously defined macros.
2.   The Permanent Symbol Table, which contains instruction mnemonics and directives.
3.   Macro Libraries, that contain externally defined macros.

If the symbol in the opcode field of the statement being processed is found in the MNT, then the invocation will be replaced by its replacement text. If we accidentally assign a name to a macro without realizing that the name is also an instruction mnemonic, our macro definition will over-ride the built-in meaning (because the Macro Name Table is searched *before* the Permanent Symbol Table). Thus, if we accidentally (or perversely) write

```
.MACRO ADD
SUB
.ENDM ADD
```

every ADD(B,W,L)[2,3] instruction following this definition will be assembled as if it were a SUB(B,W,L)[2,3] instruction.

If we define a macro but don't use it, no harm is done, and the assembler will not complain. If we invoke a macro and it happens to have some nonsense in the midst of its definition, then (since the default listing option is *not* to list macro expansion) the assembler will produce an error diagnostic, but it will appear "out of the blue": only the machine language will be shown above the error diagnostic, and we may be confused as to what went wrong. Consider the following fragment:

```
        MOVL #1, R1        ;ordinary instruction
        BLAH               ;macro invocation
        MOVL R1, ABC       ;ordinary instruction
```

We would be at least a little surprised if the assembly listing showed us:

```
          51 01 D0  0000  1 X:   MOVL #1, R1  ;ordinary instruction
                    0003  2      BLAH               ;macro invocation
                 D6 0003  3
%MACRO-E-MCHINSTSYN, Machine instruction syntax error
                    0004  4
%MACRO-E-NOTENUFOPR, Not enough operands supplied
  0000000C'EF 51 D0 0004  5 Y:   MOVL R1, ABC ;ordinary instruction
```

Looking back at our source module, we would notice that the only statement between the two MOVL instructions is BLAH, and so we would draw the correct conclusion: BLAH is a macro, and its expansion generated an instruction using illegal syntax. If we reassembled the program and included the .SHOW ME directive, we would see the macro's replacement text, and notice that we somehow wrote INCL #R1 in the body of BLAH.

.LIBRARY

As we saw in chapter 4, certain macros are available to our programs because the library containing those macro definitions (STARLET.MLB) is automatically searched by the assembler when it assembles our program; we need do nothing other than invoke them to use those macros. What if we have some macros that we defined ourselves, and that we use in many of our programs? We could include those macros' definitions in each program in which we use them, but that makes our programs much longer than necessary. Rather, we can use VMS's LIBRARIAN service to create our own macro library. Then we inform the assembler to search that library by using the .LIBRARY directive in our source module. If we had created a macro library called MYMACS.MLB, then we would include the following line to have the assembler search that library:

    .LIBRARY /MYMACS.MLB/

Note that the library name must be surrounded by delimiters; this is similar to the argument of the .ASCIZ directive. It is also possible to specify a macro library on the command line when we invoke the assembler, typing

    MACRO FILE+MYMACS.MLB/LIBRARY

This will assemble our file, FILE, and search for macro definitions in the macro library, MYMACS.MLB. We may omit the .MLB extension, because VMS assumes that we use that extension for a macro library.

If we use both the .LIBRARY directive and the /LIBRARY option, and specify different libraries with them, the macro library specified with the .LIBRARY directive is searched before the one specified with the /LIBRARY option, which is searched before the system library, STARLET.MLB. Thus, we may redefine system-defined macros, and the assembler will use our (new) definitions.

Macros with Arguments

The motivation for creating and using macros is to reduce *our* effort: let the assembler do the writing (of the macro's expansion). Writing macros does *not* reduce the work done by the assembler, and it may or may not--depending on the particular macros--have much effect on what is done at run time.

When we have a recurring pattern of text in a source module, a macro might simplify our lives. Suppose we performed extended-range arithmetic frequently with the following instruction sequence:

```
MOVL LOW1, R0    ;low part 1
MOVL LOW2, R2    ;low part 2
MOVL HIGH1, R1   ;high part 1
MOVL HIGH2, R3   ;high part 2
ADDL2 R0, R2     ;low parts
ADWC R1, R3      ;high parts, with C
```

We might consider defining a macro called EXADD:

```
.MACRO EXADD    ;extended-range add
ADDL2 R0, R2    ;low parts
ADWC R1, R3     ;high parts
.ENDM EXADD
```

Then any time we wish to use extended-range arithmetic, we can place the operands in R0 through R3 and write EXADD instead of the ADDL2-ADWC pair of instructions. However, what if we sometimes wanted to perform extended-range arithmetic with operands in R4 through R7? Rather than define another macro for this particular situation (and, extending that idea, a set of macros for *all* groups of 4 registers), we can make use of an idea that is a logical extension of the simple idea of writing a macro's name and having it replaced by its replacement text, and write macros with arguments.

Macro Arguments

VAX Macro permits macro definitions to use **formal** arguments. Each formal argument is represented by a symbolic label, subject to the same spelling rules that apply to any symbolic label. The argument names are written following the macro's name on the line with the .MACRO directive. We can now write a single definition to take care of the extended-range arithmetic using *any* group of 4 registers (or, it turns out, any 4 memory locations, as well):

```
.MACRO EXTRADD RA, RB, RC, RD    ;better extended-range add
ADDL2 RA, RC                     ;low parts
ADWC RB, RD                      ;high parts
.ENDM EXTRADD
```

It does not matter whether the names RA, RB, and so on are used anywhere else in this module; they may even be used as arguments in another macro. A macro's formal arguments are *local* to that macro (this is similar to the formal parameters of a subroutine in a high-level language).

So, rather than invoke the macro EXADD, we can now invoke EXTRADD, with the arguments R0, R1, R2, and R3 (or, R4, R5, R6, and R7, etc.). If use the invocation

    EXTRADD R6, R7, R8, R9

for example, the assembler will replace it with the following code:

    ADDL2 R6, R8
    ADWC R7, R9

Whatever the **actual** arguments provided with the macro's invocation, each occurrence of a formal argument will be replaced by the corresponding actual argument--just as each occurrence of a macro's name will be replaced by its replacement text.

Notice that we can just as easily use EXTRADD with symbolic labels as with registers. Thus, if we write

    EXTRADD LOW1, HIGH1, LOW2, HIGH2

the macro will be expanded to the following replacement text:

    ADDL2 LOW1, LOW2
    ADWC HIGH1, HIGH2

As long as LOW1, LOW2, HIGH1 and HIGH2 are properly defined symbolic labels, the assembler will just as easily generate machine language for adding operands in memory as it will for adding operands in registers.

There is nothing wrong with using the same argument names again and again. For example, we could write

    .MACRO DOUBLE X
    ADDL2 X, X
    .ENDM DOUBLE

and then, later on in the same program, we could write

    .MACRO ADDONE X
    INCL X
    .ENDM ADDONE

We can also use X as a label in the same module with no confusion on the part of the assembler and no surprises for us.

Sometimes macros are used simply to provide better mnemonics. We think of MOVL (SP)+, ABC as popping the system stack into ABC. There is a PUSHL instruction, but no POPL instruction, so why not create one:

    .MACRO POPL ARG   ;pop system stack
    MOVL (SP)+, ARG
    .ENDM POPL

Then we can write

    POPL ABC, or
    POPL (R2)

instead of

    MOVL (SP)+, ABC, or
    MOVL (SP)+, (R2)

In fact, such a macro already exists, as part of VAX Macro! If we type POPL R7 in our program and surround it with the pair of directives .SHOW ME and .NOSHOW ME, we will see that the machine language generated is that expected for MOVL (SP)+, R7.

The use of macros is not restricted to generating instructions. Any reasonable text can be included. Suppose we are testing a program, and we need several test cases. We could write a macro to help provide the test input and what we consider the correct result. Suppose the program being tested is one which transforms binary numbers (stored as words) and produces their representation as ASCII coded decimal digit strings.

The following macro will provide us with the desired test pairs:

    .MACRO TEST Y
    .WORD Y
    .ASCIZ /Y/
    .ENDM TEST

Then, we can invoke the macro with the following formal arguments:

    TST: TEST 1
    X: TEST 12

The expansion of those invocations will be as follows:

    TST: .WORD 1
         .ASCIZ /1/
    X: .WORD 12
         .ASCIZ /12/

This simply saves us typing. Note that a macro invocation can have a label, just as if it were an ordinary opcode.

Nested Macro Use

Suppose we had the following macro definition for POPL:

    .MACRO POPL ARG1
    MOVL (SP)+, ARG1
    .ENDM POPL

Then we could define an additional macro, P, as follows:

```
.MACRO P ARG
POPL ARG
.ENDM P
```

Then, if we type P R6, the assembler processes it as follows: it looks for P, and finds that it is a macro, and so expands it to POPL R6. In processing POPL R6, it finds that this, too, is a macro, and so expands it to MOVL (SP)+, R6. This could go on for many more levels, if MOVL were another macro name, whose replacement text were another macro name, and so on.

   Nesting names of previously defined macros inside macro replacement texts may sound like nesting subroutine calls inside subroutine bodies--and there are some similarities. The difference, however, is related to the difference between macros and subroutines in general: nested subroutine calls, like un-nested subroutine calls, are visible--and have their major effect--at run time. Nested use of macros, like un-nested use of macros, is completely an assemble-time phenomenon: all macro expansion takes place at assemble time, and we can't tell by examining the machine language whether it was generated by the expansion of a single macro, by the expansion of several non-nested macros, by the expansion of a series of nested macros, or by the expansion of no macros at all.

What Can Go Wrong?

The key rule in using macros is to ensure that the macro definitions are physically seen by the assembler before those macros are used. Why? Let's pretend, for a minute, that we are an assembler; if we saw

```
        TSTL X
        BLAH
   X:    .
        .
        .
```

how would we assemble it? If we had no definition for BLAH yet, we might guess "It probably needs 4 bytes, so we now know how to update the location counter." We could then set aside a 1 longword *hole* for the BLAH code, update the location counter by four, assign an address to X, and so forth. This is exactly how we would proceed to assemble the reference to X in TSTL X, since we will not have seen its definition yet. The two cases are not necessarily comparable, however: we know that the X in TSTL X will be assembled using relative addressing (displacement mode on the PC), and we know that a longword displacement will be sufficient for the PC-relative offset, no matter how far away the use of X is from its definition. And if, when we see the definition for BLAH, it generates 4 bytes of code, all will be well. If it generates any other amount of machine language, however, then the hole that we left will be either too large or too small. In that event, *all* labels defined following the first invocation of BLAH will have incorrect addresses assigned to them by the assembler. For each such label, Macro will produce a **phase error** diagnostic; it will have two different addresses for those labels: one generated assuming that BLAH occupies 4 bytes, and another now that it knows that BLAH occupies some other amount of memory. A single misplaced macro definition can trigger dozens of phase errors.

What else can go wrong? A simple typographical error can cause the assembler to fail dramatically and leave us without even a listing to look at. Consider

```
.MACRO P ARG
P ARG
.ENDM P
```

Due to a momentary lapse of attention, we typed P ARG instead of POPL ARG. When we invoke the macro P, it is expanded to P, which the assembler discovers is the name of a macro. It then expands P to P, and discovers that P is the name of a macro. The assembler continues to replace P with its replacement text, which is P. This expansion will go on indefinitely, because we inadvertently created a circular definition. Eventually, we will run out of patience with the assembler; we will stop it and find no listing produced. The assembler couldn't manage to reach the end of a circular macro definition, because (by its nature as a *circular* definition) it has no end! If we don't run out of patience, VMS will eventually abort our program, most likely with the message,

%MACRO-F-INSVIRMEM, insufficient virtual memory

This means that the assembler didn't have enough memory to store the (ever-expanding) macro expansion. This is not surprising, for the macro expansion is infinite, and so requires an infinite amount of memory; the VAX has only a finite amount--2^{32} bytes!)

What if we invoke a macro using more arguments than it expects? For example, we might write

POPL ABC, SUM

while POPL was defined with only one argument. The assembler will ignore the unexpected arguments following the first one (it will use ABC, but ignore SUM), and warn us that we have used too many arguments.

If we use a macro and provide fewer arguments than expected, the positions used by the missing arguments are left empty; this will, most likely, create a statement with illegal syntax, and so the assembler will flag the expansion with an error message. Consider our previous example: POPL, not followed by any arguments, will be expanded to

MOVL (SP)+,

which the assembler will complain about.

Every .MACRO directive must have a matching .ENDM directive. If we misspell the .ENDM or forget it, all the text following the (unmatched) .MACRO directive will be *swallowed up* as part of that macro definition--up to and including the module's final line, containing the .END directive. Since even the invocation of the macro will be considered part of the macro's definition, the assembler has no code to assemble (as far as the assembler is concerned, it has only a macro definition to store in its macro name table), so our assembly listing won't show any machine language being generated following the unmatched .MACRO directive. The assembler will, however, complain about a missing .END directive.

Summary

Some directives are provided to facilitate documenting programs; these include .TITLE, .SUBTITLE, .IDENT, .SHOW, and .NOSHOW. **Conditional assembly** directives allow us to write statements within an assembly language program and subsequently to request that the assembler include or exclude these statements, as we wish. Conditional assembly is supported by the directives .IF and .ENDC which are used to enclose the statements to be conditionally assembled. The conditions which can be specified include EQUAL, NOT_EQUAL, GREATER, LESS_THAN, GREATER_EQUAL and LESS_EQUAL. The values tested by these conditional assembly statements must be known at assemble time.

Local labels of the form 1$ through 65535$ can each be defined several times within the same module and used unambiguously, as long as repeated uses are not in the same **local label block**. A local label block is terminated by the use of a symbolic label, unless the block was begun with the .ENABLE LOCAL_BLOCK directive, in which case it is terminated by the .DISABLE LOCAL_BLOCK directive.

The assembler **location counter** has the symbolic name "."; it can be used as any other name is used. Since it is difficult to use "." correctly, and since we rarely need to use it, we are wise to avoid it unless absolutely necessary.

A **macro** is a set of assembly language statements which has been assigned a **name**. When we define macros, we use the .MACRO and .ENDM directives to associate a macro's **replacement text** with its name. The macro may or may not involve the use of arguments. A macro may already have been defined elsewhere and placed in a **macro library**; it can be made available using the .LIBRARY directive, or by including /LIBRARY on the command line.

A macro is **invoked** by using its name as if it were an opcode. At assemble time, the assembler looks up the name in its Macro Name Table, finds the definition, and replaces the macro's name with the statements which are the macro's replacement text. If the macro invocation has arguments, they are substituted in place of the formal arguments in the macro's definition. When defining a macro, we can use previously defined macros. A macro can only be used (invoked) after it has been defined, or after its definition has otherwise been made available--for example, with the .LIBRARY directive.

Exercises for Chapter 15

1. Obtain a printout of the expansion of the system macros you are using for input of data. Reconstruct from the expansion what you guess is a reasonable macro definition. If the system macro has optional arguments, explain how the definition supports the various expansion possibilities.

2. Write a macro which generates a sequence of instructions to subtract two signed integers. It *cannot* use any of the SUB(B,W,L)[2,3] instructions. To what extent is your code's action equivalent or not equivalent to that of the SUB(B,W,L)[2,3] instructions (consider, especially, the setting of the CC bits)?

3. After execution of the following program, what is in M3, M4, and T1? In one sentence, what does this program do?

```
        .ENTRY START, 0
S3:     CLRL R5
        .MACRO M1 S1, S2
        MOVAL S1, R0
        MOVAL S2, R1
        JSB M2
        .ENDM
        M1 M3, M4
        M1 M3, M4
        HALT
M3:     .LONG 26
M4:     .LONG 28
```

```
M2:   MOVL (R0), R6
      MOVL (R1), R7
      MOVL R6, T1
      MOVL R7, R6
      MOVL T1, R7
      RSB
T1:   .BLKL 1
      .END START
```

4. Does the use of macros speed up program *execution*? Explain why, if it does, and why not, if it doesn't.

5. Does the use of macros speed up program *development*? Explain why, if it does, and why not, if it doesn't.

6. Suppose that you have a (new) model of the VAX that has an instruction for **quadword** addition, which can add 8-byte quantities just as a longword instruction can add 4-byte quantities. Suppose, in addition, that you also have an older VAX, on which the best way to perform 8-byte integer arithmetic is by using the ADWC instruction. Use an assemble-time *switch,* and write those parts of a program that will allow you to assemble a program for *either* your new VAX or your old one, depending on the value of the switch. Explain what a user of your program should do in order to perform addition on 8-byte quantities on either machine. Also, show what machine language the assembler will generate in both cases. Do not use macros.

7. Repeat the previous exercise, but this time make (appropriate) use of macros.

8. Pretend that you are working on a model of the VAX which has no character string instructions. Write a macro to copy a character string from one location to another. You may choose to create the MOVC3 instruction, or (if you are more ambitious) the MOVC5 instruction; review chapter 10 if you do not remember them.

9. Suppose you have written such a long program that you forgot that a macro named AHA was defined on page 1, and you provided another definition on page 3. Will the assembler flag this? Are any other assembler error messages triggered by this event? Under what circumstances? What other reasonable choices of action could the assembler's designer(s) have implemented?

10. Write a macro called BLOCK which will work just like the .BLKW directive, but which does not use .BLKW in its definition.

■ 16 ■

High Speed I/O

Introduction

In chapters 11 and 12 we discussed character-oriented I/O; the techniques we examined are suitable for handling low- to moderate-speed devices such as CRT terminals, character printers, and so forth. Even with low-speed devices, however, the overhead for just a few CRTs running at 9600 baud may overwhelm a CPU. Consider the processing required to handle an interrupt resulting from sending one byte to a CRT.

1.   Save PC, PSL
2.   Fetch new PC
3.   TSTW, Bxxx, MOVB, INCL
4.   Restore PC, PSL

We can assume that each activity mentioned above takes about the time of an *average* instruction; this is not an unreasonable estimation, for although no instructions are executed to save the PC and PSL (for example), they are saved as part of the interrupt handling process, and their saving requires sending them to memory, to be saved on the top of the stack. So, if nothing goes wrong (there is no data overrun, no parity error, etc.) then it takes about 10 instruction times to send a byte to a CRT. The VAX model 11/780 executes about one million instructions per second, so we can estimate that it takes about 10   seconds to interrupt a program, execute the CRT's interrupt handler, and return to the interrupted program. At that rate, not quite 100,000 interrupts can be processed in a second, if the CPU has nothing else to do. How many CRTs being driven at 9600 baud can be supported? The 9600 baud rate is equivalent to a maximum data rate of 960 characters per second (recall that 1 character = 8 information bits + 2 framing bits, at that speed). About 100 CRTs can have output sent to them at this rate. Of course, the CPU can do nothing else: it can't do any computing, and it can't even process the input it is receiving!

We can look at this from another point of view: if the CPU can only handle about 100,000 interrupts per second, its I/O bandwidth (a measure of its ability to move data) cannot exceed 100 KB/sec (kilobytes per second), which is ridiculously low. It will be clear why 100 KB/sec is too low after we examine various I/O device types. Then we will examine a better way to perform I/O for high-speed devices.

Character-Oriented Devices

CRTs and other interactive terminals (e.g., hardcopy terminals) are **character-oriented** devices. Other character-oriented devices are paper tape punches and readers, character- and line-printers, and card punches and readers. These generally have a low to medium data rate. For example, a 1,000 line/minute line-printer, with 132-character lines, prints 2.2 K characters per second (cps). A 1,200 card/min card reader using 80-character (80-column) cards reads 1.6 K cps. The fastest CRTs using serial I/O run at 9600, 2*9600, or 4*9600 baud; corresponding data rates are 960, 1.92 K or 3.84 K cps. If a VAX runs CRTs at 38,400 baud (rather than 9600 baud), then, by our calculations above, it can support only about 25 terminals, rather than 100.

356

Block-Oriented Devices

Mass storage devices are an important part of virtually every modern computer system. A paper tape can store 10 characters per inch of paper tape, so that a 300-foot roll can store 36 KB; a standard magnetic tape, on the other hand, can store millions of bytes (**megabytes,** or MB), and some of the larger disk storage systems can store billions of bytes (**gigabytes,** or GB). Some disks can transfer millions of bytes of data per second.

These mass storage devices are called **block-oriented devices,** because they never transfer a single byte at a time. Rather, they transfer data in multibyte **blocks.** How big is a block? It depends on the device; some typical disk block sizes range from 512 bytes to 8K bytes. Why build block-oriented devices? The answer to this question should be clear from our previous discussion of the number of interrupts that a computer can handle per second: if a computer transfers 1 byte per interrupt, then its data transfer rate and its interrupt-handling rate are identical. If, on the other hand, a computer transfers more than 1 byte for each interrupt, then the data-transfer rate will increase (approximately) as the number of bytes per transfer increases. The increase is only approximate because handling an interrupt from a block-oriented device is more time-consuming than handling an interrupt from a character-oriented device. We will discuss how I/O is performed with these devices after looking at some of their characteristics.

Sequential Access Devices: Tape Drives

The block-oriented mass storage devices can be separated into two groups; the first group consists of **sequential** access devices. The Industry Compatible Magnetic Tape (ICMT) is the prime example of a sequential access storage medium. ICMTs come in a standard (by virtue of an ANSI standard) size of 10.5 inch diameter reels; a reel holds almost 1/2 mile (2400 feet) of 1/2 inch wide tape. The tape has a ferromagnetic coating on the side used for recording bits. A tape has two metallic markers that indicate the beginning and end of its usable section; a **tape drive** (on which the tape is mounted) senses these markers, and so knows where to read (and write) data. A tape wears fastest near the beginning-of-tape (BOT) marker; a computer operator can salvage a tape (that a tape drive has difficulty reading) by reeling off the first 30 to 40 feet of the tape, cutting it off, and gluing a new BOT marker at the new beginning of the tape.

Most tapes are certified by the manufacturer as capable of reading and writing information with a density of 6250 bits per inch (bpi). This **tape recording density** means that if we use a 6250 bpi tape on a 6250 bpi tape drive, and if we record on a full inch of tape, 6250 bytes would be recorded. Are we confusing *bits* per inch with *bytes* per inch? No: the measure, bpi, is a *linear* density, indicating the bit density on a 1-bit-wide tape channel, or **track,** of the magnetic tape; standard tapes have nine 1-bit wide channels across their 1/2 inch width, so a little (bit) more than a byte can be stored in each of the 6250 **frames** per inch. This is similar to a paper tape, which can store information with a linear density of 10 bits per inch. It has eight channels--each of which stores 10 bpi--so 1 byte of 8 bits is written in one frame, which spans all eight channels, and we can store 10 bytes per inch on a 10-bit-per-inch paper tape. The term **frames per inch** (fpi) is sometimes used in place of bits per inch; in the two cases we have just considered, they are equivalent.

Current ICMT uses nine tracks (nine channels). An 8-bit byte is recorded in one 9-bit frame; the tape drive controller attaches its own check bit (parity bit) as the ninth bit, and strips it off when the information is read. Some systems also support (older) seven-track tapes, which have densities ranging from 200 to 556 bpi. Seven- and nine-track tape *media* are the same, but the tape drives cannot read each other's tapes.

The organization of a computer system with multiple tape drives is shown in figure 16.1. As a rule, one tape controller (similar to a CRT interface controller, but more sophisticated and, therefore, more expensive) can manage several (usually some small power of 2) tape drives. It is not unusual to have several tape controllers on a large computer, with each controller managing several tape drives.

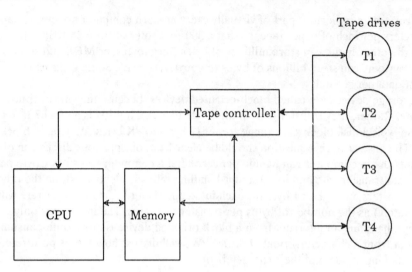

Figure 16.1 A computer system with magnetic tapes

However, only one tape drive per controller may be transferring data at one time. It is possible to have several tapes spinning simultaneously, but only one tape per controller can be actually transferring bytes; the other tapes in motion are being rewound to the BOT mark, or are performing non-data-transfer skips.

In order to record information on tape, we must present the tape drive controller with three pieces of information:

1. Memory Buffer Address (BA)
2. Word Count (WC)
3. I/O command

Some typical I/O commands are *write, read,* and *rewind.* Assuming that each of the three pieces of information is stored in a word, we can execute the following code to write (record) 512 words, at memory locations ABC, ABC+2, and so on. This code also assumes that the controller's *write* command is issued by setting bits 3, 4, and 5 in its CSR to 001_2.

```
          TWCR = ????????        ;define Word Count register
          TBAR = ????????        ;define Buffer Address register
          TCSR = ????????        ;define Control Status register
BEGIN:    MOVW #512, @#TWCR ;place Word Count in WCR
          MOVAL ABC, @#TBAR ;place address in BAR
          BISW2 #1, @#TCSR       ;select tape drive
          BISW2 #^X20, @#TCSR ;write
```

The interrupt enable bit must be set, as usual, if we want the tape's controller to interrupt the CPU; some tape controllers use a byte count rather than a word count.

Once the tape controller reads the word count, address, and command, it accelerates the tape until recording speed is reached, and then it begins transferring bytes *directly* from memory, copying them to the tape--*while the CPU continues executing instructions as usual.* The tape controller

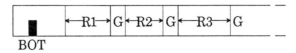

Figure 16.2 Tape record and record-gap format

decrements its word count register as it increments its buffer address register, as long as it transfers data. When the word count reaches 0, the controller writes some check bytes on the tape, to complete the block it has just written. The controller will then request an interrupt. If we repeat this process several times, the tape will look as shown in figure 16.2 (we do not show the check bytes; they are implied). Each write command generates a **record** (or **block**), R_n, on the tape, and an **inter-record gap**. Records can vary in length from record to record; that depends on the word count used when each of the records is written. The inter-record gap is never less than 1/2-inch long; its actual size varies from gap to gap, depending on variations in tape speed, tape acceleration, and so forth. The interaction between record size and record-gap size has a significant effect on a tape's storage capacity and on its data-transfer rate, as we shall soon see.

If we have written records R1, R2, and R3, as shown in figure 16.2, the next record written will follow the gap following record R3. If we try to write too many records on a tape, the tape drive will sense the EOT marker and inform the controller; the controller will abort the write operation, set the appropriate CSR error bit(s), and request an interrupt.

If we write records shorter than 18 bytes (the shortest standard ANSI record) or longer than 2048 bytes (the longest standard ANSI record), we may not be able to read them on other computers that conform to ANSI standards.

Reading a tape record involves some combination of the following operations:

1. Rewinding it to the BOT
2. Backspacing 1 record
3. Reading over 1 record

We can always add new records to a tape, but we cannot reliably replace any record except the last one. Replacing a record is called **update in place**; it is not supported by ICMT. Consider a tape with four records, as shown in figure 16.3. We can add a fifth record, R5, following R4; we can also replace R4 (before adding R5). We can replace R3 if we replace R4 at the same time, and so on. If we attempt to replace (change) any one of R1, R2, or R3, however, we cannot expect that the records following the replaced one will remain readable. Tape drives are electromechanical, and the tape medium is slightly elastic. Therefore, the gap sizes vary in length. If we try to replace R3 and the gap following R3 was exactly 1/2 inch but the new gap is slightly longer, R4 might be unreadable because the new gap overwrote the beginning of R4. Replacing the last group of records means reading them into memory, positioning the tape *in front* of that group of records, and performing another set of write operations. A write operation is automatically preceded by an erase operation.

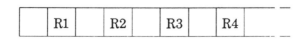

Figure 16.3 A tape with four records

How do we change a record, if we can't update it in place? First, we read records before the record to be changed and copy them onto a new tape. Then, we read and change the record to be changed, and write the new version on the new tape. Finally, we copy the records after the record that was changed from the old tape to the new one. This is a nuisance, but it has a beneficial side effect: we now have an old *master* tape as well as a new master tape. If we save the old master tape and information describing the change, we can regenerate the new master if it gets destroyed, stolen, or misplaced.

Recording Density

The three most common recording densities in use are 800, 1600, and 6250 bpi; figure 16.4 shows the influence of recording density and record size on a tape's storage capacity. The numbers in figure 16.4 are applicable to 2400-foot tape reels, with 20 feet of unused tape as a **leader** and another 20 feet of unused tape as a **trailer.** They also assume that 1/2-inch inter-record gaps are used. From this figure we can see that with small records, most of the tape is used for record gaps, and higher recording densities have little effect on the total amount of information stored on the tape. Increasing record size leads to increased information storage, but if we use records that are too long, other problems--one of which was mentioned above, and others of which will be discussed shortly-- may occur. Tape drives capable of reading and writing at higher densities are more expensive than those capable of only lower density recording, so many smaller VAX systems have drives which support only 800 and 1600 bpi.

Tape Data-Transfer Speeds

Tape drive speed is measured by the number of inches of tape which pass by the read/write head in one second. Typical tape drive speeds range from 45 ips (inches per second) to 125 ips. Since the cost of a tape drive increases rapidly with its speed, the most popular speeds are 45 and 75 ips. These speeds provide an acceptable price/performance tradeoff. The influence of recording density, tape speed, and record size on data-transfer rates is shown in figure 16.5. Figures 16.4 and 16.5 show that larger record sizes result in larger storage capacity and higher data-transfer rates. What happens if we use *huge* records? Clearly, storage capacity and transfer rates continue to increase. There are several problems associated with huge records, however:

1.   The probability of a speck of dust or a tape defect in a given record increases with the record length, and if any part of a record is unreadable, the whole record is unreadable. Thus, larger records are more likely to be unreadable than small records, and when a large record is unreadable more information is lost than when a small record is unreadable.
2.   Since reading a record involves copying it into a memory buffer, huge records require huge buffers. A memory buffer large enough to store a huge record may not available when we try to read such a record.
3.   Other systems may not be to able read our tapes if their record lengths exceed 2048 bytes. This is a software-imposed standard size limitation, designed to promote information transfer by tape.

Record size typically depends on the operating system (and situation). The VMS operating system, for example, uses variable-size records for text files, 512-byte records for binary files (such as executable files and object modules), and 8192-byte records for backing up disk files (this topic is discussed in the exercises for chapter 16).

Density (bpi)	Record Size (bytes)	Capacity (MB)
800	128	6
	256	9
	512	13
	1024	16
	2048	19
	4096	21
	8192	22
	16384	22
	32768	23
1600	128	6
	256	11
	512	18
	1024	26
	2048	33
	4096	38
	8192	42
	16384	44
	32768	45
6250	128	7
	256	14
	512	25
	1024	44
	2048	71
	4096	101
	8192	129
	16384	150
	32768	163

Figure 16.4 Recording density, record size, and tape capacity

Records and Files

There is another kind of object which can be recorded on and read from tape. This object is called a **file mark,** or a **tape mark.** A tape controller can distinguish a file mark from a record, and from the BOT and EOT marks. A tape controller creates a file mark upon receipt of a *write file mark* request. A file mark is a 3-inch block of tape, which is recognized as a file mark. The file mark allows us to organize the contents of a tape much as we would organize the contents of filing cabinets. Suppose, for example, we want to store 80-column lines from a text file on tape. The first 32 records of the tape might be images of the 32 lines in our source module, S1. If we write a file mark, FM, following record 32, the first 32 records can then be thought of as "file 1." If we then write 77 more records and follow them by another file mark (indicating "file 2"), our tape will look like that shown in figure 16.6. If we write too many small files on a tape, the 3-inch file mark will use up valuable storage space and will lower the data-transfer rate.

Tape Density	Record Size (bytes)	Data-Transfer Rates (KB/s)		
		Tape Drive Speeds (ips)		
		45	75	125
1600 bpi	128	10	17	28
	256	17	29	48
	512	28	47	78
	1024	40	67	112
	2048	52	86	144
	4096	60	100	167
	8192	66	109	182
	16384	69	114	191
	32768	70	117	195
6250 bpi	128	11	18	31
	256	21	35	59
	512	40	66	110
	1024	69	116	193
	2048	111	186	309
	4096	160	266	443
	8192	204	339	566
	16384	236	394	656
	32768	257	428	713

Figure 16.5 Data-transfer rates for 1600 and 6250 bpi tapes

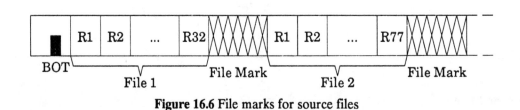

Figure 16.6 File marks for source files

Tape Compatibility

If we use an ICMT and record on it using a nine-track tape drive set at a standard density (say, 800 bpi) at 75 ips, we can, in principle, read that tape on any ICMT drive which supports the same density we used to record, at any speed the drive supports. Things are not necessarily so straightforward, however: some low-speed drives (12.5 ips) can only mount *mini* tape reels, 7 inches in diameter, which hold 600 feet of tape. We might also have written records which are either too small or too large for the software or the tape controller of the target computer. If the target computer is not another VAX, and if we wrote our tape on a VAX using a controller that writes 1 word or longword at a time, then the target computer's software might have to interchange bytes, because not all computers store bytes in words and longwords in the same order as does the VAX.

As an example of this byte-ordering problem, consider first the case in which we have stored ASCII codes for the letters, ABCD . . ., in consecutive memory locations. We could write them on a tape using a controller which fetches from memory and writes to tape 1 byte at a time (this, of course, would be wasteful from the perspective of interrupt handling overhead). In this case, the codes for ABCD . . . will be written out on tape in that sequence, and all will be well. Second, let us consider a tape controller which fetches from memory and writes to tape 1 *word* at a time. In this case, the codes may be written on the tape as if they had been the sequence BADC . . .; clearly, the target computer's software must know about the *reordering* that occurred, and it must restore the original order when reading the tape.

Binary Data

The character-oriented devices that people interact with typically send and receive only the codes of some character set (usually ASCII or EBCDIC). Paper tape is not subject to this restriction: we can record arbitrary patterns in each 8-bit frame. For example, we can record machine-language instructions and binary (numeric) data by using consecutive 8-bit frames of a paper tape.

Magnetic tape is similar to paper tape in this respect. It is not **code sensitive**: we can record and read arbitrary bit patterns. This is very important in some situations. For large-scale applications--for example, processing the U.S. census data--the processing sequence may be:

1. Input census forms, using a human keyboard operator or an optical character recognition system that produces ASCII codes corresponding to the letters it recognizes on the form.
2. Display each form for verification and correction, if necessary.
3. Convert all numeric data from ASCII coded numeric strings to binary form--integer or floating-point formats, as appropriate.
4. Record all data as-is, and store on magnetic tape.

In this case, some of the data are stored on tape in what we consider the computer's *internal representation* format. We would have a similar situation if we were to *dump* memory onto tape, bit by bit, *without* converting to ASCII character codes. We call this a *binary* record, as distinct from other records which use some standard code. Binary tape records save both space and time. They save space because, for example, the decimal number -12.345678E-12, stored as an ASCII coded string, takes 14 bytes of memory, but it can also be stored as a 4-byte F_format floating-point number. They save time because it takes time to convert from the 32-bit F_format representation, which is how the number is (most likely) manipulated by the computer, to the character string, which is how it is probably displayed to a user.

Tapes such as those used to record census data are written and verified and then never changed. In fact, they constitute a document which by law must be kept intact. We call these **archival** tapes. In order to prevent accidental overwriting of the information on such tapes (or any others), which we only intend to *read,* a removable ring in the tape hub serves as a **write-protect** interlock: even if our program had a bug and asked that the tape be written instead of read, or if our tape were accidentally mounted in place of another, a tape controller will refuse to write on a tape that has its write-protect ring in place.

Tape Labels

When we file personal papers in old shoe boxes, we usually label the boxes. With a collection of magnetic tapes, likewise, we expect to see labels on each one of them. The label is read by us or by a computer operator, in order to find the correct tape for a given job. There is another kind of label, an *internal* label, which is the first thing (the first record) written on the tape. When a tape is mounted, we are expected to type in its external label identification. Then the operating system reads the first record of the tape and verifies that the tape's internal and external identification labels match. The internal label contains additional information, such as who owns the tape, when it was first used, and so forth. There is an ANSI standard for these internal labels which specifies their format and content. Many computing installations insist that all tapes handled by them have such an internal label. If we write an ordinary tape with nothing but data on it and carry it over to a site which insists on reading labeled tapes, we will have to rewrite our tape to conform with their standard in order for them to read it. This may seem like a nuisance, but at sites where thousands of tapes are in use, the chances of using the wrong tape are high. Requiring internal labels on all tapes is a sound management practice.

Other Tape Devices

ICMT controllers and drives were once too expensive (over $50,000 each) for many smaller systems. Digital Equipment Corporation (DEC), which once built only small systems, took the initiative in this regard in the 1960s and developed a relatively inexpensive tape drive called *DECtape*. The objective of low cost and high reliability in a dirty environment (DEC's early systems were designed particularly to be used in laboratories) was met by sacrificing compatibility with ICMT and by also sacrificing capacity and performance, compared with ICMT. However, for many of DEC's customers, DECtape offered an *increase* in capacity and performance, since the only economical alternative at the time was *paper* tape (lots of it, since it is not easily erasable).

DECtape used fixed-size blocks with prerecorded block numbers and a controller which could find any block, given the block's number. Tape records could even be read backward to save time, although they appeared forward in memory (read-backward is an infrequent option on ICMT). The use of block numbers for each tape block made it possible for a DECtape to simulate a disk system (which we will discuss shortly). With the advent of floppy disks (also to be discussed shortly) DECtape systems were phased out.

DEC still supports a nonindustry standard tape format, called *CompacTape,* designed primarily for disk back-up on its smaller MicroVAX systems, and for software distribution. This tape format uses a cartridge tape based on one pioneered by the 3M Company, specifically for digital recording. DEC's cartridge tape is incompatible with ICMT in nearly every feature: it comes in nonstandard lengths, records with a nonstandard density on a nonstandard number of channels in a nonstandard pattern, and uses nonstandard record sizes (up to 64K bytes). These cartridge tape drives are nonstandard because cost is a major consideration in smaller installations: customers are often unwilling to pay more for a tape drive than for the rest of their system combined. DECtape and CompacTape are physically and conceptually different from ICMT.

Interrupts and DMA Transfers

Once we initiate a data-transfer operation (read or write) with a tape, the entire record (block) may be transferred into memory from the tape, or to the tape from memory, without any further CPU intervention. This is called **Direct Memory Access** (DMA). If a device has a DMA controller, then it is likely to have a higher data rate than a device without a DMA controller.

If we read or write *blocks* of data, we would like to have only one interrupt per block. If we transfer 512-byte blocks *without* DMA, we need 512 interrupts per block--one for each byte; if we use a DMA controller to read or write these blocks of 512 bytes, we need only one interrupt for the whole block. For a given level of I/O activity, the interrupt overhead of our system has just been reduced by a factor of 512.

DMA controllers such as those used by a tape drive are much more complicated and expensive than the simple serial interface controller used by a CRT that we discussed earlier. It takes over 10 pages of small print to describe the registers and functions of some of the ICMT DMA controllers available for the VAX. Tape controllers such as DEC's TU78 series have 16 or more control, status, buffer, and count registers. The interested reader can find more information in DEC's *Peripherals Handbook* and, of course, in each controller's reference manual.

Since a DMA device controller is considerably more complicated than a serial device controller, processing one interrupt for it takes longer than processing one for a simpler controller--one or two hundred instructions executed per interrupt handler is typical. If we assume 200 instructions, each of which takes about 1 μsec to execute on a VAX 11/780, then we can handle an interrupt in about 200 μsec, and so we can handle about 5000 interrupts per second. This results in a data-transfer rate of about 2,500 KB per second. If we execute only 100 instructions per interrupt, or if we transfer a 1024-byte block per interrupt, we double the data-transfer rate to about 5 MB per second.

Direct Access Devices: Disks

Tapes are considered sequential access devices because accessing any record requires traversing all records which separate the current record from the desired record. If we begin at the BOT mark and want to read the last record on a 2400 foot tape, we will wait at least 10 minutes (on a 45 ips drive) to reach that record. Ironically, if we were at the end of the tape and wished to read the tape's *first* record, we could get to the BOT mark in 2 minutes or less, if we requested the tape to rewind at high speed (*fast forward* is an uncommon option).

The delay in reaching the desired record is called the **access time.** For a magnetic tape, the **worst-case** access time is measured in minutes; even the *average* access time is measured in minutes. Tapes are practical when we access consecutive records. What can we do if we need to access information in nonconsecutive order? Some of the distinctions that are relevant to the various addressing modes are also relevant to tapes: autoincrement and autodecrement addressing are marvelous for sequential access to consecutive array elements, but we use displacement addressing for *random* access to array elements. Similarly, we would like a **direct access,** or **random access,** device.

Disk Drives

We can think of a disk as having one more dimension than a tape. Figure 16.7 shows a disk as an array of looped magnetic tapes. The tracks are circular, so for each track, item S_n is immediately followed by item S_0. Disks are different from tapes: when a byte is recorded on tape, a 9-bit frame cutting across all nine tape channels is used. When a byte is recorded on disk, however, the bits are placed sequentially on a single track; instead of providing each byte with a check bit, a larger set of check bits is attached at the end of each block.

Most disks are organized in fixed-size records called **sectors** or **blocks.** For the VAX, disk blocks are typically 512 bytes. Disk drives usually have at least two recording surfaces (the top and the bottom), but many have more than that, because they *stack* several disks (called **platters**) on top of each other. Let us first examine a simple drive which only uses one side of its single disk: in this

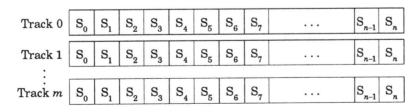

Figure 16.7 A disk viewed as an array of looped magnetic tapes

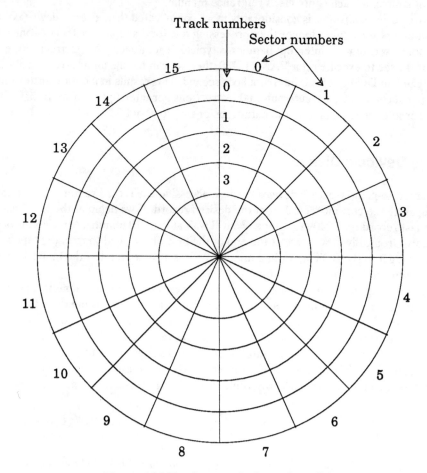

Figure 16.8 Tracks on a single-surface disk

situation, the tracks are arranged as a series of concentric circles, as shown in figure 16.8. In figure 16.8, sector numbers are shown around the outside of the disk, and track numbers are shown on each track. A single-surface disk drive uses a single read/write head, mounted on a moving arm; this arrangement is similar to an audio turntable and its tone-arm, except that a disk has no grooves, and it has several concentric tracks rather than a single spiral groove.

Disk Operating Speed

The characteristics of a disk drive which affect its data transfer rate are:

1. The speed with which the arm can be moved so that it is over the track from which data are to be read.
2. The time it takes for the disk to rotate so that the sector from which data are to be read is under the read/write head.

The time it takes for the arm to be placed over the desired track is called the **seek time** (the arm *seeks* the desired track). The seek time varies with the number of tracks separating the current arm position from the desired arm position; because of the arm's inertia, it takes only slightly longer to seek from track n to track $n + 2$ than it does to seek from track n to track $n + 1$. When specifying a disk drive's seek time, we can use any combination of three terms:

1. The **maximum seek time** is the time required to seek from the innermost track to the outermost one, or from the outermost track to the innermost one.
2. The **single-track seek time** is the time required to seek from track n to track $n + 1$ or to track $n - 1$.
3. The **average seek time** is the time required to seek halfway way across the disk. This is based on the assumption that sometimes the arm will happen to be already positioned over the correct track, sometimes it will be positioned over the innermost (or outermost) track and will have to seek the outermost (or innermost) track, and sometimes it will be somewhere in between. (These are not necessarily valid assumptions, so average seek time is more useful for comparing the performance of different disk drives than for predicting the performance of any particular disk drive in any particular situation.)

Before a disk can begin transferring data, it must wait for the seek time to elapse; however, even after the arm is positioned over the correct track, data transfer cannot begin until the desired sector has rotated under the disk's read/write head. The time required for the desired sector to rotate under the read/write head is called the **latency time,** or the **rotational latency,** of the disk. The latency time depends on the disk's speed of rotation; for any given read/write request, it also depends on the distance between the heads and the sector on which the data for this request are stored. We typically describe a disk drive's latency delay with two terms:

1. The **maximum latency** is the amount of time the disk takes to make one complete revolution. This is 1 divided by the number of revolutions per second.
2. The **average latency,** which is one-half the maximum latency. This calculation is based on the assumption that sometimes the desired sector will be exactly under the read/write head, sometimes it will have just passed the read/write head, and sometimes it will be in between these two extremes.

The *total* time required to begin data transfer is called the **access time.** The worst-case access time is calculated in a straightforward manner:

maximum access time = maximum seek time + maximum latency time

The *average* access time is calculated in a similar manner:

average access time = average seek time + average latency time

A very slow disk drive for the VAX--a **floppy disk,** or **diskette** drive--has a worst-case access time of about 1/2 second (524 milliseconds), and a high-performance disk drive for a VAX has a worst-case access time of about 1/15 second (72.6 milliseconds). In comparison, a 25 ips tape drive has a worst-case access time of about 20 minutes, and a 125 ips tape drive has a worst-case access time of about 4 minutes. A high-performance disk system's worst-case access time is, thus, more than 3000 times faster than that of a high-performance tape drive.

Since a disk by its nature has two surfaces, it is cost-effective to use both for storage. On a two-sided disk, track addresses are assigned so that even-numbered tracks are on the top surface (surface 0), and odd-numbered tracks are on the bottom surface (surface 1). This is shown schematically in figure 16.9. Such a disk needs two moving arms, and each has a read/write head

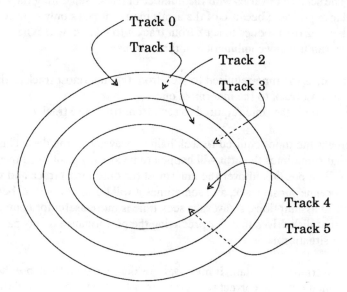

Figure 16.9 Track addresses on a double-sided disk

mounted on it. However, the two arms move as a unit, so if the top read/write head is positioned over track 4, the bottom arm is positioned over track 5. Tracks numbered 0 and 1, 2 and 3, . . . , $2n$ and $2n + 1$ are thought of as belonging to a series of concentric **cylinders.** The outer cylinder is numbered 0, and it contains tracks 0 and 1; the next cylinder is numbered 1, and it contains tracks 2 and 3. If the last cylinder is numbered x, it contains tracks $2x$ and $2x + 1$ (figure 16.10).

Tracks on different surfaces are organized as cylinders for efficiency: a disk drive transfers only a single sector (block) at a time. However, if we need to read (or write) several consecutive sectors, we can avoid any seek time or latency time between sectors if we read or write *contiguous* sectors. This is because, in the general case, when a disk finishes reading or writing sector n--if sectors with adjacent numbers are stored adjacently, on the same track--then the arm and head will be perfectly positioned to read or write sector $n + 1$. What if we request a disk transfer that goes beyond the last sector of track 0? The disk's controller need only activate the lower read/write head and continue reading or writing from track 1, which is on the other side of the disk; going from even- to odd-numbered tracks, there is no additional seek time or latency time. If, however, we are going from odd- to even-numbered tracks, then the arms will have to seek one track over; by the time this happens, the heads will no longer be positioned over the correct sector (if we are trying to read the first sector of the even-numbered track just after reading the last sector of the odd-numbered track).

By assigning consecutive numbers (addresses) to those tracks which belong to a single cylinder, we have effectively doubled the length of the disk's tracks. As long as we read from a single cylinder, there will be *no* seek delay for data-transfer operations.

The cost per byte of storage for building a disk with two data surfaces is lower than the cost per byte for building a disk with only one data surface. Similarly, the cost per byte of storage is even lower for a disk with more than two data surfaces; disks with several **platters** are common. The track numbering for such a disk is a logical extension of that for a two sided disk; it is shown schematically for a six-sided disk, comprised of three platters *stacked* on a single spindle, in figure 16.10. A multisurface disk drive has a moving arm and read/write head for each surface; as with two-sided disks, the arms and heads move together, so the idea of a cylinder is maintained and extended.

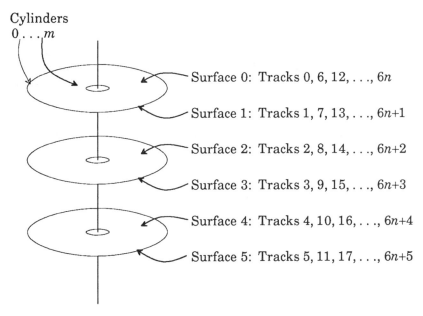

Cylinders
$0 \ldots m$

Surface 0: Tracks $0, 6, 12, \ldots, 6n$

Surface 1: Tracks $1, 7, 13, \ldots, 6n+1$

Surface 2: Tracks $2, 8, 14, \ldots, 6n+2$

Surface 3: Tracks $3, 9, 15, \ldots, 6n+3$

Surface 4: Tracks $4, 10, 16, \ldots, 6n+4$

Surface 5: Tracks $5, 11, 17, \ldots, 6n+5$

Figure 16.10 Track addresses on a six-sided disk

Switching from one track to another within a cylinder is done, as before, with *no* seek time. The worst-case access time within a cylinder is the worst-case latency delay; it occurs if the desired sector has just passed under the read/write head, necessitating a one-revolution delay until it reaches the head again.

Winchester Disks

Some disks (**disk packs**) are removable; as with tape drives, the moving arm and the read/write head(s) are part of the disk drive, and only the platter assembly is mounted and dismounted. In the last ten years, **Winchester disks** have become popular. These disks have a sealed package containing the arm(s), head(s) and platter(s); because such a package is more expensive than one that includes only the platters, Winchester disks are not usually considered removable--although it is possible to replace the disk/head package. Because of their sealed environment, Winchester disks are more reliable than removable disks, and they also typically have a higher recording density than removable disks.

Winchester disks are more reliable because the head/platter assembly is manufactured in a carefully controlled, dust-free environment and then sealed. Although removable disks are kept tightly covered, and although the disk drives that use them have sophisticated filtering systems, specks of dirt inevitably appear on the surface(s) of such disks. A very tiny speck indeed may suffice to destroy the disk platter or the read/write head: disk heads typically *fly* over the disk surface on a cushion of air that is only a few millionths of an inch thick.

Winchester disks often record at a higher density than do removable disks because their heads fly closer to the disk's surface than do those of removable disks; they can, therefore, read and write smaller areas, and so can store a single bit in a smaller area. (A more complete explanation of this phenomenon requires an understanding of electromagnetism that is beyond the scope of this book.)

Why don't removable-pack disk drives have heads that fly as close to the disks as those of Winchester disks? There are two reasons. First, dirt is more likely to be deposited on the surfaces of a removable-pack disk than of a Winchester disk; as the heads fly closer to the disk, smaller specks of dirt become bigger problems. Second, before the disk pack of a removable disk can be removed, the disk heads must be retracted (**parked**) so that they are no longer over the surface of the disk. After a new pack is mounted, the disk must come up to speed (typically 3600 rpm) before the heads can be moved back over the surface of the disk, because the air cushion that keeps the heads from contacting the disk is generated by the interaction between the air that *sticks* to the surface of the rapidly rotating disk, and the shape of the read/write heads. However, there is turbulence at the edge of the disk, so the arms must keep the heads far enough away from the disk's surface that, when they are first moved back over the surface of the disk, this turbulence won't cause them to crash into the disk. With a Winchester disk, however, the heads needn't be retracted when the disk drive is turned off (if it is ever turned off), because the heads and the disk are never separated. (The surface of a Winchester disk is lubricated so that the heads won't scratch it when they slide over it as the disk slows down and the air cushion dissipates.) Therefore, the heads of a Winchester disk can be designed to fly closer to the surface of the disk.

Some smaller Winchester disks are sold as cartridges, and are meant to be replaced, heads and all, for safe storage of information, or just when they are full. There are many different types of disk packs; even when two different computers use the same type of disk pack or cartridge, it may not be possible to transfer information from one to the other by carrying a disk pack written on one computer to be read on another. Differences in the file structure and the way different disk controllers organize the blocks may make it difficult to read a disk written on another computer, running a different operating system.

Disk I/O

When we use a disk on a bare machine, it appears similar to other I/O devices: the disk's interface controller has a set of register addresses in the I/O address space, an interrupt vector address, and a hardware priority. It may have as few as 5 or as many as 20 device registers.

Most disk controllers use DMA access to memory. As with tape drives, several disk drives of the same type may share one disk controller--often as many as eight drives per controller. One controller has only one set of registers, however, and so it can support only a single data transfer at any time.

The major differences between disk I/O and, for example, tape I/O, are that a disk may be thought of as having an extra dimension and that a disk's sectors have explicit addresses. In addition, disks are designed to permit update-in-place: any sector can be rewritten without damaging the information in adjacent sectors. If we have a computer system such as that shown in figure 16.11, then the following steps would be taken to read or write a given sector on disk D3:

1.   Use the device registers for controller C2
2.   Send to those registers the following information:

    a.   drive number
    b.   cylinder address
    c.   track address
    d.   sector address
    e.   memory-buffer address
    f.   word count

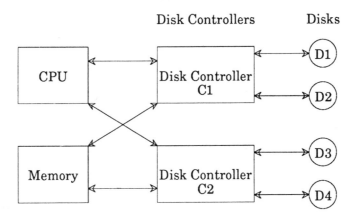

Figure 16.11 Multiple controller, multiple disk drive computer system

Model:	RX50	RA60	RA70	RA82
Type:	Floppy	Removable	Winchester	Winchester
Bytes/sector:	512	512	512	512
Sectors/track:	10	42	33	57
Tracks/surface:	80	1600	1507	2870
Data Surfaces:	1	6	11	7
Capacity (MB):	.409	205	280	622
Average access time (msec):	528	50	27	32.3
Peak transfer rate (B/sec):	31.25K	1.98M	1.4M	2.4M

Figure 16.12 Characteristics of selected disk drives

If all the bits for items (a) through (f) would fit in 1 16-bit word, and if the disk's sector size were 512 bytes, then a single controller could access no more than 64 K (2^{16}) $\cdot$ 512 = 32 MB. Thirty-two million bytes stored on the disk drives of one controller may sound like a lot of storage, but it would not accommodate even a single 67 MB disk drive; medium size VAXes often have several disk drives with 450 MB capacity or more, and large installations often have billions of bytes (gigabytes, or GB) of disk storage. Usually, therefore, a disk controller needs several registers to specify the information for items (a) through (f).

Disk Capacity and Performance

A wide variety of disk drives, built by DEC and other manufacturers, are used on VAX computers; even a summary of their characteristics would be overwhelming. Figure 16.12 provides a summary of the characteristics of four disk drives available from DEC; these were chosen because they illustrate the variety of different sizes and types of available disk drives. In figure 16.12, the labeled *capacity* row indicates *formatted* capacity rather than unformatted capacity; what is the difference? The unformatted capacity is similar to the capacity of a tape if we ignore record gaps and file marks.

When a disk is formatted, space is lost for storing track and sector addresses, as well as for each sector's check bits. The formatted capacity of a disk is often only 85% or less of its unformatted capacity.

Fixed-Head Disks

Normally, a disk drive uses a single moving arm and a read/write head for each surface of the disk pack. Very high performance disks have been manufactured which have one head per *track*. The arms of these disks never move, since there is always an arm positioned over the desired track; such disks are called **fixed-head** disks. These disks have no seek time, so their average access time is simply a function of their rotational speed. However, fixed-head disks are very expensive, because arms and read/write heads are expensive.

One particularly appropriate use for a fixed-head disk is as a **swapping device**: on a multiuser system, a single CPU is often shared among many users' programs; each program gets its turn to run. When a program isn't running, what happens to it? If there is sufficient main memory, it merely *waits* for its turn again. However, if the program whose turn it is to run needs more main memory than is available with other programs remaining in memory, those programs are **swapped out**: they are copied to a disk. When a program that has been swapped out gets its next turn to run, it must be swapped back in. Since the new program can't run until it is loaded in memory, and since it can't be loaded into memory until the old one is swapped out, a system with a fast swapping device will perform better than one with a slow swapping device, all other things being equal.

Solid-State Disks

As the cost of semiconductor memory chips has dropped, **solid-state disks** have become practical. Such disks use ordinary memory chips (ones similar to those from which a computer's main memory system is constructed), organized to simulate a disk's track. A solid-state disk, like a fixed-head disk, has no seek time; in addition, since it only *simulates* a disk, it has a latency time in the microsecond range rather than in the millisecond range. Solid state disks can have about as much storage as we can pay for. One might ask, then, "Why put all those memory chips in a box--and make them slower than the nanosecond (billionths of a second) access time of main memory--rather than adding them to main memory?" There are two reasons: first, memory chips with faster access time are, all other things being equal, more expensive than those with slower access time, so using chips that are slower than those tolerable for main memory can significantly reduce the cost. Second, the VAX has 32-bit addresses, and so it has a main memory address space of (only) about 4 billion bytes; if we wish to have more total storage (disks and main memory) than that--as many large systems do--we can't organize it as main memory.

Direct Access Storage Devices

Disk storage devices are often called **direct access storage devices** (DASD), or *random access* devices. The term DASD is used because of a disk's ability to access a record on disk more or less directly-- at least without traversing the whole disk, as is required with a **sequential access storage device** (SASD) such as a tape drive. The term *random access* is used because access times for randomly located records on a disk are more or less independent of their position--once more, at least in comparison with a SASD. We should not confuse the *random* in "random access disks" with that in "random access memory" (RAM): only the latter has truly equal access time, regardless of location.

Spooling

Spool is an acronym for Simultaneous Peripheral (device) Operations On-Line. The acronym became a noun and then a verb, so we talk of *spooling* output. Almost any disk-based system allows us to *spool* output to a printer. We identify the file we wish to print, and the spooling software takes care of our print request while we continue with our other computing tasks. This is yet another level at which I/O can overlap with other activities (our *own* tasks, in addition to operating system tasks, or other users' tasks). The evolution of computing systems to support spooling illustrates the interaction between the right kinds of devices, the right kinds of control mechanisms, and appropriate user services.

Prior to the introduction of affordable disks in the mid-1960s, users would interact with many large computing systems as follows:

1. Prepare a *job* (of program and/or data) on punched cards, using a keypunch, off line.
2. Use a card-to-magnetic-tape machine to copy a *batch* of job cards onto magnetic tape. This tape is a *job input tape*; it contains several jobs, from several different users.
3. Mount the job input tape on one of the (dozen or more) tape drives connected to the computer.
4. Process the jobs on the input tape sequentially. When a job requests that output be printed, copy that *print output* to a file on a tape designated as the *print tape*.
5. When the processing for all the jobs on the job input tape is complete, mount the print tape on another machine, which reads the tape and drives a printer (a tape-to-print machine).

In this mode of computing, jobs are processed one at a time, and the next job isn't started until the current one is completed. Jobs complete in a first-in/first-out order; this is called **batch processing.** Because much I/O is performed off-line, it is possible to overlap I/O and CPU operations--at the cost of having dedicated off-line machines for the card-to-tape and tape-to-print operations. Batch systems overlapped CPU processing and I/O by using auxiliary machines because they did not have affordable direct access storage devices such as disks.

When disks became practical, the off-line auxiliary I/O machines were retired, and punched card input began to be displaced by on-line CRTs. However, batch processing has not disappeared, although punched cards nearly have. Let us assume, for ease of comparison, that cards are still used in preparing batch jobs. Our computer system would now have an *on line* card reader, an *on-line* printer, and sufficient (on-line) disk storage. Because of these on-line devices, and because interrupts allow spooling, the flow of a batch job is now:

1. An on-line card reader reads cards and copies the information on them to memory.
2. Card images in memory are appended to a job input file on disk.
3. A system scheduler reads the next available job from the disk's job input file.
4. Running jobs build their print file on disk. When a job completes, its disk print file is appended to the print output queue on disk.
5. The printer's software prints the next item in the disk's printer queue. As long as the queue is not empty, the printer runs at full speed.

This system provides overlapped input, CPU processing, and output that is only one step away from actually *timesharing* the CPU among the batch jobs.

When we use a disk as a job input buffer and as a print output buffer (a queue and a buffer may serve the same function), a job's input and its output may be physically disassociated from the job. When our program executes instructions that say "read a card," the actual card may have been read some time ago; our program's request causes a card-image to be read from disk into main memory. Similarly, when our program executes instructions that say "print a line," the actual printing will be done some time later--how much later depends on the length of the print queue and the speed of the printer. If the system *crashes* after our job runs but before our output reaches the head of

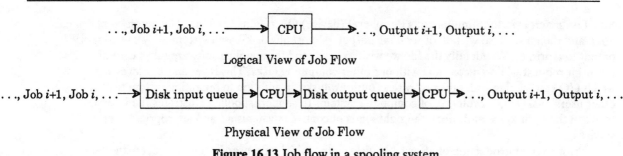

Figure 16.13 Job flow in a spooling system

the print queue, and if the print queue is not recovered when the system is rebooted, then our output may never appear. Figure 16.13 shows the logical and physical views of job flow in a spooling system. Spooling clearly requires more work from the CPU than does an ordinary batch system, and it requires greater disk capacity than would otherwise be the case. These extra costs are considered worthwhile because of the increased performance provided by spooling.

Performance

To some extent, performance is in the eyes of the beholder; there are several common measures of performance of a computer system. The subject is a vast one; we will examine only a few of its aspects that are relevant to our previous discussion.

Turnaround Time

In a batch system, the time interval from the submission of a job in machine-readable form (as a card deck, or as a set of commands at a CRT) to the time of its completion (including any output) is called the **turnaround time.** In a college computing center, the average turnaround time measured over a whole year might be under an hour, but at the end of the semester, when a considerable amount of last-minute work is typically done, the turnaround time may increase dramatically. As with disk and tape performance, the average access time is helpful, but rarely tells us all we want to know; best-case and worst-case times are also of interest to a user, or potential user, of a system. The managers of a computer center are certainly interested in maintaining the turnaround time at a reasonable level, but they are also interested in how many jobs are actually completed in a given time period.

Throughput

The average number of jobs executed per unit of time is a measure of performance which relates to the efficient use of computing resources. This measure is called **throughput.** All other things being equal, if system X can process 200 *typical* jobs per hour while another comparably priced system, Y, can process only 150 of the same kind of jobs in an hour, system X is a better system. Throughput and turnaround time can be opposing forces: the *throughput* of a Boeing 747 is much higher than that of a Piper Cub, but the *turnaround time* of the latter may be much lower.

Turnaround time and throughput are useful measures of performance in a batch system. When we deal with time-sharing systems, however, a different (or, at least, an *additional*) measure of the system's performance is also appropriate.

Response Time

The time between typing the last character of a request at a CRT and receiving a response from the computer is called the system's **response time.** For example, if we are using a text editor, how long do we usually have to wait for,

> The first prompt from the editor?
> Display of a given line?
> A response to a search request?
> Return to the operating system, after editing?

By measuring the system's response time, an average response time and a distribution can be calculated. In a general-purpose time-sharing system, the average may not be useful, because different users execute different tasks. In a special-purpose time-sharing system, the designer(s) of the system may be required to guarantee that their system can perform at certain levels. For example, an airline company may purchase a reservation system from a vendor only if the vendor can provide guarantees concerning both the average response time and worst-case response time.

Response time may be thought of as an action-by-action measure of turnaround time. The time-sharing system's counterpart of throughput is the number of concurrent users the system can support. If a time-sharing system has physical connections for, say, 50 CRTs, and if its operating system allows all 50 CRTs to be in use simultaneously, then that system is said to "support 50 concurrentusers." All other things being equal, if a 50-user system, X, provides average and worst-case response times of 1 and 5 seconds respectively, while system Y supports 50 users with average and worst-case response times of 2 and 20 seconds, system X is the better system. However, one system's performance might degrade slowly, and another's much more rapidly, with increases in user work load.

Measures of performance appropriate for batch systems or for time-sharing systems may be of little interest to the owner and user of a single-user system. If the performance is adequate, the user of such a system may care primarily about ease of programming, debugging and operating, about hardware and software reliability, about purchase price, upkeep cost, and so forth. This is partly because the performance of single-user system hardware has, by and large, made larger gains than has the quality and ease of use of single-user operating systems.

Blocking

In few instances in life do we find a better match between a container and its contents than with eggs and egg crates. The crates are designed to hold eggs, and they do that well. Computer systems are designed to be used by many applications, and so there is often a much less neat match between tape and disk storage devices and the information they hold.

Disks store and transfer records whose sizes are multiples of the disks' sector size: even if we create a file and store only a single character in it, the file takes up one complete sector on the disk. It is poor use of a disk's space to store, for example, one 80-character line in each 512-byte sector.

With magnetic tape, we can record blocks of varying size. However, doing so makes for poor use of the tape's storage capacity. If we stored a series of records whose lengths were 100, 36, 57, and 24 bytes, respectively, the record gaps on an 800 bpi tape would occupy more space than would the actual data. Using a higher recording density does not allow us to use smaller gaps, so the percentage of tape used for gaps actually increases.

The technique developed to alleviate this general problem involves *packing* several of our records--which we will now call **logical records**--into a single, larger, more efficiently handled record--which we will now call a **physical record.** If we have the logical records shown in the upper

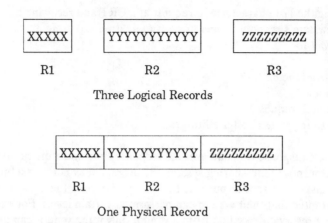

Figure 16.14 Three logical records and one physical record

part of figure 16.14, we could store them as a single physical record, as shown in the lower part of figure 16.14.

If the last logical record does not exactly fill out the physical record, then a suitable number of padding characters may be appended to it. If the last logical record is too large for a single physical record, then the excess may be stored in a new physical record. We must have some way of distinguishing between logical records, if they are not all the same length. This information can be provided either by preceding each logical record with a byte count field, or by using an end-of-record marker (such as the "|" shown in figure 16.14) between each pair of logical records.

Consider an application which deals with 80-character records. One thousand such records on an 800 bpi tape occupy 1,000 * (80/800 + .5) = 600 inches. If we pack the 80-character logical records into 512-byte physical records, we can reduce the amount of tape used as follows:

1. Each logical record consists of an 80-character record followed by an end-of-record byte, so each logical record consists of 81 bytes.
2. There are 1,000 logical records of 81 bytes each, for a total of 81,000 total bytes.
3. If we store the logical records in physical records (blocks) of 512 bytes each, we will need 81,000/512 = 158.2 physical records.
4. We need 158.2 physical records; each record consists of a 512-byte block stored in 512/800 inches of tape, plus .5-inch gap. Thus, we need 158.2 * (512/800 + .5) = 180.4 inches of tape.

Thus, if we pack logical records into physical records we use only one-third as much tape as when we don't do such packing. It also means, all other things being equal, we will be able to read the data considerably faster. The ratio between the lengths of the physical and logical records is called the **blocking factor.** In the above example, the blocking factor is 512/80, or 6.4. (We often ignore the extra end-of-record character in computing the blocking factor.) When the logical records are not all the same length, we can use an average length to compute the blocking factor.

With a disk, the physical record size typically can be no smaller than the disk's sector size; it can be larger by some whole number multiple of the sector size. With disk files, the operating system often requires use of a standard physical record size, but with tapes it is not uncommon for the operating system to allow the user a choice of block size. There is often a default block size for tape files; if a user chooses not to specify the block size, the operating system will use the default size, and then will *unblock* the file when the user reads the file.

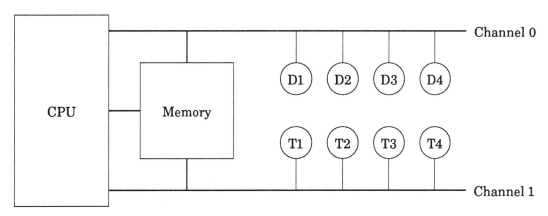

Figure 16.15 A computer with I/O channels

Computers and Buses

When a computer has several distinct functional units (such as memory and a CPU), they must be connected to each other in order to communicate in the process of executing a program. Usually, a set of wires is used for interconnecting the various parts of a computer; we call such a set of wires **a bus.** There are many different ways of designing the bus(es) of a computer; in this section we will discuss several of them, with particular consideration for the implications of bus design on I/O.

I/O Channels

In the 1960s, most computers had a set of wires connecting their CPU with memory, and additional wires connecting their I/O devices to the CPU and memory. The wires connecting I/O devices with memory and the CPU were called **channels.** Figure 16.15 shows a schematic view of a computer with I/O channels. A channel performs the functions of device controllers (that we have already discussed); in addition, as we can see from figure 16.15, a channel also has a direct connection to the memory. This provides for extremely high data transfer rates, since a system with multiple channels can have all of them actively transferring data simultaneously.

Single-Bus Computer Organization

A computer with several channels and a memory system capable of supporting them is expensive to build. In the late 1960s, Digital Equipment Corporation (which manufactures the VAX) designed the PDP-11 (the direct predecessor of the VAX). The PDP-11 has no channels, and only a single bus, which interconnects all of the PDP-11's elements--CPU, memory, and I/O devices. This bus is called a UNIBUS.[1] [TM] Recall that the VAX has no I/O instructions; the registers of device controllers are assigned addresses, and so they appear to the CPU as if they were ordinary memory locations. This technique of **memory mapped I/O** was used in the PDP-11 before it was used in the VAX; it is a natural outgrowth of the fact that *all* communication between the CPU, memory, and I/O devices is

---

[1] [TM] UNIBUS is a registered trademark of Digital Equipment Corporation.

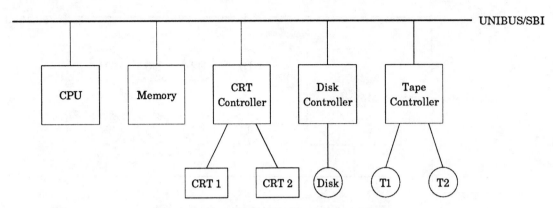

Figure 16.16 A single bus PDP-11 or VAX system

done on the UNIBUS. For example, when a PDP-11's CPU fetches the next instruction, or the current instruction's next operand, from memory, it sends the address along the UNIBUS, and it gets back some value from the memory system on the UNIBUS. Similarly, when a user types a key on a CRT, the CRT's controller sends the byte to the CPU along the UNIBUS; when a disk performs DMA input to memory, it sends the information directly to memory (without involvement of the CPU) along the UNIBUS.

A computer with a single bus is less expensive than one with several channels, and price was a major motivating factor behind the design of the PDP-11 and its UNIBUS. However, reduced cost is accompanied (as usual) by reduced performance: there are no longer multiple paths along which several I/O devices can transfer data simultaneously.

The first model of the VAX, the model 11/780, is organized around a single bus, as is the PDP-11. On the VAX, this bus is called a Synchronous Backplane Interconnect (SBI) to emphasize the fact that it is a higher performance bus than the UNIBUS, in part because it operates **synchronously** with the CPU. (The UNIBUS, and many lower performance buses, operate **asynchronously** with the CPU; this topic is beyond the scope of the present discussion.) What does it mean for the SBI to be a higher performance bus? It has a higher peak transfer rate and, therefore, (we hope) higher throughput: the PDP-11's UNIBUS is capable of transferring data at a rate of 2.6 MB per second, while the VAX's SBI has a data rate of about 13 MB per second. A schematic view of a PDP-11 and its UNIBUS, or of a VAX and its SBI, is shown in figure 16.16.

Stealing Memory Cycles

Suppose that the CPU has just initiated an I/O transfer from disk to memory, using a disk with a DMA controller. The CPU then continues executing whatever program is in progress. At the same time that the control unit is fetching instructions and storing results in memory, the disk controller is also sending data to memory. The CPU and the disk are making **interleaved** use of the bus and the memory system. In some memory systems, only one memory store or fetch can be made at one time (in the same **memory cycle**); what if both the CPU and the disk want to use the memory at the same instant?

This issue is similar in some ways to that involving simultaneous interrupts. Interrupt conflicts are resolved on the basis of priorities, but memory access conflicts are resolved more simply: the CPU waits, while the disk fetches or stores an item in that memory cycle. Then the CPU can use the next memory cycle--providing that the same device doesn't need it as well and providing that no other DMA device has requested it in the interim. This phenomenon is called **stealing memory cycles** (from the CPU). If it happens too often, the CPU will run very slowly; it will, in effect, be using very slow memory because it will only have access to every n^{th} memory cycle.

Why should the CPU wait while an I/O device gets immediate access to memory? The alternative is to force the I/O device to wait, and this could lead to data loss. Even a slow device such as a floppy disk can transfer one byte about every 30 sec; some DMA devices can transfer a byte every .5 sec. If a read from disk is in progress, and the disk has a byte to store in memory but cannot gain access to memory fast enough, then the next byte being transferred by the disk would overwrite the current byte (in the disk's DBR) before it can be stored in memory. Data overrun from a disk requires that we wait one whole disk revolution to retrieve the lost data; for a disk rotating at 3600 RPM, one revolution takes nearly 17,000 sec. Therefore, it seems wiser to force the CPU to pause for a memory cycle every .5 second rather than wait several thousand microseconds to reread or rewrite a disk sector. Missing a byte on tape would take even longer, because repositioning operations for a tape are considerably slower than those for a disk.

In order to decrease cycle stealing without increasing the likelihood of data overrun, controllers for high-performance disk drives often have a considerable amount of *buffer memory* in which data just transferred from the disk can be stored. The data can then be transferred from the controller's memory to the computer system's memory at memory speed--which is higher than disk speed--and reduce the number of memory cycles needed by the disk and, therefore, unavailable to the CPU.

Transferring all data and instructions over one shared path (a single bus) can result in the bus becoming a bottleneck for overall system performance. Thus, some of the higher performance VAXes-- the 8600/8650 and the 8800 models--achieve higher performance because they have multiple buses. For example, the 8600/8650 models have two buses: one from the CPU to memory and one from the CPU to I/O device controllers (a special part of the control unit, called the *M Box,* performs the necessary coordination of CPU and I/O demands on memory). The highest performance VAXes (the 8500, 8550, and 8800 series) also have different buses for communication with memory and I/O devices. They use a VAXBI bus (with a data-transfer rate of about 13 MB/sec) for I/O devices, but they have a much higher speed bus, the NMI bus, between the CPU and memory system. These high performance VAXes can read 71 MB/sec from memory, and they can write 59 MB/sec to memory.

Analog Data

All the I/O we have discussed so far involves digital data. Most naturally occurring phenomena, however, are analog in nature. How can a computer which performs all operations on digital values use analog inputs or produce analog outputs? How can a computer sense that a temperature is too high or that a seismic tremor is of a particular magnitude? How can a computer make a subway car go faster or slower?

The answer to these questions comes in the form of two black boxes. One box converts mechanical movement to an electrical signal and is called a **transducer.** The second device, when it converts analog information to its digital equivalent, is called an **analog-to-digital converter** (or ADC, or A-to-D); when it converts digital information to its analog equivalent, it is called a **digital-to-analog converter** (or DAC, or D-to-A). Transducers may be built in any of a variety of ways; ultimately, however, a transducer produces a voltage level, which is the input to an ADC. Conceptually, this transformation is similar to the one we saw when we converted ASCII coded digit strings into their binary, numeric equivalents.

Any quantity that can be measured can be converted into a voltage level proportional to the measured value. Temperature, weight, speed, sound level, brightness, vibration, humidity--these are just a few of the quantities that can be processed by a computer. An analog input reaches the CPU after it has been converted to a binary number (often 12 or 16 bits long); the ADC *samples* the variable it is measuring at a particular rate, and it sends a binary number to the CPU at that sampling rate. When we write programs that deal with analog data, we must know the correspondence between the high and low input values and the measured variable, and how the digital numbers produced by the ADC correspond to changes in the measured variable. The programming for analog input is otherwise similar to that for character-oriented input--provided that we have confidence concerning the consistency between the analog data source and the (converted) digital input.

One recent application of analog-to-digital conversion is the compact disk (CD) music format: the analog output of one or more microphone(s) (the transducer) is sampled at a sufficiently high rate (we hope), and that analog output is converted to a digital signal, which is stored as a series of hole/no-hole "bits" on an optical disk. When we play a CD, the digital information is read from the surface of the disk, converted back to analog form, amplified, and used to drive speakers which, in turn, produce air movement that closely matches the air movement that the microphone originally converted into an analog signal.

Digital I/O

It may seem strange to be discussing *digital* I/O on a digital computer, as if it were a special case--what else have we been discussing all along? The phrase "digital I/O" is used for what we might otherwise call *logical* I/O. We speak of digital I/O when the data transferred are independent single-bit values. A typical digital input interface may have 16 signal lines connected to it. Suppose that each input line is connected to an intrusion detector (for example, a piece of silver foil glued to a window). If an intrusion detector is triggered (by a burglar?), the signal line connected to it changes its state; the digital I/O interface senses this and requests an interrupt. The interface's interrupt handler will then examine the interface's 16-bit buffer to see which of the signal lines went high (or low).

A counter watching some experiment can be connected as a digital input source. Whenever the counter reaches a preset value, it sends a signal on its digital input line to the CPU and resets itself; the CPU increments the contents of some memory location. In this way, a computer only has to deal with each nth occurrence of a frequent event; responsibility for handling the event at its high rate is *off-loaded* to a special piece of hardware--the counter--which the CPU services only periodically.

Digital outputs often control other switches (relays). A digital output signal is usually too weak to do any useful work directly, but it is adequate for controlling a relay, which is a switch that can, in turn, control as powerful an electric source as we might wish. For instance, a computer controlled parking lot gate system uses digital outputs to raise an access gate. A sensor in the roadway detects that a vehicle has gone beyond the gate, and it sends a digital input signal so that the CPU can in turn send a digital output signal to lower the gate. From the programming point of view, digital I/O is also similar to byte-at-a-time character I/O. The exceptions are that several bytes may be involved, and that no character code is used; the data items are merely strings of bits.

Summary

We have seen how high-speed data transfers require reducing the CPU's involvement from handling one interrupt per *byte* of data transferred to handling one interrupt per *block* of data transferred. Data are transferred directly to memory from the device, or to the device from memory, when the I/O device has a **Direct Memory Access** (DMA) controller. Two major categories of device which typically have DMA controllers are the **sequential access** and the **direct access** devices.

The most commonly used of the sequential access devices is the industry-compatible magnetic tape drive. ICMT tapes and tape drives are characterized by their recording density (bpi), tape speed (ips) and record (block) sizes. The average access time to a tape record is measured in minutes; sequential access to tape records is much faster than that.

The magnetic disk is the most common type of direct access storage device. As distinct from most tapes, it is designed to support update-in-place. As with tapes, disks are not code sensitive, so binary information can be stored on them. The major physical characteristics of a disk are the number of recording surfaces, the number of tracks per surface, the number of sectors per track, the number of bytes per sector, the rotation speed (rpm), and the single track, maximum, and average seek times.

We also discussed several measures of performance. These included **turnaround time, throughput, response time,** and the number of concurrent users.

The processing of **analog data** is made possible by use of an **analog-to-digital converter.** Conversely, a computer can send analog signals to a device by using a **digital-to-analog converter.** From the programmer's point of view, handling analog I/O is not much different from handling character I/O. Similarly, **digital I/O,** in which bits are treated as independent logical signals, is also much like character I/O.

The role of I/O channels in supporting high speed data transfers was discussed and contrasted with bus-organized computers such as the PDP-11 and VAX. We saw, however, that the earlier VAX models' SBI has been replaced by multiple buses--this is reminiscent of the I/O channels of other computers.

Exercises for Chapter 16

1. An application program takes 50 milliseconds to process a 100 character record, once the record is in memory. Characters can be read from a device at the rate of 1,000 characters per second.

    a. How long will it take to read and process 20 records using busy-wait input?
    b. How long will it take to read and process 20 records using interrupts and direct memory access input?

2. Outline the steps necessary to handle an interrupt for a disk controller; be sure to consider errors that might occur. Then, if you have access to the reference manual for a disk controller, see if you have thought of everything you should have.

3. True or False?

    a. An interrupt handler cannot call a subroutine.
    b. DMA devices have higher data rates than non-DMA devices.
    c. Array descriptors or dope vectors are used to speed up array references.
    d. The average seek time for a fixed-head disk is typically between 10 and 50 milliseconds.
    e. An interrupt handler can never be interrupted.
    f. Latency time is virtually eliminated with fixed-head disks.
    g. The highest interrupt priority is automatically assigned to the device that interrupts most frequently.
    h. Nested macro definitions usually reduce a program's memory requirements.

4. If a program is run a second time with exactly the same results, which of the following is true?

    a. All I/O interrupts must occur at exactly the same points in the program;
    b. All non-I/O interrupts must occur at exactly the same points in the program;
    c. Both (a) and (b).
    d. Neither (a) nor (b).

5.   At the beginning of this chapter, we discussed saving the PC and PSL to execute an interrupt handler and then restoring them. Explain why saving them requires two memory references, but restoring them requires three memory references.

6.   It is common practice to copy periodically all the information from a computer system's disks onto magnetic tapes, for secure storage elsewhere. This practice is called creating **backup files.** Suppose you created backup files once a week. Assuming that it takes one minute to mount a magnetic tape (place it on a tape drive), and five minutes to rewind and remove a magnetic tape, how long would the backup operation take, given the following configurations, if you used 512-byte records:

a.   One 800 bpi, 45 ips tape drive; two RA60 disks
b.   Same tape and drive; one RA82 disk
c.   One 1600 bpi, 75 ips tape drive; four RA60 disks
d.   One 6250 bpi, 125 ips tape drive; four RA82 disks

7.   Recalculate the answers to the previous problem, assuming that 16 KB records are written on the tape.

8.   At some installations, creating backup tapes takes significantly longer than the preceding calculations suggest it should. What operation may be performed in conjunction with the backup that would be worth the extra time?

9.   Suppose that a system that supports spooling has 10,000 records of 80 characters each in the spool input file, and 4,000 print lines of 132 characters each in the spool output file. Spool files on this system are maintained on a disk with 512 byte sectors.

a.   Calculate the number of sectors required for the spool files with a blocking factor of 1.
b.   How many sectors are required for the spool files if they use 1 KB physical records? What is the blocking factor in this case?

■ 17 ■

Selected Topics

Introduction

We will discuss a number of topics in this chapter; some of them are primarily software oriented, and others are more architecture oriented. We will see that each one contributes to our understanding of computers and computing.

Variable-Length Macros

All the macros we have written so far have had predictable lengths. Consider, for example, a macro to multiply its argument by 4:

```
.MACRO FOUR X
ASHL #2, X, X
.ENDM FOUR
```

If invoked as FOUR R0, this macro will be expanded to the single line, ASHL #2, R0, R0--as indicated by the body of the macro. This is a fixed-length macro. What if we wanted to generate, at assemble time, varying numbers of instructions or directives? Suppose, for example, we have a program in which we save various combinations of registers at different times. We could define a set of fixed-length register-saving macros--each of which saves one of the combinations of registers we may wish to save--and use the appropriate macro at the appropriate place.

However, there is a better way: we can use a conditional assembly directive *within* the macro definition, and have the assembler expand the macro with different replacement texts, depending on the value of the conditional assembly variable. For example:

```
.MACRO SAVE NUM
.IF EQUAL NUM-1
        MOVL R1, -(SP)
.ENDC
;else
.IF EQUAL NUM-2
        MOVL R1, -(SP)
        MOVL R2, -(SP)
.ENDC
.ENDM SAVE
```

Then, the two valid invocations of this macro, and their corresponding expansions, are:

Invocation		Expansion
SAVE 1	→	MOVL R1, –(SP)
SAVE 2	→	MOVL R1, –(SP)
		MOVL R2, –(SP)

383

In the general case, we could use a sequence of mutually exclusive conditional assembly blocks within a macro definition:

```
.MACRO M ARG
.IF EQUAL ARG-1
    Block 1
.ENDC
;else
.IF EQUAL ARG-2
    Block 2
.ENDC
;else, some more conditions
.IF EQUAL ARG-n
    Block n
.ENDC
.ENDM M
```

In this example, we use the formal parameter ARG to select which statements to include and which to exclude when the macro is expanded. In the following example, we will examine ways to extend this idea of variable-length macros; in the course of our examination, we will also introduce some new assembler directives.

Consider writing a debugging procedure, HELP. We would like it to display (in hexadecimal, probably) the address and the contents of each memory location in its argument list; we'll use a procedure call instruction, and the argument pointer will contain the address of the number of memory locations to examine. Some typical calls to HELP are:

```
A:    PUSHL X1
      CALLS #1, HELP
      ;do other work
B:    PUSHL Y1
      PUSHL Y2
      CALLS #2, HELP
```

The first call, at A, will display X1 and (X1); the second call, at B, will display Y1, (Y1), Y2, and (Y2). We could control the inclusion of these subroutine calls by using a conditional assembly block:

```
SWITCH = 1   ;include debug code
;some code
.IF NOT_EQUAL SWITCH
    PUSHL X1
    CALLS #1, HELP
.ENDC
;some more code
.IF NOT_EQUAL SWITCH
    PUSHL Y1
    PUSHL Y2
    CALLS #2, HELP
.ENDC
;continue
```

We may find ourselves writing these sets of statements frequently and decide to create a macro,

HELPM:

```
.MACRO HELPM NUM, A, B, C, D, E
PUSHL A
PUSHL B
PUSHL C
PUSHL D
PUSHL E
CALLS #NUM, HELP
.ENDM HELPM
```

Then, the previous code sequence becomes:

```
SWITCH = 1    ;include debug code
;some code
.IF NOT_EQUAL SWITCH
    HELPM 1, X1
.ENDC
;other code
.IF NOT_EQUAL SWITCH
    HELPM, 2, Y1, Y2
.ENDC
;continue
```

Unfortunately, this will not work: we have defined macro HELPM with six arguments, but we have invoked it with two and three arguments. The assembler doesn't object when we invoke a macro with too few arguments, but it *does* object when a PUSHL instruction has no operand--which is what will happen to the last four and three PUSHL instructions in the above two invocations of HELPM. What can we do?

The .IRP Directive

The .IRP directive allows us to create an **indefinite repeat** block. It has a single formal argument, and replaces it once for each of a list of actual arguments. The format of the .IRP directive is:

```
.IRP symbol, <argument list>
    block of text
.ENDR
```

The symbol is the formal argument, and the argument list contains the actual arguments, separated by commas and surrounded by angle brackets. The block of text is repeated once for each argument in the argument list; for each repetition, a different actual argument is substituted for each occurrence of the formal argument.

Let's see how we can use this directive to solve our problem. If we wish to save registers, we can use the .IRP directive in a very simple manner. To save R1 and R2, we write:

```
.IRP X, <R1, R2>
    PUSHL X
.ENDR
```

The assembler generates

        PUSHL R1
        PUSHL R2

If we write

        .IRP X <R1, R2, R3, R4, R5, SUM>
            PUSHL X
        .ENDR

then the assembler will generate code to push the contents of 5 registers and 1 memory location on the stack.

   To return to our debugging macro, we can rewrite it as HELP2, using the .IRP directive, as follows:

        .MACRO HELP2 NUM, LIST
        .IRP EACH, <LIST>
            PUSHL EACH
        .ENDR
        CALLS #NUM, HELP
        .ENDM

If we wish to invoke the macro to provide us with debugging information concerning X1, X2, and X3, we type

        D: HELP2   3, <X1, X2, X3>

The assembler expands this to

        .IRP EACH <X1, X2, X3>
            PUSHL EACH
        .ENDR
        CALLS #3, HELP

The repeat block is then *expanded,* and so machine language is ultimately generated for the following assembly language statements:

        PUSHL X1
        PUSHL X2
        PUSHL X3
        CALLS #3, HELP

This is, of course, exactly what we wanted in the first place: it has exactly the correct number of PUSHL instructions--one for each argument in LIST.

   Note that the macro was invoked with the actual arguments to the .IRP directive enclosed by angle brackets (< and >). This may seem redundant, since the definition of HELP2 included the angle brackets in the argument list of the .IRP directive. It is necessary to use the brackets, however, because whenever they are used to provide an argument to a macro, the assembler strips off the outermost pair as expansion proceeds to the next level of nested macros (or directives such as .IRP, which have their own arguments). Thus, if we define HELP2 without brackets, as follows:

```
.MACRO HELP2 NUM, LIST
.IRP EACH, LIST
        PUSHL EACH
.ENDR
CALLS #NUM, HELP
.ENDM
```

then the correct invocation is with *two* pairs of brackets:

```
HELP2 NUM, < <X1, X2, X3> >
```

The assembler will strip off the first pair of brackets when it expands the macro HELP2, but there will still be one pair of brackets left, for the .IRP directive--as there should be.

The .IIF Directive

We have omitted the conditional assembly block in the version of our debugging macro that uses the .IRP directive. We can rewrite it in a straightforward way, merely substituting our new HELP2 macro for our previous HELPM one, but we can also use the .IIF directive. .IIF is an **Immediate .IF**; it is called *immediate* because it is for one-line conditional blocks, and (therefore) needs no terminating .ENDC. The general form of .IIF is

```
.IIF condition, argument(s), statement
```

The conditions used with the .IIF directive are the same ones used with the .IF directive; they were described in chapter 15 (figure 15.1). The conditional block for .IIF is *statement*, which must be on the same line as the directive, condition, and argument(s). The statement may include a label, and the line with the .IIF directive may also have a label. For example, consider the following two .IIF statements:

(a)	(b)
ABC: .IIF NOT_EQUAL, XYZ, HALT	.IIF NOT_EQUAL XYZ, ABC: HALT

They will both produce the HALT instruction, or nothing at all, depending on the assemble-time value of XYZ. However, there is a subtle difference between them: in case (*a*), the label ABC will always appear in the symbol table, while in case (*b*), ABC will only appear if XYZ has a nonzero value.

If we apply this new directive to our debugging macro, we can define yet another macro, HELP3, as follows:

```
.MACRO HELP3 NUM, LIST
.IIF NOT_EQUAL SWITCH, HELP2 NUM, LIST
.ENDM
```

This may be a little obscure (as macro invocations within macro definitions tend to be); we can also write it as follows:

```
        .MACRO HELP3 NUM, LIST
        .IF NOT_EQUAL SWITCH
            .IRP EACH, <LIST>
            PUSHL EACH
            .ENDR
            CALLS #NUM, HELP
        .ENDC
        .ENDM
```

The two versions of HELP3 generate the same code; what would happen if they (accidentally) both appeared in the same source file--would the assembler complain? No: it would use the first definition until it encountered the second definition, at which point it would redefine the macro, and begin using the second definition.

Note that HELP3 is a variable-length macro, and that it calls a procedure, HELP, with a variable number of arguments. It is not difficult to write a procedure that works correctly with a variable number of arguments. Recall that both the CALLS and CALLG instructions initialize the argument point (R12, or AP) to contain the address of the argument list--and the first longword of such an argument list contains the number of arguments following it in the list.

Other Assembler Features

Many of the features we will discuss in this section are used primarily by system programmers. Those readers who expect to be primarily *users* will probably never need to use them. We discuss them so that--should the occasion arise--they will be part of our programming repertoire.

Assembler-Generated Labels

It is sometimes useful, and sometimes necessary, to use labels within a macro definition. Suppose we use the macro, MX, as part of the definition of another macro, SAM:

```
        .MACRO SAM A, B, C
        MOVL A, R0
        BEQL HERE
        MX B                        ;nested macro invocation
HERE:   MOVL R0, C
        .ENDM SAM
```

If we invoke SAM more than once, the assembler will complain that HERE is multiply defined. We could try using a local label, say 2$, rather than HERE. But we would still run the risk of the macro's use of 2$ conflicting with other uses of 2$ in the surrounding code. We might think that this is exactly the place to address the location counter by its name, and use the (dangerous) format, ".+n". However, even this may not work: what if the length of MX (the number of bytes of machine language generated by its expansion) depends on the value of B at the time that SAM is invoked?

We could solve this problem by making HERE a formal argument of the macro: we could redefine SAM as SAMMY, as follows:

```
              .MACRO SAM A, B, C
              MOVL A, R0
              BEQL HERE
              MX B                         ;nested macro invocation
HERE:         MOVL R0, C
              .ENDM SAM
```

However, now each invocation of SAMMY will require us to provide an additional argument--a symbolic label that is not otherwise being used. We could write

```
SAMMY X, Y, Z, NNN
;other code
SAMMY P, Q, R, MMM
;continue
```

We have avoided one problem and created another one--just the problem that local labels are supposed to eliminate. We can do better, because Macro can create local labels for us.

If we precede a macro's formal argument with the character "?," nothing unusual will happen unless we invoke the macro without specifying an actual argument for that formal argument. In that case, the assembler will assign a value to that argument for us: it will choose the next available local label in the range 30000$, 30001$, . . . , 65535$. Each occurrence of the formal argument in the replacement text of the macro will be replaced by the same local label when the macro is expanded. What makes a local label *available*? The fact that it has not yet been used. Therefore, if we have several different formal arguments preceded by "?," the assembler will generate a new local label for each one--if we don't provide an actual argument when the macro is invoked. Thus, we can rewrite the SAMMY macro as follows:

```
              .MACRO SAMMY A, B, C, ?HERE ;note the "?"
              MOVL A, R0
              BEQL HERE                    ;no question mark
              MX B                         ;nested macro invocation
HERE:         MOVL R0, C                   ;no question mark
              .ENDM SAMMY
```

Notice that the "?" is used only in the list of formal arguments, on the .MACRO line. Each new invocation of a macro which needs assembler-generated labels will get a new value between 30000$ and 65535$. When the list is exhausted, the assembler will start over again with 30000$.

The .REPEAT Directive

The .REPEAT directive is related to the .IRP directive: .IRP is used to repeat a block of statements an *indefinite* (variable) number of times--once for each argument in its argument list; .REPEAT is used to repeat a block of statements a specified number of times--specified by its argument. The format of .REPEAT is similar to .IRP:

```
.REPEAT expression
     block of text
.ENDR
```

The argument, *expression,* must have an assemble-time value. Consider the following example:

```
.REPEAT 3
    .WORD 0
.ENDR
```

This is a hard way of writing the equivalent,

```
.WORD 0, 0, 0
```

However, any legal statement may appear in a repeat block; therefore, we can also write

```
.REPEAT 3
    .LONG N
    N = N + 4
.ENDR
```

If N had the value 10_{16} prior to the assembler's encountering the .REPEAT directive, then the repeat block will expand to

```
.LONG 10      ;N   =    10 before, 14 after
.LONG 14      ;N   =    14 before, 18 after
.LONG 18      ;N   =    18 before, 1C after
```

The argument to .REPEAT may be a more complicated expression. If, for example, we wrote

```
.REPEAT M-2
    BLAH
.ENDR
```

then the assembler will duplicate BLAH M-2 times. If M-2 evaluates to 0 or less, then the repeat block will not be assembled at all.

We can use the .REPEAT directive as part of a macro definition. For example, we can use a simple macro, with a repeat block, to create the header for subroutines that we write:

```
;*****************************
;*****************************
;*****************************
;*
;* Subroutine TITLE
;*
;*****************************
;*****************************
;*****************************
```

The following macro would produce that header:

```
.MACRO SUBHEADER TITLE
.REPEAT 3
;******************************
.ENDR
;*
;* Subroutine TITLE
;*
.REPEAT 3
;******************************
.ENDR
.ENDM SUBHEADER
```

Then, if we use the .SHOW ME directive, the assembler will list the expansion of the macro each time we use it, and we will have a subroutine header similar to the one shown, with minimal typing. Why will the header only be *similar* to the one shown? Because the assembler lists each step in the expansion of the macro, so we will see, in addition to the lines of the header, the text of the macro, including the .REPEAT directive and the text of its repeat block before the repeat block has been repeated.

This example may not be a useful one for writing programs: most editors provide for duplicating lines as easily (or, almost as easily) as invoking a macro, and we may not be pleased with the extra output for our subroutine headers. However, the example emphasizes the fact that macro expansion is merely a process of text substitution. The above macro generates *nothing* that exists at run time; in fact, all of its replacement text is commented out, and so hardly even exists after the macro has been expanded. It exists only to the extent that the assembler generates it, and copies it into the listing file; the assembler never *processes* it in any other way.

Nested Macro Definitions

The body of a macro may contain arbitrary (almost) text--it may, for example, contain another macro definition. Haven't we already seen several examples of a macro containing another macro? We have seen macro definitions that contain the *invocation* of previously defined macros, but here we are talking about a macro definition that contains the *definition* of another macro; the two things are very different.

Suppose we are writing macro definitions to facilitate the use of the mathematical subroutine library. The library contains subroutines with entry point names such as SIN, COS, TAN, etc. for mathematical functions sine, cosine, tangent, and so on. The mathematical library might have 150 functions, each with its own entry point in the library. So, we begin defining the following macros:

```
.MACRO SIN A
PUSHL A
CALLS #1, SIN
.ENDM SIN
;
.MACRO COS B
PUSHL B
CALLS #1, COS
.ENDM COS
```

```
;
            .MACRO TAN C
            PUSHL C
            CALLS #1, TAN
            .ENDM TAN
```

After a while, we realize that there is no need to use different formal argument names (A, B, C) for each macro, so we write:

```
            .MACRO SIN X
            PUSHL X
            CALLS #1, SIN
            .ENDM SIN
;
            .MACRO COS X
            PUSHL X
            CALLS #1, COS
        .ENDM COS
;
            .MACRO TAN X
            PUSHL X
            CALLS #1, TAN
            .ENDM TAN
```

Still later, we realize that these sets of four-line definitions hardly differ from each other at all-- only in those places shown by the bold face text, below:

```
    .MACRO SIN X      .MACRO COS X      .MACRO TAN X
    PUSHL X           PUSHL X           PUSHL X
    CALLS #1, SIN     CALLS #1, COS     CALLS #1, TAN
    .ENDM SIN         .ENDM COS         .ENDM TAN
```

What do we normally do when we have a set of lines which recur frequently and which differ in some systematic fashion? We consider using a macro to generate those lines. So, let's try the following macro:

```
    .MACRO DEFINE NAME
        .MACRO NAME X
        PUSHL X
        CALLS #1, NAME
        .ENDM NAME
    .ENDM DEFINE
```

NAME is a formal argument just as X is a formal argument. When the assembler first sees the definition of the macro DEFINE, it will store that name (and a way to find its replacement text) in the Macro Name Table. If, at some later place in our program, we invoke DEFINE, then the macro will be expanded. If, for example, the following two lines appear in our program,

```
    DEFINE SIN
        .
        .
        .
```

DEFINE COS

.
.
.

then the following text will result from the expansion of these invocations of the macro DEFINE:

```
.MACRO SIN X
PUSHL X
CALLS #1, SIN
.ENDM SIN
```

.
.
.

```
.MACRO COS X
PUSHL X
CALLS #1, COS
.ENDM COS
```

.
.
.

As usual, the assembler processes the code that it generates in expanding a macro. In this case, the assembler is generating some new macro definitions, so it associates the names SIN and COS with their replacement texts and places the names SIN and COS in the Macro Name Table (only when we invoke SIN and COS will the assembler generate the PUSHL and CALLS instructions).

So, we have reduced our writing from 4 lines for each of 150 needed macro definitions--a total of 600 lines--to 6 lines for the macro, plus 150 invocations of DEFINE, for a total of 156 lines. We can, if we wish, let the assembler do even more for us; consider the following macro definition:

```
.MACRO DEFINE2 LIST
.IRP NAME, <LIST>
    DEFINE NAME
.ENDR
.ENDM DEFINE2
```

Now, we can write

```
DEFINE2 <SIN, COS, TAN>
```

and the assembler will generate

```
.IRP NAME, <SIN,COS,TAN>
    DEFINE NAME
.ENDR
```

This, in turn, is expanded to

```
DEFINE SIN
DEFINE COS
DEFINE TAN
```

and that, in turn, generates the definition of the three desired macros.

Recall that each .IRP and .REPEAT must have a corresponding .ENDR, and that each .MACRO must have a matching .ENDM. Forgetting this can be a disaster (relatively speaking): too many .ENDMs or .ENDRs is a minor problem, but too few causes all the text following the missing .ENDM or .ENDR to be included as part of the body of a macro definition or repeat block. Nothing beyond the missing .ENDM or .ENDR will be assembled. Note, also, that the assembler's understanding of which directive is missing may not coincide with ours (this is similar to what happens when we leave out an **end** statement in Pascal).

Tables, Lists, Queues, and Trees

One of the identifying characteristics of an array is uniformity: its elements are alike. Because an array's elements are homogeneous, it is relatively straightforward to calculate the offset of an element (from the beginning of the array), given its subscript(s). A table, on the other hand, has rows and columns, with nonhomogeneous elements. One column of a table, for example, might be a list of names, while another column is a set of addresses. A restaurant menu can be thought of as a table, as shown in figure 17.1. A sales report, with monthly and year-to-date data, may include tables such as the one shown in figure 17.2. As we see, alphabetic entries may vary considerably in length. A simple way to store the item names and monthly sales columns of the table in figure 17.2 is as follows:

```
.ASCII /Nuts                 /
.LONG 12
.ASCII /Bolts                /
.LONG 1
.ASCII /Solid-Fuel Rockets   /
.LONG 8
```

At the cost of setting aside about 20 bytes for each name, we can ensure adequate space is provided for the longest name we anticipate, and provide uniform-length entries to facilitate rapid access. This may work well for small tables, but it would be a disaster for a firm with thousands of products, or for a student record system with a student population in the tens of thousands.

Let us consider packing the names in contiguous bytes and not wasting any space for blanks. Then, the quantities could be paired with *pointers*[1] to the corresponding names. We used this technique in our discussion of a hybrid approach for fast access to a multi-dimensional array's elements; an example applying it to the sales report table is shown in figure 17.3. If we wished to sort this table alphabetically, based on item names, we would leave the names where they are, and simply reorder the item addresses (ITEM1, ITEM2, and ITEM3) as they appear in COLUMN1. The values in COLUMN2, then, should also be reordered, to maintain consistency.

We could avoid moving anything, however, if we created yet another array--one which has its pointers arranged so that, if we follow the first pointer we will find the alphabetically first item. We could create this array as follows:

ORDERED: .ADDRESS ITEM2, ITEM1, ITEM3

---

[1]We can think of an item's address as a pointer to that item, bevause it tells us how to find the item. Higher level languages that support pointers typically implement them as addresses.

Item	Price
Coffee	.50
Tea	.50
Milk shake	1.25
Beer	.90

Figure 17.1 A menu as a table

Item	Monthly sales	Year-to-Date	Goal	% of Goal
Nuts	12	102	114	89
Bolts	1	2	3	67
Solid-Fuel Rockets	8	89	106	84

Figure 17.2 A sales report as a table

```
ITEM1:        .ASCIZ /Nuts/
ITEM2:        .ASCIZ /Bolts/
ITEM3:        .ASCIZ /Solid-Fuel Rockets/
;
TABLE:
COLUMN1:      .ADDRESS ITEM1, ITEM2, ITEM3      ;addresses of items
COLUMN2:      .LONG 12, 1, 8                     ;monthly sales
```

Figure 17.3 Using row addresses

Lists

What we have just constructed above, in our array of pointers, is a kind of **list**. It is only a kind of list because we stored the pointers in an array; with an array, we know where the *next* element is because its address is the address of the memory location immediately following that of the *current* element. In a list, however, the next element could be anywhere: we don't just use a pointer to find the next element--we use a pointer to find the next pointer, as well.

A **linked list** is made of a series of **nodes** (or elements), each of which contains two items: a **data field** and a **pointer**. The data field contains the data that we care about; this is the equivalent of an array element. The pointer is the address of the next node in the list. With an array, we must know the *name* of the array (the address of its first element) and how large each element is (in the general case, we must also know well how many dimensions an array has and the size of each dimension). With a linked list, all we need to know is the address of its first node, which is the **head** of the list (the last node is called the **tail**) and where in each node the pointer to the next node is stored. We can find any other node by following a series of pointers: the head pointer tells us where the head of the list is; that node's pointer tells us where the next item is; the pointer in the next item tells us where *its* next item is, and so on. We must know when we get to the end of a list;

typically, the tail element's pointer contains a special value which we understand to mean that there are no more elements in the list. In our examples, we will store 0 as the end-of-list indicator; we must remember, however, that there is nothing magic about 0: it is just as good an address as any other 32-bit number. We could just as well use $FFFFFFFF_{16}$, or 80000000_{16}; we must make sure, however, that whatever programs we write understand the difference between this special value and all others.[2] Depending on how we use a list, we may wish to keep track of the tail as well as the head.

The most important feature of a list is that its nodes need not occupy consecutive memory locations. We do not need a large block of contiguous memory to store a large linked list, since each node needs only enough space for a single node. This is the reason that there is a pointer in each node: each node points to its successor node--wherever it may be. Note, however, that we pay a price for this flexibility: we need to store only data in an array, while we must store both data and the address of the next node in a linked list.

A linked list can be used in place of an array: instead of having the array RR:

    RR: .LONG 12, 1, 8

we could construct a one-way linked list, LIST:

    LIST: .LONG 12, 1$;value, pointer
    1$:   .LONG 1, 2$;value, pointer
    2$:   .LONG 8, 0   ;value, pointer

The pointer to the head of this list will have the value of LIST; if we also store a pointer to the tail of the list, it will have the value of 2$. We can draw the list schematically, as shown in figure 17.4.

Why use a linked list? There is no reason to, if an array will work just as well. However, if we expect that the number of items we must store will change at run time, then we might wish to use a list. Finding an element in an array is straightforward if we know its subscript(s); finding an element in a linked list is time-consuming because we must follow a series of pointers, one at a time. However, if we wish to insert or delete an item from an array, we must move all of the items following a new one over to make room for it, or move all of the items following a deleted one over so there is no "hole" where it was; insertion and deletion are much simpler in a linked list.

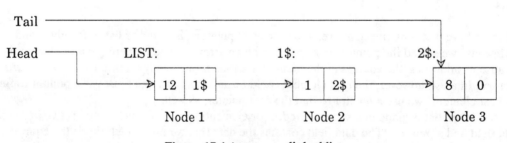

Figure 17.4 A one-way linked list

---

[2]Pascal's *nil* is a high-level implementation of this idea of a special value that indicates the absence of a next element.

Before insertion:

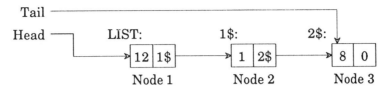

After insertion:

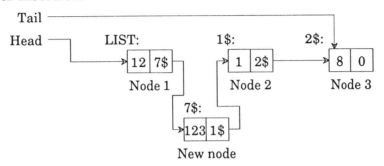

Figure 17.5 Inserting a new node in a linked list

Consider inserting a node with the value 123, immediately following the first node of our example list, LIST. Before insertion, our list looks as follows (as we have already seen):

```
LIST:     .LONG 12, 1$      ;value, pointer
1$:       .LONG 1, 2$       ;value, pointer
2$:       .LONG 8, 0        ;value, pointer
```

After inserting the new node, our list looks like this:

```
LIST:     .LONG 12, 7$      ;value, pointer
1$:       .LONG 1, 2$       ;value, pointer
2$:       .LONG 8, 0        ;value, pointer
;
7$:       .LONG 123, 1$     ;value, pointer (new node follows node 1)
```

We can use any available space to store the new node; we initialize its data field to 123 and its pointer field to the same value that is in the first node's pointer field, and then we update the first node's pointer field so that it points to the new node. Schematically, this is shown in figure 17.5.

Deleting a node is also simple: we need only find the node to be deleted and the node *before* that one, and change the pointer field in the node before the node to be deleted so that it points to the node *after* the node to be deleted. We can now reuse the memory that was allocated to the node that was just deleted. Keeping track of memory that is available to allocate new nodes is often done by using a list called a **free list**--so called because it tells us which memory locations are in use and which are *free*. When we delete a node from a list we don't just "throw it away"; we replace it on the free list, so we can reuse it when we need to create (and insert) a new node.

Finding an item in a one-way linked list requires searching each node, beginning with the head node; if we forget to keep track of the node preceding the one we wish to delete, we must start

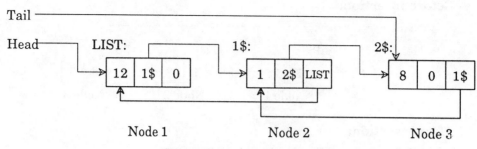

Figure 17.6 A two-way linked list

again at the beginning to find it. We can only traverse a one-way linked list in one direction--forward, from head to tail (this is why it is called a *one* way linked list). In some cases, it is useful to be able to traverse the list in both directions; in these cases, we create a **two-way linked list.** Each node in a two-way linked list has three fields: a data field, and *two* pointers--one to the node after it (the *forward* pointer), and one to the node *preceding* it (the *backward* pointer).

We can modify the one-way linked list of our examples to make a two-way linked list as follows:

```
LIST:     .LONG 12, 1$, 0      ;value, forward pointer, backward pointer
1$:       .LONG 1, 2$, LIST    ;value, forward pointer, backward pointer
2$:       .LONG 8, 0, 1$       ;value, forward pointer, backward pointer
```

Schematically, we can draw a two way linked list as shown in figure 17.6. Note that, once again, we pay--with increased memory requirements--for the additional flexibility: with a one-way linked list, each node stores only one address--that of the next node; with a two-way linked list, each node stores two addresses--that of the next node and that of the previous node. With a two-way linked list, we typically keep track of both the head and the tail of the list; they may well change, at run time, as items are inserted into the list and deleted from it.

Queues

A **queue** is the reverse of a stack: a stack obeys the Last In/First Out (LIFO) discipline, while a queue obeys the First In/First Out (FIFO) discipline (in everyday life, we call this "waiting in line"). A queue is shown schematically in figure 17.7; a queue may be implemented conveniently as a one-way linked list. Items are always inserted into this list at its tail, and items are always removed from the

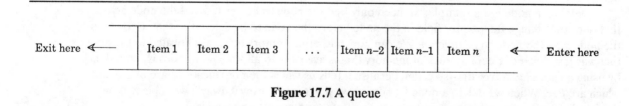

Figure 17.7 A queue

list at its head. One common example of such a queue is a line-printer queue: the spooler maintains a queue of files that are waiting for the line printer, and the file that has been in the queue the longest is the next file that will get printed.

A linked list can also be used to implement a queue whose elements are ordered according to their priority. Suppose that each queue element contains the disk addresses of a print file (it is easier to move the addresses than the files themselves), a priority, and a pointer to the next queue element. Priorities can be assigned to print files according to the urgency of the task, so instead of printing in a First In/First Out order, we will print the file with the highest priority first. In this case, a new item is placed in the queue in order of its priority; if two items have the same priority, we can order them according to time of arrival (FIFO). To insert a new item into the queue, we must search the queue (traverse list) until we find the first item with *lower* priority than the item we wish to insert. The new item goes immediately *before* this item, or immediately *after* the last item with a priority higher than or equal to that of the item we wish to insert.

If we implement a queue as a one-way linked list and arrange for the pointer of the last node of the queue to point to the first node of the queue, we can create a **circular queue.** If we implement a queue as a two-way linked list, then we create a circular queue by having the forward pointer of the last node point to the first node, and the backward pointer of the first node point to the last node. With a circular queue, we need keep track of only the head of the queue, since we can easily find the tail from the head (and the head from the tail--which is impossible with a one-way linked list that is *not* circular).

The QUEUE Instructions

Queues are useful for a variety of operating system functions (such as spooling print files). The VAX has a series of instructions for inserting and deleting items into queues that are implemented as circular, two-way linked lists. There are queue instructions for two types of queues: **absolute queues,** where the forward and backward pointers specify the following and preceding elements by their addresses; and **self-relative queues,** where the forward and backward pointers specify the following and preceding elements by their displacement from the current element. The forward and backward pointers of both types of queues are longwords; the forward pointer is the first (lowest address) longword of a queue element and the backward pointer is the second (next lowest address) longword of a queue element. Both types of queues are specified by a **header,** which contains a forward pointer to the queue's head and a backward pointer to the queue's tail; the forward pointer of the tail element of the queue points to the queue's header.

The VAX queue instructions allow insertion and deletion in arbitrary items of an absolute queue, but only at the head and tail of a self-relative queue. The queue instructions are complex instructions; they are summarized in figure 17.8, but the interested reader is referred to the *Architecture Reference Manual* for a more complete description of their function and use.

Instruction	Mnemonic	Opcode
Insert at queue head	INSQHI ENTRY, HEADER	5C
Insert at queue tail	INSQTI ENTRY, HEADER	5D
Remove from queue head	REMQHI ENTRY, ADDRESS	5E
Remove from queue tail	REMQTI ENTRY, ADDRESS	5F
Insert entry in queue	INSQUE ENTRY, PREDECESSOR	0E
Remove entry from queue	REMQUE ENTRY, ADDRESS	0F

Figure 17.8 Queue instruction summary

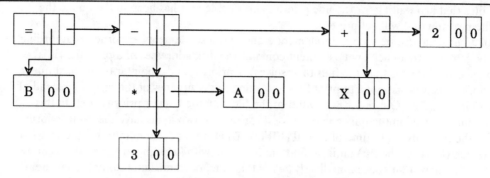

Figure 17.9 A two-dimensional linked list

Two-Dimensional Linked Lists

Up to now, we have been considering one-dimensional linked lists: each node has at most a single successor and a single predecessor. A two-dimensional linked list can be used to represent two-dimensional structures. When we consider the expression $B = 3 * A - (X + 2)$ as an ASCII character string, we think of it as a one dimensional array of bytes. But we can also interpret it as an arithmetic statement in a high-level programming language, with the meaning "Multiply the current value of A by 3, subtract from that product the sum of the current value of X and 2, and store that difference in location B." In this case, we might represent the expression, and its order of evaluation, as the two-dimensional linked list shown in figure 17.9.

This two-dimensional linked list uses two forward pointers per node; this is a a linked list representation of a data structure that computer scientists are particularly fond of. It is called a **binary tree**; each node in a binary tree can have at most two successor nodes. Figure 17.10 represents the arithmetic expression shown as a two-dimensional linked list in figure 17.9 as a binary tree. A binary tree consists of a finite set of nodes. This set may be empty, or it may consist of a **root node,** and two disjoint binary trees stemming from this root node (**subtrees**). Since each of the root node's subtrees is a tree, each consists of a set of nodes that may be empty, or may consist of a root node and two disjoint binary trees stemming from this root node. This definition is **recursive--** the term *recurs* in its definition. Some small binary trees are shown in figure 17.11.

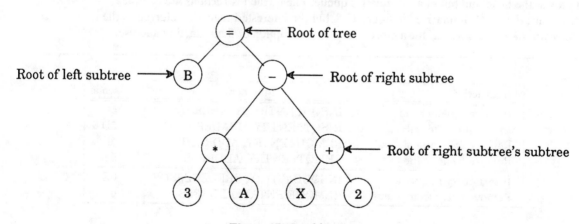

Figure 17.10 A binary tree

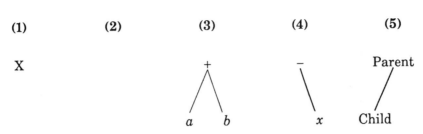

Figure 17.11 Some small binary trees

Recursion

Recursion is important in mathematics. One simple application is to define a function that is vital to probability theory and practice: the **factorial** function. Factorial has one argument, which must be a positive integer. It is common to write *factorial(n)* as *n!*. A common (recursive) definition for *n!* is

$$n! = n * (n\text{-}1)!$$
$$1! = 1$$

We can read this as, "Given some integer, *n,* where $n > 0$, *factorial(n)* is found by multiplying *n* by *factorial* (*n*-1); if *n* is 1, then the value of *factorial* (*n*) is also 1.

We say that something is defined *recursively* when it is defined in terms of itself, in a manner which terminates. If we defined *factorial(n)* as *n * factorial(n*-1), we would be providing a recursive definition that does *not* terminate. However, when we add the terminating condition, *factorial(1)* = 1, we guarantee that, for any integer, *n,* as long as $n > 0$, the sequence *n, n*-1, . . . , 2, 1 is finite. Thus, *factorial(n)* can be evaluated in a finite number of steps, and so the expansion of the definition terminates. We can illustrate the solution of *n!* by tracing the partial calculations:

n!	=	*n * (n*-1)!
(*n*-1)!	=	(*n*-1) * (*n*-2)!
(*n*-2)!	=	(*n*-2) * (*n*-3)!
.		
.		
.		
3!	=	3 * 2!
2!	=	2 * 1!
1!	=	1 (AHA)

Since we know that 1! is 1, we can start reversing our path, and substituting values for expressions:

1! = 1
2! = 2 * 1
3! = 3 * 2
.
.
.
n! = *n * (n*-1)!

Recursion also appears frequently in computing. It is used for at least all of the following:

1.   To define some mathematical functions;
2.   To write recursive subroutines;
3.   To manipulate recursively defined data structures;
4.   To write recursive definitions of macros.

Consider a simple arithmetic expression, such as $a + 2$, or $(b - 2 * (c + 3)$, and so forth. We can create a formal definition for a general arithmetic expression (AE):

1.   A **term** is either a variable, a constant or a parenthesized AE;
2.   An AE is either a term or a signed term or an AE + term or an AE - term.

Leaving out the English, and using | to indicate alternatives, we can write the above AE definition as follows:

1.   Term := variable | constant | (AE)
2.   AE := term | + term | - term | AE + term | AE - term

This is clearly a recursive definition; we have been using (implicitly, most likely) such a definition each time we have evaluated (by hand) expressions such as

   3 * (7 - 2)

As we process this, we say to ourselves, "3 times whatever the (. . .) evaluates to". This is a recursive process.

Recursively Defined Macros

Recall the caution about the consequences of certain typographical errors when we define macros. If, for example, while defining the macro, P, we accidentally wrote

   .MACRO P argument list
   ;macro body
   P operands
   ;more macro body
   .ENDM P

Macro would assume that we were defining P recursively; when we then invoked P, an infinite process would begin, because the P expansion leads to the invocation of P, whose expansion, in turn, leads to another invocation of P, whose expansion leads to yet another invocation of P until the assembler runs out of memory.

   We *can* write recursively defined macros--as long as we remember to provide a terminating condition. The assembler printout in figure 17.12 shows the definition of macro INTEGERS, which recursively generates a series of .BYTE directives with arguments n, n-1, n-2, . . . , 1, 0. Figure 17.12 also shows the macro invoked with the argument 3, and the assembler's output.

```
 00000004  1   .MACRO INTEGERS N                  ;recursive macro
    0004   2   .IIF EQUAL N, .BYTE N              ;terminating condition
    0004   3 ;else, N not 0
    0004   4   .IF NOT_EQUAL N
    0004   5   .BYTE N
    0004   6   INTEGERS N-1
    0004   7   .ENDC
    0004   8   .ENDM INTEGERS
    0004   9   ;
    0004  10   .SHOW ME
    0004  11   INTEGERS 3                         ;invocation
    0004       .IIF EQUAL 3, .BYTE 3              ;terminating condition
    0004     ;else, 3 not 0
00000003  0004       .IF NOT_EQUAL 3
   03   0004       .BYTE 3
         0005       INTEGERS 3-1
         0005       .IIF EQUAL 3-1, .BYTE 3-1      ;terminating condition
         0005     ;else, 3-1 not 0
00000002  0005       .IF NOT_EQUAL 3-1
   02   0005       .BYTE 3-1
         0006       INTEGERS 3-1-1
         0006       .IIF EQUAL 3-1-1, .BYTE 3-1-1  ;terminating condition
         0006     ;else, 3-1-1 not 0
00000001  0006       .IF NOT_EQUAL 3-1-1
   01   0006       .BYTE 3-1-1
         0007       INTEGERS 3-1-1-1
   00   0007       .IIF EQUAL 3-1-1-1, .BYTE 3-1-1-1  ;terminating condition
         0008     ;else, 3-1-1-1 not 0
00000000  0008       .IF NOT_EQUAL 3-1-1-1
         0008       .BYTE 3-1-1-1
         0008       INTEGERS 3-1-1-1-1
         0008       .ENDC
         0008       .ENDC
         0008       .ENDC
         0008       .ENDC
         0008  12   .END
```

Figure 17.12 A recursive macro

Using Binary Trees

Binary trees are common data structures, because they have many uses. One use is to maintain items in a way that facilitates rapid access to them. If we have a fixed number of items, we can store them in an array, then sort them, and locate any item (given some key, k, identifying it) using a **binary search.** With a binary search, we need examine at most n items in an array with 2^n entries; by then we will either have found the item we are looking for, or we will know that it is not in the array. Briefly, a binary search involves looking at the middle element of an array; if its key matches the one we're looking for, then we've found the item. If its key is smaller than the one we're looking for, then we look at the middle item in the upper half of the array; if the middle element's key is larger than the one we're looking for, then we look at the middle item in the lower half of the array. Thus, with each item examined, we either find what we're looking for, or halve the size of the array still to be searched. Given an array of size 2^n, we can halve it only n times before there will be nothing left--and we will either have found what we are looking for or know that it is not in the array.

If binary search on a sorted array is such a good technique, why use a tree? Since an array's elements are stored in consecutive memory locations, we can calculate the address of an element in an array by knowing the array's base address and the element's subscript(s). However, if elements must be stored in consecutive memory locations, then an array has a maximum size; once all the memory locations reserved for the array are full, we can't store any new elements in the array. A tree, on the other hand, is particularly useful for storing items when we don't know how many there will be--or, when we expect items to be frequently inserted and deleted.

Consider the following approach: suppose that items to be inserted arrive in a random sequence; as each item arrives (perhaps because some user has typed it from a keyboard), we construct a binary tree by storing the items such that all nodes in a given node's left subtree have values smaller than any value in that node's right subtree. If numeric items arrive in the sequence 18, 7, 25, 3, 19, we would construct a tree beginning with the first value (18), and add a new node as each of the following items arrives. The growth of our tree is shown as a series of snapshots after each item arrives in figure 17.13. As usual, computer scientists grow trees with the root up and the leaves down.

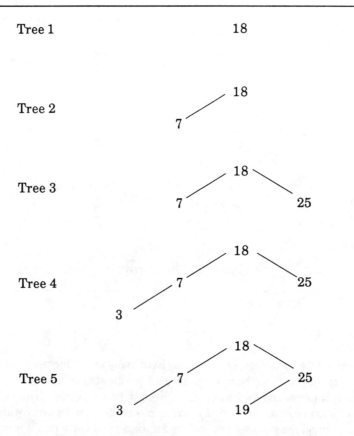

Figure 17.13 Building an ordered binary tree

We can build this tree at assemble time, by writing the following:

```
ROOT:   .LONG 18, 1$, 2$       ;value, left ptr, right ptr
1$:     .LONG 7, 3$, 0
3$:     .LONG 3, 0, 0
2$:     .LONG 25, 5$, 0
5$:     .LONG 19, 0, 0
```

This tree is sorted, and any new item can be inserted in the correct place so that the new tree remains sorted. Lookup is rapid: because of the tree's structure, we compare the key we are searching for with that of the current node, and choose which pointer to follow according to the outcome of this comparison. The best-case performance of a search of a binary tree is the same as a binary search of an array, but its performance can degenerate to that of sequential search of a linear linked list.

After all elements have been inserted into the tree, we can write a recursive subroutine to traverse the tree and print, in numeric order, the key stored in each node. The algorithm that such a subroutine would implement for **in-order** traversal of a binary tree may be stated as follows:

1. Traverse the left subtree and display the node keys;
2. Display the root key;
3. Traverse the right subtree and display the node keys.

Another Example of Recursion

Horizontal tabs are represented by the ASCII character code 09_{16} (Control I). Some CRTs and printers can, upon receipt of a tab character code, space to the next tab stop, but others respond to a tab code as if it were a space code--which, effectively, ignores the tab. Terminals that respond to tabs as we would expect are said to have hardware-supported tabs. With these terminals, tab stops are typically set at columns 9, 17, 25, and so on. Some smarter terminals have soft tabs; we can change their setting if we don't like the default. How does a multi-user operating system deal with a variety of terminals, each of which may have different characteristics? We would like to be able to describe our terminal to the operating system by saying, for example, "I have a VT100," and letting *it* do the work; the alternative is to define a multitude of parameters--such as line length, screen capacity, type of tab support, and so forth. Let's consider, briefly, how an operating system can support tabs on a terminal which ignores them.

The common way to create tabs for a terminal that has no hardware support for them is for the operating system's **terminal driver** to replace each tab code sent by a program to the terminal with the appropriate number of spaces. This can be done iteratively (using a loop and a loop-control variable to count), but it can also be done recursively, as we will soon see. Suppose the tab stops are set at columns 9, 17, 25, and so on. If the string "THIS>IS>A>TEST" were being sent to a CRT, then each ">" (a symbol we are using to indicate the tab code) would be replaced by an appropriate number of blanks. The CRT display would show:

Columns:	1	9	17	25	33	41
	THIS	IS	A	TEST		

The first tab is replaced by four spaces, the next one by six, and so on. Let's outline how the software driver sends output to the terminal:

1.   Get next character (if none left: call end-of-line subroutine)
2.   Examine character.
          not a tab: emit character; increment character count; goto (1).
          found a tab code: call tab subroutine; goto (1)

Tab subroutine:
          Are we already at a tab stop?
              if so, exit.
              if not, emit space code; increment character count; call tab subroutine.

Once we understand the nature of the task, we can describe it in a few lines of English; at this point, writing the recursive subroutine is straightforward:

```
TAB:      CMPB R3, COUNT        ;check for tab stop
          BNEQ 1$               ;if not there, output space
          ;else, done
          RSB
;
1$:       MOVB #^A/ /, (R2)+    ;output one space
          INCB COUNT            ;keep track of how many
          JSB TAB               ;keep processing
          RSB
```

The caller of the TAB subroutine uses R2 as the address in the buffer for the output string it is creating. It uses R3 to specify where the next tab stop should be. The RSB instruction following the JSB instruction may look strange; the intrigued reader is invited to pick a small example and keep track of the stack history as TAB is recursively called and then, returned from.

Cross Assembly

Back in chapter 1, we discussed the possibility of combining the advantages of both multiuser and single-user systems. It is common to prepare, assemble, and test programs on a multiuser **host** computer--taking advantage of the convenient programming environment most multiuser systems offer--with the intention of executing those programs on a single-user **target** computer, to take advantage of the constant response time and dedicated hardware available on a single-user system.

It is straightforward to develop software on one system and run it on another if the CPUs of both systems execute the same instruction set: a **download link** is used to transfer the bytes of the executable program from the host CPU to the target CPU. The link can be implemented in a variety of ways, including as a pair of serial interfaces, with the host's software treating the target CPU as an intelligent terminal. Sometimes executable programs are transferred using a removable storage medium such as a floppy disk. In automobile production, programs (to control automobile fuel injection systems, for example) are stored in Read Only Memory (ROM) chips, which are then plugged into the hundreds of thousands of automobiles that use them.

What if the host and target CPUs execute different instruction sets? Suppose we are developing software on a VAX, but the target is an Intel 8080 microprocessor (the 8080 is a predecessor to Intel's 8086, 8088, 80186, 80286 and 80386 microprocessors). We could write an 8080 assembler, which translates symbolic programs into 8080 object modules, but which itself (the 8080 assembler) executes on a VAX; this kind of program is called a **cross assembler.** If the host and target CPUs execute sufficiently similar instruction sets, we may be able to avoid writing a complete assembler by making careful use of the host computer's macro facility. Consider the following example.

The 8080 has 16-bit addresses for 8-bit data items; its memory is byte addressable. An 8080 ADD instruction has the generic form

    ADD REG

In particular, the use of the ADD instruction with one of 8 registers (R0 through R7)--for example

    ADD R1

should generate the machine language 81_{16}, as a single-byte instruction. At run time, the contents of R1 will be added to the 8080's accumulator register. If we define some macros, we can have VAX Macro seem to understand 8080 instructions:

    .MACRO ADD REG   ;redefining ADD for 8080
    .BYTE ^X80+REG
    .ENDM ADD

We can make life easier for ourselves by using some assemble-time constants:

    REG1 = 1
    REG2 = 2
    REG3 = 3
    REG4 = 4
    REG5 = 5
    REG6 = 6
    REG7 = 7

Now, if we type ADD REG3, the macro will be expanded to .BYTE ^X83, which is just what we want.

VAX Macro does more than just translate assembly language to machine language; it also does some (primitive) assembly language syntax checking. Can we use it to check 8080 syntax, too? There is an assemble-time message function which Macro provides; we can use it for just this purpose. The .ERROR directive prints the message that is its argument; the printing occurs at assemble time, so if we wish to conditionally print an error message (which we do, assuming that we won't *always* use incorrect syntax), we must use conditional assembly directives. For example, we may wish to make sure that we haven't forgotten that the 8080 has only 8 registers (which is easy to do, since the VAX has 16). We could write the following pair of macros to make sure that we know if we do:

    .MACRO ADD REG   ;improved, syntax checking, ADD
    CHECK REG   ;make sure 0 $\leq$ REG $\leq$ 7
    .BYTE ^X80+REG
    .ENDM ADD

CHECK is a macro that generates an assemble-time message (an *error* message) if the argument to ADD is inappropriate as a register name for the 8080. We can define CHECK as follows:

    .MACRO CHECK R ?TEMP   ;check for legal 8080 register
    TEMP = 2
    .IIF GREATER_EQUAL R, TEMP = TEMP-1   ;> 0?
    .IIF LESS_EQUAL <R-^X7>, TEMP = TEMP-1 ;< 0?
    .IIF NOT_EQUAL TEMP, .ERROR; illegal 8080 register use
    .ENDM CHECK

The first .IIF condition subtracts 1 from the (assembler-generated) symbol TEMP only if the register number being checked is not negative. The second .IIF condition subtracts 1 from TEMP only if the register number being checked is not larger than 7. Finally, the third .IIF condition causes the argument of the .ERROR directive to be printed only if TEMP is not equal to 0. TEMP would be 0 if the register number is valid, because it was initialized to 2, decremented to 1 when the register number was found to be greater than 0, and decremented once more to 0 when the register number minus 7 was found to be less than or equal to 0.

If we invoke ADD with the argument 15, and have used the .SHOW ME directive, then the following is an edited excerpt of the assembler printout:

```
ADD   15
CHECK 15
30000$ = 2
%MACRO-E-GENERR, Generated ERROR:  illegal 8080 register use
```

The byte $8F_{16}$ is generated, even though the error message is printed; this is because only the .ERROR directive is in the range of the .IIF directive in the CHECK macro. If we had not used the .SHOW ME, our listing would have included only the line

```
%MACRO-E-GENERR, Generated ERROR:  illegal 8080 register use
```

In addition, the assembler will report the "Generated ERROR," along with any other errors it finds, as part of its summary of the assembly process--even if we have not requested an assembler printout. If we invoke ADD with the argument 2, and we have used the .SHOW ME directive, then the assembler produces the following output:

```
ADD  2
CHECK 2
30001$ = 2
.IIF GREATER_EQUAL 2, 30001$=30001$-1
.IIF LESS_EQUAL <2-^X7>, 30001$=30001$-1
.IIF NOT_EQUAL 30001$, .ERROR; illegal 8080 register use
.BYTE ^X80+2
```

In this case, the assembler-generated symbol 30001$ has been decremented to 0, so the .IIF NOT_EQUAL 30001$ condition is not met, and the .ERROR directive is not assembled. Note that the .ERROR directive must be separated by a semicolon from its argument. The .ERROR directive can also have a number preceding the semicolon; this number will be treated as an error number and will be printed just before the message if the .ERROR directive is assembled.

The 8080 has a jump-if-zero instruction that is similar to the TZE instruction of the hypothetical computer we discussed in chapter 2. It has the symbolic form

```
JZ ADR   ;16-bit address
```

We can define a macro that uses the assemble-time division operator, "/", and the assemble-time logical **and** operator, "&", to create a JZ instruction:

```
.MACRO JZ ADR        ;8080 JZ instruction
.BYTE ^XCA           ;opcode
.BYTE ^X<FF&ADR>     ;low-order 8 bits of address
.BYTE ^X<ADR/100>    ;high-order 8 bits of address
.ENDM JZ
```

Given the invocation JZ <^X1234>, the assembler will generate the following code

```
.BYTE ^XCA           ;opcode
.BYTE ^X34           ;low-order 8 bits of address
.BYTE ^X12           ;high-order 8 bits of address
```

Why is the argument to JZ in angle brackets; why don't we write JZ ^X1234? When it is used in a macro argument, the assembler interprets the circumflex (^) as an indicator that whatever immediately follows it is a string delimiter, so if we want it to treat the circumflex as part of the hexadecimal radix control sequence, "^X" we must enclose it in its own delimiters.

We discussed the use of assemble-time arithmetic operators (+, -, *, and /) in expressions such as

```
.WORD  A+2, B-1
.LONG TEN/2, TEN*3
```

in chapter 6. There are also assemble-time logical operators, for **and** (&), **inclusive or** (!) and **exclusive or** (/). In the JZ macro, we need to treat the 16-bit address as a string of bits at assemble time, and divide it into two 8-bit numbers. We use the logical **and** with a *mask* of FF_{16} (which is, of course, 11111111_2 to extract the low-order 8 bits from the 16-bit address. We use (hexadecimal) division to *shift* the address 8 bits to the right, and store the high-order 8 bits in the second byte.

The assemble-time arithmetic and logical operators we have used are **binary** operators, because each requires 2 operands (*not* because they operate on binary numbers!). In mathematics (and in most high-level programming languages), different binary operators have different **precedence**: some are evaluated before others. Thus, if we wrote

```
2 + 3 * 4
```

we would expect the multiplication to be performed before the addition, because it has higher precedence. So,

$$2 + 3 * 4 \equiv 2 + 12 \equiv 14$$

As far as the VAX's assembler is concerned, however, all binary operators have equal precedence; expressions are evaluated strictly from left to right, so

$$2 + 3 * 4 \equiv 5 * 4 \equiv 20$$

If we want the assembler to evaluate expressions in any other order, we must use angle brackets to group the terms:

```
.LONG 4+5*6       ;36₁₆
.LONG 4+<5*6>     ;22₁₆
```

It turns out that, without too much work, we can write macros for the VAX's assembler, Macro, to translate 8080 assembly language programs into 8080 machine-language programs: we can create an 8080 cross assembler out of VAX Macro and a collection of macro definitions. It would be more difficult to create a cross assembler for a more complex computer out of VAX Macro, however. Cross assemblers are, therefore, often written in a higher level language such as FORTRAN or C.

BLANK and NOT_BLANK

Sometimes we would like to write a macro that allows us to provide it with a particular argument if we so desire but allows us to use a default argument if that suits our purposes. We can use BLANK and NOT_BLANK as conditions for the .IF and .IIF directives to test whether an argument is *blank* or *not blank*. These conditions are only useful in a macro definition, since they check whether the macro's argument has a value or not. Consider the following macro invocations:

```
TTYIN                   ;read a byte, put it in R0
TTYIN (R1)              ;get a byte, put it in memory
```

We could write these macros to make use of the GETC macros we have already seen. We could write the first macro to expand to

```
GETC R0
```

and the second one to expand to
```
GETC R0
MOVB R0, (R1)
```

If we use the BLANK and NOT_BLANK conditions, then we could write TTYIN as follows:

```
.MACRO TTYIN ARG    ;read a character
GETC R0                 ;use R0 by default
.IF NOT_BLANK <ARG>
     MOVB R0, ARG
.ENDC
.ENDM TTYIN
```

Alternatively, we could replace the three-line conditional block with an immediate conditional test:

```
.IIF NOT_BLANK <ARG>, MOVB R0, ARG
```

Concatenation

The apostrophe, or single quote character (') can be used in a special way in a macro definition. When it immediately precedes or immediately follows a formal argument in the body of a macro definition, it is treated by the assembler as a **concatenation** operator. In this role, it serves initially to separate (*delimit*) its left or right neighbor from the adjoining argument. When the macro is invoked, however, the " ' " is removed during macro expansion, and the current value of the adjoining argument replaces it. Suppose, for example, we wrote:

```
        .MACRO EX A
L'A:    .WORD           A'M
        .ENDM EX
```

The invocation EX BBB generates the following expansion:

```
LBBB:   .WORD BBBM
```

Since any field of an assembly language statement can be specified by a macro argument, we can even use a macro to "build" directives. For example,

```
.MACRO BLOCK ARG, COUNT
.BLK' ARG COUNT
.ENDM BLOCK
```

Thus, if we invoke BLOCK as follows:

```
X:    BLOCK B 5
Y:    BLOCK W 6
Z:    BLOCK L 9
```

the assembler will expand these invocations to the following replacement texts:

```
X:    .BLKB 5
Y:    .BLKW 6
Z:    .BLKL 9
```

It is also possible to concatenate two macro arguments; we separate them by *two* apostrophes. Thus, a macro to generate arbitrary instructions can be written as follows:

```
.MACRO INSTRUCTION OPERATION, OPERAND
OPERATION' ' OPERAND R0
.ENDM INSTRUCTION
```

We can use this macro to generate the CLRL R0 instruction with the invocation:

```
INSTRUCTION CLR, L
```

which will expand to

```
CLRL R0
```

Threaded Code

Sometimes a main program is simply a list of subroutine calls, one after another. For example, if we wish to perform 256-bit integer arithmetic, we might have long sequences of code such as the following:

```
MOVAL A, ARGLIST      ;number in A, A+4, A+8, A+12, A+16, A+20, A+24, A+28
MOVAL B, ARGLIST+4    ;number in B, B+4, B+8, B+12, B+16, B+20, B+24, B+28
MOVAL C, ARGLIST+8    ;result in C, C+4, C+8, C+12, C+16, C+20, C+24, C+28
JSB BIGADD            ;add As and Bs, result in Cs
MOVAL C, ARGLIST      ;number in C, C+4, C+8, C+12, C+16, C+20, C+24, C+28
MOVAL X, ARGLIST+4    ;number in X, X+4, X+8, X+12, X+16, X+20, X+24, X+28
MOVAL Y, ARGLIST+8    ;result in Y, Y+4, Y+8, Y+12, Y+16, Y+20, Y+24, Y+28
JSB BIGSUB            ;subtract Cs from Xs, result in Ys
MOVAL Y, ARGLIST      ;number in Y, Y+4, Y+8, Y+12, Y+16, Y+20, Y+24, Y+28
MOVAL H, ARGLIST+4    ;number in H, H+4, H+8, H+12, H+16, H+20, H+24, H+28
```

```
MOVAL M, ARGLIST + 8 ;result in M, M + 4, M + 8, M + 12, M + 16, M + 20, M + 24, M + 28
JSB BIGMUL              ;multiply Ys and Hs, result in Ms
;etc.
```

In an attempt to reduce the memory requirements for such a program, we might consider revising each of the subroutines slightly, and rewriting the invocations *without* the explicit JSB instruction. The main program would then become:

```
PROG:   .ADDRESS LONGADD    ;extended-range addition subroutine
        .ADDRESS A, B, C     ;arguments for LONGADD
        .ADDRESS LONGSUB    ;extended-range subtraction subroutine
        .ADDRESS B, X, Y     ;arguments for LONGSUB
        .ADDRESS LONGMUL    ;extended-range multiply subroutine
        .ADDRESS Y, C, M     ;arguments for LONGMUL
```

The subroutine names have been changed to remind us that if we write our main program this way, then the subroutines will also have to change. The "code" at PROG has no instructions. We turn it into a program by executing a few *initializing instructions,* such as:

```
INIT:   MOVAL PROG, R5      ;use R5 as pointer
        JMP @(R5)+          ;call first subroutine
```

These two instructions call LONGADD, and leave R5 pointing to PROG + 4, which is the address of LONGADD's first argument. If we write the subroutines to use R5 as their *argument pointers,* then the only unusual feature in each will be the instruction JMP @(R5)+, instead of the usual RSB, to return control to the caller. In this case, however, control will not return to the caller--it will go directly to the next subroutine. Each subroutine, when it is done, finishes its work by calling the next subroutine we would have called if we had used the traditional technique with subroutines BIGADD, and so forth. The compact representation of the code, beginning at PROG, is called a **thread.** The main parts of the subroutines which work with this thread are shown here:

```
INIT:           MOVAL PROG, R5          ;set thread pointer
                JMP @(R5)+
;
LONGADD:        MOVL @(R5)+, R1          ;get 1st arg in R1
                MOVL @(R5)+, R2          ;get 2nd arg in R2
                ;perform 256-bit addition
                MOVL @(R5)+, R3          ;get 3rd arg
                ;R3 contains address of destination
                JMP @(R5)+               ;return--actually, go to next subroutine
LONGSUB:        MOVL @(R5)+, R1          ;get 1st arg in R1
                ;etc.
                JMP @(R5)+               ;go to next subroutine
                ;similarly for other subroutines
```

Register 5 is initialized so that it points to the thread we intend to execute. The first entry in the thread is the entry point of the first subroutine we plan to call. From then on, R5 is either pointing to a subroutine's argument or to a subroutine's entry point. We need to do something different when the thread ends: we need to return control to the main program. This is not complex; it's similar to the other indirect JMP instructions we have been executing:

;begin thread here

```
    INIT:           MOVAL THREAD, R5
                    JMP @(R5)+
    RESUME:                              ;return here, after executing thread
                    ;done calling subroutines--do whatever needs doing
                    .EXIT
;
    THREAD:         .ADDRESS LONGADD
                    .ADDRESS A, B, C
                    ;more addresses
                    .ADDRESS RESUME    ;leave the thread
```

The idea behind threaded code can be extended; doing so can lead us to **knotted code,** which is discussed in an exercise at the end of this chapter.

The original motivation for threaded code was to reduce the amount of memory used. However, it also eliminates the overhead of subroutine linkage. Subtroutine linkage merely involves saving and restoring the PC, for the JSB instruction, but there is much more linkage overhead for the CALLS and CALLG instructions. When we use threaded code, we do more work at assemble time in order to do less work at run time; this places an increased burden on an assembly language programmer (or compiler writer), but it can lead to dramatic reductions in program execution time. There is yet another benefit of threaded code that was probably not foreseen when it was first used; this benefit is obtainable when we execute small (in terms of memory requirements) programs on most models of the VAX, which have a small amount of very high speed memory, called a **cache memory.** We will discuss this method of speeding up program execution, and others, in the next section.

Speeding Up Program Execution

The flow of instructions and data between the ALU, the registers, the control unit, and the memory system of a typical computer is shown in figure 17.14. Clearly, memory is central in the path along which information flows to the various parts of a computer. All instructions and data are stored in memory; instructions must be fetched to be executed, and data must be fetched from memory, computed with, and then stored in memory. (Even when we place frequently used data in registers, we typically store final results in memory after intermediate results have been computed.)

It is often straightforward to predict what the relative execution times of two different versions of a code segment will be. Such prediction is more complicated if the computer has virtual memory (and uses virtual addresses, that must be translated into physical addresses), and if our code segment performs input or output. However, often we can tell just by looking at a particular code segment what can be done to speed it up. For example, consider the following loop:

```
        MOVL #3, R0     ;initialize loop count
        MOVAL A, R1     ;base address
1$:     CLRL (R1)+
        SOBGTR R0,1$
```

If we write out by hand each instruction that is executed at run time, we see the following trace:

```
    MOVL#3, R0      ;initialize loop count
    MOVAL A, R1     ;base address
    CLRL (R1)+      ;A ← 0
    SOBGTR R0, 1$   ;R0 ← 3 − 1 = 2; 2 > 0, so branch
```

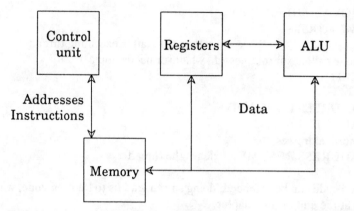

Figure 17.14 Flow of instructions and data for a typical computer

```
CLRL (R1)+         ;A+4 ← 0
SOBGTR R0, 1$      ;R0 ← 2 − 1 = 1; 1 > 0, so branch
CLRL (R1)+         ;A+8 ← 0
SOBGTR R0, 1$      ;R0 ← 1 − 1 = 0; 0 is not > 0, so fall through
```

Obviously, it is more efficient to write,

```
CLRL A
CLRL A+4
CLRL A+8
```

Here, only three instructions, occupying a maximum of 18 bytes of memory (if A is assembled using longword displacement), must be executed. In the previous example, 8 instructions, occupying 25 bytes of memory, must be executed. It is even faster to write this program as follows:

```
MOVAL A, R0
CLRL (R0)+
CLRL (R0)+
CLRL (R0)+
```

In this case, four instructions, occupying only 13 bytes of memory, are executed. We examined a similar situation in chapter 2, when we analyzed a looping program for the hypothetical computer, and compared it with a straight-line program.

Let us consider another example. We can add 1 to the contents of 1000 different memory locations by writing a program consisting of 1001 instructions, occupying 2007 bytes of memory (assuming longword displacement for B), as follows:

```
MOVAL B, R8       ;address of first byte
INCB (R8)+        ;first byte
INCB (R8)+        ;second byte
;etc.
```

```
INCB (R8)+          ;998th byte
INCB (R8)+          ;999th byte
INCB (R8)+          ;1000th byte
```

Alternatively, we can write a program consisting of only 4 instructions, occupying only 19 bytes of memory:

```
        MOVL #1000, R7    ;loop count
        MOVAL B, R8       ;address of first byte
2$:     INCB (R8)+        ;increment
        SOBGTR R7, 2$     ;do 1000 times
```

Which is faster? Although we only *write* 4 instructions using the second method, 2002 instructions are executed--twice as many as with the first method. If we count the number of memory references each technique requires to fetch and execute the programs, the former requires about 4000 (4 memory references for each of 1000 instructions), while the latter requires about 7000 (4 for the INCB instruction and 3 for the SOBGTR instruction, 1000 times through the loop). Thus, here are two situations in which we can trade time for space. If we are willing to use 100 times as much memory, we can get a speedup of about a factor of 2 in principle: we will see, when we discuss cache memory, that this analysis is not as simple as it may seem.

What about subroutine linkage overhead? Is it better to write slightly longer programs than to pay the price in extra execution time to call and return from subroutines? Consider the following program fragment:

```
        ;some code
        MOVL #500, R4
10$:    MOVL A, ARGLIST       ;first arg in list
        MOVL B, ARGLIST+4     ;second arg
        MOVL C, ARGLIST+8     ;third arg
        MOVAL ARGLIST, R0
        JSB SUB1
        MOVL L, ARGLIST       ;first arg in list
        MOVL M, ARGLIST+4     ;second arg
        MOVAL ARGLIST, R0
        JSB SUB2
        MOVL Q, ARGLIST       ;first arg in list
        MOVL X, ARGLIST+4     ;second arg
        MOVL Z, ARGLIST+8     ;third arg
        MOVAL ARGLIST, R0
        JSB SUB1
        SOBGTR R4, 10$
```

Would it be better to write out the bodies of subroutines SUB1 and SUB2 as in-line code in order to avoid executing 18 subroutine linkage instructions (15 in the loop, plus 3 RSB instructions), 500 times each? Many VAX systems have sufficient memory so that the increase in speed is worth the additional memory requirements. However, expanding subroutine calls in-line makes programs significantly less readable by humans.

We can have the best of both worlds if we define macros to make our program *look* like it is written as a series of subroutine calls while it is actually a large straight-line program (the .REPEAT directive would work very well for this task). If we are working in a high-level language, we might be able to take advantage of a compiler that is sufficiently sophisticated to treat subroutine calls as if they were macro invocations; such a compiler would replace the subroutine call statement with the subroutine's body, rather than generate call, return, and argument-passing instructions.

If everything else is equal, a program that executes fewer instructions will run faster than one that executes more instructions. However, everything else is rarely equal: if we can write two programs that do the same thing in different ways, we will be unlikely to use the same instructions, or the same number of instructions, in both programs. This is a significant consideration for modern computers, where special-purpose hardware has been added to make program execution faster.

Cache Memory

If we are designing a computer, how can we make it fast? There are many possibilities--for example:

1. **Use more registers.** This is useful, up to a point; registers are fast because they are built out of fast hardware and because they are very close to the CPU. Fast hardware is expensive and registers are affordable exactly because there aren't too many of them. Also, not *everything* can be close to the CPU; if there are too many registers, they will no longer be close to the CPU.
2. **Use faster hardware.** This is the one sure way to make a computer go faster. Unfortunately, faster hardware is more expensive; not everyone can afford it. In addition, once we use the fastest hardware available, it is still possible to build two computers that perform the same task in very different amounts of time.
3. **Use faster memory.** This is also possible only up to a certain point. As with other hardware, faster memory is more expensive. In addition, most computer users want large memory, and there is generally an inverse relationship between the size of the memory system and its effective speed.
4. **Use a wider bus.** Since everything must come from memory, if we can get more bits at a time, our computer should run faster. At one extreme, we could build a VAX with a 1-bit wide bus; fetching a single longword would require 32 bus cycles. At the other extreme, we could fetch a whole program at once--but then we would need another memory system in the control unit to store instructions until they are actually executed.
5. **Use a faster bus.** This, also, is effective, but only up to a point. If the CPU executes instructions slowly, then it does little good to fetch them and their operands quickly.

The above is only a short list of possibilities; each one interacts with the others, and many other possibilities have been omitted. Computer architects spend their lives trying to invent new ways (or new combinations of old ways) to make computers go faster, and there are many advanced books on computer architecture that discuss some of those ways. A complete discussion of this issue is beyond the scope of this book. However, in this section we will discuss a technique that is commonly used on middle- and high-performance computers: **cache memory.**

A **cache** is a relatively small, very high speed memory through which all CPU fetches and stores to main memory flow. How small is it? Different model VAXes have between 4K and 64K bytes of cache memory. How fast is it? The main memory system can provide information at a rate that is about 5 to 10 times slower than a register can supply information; the cache can supply information at about the same speed as a register. After we understand something of how a cache is built, we will be in a better position to understand why a small cache memory can have a large impact on the performance of a computer system.

Consider the five entry cache shown in figure 17.15. Each cache entry has three fields; the *address* field is 32 bits wide and contains the address in main memory from which the 32-bit item in the *contents* field has been fetched. The *valid* field is a single bit; it indicates whether or not this cache entry may be used by the program that is currently running. How is the cache used? When the computer is turned on, all the valid bits are cleared--which means that none of the cache entries may be used. Whenever the CPU initiates a memory read, the memory address is sent to the cache as

Entry #	Address	Contents	Valid
0			
1			
2			
3			
4			

Figure 17.15 Simple, five-entry cache memory

well as to main memory. The address is compared with the address in each cache entry's address field, if that entry's valid bit is set. If no match is found (a **cache miss**)--as will be the case when the computer has just been turned on, and all items in the cache are invalid--the CPU must wait for the item to be supplied from main memory. When the item is supplied from the memory, it is sent to the CPU, of course, but it is also copied into the cache (on the assumption that what was used once is likely to be used again) and that row's valid bit is set.

A subsequent request by the CPU for the same item might find it still in the cache. In this case, a match will be found between the address of the item being requested and the address field of one of the items in the cache. If the items valid bit is set, this is a **cache hit**: the cache will send the item to the CPU, and the CPU won't have to wait for the much slower main memory to supply it. The cache's **hit ratio** is the number of memory requests supplied by the cache divided by the total number of memory requests. The larger the hit ratio, the less the CPU must wait for the slower main memory.

What happens when the CPU changes a data item that is also in the cache? Since there are two copies of the same item (one in memory and one in the cache), we must decide whether to change both of them or just one. Clearly, it would be a disaster if we had two different values--one in the cache and one in main memory--for the *same* item; this is the **cache consistency** (or **cache coherency**) problem: the cache and main memory must be consistent about the value stored in every location. The simplest way to handle the problem of stores (or *writes*) is to change the item in the cache and also change the item in memory; this is called **write through,** because every write goes *through* the cache, to main memory. Write through has the disadvantage of potentially conflicting with a request from the CPU to read a different item from memory: if the memory system is busy writing something, it can't respond to a read request until it is done.

Some cache memories solve the consistency problem by using **write back**: as long as an item remains in the cache, there is no need to change its value in main memory, because the cache (and not main memory) will always supply the item in response to a read request. Only when an item in the cache is about to be discarded from the cache must it be written *back* to main memory. A cache memory that implements write back is more complex than one that implements write through, but write back usually provides better performance than write through.

Why would an item in the cache need to be discarded? Sooner or later the cache will be full (with a five-entry cache, this will occur much sooner than later!). The cache is built with a **replacement algorithm** to decide which item should be overwritten when a memory request causes a miss in a full cache. One common replacement algorithm is **least recently used**: the new entry replaces the entry that was used the longest ago of all entries in the cache (an additional field is needed to implement this algorithm; it has been omitted from figure 17.15 for simplicity's sake). If the cache uses write through, then the discarded item is simply overwritten; if it uses write back, then the discarded item may have to be written to memory before it is overwritten. When does an item have to be written to memory? When it has been changed since it was read from memory. Thus, each row in a cache that uses write back has an additional bit called a **dirty bit**; the dirty bit is set if the item has been changed and, therefore, must be written back to memory before it is overwritten by a new entry.

Although we have described the VAX's instruction fetch-execute cycle as if it fetches a 1-byte opcode, then a 1-byte operand specifier, then the next 1-byte operand specifier, and so on, in fact many models of the VAX fetch 4 or 8 bytes at a time into the cache. This is because the designers of a cache assume that if we are requesting the contents of memory location n, we are likely to soon request the contents of memory location $n + 1$. This assumption is supported by many empirical studies of the memory-reference patterns of programs as they actually execute: most programs exhibit a considerable degree of **spatial locality.** This assumption is also supported by studies of cache hit ratios, which find that they are often above 90%.

A cache hit speeds up a memory reference by a factor of 5 to 10; a relatively small amount of fast memory can make a big difference, when it is used as a cache. What are the factors that limit the size of a cache? Recall that the cache must not only supply the requested item, but it must also determine whether or not the item is present. Thus, the address of the memory reference is *simultaneously* compared with the address fields of *all* the entries in the cache! This requires a large amount of expensive hardware. We must also consider the benefit attainable: if a system has a 64K-byte cache and a 5% cache miss ratio, that miss ratio will not necessarily drop to 2.5% simply by increasing the cache size to 128K bytes; operating system service requests, and multiuser context switches (a context switch occurs when one user's time limit is up, and the operating system begins executing another user's program, because it is that program's turn to run) may cause cache misses that are nearly unavoidable.

On the other hand, if the cache is large enough for a whole program, then the hit ratio may, in principle, reach 100%; this is why we have qualified our analysis of the time/space tradeoff of looping vs in-line code in the preceding section. Even though a straight-line program may execute many fewer instructions than a looping program, the looping program's smaller memory requirements may allow it to all fit in the cache. So, the looping program will execute a large number of instructions, but only a few *different* ones, so it will fetch them all from the cache; the straight line program will execute fewer instructions, but (by definition) each one will be different (and in a different memory location), so it may cause many more cache misses, and so the CPU may have to wait much longer for the (fewer) instructions.

Although we may write the same program two different ways if we know that one will run on a VAX with a cache and the other will run on a VAX without a cache, the use of a cache is, in principle, transparent to the user. No program changes are *required,* so we don't *have* to rewrite our programs if we wish to move them from a small VAX system to a large one--even though we may be able to decrease their execution time by rewriting them. In fact, a cache often can be disabled, which effectively removes it from the CPU-memory data flow path. When a cache is disabled, programs continue to execute correctly. We would notice the difference, however, because our programs would execute slower with the cache disabled than with it enabled.

A cache is standard on most VAXes (with the exception of the microVAX line), and most other medium- and high-performance computer systems. It is interesting to note, however, that some very high performance computers--such as the Cray I--don't have a cache; instead, they have a very large number of registers, which programmers must explicitly manage, that perform some of the functions that a cache is designed to perform automatically.

Pipelining

Typically, we think of a computer as executing one instruction at a time--in the order in which a programmer writes them. However, high performance computers often execute several instructions "at the same time," using a technique called **pipelining,** which we will briefly discuss in this section.

We introduced the basis for the idea of pipelining when we discussed overlapped processing and I/O and when we discussed I/O with a DMA controller. In those cases, we saw that it is possible to

Time:	t_0	t_1	t_2	t_3	t_4
Instruction fetch	n	$n+1$	$n+2$	$n+3$	$n+4$
Instruction decode		n	$n+1$	$n+2$	$n+3$
Operand fetch			n	$n+1$	$n+2$
Execute				n	$n+1$
Result store					n

Figure 17.16 A five-stage pipeline

free the CPU to continue computing--if we build I/O controllers that are smart enough to do the necessary work (such controllers may be considered special-purpose computers). The basic idea of pipelining is to avoid having *most* of our processor hardware sitting idle, waiting for a task that is performed by only a small part of that hardware. Pipelining involves dividing the fetching and execution of an instruction into several parts, and separating the pieces of hardware that are in charge of each part.

Pipelining a computer is similar to using an assembly line in an automobile manufacturing plant, for example. Automobile manufacturers don't finish building one automobile before beginning the next one; rather, they divide the process of building an automobile into many steps, and have a worker perform each step. Thus, as soon as the first automobile has completed step 1 it moves on to step 2, and the second one can begin step 1, and so on. With a computer, the instruction fetch-execute cycle is also divided into a series of steps (each is called a **stage** in the pipeline); as soon as one instruction has left the first pipeline stage--and gone on to the next stage--the next instruction can enter the first stage.

What are the stages in a computer's pipeline? There is no fixed number of stages, but it is common to have a stage for instruction fetch, instruction decode, operand fetch, execution, and result store. Thus, when instruction n is in the result-store stage, we can expect that instruction $n+1$ is in the execute stage, instruction $n+2$ is in the operand-fetch stage, instruction $n+3$ is in the instruction decode stage, and instruction $n+4$ is in the instruction fetch stage. Figure 17.16 shows such a five-stage pipeline, with a different instruction in each stage.

No single instruction executes more quickly on a pipelined computer than on a nonpipelined computer, just as no single automobile is built more quickly on an assembly line than it would be off an assembly line. In an automobile assembly line, a new "car" enters the assembly line as a completed car exits it, and as all the in-between "cars" move to the next step. If each step takes five minutes, then one automobile can be finished every five minutes, even though it may take several hours to complete a given automobile. Similarly, as a new instruction enters the computer's pipeline, a completed instruction exits. A nonpipelined computer that can execute one million instructions per second, completes one instruction every millionth of a second. A computer with hardware of comparable speed, but with a five-stage pipeline, can also execute one entire instruction every millionth of a second, but it can complete *five* instructions in that same millionth of a second.

Why aren't all computers pipelined? First, additional hardware is required to separate the pieces of the CPU into pipeline stages, and additional hardware means additional expense. Second, pipelines don't always speed up instruction execution: consider a program that uses self-modifying code. If we execute such a program on a computer with the five-stage pipeline described above, it will not execute any faster than it will on a nonpipelined computer. Why is this? Because the last pipeline stage is the storing of results into memory, and the first pipeline stage is fetching the next instruction. If the preceding instruction *creates* the next instruction, then we can't begin execution of the next instruction until the preceding one creates it, and stores it in memory.

Self-modifying code is, perhaps, uncommon; a more common situation is that in which the current instruction produces results that the next instruction uses as an operand. In this case, the instruction in stage 3 (operand fetch) would not be able to move on to stage 4 (execution) until the preceding instruction completed (rather than when it moved on to stage 5). Detecting and/or preventing such pipeline **hazards** requires additional hardware and/or software complexity; these are topics of active interest to researchers and computer manufacturers. We have presented only a brief introduction to pipelined computers; once more, additional details are beyond the scope of this book.

On-Line, Real-Time Computing

We used the phrase *on-line* when we discussed spooling in chapter 16: when I/O devices are attached to the CPU, they are **on-line.** In data processing circles, an **on-line system** is what computer scientists usually call an **interactive system**--as opposed to a batch system. The distinction is based on where data preparation takes place: on-line (at a terminal, for example) or off-line--on a key-to-disk machine, for example.

Real-time computing also has two different meanings. In scientific and engineering applications, a piece of equipment which is on-line may require **real-time** response from the CPU: the CPU must honor the equipment's interrupt request when it is received. A computer in an airborne navigation system, one controlling an automobile's fuel system, and one monitoring coolant temperature in a nuclear power plant, are all examples of equipment that demands real-time response from the computer. (Real-time is distinguished from the kind of time in which the computer responds to, for example, interactive human users of CRTs: the computer responds to them *whenever it can.*)

When we describe a data processing installation as an *on-line, real-time* system, we mean something quite different: no special equipment is involved, and the real-time response requirements are typically specified in seconds rather than in milliseconds or microseconds. Consider a banking system: on-line terminals may be used to record customer transactions as they occur, which makes the system an on-line system. Such a system is real-time if all the relevant files and balances are immediately updated. Until recently, it was common to compute new account balances only *after* the close of the banking day (which is why banks used to close at 3:00 p.m.). The transactions recorded during the day were totaled late in the afternoon, and all changes were made in a batch, so that everything was current for the opening of the next banking day. In this sense of real-time, an airline reservation system must be real-time--otherwise, travelers would not know if their reservations were successful or not until the next day.

An interesting anomaly can occur with scientific real-time systems. One might think that the fastest computer available is the best choice for real-time computing, when a millisecond's delay can be critical. Suppose, however, that three scientists, each with their own laboratory, want to pool their resources and (finally) begin using computers in their laboratories. They had been using a computing service for data analysis, but they now want to use computers in data collection, as well. Should these scientists buy their own small computers, or would it be better for them to buy a larger, faster, shared computer?

This is not an easy question to answer; bigger and faster is not necessarily better, when it involves sharing of resources. Wiring several laboratories so that they can share a single CPU is expensive. It is expensive to connect high-speed devices to a computer over long distances. A shared computer may be fine for data analysis, but it may not be responsive enough for real-time data collection. There are many other issues involved in choosing between multiple, dedicated computers and a single, shared one. Fortunately, networking (as shown in figure 17.17) makes it possible to have (nearly) the best of both worlds. It is not unusual to have several dedicated computers in a single laboratory; each is devoted to the real-time monitoring of some apparatus. A modest amount of disk

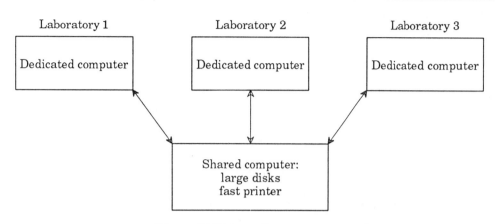

Figure 17.17 A small computer network

User	Activity	Memory (KB)
1	edit	128
2	edit	128
3	edit	128
4	edit	128
5	edit	128
6	Pascal	40
7	Pascal	40
8	FORTRAN	18
9	FORTRAN	18
10	word processing	64
11	word processing	64
12	word processing	64
13	user program	20
14	user program	100
	Total:	1068

Figure 17.18 Memory requirements without reentrant code

storage is provided on each of the dedicated computers, and they each rely on a larger, shared, system for the less time-dependent activities, such as data analysis and word processing.

Reentrant Code

When several users can share a single executable program--by using one copy of it in memory--we call that program **reentrant**. In order for a program to be reentrant, each user must have a private data space (uninitialized memory), and no part of the reentrant program itself must ever be modified. The program is then **read-only**, or **pure code**; clearly, a reentrant program cannot use self-modifying code. Reentrancy is important for two classes of users that have almost nothing in common: users of very large systems and users of very small systems.

Reentrancy on Large Systems

It almost goes without saying that a large system, because of its high cost, must be a multiuser system. Most programs which run on a multi-user system are (or should be) reentrant. The editing program, the FORTRAN, Pascal, and C compilers, the text-formatting program, for example, should all be reentrant. If this were not the case, consider the consequences: when we configure a computer system, we specify how much memory it will have, how many disks of what type, and other options and peripheral devices we wish to purchase. In order to do this we need to know how the computer will be used, so we describe a (hypothetical) typical day in the life of the proposed computer. The scenario we outline represents our best guess as to what constitutes a typical work mix under reasonably heavy load conditions; it might look like that shown in figure 17.18. This typical snapshot shows 14 users, each involved in the indicated activity. The memory requirement for each activity is system-dependent; the figures shown are reasonable estimates, and the total requirements are about 1 MB of memory. The operating system itself needs a significant amount of memory, so we will probably decide that we need at least 2 MB of memory for this system.

If the editor, the compilers, and the text-formatting program were reentrant, we could either get by with much less memory, or we could support more concurrent users. Consider how reentrant code can reduce memory requirements, as shown in figure 17.19. The first user of a reentrant program requires that the program be in memory, so the first user's copy of the editor requires the full 128 KB of memory. Additional users of the same editor, however, need only their own workspaces, which we assume is 40 KB per user. In this example, we have reduced our memory requirements by about 50%, not counting the operating system. When memory was very expensive, this would have been a significant cost reduction. Today, reentrancy allows us to have lower memory requirements per user, and so we can support more users, with a given amount of memory.

User	Activity	Memory (KB)
1	edit	128
2	edit	40
3	edit	40
4	edit	40
5	edit	40
6	Pascal	40
7	Pascal	10
8	FORTRAN	18
9	FORTRAN	10
10	word processing	64
11	word processing	20
12	word processing	20
13	user program	20
14	user program	100
	Total:	590

Figure 17.19 Memory requirements with reentrant code

Reentrancy on Dedicated Computers

A dedicated computer is a single-user computer which always has the same user; that user is usually a thing rather than a person. For example, the microcomputer in a microwave oven is a dedicated computer. Since such a computer never shares programs among multiple users, how can reentrancy be useful on a single-user, dedicated computer?

Dedicated computers are sometimes used in hostile environments. For example, the computer that controls an automobile's fuel injection system is subject to temperature extremes, vibration, and dirt that would destroy many delicate computer peripherals (such as a tape or disk drive) in short order. Microwave ovens, on the other hand, are typically used in clean, comfortable kitchens. In both cases, the one and only program the dedicated computer executes must be in **nonvolatile** memory--memory which does not lose information when its power is turned off and then back on. Why not use ordinary (volatile) RAM, with a battery for backup power? Imagine our car breaking down somewhere, and our discovering that the battery failed. We can call a mechanic and have the battery replaced, but will the mechanic also be able to reload the program into our car's RAM? Which program? Which version?

So, some dedicated computers must use ROM (Read Only Memory) so that their program will never be destroyed--unless the whole computer goes up in flames; what does this have to do with reentrancy? Reentrant programs are pure code, so they can reside in ROM. The dedicated computer uses its registers and RAM as a workspace; in the event of a power loss, when power is restored a power-up sequence is begun, which includes execution of some re-initialization code which is part of the reentrant program in the ROM. Such a program is usually developed on a development system (host computer), where it is tested and debugged. When it is considered free of bugs, the program is *burned in* to the ROM (bit by bit, or word by word) with a ROM programming machine.

Coroutines

The combination of a main program and a subroutine is based on the idea of a hierarchical relationship between one piece of code and another: the main program has a problem to solve, and it requests the assistance of a subroutine (or, of several subroutines) to solve that problem. We tend to solve problems in a top-down manner, and so we think of the relationship between the main program and its subroutines as asymmetrical, in the direction that their names indicate. However, it is possible to write a program in which a pair of routines call *each other* in a symmetrical manner: neither may appropriately be considered a main program or a subroutine. We call such routines **coroutines.**

The symmetry of the relationship between coroutines is also seen in the syntax of their execution: when one coroutine calls another, the callee is resumed at the point where it left off; when the callee ends, its caller is resumed at the point where it left off. This, also, is different from main programs and subroutines: when a subroutine returns, the main program is resumed at the point where it left off, but a subroutine always starts at its beginning, and executes until its end. It is difficult to provide a simple example of coroutines, but we can think of writing a chess playing program as a pair of coroutines--one for black and one for white. After white moves, it calls black; after black moves, it calls white, which resumes at the point where it left off after its last move.

How can we implement coroutines in the VAX? It is not especially difficult. With subroutines, we need to save the address of the caller during the subroutine call, but not the address of the callee after it returns. Therefore, we use the JSB instruction--which saves the PC on the system stack--to call a subroutine, and the RSB instruction--which simply pops the system stack into the PC--to return from it. With coroutines, we need to do a little more work: we need to save each coroutine's return address when we call the other coroutine. We want to place what's in the PC on the top of the stack, and what's on the top of the stack in the PC; how can we do that? We can *exchange* the contents of the PC and the top of the stack by using the JSB instruction, with autoincrement deferred addressing: if the top of the stack contains the address of the next instruction of a coroutine that we wish to execute, then we can execute the instruction

        JSB @(SP)+

to place what's in the PC on the top of the stack, and what's on the top of the stack in the PC. Thus, we could initialize a pair of coroutines with the following code:

```
            ;do some processing
            MOVAL CO2, -(SP)        ;entry point for coroutine
            JSB @(SP)+              ;call coroutine: swap PC and top of stack
CO1:;continue processing, etc.
```

This initialization sequence will invoke the coroutine whose entry point is CO2; when CO2 terminates by executing the JSB @(SP)+ instruction, its return address will be saved on the stack, and CO1 will be placed in the PC. We can make the example more involved, as follows:

```
            .ENTRY START, 0
CO0:        MOVAL CO2, -(SP)        ;entry point for CO2
            JSB @(SP)+              ;begin CO2
;
CO1:        ;coroutine CO1 starts here
            ;process CO1
            JSB @(SP)+                  ;resume CO2
CO11:       ;process CO1
            ;etc.
            JSB @(SP)+                  ;resume CO2
CO12        ;process CO1
            ;etc.
            JSB @(SP)+                  ;resume CO2
;
;CO2 starts here
;
CO2:        ;process CO2
            ;etc.
            JSB @(SP)+          resume CO1
CO21:       ;process CO2
            ;etc.
            JSB @(SP)+          resume CO1
CO22:       ;process CO2
            ;etc.
            JSB @(SP)+          resume CO1
C2END:      EXIT
```

At run time, the coroutines alternate: execution is begun with the initialization code, which jumps to CO2. After processing, control is transferred to CO1, which processes and then returns to CO21. Once more, the CO2 coroutine processes and then transfers control to CO11, which processes and then transfers control to CO22, which transfers back to CO12, which then transfers back to C2END, where the program terminates. In order to transfer control from one coroutine to the next, a JSB @(SP)+ instruction is executed, which saves the current PC on the top of the stack and pops the top of the stack (the other coroutine's saved PC) into the PC--thereby causing CO1 and CO2 to alternate in their execution.

Character	Hex	Binary
A	41	100 0001
C	43	100 0011
B	42	100 0010
C	43	100 0011
d	64	110 0100
e	65	110 0101

Figure 17.20 Some ASCII character codes

Sometimes we need to perform complex processing on a large data file. It is often intuitively straightforward to write a program that does such processing as a series of passes over the data file, with each pass doing a part of the total work and writing its intermediate results to another file. However, it can be inefficient to make several passes over a large data file; if we use coroutines, we can sometimes do the same complex processing with only a single pass.

Error Detection and Correction

We have already seen that since ASCII codes are only 7 bits long, and since bytes are typically 8-bit quantities, the eighth bit can be used as a **parity** bit (**check** bit). We will now consider in greater detail how a parity bit can be used; we will also consider another technique that allows us to actually *correct* some errors.

A Single Parity Bit

Given a code set, such as ASCII, we can write down all of the character code pairs which differ by only 1 bit; three such pairs are shown in figure 17.20. A single bit error in bit 1 can transform an *A* into a *C*; a single bit error in bit 0 can transform a *B* into a *C*, or a *d* into an *e*--or vice versa.

When we add the parity bit to an ASCII code, we choose it so that it increases the separation, the **distance**, between that code and all other members of the ASCII character set. We can define the distance (*d*) between two binary codes, *x* and *y*, as the number of 1s in the bit-wise **exclusive or** of the codes. We can write this as follows:

$$d(x,y) = \text{sum}(x \neq y)$$

Accordingly, for the ASCII codes for *A* and *B*, the distance is 2:

$$\neq \quad \frac{\begin{array}{c} 100\ 0001 \\ 100\ 0010 \end{array}}{000\ 0011}$$

If the distance between *x* and *y* is *n* then it will take *n* simultaneous single-bit errors to transform *x* into *y*, or *y* into *x*.

If we do not use a parity bit, the minimum distance between any pair of ASCII codes is 1: some single-bit errors will not be detected, because they will transform one valid ASCII code into another one. If we add a parity bit to each ASCII code, we increase the minimum distance between any pair of codes to 2. Suppose, for example, we use even parity: the parity bit is assigned so that there is an even number of 1 bits in each byte. It is clear that adding a bit cannot *decrease* an ASCII code's distance from the other codes. If we consider the effect of an even parity bit on two codes that were distance 1 apart, it is easy to see that the parity bit will cause them to be distance 2 apart. This is true for all such *close* codes; with a parity bit, the ASCII code's minimum distance is increased from 1 to 2, which guarantees that all single-bit errors--but no two-bit errors--can be detected. (Because the parity bit tells us if there was an even or an odd number of 1s in the byte, we can detect any *odd* number of errors, but we can't detect any *even* number of errors.)

Row and Column Parity

With 1 parity bit for each 7 information bits, we can detect a single bit error, but we have no idea *which* bit is wrong. If we extend the idea of parity, we can detect *where* the error is; if we know which bit is wrong, we can make it right, of course: if one of two possible values is the wrong value, then the other is the correct value. How do we extend the idea of parity? We use an extra parity *byte,* where each bit is a parity bit for the corresponding column of bits in the *n* preceding bytes. Consider the case where *n* is 7: we transmit 7 ASCII codes--each with a single parity bit--and then a parity byte. For example, with even parity, we can send the following 8 bytes:

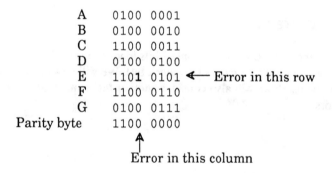

```
             A             0100 0001
             B             0100 0010
             C             1100 0011
             D             0100 0100
             E             1101 0101  ←— Error in this row
             F             1100 0110
             G             0100 0111
   Parity byte             1100 0000
                              ↑
                        Error in this column
```

Each bit in the parity byte is a parity bit (even, in this case) for its column of bits; bit 0 of the parity byte is the parity bit for each of the bit 0s of the 7 preceding bytes, and so on.

How does this allow us to correct errors? Consider the possibility that an error occurred in the transmission of the ASCII code for *E*; $1100\ 0101_2$ was sent, but $1101\ 0101_2$ was received. The situation on the receiver's end will be as follows:

```
             A             0100 0001
             B             0100 0010
             C             1100 0011
             D             0100 0100
             E             1100 0101
             F             1100 0110
             G             0100 0111
   Parity byte             1100 0000
                              ↑
                         Parity bits
```

The receiver, in computing the parity of each byte that is sent, will notice that the fifth byte sent--what should be the code for E--has odd parity while it should have even parity. The receiver will know that an error occurred in the transmission. In addition, after the block of 8 bytes is received, the sender will notice that the fifth column from the right also has odd rather than even parity. The intersection of the fifth row and the fifth column is the erroneous bit; if we complement the 1 in that position, we turn 1101 0101 back into 1100 0101, and we have corrected the transmission error.

Hamming Codes

Richard Hamming is credited with developing the idea of the *distance* between the members of a code set like ASCII; he developed this idea further, beyond the use of a single parity bit, and he found another way in which errors can be both detected and corrected. Hamming developed a method whereby all single-bit errors are correctable, and all two-bit errors are detectable. This is sufficient, in most cases: if there is a low probability of occurrence of single-bit errors (say one in 100 million --10^{-8}), and if errors in different bits of the same byte are independent of one another, then the probability of n errors is the product of each one's individual probability. The probability of two errors is 10^{-16}; this is such a small probability that we can almost ignore it. However, even if individual bit errors are not independent, and the probability of a two-bit error is greater than the product of the probabilities of two single-bit errors, it is still safe to assume that it is considerably smaller than the probability of a single-bit error.

So, how did Hamming develop a *self-correcting* code? Suppose we have a very small code set, consisting of the single-bit codes 0 and 1. In this situation, the distance between the different codes is 1 ($d(0,1) = 1$), and we cannot even *detect* single-bit errors. What happens if we add an even parity bit to each code, writing it to the left of the code bit? The 0 and 1 codes now look as follows:

$$
\begin{array}{lll}
0 & \rightarrow & 0\ 0 \\
1 & \rightarrow & 1\ 1 \\
\text{bit positions:} & & 1\ 2
\end{array}
$$

Now, $d(00,11) = 2$, which is better. Suppose we add a third bit, and use it as another even parity bit, but only for itself and the original information bit. If we add it, too, on the left, then our codes are transformed once more:

$$
\begin{array}{llllccc}
 & & & & c1 & c2 & i \\
0 & \rightarrow & 00 & \rightarrow & 0 & 0 & 0 \\
1 & \rightarrow & 11 & \rightarrow & 1 & 1 & 1 \\
\text{bit positions:} & & & & 1 & 2 & 3
\end{array}
$$

And, $d(000,111) = 3$. We have a three-bit code "word", $(c1,c2,i)$, with two check bits--c1 and c2--and one information bit--i. The relationships between the groups of bits are as follows:

parity($c1,i$) = even
parity($c2,i$) = even

Suppose we introduce a single-bit error in one of these three-bit code words:

$111 \rightarrow 110$

If we calculate the parity of c1 and i ($p(c1, i)$), and call it $p1$ (it is the modulo 2 sum of the 2 bits); and if we calculate the parity of c2 and i ($p(c2, i)$), and call it $p2$; then we have the following situation:

$$p1 \leftarrow p(c1, i) = p(1,0) = 1$$
$$p2 \leftarrow p(c2, i) = p(1,0) = 1$$

If no error had occurred, then p1 and p2 would both be 0, because we assigned c1 and c2 to produce even parity. If a single-bit error occurs, one or both of p1 and p2 will be nonzero, and the binary number (p2,p1) is used to locate the erroneous bit, which is complemented, and thereby corrected. Since (p2,p1) is 11, bit 3 from the left (note that we are numbering bits in reverse of our normal order) must be wrong. Complementing this bit, we get 111, which is the correct code word.

Hamming's technique can be generalized to code sets with any number of information bits. Recall that when we had only a single information bit we needed 2 check bits to correct an error: there were twice as many check bits as information bits! However, with 64 information bits, we need only 8 check bits to correct any single-bit error; this is less overhead than even a single parity bit for each 7 information bits, which allows us merely to detect an odd number of errors. An explanation of generalized Hamming codes is beyond the scope of this book. Most VAXes (and many other medium and large computers) use a Hamming code generator and checker, implemented in hardware, to correct single-bit errors and detect two-bit errors; the interested reader is referred to the extensive literature on error detection and correction schemes.

Historically, it was both too expensive and unnecessary to perform error correction. It was too expensive because memory and hardware were expensive, and we need more memory to store the check bits and more hardware to implement the algorithm that sets and checks them. It was unnecessary because the likelihood of even single-bit errors in a memory system using magnetic cores is very low. Only more recently, as computers began using large semiconductor memory systems (which often have components with hundreds of thousands, or even millions, of bits on a single integrated circuit chip), has error correction become feasible and necessary.

Traps and Program Debugging

The VAX has hardware that allows us to perform extremely powerful--and extremely time-consuming-- tracing of a program's execution: we may interrupt a program after the execution of each one of its instructions and examine memory, register values, or anything else of interest. How is it possible to do this? The PSL contains 2 bits, the T (*trace enable*) bit, bit 4, and the TP (*trace pending*) bit, bit 30. The PSL, including the T and TP bits, is shown in figure 17.21. If the T bit is set, then a **trace fault** will occur before the next instruction begins: control will be transferred to a **trace handler** whose vector is 28_{16} in the System Control Block (SCB). How does the T bit get set? By executing the BISPSW (BIt Set PSW) instruction, which has a mask operand just like the BIS(B,W,L)[2,3] instructions, but whose destination operand is always the low-order 16 bits of the PSL (which is the Processor Status Word, or PSW).

If the T bit is set, then *every* instruction generates a trace fault; what if we wish to examine the results of our program only occasionally? The VAX has another instruction that is used for tracing: the BPT (breakpoint) instruction. Whenever this instruction is executed, it causes a fault; control is transferred to the handler whose address is in vector $2C_{16}$ in the SCB. The BPT instruction (and the setting of the T bit) are typically used for debugging a program; this is how the VAX's debugger, DEBUG, can show us the contents of memory or of the registers after each instruction has been executed, *without* using a routine like SNAP or DUMP.

Why are there 2 trace bits, T and TP? It is possible that an interrupt or fault will occur during the execution of an instruction which is to be traced because the T bit is enabled. Tracing should not occur during execution of the interrupt handler, but it should resume once the interrupt has been handled and control has returned to the interrupted program. By having both a T and a TP bit, the designers of the VAX ensure that the trace handler will be executed exactly once per instruction, rather than twice or not at all, depending on the nature of interrupt, if any, that occurs

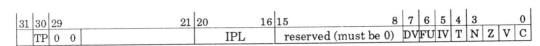

31	30	29	21	20	16	15	8	7	6	5	4	3	0
	TP	0 0		IPL		reserved (must be 0)		DV	FU	IV	T	N	Z	V	C

Figure 17.21 PSL, including T and TP bits

during an instruction's execution. This issue is dealt with in detail in the *VAX Architecture Reference Manual.*

Summary

We have seen many new ideas in this chapter, and we have reexamined some old ones--extending them and adding to our understanding of them. We have seen that macro definitions can take advantage of conditional assembly directives, which allows us to tailor macros to almost any need.

The directives .IRP and .REPEAT can be used within macro definitions or independently of macros; this allows us to generate iterative and count-controlled constructs. Each .IRP and each .REPEAT must have a matching .ENDR.

We have also discussed the design and implementation of data structures such as **lists, two-dimensional** lists, and **trees.** We briefly examined the relationship between data structures and **recursion,** and we saw how recursion can be used in subroutines. We also examined several techniques for speeding up program execution. These include replacing subroutine calls with in-line code where appropriate. However, the use of **cache memory** favors nontraditional coding techniques such as threaded code.

We investigated ways in which computers may be constructed for faster operation. In the VAX, cache memory and **pipelining,** as well as faster hardware and buses, are used to increase performance. All of these techniques are transparent to the user, but if we know of them and take them into account when we write programs, we may be able to decrease the execution time of our programs.

Reentrant code, which is sharable, is used on both large multiuser systems and dedicated microcomputers; reentrant code is incompatible with self-modifying code. We also discussed "equal" subroutines, which are called **coroutines.** Coroutines are easily supported by the VAX because of its general addressing modes.

We reexamined the use of the **parity bit** as a 1-bit error detection technique, and briefly examined methods of extending the idea of error detection to include error correction. We saw that we can use parity directly, calculated on both rows and columns, to pinpoint an error, or we can use a more complex, more powerful technique, based on Hamming codes. Error correcting hardware makes semiconductor memory as reliable as core memory.

Exercises for Chapter 17

1. Consider the following program:

```
MINUS = ^A/-/
PLUS  = ^A/+/
LEFT  = 4
RIGHT = 8
```

```
;main program starts here
;
            .ENTRY START, 0
            MOVAL EX, R0
            JSB F
            $EXIT_S
;
;data
;
EX:         .LONG MINUS, L, R
L:          .LONG PLUS, A, B
R:          .LONG PLUS, D, E
A:          .LONG 3, 0, 0
B:          .LONG 4, 0, 0
C:          .LONG 2, 0, 0
D:          .LONG 0, 0, 0
E:          .LONG 1, 0, 0
;
;Subroutine F
;
F:          MOVL TEMP, -(SP)
            MOVL XROOT, -(SP)
            MOVL R0, -(SP)
            MOVL XROOT, R0
            MOVL RIGHT(R0), XROOT
            BEQL NUM
OP:         JSB F
            MOVL VAL, TEMP
            MOVL LEFT(R0), XROOT
            JSB F
            CMPL (R0), #PLUS
            BNEQ MIN
            ADDL2 TEMP, VAL
            BRB DONE
MIN:        SUBL2 TEMP, VAL
            BRB DONE
NUM:        MOVL (R0), VAL
DONE:       MOVL (SP)+, R0
            MOVL (SP)+, XROOT
            MOVL (SP)+, TEMP
            RSB
TEMP:       .BLKL 1
VAL:        .BLKL 1
```

a. Draw a diagram of the structure that subroutine F operates on.
b. What does F compute, in the case shown in this example?
c. In general, what could subroutine F be used for?

2.

    a. Write a macro to find the largest and smallest of a list of longwords. Its invocation should be as follows:

        EXTREMES <list of things>, MAX, MIN

    MAX is the place to put the largest item, and MIN is the place to put the smallest. The macro should generate code to compute the largest and smallest items at *run* time.

    b. What code is generated by your macro for the following invocation?

        EXTREMES <A, B, (SP), 16(R7)>, R8, R9

3. Act as an assembler, and translate the following assembly language program into machine language. Assume that the entry point is location 0.

```
        .MACRO PUSH, ITEM
        MOVL ITEM, -(SP)
        .ENDM PUSH
    ;
        .MACRO POP, ITEM
        MOVL (SP)+, ITEM
        .ENDM POP
    ;
        .MACRO WRITE, ARG, ?B, ?C
        PUSH R0
        PUTS B
        JMP C
    B:  .ASCIZ / ARG /<10> <13>
    C:  POP R0
        .ENDM WRITE
    ;
        .ENTRY START, 0
        WRITE <THIS IS AN EXAMPLE>
        $EXIT_S
        .END START
```

Ignore the code generated by the PUTS system service macro.

4. Draw the binary tree that would be built by a binary tree program from the following input data:

    20, 25, 30, 10, 35, 15, 40

Is there an ordering of the data that would result in a more balanced tree? If so, write one down, and draw that tree.

5. Using only the .LONG directive (or, the .LONG and .ADDRESS directives), show how you would construct the following data structures with the items 20, 25, 30 and 10 as the values in the nodes of:

    a. A one-way linked list;
    b. A two-way linked list.

6. Suppose we want to write a macro to multiply 2 longwords and store the product. Explain briefly how the macro definition and invocation shown below will accomplish this objective. Or, if you don't think it will work, explain why not. (Ignore the potential difficulty due to the fact that the product of two n-bit numbers can be $2n$ bits long.)

```
;macro definition here:
        .MACRO MULTIPLY X, Y, RESULT, ?LOOP
        CLRL RESULT
LOOP:   .REPEAT X
        ADDL2 Y, RESULT
        .ENDR
        .ENDM MULTIPLY
;macro invocation here:
        MULTIPLY R1, R2, R3   ;R3        <-- R1 * R2
```

7. Suppose you have R records, each with 2 fields: a part number, PN, and a part description, PD. The PNs are between 0 and $50,000_{10}$; the PD's are character strings of 10 to 60 characters. Suppose, in addition, that you must write code to sort these R records by PN, using a binary tree.

    a. Describe what a typical node in your tree will contain; specify the size and purpose of each field.

    b. How could you restrict the records in order to substantially reduce the node sizes?

    c. Consider using a recursive tree traversal subroutine. In the worst-case situation, how deep must a stack be for use with such a subroutine? What would be on the stack? What kind of a tree does this worst-case situation correspond to?

    d. For $R = 31$, what is the minimum stack depth for traversing the tree?

8. Given the ordered list of numbers (25, 6, 29, 76, 24, 26), write the assembly language directives needed to represent the numbers as each of the following structures at assemble time:

    a. a one-way linked list;

    b. a two-way linked list;

    c. a binary tree in which the nodes of left subtrees are less than those of right subtrees.

9. If you could not use macros, show what you would have to write to replace the following:

```
;macro definition here:
        .MACRO SAM, A, B, ?C
        .IIF NOT_BLANK <A>, MOVL A, R0
        JSB JOAN
        .IF NOT_BLANK <B>
        BCC C
        JMP B
C:
        .ENDC
        .ENDM SAM
;macro invocations here:
        SAM ABC
        SAM #PQ, ED
```

10. True or False?

    a. Inserting an item into the middle of an ordered array of items is usually faster than inserting an item into the middle of a linked list of items.

    b. Arrays generally require more memory than linked lists do to store the same number of data items.

    c. A queue operates on the FIFO principle.

    d. The priority at which an interrupt handler executes is stored in the interrupt vector for that handler.

    e. Reentrant code should allocate work areas in read-only memory.

11. Rewrite the string-copy macro from the exercises for chapter 15, with the following improvement: use the MOVL instruction to copy longwords, and use MOVW and MOVB instructions only if necessary.

12. True or false?

    a. A queue is a linear linked list with a last-in, first-out discipline.

    b. A queue is a linear list with a first-in, last-out discipline.

    c. A circular queue cannot overflow.

    d. Arbitrary references to elements of a multi-dimensional array are faster than sequential references.

    e. Programs written using macros usually assemble and run faster than programs written without macros.

    f. If an interrupt handler is to perform correctly, it must not be interrupted.

    g. Floating point operations are extensively used in scientific applications because they are more accurate than integer operations.

    h. All the information in a device's control and status register may be modified by user programs.

    i. Interrupt handlers may not call subroutines, because subroutines also use the stack to store information.

    j. If the CPU sets the V bit in the PSL, then we can be sure that an arithmetic error has occurred.

13. Assume that each memory reference (for the fetching of an item from memory, or for storing it in memory) takes .5 μsec, and that instruction execution takes no time.

    a. What does the assembler generate when it processes the following statements?

    b. How long does the code it produces (if any) take to execute?

```
FISH = 0
.REPEAT 3
.IF EQUAL FISH
CLRL FISH
FISH = FISH + 1
.ENDC
.ENDR
```

14. Suppose that a computer has a subroutine call instruction with the format JSB REG, LOC, which stores the current value of the PC in REG and then transfers control to LOC. This computer has a subroutine return instruction with the format RSB REG, which is equivalent to JMP @REG. Will recursive programs run correctly on this computer? Explain your answer.

15. What can the following macro be used for? Discuss different invocations.

```
                .MACRO DB A, B
                .IF NOT_BLANK <A>    ;test for not blank
        PUSHL A
                PUSHL B
                CALLS #2, DUMP
                .ENDC
                .IF BLANK <A>         ;test for blank
                SNAP
                .ENDC
                .ENDM DB
```

16. Consider the following macro definition:

```
                .MACRO ARRAYCLEAR ABC, COUNT, ?LOOP
                MOVAL ABC, R0
        LOOP:   CLRL (R0)+
                DECL COUNT
                BNEQ LOOP
                .ENDM ARRAYCLEAR
```

   a. Assume that ARRAYCLEAR is the only macro in your program. Show the assembly language that it would expand to, given the following invocation:

   ARRAYCLEAR FOO, XYZ

   b. Suppose we invoked ARRAYCLEAR a second time in the same program, using the same invocation as above. Would the assembly language generated be the same? If not, explain any differences.

17. What is the difference between a macro and a subroutine?

18. What does the following macro do? Be sure to discuss what happens with different invocations.

```
                .MACRO SOLVE PROB ?X
                .IIF NOT_BLANK <PROB>, JSB PROB'IT
                BRB  X
                SNAP
        X:
                .ENDM SOLVE
```

19. Briefly describe what reentrant code is and what it is good for.

20.   True or False?

    a.   All high-level languages use the same, standard format for storing the rows and columns of multidimensional arrays in memory.

    b.   It is good programming practice to make sure that for every PUSH onto a stack, there is, at least eventually, a corresponding POP.

    c.   The use of conditional assembly statements can affect how long a program is after it is assembled.

    d.   Each macro that is defined in a given source module must be invoked at least once in that source module.

    e.   It is important to know the size of the elements when calculating offsets in multidimensional arrays.

    f.   The system stack is the only acceptable way to pass parameters to subroutines.

    g.   Arrays accessed by assembly language programs cannot have more than five dimensions.

    h.   A subroutine cannot redefine labels defined as part of itself, but it can redefine labels that are defined in its calling program.

    i.   It is illegal for a subroutine to call itself.

    j.   It is illegal for a macro to invoke itself.

21.   What is the following macro being used for? Why is this poor programming practice?

```
;macro definition:
        .MACRO ZERO ARRAY N
        MOVAL ARRAY, R0
        .REPEAT N
        CLRL (R0)+
        .ENDR
        .ENDM
;macro invocations:
        ZERO ABC, 100

            .
            .
            .

        ZERO PQR,50

            .
            .
            .

ABC:    .BLKL 100
PQR:    .BLKL 50
```

22.   The term *overflow* is used in conjunction with operations on a variety of data types and data structures. For each of the following, explain what overflow means:

    a.   array

    b.   linked list

    c.   queue

    d.   stack

    e.   integer

    f.   floating point number.

23. Consider two programs that do the same work and that are identical in all respects except that one uses macros and the other uses subroutines:

    a.   Which program, in the general case, would require more memory while it is running? Why?
    b.   Which program, in the general case, will execute faster? Why?

24. How can we run out of memory at assemble time? (Hint: consider macros).

25. We wish to test a tree traversal program with a tree that we can guarantee is correct by creating it at assemble time.

    a.   Write the assembler directives to construct a tree with node values of 10, 15, 6, 22, and 7 hexadecimal.
    b.   Draw a picture of the tree.
    c.   Write another sequence of directives so that the tree you construct has no left sub-trees.

26. A reentrant program is usually somewhat slower than a non-reentrant version would be.

    a.   Why is this the case?
    b.   There are, nevertheless, situations in which computing proceeds more rapidly using reentrant programs than using non-reentrant programs. Explain how this is possible; resolve the apparent contradiction.

27. In some applications, we may have many consecutive invocations of the same subroutine. Show how the idea behind threaded code can be extended to avoid unnecessarily repeating consecutive subroutine invocations. For example, instead of:

```
PROG:    .ADDRESS SUB1
         .ADDRESS X, Y, Z
         .ADDRESS SUB1
         .ADDRESS  P, Q, R
         .ADDRESS SUB2
         .ADDRESS  A, B, C
         .ADDRESS SUB2
         .ADDRESS M, N, OH
```

we could write:

```
PROG:    .ADDRESS SUB1
         .LONG  X, Y, Z
         .LONG P, Q, R, 0
         .ADDRESS SUB2
         .LONG A, B, C
         .LONG M, N, OH, 0
```

What modifications would we have to make to the subroutines for this to work? What assumptions must we make regarding the arguments? Threads of this type, where multiple consecutive subroutine invocations are implied, are called **knotted** code.

28. In the simple example of a Hamming code discussed in the text, we needed 2 check bits (for only one information bit!) to be able to correct a single bit error. If we have only 1 information bit, we might think that we can use a single check bit as a parity bit, because if there is an

error, it must be in that single information bit. Is this true? If not, explain what is wrong with the reasoning.

29. Using the parity bit and parity row technique with 7 bytes of information and 1 parity byte, what is the smallest number of simultaneous errors that can *not* be detected? Give an example of such a situation.

Case Study

The following program is an example of the use of recursive subroutines to create and traverse a binary tree. Each node contains two pointers (to the left and right subtrees) and a data field of 8 bytes. The data, in this case, are names--limited to 7 characters, because the last byte is cleared so that the PUTS system service routine can be used to print the name when the tree is traversed. With only minor changes, the program could be modified to store a pointer to the name (instead of the name itself) in each node. Then, names could be of essentially unlimited length.

The program's input, consisting of an unsorted sequence of names, is shown below, as it was echoed by the program, after each name was typed from the keyboard. Note that the sentinel value, *qq*, is also echoed by the program, before it is processed, and before the tree traversal begins.

```
Unsorted Data:


ABIGAIL

MICHAEL

THOMI

JEROME

DMITRI

ALBERT

NAOMI

HAZEL

qq
```

After the program creates the tree, it produces a hexadecimal dump of the tree's first 10 nodes (only 8 of which are used in this example). After printing the memory dump, the program prints the names in sorted (lexicographic) order, as produced by the traversal subroutine. The traversal subroutine also produces an abbreviated register snapshot, which shows the address of the *current* node (the node being examined by the subroutine at that moment) and the stack pointer, as the tree is traversed.

```
;English words of 8 characters or fewer are read, one word
;per line; input is terminated with a  data field of qq.
;Each node's data field is its first 8 bytes, its left pointer
;is the next 4 bytes, and its right pointer is the last 4 bytes.
;0 is used to indicate NIL.  Each word is echoed, then it is stored
```

```
;as the leaf of a subtree, such that all left subtrees are
;alphabetically less than right subtree values.
;When input is terminated, a recursive tree traversal procedure
;is called, which prints the data, sorted.
;
;
            DATA  = 0                      ;data field offset
            LEFTP  = 8                     ;left pointer offset
            RIGHTP  = 12                   ;right pointer offset
            NODESIZE  = 16                 ;number of bytes per node
            DATASIZE  = 8                  ;number of data bytes per node
            LF = ^X0A
            CR = ^X0D
            .LIBRARY /[PB]IOMAC.MLB/       ;macro library for I/O routines
;
            .ENTRY START, 0
            IOINIT                         ;initialize I/O macros
            PUTS TITLE                     ;print unsorted data
            PUTS SPACE                     ;skip a line
            MOVAL TREE, R3                 ;put root address in R3
            GETS (R3)                      ;get root value or quit
            PUTS (R3)                      ;echo
            PUTS SPACE
            CMPW (R3), #^A/qq/             ;check for done
            BNEQ 1$                        ;if not: go on
      ;else, error:  no data
            BRW NODATA                     ;print error message
      ;else
1$:         JSB CLEAR                      ;clear pointer locations
;
NEXT:       ADDL2 #NODESIZE, R3            ;address of next available node in R3
            GETS (R3)                      ;get root value, or quit
            PUTS (R3)                      ;echo
            PUTS SPACE
            CMPW (R3), #^A/qq/             ;check for done
            BEQL NOMORE                    ;if done: traverse and print
      ;else
            JSB CLEAR                      ;if not, create a new node
            MOVAL TREE, R4                 ;R4 points to tree or subtree node
            JSB SORT                       ;insert into correct place
            BRW NEXT                       ;and continue
;
NODATA:     PUTS ERROR                     ;no data
            BRW DONE                       ;and exit
NOMORE:     DUMP TREE, TREE+160            ;hex dump of first 10 nodes
            PUTS SPACE
            PUTS TITLE2                    ;print sorted data
            PUTS SPACE
            MOVAL TREE, R4                 ;root node address in R4
            JSB TRAVERSE                   ;traverse tree
DONE:       $EXIT_S
;
```

```
;data for main program
;
TREE:           .BLKL 100
SPACE:          .ASCIZ //<LF><CR>
TITLE:          .ASCIZ /Unsorted Data:/<LF><CR>
TITLE2:         .ASCIZ /Sorted Data:/<LF><CR>
ERROR:          .ASCIZ /Error: No Data!/<LF><CR>
;
;subroutines follow
;
;The CLEAR subroutine terminates the data field of a node with a byte of
;0--the ASCII NUL character--for printing.  It also places 0 (NIL) in both
;the left pointer and the right pointer of the new node (whose address
;is in R3).  It's actually a pretty simple subroutine.
;
CLEAR:          CLRB DATASIZE-1(R3)     ;need to terminate string with 0
                CLRL LEFTP(R3)          ;left pointer
                CLRL RIGHTP(R3)         ;right pointer
                RSB                     ;and done
;
;SORT is a recursive subroutine that inserts a (newly created) node into
;the tree, according to lexicographic ordering, so that the tree remains
;sorted.  SORT expects R3 to have the address of the node to insert, and
;R4 to have the address of the root of the tree (or the subtree) in which
;to insert the node.  The subroutine compares characters in the data fields
;of the two nodes, and inserts the new node in the left subtree if it's
;smaller and in the right subtree if it's bigger.
;
SORT:           MOVL R3, R1             ;save new node's address
                MOVL R4, R2             ;save root's address, too
                ;now, R1 points to data for new node, and R2--for old node
CONTINUE:
                TSTB (R1)               ;check for end of data
                BEQL RIGHT              ;if so: go right
                ;else, continue comparing
                CMPB (R1)+, (R2)+       ;compare pair of letters
                BEQL CONTINUE           ;if same: keep comparing
                ;else, not the same, so either bigger of smaller:
                BGTRU RIGHT             ;if bigger: insert to right
                ;else, smaller, so insert to left
                TSTL LEFTP(R4)          ;check if already a left subtree
                BNEQ 1$                 ;if so, insert in left subtree
                ;else, insert here
                MOVL R3, LEFTP(R4)      ;inserted!
                BRB RETURN              ;and done
1$:             MOVL LEFTP(R4), R4      ;root of new tree to search
                JSB SORT                ;insert in left subtree
                BRB RETURN              ;return, when done inserting
RIGHT:          TSTL RIGHTP(R4)         ;is there already a right subtree?
                BNEQ 2$                 ;if so, insert in right subtree
                ;else, insert here
                MOVL R3, RIGHTP(R4)     ;inserted!
```

```
            BRB RETURN                    ;and done
2$:         MOVL RIGHTP(R4), R4           ;right subtree is root of new tree
            JSB SORT                      ;insert in right subtree
RETURN:     RSB                           ;and done
;
;
;TRAVERSE is another recursive subroutine.  It traverses a binary tree
;with its root node address in R4 and prints the data field of each node,
;in lexicographic order.  Its algorithm is traverse left subtree, then
;print root node, then traverse right subtree.
;
TRAVERSE:   SNAP                          ;produce register snapshot
            TSTL R4                       ;is this a leaf (terminating condition)?
            BEQL RETURN2                  ;if so, done
            ;else, traverse left subtree
            PUSHL R4                      ;save node address, for printing later
            MOVL LEFTP(R4), R4            ;left subtree is node to print now
            JSB TRAVERSE                  ;traverse it
            MOVL (SP)+, R4                ;now print current node value
            PUTS (R4)                     ;print node
            PUTS NEWLINE                  ;start next on next line
            MOVL RIGHTP(R4), R4           ;and traverse right subtree
            JSB TRAVERSE
RETURN2:    RSB
NEWLINE:    .ASCIZ //<CR><LF>
            .END START
```

The program inserts each name in the tree as it reads that name; when it encounters the sentinal value, *qq*, it produces a hexadecimal memory dump of the first 10 nodes of the tree, as shown below:

```
004C4941   47494241   7FFEDF40   9F01FB01   :   00000500
004C4541   4843494D   00000518   00000000   :   00000510

00000D49   4D4F4854   00000528   00000538   :   00000520
000D454D   4F52454A   00000000   00000568   :   00000530

000D4952   54494D44   00000000   00000548   :   00000540
000D5452   45424C41   00000578   00000558   :   00000550

00000D49   4D4F414E   00000000   00000000   :   00000560
00000D4C   455A4148   00000000   00000000   :   00000570

00000000   000D7171   00000000   00000000   :   00000580
00000000   00000000   00000000   00000000   :   00000590

00000000   00000000   00000000   00000000   :   000005A0
00000000   00000000   00000000   00000000   :   000005B0
```

Only eight names have been typed from the keyboard, so only the first 8 nodes of the tree are *occupied.* The address of the root of the tree (TREE) is 508_{16}; we see the ASCII codes for *ABIGAIL* in locations 508_{16} through $50F_{16}$, which comprise the data field for the first node. This node has a right child, but no left child, because all the other names processed by the program are lexicographically larger than *ABIGAIL*; examining locations 510_{16} and 514_{16}, we see that this node's left pointer (in location 510) is 0--indicating no left child--and its right pointer (in location 514) is 518--which is the address of the node that is its right child. In location 518, we see the ASCII codes for *MICHAEL*, which is the root of the root node's right (and only) subtree; this node has both a left child and a right child, in locations 538_{16} and 528_{16}, respectively. The right child of the node whose data field contains *MICHAEL* has a data field containing the ASCII codes for *THOMI*, followed by a byte $0D_{16}$, followed by a byte 00; where did the 0D come from? The ASCII code for carriage return is read by our program, along with the rest of each line of input, each time we execute the GETS system service. When we use names that are 7 characters long, the eighth character is the carriage return character, but the CLEAR subroutine overwrites it with a byte of 0 (the NUL character), so the PUTS system service will work correctly. When names are fewer than 7 characters long, the 0D is not overwritten, and so we see it stored in memory. If we continue this process of tracing the tree's nodes and left and right pointers, we can diagram the tree constructed by the program, as shown below:

The output of our program, as the TRAVERSE subroutine traverses the tree, is shown below. The SNAP output has been abbreviated so that we see only R4, SP, and PC. Notice that sometimes there is an "extra" blank line: this is caused by the ASCII code for carriage return ($0D_{16}$) that was stored whenever a name was shorter than 7 characters long.

```
Sorted Data:


R4, SP, PC:    00000508 7FF27D7C  0000070F
R4, SP, PC:    00000000 7FF27D74  0000070F
ABIGAIL

R4, SP, PC:    00000518 7FF27D78  0000070F
R4, SP, PC:    00000538 7FF27D70  0000070F
R4, SP, PC:    00000548 7FF27D68  0000070F
R4, SP, PC:    00000558 7FF27D60  0000070F
R4, SP, PC:    00000000 7FF27D58  0000070F
ALBERT



R4, SP, PC:    00000000 7FF27D5C  0000070F
DMITRI
```

```
R4, SP, PC:   00000578  7FF27D64   0000070F
R4, SP, PC:   00000000  7FF27D5C   0000070F
HAZEL


R4, SP, PC:   00000000  7FF27D60   0000070F
JEROME


R4, SP, PC:   00000000  7FF27D6C   0000070F
MICHAEL

R4, SP, PC:   00000528  7FF27D74   0000070F
R4, SP, PC:   00000568  7FF27D6C   0000070F
R4, SP, PC:   00000000  7FF27D64   0000070F
NAOMI


R4, SP, PC:   00000000  7FF27D68   0000070F
THOMI


R4, SP, PC:   00000000  7FF27D70   0000070F
```

Why are there varying numbers of register snapshots between the different names? Each register snapshot corresponds to a call of the TRAVERSE subroutine. When a given node has a *left* child, and when that *left* child, in turn, has its own *left* child, then TRAVERSE will be called several times before any printing is actually done (it only prints data fields of nodes with no left children). It is a worthwhile exercise to draw the stack and execute TRAVERSE by hand (perhaps with a simpler tree), to see exactly how it works.

▪ 18 ▪

Micros, Minis, and Mainframes

Introduction

In the process of trying to understand how computer hardware works, we'd like to avoid missing the forest for the trees. The VAX is just one of a multitude of different but related computers. The VAX is a multitude in its own right: the size of the VAX family ranges from the small MicroVAX to the multirefrigerator-sized VAX 8978. In this chapter we will consider the variety of similarities and differences between VAXes and other computers.

Features Common to All Computers

In most modern computers, the internal representations of instructions and data are based on the binary number system. The most commonly used byte size is 8 bits. The two most frequently used character code sets are ASCII and EBCDIC. Nearly every CPU has a control unit, an instruction register, a program counter (sometimes called an **instruction counter**), and an ALU. The differences in performance and capacity of different computers derive from the word size, ALU implementation, instruction set and addressing characteristics, bus or channel organization, and the component technology used. These are properly thought of as architectural *and* hardware issues; as we saw when we discussed some of the ways to increase a computer's performance, it is often difficult to draw a clear line between the two.

Distinguishing Features

We can arbitrarily classify *general-purpose* computers into three categories: (1) micro, (2) mini, (3) mainframe. There is no universally accepted definition for these terms which can be applied consistently. At one time, the U.S. Government General Services Administration (the government's major buyer of computers) ruled that, as far as the federal government was concerned, a computing system costing less than $50,000 was a minicomputer system. Such a threshold is no longer in use, in part because computer costs have changed so dramatically in recent years--as we will soon discuss. As we attempt to describe each class of computer in turn, their distinguishing features--and the arbitrariness of the classification--will become evident.

Micros

The first microprocessor, the Intel 4004, was introduced in 1971 and had a 4-bit word. In 1972, Intel introduced the 8008, with an 8-bit word. Most of the 8008's competitors, and many of its successors, also have an 8-bit word; some are listed in figure 18.1. Many newer microprocessors use 16 or 32-bit words.

Manufacturer	Model
Intel	8080, 8080A, 8084, 8085, . . .
Zilog	Z80, Z8, Z80A, . . .
Motorola	6800
RCA	Cosmac
Fairchild	F8
AMD	6502

Figure 18.1 Some early microcomputers and microprocessors

We can distinguish between a **microcomputer** on a chip (such as the Intel 8048)--which is a complete computer, with control unit, registers, ALU and even memory system on a single integrated circuit--and a **microprocessor** on a chip (such as the Intel 8080)--which contains the CPU (the ALU, control unit, and registers) on a single chip, but needs one or more additional chips (usually for memory) to complete the computer system.

Both cost and reliability of a computer system are directly related to the number of chips in the system: the fewer the chips the more reliable and less expensive the system will be, as a rule. Thus, if a single-chip microcomputer can do the job for a dedicated application, it will usually provide the lowest cost, highest reliability, solution to our computing needs, since it has a chip count of 1. Motorola's MC68HC11A8 is an example of a recent single-chip microcomputer: this 8-bit, single-chip microcomputer (which is about the size of a postage stamp) includes the following parts:

8K bytes of ROM
512 bytes of EEPROM
256 bytes of RAM
timer
serial interface
8-channel analog-to-digital converter

Its instruction set includes that of the MC6800 and an additional 91 opcodes. It is capable of addressing up to 64K bytes of off-chip memory. This, and other similar microcomputers, are well-suited for use as device controllers. Microprocessors, unlike microcomputers, need additional chips to form a complete computer. The full set of chips is usually assembled on a circuit board; if this results in a self-contained computer (except for a power supply and peripheral devices), it is called a **single-board computer** (SBC).

The 8-bit micro continues to dominate the world of micros: the fact that almost every automobile now built uses three or four 8-bit micros suggests that many millions of them will be built each year--for many years to come. The second generation of micros, typified by the the Intel 8086 and the Motorola MC68000, can be considered 16-bit micros in that they can operate on 8 and 16-bit data items. These micros are used in the most popular personal computers.

The newest generation of traditional microprocessors supports 32-bit operations and very large memories. These microprocessors often have optional memory-management chips; they approach the speed of the smaller minicomputers, in terms of program execution. The Intel 80386, Motorola MC68020 and MC68030, National Semiconductor NS32032 (and others) are used in the most powerful personal computers. They are similar to the VAX in having 32-bit addresses and instructions that deal with 8-, 16- and 32-bit data items. The term **workstation** is often used to describe what appears to be a personal computer but which--because of its higher cost due to high performance, large disks, and superior graphics--is priced beyond the range of ordinary personal computers.

The newest "conventional" microprocessors--the 32-bit micros--have instruction sets and other architectural features that are often remarkably similar to that of the VAX. However, there is another class of microprocessors that is trying to attain high performance by using a significantly different architecture. The VAX has over 300 opcodes; these new microprocessors typically have fewer than 100. Does this mean that they can only do about one-third as much as a VAX? Not in principle: recall that we described an algorithm for performing multiplication as a sequence of additions; the **Reduced Instruction Set Computers** (RISCs) have only a small number of simple instructions, but programmers can combine them to do exactly the same work that one single, complex VAX instruction can do. The philosophy behind the RISC design is that the ALU must do the same amount of work to multiply two numbers, whether it is executing a single MUL instruction or a series of ADD instructions; the only thing wrong with executing many ADD instructions is that each one must be fetched from memory. And with a cache memory and an execution pipeline, fetching many instructions can be (nearly) as fast as fetching only one.

If RISCs are only no *slower* than traditional computers, why build them? The second principle behind the RISC design is that a control unit that must execute only a few instructions is simpler than one that must execute a large number of instructions, and so its design can be optimized for the small number of instructions that it executes. Thus, a RISC may have to execute several ADDs and ASHLs while a VAX will only execute a single MUL, but (the RISC's designers hope) each of those ADDs and ASHLs will take considerably less time to execute on their RISC than it would on a VAX, so the net difference will be small, or even in the RISC's favor.

How do the designers of a RISC decide which opcodes to include and which must be "created" by a programmer? They include opcodes for performing only the most frequently used operations. Thus, there will not be a POLYF instruction on a RISC, for that instruction is probably executed very infrequently in a typical workload. In the late 1940s, computers executed small instruction sets because it was too expensive to design and build complex instruction set computers. In the late 1960s and the 1970s, when design and implementation technology had made significant progress, and complex instruction set computers were becoming popular, the highest performance computers--in particular, those designed by Seymour Cray--used small instruction sets. The designers of RISC microprocessors hope to use this philosophy to build high performance *small* computers, but the first RISC microprocessors are just beginning to be commercially available, so it is not yet clear whether they will provide increased performance compared with the more traditional 32-bit micros.

The uses of microprocessors and microcomputers are similar to those of small electric motors: it is common to find an electric motor in a vacuum cleaner, a blender, a clock, a dishwasher, a fan, a drill, and so forth. Similarly, the low cost of 8- and 16-bit micros makes it possible to use them in dedicated applications, ranging from sewing machines to fuel injection systems.

Minis

DEC popularized the minicomputer with its PDP-8 and PDP-12, which used 12-bit words; over 50,000 were sold. In 1970, DEC consolidated its minicomputer product line by introducing the PDP-11 family of computers. The PDP-11 has 16-bit addresses, and deals with 8- and 16-bit data items. The PDP-11 family includes the low-cost LSI-11s, which were also available as single-board computers. In 1978 DEC introduced the first VAX, the model 11/780; as the VAX became more popular, the PDP-11 family has been deemphasized (although several new models have been introduced in the last few years). The VAX family is now DEC's principal computer product.

The VAX family spans the range from microcomputer to mainframe; figure 18.2 shows many of the models in the VAX family. The horizontal axis represents the year that each model was introduced, and the vertical axis represents relative performance (not to scale). The lowest performance model executes about 0.5 million instructions per second (MIPs), and the highest performance system (the 8978, composed of several 8800s) executes about 50 million instructions per second: no other family of computers has such a wide performance range. The least expensive system

Performance

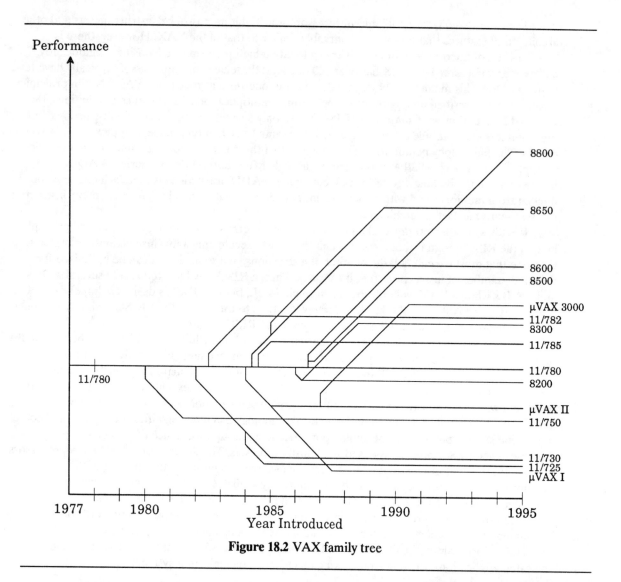

Figure 18.2 VAX family tree

costs under $5,000, and the most expensive one costs nearly $5,000,000. The price/performance ratios indicate that the small systems execute about 100 instructions per second per dollar (ips/dollar), while the very large ones execute only about 10 ips/dollar. Why do people buy machines that deliver less performance per dollar? Unfortunately, $5,000,000 worth of small computers cannot be used to solve big problems as readily as one very fast $5,000,000 computer; we will consider another aspect of this issue later in this chapter.

DEC made the minicomputer popular, but many other firms sell minicomputers. Data General (founded by former DEC employees) makes the Nova and Eclipse families of minicomputers; Prime, Hewlett-Packard, Harris, Unisys, IBM--these are just some of the companies which manufacture minis (although IBM prefers to call them *small computers* rather than minis).

The 16-bit word size once was the most common word size for minicomputers; now most have 32-bit words. The Harris Corporation (formerly Datacraft) uses 24-bit and 48-bit words on its minis. The older DEC PDP-15 used an 18-bit word; there were also some 21-bit minis.

As a rule, when buying a mini, one must buy a complete system, which includes the CPU, memory, power supply, cabinet, disk and/or tape drive(s), and some peripherals. Some of the different levels of physical organization of the components of a complete computer system, beginning with integrated circuit *chips,* are:

1. Chip sets
2. Boards
3. Cabinets
4. Complete systems

OEM (original equipment manufacturer) companies buy hardware from computer manufacturers, package the hardware (sometimes adding special hardware), add some software, and resell the packaged system. Ordinary users generally do not have as many choices as an OEM has. An OEM, despite its name, is a *buyer,* not a *manufacturer,* of hardware.

Many minis are used as dedicated processors within systems which require more computing power than a typical micro can provide. For instance, a CAT (computerized axial tomography) scanner used in medical diagnosis usually has a mini within it. Many other minis are used as general-purpose computing systems or in the support of data processing applications such as banking systems; minis are also used as *front ends* to supercomputers.

Mainframes

The typical general-purpose computer, before minis and micros evolved, was called a **mainframe.** The term *mainframe* is still used to describe the most expensive general-purpose computers. Some mainframes have a larger word size than micros or minis. Figure 18.3 lists the word sizes on some mainframes. (Burroughs and Sperry--Sperry used to be UNIVAC--have joined to become Unisys.) Mainframes are sold as complete systems, and they generally require a special computer-room environment: special power, special cooling, humidity control, dust control, fire-abatement equipment, and so forth. Minis and micros are generally less sensitive, but we expect more from mainframes in terms of performance. Expectations are not always fulfilled: some models classified by their makers as minis (for example, DEC's VAX) have mainframe characteristics and can match or exceed the performance of some mainframes. This emphasizes the (ultimately) arbitrary nature of these classifications.

Mainframe systems are found in most large firms, government agencies, or universities. They typically support large database systems, large transaction processing systems, and statistical or numerically oriented application programs. The top end of the VAX family has performance which is comparable to that of IBM's most powerful mainframe. Of course, this model (the VAX 8978) sells for a mainframe price--about $5 million.

Machine	Word size
Burroughs (Unisys) 6700	48
Cray I	64
CDC Cyber	64
IBM 370	32
IBM 4300	32
Sperry (Unisys) 1100	36

Figure 18.3 Some mainframes and their word sizes

Model:	MicroVAX II	8550	8810	8840
Minimum:	2	32	48	128
Maximum:	16	256	512	512

Figure 18.4 Minimum and maximum physical memory (MB)

Virtual Memory Revisited

Each model of the VAX family of computers has 32-bit addresses and so can address up to 2^{32} bytes (4 gigabytes, or GB) of memory. However, various models differ in the minimum and maximum **physical memory** that can actually be connected to them. Figure 18.4 shows the minimum and maximum physical memory supported by several VAX models; *all* of them, it should be emphasized, use 32-bit addresses.

A computer with virtual memory can execute programs that are too large to fit into the entire physical memory of the system, or it can execute more simultaneous programs than can fit into the system's physical memory. How is this possible? The apparent magic is due to the fact that the operating system uses **memory management hardware** to keep track of which programs are in use and where the various parts of these programs are actually located. In the VAX, programs are broken up into 512-byte units called **pages**. The operating system is responsible for maintaining a table--the **page table**--to keep track of where each page of a program is. Where can a program's pages be? Any given page might be, at any given time, in physical memory or on a disk (where programs are typically stored when they are not being executed). While a program is executing, each memory reference (for instruction fetch, operand fetch, and result store) requires that the hardware consult the page table. If the required location is not in *physical* memory, then an interrupt called a **page fault** occurs: the handler for this fault is an operating system routine that transfers the required page from disk to physical memory.

What happens if no physical memory is available? Some allocated memory will have to be *de*allocated (and, perhaps, written back to disk) so that the referenced location can be placed in physical memory. Sometimes a set of programs causes a vicious cycle of page faults: one program generates a page fault, but there is no available physical memory, so a page must be deallocated from another program. But, when the program whose page was deallocated starts executing again, it makes a reference to an item on the page that was deallocated, and the page fault handler deallocates a page from the first program. A program that has referenced a memory location on a page which is on disk cannot continue until the required page has been transferred from disk to physical memory, and transfers from disk to memory are much slower than transfers from memory to memory. Thus, it is possible for a system to spend most of its time handling page faults--transferring pages from memory to disk and from disk to memory--and have little or none left over for useful computing. Such a system is **thrashing**; the operating system's page allocation policy (how it chooses which page to replace) can help prevent thrashing, but a system that often thrashes probably has insufficient physical memory.

Virtual memory is a complex topic; we have discussed it only briefly. It is interesting, however, to consider the similarities between virtual memory and cache memory. In both cases there is a small, fast memory and a large, slow memory. In both cases information is transferred from the large memory to the small one *on demand,* and (in both cases) if more information is stored in the fast memory, the system runs faster.

Supercomputers and Minisupercomputers

Supercomputers and minisupercomputers are not listed as a separate category at the beginning of this chapter because they are not *general*-purpose computers; they are *special*-purpose, very high performance computers. The first of the modern supercomputers was the Control Data Corporation (CDC) model 6600, which was designed specifically for use in science and engineering. Shortly after designing the 6600, Seymour Cray, CDC's leading computer architect, left to form his own company, Cray Research. Cray Research does not produce general-purpose computers; they produce only supercomputers, costing from about $5 million to about $20 million. In 1987, it was estimated there were 200 supercomputers in use in the entire world, and about two-thirds of them were built by Cray. In 1987, ETA Systems, a CDC subsidiary, was formed with the goal of helping CDC regain its leadership position in supercomputers. They introduced the ETA10-P, which is claimed to be the first supercomputer system selling for less than $1 million.

Supercomputers are special-purpose computers: they are designed specifically to achieve very high performance for solving problems in which floating-point operations predominate. For this reason, the performance of a supercomputer is usually measured in **megaflops**--millions of floating-point operations per second--rather than MIPs. Floating-point operations predominate for example in aerodynamics, nuclear physics, meteorology, geophysics. Supercomputers achieve their very high performance by use of many of the techniques we have discussed: fast hardware, many registers, pipelining, and simple instruction sets. In particular, supercomputers have **floating-point units**--special hardware to execute floating point arithmetic quickly. These floating-point units are typically pipelined: recall (from chapter 13) that floating-point arithmetic can be broken into several steps--extraction of the exponent and fraction, alignment of the exponents, addition of the fractions, and renormalization, for example. In a supercomputer floating-point unit, each step might be one stage of a pipeline.

The peak performance of the Cray computers is between several hundred and about one thousand megaflops (a thousand megaflops is also called a **gigaflop,** or gflop). The ETA10-P has a peak performance of 375 megaflops, and the high-end ETA supercomputer is predicted to execute just over one gflop. We should be aware of the fact that the *peak* performance of a computer is really its *maximum* performance; there are many factors which make it unlikely that a system will sustain that performance during the course of any actual workload.

Minisupercomputers are a still newer class of computers; they can be divided in two broad subclasses. One subclass of minisupercomputers consists of machines that attempt to be to supercomputers what the minicomputers of the 1960s and 1970s were to mainframes: they try to provide a large percentage of the performance of a supercomputer, at only a small percentage of the price of a supercomputer. The second subclass of minisupercomputers is composed of a heterogeneous group of machines that use **multiprocessing**--a large number of CPUs--to provide high performance. The Connection Machine, for example, produced by Thinking Machines Corporation, uses 65,536 processors; an earlier version, in commercial use, uses about 16,000 processors. Intel, Sequent, Encore, BBN and a variety of other companies are producing--or have announced--computer systems with tens to thousands of processors. Many of the commercial multiprocessing supercomputers are based on designs from computer science and computer engineering departments of universities throughout the U.S.A.

How can thousands of processors be used? Consider searching a large file for some data item; instead of having a single processor search the entire file, each processor of a Connection Machine, for example, can be programmed to search a small portion of the file. Multiprocessor machines are clearly well-suited to special applications; a major challenge in computer science research is to find ways of rewriting programs to take advantage of multiple processors.

As we might expect, supercomputers can also take advantage of multiprocessing--and they do. The larger Cray systems have 2, 4, or 16 CPUs; we can expect that the categories of supercomputer and minisupercomputer soon will be as difficult to distinguish as is now the case with minicomputers and mainframes.

Selecting and Configuring a Computer System

We have discussed some of the choices we can make when we write a program: we can solve a given problem in many ways. Even when we have selected the best algorithm, there are many choices to make while implementing the algorithm as a program: often, we can make time vs. space, or other, trade-offs. There are almost as many different kinds of computers as there are ways of solving a particular problem; what choices do we make when selecting a computer?

First, we must define our computing needs. If we are upgrading an existing installation to provide greater capacity, then our choices are largely limited by *compatibility* considerations: users with large investments in programs and data files usually cannot afford the time and money required to convert to a new, incompatible computer. Even users who religiously use only industry-standard *machine-independent* languages such as COBOL and FORTRAN discover that machine dependencies creep in. Furthermore, many applications reflect operating system characteristics. So more often than not, conversion costs preclude switching to an incompatible computer.

If we are dealing with a new installation then compability is not an issue, so we can start by defining our computing needs. We must identify, as well as we can, factors such as transaction volume and rate--defining the peak, the average, and the distribution of the expected work load. We must forecast, as well as we can, our system's expected workload *growth* over a multiyear period. If the application involves some heavy-duty computing, we should probably prepare and run **benchmark** programs on the kinds of computers we think are suitable. A benchmark program allows us to compare the performance of different systems on the same workload, but it may not be very useful if the benchmark doesn't accurately reflect the system's actual workload. Preparing, running, and analyzing the results of benchmark programs can take a number of experienced people from a few months to well over a year.

Once we have defined our computing needs--an exhaustive exercise that can take many people a significant amount of time--we start making choices on the basis of cost. Of course, the meaning of cost itself is subject to debate; a sensible approach to cost is to consider the proposed system's life cycle. What will it cost to purchase, install, train staff, operate, maintain, and expand this system, over (say) the next five years? This establishes the system's **life cycle cost.**

To ourselves, we keep repeating, "All other things being equal, buy the least expensive system." It sounds simple, but as we might suspect, there is no algorithm for verifying that all other things are equal. For example, we may have a new application which requires nonstop operation; down time of even one hour would be catastrophic. This requirement would immediately limit our hardware selection to either the higher-cost, very-high-reliability **fault-tolerant** systems--such as those made by Tandem or Stratus--or to a system from a manufacturer who is willing to provide a resident engineer and a maintenance agreement that essentially guarantees nonstop operation. If we are located in a smaller town in a lightly-populated region, our choices may be very limited.

There are many, many choices to be made--too many to consider fully here. We will simply illustrate some of the choices involved, assuming that we have opted to base the new application on a VAX. Perhaps our choice was prompted by wanting to be compatible with the other parts of the organization we work for. It may be that once the new application is completed, we intend to package it and sell it as a **turnkey system**: a complete system for a specific application such as banking, inventory control, etc., that comes ready to use--all the user needs to do is *turn the key*. In that case, we will be particularly attracted to hardware that comes from a manufacturer with a widespread field maintenance organization.

Some Choices in Configuring a Computer System

Suppose we are about to configure a VAX system. What choices can--or must--we make? First, we must select the processor--the CPU. In 1988 there were at least ten single CPU systems, ranging from the MicroVAX to the 8810. Our choice might be influenced by the results of benchmark programs.

Having chosen a CPU, we must choose an appropriate amount of physical memory. The choices run in ranges--from 2 to 16 MB for the MicroVAX II, and from 48 to 512 MB for the 8810. Some CPUs provide battery backup for memory as a standard feature; others have it as an option. Should we choose it, if it is an option? Even the smallest VAXes support the entire VAX instruction set, but more of it may be implemented by firmware or software than is the case with the larger VAXes. In the case of the MicroVAX, a **floating-point accelerator,** to speed up floating-point operations, is available as a processor option. Do we need it?

Now we must decide on mass storage. Among other considerations, we need to consider capacity, performance, reliability, removability, and size. In some cases, availability of floor space dictates which disk storage system is selected. For the VAX, there are almost a dozen choices, ranging from 5 1/4" diskette drives, through 200 MB removable-media disks, to 600 MB fixed (nonremovable) disks. In choosing disks, both performance and cost can be greatly affected by the type of disk controller that each disk needs. For example, some controllers can only handle two drives, while others may handle up to 32 drives; some controllers support a mix of different drive types.

Next, we must consider what kind of magnetic tape we need--if any. There are at least two good reasons to include a tape drive in most configurations: they provide a low-cost, compact, high capacity, easily transported medium for software distribution, and they allow for disk file backup. Each VAX must have some device to load software (such as the operating system) from; DEC calls this the **load device,** and it is often a tape or diskette drive. In addition, each VAX must have a device that the operating system resides on and runs from; DEC calls this the **system device,** and it is usually some kind of disk.

Just as we think the end is near, we discover that some of the more difficult choices have yet to be made. What kinds of communication interfaces will be needed? Will this be an 8 user system, a 100 user system, or something in between? Will it be a laboratory system? Will any special devices--such as ADCs, DACs, or digital I/O devices be used? Will the system be part of a network? How will users interact: will CRTs suffice, or will they need intelligent workstations? What are the hardcopy output requirements? Will there be input devices such as scanners and digitizers? How will all this hardware be packaged? We will need to select mounting racks. We will need to verify that the power supplies provided are adequate for all the options we want. Have we ordered the right number of cables, with the right connectors? Will they be long enough?

The details of configuring a VAX system are sufficiently complex that DEC has written special software (an **expert system**) to assist in this task. There are so many configuration possibilities, and so many configuration prerequisites and constraints, that potential customers often find them difficult to sort out. Even a computer manufacturer's sales staff--which works full-time preparing proposals for customers--can easily make mistakes. So, proposed configurations are supplied as input to DEC's configuration-checking programs, to ensure that everything fits.

Here, we are putting at the end what often comes first: we need to select the right software. Actually, what we mean by *the right software* is *in addition* to the application software which we intend to use. We must order additional software, *with* our hardware, in order to make the hardware useful. For example, we must choose some or all of the following:

1. Operating system software (VMS, ULTRIX, UNIX)
2. Networking software
3. Programming language compilers
4. Diagnostic programs
5. Utility programs

It should be clear from this discussion that choosing and configuring a computer system is a challenging project.

Pricing Trends

Component costs in computer technology have been dropping ever since the introduction of the transistor in the 1950s. This is a remarkable phenomenon: costs in most other sectors of manufacturing have been rising, yet--despite inflation--they have been dramatically falling in the electronics area. IBM takes pride in illustrating their record over the 26 years beginning in 1953, as shown in figure 18.5. If IBM were to update this chart, progress on all six curves would continue. For instance, since 1979, memory chips have increased in capacity from 16K bits to 64K bits to 256K bits to 1M bits to 4M bits.

It is also interesting to note that, although component costs go down, system prices do not necessarily go down. Vendors always have the choice of delivering either a higher performance system

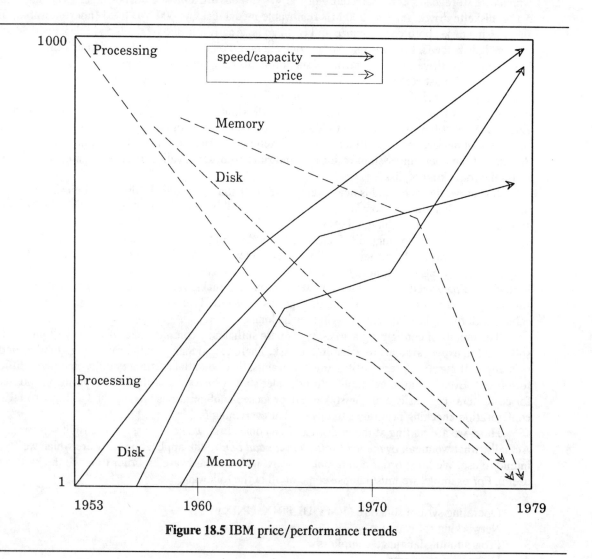

Figure 18.5 IBM price/performance trends

for the same price, or a same performance system for a lower price; they often prefer the former option. However, when we consider inflation (even single-digit inflation), we realize that even when manufacturers keep the price constant, it is actually decreasing, in terms of *real* price.

While hardware component costs are dropping, software costs are rising. Producing quality software is labor-intensive--as anyone who has completed the programming exercises in this book well knows. So software *manufacturing* costs rise with salaries; customers will likely see fewer no-charge software tools provided with computers as this trend continues.

The key to lower cost is in volume production: their first hand-held programmable calculator cost Hewlett-Packard over $1 million to produce. Their manufacturing cost today must be low indeed for them to make a profit from selling a much more powerful calculator for under $50. The reduction in cost is attributable to automated mass production; this effect is most striking in the microprocessor field. An M6800 processor chip could be bought for less than $10 a few years ago, while the M6800 reference manual cost $25. The same chip today is much cheaper, but the manual still costs $25. Volume production of books does not reduce costs to the degree that is common in the chip fabrication business.

It was inconceivable fifteen or twenty years ago that an ordinary person could have a whole computer system at home, for personal use. The average cost of an automobile--which most individuals consider a necessity, and therefore affordable--has increased over the last twenty years from around $2,000 to over $14,000. Over the same period of time, the price of small computer systems has decreased from nearly $100,000 to $1,000 or less.

Summary

We have tried to identify the differences between microcomputers, minicomputers, and mainframe computers. These distinctions are somewhat arbitrary, and they change over time. At the present time, the best distinguishing features are word size and cost: most micros still use 8- or 16-bit words, most minis use 16- or 32-bit words, and most mainframes use words of 32 bits or more. As a general rule, both the performance and the cost increase as one goes from a micro to a mini, or from a mini to a mainframe, but the performance increase is typically less than the price increase.

Micros offer the greatest flexibility in terms of packaging. They also make the greatest demands on a user's technical skills. The larger minis and most mainframes often come packaged as whole systems, ready to use.

Supercomputers are special-purpose computers, usually specialized for floating-point operations in scientific and engineering applications. Multiple processors will probably be the basis of the highest performance computers of the future.

Pricing trends in computing go counter to those found in almost every other economic field. This has been true for very large as well as very small computers. Hardware component costs will probably continue to decline as new technology evolves. While system costs may not come down, more capability at the same price level will probably continue to be offered. Software costs, on the other hand, are expected to continue to increase.

Exercises for Chapter 18

1. Many supercomputers have optimized their instruction sets and their hardware implementations to support matrix operations. One common operation is that of matrix addition. Assume that two matrices are each stored as one-dimensional arrays. With a general-purpose computer--such as the VAX--how many instructions must be executed to add two arrays of n words? Design one or more instructions that would permit a supercomputer to perform the same operation in much less time. (Hint: the VAX has instructions like these, but not for adding arrays.)

2.   The one-time, per-user, cost for a large VAX may be considerable--it may be much greater than the cost of some personal computers. Discuss the advantages and disadvantages of a single, multi-user system vs. multiple single-user systems. Compare maximum program sizes, file space, reliability, availability, predictability, performance range, and so forth.

3.   Suggest and discuss an approach to the problem of the preceding exercise which combines the best of both worlds. What would it take to implement your suggestion? What new problems would your approach introduce?

How Does the Hardware Work?

Introduction

If we want to understand computing, sooner or later we must ask ourselves, "How does the hardware work?" This is an intriguing question: if we pursue it far enough, we can make a career of computer or electrical engineering. If we pursue it further, we can end up in solid-state physics or theoretical chemistry: the properties of materials--their molecular structure, their behavior under different temperature conditions and in varying electrical fields, for example--are at the heart of what makes a computer function. Obviously, in one chapter of an introductory text we can barely scratch the surface of the answer, but it is surprising how simple (and elegant) many of the principles of computer design really are.

Historical Evolution

The earliest machines that we would call "computing machines" were entirely mechanical. We generally credit Blaise Pascal for having built the first mechanical calculator in the 1600s, but Wilhelm Schickard built a mechanical calculator in 1623--the year that Pascal was born. Charles Babbage made major contributions to the field of mechanical calculators with his Difference Engine and Analytical Engine in the mid 1800s. Another major leap forward came in the late 1800s, when electricity and the electromechanical relay came into use: calculators began to be built using electromechanical relay logic; IBM was building accounting and tabulating machines with relays, even before it was called IBM.

Vacuum tubes became commercially available in the 1910s; by the 1940s (with military support during World War II) they began replacing relays in computers. Figure 19.1 shows a time line of the revolutions in electronic components. The transition to vacuum tube computers is credited to the designers of the ENIAC, which was the world's first *electronic* computer. Earlier computers used relays; they were still computers, but **electromechanical** rather than electronic ones. What difference does it make? Speed: a relay can be used in a logic circuit (or **gate**), and it can be switched a certain number of times per second; a vacuum tube can also be used in a circuit, but the vacuum tube (unlike the relay) has no moving (mechanical) parts, so it can be switched many more times per second. The speed with which a gate can be switched is one of the major determinants of a computer's operating speed, so vacuum tube computers were much faster than relay computers.

In the late 1940s, a group of scientists at Bell Laboratories invented the **transistor.** They found that transistors could replace vacuum tubes, so they began implementing gates with transistors. Shortly thereafter the first transistorized computer was built. Transistors are much smaller than vacuum tubes: a transistor may be about the size of a pea, while a small vacuum tube is about the size of a carrot. Smaller is often faster, when electronic circuits are concerned. In addition, transistors use very little power--this is why transistor radios can be battery powered. Vacuum tubes use much more power than transistors, so they get much hotter than transistors; heat is an enemy of reliable operation. Computers that use transistors are faster, less expensive, and more reliable than computers that use vacuum tubes.

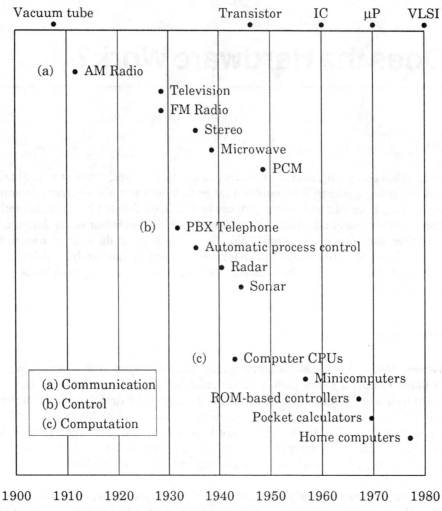

Figure 19.1 Electronic component revolutions

Early transistorized computers used **discrete components**: each part was identifiable; each transistor, resistor, capacitor, and so forth, had to be mounted by hand to create a gate or other circuit. This method of assembly is labor intensive, expensive, and error prone; engineers soon realized that an electronic device with fewer discrete components is more reliable and less expensive than one with more components. A major advance in reducing the number of discrete components was made in the early 1960s, when the first **integrated circuit** (IC) chips were built. The first ICs used **small-scale integration**; one such IC replaced tens of discrete components such as transistors and resistors. Since then the technology has progressed remarkably: from small-scale integration (SSI) to medium-scale integration (MSI), to large-scale integration (LSI), to very large-scale integration (VLSI). A VLSI chip can replace hundreds of thousands or millions of discrete components: the CPU of a MicroVAX, for example, consists of a single VLSI chip; RAM chips storing 4 million bits are also commercially available.

At every stage in this evolution from discrete components to VLSI, speed, reliability and cost have improved, because of a number of interrelated factors:

1. Smaller components
2. Fewer components
3. Fewer interconnections
4. Lower power consumption
5. Less heat dissipation

In our effort to understand how computer hardware works, we could try to describe how each chip in a VAX works, and then describe how each chip interacts with all the other parts of the hardware. We would not gain much insight using this approach; instead, we will describe the functions that a computer must perform, and then describe how hardware can be built to implement each function.

The simplest imaginable computer would use words of 1 bit; its ALU would process 1-bit data, store 1-bit results, and so forth. If we were to use such a computer, we could program it to perform extended-range arithmetic; in fact, we could program it to do anything that a VAX--or any other computer--can do. So, let us see how we can store, transmit, process, and compare single-bit words; then we will have some idea how newer technology can be used to simulate the older technology we will describe. We can then enhance our design with more parallelism--for example, we can build hardware for manipulating 2-bit operands. The pioneering work described by Stibitz, in figure 19.2, shows some of the flavor of this approach.

Functional Elements of a Computer

What functions must our 1-bit computer be able to perform? It must

1. Store a bit
2. Transmit a bit
3. Combine two one-bit operands to produce a result
4. Compare two one-bit operands

We saw how bits can be transmitted when we discussed serial communication, in chapter 11. Bit transmission *inside* a computer (from memory to a register, or from a register to the ALU) is **synchronous**. All of the parts of our 1-bit computer fit into a single box, so we can use a common clock for the memory, ALU, registers, and all other components; there is no need for framing bits. (Recall that the purpose of framing bits is to provide timing synchronization in the absence of a common clock.)

Storing a Bit

Bits are stored in **memory,** and there are two common types of memory: **volatile** and **non-volatile.** Volatile memory retains its contents only so long as power is supplied to it; non-volatile memory retains data even when disconnected from a power source. Volatile memory--using vacuum tubes, transistors or integrated circuits--can also be implemented with an electromechanical relay; all we must do is decide what voltage level corresponds to the value 1 and what voltage level corresponds to the value 0. Then, if the voltage, V, exceeds some threshold--say, $+n$ volts--it will be considered a 1 bit; if it is below a threshold--say, $-n$ volts--it will be considered a 0 bit. Any voltage level that is neither above the first threshold nor below the second has an undefined value. We can represent the storing of a bit with the "gate" shown in figure 19.3. The arm in this figure pivots around point x, and can connect I to either point a--storing a 1--or to point b--storing a 0. A control mechanism

Early Computers

George R. Stibitz

In the late fall of 1937, I was asked, as a "mathematical engineer" at Bell Telephone Laboratories (BTL), to look into the design of the magnetic elements of a relay. Until that time I had had no acquaintance with relays, and I was curious about their properties and capabilities. In particular, the logic functions that the relays embodied were interesting, and it occurred to me that binary arithmetic would be naturally compatible with the binary behavior of relay contacts.

I borrowed a few U-type relays from a junk pile the Bell Labs maintained, finding some with low-resistance windings suitable for operation on a few volts of dry battery. Late in November, I worked out the logic of binary addition of the two one-digit binary numbers, each defined by the state of a manually operated switch. The two-digit output of this adding circuit actuated a pair of flashlight bulbs. With a scrap of board, some snips of metal from a tobacco can, two relays, two flashlight bulbs, and a couple of dry cells, I assembled an adder on the kitchen table at our home.

I took this device to the Labs with me and demonstrated that binary devices like the relays were capable of performing arithmetic operations. Of course, I sketched a schematic for a multidigit binary adder, and pointed out that a relay machine could do anything a desk calculator could do.

The problem of interface between decimal computists and a binary computer next engaged my attention. It seemed impractical to persuade the computists to learn the binary notation, and the alternatives appeared to be those of making the computer convert decimal numbers into binary ones or of making the computer into a decimal device. This last alternative was abandoned at once. However, in its place I proposed a mixed binary-decimal system in which each decimal digit was converted into a binary number. Then all arithmetic operations could be performed by binary adders suitably interconnected.

The circuitry required to carry between binary adders was rather messy, and it occurred to me that if each of the digits were increased by three units before adding, then the sum would be increased by six units, and a sum equal to nine would become a binary fifteen. Any greater sums would be binary numbers of more digits. Thus in the "excess-3" notation, decimal 9 is 1111 and decimal 10 is 10000. In this notation, the decimal carry occurs if and only if there is a carry in the excess-3 adder.

An incidental advantage of the excess-3 notation is that the binary complement is the binary form of the decimal complement. A simple reversal of polarity in the relays that represent numbers in excess-3 form produces the decimal complement of the represented number.

The investigations into the excess-3 system and the relays that would embody it took place, as I recall, toward the end of that winter and in the early spring of 1938.

Figure 19.2 Reprint from Stibitz

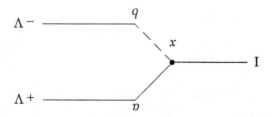

Figure 19.3 Storing one bit

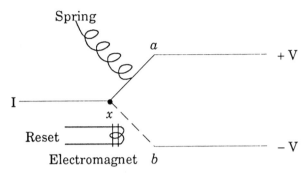

Figure 19.4 1-bit relay storage device

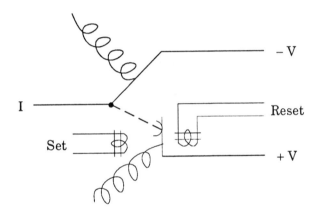

Figure 19.5 1-bit nonvolatile relay storage device

causes the arm to pivot around point x; that control mechanism determines which position the arm has at any given time.

A relay can be used to store a bit: the control mechanism is composed of a spring, attached to the arm and pulling it toward point a (in figure 19.4), and an electromagnet which pulls the arm-- against the resistance of the spring--to point b. When an electric current flows through the coil of the electromagnet, a magnetic field is induced; this magnetic field pulls the arm to position b, and it is held in this position as long as current flows through the electromagnet. When the current through the electromagnet is turned off, it releases the arm, and the spring pulls the arm back to point a-- causing the gate to *forget* the bit that was stored; we consider the bit forgotten because it will be a 1 no matter what it was before.

When current flows through the *Reset* input lines, the arm moves down and is held in the 0 bit position; when no current flows through the electromagnet, the arm position defaults to the 1 value. This is a 1-bit **volatile** storage device. We can transform it into a **nonvolatile** storage device, as shown in figure 19.5. The 1-bit storage device shown in figure 19.4 has no difficulty *remembering* a 1, because its spring pulls the movable arm into that position whenever power to the electromagnet is turned off. The storage device shown in figure 19.5 has a **latch**: if current ever flows through the *set* electromagnet, the movable arm is pulled down and latched (the lower spring in the figure holds the latch against the end of the movable arm); turning off the power will not change the setting of this storage device. If we want to store a 0 in this device, we must send current through the *reset* electromagnet: this will pull the latch away from the movable arm, so the upper spring in the figure can pull the movable arm into the 0 position. We, of course, decide which position represents 0 and which represents 1.

Most large capacity, nonvolatile storage devices use ferromagnetic recording media: a magnet has a north and a south pole, and we can use the orientation of these poles to represent binary 1 and 0. The coating material used on the surface of a magnetic tape or disk allows us to orient "miniature magnets" on the material's surface--thereby storing 1s and 0s. If we have a sequence of bar magnets, as in figure 19.6, we could arrange their north and south poles in different patterns, to represent different bit patterns. With three magnets, and a convention concerning which pole represents 1 and which 0, we can store the bit string 010 by arranging the magnets as shown in figure 19.7. With six magnets, we can store 001 and 100, as shown in figure 19.8. If we want to use magnetic alignment to store bits, we need more than just the magnets; what additional hardware is required? Basically, a **read head** containing a coil of wire moves along a line of magnets; it *intercepts* the magnetic field produced by each magnet, which induces a current in the read head's coil of wire. The direction of the current flow depends on the orientation of the magnetic field, so the head can read the bits. The spacing of the magnets on the recording medium must be carefully controlled; the closer the spacing, the higher the recording density.

Electricity and magnetism have a marvelous symmetry: on the one hand, we can use an electric current to create a magnetic field. This is what makes a relay's electromagnet work, and it is also how we write on a magnetic disk or tape: a pattern of electric currents flows through the write head, which is a small electromagnet; the pattern of currents induces a corresponding pattern of magnetic fields, which--in turn--magnetizes the medium with the appropriate pattern of 0s and 1s.

The other half of the symmetry--using a magnetic field to induce an electric current--is the basis of reading the information we have stored on a disk or tape: a magnetic field passed through a coil of wire (or a coil of wire passed through a magnetic field), induces an electric current in the coil, whose direction of flow is related to the orientation of the magnetic field. (This is also the principle upon which the operation of electric power generators is based.)

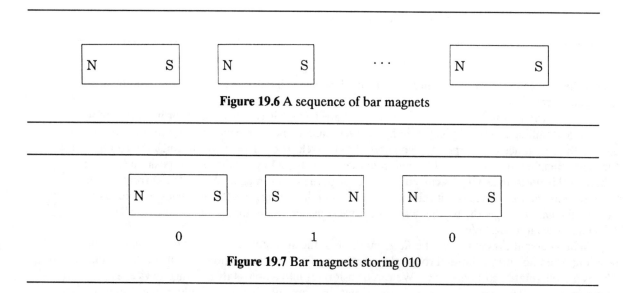

Figure 19.6 A sequence of bar magnets

Figure 19.7 Bar magnets storing 010

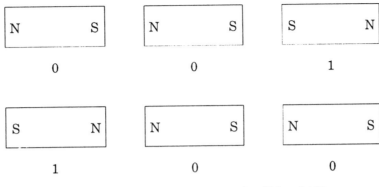

Figure 19.8 Bar magnets storing 001 and 100

With this quick course in electricity and magnetism, we can see that magnetic-media based recording and playback devices have the following characteristics:

1. The write head uses an electromagnet to create magnetic patterns on the recording medium.
2. The read head uses a coil to sense the orientation of magnetic patterns on the recording medium.
3. The recorded information is nonvolatile because the recording medium does not spontaneously change the orientation of its magnetic fields.
4. The recorded information can be erased and rewritten, because the write head can reorient the magnetic fields of the recording medium.
5. The recording medium and the read/write heads must be in relative motion in order to store or retrieve information: the tape must move, and the disk must spin.

The magnetic recording technique we have just described is similar to the one used for recording at 800 bpi; it is called Non-Return to Zero Invert (NRZI). A different technique is used for recording at 1600 bpi; it is called Phase Modulation (PM). Yet another technique is used for recording at 6250 bpi; it is called Group Code Recording (GCR). The techniques used for higher recording densities are more reliable than those used for lower densities, but the higher density techniques also require more sophisticated--and more expensive--hardware. All three techniques, however, are based on creating and then sensing magnetic patterns.

Building an ALU

Let us now consider building a simple ALU. It should be able to compute the logical **and**, the logical **or**, and the arithmetic sum of pairs of 1-bit operands; it should also be able to compare a pair of 1-bit operands. If we use relays, we can implement gates as shown in figure 19.9. This figure is simplified: it does not show the electromagnet that is controlled by the signal at x. This control signal will close the moving arm when it is turned on; when it is off, the arm will be pulled up by a spring (which is also not shown in figure 19.9). If a current is applied to the electromagnet, the gate will "close," allowing a signal to flow from the Input to the Output.

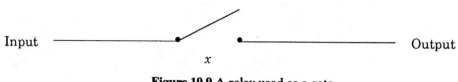

Figure 19.9 A relay used as a gate

Figure 19.10 An AND gate made of relays

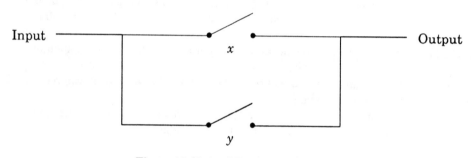

Figure 19.11 An OR gate made of relays

AND and OR Gates

If we use two gates--one controlled by signal x and the other by signal y--we can build a circuit whose output "computes" the x **and** y logic function, as shown in figure 19.10. Note that a signal sent to the Input will arrive at the Output if and only if both x and y are **set**--i.e., have current applied to their electromagnets.

A circuit to implement the logical **or** of x and y is also simple; it is shown in figure 19.11. In this case, if either x **or** y is set (or if both are set) then a signal applied to the Input will be received at the Output; this circuit, therefore, implements x **or** y.

A Comparator

What is the basis for the CMP instruction? Given inputs x and y, we want to know if they are the same--or, if they are not the same, which is greater. We can enumerate all possible outcomes of such a comparison in a table, as shown in figure 19.12. A comparator, thus, has two inputs and three possible outcomes: same, x-larger, or x-smaller. We can use an **exclusive or (xor)** circuit to

Inputs		Output
x	y	CMP
0	0	same
0	1	x-smaller
1	0	x-larger
1	1	same

Figure 19.12 All combinations of comparing 2 bits

+	0	1
0	0	1
1	1	10

XOR	0	1
0	0	1
1	1	0

Figure 19.13 Binary addition table and XOR truth table

implement a comparator: when x and y are the same, the output of the **xor** circuit is 0. When x and y are different, the output of **xor** is 1, and we can use the inputs to tell which is the larger: if the output is 1 and x is 1, then x is larger (because y must be 0)--and vice versa. We leave it as an exercise for the interested reader to build an **xor** circuit from relays.

Performing Binary Arithmetic

We saw in chapter 10 that the binary addition table is nearly identical to the truth table for **xor**. These tables are reproduced as figure 19.13, to refresh our memories. If we could build a circuit that implements **xor**, we would have most of what we need to perform binary addition--*most*, but not *all*: **xor** produces the wrong result for the sum of 1 and 1, because it doesn't indicate *carry*. Carry occurs when both addends are 1; or, rephrasing, the carry is 1 only when both inputs are 1. This sounds like the **and** function--and it is. So, we can use an **xor** circuit to calculate the sum of our two 1-bit addends, and then an **and** circuit to calculate the carry. This combined circuit is called a **half-adder**; it is shown schematically in figure 19.14. Why is this a *half*-adder? Because it has only two inputs, and--in the general case--when we add binary numbers, each addition has *three* inputs: the 2 bits in the positions we are adding, plus the carry from the previous position. (Note that, for our computer with 1-bit words, a half-adder is a full adder, because there are *no* previous bit positions.) If we want to add numbers of 2 or more bits, we can combine half-adders to make a full adder, as shown in figure 19.15. If we use the simple design shown in figure 19.15, then the sum for bit position i can't be calculated until the carry from bit position i-1 is known; the carry *ripples* from bit position to bit position, with the result that addition is slow. The design of high-speed adders is of considerable interest to manufacturers of high-performance computers; there are fascinating methods of reducing the carry ripple delays. But this topic is beyond the scope of the present book; we must move on to other matters.

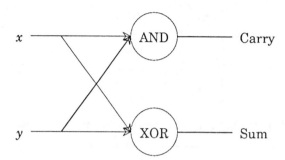

Figure 19.14 A half-adder

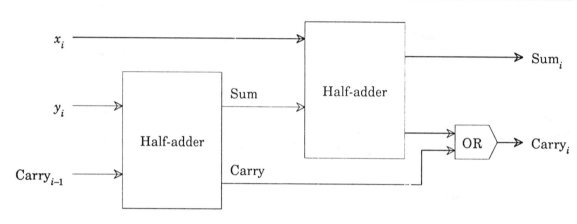

Figure 19.15 A full adder

Sequencing

The harmonious interaction of the hardware elements we have examined requires that their activation be **sequenced**: signals must arrive at the appropriate circuit(s), at the appropriate time(s). One of the simplest mechanisms used for sequencing events is found in common household machines such as washing machines and dishwashers. The user of such a machine selects an operation (e.g., heavy-duty wash cycle), and a master clock starts ticking. As time progresses, a timing disk rotates; at each instant, the timing disk determines which of the components of the machine are activated. Consider the sequence of steps for a wash cycle shown in figure 19.16; this method of displaying a sequence of events is called a **timing chart.** The event-sequencing that is depicted in this chart can be implemented by making a **timing disk** with five concentric circles; each circle is associated with a particular physical machine component that can be activated independently of the other components. Along the part of each circle that corresponds to the x's on the timing chart, there is a conductor, which allows current to flow to the corresponding machine component. The rotation of the timing disk guarantees that the current will flow to a particular component only during the prescribed period of time; a timing disk is shown schematically in figure 19.17.

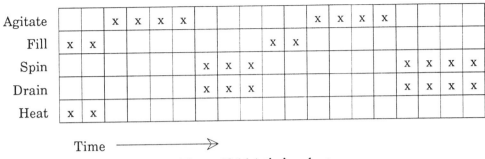

Figure 19.16 A timing chart

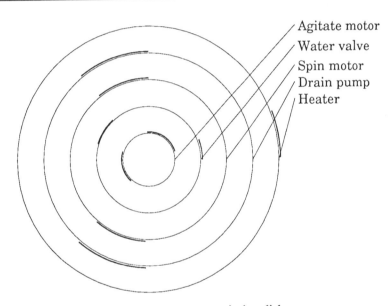

Figure 19.17 A timing disk

Each operation in a computer--such as execution of an instruction--has associated with it a timing chart to indicate the sequence of gate activations required to implement that operation. In principle, each of these sequences of activities could be implemented as a timing disk; in practice, a mechanical timing disk is much too slow for a computer, but it is conceptually similar to what computers actually use. The sequencing control signal might be one input to a circuit that implements the **and** function--called an **and** gate. In such a case, when the control signal is on it allows another signal to *pass through* the **and** gate, and when it is off it blocks the signal's passage.

From Relays to Tubes to Transistors

A relay can implement a gate, and with the right combinations of gates we can implement the **and** function, the **or** function, and so on; from these, we can build everything needed in a computer's

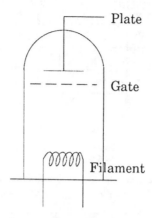

Figure 19.18 A vacuum tube simulating a relay

Figure 19.19 A transistor

ALU. If a vacuum tube could simulate a relay, it could implement a gate; we could then build an ALU as before, except that it would be a faster, electronic ALU rather than a slower, electromechanical ALU.

A vacuum tube, shown schematically in figure 19.18, can act like a relay as follows: when current is applied to the filament, the filament heats up and electrons flow through the gas inside the vacuum tube to the plate. The electrons that flow from the filament can be prevented from reaching the plate by a current that is applied to the gate of the vacuum tube. A small gate current can control a much larger filament-to-plate current.

A transistor can also simulate a relay, and so computers can be--and are--built out of transistors, as well. A transistor is shown schematically in figure 19.19; a small current at x can control the flow of current from a to b.

This is a very brief glimpse at how the hardware works. There are many texts which provide a more thorough introduction to hardware; some are understandable even by someone without an electrical engineering or physics degree. We should not frighten ourselves into thinking that the key concepts of electronics are beyond our grasp, but neither should we trick ourselves into thinking that designing and building a reliable computer is trivial. Good electrical engineers have built terrible computers because they ignored seemingly minor details such as air flow for cooling. Building a usable computer system requires expertise in almost every area of engineering--not just in electrical engineering and computer science.

Microprogramming

Microprogramming (which does not have any particular connection to programming microcomputers) is a technique that has been used since the 1960s for building most computers. Until microprogramming was invented, computers had been designed by directly implementing all the necessary functions as a series of circuits. A computer engineer would define an instruction set, sketch out the circuits to implement each instruction, and then build the hardware to implement each circuit.

In 1950, Maurice Wilkes suggested that it would be easier to build complex computers by designing circuits and building hardware for simple computers and then writing special *control programs* to implement the instruction set of the more complex computer. The end user of the computer would not care that the computer was only partly hardware and that the remainder was really software. Since the special software that implements the instruction set must be protected from being changed, it is usually stored in ROM. The term **firmware** is used for the microcode that creates a complex instruction set out of simple hardware; this name suggests that it is neither hardware nor software, but something in between.

So, a microcoded computer may be thought of as *a computer within a computer*; this organization is shown in figure 19.20. All members of the VAX family are built using an inner computer that executes firmware from the control store to implement the instructions that we human programmers write. In most VAXes the firmware is stored in ROM; for some models of the VAX we can purchase a Writable Control Store (WCS). This allows us (if we have privileged user status) to "create" new instructions, or *improve* old ones, by writing microcode sequences and placing them in the WCS--from which they are fetched and executed by the inner computer.

In principle, writing microcode programs (to implement assembly language instructions) is similar to writing machine-language programs. There are two related differences, however: first, there are even more low-level details to be concerned with, because the machine-language instructions hide some of the implementation details of the hardware. For example, the microcode for an instruction

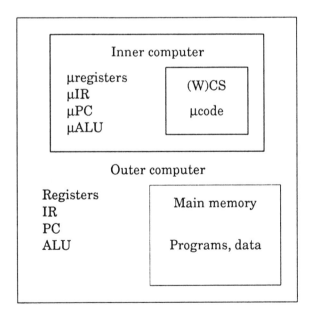

Figure 19.20 Organization of a microprogrammed computer

must include updating the PC at the correct time. Second, a microcode instruction has more fields than an assembly language instruction. For example, each microcode "word" for a VAX 11/750 is 80 bits wide, and there are 22 fields per word. The fields in a microcode word are for things like sending the ADD command to the ALU, or the READ command to memory.

Summary

People have been computing with the help of machines for over four hundred years. In the last fifty years, however, there have been enormous advances in this field: electromechanical computers were built with relays, and electronic computers have been built with vacuum tubes, transistors, and (now) integrated circuit chips. No matter what components we build a computer from, it is based on a few simple ideas: numbers can be stored as sequences of bits and bits can be stored and manipulated using circuits that can be constructed in many different ways. We described the storing of bits using relays (as Dr. Stibitz did over fifty years ago) because relays are easier to visualize than vacuum tubes, transistors or integrated circuits.

The basic operations of a computer are adding bits, transmitting bits, and comparing bits. We have discussed implementation of each of these functions. Relays can be replaced by tubes, tubes by transistors, and so on; each substitution results in increased speed and greater reliability. Modern digital computers are based on the simple ideas we have seen.

Microprogramming is a technique which lets computer designers build simple hardware and provides for sophisticated instruction sets by microcoding them either in writable control store (WCS) or read only memory (ROM).

Exercises for Chapter 19

1. A **not** gate inverts its input: if the input is 0 the output is 1, and if the input is 1 the output is 0. Sketch the schematic for building a **not** gate with relays.
2. Sketch the schematic for building an **exclusive or** gate with relays.
3. When we want an n-bit full adder, we can construct it from a series of single-bit full adders, but we need to delay the carry out from each full adder by the time it takes to complete one stage of the multibit adder. How can we implement a such a delay?
4. When an ADD instruction is implemented as a microprogram, it is broken into a series of **microinstructions**; when the whole program is executed, the ADD instruction has completed. What are some of the steps that a VAX ADD instruction can be broken into?
5. Consider the VAX's addressing modes--the "execution" of the addressing modes is also implemented as a microprogram. What are some of the steps that the interpretation of the different addressing modes can be broken into?
6. RISCs (Reduced Instruction Set Computers) are usually not microprogrammed; the designers of RISCs claim that microprogramming a computer makes it run slower. What is the relationship between RISCs and microprogramming? What is the relationship between microprogramming and performance?

■ 20 ■

Telecommunication and Networking

Introduction

We take it for granted that a computer can be used at a distance, because it is so common for computers to be connected to telecommunication networks. Accessing a computer over a telecommunication link is called **teleprocessing**. Many people use personal computers and home telephones as a link into the largest telecommunication network in the world--the one provided by our telephone companies.

The operation of an ordinary telephone is shown in a schematic manner in figure 20.1; how can something designed to transmit voices be used to transmit bits? The telephone system most of us use is an analog system; an analog telephone transmits voice information by converting changes in air pressure (produced by our speaking) into continuously varying voltage levels. The mechanical energy generated by our vocal cords (which cause air vibration) is converted into electrical energy by a microphone. Telephone lines carry this analog electrical signal; it is used to reconstruct the original audio signal when it reaches an earphone. Microphones and earphones are analog-to-analog signal converters: microphones transform mechanical energy (vibrating air) into electrical energy, and earphones (or loudspeakers) perform the inverse transformation. The phone system is in the process of being changed into a digital system, but such a massive undertaking will probably take many more years to complete.

In this chapter we will discuss some of the many ways in which computers communicate--with users and with each other--over distances ranging from a few feet to thousands of miles. We will discover that the telephone system is intimately involved in much of this communication.

Telephone Dialup Access

If we want a computer (or a computer terminal) to communicate over the telephone system with another computer, then we need a pair of converters--one at each end. Each converter itself implements two conversion functions, as shown in figure 20.2. When a converter's input is the telephone's audio signal, the converter is called an **acoustic coupler**; acoustic couplers are convenient because they require no changes to the telephone system's wiring. Most converters skip the audio conversion entirely, however: they directly generate electrical signals acceptable to the telephone system, and they convert incoming telephone electrical signals back into bit streams. These converters

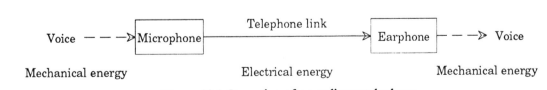

Figure 20.1 Operation of an ordinary telephone

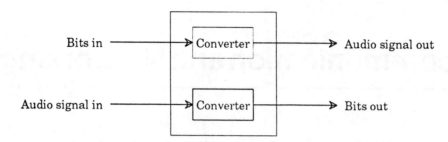

Figure 20.2 Conversion functions for telephone-computer hookups

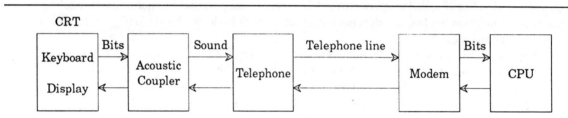

Figure 20.3 Using a modem to access a computer

are called **modems** (modulator--demodulators); a modem must be electrically connected to the telephone system. In telephone terminology, a modem is called a **data set** and the modem connection to a CRT or CPU is called its **business machine interface.** The modem's other connection, linking it to the telephone system, is called its **switched network interface.**

Direct connection using a modem used to be a nuisance; now that most telephones have modular jacks, however, it is easy to hook up a modem. The typical use of a modem or an acoustic coupler to access a computer with a modem is shown in figure 20.3. The most popular acoustic couplers operate at baud rates from 110 to 300 baud; some can operate at 1200 baud. The most common baud rates for modems are 1200 and 2400 baud; higher rates--9600 and above--are also available. Many of the higher speed modems can also operate at lower speeds, such as 300 or 1200 baud. When a multispeed modem answers an incoming call, it switches itself to the correct speed.

Modems and acoustic couplers have two connections--one to the telephone network (electrical or audio), and one to a communicating device (such as a terminal) or the computer. The connection to the terminal or computer is often through a serial interface conforming to the RS-232C standard.

The occasional user of remote access computer services can use an ordinary telephone to connect a CRT or workstation to the computer, provided that:

1. the user has an originate-modem or coupler,
2. the computer has an auto-answer modem,
3. the modems are compatible.

Modems are compatible when they both operate at the same speed, and they are both asynchronous (or both synchronous). A computer's auto-answer modem is usually permanently connected to the telephone system. The telephone subscriber is the computer's serial port to which the modem is connected. When an auto-answer modem receives a telephone ring signal, its serial interface interrupts the CPU, and the software handler is executed so that communication can take place.

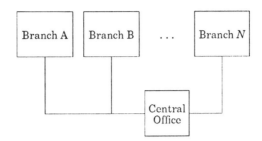

Figure 20.4 A company with many branch offices

Modems usually provide other features, such as **auto-dial** capability. A modem with auto-dial will interpret predefined character sequences coming from its serial port connection as commands to dial the telephone number encoded in the character sequence it received.

When using a hardwired CRT, turning it off may have no significance for the CPU; the CRT is probably connected to a dedicated port, and can be used as much or as little as we like. With telephone access, however--particularly on a dialup basis--there may be a great deal of contention for a telephone line. For example, a company might have several branch offices, as shown in figure 20.4. Each branch office has a minicomputer or microcomputer equipped with an auto-dialing modem, and each branch office computer automatically calls the central office each night to transmit a summary of the day's transactions to the central office's large file system. During the same call, the branch office computer receives messages, orders, and so forth, that are waiting for it on the central office's computer system. A branch computer can be programmed to call the main office's computer at a given time and to keep trying every 15 minutes thereafter if it gets a busy signal. In this way, a single telephone line connected to a modem at the main office suffices for many branch offices.

It is important for a computer to know whether a telephone line is still in use, especially if there happen to be no data transmitted over it at a particular time. How does a computer know if a caller is still on the line? This information is provided by the telephone **carrier signal**: when two modems begin to communicate, a high-pitched whistle tone is established, which is maintained until either side disconnects. If loss of the carrier signal is detected by the modem connected to the CPU, it waits a short time (about 5 to 10 ms), and if the carrier is not reestablished, the modem triggers an on-hook condition which terminates the telephone call. This both frees the telephone line and interrupts the CPU; the latter is done so the operating system can either initiate a "logout the previous user of this telephone line" procedure or try to reestablish the call by using its auto-dial modem to call the user back.

Organizations which provide dialup access for their employees or clients are concerned about system security. What security measures can be provided in addition to the password protection that is standard on most multiuser operating systems? How can we complicate life for ill-behaved "hackers?" If we remember that both call-originate and auto-answer capabilities are standard features of most modems, we can arrange for dialup access to involve a two-step procedure: first, when a user's modem originates a call, the user identifies himself or herself to the remote computer and then hangs up. Then the remote computer calls the user back. This **call-back** scheme requires an established list of authorized users and their telephone numbers.

Organizations concerned with eavesdropping or with illegal telephone wire tapping, can purchase modems that perform **encryption**: the sender's modem encrypts (encodes) everything it sends, and the receiver's modem decodes everything it receives.

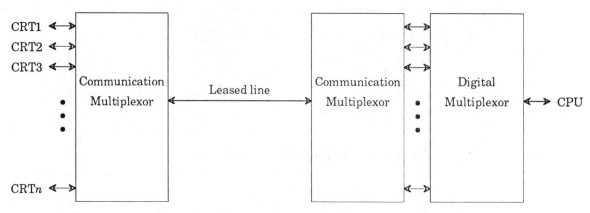

Figure 20.5 A communication multiplexor and a serial multiplexor

Leased Lines

Heavy users of remote access services often want a dedicated communication link. Such a link can be leased from the telephone company or from another firm licensed as a common carrier. As a rule, a leased line is not only a line dedicated to the lessor, but it also supports a higher maximum baud rate and has fewer transmission errors than an ordinary line. Since the cost of a leased line is substantial, it makes sense for several CRTs at one site to share a single leased line going to a remote CPU. This can be done with a **communication multiplexor.** Such a multiplexor differs from multiplexors which connect directly to a CPU. For example, the VAX's DHU11 multiplexor provides 16 connections to a single VAX serial interface, while a communication multiplexor allows many CRTs to share a single leased telephone line. We can use a communication multiplexor with a computer's serial multiplexor, as shown in figure 20.5. The CPU is not necessarily aware of the pair of communication multiplexors; the CPU interacts with each remote CRT as if it had its own modem and dedicated communication line. Once again, a service is provided that is **transparent**; the same software will work with or without a communication multiplexor.

The start-stop, **asynchronous** communication we saw earlier (in chapter 11) is adequate for relatively low-speed traffic on either hardwired or dedicated lines. But when we share a leased line, we want to get the most out of it; the start and stop bits are a waste of time and money. We can eliminate them by using a common clock for the sender and the receiver, in which case we are no longer restricted to sending one character at a time. We can send groups of characters with a **synchronous** communication protocol. In synchronous communication, we always transmit a group, or **block,** of characters. A block may be composed of several lines of text or whole screenfuls. The format of the block must be agreed upon by the sender and receiver; the general format is:

SOM <header> block of message bytes <trailer> EOM

No framing bits are used; instead, we use framing *bytes*--one set at the beginning of the message and another at its end. The ASCII codes for start-of-message (SOM) and end-of-message (EOM) are used for this purpose. Once message transmission starts, it proceeds at a uniform rate until all the bits have been sent: it is transmitted synchronously. Many more bits of information can be transmitted each second when we don't use framing bits for each byte. The header might include identification of the originator, and the trailer might include a message checksum for detecting transmission errors.

Data processing systems often do things one screen at a time: filling in the blank fields on the screen corresponds to filling out a form; when the completed form is transmitted, it is called a **transaction.** After any local (off-line) editing to correct typing errors has been performed, the *enter* key on the CRT is pressed. This informs the CPU that the CRT is ready to transmit a screenful; if it receives a signal from the CPU, the CRT transmits its entire screen synchronously. In some cases, the CRT can distinguish between the information which defines the *form* on the screen and those items that have been keyed in (that represent data); only data need be transmitted, which saves additional time.

Line-sharing can take place at another level. When a computer uses vectored interrupts, an interrupt vector is dedicated to each device--so when a device requests an interrupt that is granted, the vector contains the address of the device's interrupt handler. In data processing, we can trade off line costs and interface costs against CRT memory cost. Since a synchronous CRT has enough memory to store a full screen of text, there is less danger of data loss if an interrupt is serviced a little more slowly than with asynchronous CRTs. If several CRTs share a single line to the CPU, then when the CPU receives an interrupt request, it can **poll** the line to find out which CRT needs service. Servicing a CRT this way takes longer than it would if each CRT had a dedicated interrupt line, but it is also less expensive. The interrupt response time is usually adequate--unless there are too many heavily used CRTs sharing a single interrupt line.

Historically, asynchronous communication has been common on scientific and engineering computer systems, while synchronous communication has been common on business data processing systems.

Communication Interfaces

We are accustomed to seeing two kinds of electrical power plugs in North America: the older two-prong plug and the newer three-prong (grounded) plug. Fortunately, the newer type is *upward compatible* with the older type. In most respects, the RS-232C ANSI standard for the communication interface is analogous to the power plug standard: the ANSI standard specifies how many prongs are provided (in this case they are called **pins**), how each is used (for all 25 of them!), their physical layout (the pin to pin spacing), and the voltage levels involved. The RS-232C standard prescribes mechanical, electrical, and logical requirements; what does it have to do with computing? That standard is the most widely supported interface standard for dealing with CRTs, serial printers, serial computer interfaces, modems, couplers, and so forth.

The RS-232C standard is slowly being supplanted by the upward compatible RS-422 and RS-423 interconnect standards. These newer standards allow for longer cable lengths than were anticipated when the older standard was adopted: with the old standard, the maximum distance between a CRT and serial interface is several hundred meters, but the new standard permits much longer distances. In principle, RS-232C only supports distances up to 50 feet at data rates of 20 Kbaud (distances are shorter at higher speeds). The RS-422 and RS-423 interface standards support distances up to 4,000 feet, or data rates as high as 10 Mbaud. Upward compatibility means that existing systems can be upgraded over a period of time.

The only other common asynchronous serial interface standard is the old one established by the model 33 Teletype. It uses a 20 milliampere current loop interface. Loss of current for whatever reason is detected by the sender and receiver immediately--just like loss of the carrier signal with a modem. When current loss is detected, the TTY "chatters" until the broken communication link is reestablished, or until the TTY is turned off. This was a good way to detect breaks in communication lines due to storms, acts of war, etc. Sometimes an interface is referred to as an *EIA interface*; this is an incomplete specification (EIA is the Electronics Industries Association), and the specifier is likely referring to the RS-232C interface.

Modem Control

When we discussed character I/O, we looked at a simple serial interface. Its control/status register (CSR) had just a few status bits, because it was designed for a hard-wired terminal, which is directly connected to the interface. When our serial interface is connected to a modem which is connected to the telephone system, we need an enhanced CSR. If we install an RS-232C serial interface, we must specify if we want modem controls included. If we do, then the CSR will have a number of extra status bits for events such as **ring detect** and **carrier loss**; these allow the interrupt handler to know what event caused the interrupt it is handling.

Networks

We briefly discussed a small laboratory network earlier, in chapter 17, but we made no mention of how several computers can be physically linked together. One simple way involves directly connecting every computer to every other one in the network; if very high speed communication is not required, we can use a pair of asynchronous serial interfaces for each direct connection. If the distances are a little too long for RS-232C interfaces, we can use a pair of modems on a private telephone line. We can get a higher baud rate, if necessary, by using synchronous interfaces instead. Finally, we can buy **parallel interfaces** and add sufficient wire for 8- or 16-bit parallel transmission (along 16 or 32 wires). This is more expensive than the preceding options and is limited to distances of about 1 kilometer. How do people set up nationwide, or international, computer networks?

There are many large computer networks in use today; many large corporations have their own networks, as do universities and government institutions. The communication network appropriate for use in a single building is probably not appropriate for use over long distances. A localized network is called a **local area network** (LAN), and a geographically dispersed network is called a **long-haul network,** or a **wide area network.** We will briefly discuss some communication schemes for these networks.

Packet Switching

When using a telephone, we are using a **circuit-switched** network. Each time we make a long distance call, a unique circuit, with many links, is switched into existence for our exclusive use for the duration of the call. With computer-to-computer communication, the information transmission is typically unevenly distributed over time: it tends to come in bursts, with long pauses. If we used the same type of network for computer communication that we use for voice communication, we would maintain expensive point-to-point connections for long periods of time when no information was being transmitted. Designers of computer networks wanted a better way.

The ARPANET, sponsored by the Department of Defense's Advanced Research Projects Agency, pioneered the use of the **packet-switching** communication scheme. Computers on a packet-switching communication network do not use direct point-to-point links to communicate with each other, nor do they use a switched network: either one would be too expensive. Instead, the computers share a network in which any computer can reach any other computer over at least two different paths. When CPU A sends a message (or a whole file) to CPU B, it passes the message to its network interface controller, which is called an IMP (Interface Message Processor). The IMP breaks the message into a series of **packets** of approximately 1K bits each. These packets are sent by whatever route seems best at the time. If a message is broken up into several packets, each packet could conceivably travel over a different path. It is the responsibility of the IMP that communicates with CPU B to reassemble the message originally sent from CPU A--or to find out why part of it was lost, and negotiate with the

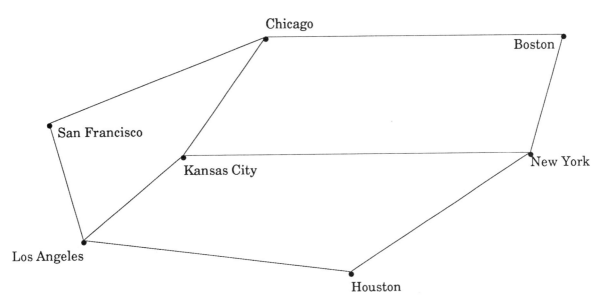

Chicago

Boston

San Francisco

Kansas City

New York

Los Angeles

Houston

Figure 20.6 A packet-switching network

IMP that communicates with CPU A to resend the missing part. As far as computers A and B are concerned, the path between them is error-free, but messages sometimes take longer than usual to arrive. Any pair of cities in figure 20.6 could be the points A and B we have described.

The common speed used on packet-switching systems is 50 Kbaud. An IMP is a special-purpose computer, with computing power comparable to a small MicroVAX. If an IMP fails, the computers connected to it are disconnected from the network, but the network is otherwise unaffected--because there are alternate paths to every IMP.

There are also commercial packet-switched networks that are available to the public. One of the largest is TELENET, which operates as a subsidiary of GTE (General Telephone and Electronics). It has many hundreds of CPUs of all makes connected to it, located in over 250 cities in North America and elsewhere. The computers do not belong to TELENET; they belong to the customers who pay TELENET for the privilege of being part of the network.

Local Networks, Ethernet, DECNET

If we wish to connect all the personal computers, telex terminals, laser printers, micros, minis, and mainframes in our building, we should consider something other than a point-to-point system, for obvious reasons. A switched-circuit system will most likely not make much sense, and packet switching is too expensive (since we need an IMP for each machine we want to connect). Instead, we can use the kind of cable that cable television companies use. This is **coaxial** cable (*coax* for short); it has a thick, shielded, central conductor. An ordinary twisted pair usually cannot send bits reliably at much more than 50 Kbaud over distances of 1 to 2 kilometers, but coaxial cable can support 10,000 Kbaud over those distances.

Let's call the devices we connect to our local network D1, D2, . . ., Dn, and let's use an interface, T (for Tap), to connect each device to the cable; we can illustrate the network we have created as shown in figure 20.7. Each tap must be compatible with its device's communication

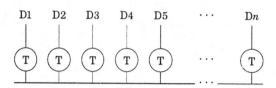

Figure 20.7 A local area network

interface. A local area network's taps are similar to the ARPANET's IMPs, but there is an important difference: the IMPs must keep track of which links are operative and which are inoperative, which links were heavily used and which are underused--at any given time. We assume, however, that the coaxial cable is indestructible, and so we don't worry about routing messages. A tap is passive; if one fails, only the device connected to it is isolated from the network. A message being sent from device *A* to device *B* is broken up by the device's software driver into packets. The packets are broadcast by the tap, and all other taps receive it. When tap *B* recognizes that the packet is for its device, it copies the packet and passes it on to device *B*. Every device must be "smart" enough to support the packet assembly/disassembly process.

Ethernet

The Ethernet system developed at Xerox works as described above. It is as easy to connect to an Ethernet-like local area network as it is to plug in a toaster. Figure 20.8 is an advertisement for Ethernet that was printed nearly ten years ago; it is still current today.

Network Architecture

It is difficult to understand how computer networks work without understanding how they fit into the larger scheme of things. A good network can make us believe that the remote computer we are connected with is the one we see sitting in the same room with us; creating this illusion requires considerable cooperation between hardware and software. Network designers use one of the rules that has been so successfully applied to other large problems: divide and conquer. Thus, network hardware and software--the network architecture--is divided into a number of **layers,** each of which performs a particular function; the sum of the functions provided by each layer implements a complete network.

The International Standards Organization (ISO) recently adopted the Open Systems Interconnection (OSI) network architecture, which specifies what functions a computer network should perform and which layer is responsible for which function. In the meantime, DEC had been working for many years with the needs of its customers for better networking; this work culminated in DEC's Digital Network Architecture, or DNA. There is a close correspondence between the DNA model and the OSI model. Figure 20.9 shows that although the ISO model describes seven layers and the DNA model five, the major differences are ones of terminology. In addition, DEC has announced that it will modify DNA by 1990 so that it is fully compatible with the OSI standard.

THE LEADING EDGE

#1 in a series of reports on new technology from Xerox

About a year ago, Xerox introduced the Ethernet network—a pioneering new development that makes it possible to link different office machines into a single network that's reliable, flexible and easily expandable.

The following are some notes explaining the technological underpinnings of this development. They are contributed by Xerox research scientist David Boggs.

The Ethernet system was designed to meet several rather ambitious objectives.

First, it had to allow many users within a given organization to access the same data. Next, it had to allow the organization the economies that come from resource sharing; that is, if several people could share the same information processing equipment, it would cut down on the amount and expense of hardware needed. In addition, the resulting network had to be flexible; users had to be able to change components easily so the network could grow smoothly as new capability was needed. Finally, it had to have maximum reliability—a system based on the notion of shared information would look pretty silly if users couldn't get at the information because the network was broken.

Collision Detection

The Ethernet network uses a coaxial cable to connect various pieces of information equipment. Information travels over the cable in packets which are sent from one machine to another.

A key problem in any system of this type is how to control access to the cable: what are the rules determining when a piece of equipment can talk? Ethernet's method resembles the unwritten rules used by people at a party to decide who gets to tell the next story.

While someone is speaking, everyone else waits. When the current speaker stops, those who want to say something pause, and then launch into their speeches. If they *collide* with each other (hear someone else talking, too), they all stop and wait to start up again. Eventually one pauses the shortest time and starts talking so soon that everyone else hears him and waits.

When a piece of equipment wants to use the Ethernet cable, it listens first to hear if any other station is talking. When it hears silence on the cable, the station starts talking, but it also listens. If it hears other stations sending too, it stops, as do the other stations. Then it waits a

random amount of time, on the order of micro-seconds, and tries again. The more times a station collides, the longer, on the average, it waits before trying again.

In the technical literature, this technique is called carrier-sense multiple-access with collision detection. It is a modification of a method developed by researchers at the University of Hawaii and further refined by my colleague Dr. Robert Metcalfe. As long as the interval during which stations elbow each other for control of the cable is short relative to the interval during which the winner uses the cable, it is very efficient. Just as important, it requires no central

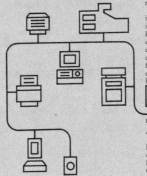

control—there is no distinguished station to break or become overloaded.

The System

With the foregoing problems solved, Ethernet was ready for introduction. It consists of a few relatively simple components:

Ether. This is the cable referred to earlier. Since it consists of just copper and plastic, its reliability is high and its cost is low.

Transceivers. These are small boxes that insert and extract bits of information as they pass by on the cable.

Controllers. These are large scale integrated circuit chips which enable all sorts of equipment, from communicating typewriters to mainframe computers, regardless of the manufacturer, to connect to the Ethernet.

The resulting system is not only fast (transmitting millions of bits of information per second), it's essentially modular in design. It's largely because of this modularity that Ethernet succeeds in meeting its objectives of economy, reliability and expandability.

The system is economical simply because it enables users to share both equipment and information, cutting down on hardware costs. It is reliable because control of the system is distributed over many pieces of communicating equipment, instead of being vested in a single central controller where a single piece of malfunctioning equipment can immobilize an entire system. And Ethernet is expandable because it readily accepts new pieces of information processing equipment.

This enables an organization to plug in new machines gradually, as its needs dictate, or as technology develops new and better ones.

About The Author

David Boggs is one of the inventors of Ethernet. He is a member of the research staff of the Computer Science Laboratory at Xerox's Palo Alto Research Center.

He holds a Bachelor's degree in Electrical Engineering from Princeton University and a Master's degree from Stanford University, where he is currently pursuing a Ph.D.

XEROX

XEROX® and Ethernet are trademarks of XEROX CORPORATION.

Xerox introduces the Information Outlet.

If you're wondering how business will handle information in the '80s, the handwriting is clearly on the wall.

We call it the Information Outlet—a new way for you to custom design an information management system that will give you maximum flexibility with minimum expense.

Here's how it works:
The Information Outlet gives you access to a special Xerox Ethernet cable that can link a variety of office machines. Including information processors like the Xerox 860, various electronic printers and files, and, of course, computers.

The Xerox Ethernet network will enable people throughout your company to create,

store, retrieve, print and send information to other people in other places—instantaneously.

This network wasn't designed to work exclusively with our equipment. Other companies' products can be connected as well.

As your needs change, so can your network. You'll simply plug in new machines as you need them—or as technology develops better ones.

So, through the Xerox Information Outlet, you'll get to the future the way the future itself will get here.

One step at a time.

XEROX

If you'd like more information on the Information Outlet, write us and we'll send you a booklet: Xerox Corporation, P.O. Box 470065, Dallas, Texas 75247.

Figure 20.8 Xerox Ethernet

	ISO	DNA
Software	Application	Application
	Presentation	
	Session	(None)
	Transport	Network services
	Network	Transport
Hardware	Data-link	Data-link control
	Physical	Physical

Figure 20.9 Comparison of the ISO and DNA models

In this discussion, we are particularly interested in the hardware section of figure 20.9. The layers above that section represent the layers of software provided by application programs, operating systems, and special-purpose network software. The bottom two layers are the hardware--the **physical interface**--which actually moves the bits back and forth. There are many ways of implementing these physical links; we will discuss two of the leading kinds of physical channels--**broadband** and **baseband.**

Broadband Networks

Broadband networks grew out of the technology used in the cable television industry. A single coaxial cable carries over one hundred television channels to home television sets; if a home has several television receivers, each one can be tuned to a different channel, although they are all connected to the same cable. Data as well as video (or voice) can be transmitted on such a broadband cable, and some local area networks use a broadband link.

Baseband Networks

Broadband networks share a cable among varied, simultaneous uses; baseband networks devote the cable to a single use--data transmission--in order to transmit the data at the highest possible speed. Baseband channels eliminate the complications introduced by sharing a cable with video and voice traffic.

Baseband channels eliminate some problems, but not *all* problems; baseband and broadband networks have in common the problem of **collisions**: when several computers share a communication channel, they must establish a protocol to determine which one gets to use the channel at any given instant. A simple protocol is for a computer, when it wants to send a message, to listen to the channel; if no one is currently sending, then the channel is available and the computer can send its message. If two computers listen at the same time and find the channel available, they may begin sending at the same time, and a collision will occur: both messages are garbled and must be resent--which could lead to another collision! Good networking hardware and software are designed to reduce collisions to a manageable level; if a high rate of collisions persists, then the network probably needs a faster cable, or has too many computers connected to it.

Network hardware is evolving rapidly: in addition to coaxial cable, it is also possible to use **fiber optic** cable. Fiber optic cable has many attractive properties: it can support very high speed transmission, it is easy to install, it is light, and it is immune to electronic *noise,* for example.

However, old-fashioned telephone wiring also works well for some things--such as connecting CRTs, personal computers, and workstations to the nearest connection to the local area network.

The subject of local and wide area computer networks is a large one; some knowledge of how they work is necessary for an understanding of computing in large organizations.

Remote Diagnosis

Remote access to computers is now common; methods for remote access are well enough established that computer manufacturers use remote access to help alleviate what might otherwise be a critical problem: timely service. Most medium-to-large computer systems make use of contracted maintenance service, usually (but not necessarily) provided by the computer's manufacturer; most service contracts provide service during the business day. It is a major challenge for service providers to guarantee each customer prompt *and* affordable service: prompt service can be guaranteed by having a large maintenance staff, but affordable service cannot be provided if a maintenance staff large enough for prompt service means that most workers are idle much of the time.

Some computer service firms solve this problem by setting up telephone *hot lines* that allow their customers to contact diagnostic centers which are staffed 24 hours a day. A customer with an ailing computer system calls the hot-line number and explains the problem; a technician at the diagnostic center then instructs the customer to load a particular diagnostic program and to enable the computer's **remote diagnosis** module. The technician can then call the computer's diagnostic module, feed it appropriate commands, and examine its responses. The customer and the technician can still communicate by using the computer's console as a telecommunication device--the technician might ask the customer to load another diagnostic program, for example.

On the VAX-11/780, an LSI-11 (a member of the PDP-11 family) is used as a remote diagnosis module; the LSI-11 comes as part of the VAX. The diagnostic programs are read on the floppy disk drive which comes with this LSI-11; the same floppy disk drive is also used to read in the microcode that defines the VAX's instruction set.

Remote diagnosis is dependent upon the remote diagnosis hardware of a malfunctioning computer; is this wise? In the case of the VAX, the LSI-11 is an independent computer, and there is no particular reason to suppose that a hardware failure in the VAX will cause a failure in the LSI-11. In addition, the LSI-11 is much simpler than the VAX; it may, therefore, be less likely to fail.

A typical result of a remote diagnosis session is a final message from the diagnostic center, such as, "The problem is with circuit board such-and-such; have your local service office replace it."

Impact of Computer Networks

Computer networks are a major force in the world--more than many people suspect. Two recent incidents dramatize the role of computer networks; one shook the political framework of the U.S., and the other had--and will continue to have--global economic consequences.

In the spring and summer of 1987, a joint U.S. Senate and House committee conducted hearings on the "Iran-Contra affair." The investigation upon which these hearings depended was making little progress because critical documents had been shredded and important computer files had been erased. A breakthrough occurred when a previous National Security Agency (NSA) Director, Robert McFarlane, pointed out that the staff of the NSA made use of electronic mail to exchange messages and to prepare and circulate drafts of various position and policy papers. The IBM system they used, called PROFS (Professional Office System), provided networking services such as electronic mail. Principal witnesses in the investigation (such as Colonel Oliver North) acknowledged frequent use of PROFS, but North and others also indicated that they immediately destroyed their sensitive electronic mail messages. However, North and others failed to realize the extent to which good networking software anticipates and guards against system failure. The PROFS software automatically creates archival copies of all electronic mail messages--in case the system should fail. If the system does fail, then when it is restarted, undelivered or unread mail is retransmitted from the archival copy. Meanwhile, computer administrators routinely made backup copies of all files--including the archival copies of mail messages. Thus, even though users of the electronic mail service were careful not to save sensitive messages, the investigators were able to retrieve these messages from the backup tapes. One of the principals--Admiral Poindexter, McFarlane's successor as NSA director, and a computer hobbyist--knew that PROFS makes archival copies of mail messages. As a result, Pointdexter erased the archival copies of his sensitive messages *before* backups were made, so none of his PROFS messages were retrieved.

The second incident began on Monday, 19 October 1987; this day has been called "Black Monday" because of the stock market crash in Wall Street. Some years ago, the New York Stock Exchange (NYSE) and most stock brokerage firms began automating their operations. It was obvious to all involved that brokerage-firm computers should be linked to the NYSE computers to execute buy and sell orders. Other financial markets in the country also began automating.

Meanwhile, new investment products were developed. For example, stock index funds were invented, which guaranteed that an investor would do as well as the Dow-Jones Industrial Average (DJIA), because these funds hold the same proportional mix of stocks that is used to calculate the DJIA. Similar index funds were created to match the Standard and Poor's 500 (which includes stocks from 500 companies). In addition, stock index *futures* funds were established. One feature of these new investment products is that the only efficient way to manage them is by computer; networked computers transfer buy and sell orders quickly.

The speed of the computers and their network made it feasible for a brokerage firm to monitor the market's fluctuations in real time, and to have the firm's computer *automatically* transmit buy or sell orders for hundreds of different stocks at once. This activity, called **program trading,** is considered a major contributor to the market's crash; the crash is likely to influence the world economy for months or even years.

The NYSE, the U.S. Securities and Exchange Commission (which regulates the NYSE and other exchanges,) and the U.S. Congress have begun looking into restricting or regulating program trading. It is unlikely that we will ever know the exact contribution of program trading to the crash, because no system like PROFS was used, and so there is no way of knowing which transactions were carried out by computers and which were not. However, this is a case where too much automation (or, perhaps, too little regulation), combined with use of extensive computer networks, may have contributed to a financial and economic disaster.

Trends

In many countries, the telephone service is provided directly by the government: in France and England, as in many other countries, the government provides postal, telephone, telegraph, radio, and television services. In the U.S.A., the government provides postal service, but not telephone service. (Even postal service may soon be privately operated.) Telephone service is a regulated industry: each provider has a monopoly in its service area, which is subject to a commission that oversees the quality and cost of telephone services.

At the national level, the Federal Communications Commission (FCC) of the U.S. government regulates all forms of electrical or electronic communication, including the following:

Telephone
Telegraph
Radio
Broadcast television
Cable television

Microwave communication
Satellite communication

What does all of this have to do with computing? The FCC has come to have more day-to-day influence on computing than any other federal agency (except for the the Department of Defense, which is largely a consumer--of enormous quantities--of both hardware and software). The interaction between federal agencies, private enterprise, and judicial rulings has led the world of computing to the threshold of a new era: for many years the FCC held that the telephone companies (in particular, the American Telephone and Telegraph Company, AT&T) could provide communication services, but that antitrust law prohibited them from providing computer hardware or software--despite the fact that computers are, and have been for many years, extensively used by the telephone companies. Similarly, computer companies (notably IBM) were permitted to provide computing equipment and services, but antitrust law prohibited them from providing communication services. The FCC reversed itself a few years ago on the separation of computing and communication services. The consequences of this decision are still unfolding, so its outcome is not yet clear. However, **deregulation** has resulted in AT&T's entering computer manufacturing and sales, and it has resulted in IBM's getting involved in telecommunication--for example, it purchased ROLM, an AT&T competitor.

Summary

Remote access to computing services is afforded by telephone lines. These services may be accessed on a dial-up basis or continuously, using leased lines. Computer interfaces to remote terminals need more status bits to indicate the state of the communications process; these extra bits are called *modem-control and status* bits.

Computer networks are a generalization of remote access to computing services. We have discussed the difference between circuit-switched and packet-switched networks. We have also discussed the difference between local and geographically distributed networks.

The interplay between communication and computing is intensifying; this is evident from recent judicial rulings, as well as from recent economic and political events in the U.S. and around the world.

Exercises for Chapter 20

1. Providing dialup access to a computer introduces security problems. Briefly describe what these problems are and what measures can be taken to control them.

2. How efficient is it to use a 1200-baud line with asynchronous communication of ASCII codes? How efficient is it to use synchronous communication with 1 KB message blocks, using 20 bytes for the header and trailer? In both cases, express efficiency as the ratio of information bits to total bits transmitted.

3. In some areas of the country, dialup lines are almost always noisy--and noise may cause transmission errors. Suppose the detection of an error requires retransmission. With asynchronous communication, if a bad character is received, it must be retransmitted. With synchronous communication, however, when an error is detected, the whole block must be retransmitted (there is no way of knowing which character was bad). Using the standard asynchronous protocol and the synchronous parameters described in the preceding question, how high would the error rate have to be (1 error bit for every n transmitted bits) before it would be as efficient to use asynchronous as synchronous communication?

4.   Providing dialup access introduces other problems in addition to those of security. For example, what if a user is accidentally disconnected? What might happen? What can the operating system do to help? Which hardware feature assists in this situation?

5.   Suppose you are the designer of a credit-card reading machine which will be used in retail outlets, motels, and other places where credit cards are typically accepted. The machine reads the card number, the clerk types the sales amount using the machine's keyboard, and the machine then dials the credit card processing center and transmits this information in order to obtain authorization for the charge. The processing center then responds in one of three ways:

   a.   It sends an authorization code.
   b.   It states that the charge cannot be accepted.
   c.   It sends a code indicating that the card should be held for it has been reported lost or stolen.

   The maximum number of bytes transmitted in any of these transaction is 30; the maximum tolerable delay for a response from the credit-card processing center is 20 seconds.
   You have to make the following decision: if you build the machine with an internal 300-baud modem, you can lease it to outlets for $20 per month, but if you build it with an internal 2400-baud modem, you can lease it for $60 per month. Explain which choice is least expensive for a user who makes 500 authorization transactions per month, when each transaction involves a telephone charge of $0.50 plus $1.80 per minute (30-second minimum).
   You should respond with more than just, "Choose this one"; you should explain the technical basis of your choice.

∎ 21 ∎

Beyond Machine and Assembly Language

Introduction

Writing assembly language programs gives one a feeling of great power; interpreting a hexadecimal memory dump is an amazing feat in the eyes of the uninitiated. Any program that can be written in a high-level language can also be written in machine or assembly language. So, why have--and why use--high-level languages? In this last chapter of a book that uses machine and assembly language programming to explain a computer's architecture, we will try to answer this question.

Looking back at the programs we have written, we can compile a catalog, listing all of the ways in which things can go wrong when we use assembly language. For example, a seemingly innocuous typographical error can have snowballing consequences--because the assembler has (almost) no idea of what we are trying to do when we write a program. It cannot tell the difference between an array, a tree, a list or a buffer; it cannot even tell the difference between an integer and a character, in any useful way. We might agree, but say, "What if we enhance the assembler, so that it has built-in data types--and the directives to support them?"

This may be possible, but what about assembly language's minimal power of expression? It takes several lines of assembly language to write

$$A = \frac{B + C * (D - 3)}{\sin(x)}$$

and we would be unlikely to get it right the first time. We might respond, "What about writing macros that allow for infix operations, with precedence?" The macros we have used up to now have had the macro name *followed* by the operand list, which is called **postfix** form. If we could use **infix** form, then instead of writing ADD A, B, we could define a macro, CADD, to be an infix operator with its arguments on either side of it. Then we could use the invocation A CADD B. We could redesign the assembler, so that if we write $A = B + C$, it is interpreted as an invocation of the "=" and "+" macros. $A = B + C$ would then be expanded to ADDL3 B, C, A, assuming we are dealing with 32-bit numbers.

This dialog can continue indefinitely: for every objection regarding the use of assembly language, there is some technique--some preprocessor, perhaps--which can be used to counter the objection. In the process of adopting all these techniques, we will have transformed what was a simple (and simple-minded) assembler into a very powerful program which is practically indistinguishable from a good high-level language compiler. In that case, why not use the best available tools for the job--ones that were designed for it from the beginning? For these reasons (and many others, some of which will be discussed shortly), high-level languages have largely replaced assembly language in the programmer's repertoire. We reiterate, however, that the study of machine and assembly language is still an excellent way to develop an understanding of computers and computing.

Most programmers agree that a high-level language is easier to learn and use than is an assembly language. Assembly language requires constant attention to many details--exactly those details which high-level languages are designed to hide from (human) programmers. Because a high-level language is easier to learn, more people can be trained in its use. That makes it easier for an employer to find a high-level language programmer than an assembly language programmer (because of this, an assembly language programmer can be very valuable, should his or her services be required).

483

We can be far more productive when using an appropriate high-level language than when using machine or assembly language. In addition, high-level language programs are much easier to understand than are assembly language programs. This makes program debugging, maintenance, and enhancement easier--and, therefore, less costly. We will not review all of the reasons for using high-level languages; the most important one, we believe, is that they help prevent incorrect programs from being written. When we have to use a computer, we should use the best available software tools we have access to--which will almost certainly not include assembly language. A well-designed high-level language--with a compiler that performs thorough and helpful compile-time error checking, and with a suitable run-time support package--will go a long way toward preventing the use of erroneous programs.

When we write assembly language programs, we can write almost anything that comes to mind-- no matter how foolish it may seem to someone else (or to ourselves, on second thought). In a well-designed high-level language--such as Pascal--we cannot succeed in writing some kinds of nonsense: we can compare apples with apples, but the compiler won't let us compare apples with bananas, for example.

Software should be correct the first time it is used. Any error which can conceivably be detected at compile time (such as adding an integer to a floating-point number) should be reported at compile time. Anything that cannot be checked before run time should be checked at run time. If an array subscript cannot be guaranteed to be in bounds at compile time, then run-time checking should be enforced. Someone might object, "Won't run-time checking slow things down?" It certainly will, but is it better to get a correct answer a little later, or an incorrect answer a little sooner? If a program produces incorrect results, we might as well not have run it at all.

We can summarize some of the principal reasons why high-level programming languages are used in preference to assembly language: they are easier to learn, easier to write, easier to read, and easier to maintain or modify; they provide better compile-time error detection and better run-time error detection, and they are (almost) machine-independent. If an application written in a high-level language is too slow or too large (or both), then the few program modules that contribute most to the inadequacy can be rewritten. If necessary, they can be rewritten in assembly language.

When a scientist reports a new result, other scientists try to replicate that result; if they can't, they consider the originator either a fraud or an incompetent. Software, however, is simply too expensive to replicate; the idea that someone else should write an independent version of a program in order to confirm the program's correctness staggers the mind. Consider, for example, the real-time programs which implement the North American Air Defense system, or the software which is supposed to implement the Strategic Defense Initiative. Such programs must be written so they are correct the first time they are used; we may not get a second chance, when military applications are involved.

The cost of developing software is so high that it is common to link computers together in networks, so that the software which runs on one computer can be shared by all users of the network. This is the kind of computer network access that facilitated the research done, for example, by Dr. Lawrence R. Klein, who was awarded the 1980 Nobel Prize in economics. He shared the computer program implementing his econometric model (running at the University of Pennsylvania) in exchange for access to programs running on computers elsewhere--in the U.S.A. and abroad.

High-Level Programming Languages

Any reader of this book has probably used one or more of the following high-level languages: Ada, APL, BASIC, C, COBOL, FORTRAN, Modula-2, Pascal, PL/I. These are all considered general-purpose

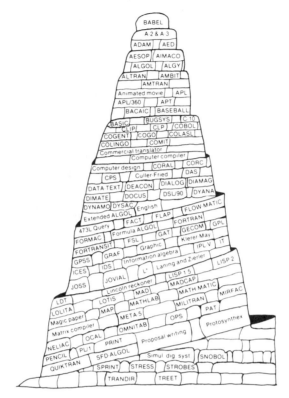

Figure 21.1 The Babel of programming languages

languages: each one can be used to implement algorithms to solve almost any kind of problem. Although some were designed for particular applications--COBOL for business, FORTRAN for science and engineering, Pascal for teaching--each one of the above languages can be used as a general-purpose tool. Figure 21.1 depicts the profusion of programming languages in use in the U.S.A. in 1960; computer languages seem to be created faster than they vanish.

There are other computer languages that are *not* general-purpose; each is designed to solve problems of a particular type. Some of these are best described by naming the kind of object they manipulate:

LISP	List processing
SNOBOL4	String processing
FORMAC	Formula manipulation
APT	Numerical tool control
Prolog	Logic programming

A roster of high-level languages in use in the U.S.A. was published in 1969; it listed 120 computer languages, in 17 categories such as machine-tool control, compiler writing, simulation, and graphics. By 1973, the roster had 171 computer languages in 26 categories--after many languages from the older list had been deleted. If anyone were to count high-level languages in use today, both the language

485

The Pentagon's National Military Command Center; Augusta Ada Byron (inset).

Pentagon pins its hopes on Ada; just ask any computer

By RICHARD HALLORAN

WASHINGTON—Ada lives. Not Augusta Ada Byron, the legitimate daughter of the English poet Lord Byron, Countess of Lovelace and, in the mid-1800's, the world's first computer programmer, but the lady's namesake. Some 128 years after her death, she whom Byron poeticized in "Childe Harold" as the "sole daughter of (his) house and heart" has "turned to battle's magnificent stern array," coming alive as a highly sophisticated computer language developed under the auspices of the Defense Department. Testing is scheduled to end today.

Just as human language conveys information and ideas from one mind to another, so a computer language communicates between the human mind and a computer's memory. The language allows a person to put questions to the computer, order it to perform various functions and extract answers from it. In computer jargon, a language is part of the software as compared with the machinery, the hardware.

Ada is one language the Defense Department needs, and needs so badly that though working the bugs out of a computer language usually takes years, Ada's project managers put it through an intensified testing program in 14 months. The completed language was delivered in July. The Defense Department has been refining it ever since, making Ada what department experts consider a remarkable "high-order language," one that closely approximates human language by using recognizable words and phrases in its programming and printed answers. Computations using a binary number code are left to languages of a lower level. In languages like Ada, a single command will initiate a series of operations, much as the general command "walk" will lead a child to perform a series of muscle movements. These languages are easier to learn and use than their lower-level cousins. The New York Times computerized information bank, for instance, has such a high-level language that even the most obtuse reporter can master it in a few hours.

Computer specialists say designing a language is not a mechanical matter, but one of imagination and taste. Ada, they explain, is an advance over earlier languages because its structure—the manner in which questions are put, answers are returned, programs are designed—incorporates the most modern concepts of logic. It takes a highly skilled programmer to write a program in Ada. More important, however, it does not take so highly skilled an individual to use it. And this language can be used in a variety of computers, with minor adjustments. Older languages are keyed to specific machines.

Five years ago, the Pentagon decided to standardize the more than 1,000 languages used by the Defense Department. The annual cost of this software proliferation ran to more than $3 billion last year, not including the cost of training people to use it all.

Figure 21.2 Hopes for Ada

count and the category count likely would be higher. The U.S. Department of Defense found the situation so chaotic that it commissioned the development of a new, single, programming language-- Ada. Ada, the Defense Department hopes, will be the single language that satisfies all users. The article, "Pentagon Pins Its Hopes on Ada," which is reproduced as figure 21.2, provides some historical background to the development of Ada.

High-Level Programming Languages on the VAX

Which high-level programming languages are available on a VAX? VAX high-level languages can be divided into two categories: those available from DEC, and those available from other sources. A partial list of the programming languages available from DEC and a brief description of each one follow:

Ada	the Dept. of Defense language for mission-oriented applications
APL	a powerful, vector-oriented, scientific language
BASIC	an interactive, general-purpose language
BLISS	a systems-implementation language
C	a general-purpose language, also suitable for system-implementation
COBOL	the most widely used business data processing language
DIBOL	Digital Interactive Business Language, an alternative to COBOL
FORTRAN	the FORTRAN-77 implementation, for scientific and engineering applications
OPS5	a language for artificial intelligence applications
Pascal	a modular, general-purpose language
PL/I	a comprehensive language for scientific and business applications
RPG	a Report Generator language
SCAN	a language for pattern matching and text manipulation

There are many other languages available from other sources. They include

LISP	a language for artificial intelligence
Modula-2	a general-purpose language for system programming
Prolog	a language for artificial intelligence applications
SNOBOL4	a string-processing language

In addition to programming languages, there are numerous **application packages** available for the VAX. An application package is problem-specific; for example, there are application packages to help manage large VAX installations, to perform statistical analysis of data, to provide publishing services, and more.

Database Management Systems

In an ordinary, general-purpose, high-level language, we must explicitly describe an algorithm we wish to implement. In an application-oriented high-level language, there are typically built-in operators and data structures suitable for that application area, so we merely provide input data (in some prescribed format) and *call* predefined operations. (This is how most statistical program packages are used, for example.)

In all of the cases we have considered so far, there is an intimate relationship between a program and its data files: the data file's format must match the format expected by the program.

After a few years, a computer facility may have a collection of several hundred programs, each of which uses a (perhaps only slightly) different file format. This is tolerable--although it may represent considerable duplication of effort--if the programs are used independently of each other for solving unrelated problems. However, when a computing facility is set up to provide services to a single firm, it makes sense for different programs to be able to share data files.

The idea of making data files sharable has evolved to the point where a Database Management System (DBMS) provides the program interface to data files. Each data item in a data base has a machine-readable description, which is stored on-line in a **data dictionary.** All programs which use the data do so via DBMS service requests; no user program knows what *format* the data are stored in-- nor does it need to. All a user program needs to know is the *name* of the desired data item in the data dictionary. Therefore, all user programs are independent of the data format; if it is changed, only the data dictionary--and not all of the user programs--must be changed.

The indirection of accessing data via its description in a data dictionary adds overhead to a user program. However, it is much easier--and faster--to construct a new program that uses the database than one that must deal with data directly. In addition, it is often straightforward to enhance a program that accesses data using a DBMS--even to provide functions that were unforeseen when the program was first written. This increased ease of programming and program changing is similar to what we find when we move from machine language--where all addresses and offsets must be calculated by hand--to assembly language--where we use symbolic labels in place of addresses and offsets--to higher level languages where we use variable names and needn't have any notion of addresses or offsets at all.

There are many DBMS packages available for the VAX; a few of them are listed here:

Focus
IDMS/SQL
Informix-SQL
INGRES
Oracle
PowerHouse
System/2000
Unify

It is common for a DBMS package to have a *terminal interface,* so that a user can sit at a terminal and **run a query** on the database. It is also common for a DBMS package to have a software interface to popular programming languages available on a VAX, so that users may embed their queries in programs. If a DBMS allows user-defined functions, then the DBMS will usually allow users to write these functions using a standard high-level programming language. Conversely, when writing a program using a standard high-level programming language, we would like to be able to call upon the DBMS to provide support for storing data in and retrieving data from the database.

One Last Look

This leads us to take one final look at a computing system, so we can put the hardware and software in perspective.

Hardware	Microcoded CPU
Bare machine	Preceding + control store + memory
Minimal system	Preceding + peripherals

Minimal usable system	Preceding + I/O software
Effective system	Preceding + operating system
Useful system	Preceding + compilers + library
Flexible system	Preceding + DBMS
Application-oriented system	Preceding + application packages

The world of computing is a fast-changing one; it is fascinating--and of considerable practical use, for most people--to try to keep up with that world's developments.

Summary

Assembly language programmers have access to every feature of a computing system; assembly language programming, therefore, is an excellent way to learn what computers do and how they do it. However, it is easy to make mistakes when using a low-level language; high-level languages help us avoid programming errors and should be used whenever possible. There are also many application-oriented languages that may be used instead of traditional high-level languages. There is a class of applications that has led to the development of what can almost be regarded as another operating system: **database management systems** (DBMSs). A DBMS is an additional step in the ascent from machine language to assembly language to high-level language; each step helps reduce the likelihood that our efforts will result in the execution of a nonsense program, which produces nonsense results.

Exercises for Chapter 21

1. For the high-level language of your choice, prepare a list of five different programming errors which the language's compiler or run-time system would detect, but which would go undetected if you had been using assembly language. Consider, for example, the following incorrect program fragment:

```
        MOVL #100, R1
        ADDL2 X, A(R1)
        ;continue computing
    A:  .BLKL 10
```

Why is it incorrect? Its Pascal counterpart would be flagged as a compile-time error.

2. Continuing with the topic from question 1, are there situations which cause Macro to detect an error which a high-level language compiler would not detect?

3. Some programs have been in use for a long time and their source code has been lost: all that remains is the binary load module. In some of these cases it may not even be known if the binary was generated by a compiler or by an assembler. Sketch how you would implement a **disassembler**: the disassembler's input is a binary load module, and its output is a symbolic assembly language program. What problems are you likely to encounter?

4. Can we generalize the previous problem involving a disassembler to a **decompiler**? The input to a decompiler is a load module, and its output is a source module in a high-level language; the source module, if compiled, would generate the original load module. Sketch an approach to doing this. What problems are you likely to encounter?

System Services

Introduction

System services are *services* provided by *the system*. They include input/output routines, and a variety of other *macros* (abbreviations) that make our lives as programmers easier. When creating a source module in a file (e.g., FILENAME.MAR), we can use the system services as they are described in this appendix. These system services are macros; since, by default, macro expansion is not listed in the assembler's printout (FILENAME.LIS), we will notice only the single line that is the macro's invocation and a larger-than-expected difference between the addresses of the instructions preceding and following the system service request.

Examining Memory and Registers

When we write a program, it is fine if the program performs correctly, performs the desired computations, but we need more than that. If a program doesn't produce any output, it is unlikely to be a useful program. There are two system services that provide detailed output: a hexadecimal memory dump, and a hexadecimal register snapshot.

DUMP

The DUMP system service provides a hexadecimal memory dump of specified memory locations. DUMP has two arguments: a starting address and a stopping address; the memory dump is from the location specified by its first argument to the location specified by its second argument. DUMP is a macro; its arguments are placed on the same line as its name, separated by white space.

The following excerpt from an assembler listing shows a sample use of the DUMP macro, and its output:

```
                         0000   1      .LIBRARY /[PB]IOMAC.MLB/
             00000004    0000   2 A:   .BLKL 1
             00000008    0004   3 B:   .BLKL 1
                         0008   4      .ENTRY START, 0
                         000A   5      IOINIT
A6 AF   04   03   C1     0055   6      ADDL3 #3, #4, A
A5 AF   08   09   C3     005A   7      SUBL3 #9, #8, B
                         005F   8      DUMP A, B
                         006C   9      $EXIT_S
                         0075  10      .END START


010E000A  2B110000  FFFFFFFF  00000007  :  00000200
00097475  7074756F  24737973  00000214  :  00000210
```

Note that although the arguments to DUMP are A and B (with addresses 00000000 and 00000004, which will be relocated to 00000200 and 00000204), the output of DUMP is 8 longwords. This is because DUMP's output begins with a location whose address is evenly divisible by 10_{16} and always consists of at least 20_{16} bytes. In the above example, the instruction on line 6 adds 3 and 4 and stores the sum (7) in location A, and the instruction on line 7 subtracts 9 from 8 and stores the difference (-1) in location B. The address of A is 00000200 and the address of B is 00000204; we see from the output of DUMP that A contains 00000007_{16} and that B contains $FFFFFFFF_{16}$--just as they should.

It is important to realize that the arguments of DUMP are the starting and stopping addresses themselves, and not the addresses of the locations containing the starting and stopping locations. If we wish, we may use other addressing modes to specify the arguments for DUMP, but we must be aware that, in general, DUMP's arguments are specified with one *less* level of indirection than are the operands of most of the VAX's instructions. For example, if we put the starting address in R0 and the stopping address in R1, then DUMP R0, R1 will not work, but DUMP (R0), (R1) will.

There are three additional comments with regard to using the DUMP (and SNAP--see below) system services. First, in order to use DUMP (or SNAP), you must first invoke the macro IOINIT in your program (see below). Both DUMP and SNAP use other macros (described below) that send output to the screen of your terminal, and IOINIT performs operations necessary for sending output to a terminal.

Second, note the .LIBRARY directive on line 1 of the sample program listing, above. As described in chapter 15, the .LIBRARY directive tells the assembler to search in a particular macro library for macros that are used in this program. In the example shown above, the library is called [PB]IOMAC.MLB; if you are using the software available with this book, it is likely that the library containing these macros will have a different name. You should ask your instructor or system administrator what the name of the library is, so you can provide it as the argument to the .Library directive. (You may wish to avoid use of the .LIBRARY directive by specifying the/LIBRARY option to MACRO; this is also described in chapter 15.)

Third, both the DUMP and SNAP (described below) macros expand to subroutine calls (and some other instructions). The subroutines themselves are provided (of course) as part of the software package available with this book, and their object modules must be linked to the object module created by MACRO for the program that calls them. In the ordinary case, after assembling a program (by typing MACRO PROG1, for example), you must link it (by typing LINK PROG1). If you have used the DUMP system service, however, you will have to type LINK PROG1,DUMPR. DUMPR is the name of the file containing the subroutine that the DUMP macro calls. Its *complete name* must be supplied to the linker, and that complete name will depend on exactly where (in what directory) the software has been installed. Just as you must check with your instructor or system administrator to find out where the macro library containing the macros is (for use in the .LIBRARY directive), so you must find out where the DUMPR (and SNAPR--see below) object modules are installed, so you can list them on the command line to LINK.

SNAP

Sometimes we want a register snapshot as well as--or instead of--a memory dump; in those cases, we can use the SNAP system service. If we write a program that places 1 in R0, 2 in R1, 3 in R2, and so on, and then request a register snapshot, we will see the following output:

```
PC:   00000271     PSL:   03C00000

R0-R11, AP, FP, SP, PC:

00000001 00000002 00000003 00000004 00000005 00000006 00000007 00000008
00000009 0000000A 0000000B 0000000C 7FF27DCC 7FF27D84 7FF27D80 00000271
```

The first line of the snap shows the contents of the program counter (PC) and the processor status longword (PSL). The last two lines are the registers, from R0 through R7 (left to right) on one line, and from R8 through R15 on the next line. Note that register 15 has the same contents as the PC--because R15 *is* the PC.

The first line of SNAP's output shows us the PSL, whose low-order hex digit contains the condition code bits, N, Z, V, and C (high-order to low-order). However, since SNAP is a macro that expands to a series of instructions (recall that most instructions *change* the CC bits), SNAP shows us the CC bit settings prior to the SNAP, but it also changes the CC bit settings. It is wrong, therefore, to separate an instruction that sets the CC bits from one that tests them with a SNAP system service request--although we may sometimes be tempted to do so.

Other I/O Services

SNAP and DUMP are indispensable for providing a run-time picture of the contents of memory and registers. However, we often write programs that read input (from the keyboard, perhaps), and/or produce output (such as printing messages on the screen). In this section, we will describe system services designed to print ASCII characters and to read them; these system services are similar to Pascal's **read** and **write** functions.

IOINIT

Before using any of the system services (other than SNAP and DUMP), we must invoke the IOINIT macro. This macro performs some *initialization* functions that are necessary for VMS to perform the I/O functions that the following system services provide. IOINIT generates instructions that must be executed, so it should appear *after* the .ENTRY macro. The skeleton of the instruction part of a program that uses I/O system services, thus, might look like this:

```
.ENTRY START, 0
IOINIT
;instructions here
$EXIT_S
.END START
```

GETC

GETC reads a character from the keyboard and places it in the location that its argument specifies. Thus, if we wish to read a character and place it in R6, we would type GETC R6. If we wish to read a series of characters and store them in a series of locations with addresses BUFFER, BUFFER+1, etc. (declared with the .BLKB directive, perhaps), we might write the following program segment:

```
                MOVAB BUFFER, R6
                MOVL COUNT, R5          ;how many bytes to get
    MORE:       GETC (R6)+
                DECL R5                 ;decrement count
                BNEQ MORE               ;if not done, get another byte
```

Note that we can use the autoincrement addressing mode (mode 8) with GETC and that the register is incremented by 1--as we would expect.

It is important to understand how GETC interacts with the VMS operating system. Nothing is actually available to our program until we press *return*--thereby sending the ASCII code $0D_{16}$ to the CPU. Once we have pressed *return,* the GETC request in our program asks the operating system for one character at a time; if we wish to get more than one character, we must execute GETC more than once--typically, by putting it in a loop (as in the example above). The ASCII code for the return character (0D) will be the last character sent to our program. If our program doesn't get that character at the end of a line, it will still "be there" (stored for us by the operating system) and will be the first character gotten when our program uses GETC next.

If we wish to get a whole line and put it in an array of bytes starting at BUFFER, we can write the following code:

```
                MOVAB BUFFER, R4        ;where to put the characters
    MORE:       GETC R5                 ;get a character
                MOVB R5, (R4)+          ;put it in BUFFER
                CMPB R5, #^XD           ;check for return
                BNEQ MORE               ;if not, get another character
```

PUTC

PUTC is the *opposite* of GETC: it sends the character whose address is its argument to the screen of a terminal. PUTC is used like GETC; if we wish to echo each character typed, we might write a program fragment like this:

```
    AGAIN:      GETC R5                 ;get the character
                PUTC R5                 ;echo it
                CMPB R5, #^XD           ;check for return
                BNEQ AGAIN              ;if not, echo next character
```

Note that in the echoing program fragment, nothing is saved in memory. If we wish to print characters stored in memory, we may use deferred addressing modes, as with GETC. For example, if we wish to print a character string whose address is STRING and whose first byte is the number of characters in it, we might use the following program fragment:

```
                MOVB STRING, R6         ;number of bytes to print
                MOVAB STRING+1, R7      ;address of 1st char
    LOOP:       PUTC (R7)+              ;print the character
                DECB R6
                BNEQ LOOP               ;if not done, print more
```

We can store a string in memory (compute with it) and then print it by using PUTC and GETC, as follows:

```
            MOVAB BUFFER, R0      ;address to store string
INPUT:   GETC (R0)+               get a byte
            CMPB -1(R0), #^X0D     ;return?
            BNEQ INPUT            ;if not--get another
            ;else: finished reading line--compute, and then print results
            MOVAB RESULTS, R1     ;address of string to print
OUTPUT:PUTC (R1)+                 ;print a byte
            CMPB -1(R1), #^X0D    ;last one?
            BNEQ OUTPUT           ;if not--print another
```

PUTS

PUTC prints one character at a time; PUTS prints a *string* at a time. A string, in the case of PUTS, is a null-terminated series of ASCII character codes; the .ASCIZ directive is a convenient way to create a string. The following program shows how to print the message "Hello, world" to standard output, using the PUTS system service.

```
            CR = ^X0A
            LF = ^X0D
            .ENTRY START, 0
            IOINIT                      ;initialize channels for I/O
            PUTS STRING                 ;print string
            $EXIT_S
STRING:  .ASCIZ "Hello, world" <LF><CR>
```

GETS

Just as PUTC prints a character and PUTS prints a string, so GETC *reads* a character and GETS *reads* a string. GETS reads a series of bytes from the keyboard, places them in successive locations beginning with the one specified by its argument, and null-terminates the string--it places a byte of 0 after the last ASCII code read from the keyboard. Thus, if we store a series of character codes by using the GETS system service, then we can print them (with PUTS) without writing code to place the null character (necessary for terminating PUTS) after the last character in the string.

Using GETS is similar to using the other system services; if we wish to echo input by using GETS and PUTS, we might write a program fragment as follows:

```
            GETS BUFFER      ;read string
            PUTS BUFFER      ;print string
            ;continue
BUFFER: .BLKB 20             ;place for string
```

VAX Opcodes in Numeric Order

00	HALT	10	BSBB	20	ADDP4	30	BSBW
01	NOP	11	BRB	21	ADDP6	31	BRW
02	REI	12	BNEQ	22	SUBP4	32	CVTWL
03	BPT	13	BEQL	23	SUBP6	33	CVTWB
04	RET	14	BGTR	24	CVTPT	34	MOVP
05	RSB	15	BLEQ	25	MULP	35	CMPP3
06	LDPCTX	16	JSB	26	CVTTP	36	CVTPL
07	SVPCTX	17	JMP	27	DIVP	37	CMPP4
08	CVTPS	18	BGEQ	28	MOVC3	38	EDITPC
09	CVTSP	19	BLSS	29	CMPC3	39	MATCHC
0A	INDEX	1A	BGTRU	2A	SCANC	3A	LOCC
0B	CRC	1B	BLEQU	2B	SPANC	3B	SKPC
0C	PROBER	1C	BVC	2C	MOVC5	3C	MOVZWL
0D	PROBEW	1D	BVS	2D	CMPC5	3D	ACBW
0E	INSQUE	1E	BGEQU, BCC	2E	MOVTC	3E	MOVAW
0F	REMQUE	1F	BLSSU, BCS	2F	MOVTUC	3F	PUSHAW
40	ADDF2	50	MOVF	60	ADDD2	70	MOVD
40FD	ADDG2	50FD	MOVG	60FD	ADDH2	70FD	MOVH
41	ADDF3	51	CMPF	61	ADDD3	71	CMPD
41FD	ADDG3	51FD	CMPG	61FD	ADDH3	71FD	CMPH
42	SUBF2	52	MNEGF	62	SUBD2	72	MNEGD
42FD	SUBG2	52FD	MNEGG	62FD	SUBH2	72FD	MNEGH
43	SUBF3	53	TSTF	63	SUBD3	73	TSTD
43FD	SUBG3	53FD	TSTG	63FD	SUBH3	73FD	TSTH
44	MULF2	54	EMODF	64	MULD2	74	EMODD
44FD	MULG2	54FD	EMODG	64FD	MULH2	74FD	EMODH
45	MULF3	55	POLYF	65	MULD3	75	POLYD
45FD	MULG3	55FD	POLYG	65FD	MULH3	75FD	POLYH
46	DIVF2	56	CVTFD	66	DIVD2	76	CVTDF
46FD	DIVG2	56FD	CVTGH	66FD	DIVH2	76FD	CVTHG
47	DIVF3	57	reserved	67	DIVD3	77	reserved
47FD	DIVG3	57FD	reserved	67FD	DIVH3	77FD	reserved
48	CVTFB	58	ADAWI	68	CVTDB	78	ASHL
48FD	CVTGB	58FD	reserved	68FD	CVTHB	78FD	reserved
49	CVTFW	59	reserved	69	CVTDW	79	ASHQ
49FD	CVTGW	59FD	reserved	69FD	CVTHW	79FD	reserved
4A	CVTFL	5A	reserved	6A	CVTDL	7A	EMUL
4AFD	CVTGL	5AFD	reserved	6AFD	CVTHL	7AFD	reserved
4B	CVTRFL	5B	reserved	6B	CVTRDL	7B	EDIV
4BFD	CVTRGL	5BFD	reserved	6BFD	CVTRHL	7BFD	reserved
4C	CVTBF	5C	INSQHI	6C	CVTBD	7C	CLR(Q,D,G)
4CFD	CVTBG	5CFD	reserved	6CFD	CVTBH	7CFD	CLR(H,O)
4D	CVTWF	5D	INSQTI	6D	CVTWD	7D	MOVQ
4DFD	CVTWG	5DFD	reserved	6DFD	CVTWH	7DFD	MOVO
4E	CVTLF	5E	REMQHI	6E	CVTLD	7E	MOVA(Q,D,G)
4EFD	CVTLG	5EFD	reserved	6EFD	CVTLH	7EFD	MOVA(H,O)
4F	ACBF	5F	REMQTI	6F	ACVD	7F	PUSHA(Q,D,G)
4FFD	ACBG	5FFD	reserved	6FFD	ACBH	7FFD	PUSHA(H,O)

80	ADDB2	90	MOVB	A0	ADDW2	B0	MOVW
81	ADDB3	91	CMPB	A1	ADDW3	B1	CMPW
82	SUBB2	92	MCOMB	A2	SUBW2	B2	MCOMW
83	SUBB3	93	BITB	A3	SUBW3	B3	BITW
84	MULB2	94	CLRB	A4	MULW2	B4	CLRW
85	MULB3	95	TSTB	A5	MULW3	B5	TSTW
86	DIVB2	96	INCB	A6	DIVW2	B6	INCW
87	DIVB3	97	DECB	A7	DIVW3	B7	DECW
88	BISB2	98	CVTBL	A8	BISW2	B8	BISPSW
88FD	reserved	98FD	CVTFH	A8FD	reserved	B8FD	reserved
89	BISB3	99	CVTBW	A9	BISW3	B9	BICPSW
89FD	reserved	99FD	CVTFG	A9FD	reserved	B9FD	reserved
8A	BICB2	9A	MOVZBL	AA	BICW2	BA	POPR
8B	BICB3	9B	MOVZBW	AB	BICW3	BB	PUSHR
8C	XORB2	9C	ROTL	AC	XORW2	BC	CHMK
8D	XORB3	9D	ACBB	AD	XORW3	BD	CHME
8E	MNEGB	9E	MOVAB	AE	MNEGW	BE	CHMS
8F	CASEB	9F	PUSHAB	AF	CASEW	BF	CHMU

C0	ADDL2	D0	MOVL	E0	BBS	F0	INSV
C1	ADDL3	D1	CMPL	E1	BBC	F1	ACBL
C2	SUBL2	D2	MCOML	E2	BBSS	F2	AOBLSS
C3	SUBL3	D3	BITL	E3	BBCS	F3	AOBLEQ
C4	MULL2	D4	CLRL, CLRF	E4	BBSC	F4	SOBGEQ
C5	MULL3	D5	TSTL	E5	BBCC	F5	SOBGTR
C6	DIVL2	D6	INCL	E6	BBSSI	F6	CVTLB
C6FD	reserved	D6FD	reserved	E6FD	reserved	F6FD	CVTHF
C7	DIVL3	D7	DECL	E7	BBCCI	F7	CVTLW
C7FD	reserved	D7FD	reserved	E7FD	reserved	F7FD	CVTHD
C8	BISL2	D8	ADWC	E8	BLBS	F8	ASHP
C9	BISL3	D9	SBWC	E9	BLBC	F9	CVTLP
CA	BICL2	DA	MTPR	EA	FFS	FA	CALLG
CB	BICL3	DB	MFPR	EB	FFC	FB	CALLS
CC	XORL2	DC	MOVPSL	EC	CMPV	FC	XFC
CD	XORL3	DD	PUSHL	ED	CMPZV	FD	2-byte opcode
CDFF	reserved	DDFF	reserved	EDFF	reserved	FDFF	BUGL
CE	MNEGL	DE	MOVA(L,F)	EE	EXTV	FE	2-byte opcode
CEFF	reserved	DEFF	reserved	EEFF	reserved	FEFF	BUGW
CF	CASEL	DF	PUSHA(L,F)	EF	EXTZV	FF	2-byte opcode

VAX Opcodes in Alphabetical Order

Mnemonic	Opcode	Description	N	Z	V	C[1]
ACBB	9D	Add Compare and Branch Byte	*	*	*	-
ACBD	6F	Add Compare and Branch D_floating	*	*	*	-
ACBF	4F	Add Compare and Branch F_floating	*	*	*	-
ACBG	4FFD	Add Compare and Branch G_floating	*	*	*	-
ACBH	6FFD	Add Compare and Branch H_floating	*	*	*	-
ACBL	F1	Add Compare and Branch Long	*	*	*	-
ACBW	3D	Add Compare and Branch Word	*	*	*	-
ADAWI	58	Add Aligned Word Interlocked	*	*	*	*
ADDB2	80	Add Byte 2-Operand	*	*	*	*
ADDB3	81	Add Byte 3-Operand	*	*	*	*
ADDD2	60	Add D_floating 2-Operand	*	*	0	0
ADDD3	61	Add D_floating 3-Operand	*	*	0	0
ADDF2	40	Add F_floating 2-Operand	*	*	0	0
ADDF3	41	Add F_floating 3-Operand	*	*	0	0
ADDG2	40FD	Add G_Floating 2-Operand	*	*	0	0
ADDG3	41FD	Add G_Floating 3-Operand	*	*	0	0
ADDH2	60FD	Add H_Floating 2-Operand	*	*	0	0
ADDH3	61FD	Add H_Floating 3-Operand	*	*	0	0
ADDL2	C0	Add Long 2-Operand	*	*	*	*
ADDL3	C1	Add Long 3-Operand	*	*	*	*
ADDP4	20	Add Packed 4-Operand	*	*	*	0
ADDP6	21	Add packed 6-Operand	*	*	*	0
ADDW2	A0	Add Word 2-Operand	*	*	*	*
ADDW3	A1	Add Word 3-Operand	*	*	*	*
ADWC	D8	Add with Carry	*	*	*	*
AOBLEQ	F3	Add One and Branch Less Than or Equal	*	*	*	-
AOBLSS	F2	Add One and Branch Less Than	*	*	*	-
ASHL	78	Arithmetic Shift Long	*	*	*	0
ASHP	F8	Arithmetic Shift and Round Packed	*	*	*	0
ASHQ	79	Arithmetic Shift Quad	*	*	*	0
BBC	E1	Branch on Bit Clear	-	-	-	-
BBCC	E5	Branch on Bit Clear and Clear	-	-	-	-
BBCCI	E7	Branch on Bit Clear and Clear Interlocked	-	-	-	-
BBCS	E3	Branch on Bit Clear and Set	-	-	-	-
BBS	E0	Branch on Bit Set	-	-	-	-
BBSC	E4	Branch on Bit Set and Clear	-	-	-	-
BBSS	E2	Branch on Bit Set and Set	-	-	-	-

[1]*Asterisk* = CC bit set according to result; *dash* = CC bit unchanged

Mnemonic	Opcode	Description	N	Z	V	C
BBSSI	E6	Branch on Bit Set and Set Interlocked	-	-	-	-
BCC	1E	Branch on Carry Clear	-	-	-	-
BCS	1F	Branch on Carry Set	-	-	-	-
BEQL	13	Branch on Equal (signed)	-	-	-	-
BEQLU	13	Branch on Equal Unsigned	-	-	-	-
BGEQ	18	Branch on Greater Than or Equal (signed)	-	-	-	-
BGEQU	1E	Branch on Greater Than or Equal Unsigned	-	-	-	
BGTR	14	Branch on Greater Than (signed)	-	-	-	-
BGTRU	1A	Branch on Greater Than Unsigned	-	-	-	-
BICB2	8A	Bit Clear Byte 2-Operand	*	*	0	-
BICB3	8B	Bit Clear Byte 3-Operand	*	*	0	-
BICL2	CA	Bit Clear Long 2-Operand	*	*	0	-
BICL3	CB	Bit Clear Long 3-Operand	*	*	0	-
BICPSW	B9	Bit Clear PSW	*	*	*	*
BICW2	AA	Bit Clear Word 2-Operand	*	*	0	-
BICW3	AB	Bit Clear Word 3-Operand	*	*	0	-
BISB2	88	Bit Set Byte 2-Operand	*	*	0	-
BISB3	89	Bit Set Byte 3-Operand	*	*	0	-
BISL2	C8	Bit Set Long 2-Operand	*	*	0	-
BISL3	C9	Bit Set Long 3-Operand	*	*	0	-
BISPSW	B8	Bit Set PSW	*	*	*	*
BISW2	A8	Bit Set Word 2-Operand	*	*	0	-
BISW3	A9	Bit Set Word 3-Operand	*	*	0	-
BITB	93	Bit Test Byte	*	*	0	-
BITL	D3	Bit Test Long	*	*	0	-
BITW	B3	Bit Test Word	*	*	0	-
BLBC	E9	Branch on Low Bit Clear	-	-	-	-
BLBS	E8	Branch on Low Bit Set	-	-	-	-
BLEQ	15	Branch on Less Than or Equal (signed)	-	-	-	-
BLEQU	1B	Branch on Less Than or Equal Unsigned	-	-	-	-
BLSS	19	Branch on Less Than (signed)	-	-	-	-
BLSSU	1F	Branch on Less Than Unsigned	-	-	-	-
BNEQ	12	Branch on Not Equal (signed)	-	-	-	-
BNEQU	12	Branch on Not Equal Unsigned	-	-	-	-
BPT	03	Breakpoint	0	0	0	0
BRB	11	Branch with Byte Displacement	-	-	-	-
BRW	31	Branch with Word Displacement	-	-	-	-
BSBB	10	Branch to Subroutine With Byte Displacement	-	-	-	-
BSBW	30	Branch to Subroutine With Word Displacement	-	-	-	-

Mnemonic	Opcode	Description	N	Z	V	C
BUGL	FEFF	Bugcheck with Longword Message Identifier	-	-	-	-
BUGW	FDFF	Bugcheck with Word Message Identifier	-	-	-	-
BVC	1C	Branch on Overflow Clear	-	-	-	-
BVS	1D	Branch on Overflow Set	-	-	-	-
CALLG	FA	Call Procedure with General Argument List	0	0	0	0
CALLS	FB	Call Procedure with Stack Argument List	0	0	0	0
CASEB	8F	Case Byte	*	*	0	*
CASEL	CF	Case Long	*	*	0	*
CASEW	AF	Case Word	*	*	0	*
CHME	BD	Change Mode to Executive	0	0	0	0
CHMK	BC	Change Mode to Kernel	0	0	0	0
CHMS	BE	Change Mode to Supervisor	0	0	0	0
CHMU	BF	Change Mode to User	0	0	0	0
CLRB	94	Clear Byte	0	1	0	-
CLRD	7C	Clear D_floating	0	1	0	-
CLRF	D4	Clear F_floating	0	1	0	-
CLRG	7C	Clear G_floating	0	1	0	-
CLRH	7CFD	Clear H_floating	0	1	0	-
CLRL	D4	Clear Long	0	1	0	-
CLRO	7CFD	Clear Octa	0	1	0	-
CLRQ	7C	Clear Quad	0	1	0	-
CLRW	B4	Clear Word	0	1	0	-
CMPB	91	Compare Byte	*	*	0	*
CMPC3	29	Compare Characters 3-Operand	*	*	0	*
CMPC5	2D	Compare Characters 5-Operand	*	*	0	*
CMPD	71	Compare D_floating	*	*	0	0
CMPF	51	Compare F_floating	*	*	0	0
CMPG	51FD	Compare G_floating	*	*	0	0
CMPH	71FD	Compare H_floating	*	*	0	0
CMPL	D1	Compare Long	*	*	0	*
CMPP3	35	Compare Packed 3-Operand	*	*	0	0
CMPP4	37	Compare Packed 4-Operand	*	*	0	0
CMPV	EC	Compare Field	*	*	0	*
CMPW	B1	Compare Word	*	*	0	*
CMPZV	ED	Compare Zero-Extended Field	*	*	0	*
CRC	0B	Calculate Cyclic Redundancy Check	*	*	0	0
CVTBD	6C	Convert Byte to D_floating	*	*	0	0
CVTBF	4C	Convert Byte to F_floating	*	*	0	0
CVTBG	4CFD	Convert Byte to G_floating	*	*	0	0
CVTBH	6CFD	Convert Byte to H_floating	*	*	0	0
CVTBL	98	Convert Byte to Long	*	*	0	0
CVTBW	99	Convert Byte to Word	*	*	0	0
CVTDB	68	Convert D_floating to Byte	*	*	*	0

Mnemonic	Opcode	Description	N	Z	V	C
CVTDF	76	Convert D_floating to F_floating	*	*	*	0
CVTDH	32FD	Convert D_floating to H_floating	*	*	*	0
CVTDL	6A	Convert D_floating to Long	*	*	*	0
CVTDW	69	Convert D_floating to Word	*	*	*	0
CVTFB	48	Convert F_floating to Byte	*	*	*	0
CVTFD	56	Convert F_floating to D_floating	*	*	*	0
CVTFG	99FD	Convert F_floating to G_floating	*	*	*	0
CVTFH	98FD	Convert F_floating to H_floating	*	*	*	0
CVTFL	4A	Convert F_floating to Long	*	*	*	0
CVTFW	49	Convert F_floating to Word	*	*	*	0
CVTGB	48FD	Convert G_floating to Byte	*	*	*	0
CVTGF	33FD	Convert G_floating to F_floating	*	*	*	0
CVTGH	56FD	Convert G_floating to H_floating	*	*	*	0
CVTGL	4AFD	Convert G_floating to Long	*	*	*	0
CVTGW	49FD	Convert G_floating to Word	*	*	*	0
CVTHB	68FD	Convert H_floating to Byte	*	*	*	0
CVTHD	F7FD	Convert H_floating to D_floating	*	*	*	0
CVTHF	F6FD	Convert H_floating to F_floating	*	*	*	0
CVTHG	76FD	Convert H_floating to G_floating	*	*	*	0
CVTHL	6AFD	Convert H_floating to Long	*	*	*	0
CVTHW	69FD	Convert H_floating to Word	*	*	*	0
CVTLB	F6	Convert Long to Byte	*	*	*	0
CVTLD	6E	Convert Long to D_floating	*	*	0	0
CVTLF	4e	Convert Long to F_floating	*	*	*	0
CVTLG	4EFD	Convert Long to G_Floating	*	*	0	0
CVTLH	6EFD	Convert Long to H_Floating	*	*	0	0
CVTLP	F9	Convert Long to Packed	*	*	*	0
CVTLW	F7	Convert Long to Word	*	*	*	0
CVTPL	36	Convert Packed to Long	*	*	*	0
CVTPS	08	Convert Packed to Leading Separate Numeric	*	*	*	0
CVTPT	24	Convert Packed to Trailing Numeric	*	*	*	0
CVTRDL	6B	Convert Rounded D_floating to Long	*	*	*	0
CVTRFL	4B	Convert Rounded F_floating to Long	*	*	*	0
CVTRGL	4BFD	Convert Rounded G_floating to Long	*	*	*	0
CVTRHL	6BFD	Convert Rounded H_floating to Long	*	*	*	0
CVTSP	09	Convert Leading Separate Numeric to Packed	*	*	*	0
CVTTP	26	Convert Trailing Numeric to Packed	*	*	*	0
CVTWB	33	Convert Word to Byte	*	*	*	0
CVTWD	6D	Convert Word to D_floating	*	*	0	0
CVTWF	4D	Convert Word to F_floating	*	*	0	0
CVTWG	4DFD	Convert Word to G_floating	*	*	0	0
CVTWH	6DFD	Convert Word to H_floating	*	*	0	0
CVTWL	32	Convert Word to Long	*	*	0	0
DECB	97	Decrement Byte	*	*	*	*
DECL	D7	Decrement Long	*	*	*	*
DECW	B7	Decrement Word	*	*	*	*

Mnemonic	Opcode	Description	N	Z	V	C
DIVB2	86	Divide Byte 2-Operand	*	*	*	0
DIVB3	87	Divide Byte 3-Operand	*	*	*	0
DIVD2	66	Divide D_floating 2-Operand	*	*	0	0
DIVD3	67	Divide D_floating 3-Operand	*	*	0	0
DIVF2	46	Divide F_floating 2-Operand	*	*	0	0
DIVF3	47	Divide F_floating 3-Operand	*	*	0	0
DIVG2	46FD	Divide G_floating 2-Operand	*	*	0	0
DIVG3	47FD	Divide G_floating 3-Operand	*	*	0	0
DIVH2	66FD	Divide H_floating 2-Operand	*	*	0	0
DIVH3	67FD	Divide H_floating 3-Operand	*	*	0	0
DIVL2	C6	Divide Long 2-Operand	*	*	*	0
DIVL3	C7	Divide Long 3-Operand	*	*	*	0
DIVP	27	Divide Packed	*	*	*	0
DIVW2	A6	Divide Word 2-Operand	*	*	*	0
DIVW3	A7	Divide Word 3-Operand	*	*	*	0
EDITPC	38	Edit Packed to Character String	*	*	*	*
EDIV	7B	Extended Divide	*	*	*	0
EMODD	74	Extended Multiply and Integerize D_floating	*	*	*	0
EMODF	54	Extended Multiply and Integerize F_floating	*	*	*	0
EMODG	54FD	Extended Multiply and Integerize G_floating	*	*	*	0
EMODH	74FD	Extended Multiply and Integerize H_floating	*	*	*	0
EMUL	7A	Extended Multiply	*	*	0	0
EXTV	EE	Extract Field	*	*	0	-
EXTZV	EF	Extract Zero-Extended Field	*	*	0	-
FFC	EB	Find First Clear	0	*	0	0
FFS	EA	Find First Set	0	*	0	0
HALT	00	Halt (kernel mode)	-	-	-	-
INCB	96	Increment Byte	*	*	*	*
INCL	D6	Increment Long	*	*	*	*
INCW	B6	Increment Word	*	*	*	*
INDEX	0A	Compute Index	*	*	0	0
INSQHI	5C	Insert Entry into Queue at Head, Interlocked	0	*	0	*
INSQTI	5D	Insert Entry into Queue at Tail, Interlocked	0	*	0	*
INSQUE	0E	Insert Entry in Queue	*	*	0	*
INSV	F0	Insert Field	-	-	-	-
JMP	17	Jump	-	-	-	-
JSB	16	Jump to Subroutine	-	-	-	-

Mnemonic	Opcode	Description	N	Z	V	C
LDPCTX	06	Load Process Context	-	-	-	-
LOCC	3A	Locate Character	0	*	0	0
MATCHC	39	Match Characters	0	*	0	0
MCOMB	92	Move Complemented Byte	*	*	0	-
MCOML	D2	Move Complemented Long	*	*	0	-
MCOMW	B2	Move Complemented Word	*	*	0	-
MFPR	DB	Move From Processor Register	*	*	0	-
MNEGB	8E	Move Negated Byte	*	*	*	*
MNEGD	72	Move Negated D_floating	*	*	0	0
MNEGF	52	Move Negated F_floating	*	*	0	0
MNEGG	52FD	Move Negated G_floating	*	*	0	0
MNEGH	72FD	Move Negated H_floating	*	*	0	0
MNEGL	CE	Move Negated Long	*	*	*	*
MNEGW	AE	Move Negated Word	*	*	*	*
MOVAB	9E	Move Address Byte	*	*	0	-
MOVAD	7E	Move Address D_floating	*	*	0	-
MOVAF	DE	Move Address F_floating	*	*	0	-
MOVAG	7E	Move Address G_floating	*	*	0	-
MOVAH	7EFD	Mova Address H_floating	*	*	0	-
MOVAL	DE	Move Address Long	*	*	0	-
MOVAO	7EFD	Mova Address Octa	*	*	0	-
MOVAQ	7E	Move Address Quad	*	*	0	-
MOVAW	3E	Move Address Word	*	*	0	-
MOVB	90	Move Byte	*	*	0	-
MOVC3	28	Move Character 3-Operand	0	1	0	0
MOVC5	2C	Move Character 5-Operand	*	*	0	*
MOVD	70	Move D_floating	*	*	0	-
MOVF	50	Move F_floating	*	*	0	-
MOVG	50FD	Move G_floating	*	*	0	-
MOVH	70FD	Move H_floating	*	*	0	-
MOVL	D0	Move Long	*	*	0	-
MOVO	7DFD	Move Octa	*	*	0	-
MOVP	34	Move Packed	*	*	0	-
MOVPSL	DC	Move from PSL	-	-	-	-
MOVQ	7D	Move Quad	*	*	0	-
MOVTC	2E	Move Translated Characters	*	*	0	*
MOVTUC	2F	Move Translated Until Character	*	*	*	*
MOVW	B0	Move Word	*	*	0	-
MOVZBL	9A	Move Zero-Extended Byte to Long	0	*	0	-
MOVZBW	9B	Move Zero-Extended Byte to Word	0	*	0	-
MOVZWL	3C	Move Zero-Extended Word to Long	0	*	0	-
MTPR	DA	Move to Processor Register	*	*	0	-
MULB2	84	Multiply Byte 2-Operand	*	*	*	0
MULB3	85	Multiply Byte 3-Operand	*	*	*	0
MULD2	64	Multiply D_floating 2-Operand	*	*	0	0
MULD3	65	Multiply D_floating 3-Operand	*	*	0	0

Mnemonic	*Opcode*	*Description*	*N*	*Z*	*V*	*C*
MULF2	44	Multiply F_floating 2-Operand	*	*	0	0
MULF3	45	Multiply F_floating 3-Operand	*	*	0	0
MULG2	44FD	Multiply G_floating 2-Operand	*	*	0	0
MULG3	45FD	Multiply G_floating 3-Operand	*	*	0	0
MULH2	64FD	Multiply H_floating 2-Operand	*	*	0	0
MULH2	65FD	Multiply H_floating 3-Operand	*	*	0	0
MULL2	C4	Multiply Long 2-Operand	*	*	*	0
MULL3	C5	Multiply Long 3-Operand	*	*	*	0
MULP	25	Multiply Packed	*	*	*	0
MULW2	A4	Multiply Word 2-Operand	*	*	*	0
MULW3	A5	Multiply Word 3-Operand	*	*	*	0
NOP	01	No Operation	-	-	-	-
POLYD	75	Polynomial Evaluation D_floating	*	*	0	0
POLYF	55	Polynomial Evaluation F_floating	*	*	0	0
POLYG	55FD	Polynomial Evaluation G_floating	*	*	0	0
POLYH	75FD	Polynomial Evaluation H_floating	*	*	0	0
POPR	BA	Pop Registers	-	-	-	-
PROBER	0C	Probe Read Accessibility	0	*	0	-
PROBEW	0D	Probe Write Accessibility	0	*	0	-
PUSHAB	9F	Push Address Byte	*	*	0	-
PUSHAD	7F	Push Address D_floating	*	*	0	-
PUSHAF	DF	Push Address F_floating	*	*	0	-
PUSHAG	7F	Push Address G_floating	*	*	0	-
PUSHAH	7FFD	Push Address H_floating	*	*	0	-
PUSHAL	DF	Push Address Long	*	*	0	-
PUSHAO	7FFD	Push Address Octa	*	*	0	-
PUSHAQ	7F	Push Address Quad	*	*	0	-
PUSHAW	3F	Push Address Word	*	*	0	-
PUSHL	DD	Push Long	*	*	0	-
PUSHR	BB	Push Registers	-	-	-	-
REI	02	Return from Exception or Interrupt	*	*	*	*
REMQHI	5E	Remove Entry from Queue at Head, Interlocked	0	*	*	*
REMQTI	5F	Remove Entry from Queue at Tail, Interlocked	0	*	*	
REMQUE	0F	Remove Entry from Queue	*	*	*	*
RET	04	Return from Procedure	*	*	*	*
ROTL	9C	Rotate Long	*	*	0	-
RSB	05	Return from Subroutine	-	-	-	-
SBWC	D9	Subtract with Carry	*	*	*	*
SCANC	2A	Scan Characters	0	*	0	0
SKPC	3B	Skip Character	0	*	0	0
SOBGEQ	F4	Subtract One and Branch Greater Than or Equal	*	*	*	-

Mnemonic	Opcode	Description	N	Z	V	C
SOBGTR	F5	Subtract One and Branch Greater Than	*	*	*	-
SPANC	2B	Span Characters	0	*	0	0
SUBB2	82	Subtract Byte 2-Operand	*	*	*	*
SUBB3	83	Subtract Byte 3-Operand	*	*	*	*
SUBD2	62	Subtract D_floating 2-Operand	*	*	0	0
SUBD3	63	Subtract D_floating 3-Operand	*	*	0	0
SUBF2	42	Subtract F_floating 2-Operand	*	*	0	0
SUBF3	43	Subtract F_floating 3-Operand	*	*	0	0
SUBG2	42FD	Subtract G_floating 2-Operand	*	*	0	0
SUBG3	43FD	Subtract G_floating 3-Operand	*	*	0	0
SUBH2	62FD	Subtract H_floating 2-Operand	*	*	0	0
SUBH3	63FD	Subtract H_floating 3-Operand	*	*	0	0
SUBL2	C2	Subtract Long 2-Operand	*	*	*	*
SUBL3	C3	Subtract Long 3-Operand	*	*	*	*
SUBP4	22	Subtract Packed 4-Operand	*	*	*	-
SUBP6	23	Subtract Packed 6-Operand	*	*	*	-
SUBW2	A2	Subtract Word 2-Operand	*	*	*	*
SUBW3	A3	Subtract Word 3-Operand	*	*	*	*
SVPCTX	07	Save Process Context	-	-	-	-
TSTB	95	Test Byte	*	*	0	0
TSTD	73	Test D_floating	*	*	0	0
TSTF	53	Test F_floating	*	*	0	0
TSTG	53FD	Test G_floating	*	*	0	0
TSTH	73FD	Test H_floating	*	*	0	0
TSTL	D5	Test Long	*	*	0	0
TSTW	B5	Test Word	*	*	0	0
XFC	FC	Extended Function Call	0	0	0	0
XORB2	8C	Exclusive-OR Byte 2-Operand	*	*	0	-
XORB3	8D	Exclusive-OR Byte 3-Operand	*	*	0	-
XORL2	CC	Exclusive-OR Long 2-Operand	*	*	0	-
XORL3	CD	Exclusive-OR Long 3-Operand	*	*	0	-
XORW2	AC	Exclusive-OR Word 2-Operand	*	*	0	-
XORW3	AD	Exclusive-OR Word 3-Operand	*	*	0	-

Addressing Mode Summary

General Register Addressing Modes

Mode	Name	Format	Explanation
0-3	Short Literal	#X	Operand is operand specifier.
4	Index	BOS[Rn]	**B**ase **O**perand **S**pecifier specifies Base Operand Address. Operand address is BOA + [size * (Rn)].
5	Register	Rn	Operand is in Rn.
6	Register Deferred	(Rn)	Operand address is in Rn.
7	Auto-Decrement	−(Rn)	Rn←Rn−dec before address is computed; *then* operand address is in Rn.[†]
8	Auto-Increment	(Rn)+	Operand address is in Rn; Rn←Rn+inc *after* operand is fetched.[‡]
9	Auto-Increment Deferred	@(Rn)+	Address of operand address is in Rn; Rn←Rn+4 *after* operand is fetched.
A (C, E)	Byte, (Word, Longword) Displacement	X(Rn)	Operand address is X+Rn; X follows operand specifier.
B (D, F)	Byte (Word, Longword) Displacement Deferred	@X(Rn)	Address of operand address is X+Rn; X follows operand specifier.

[†]dec = 1 for byte, 2 for word, 4 for longword instruction.
[‡]inc = 1 for byte, 2 for word, 4 for longword instruction.

General Register Addressing Modes in Action

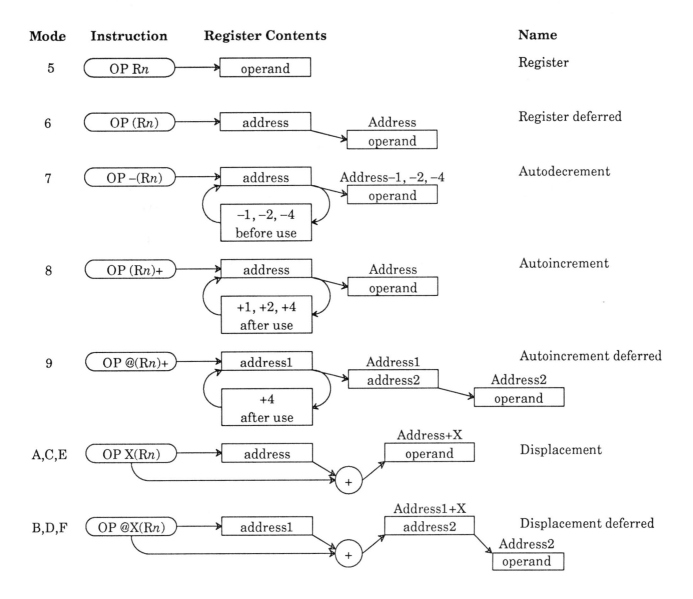

Mode	Instruction	Register Contents		Name
5	OP Rn	operand		Register
6	OP (Rn)	address	Address / operand	Register deferred
7	OP −(Rn)	address / −1, −2, −4 before use	Address−1, −2, −4 / operand	Autodecrement
8	OP (Rn)+	address / +1, +2, +4 after use	Address / operand	Autoincrement
9	OP @(Rn)+	address1 / +4 after use	Address1 / address2 → Address2 / operand	Autoincrement deferred
A,C,E	OP X(Rn)	address +	Address+X / operand	Displacement
B,D,F	OP @X(Rn)	address1 +	Address1+X / address2 → Address2 / operand	Displacement deferred

Program Counter Addressing Modes

Mode	Name	Format	Explanation
8	Immediate	#X	Operand is X; X follows operand specifier.
9	Absolute	@#X	Operand address is X; X follows operand specifier.
A (C, E)	Relative	X	Operand address is X; X–PC follows operand specifier.
B (D, F)	Relative Deferred	@X	Address of operand address is X; X–PC follows operand specifier.

Powers of 2 and Powers of 16

Powers of 2		Powers of 16	
n	2^n	n	16^n
0	1	0	1
1	2	1	16
2	4	2	256
4	16	3	4,096
8	256	4	65,536
10	1,024	5	1,048,576
12	4,096	6	16,777,216
14	16,384	7	268,435,456
15	32,768	8	4,294,967,296
16	65,536	9	68,719,476,736
18	262,144	10	1,099,511,627,776
20	1,048,576	11	17,592,186,044,416
22	4,194,304	12	281,474,976,710,656
24	16,777,216	13	4,503,599,627,370,496
26	67,108,864	14	72,057,594,037,927,936
28	268,435,456	15	1,152,921,504,606,846,976
30	1,073,741,824	16	18,446,744,073,709,551,616
32	4,294,967,296	17	295,147,905,179,352,825,856
40	1,099,511,627,776	18	4,722,366,482,869,645,213,696
48	281,474,976,710,656	19	75,557,863,725,914,323,419,136
52	4,503,599,627,370,496	20	1,208,925,819,614,629,174,706,176
56	72,057,594,037,927,936	21	19,342,813,113,834,066,795,298,816
64	18,446,744,073,709,551,616	22	309,485,009,821,345,068,724,781,056

Hexadecimal and Decimal ASCII Character Codes

Hex	ASCII	Dec	Hex	ASCII	Dec	Hex	ASCII	Dec	Hex	ASCII	Dec
00	nul	0	20	space	32	40	@	64	60		96
01	soh	1	21	!	33	41	A	65	61	a	97
02	stx	2	22	"	34	42	B	66	62	b	98
03	etx	3	23	#	35	43	C	67	63	c	99
04	eot	4	24	$	36	44	D	68	64	d	100
05	enq	5	25	%	37	45	E	69	65	e	101
06	ack	6	26	&	38	46	F	70	66	f	102
07	bell	7	27	'	39	47	G	71	67	g	103
08	bs	8	28	(	40	48	H	72	68	h	104
09	ht	9	29	)	41	49	I	73	69	i	105
0A	lf	10	2A	*	42	4A	J	74	6A	j	106
0B	vt	11	2B	+	43	4B	K	75	6B	k	107
0C	ff	12	2C	,	44	4C	L	76	6C	l	108
0D	cr	13	2D	-	45	4D	M	77	6D	m	109
0E	so	14	2E	.	46	4E	N	78	6E	n	110
0F	si	15	2F	/	47	4F	O	79	6F	o	111
10	dle	16	30	0	48	50	P	80	70	p	112
11	dc1	17	31	1	49	51	Q	81	71	q	113
12	dc2	18	32	2	50	52	R	82	72	r	114
13	dc3	19	33	3	51	53	S	83	73	s	115
14	dc4	20	34	4	52	54	T	84	74	t	116
15	nak	21	35	5	53	55	U	85	75	u	117
16	syn	22	36	6	54	56	V	86	76	v	118
17	etb	23	37	7	55	57	W	87	77	w	119
18	can	24	38	8	56	58	X	88	78	x	120
19	em	25	39	9	57	59	Y	89	79	y	121
1A	sub	26	3A	:	58	5A	Z	90	7a	z	122
1B	esc	27	3B	;	59	5B	[	91	7B	{	123
1C	fs	28	3C	<	60	5C	\	92	7C			124
1D	gs	29	3D	=	61	5D	]	93	7D	}	125
1E	rs	30	3E	>	62	5E	^	94	7E	~	126
1F	us	31	3F	?	63	5F	_	95	7F	del	127

Debugging Assembly Language Programs With DEBUG

Using DEBUG

In chapter 4 we presented a brief introduction to the VMS debugger, DEBUG. In this appendix we will elaborate on that introduction, but we will make no attempt to provide a complete description of DEBUG. DEBUG is a complex and sophisticated program; it can be used with high-level language programs as well as assembly language programs. The reader interested in greater detail should consult the *VMS Debugger Reference Manual*. (The other common operating system for VAXes--UNIX--also provides debugging software; there is an assembly language debugger called **adb** and a symbolic debugger called **dbx**. The interested reader should consult the appropriate documentation.)

When we write assembly language programs, we pass on to the assembler the task of assigning addresses and keeping track of memory locations; we use symbolic labels rather than addresses. The assembler produces a symbol table in its listing, but this symbol table is only for our information as programmers: it is not passed on to the linker. The linker doesn't need information about any symbols that are local to our program (symbols that are defined in a module and referenced only in that module), so the assembler only passes information concerning global labels to the linker. However, when we use DEBUG, we would like to specify memory locations to examine by using their symbolic labels rather than their addresses, so we need to instruct the assembler and linker to pass *all* symbols in the symbol table to the debugger.

How do we inform the assembler and linker to pass on the complete symbol table? When we assemble a program (PROG1, say), we normally type

MACRO PROG1

or

MACRO/LIST PROG1

but if we wish to use the debugger, we would type

MACRO/DEBUG PROG1

Similarly, when we link our program, we would type

LINK/DEBUG PROG1

Then, when we run our program (by typing RUN PROG1), the debugger will be automatically invoked.

DEBUG Statements

The general format of a statement for DEBUG is

command </qualifier>   <parameter>   <address>   <!comment>

The following sections describe some of the more useful DEBUG statements.

EXAMINE

In chapter 4 we saw that we can examine (using the EXAMINE command, or E for short) the contents of the memory location referred to by the label LABEL by typing

E LABEL.[1]

By default, DEBUG will show us the hexadecimal value of a memory location when we use EXAMINE. However, as we also saw in chapter 4, if we wish to have the contents of some location *disassembled*, we can use the INST qualifier. If we type

E/INST LABEL

DEBUG will interpret the contents of location LABEL as an instruction and show us the assembly language instruction that generated the machine language stored at location LABEL.

We can also use the EXAMINE command to examine register contents. If we want to see the contents of R3, we can type

E R3

If we want to see the contents of R3, R4, R5, and R6, we can type

E R3:R6

By default, DEBUG produces output in hexadecimal. If we wish to have DEBUG show us the contents of some location in decimal, we can use the DECIMAL (or DEC) qualifier, and type

E/DEC LOCATION

DEPOSIT

DEBUG will *initialize* memory locations if we instruct it to do so with the DEPOSIT command. Thus, if we are using the debugger to run a program in which we have found that we forgot the initialize R7 to 100_{16} before we used it, we can, in the debugger, type

D R7=100

---

[1]Recall that VMS is case insensitive: it doesn't distinguish between upper- and lowercase. Thus, it is just as correct to type "E LABEL" as "e label."

Unfortunately, the /DEC qualifier does not work with DEPOSIT; if we wish to initialize memory location JUNK to 10_{10}, we must type

    D JUNK=A

Our only alternative is to type

    SET RADIX DECIMAL

which will cause DEBUG to interpret all of the numbers we type as decimal numbers.

STEP

We saw that executing a program in the debugger is done by typing GO. However, we sometimes want to execute only one instruction at a time. If we use the STEP command, the next instruction will be executed, and then the debugger will stop program execution and wait for our next command. We can examine some memory location or register or deposit a value in a memory location or register, and then execute the next instruction or instructions, or execute all the remaining instructions in the program. By default, the STEP command causes only one instruction to be executed. If we give it an integer parameter, then the number of instructions specified by the parameter will be executed. Thus, if we type

    STEP 3

the next three instructions will be executed; if we use the parameter *n*, the next *n* instructions will be executed.

SET

There is a large class of SET commands; we will briefly describe one subclass of the SET commands which is particularly useful for debugging large assembly language programs. If we know that the value of some particular variable is incorrect, but we don't know why, we can use the SET WATCH command. If we are interested in watching the variable whose label is VALUE1, we can type

    SET WATCH VALUE1

and the debugger will halt execution of our program every time the contents of location VALUE1 change. When it halts execution, DEBUG will also inform us of the address of the instruction that changed the contents of that location, and its old and new contents.

We can also use the SET command to stop execution when a certain instruction in our program is reached. We call this point in our program--just before the instruction is executed--a **breakpoint.** If we type

    SET BREAK SKIP

then the debugger will stop our program just before the instruction at location SKIP is executed. We can use a qualifier with the SET BREAK command: if we type

    SET BREAK/AFTER:3 LOOP

then the debugger will stop execution when the instruction at location LOOP is reached the third time--as usual, just before it is executed. In all of these cases, after the debugger stops execution of our program, we can examine or initialize any memory location we wish to, and then continue execution of our program using either the STEP command or the GO command.

Sample DEBUG Session

Below, we present a trace of a DEBUG session, illustrating some of the commands described. DEBUG recognizes the exclamation mark (!) as a comment delimiter, and ignores everything on the line after it. The assembler's listing of the program used for this DEBUG session is shown in figure 1. The observant reader will notice that, in the sample session, when R5 contains 0 and then gets decremented, DEBUG shows us that it contains $0FFFFFFFF_{16}$. This is because DEBUG requires that, when we type a hexadecimal number beginning with a digit between A and F, we must use a leading 0. Similarly, when DEBUG shows us a hexadecimal value beginning with a digit between A and F, it prints a leading 0.

```
$ MACRO/DEBUG PROG1

$ LINK/DEBUG PROG1

$ RUN PROG1

        VAX DEBUG Version V4.5-6


%DEBUG-I-INITIAL, language is MACRO, module set to 'PROGRAM1'

DBG> E A                         !Examine contents of A

PROGRAM1\A:     00000006

DBG> E B                         !Examine contents of B

PROGRAM1\B:     00000007

DBG> E/INST LOOP                 !Disassemble instruction at LOOP

PROGRAM1\LOOP:  DECL    R5

DBG> S                           !Step one instruction

stepped to PROGRAM1\START+0D: MOVL I^#00000100,R8

DBG> E A

PROGRAM1\A:     00000006

DBG> E B                         !B should have changed

PROGRAM1\B:     0000000D

DBG> E R5:R8                     !Registers still uninitialized
```

```
PROGRAM1        5-MAR-1988 16:33:31  VAX/VMS Macro V04-00        Page   1
                5-MAR-1988 16:33:23  [PB.APPENDICES]PROG1.MAR;2         (1)

                              0000    1           .TITLE PROGRAM1
                      0000    0000    2           .ENTRY START, 0
  0000002C'EF   00000028'EF   C0 0002    3           ADDL2 A, B
         58     00000100 8F   D0 000D    4           MOVL #^X100, R8
                   57    04   D0 0014    5           MOVL #4, R7
                   55    03   D0 0017    6           MOVL #3, R5
                         55   D7 001A    7 LOOP: DECL R5
                   FB 57      F5 001C    8           SOBGTR R7, LOOP
                              001F    9           $EXIT_S
                   00000006    0028   10 A:   .LONG 6
                   00000007    002C   11 B:   .LONG 7
                              0030   12           .END START
PROGRAM1        5-MAR-1988 16:33:31  VAX/VMS Macro V04-00        Page   2
Symbol table    5-MAR-1988 16:33:23  [PB.APPENDICES]PROG1.MAR;2         (1)

A               00000028 R  D   01
B               0000002C R  D   01
LOOP            0000001A R  D   01
START           00000000 RG D   01
SYS$EXIT        ********  GX     01
```

Figure A7.1: Assembler listing for DEBUG session

```
0\%R5:   00000000
0\%R6:   7FF27849
0\%R7:   8001E4DD
0\%R8:   7FFED052

DBG> S                          !Step another instruction

stepped to PROGRAM1\START+14: MOVL S^#04,R7

DBG> E R5:R8                    !R8 should be initialized now

0\%R5:   00000000
0\%R6:   7FF27849
0\%R7:   8001E4DD
0\%R8:   00000100

DBG> S

stepped to PROGRAM1\START+17: MOVL S^#03,R5

DBG> E R5:R8                    !R7 should be initialized now
```

```
0\%R5:   00000000
0\%R6:   7FF27849
0\%R7:   00000004
0\%R8:   00000100

DBG> S

stepped to PROGRAM1\LOOP: DECL R5

DBG> E R5:R8                    !R5 should be initialized now

0\%R5:   00000003
0\%R6:   7FF27849
0\%R7:   00000004
0\%R8:   00000100

DBG> S

stepped to PROGRAM1\LOOP+2: SOBGTR R7,PROGRAM1\LOOP

DBG> E R5:R8                    !R5 should be 1 less

0\%R5:   00000002
0\%R6:   7FF27849
0\%R7:   00000004
0\%R8:   00000100

DBG> S

stepped to PROGRAM1\LOOP: DECL R5

DBG> E R5:R8                    !R7 should be 1 less

0\%R5:   00000002
0\%R6:   7FF27849
0\%R7:   00000003
0\%R8:   00000100

DBG> S

stepped to PROGRAM1\LOOP+2: SOBGTR R7,PROGRAM1\LOOP

DBG> E R5:R8                    !R5 1 less

0\%R5:   00000001
0\%R6:   7FF27849
0\%R7:   00000003
0\%R8:   00000100

DBG> S

stepped to PROGRAM1\LOOP: DECL R5
```

```
DBG> E R5:R8                          !R7 1 less

0\%R5:   00000001
0\%R6:   7FF27849
0\%R7:   00000002
0\%R8:   00000100

DBG> S

stepped to PROGRAM1\LOOP+2: SOBGTR R7,PROGRAM1\LOOP

DBG> E R5:R8                          !R5 1 less

0\%R5:   00000000
0\%R6:   7FF27849
0\%R7:   00000002
0\%R8:   00000100

DBG> S

stepped to PROGRAM1\LOOP: DECL R5

DBG> E R5:R8                          !R7 1 less

0\%R5:   00000000
0\%R6:   7FF27849
0\%R7:   00000001
0\%R8:   00000100

DBG> S

stepped to PROGRAM1\LOOP+2: SOBGTR R7,PROGRAM1\LOOP

DBG> E R5:R8                          !R5 1 less; note leading 0

0\%R5:   0FFFFFFF
0\%R6:   7FF27849
0\%R7:   00000001
0\%R8:   00000100

DBG> S

stepped to PROGRAM1\LOOP+5: PUSHL S^#01

DBG> E R5:R8                          !R7 <= 0, so branch not taken

0\%R5:   0FFFFFFF
0\%R6:   7FF27849
0\%R7:   00000000
0\%R8:   00000100

DBG> S
```

```
stepped to PROGRAM1\LOOP+7: CALLS S^#01,@#SYS$EXIT

DBG> S

%DEBUG-I-EXITSTATUS, is '%SYSTEM-S-NORMAL, normal successful completion'

DBG> E A

PROGRAM1\A:        00000006

DBG> E B

PROGRAM1\B:        0000000D

DBG> D B=7                         !Reinitialize B, and execute again

DBG> E B

PROGRAM1\B:        00000007

DBG> SET WATCH B                   !Stop when B changes

DBG> GO START                      !Begin execution at START

watch of PROGRAM1\B at routine PROGRAM1\START: ADDL2 L^PROGRAM1\A,L^PROGRAM1\
  ?
B
   old value: 00000007
   new value: 0000000D
break at PROGRAM1\START+0D: MOVL I^#00000100,R8

DBG> SET BREAK LOOP                !Stop when LOOP is reached

DBG> GO                            !continue execution

break at PROGRAM1\LOOP: DECL R5

DBG> E R5:R7                       !just before R5 changes

0\%R5:   00000003
0\%R6:   7FF27849
0\%R7:   00000004

DBG> GO                            !continue execution

break at PROGRAM1\LOOP: DECL R5

DBG> E R5:R7                       !R5 and R7 should have changed

0\%R5:   00000002
0\%R6:   7FF27849
0\%R7:   00000003
```

```
DBG> GO                          !continue

break at PROGRAM1\LOOP: DECL R5

DBG> E R5:R7                      !R5 and R7 changed again

0\%R5:   00000001
0\%R6:   7FF27849
0\%R7:   00000002

DBG> GO                          !continue

break at PROGRAM1\LOOP: DECL R5

DBG> E R5:R7                      !R5 and R7 changed again

0\%R5:   00000000
0\%R6:   7FF27849
0\%R7:   00000001

DBG> GO                          !continue, but LOOP won't be reached

%DEBUG-I-EXITSTATUS, is '%SYSTEM-S-NORMAL, normal successful completion'

DBG> EXIT                        !end debugging session

$
```

Solutions to Selected Exercises

This appendix contains solutions to some of the end-of-chapter exercises. The solutions not presented here are marked with asterisks (*), and they are in the instructor's manual.

Programming exercises rarely have unique solutions; the ones presented in this appendix are meant only to be illustrative of what constitutes a good solution. However, the fact that two solutions may be equally correct does not mean that they are equally good. In general, a clearer solution is a better one, unless other constraints (such as code size or execution efficiency) are of great importance. The solutions presented here are intended to be correct, but not to be the best possible solutions. You may find it educational to try to improve these solutions.

Selected Solutions for Chapter 1

1.   The surface area program can be rewritten to use fewer memory locations as follows:

```
  S 0    Store height in location 0
  S 1    Store length in location 1
  S 2    Store width in location 2
  R 0    Recall H
* R 1    H * L
  S 7    Store H * L in location 7
  R 1    Recall L
* R 2    L * W
+ R 7    L * W + H * L
  S 7    Store L * W + H * L in location 7
  R 0    Recall H
* R 2    H * W
+ R 7    (L * W + H * L) + H * W
```

In this program, we use location 7 to accumulate the result, and eliminate the need for location 8.

2. The program to compute $a + bx + cx^2$:

```
  S 0    Store value for a
  S 1    Store value for b
  S 2    Store value for c
  S 9    Store value for x
* R 2    c * x
+ R 1    b + c * x
* R 9    (b + c * x) * x
+ R 0    a + ( b * x + c * x * x)
```

For each new value of x, repeat from the line where we store the value of x in location 9.

3. *

4. With a 5 bit code you can normally only represent 2^5, or 32, distinct items. However, if you designate one of these as a mode indicator (similar to the role played by a shift key on a typewriter), you can assign two meanings to each of the other 31 codes. In the absence of use of the mode code—mode 0, let's say—each code has its default interpretation. The appearance of a mode code, however, means that mode 1 is now entered, and we return to mode 0 when next encountering the mode code. For example, let the mode code be represented by "$". The character string

   THIS IS $A TEST $OF P$A$TIENCE

could be interpreted as

   THIS IS a test OF PaTIENCE.

520

The Baudot code uses two mode codes instead of one. It has a "figures" code and a "letters" code. Thus, with the Baudot code you explicitly state what mode you're in, rather than toggling back and forth between the two modes.

5. *

6. The Hollerith code for the characters +, −, 0, 1, · · · , 9 uses one hole per column for each of these characters. Each column can accommodate up to 12 holes, with one per row. The rows are identified with the names of the characters.

The (upper case) letters of the alphabet each use two holes per column. The letter *A* uses the + and 1 holes, *B* uses the + and 2 holes, · · ·, *I* uses the + and 9 holes. Similarly, the letters *J* through *R* use − and 1 through − and 9, and the letters *S* through *Z* use 0 and 2 through 0 and 9. The other characters use more than two holes each. For example, the decimal point (period) uses the +, 3 and 8 holes. Typically, card reader hardware or software converts the 12-bit Hollerith code from a punched card to a more convenient 6 or 8 bit code.

7. A 91 bit wide binary code can accommodate the 88 keys and three pedals of a piano. Since almost any combination of these may occur (you can play more than one key simultaneously), you can't reduce the 91 without constraining future composers. We were able to replace the 17 bit wide calculator code by a five bit code only because only one of 17 keys is pushed simultaneously. This is not true with a piano.

8. *

9.
a. (1) The parity of 1100 is even, (2) the parity of 100010 is even, and (3) the parity of 011001 is odd.
b. (1) 111000 has odd parity, (2) 1100010 has odd parity, and (3) 0011001 has odd parity.
c. (1) 01100 has even parity, (2) 100010 has even parity, and (3) 1011001 has even parity.

Selected Solutions for Chapter 2

1.   The pay program, in contiguous memory locations:

Address	Contents		Comments
00	0127	LAC 27	Get hours
01	0420	SUB 20	hours − 40
02	09 ?	TPL ?	hours > 40?
03	0121	LAC 21	Get 0
04	0225	STO 25	overtime ← 0
05	0127	LAC 27	Get hours
06	0523	MPY 23	mult hours * rate
07	0224	STO 24	store regular pay
08	0226	STO 26	store total pay
09	0000	HLT	stop
10	0523	MPY 23	Extra hours * rate
11	0522	MPY 22	mult * 2 (double time)
12	0225	STO 25	store overtime pay
13	0140	LAC 40	get 40 (regular hours)
14	0523	MPY 23	mult * rate
15	0224	STO 24	store in regular pay
16	0325	ADD 25	add overtime pay
17	0226	STO 26	store in total pay

```
18          0000      HLT         stop
                       .
                       .
                       .
            Constants
20          0040                  40 regular hours
21          0000
22          0002                  double time for overtime

23          ____                  rate per hour
24          ____                  regular pay
25          ____                  overtime pay
26          ____                  total pay
27          ____                  hours worked
```

2. *

3. *

4. If location 70 held 0170 instead of 0150, the program would use its own first instruction as if it were the number of hours worked!

5. If we assume that each character corresponds to a single instruction, then at 500 CPS we are fetching (and executing) 500 instructions per second, or .0005 MIPS.

6. The arithmetic instructions require either 2 fetches/instruction or 1 fetch and 1 store per instruction; thus 2 memory accesses per arithmetic instruction are required. If each memory access requires 1 μs per memory access, we can execute .5 MIPS. The branch (transfer) instructions execute at the rate of 1 MIPS, so a typical program would execute between .5 and 1 MIPS (ignoring I/O and other, similar events).

7. *

8. A program to place 0 in ten consecutive locations can be written as follows:

Address	Contents	Comments
00	0113	LAC zero
01	0290	STO 90, 91, etc. ← 0
02	0111	LAC count
03	0412	SUB one
04	0211	STO count
05	0710	TZE done
06	0101	LAC instruction
07	0312	ADD one
08	0201	STO instruction (change address)
09	0600	TRA 00 (go back and execute again)
10	0000	HALT (done)
11	0010	count
12	0001	one
13	0000	zero

9. *

10. *

11. It is *not* necessary for data to be placed in low memory, or for instructions to be placed in high memory.

To fit the sample program into locations 20 through 26, we can write it as follows:

Address	Contents
20	0123
21	0634
22	0221
23	0120
24	0321
25	0322
26	0000

12. To fit the sample program into locations 50 through 56, we can write it as follows:

Address	Contents
50	0123
51	0634
52	0221
53	0150
54	0351
55	0352
56	0000

13. *

14. *

15. *

16. The following program creates a table of 20 items, with each item being the address of the location in which it is stored. The table begins at location 50.

Address	Contents	Comments
00	0108	LAC address
01	0250	STO 50
02	0307	ADD one
03	0208	STO address
04	0409	SUB max
05	0800	TMI loop
06	0000	HALT
07	0001	one
08	0050	address
09	0070	max

17. The program of figure 2.13, testing for completion before the key addition:

Address	Contents	Comments	
83	____	sum	
84	0100	LAC 00	get 1st item
85	0284	STO 84	initialize sum
86	0199	LAC 99	decrement count
87	0498	SUB 98	
88	0299	STO 99	

```
89        0797        TZE ??  stop if count is 0
90        0184        LAC 84  get sum
91        0301        ADD 01
92        0284        STO 84
93        0191        LAC 91 modify address
94        0397        ADD 98
95        0291        STO 91
96        0690        TRA 90
97        0000        HALT
98        0001        constant, 1
99        0010        constant, 10
```

18. *

19. Adding ten numbers using straight-line code requires one LAC, nine ADDs, and one HALT, for a total of 11 instructions; it also requires 11 other memory accesses for data.

The program in figure 2.13 has 13 instructions, of which 3 will be executed once. The other 10 instructions will be executed 9 times each, requiring ten instruction fetches and nine data transfers. This adds up to $3 + 9(10 + 9)$, or $6 + 171$, or 174 memory references.

The straight-line program makes 22 memory references, while the looping (self-modifying) program makes 174 memory references; the straight-line program will execute about 8.5 times faster.

20. *

21. *

22. *

23. It is possible for a program to use the 0000 value associated with the HALT instruction as a constant with the value zero. The computer won't mind, but you (the programmer) may regret it later, if you make any changes to your program and forget that an instruction was also being used as a numeric constant. It is good practice to use instructions only as instructions, and data only as data.

Selected Solutions for Chapter 3

1. *

2. We use K to represent the number 1024 rather than 1000 because computers use binary, and 1024 is a power of 2 (2^{10}), while 1000 is not.

3.

a.   1111 1111 1111 1111 1111 1111 1111 1111

b.   4,294,967,295

c.   FFFFFFFF

d.   4,194,304

4. *

5.

```
a.    11001     b.    10101     c.    11001
      10101           10001           10001
     _____          _____          _____
     101110          100110          101010
```

6. *

7. The BGEQ instruction is often followed by instructions which we which wish to execute if the result of the last arithmetic computation was *not* positive, as follows:

```
        BGEQ count
    ;else, result zero or negative
        ;instructions for zero or negative result
        JMP A
        ;instructions for positive result
    A:  ;continue
```

We could replace that sequence with the following one:

```
        BLSS count  ;if negative, go somewhere else
        BEQL count  ;if zero, go somewhere else
    ;else, result positive
        ;instructions for positive result
        JMP A
        ;instructions for zero or negative result
    A:  ;continue
```

8. Consider the following hypothetical computer instruction sequence:

```
LAC X
ADD Y
STO Z
```

The ADD instructions are *not* essential. If we had no ADD instruction, we could replace it with the following sequence of instructions:

```
STO TEMPA       save AC
LAC ZERO        AC ← 0
SUB Y           AC ← -(Y)
STO TEMPB       store -(Y)
LAC TEMPA       replace (X) in AC
SUB TEMPB       AC ← (X) - (-(Y))
```

Clearly, subtracting a number's negation is equivalent to adding that number.

9. *

10. *

11. *

12. The largest hexadecimal numbers representable in a VAX byte, word and longword are, respectively, FF, FFFF, and FFFFFFFF. Their decimal equivalents are 255, 65,535, and 4,294,967,295. In K units, they are .25K, 64K, and 4,194,304K.

13.

```
200: 11
201: 12
202: 01
203: 02
204: 03
205: ??
206: 06
207: 13
208: 10
```

14. The VAX knows whether an address that it fetches, following an operand specifier of 9F, is the address of a bye, word, or longword by looking at the opcode (in the IR), which indicates whether the instruction is a byte, word or longword instruction.

15. *

16. *

17.

; Address	Contents	Comments
250:	00000001	;data item #1
254:	00000004	;data item #2
258:	00000010	;data item #3
25C:	00000014	;data item #4
;		
200:	D0	;MOVL opcode
201:	9F	;operand specifier
202:	00000050	;source address
206:	9F	;operand specifier
207:	00000060	;destination address
;		
20B:	C0	;ADDL2 opcode
20C:	9F	;operand specifier
20D:	00000054	;source address
211:	9F	;operand specifier
212:	00000060	;destination address
;		
216:	C0	;ADDL2 opcode
217:	9F	;operand specifier
218:	00000058	;source address
21C:	9F	;operand specifier
21D:	00000060	;destination address
;		
221:	C0	;ADDL2 opcode
222:	9F	;operand specifier
223:	0000005C	;source address
227:	9F	;operand specifier
228:	00000060	;destination address
;		
22C:	00	;HALT instruction
0		;entry point

18. If you ask the loader to place a three digit number in a byte, it will place it in *two* bytes, with the low order digits to the right. The control unit will fetch a single byte for the branch count, and treat the high order digit(s) of the count as the opcode of the next instruction.

19. *

20. *

21. MOVB instruction:

opcode:	read 1 byte
operand specifier:	read 1 byte
source address:	read 4 bytes
source operand:	read 1 byte
operand specifier:	read 1 byte
destination address:	read 4 bytes
destination operand:	write 1 byte

The total is: read 11 bytes to fetch the instruction, read 1 byte and write 1 byte in executing the instruction, for a total of 13 bytes read and written.

22. If your operating system doesn't impose an execution limit, then you can usually type CTRL-C to terminate a program.

23. The pay program of chapter 2 can be written for the VAX as follows:

```
 0:    00000028      ;40₁₀ hours per week
 4:    00000000
 8:                  ;X, for overtime calculation
 C:                  ;overtime pay
10:                  ;regular pay
14:                  ;total pay
18:                  ;hours
1C:                  ;XX, for overtime calculation
;
20:  D0 9F 00000004 9F 0000000C    ;MOVL 0 to overtime
2B:  D1 9F 00000018 9F 00000000    ;CMPL hours to 40
36:  13 08                         ;if hours = 40: no overtime
38:  19 06                         ;if hours < 40: no overtime
3A:  17 9F 0000008E                ;else: overtime!
;no overtime portion of the code
40:  D0 9F 00000018 9F 00000010    ;MOVL hours to pay
4B:  C0 9F 00000018 9F 00000010    ;ADDL2 hours to pay (*2)
51:  C0 9F 00000018 9F 00000010    ;ADDL2 hours to pay (*3)
5C:  C0 9F 00000018 9F 00000010    ;ADDL2 hours to pay (*4)
67:  C0 9F 00000018 9F 00000010    ;ADDL2 hours to pay (*5)
72:  D0 9F 00000010 9F 00000014    ;MOVL pay to total
7D:  C0 9F 0000000C 9F 00000014    ;ADDL2 overtime to total
88:  17 9F 000000F7                ;done: JMP to HALT
;overtime portion of the code
8E:  D0 9F 00000018 9F 0000001C    ;MOVL hours to X
99:  C2 9F 00000000 9F 0000001C    ;SUBL2 hours from X (overtime hours)
A4:  C0 9F 0000001C 9F 0000001C    ;double hours (overtime: double time)
AF:  D0 9F 0000001C 9F 00000008    ;MOVL X to XX, to save it
BA:  C0 9F 0000001C 9F 0000001C    ;need to compute 10 * X; have 4 * X
C5:  C0 9F 0000001C 9F 0000001C    ;8 * X
```

```
D0:   C0 9F 00000008 9F 0000001C    ;10 * X (5 * 2 = 10)
DB:   D0 9F 0000001C 9F 0000000C    ;MOVL overtime pay to overtime
E6:   D0 9F 00000000 9F 00000018    ;MOVL 40 to regular hours
F1:   A7 9F 00000040               ;calculate regular pay
F7:   00                           ;HALT
```

This program is inefficient for large pay rates because it multiplies hours worked times rate by repeated addition.

24. No, the VAX program is much longer than the hypothetical computer program. The major difference in program size is due to the difference in address length of the hypothetical computer compared with the VAX. However, if the VAX used a one-address format, its instructions would be considerably shorter.

25.

```
      ;This program uses self-modifying code to move an array of words stored
      ;beginning at location 200, to location 300.
      200:                 ;data to move go here
      300:                 ;this is where the data get moved to
      400:    00000002     ;2, for changing addresses (of words)
      ;
      ;Program starts here
      ;
      420:    B0           ;MOVW from 200 to 300
      421:    9F           ;operand specifier
      422:    00000200     ;source address (this will change!)
      426:    9F           ;operand specifier
      427:    00000300     ;destination address (this will also change!)
      42B:    13 1D        ;if moved 0: branch to RSB
      ; else, change address and continue
      42D:    C0           ;ADDL2
      42E:    9F           ;operand specifier
      42F:    00000400     ;address of number 2
      433:    9F           ;operand specifier
      434:    00000422     ;address of source address of MOVW
      438:    C0           ;ADDL2 again
      439:    9F           ;operand specifier
      43A:    00000400     ;address of number 2
      43E:    9F           ;operand specifier
      43F:    00000427     ;address of destination address of MOVW
      443:    17           ;JMP
      444:    9F           ;operand specifier
      445:    00000420     ;to do again
      449:    05           ;RSB ("HALT")
      ;
      420                  ;entry point
```

The program "knows" when it encounters a word of 0 because the Z bit of the condition code is set. It needn't use a CMPW instruction, because the MOVW instruction sets the condition code bits.

26. *

27. *

28. *

29. *

30. In fact, nothing different would happen. However, something different *could* happen: 80 is the opcode for the ADDB instruction; we would be changing only the low order eight bits of the address. If the address happened to be, for example, 000000FF, then when we changed it, it would not be correct, for only the low order eight bits would change.

Selected Solutions for Chapter 4

1.   The first four exercises are system specific; they have no answers, as such, and are provided to encourage "hands-on" experience.

5.   The first two instructions will occupy 11 bytes each, the third instruction will occupy 16 bytes, and the HALT instruction will occupy a single byte, so data will begin at address 39_{10}, or 27_{16}. Thus, the address of PLACE1 will be 27, of PLACE2 will be 2B, of NUM1 will be 2D, of NUM2 will be 31, NUM2 32, NUM3 33, NUM4 34, and num5 36. The assembler will generate the following code for this program fragment is as follows:

```
FIRST:   D0 9F 0000002D 9F 00000027
NEXT:    80 9F 00000031 9F 00000032
THIRD:   A3 9F 00000033 9F 00000035 9F 0000002B
DONE:    00
PLACE1:  ????????
PLACE2:  ????
NUM1:    0000002B
NUM2:    0C
NUM3:    11
NUM4:    0101
NUM5:    0102
```

In memory, the program will look as follows:

+3	+2	+1	+0	address
00	2D	9F	D0	00000000
27	9F	00	00	00000004
80	00	00	00	00000008
00	00	31	9F	0000000c
00	32	9F	00	00000010
9F	A3	00	00	00000014
00	00	00	33	00000018
00	00	35	9F	0000001c
00	2B	9F	00	00000020
??	00	00	00	00000024
??	??	??	??	00000028
00	00	2B	??	0000002c
01	11	0C	00	00000030
	01	02	01	00000034

6. *

7. The correct order of events is (d): expand macros, assemble, link, load, run.

8. *

9. The machine language program for moving an array of words can be written as follows:

```
        .LIBRARY /[PB]IOMAC.MLB/
SOURCE: .BLKW 100                    ;source array
DEST:   .BLKW 100                    ;destination array
TWO:    .LONG 2                      ;for changing addresses
        .ENTRY START, 0
CHANGE: MOVW @#SOURCE, @#DEST        ;move first word
        BEQL DONE                    ;if 0: done
     ;else, change addresses, and keep moving
        ADDL2 @#TWO, @#CHANGE+2      ;address of source address
        ADDL2 @#TWO, @#CHANGE+7      ;address of destination address
        JMP @#CHANGE                 ;and move another
     ;else, done
DONE:   $EXIT_S
        .END START
```

Selected Solutions for Chapter 5

1.

```
        CMPL @#C, @#A          ;C - A
        BLSS CHECKMORE
   ;else, C > A, so do "else" part
        JMP @#ELSEPART
CHECKMORE:CMPL @#C, @#D        ;C - D
        BLSS IFPART            ;if C < D, go to "if" part
   ;else, do "else" part
ELSEPART: SUBL3 @#B, @#A, @#X ;X := A - B
        JMP @#CONTINUE
IFPART:   ADDL3 @#C, @#D, @#X ;X := C + D
CONTINUE: ;continue executing instructions
```

2. Pay program, written using registers:

```
HOURS:  .BLKL 1                   ;number of hours worked
RATE:   .BLKL 1                   ;pay rate
FORTY:  .LONG 40                  ;forty regular hours
ZERO:   .LONG 0
ONE:    .LONG 1
;use R0 for regular pay, R1 for overtime pay, R2 for total pay
        .ENTRY START, 0
        MOVL @#ZERO, R1           ;start with overtime = 0
        MOVL @#HOURS, R5
        CMPL R5, @#FORTY
        BLSS NONE                 ;no overtime pay
        BEQL NONE                 ;no overtime pay
    ;else, compute overtime pay
        SUBL2 @#FORTY, R5         ;overtime hours in R5
        ADDL2 R5, R5             ;double time for overtime
        MOVL R5, R6              ;accumulate overtime pay in R6
        MOVL @#RATE, R4
```

```
MULA:       SUBL2 @#ONE, R4       ;R4: loop count
            BEQL REGPAY
            ADDL2 R5, R6          ;multiply by adding
            JMP @#MULA
        ;here, compute regular pay
REGPAY:     MOVL @#FORTY, R5      ;if overtime: 40 regular hours
NONE:       MOVL R5, R0           ;R5 has hours worked
            MOVL @#RATE, R4       ;loop count
MULB:       SUBL2 @#ONE, R4       ;decrement loop count
            BEQL DONE
        ;else, add again
            ADDL2 R5, R0
            JMP MULB
DONE:       ADDL3 R0, R6, R2      ;R6 ← regular pay + overtime pay
            $EXIT_S
            .END START
```

3. *

4. *

5. There are many single bit errors that would be undetectable if we were sending or receiving 7 bit ASCII codes. For example, if we sent the code for B (100 0010) followed by the codes for A and T, and the least significant bit of the code for B happened to be changed from 0 to 1, we would send the wrong animal.

If we are using eight bit codes (with the eighth bit functioning as a parity bit), there is no single bit error in transmission that we would not be able to detect.

6. *

7. *

8. The string contains the codes for the sentence, "VAX assembly language is fun". This is the correct way to allocate longwords because the PUTS system service prints from lowest address byte to highest address byte.

9.

a.   The PSL is the Processor Status Longword. So far, we have seen only that it contains the condition code bits.

b.   The PC is the Program Counter (also register 15), which contains the address of the next instruction or part of instruction that will be fetched from memory.

c.   BNEQ is a conditional branch instruction, that is taken if the Z bit of the condition code is 0.

d.   CC is condition code bits. These bits indicate certain things about the results of the last data-oriented instruction.

e.   A **branch offset** is the operand of the VAX conditional branch instructions. It is a number which, when added to the PC, will produce the address of the instruction to be executed if the branch condition is true.

f.   A **register** is a special place for storing operands. It is made out of high speed hardware and is close to the CPU.

g.   An **operand specifier** is an eight bit quantity, containing a mode field and a register field. All operands of VAX instructions (except for the branch instructions) have operand specifiers.

h. The **assembler listing** is a file of ASCII characters that is produced by the assembler, and shows the machine language that it generated, and the addresses that it assigned, in translating an assembly language program.

10. *

11. *

Selected Solutions for Chapter 6

1. *

2.

```
STRING1:   .ASCIZ "TEST O NE     TWO"
STRING2:   .BLKB 40                 ;or, may need to be bigger
BLANK:     .BYTE ^X20               ;ASCII code for space
           .ENTRY START, 0
           MOVAB @#STRING1, R0      ;initialize registers
           MOVAB @#STRING2, R1
CHECK:     MOVB (R0)+, R2           ;get a byte
           BEQL DONE                ;if 0: done
       ;else, check for blank
           CMPB R2, @#BLANK         ;check for blanks
           BEQL CHECK               ;if so, check next character
       ;else, copy the non-blank
           MOVB R2, (R1)+           ;copy the byte
           BRB CHECK                ;and continue
DONE:      $EXIT_S
           .END START
```

3. *

4. The machine language generated by the assembler is as follows:

```
       50   60   90   BEGIN:  MOVB (R0), R0
            2C   A1   94            CLRB 44(R1)
   80   00000040 8F   C0            ADDL2 #CONST, (R0)+
                      00            HALT
                    001B   STORE:  .WORD 27
```

5. *

6. a. false; b. false; c. false; d. false; e. true.

7.

```
LIST:   .ADDRESS L0, L1, L2, L3, L4
        .ENTRY START, 0
          .
          .
          .
ABC:    ADDL2 R1, R1          ;double value
        ADDL2 R1, R1          ;*4
        MOVL LIST(R1), R1     ;get address
        JMP (R1)              ;indirect addressing
```

```
            $EXIT_S
            .END START
```

8. *

9. MOVL #1, @#ABC places 00000001_{16} in the memory location corresponding to label ABC. On the other hand, MVOL @#ABC, #1 will be flagged by the assembler as illegal use of immediate operands.

10. *

11. *

12. *

13. The program compares the first character of the string at ABC with each of the characters in the string STRING. It doesn't find a match, and so does the same thing with the second character in ABC, etc. If it ever finds matching characters, it replaces them with blanks, prints both strings, and stops. The output for the program as shown will be AN WER and QUE TION. When LOOK OUT is substituted for QUESTION, nothing is printed, because the two strings then have no letters in common.

14. A machine language program loading program could be written as follows: First, read a line of the machine language program, using a system service routine (such as GETS; see Appendix 1). Search the line for a colon; if it isn't found, then assume that this line is the entry point. Convert the ASCII character codes in that line into the integer that they represent, say X, and transfer control to location X, since it is the entry point. If the line contains a colon, convert the ASCII characters preceding it into an integer, say Y, and then convert the group(s) ASCII characters following it into one or more integers, say A, B and C. Then, store A, B, and C at locations Y, Y+1 and Y+2 (depending on the sizes of the integers). Then read the next line, etc, until encountering a line without a colon.

It is obvious from this outline that we can benefit greatly from instructions to help with the conversion from ASCII codes to integers, and from structuring methods such as subroutines. By the time we get to chapter 10, we will have seen all we need to write such a loader, and an implementation of a loader is provided as a case study, at the end of chapter 10.

15. *

16. *

Selected Solutions for Chapter 7

1. The parity of a 3-bit nibble, in the low order 3 bits of a byte, can be calculated as follows (assuming that the high order 5 bits are all 0):

```
            .ENTRY START, 0
            CLR R2                ;parity will go in R2
            MOVB @#DATA, R1        ;compute parity of this nibble
            BEQL DONE             ;if whole byte is 0, nibble has even parity
            SUBB2 @#BIT2, R1      ;check if bit #2 is set
            BGEQU BIT2SET
        ;else, bit #2 not set
            ADDB2 @#BIT2, R1      ;restore to original value
            BRB DOBIT1
BIT2SET:    INCL R2               ;bit 2 is set
```

```
DOBIT1: SUBB2 @#BIT1, R1     ;now, check if bit #1 is set
        BGEQU BIT1SET
    ;else, bit #2 not set
        ADDB2 @#BIT1, R1     ;restore to original value
        BRB DOBIT0
BIT1SET:INCL R2              ;bit 1 is set
DOBIT0: DECB R1              ;DEC rather than SUB
        BGEQU BIT0SET
    ;else, bit #0 not set, so done (almost)
        BRB DONE
BIT0SET:INCL R2             ;bit 0 is set
DONE:   CMPL R2, #2         ;if 2, then 2 bits were set:  even parity
        BNEQ EXIT
    ;else, 2 bits set, so even parity, so clear R2
        CLRL R2             ;0 for even, 1 or 3 for odd parity
EXIT:   $EXIT_S
BIT2:   .BYTE 4             ;or, 100 binary
BIT1:   .BYTE 2             ;or, 10 binary
DATA:   .BYTE ???           ;the byte to compute parity on
        .END START
```

2. The parity of the high order three bits of a byte can be computed in a manner very similar to that in which we computed the parity of the low order three bits, using the same idea of counting the number of bits set. Again, we assume that all bits but the three high order ones are zero.

```
        .ENTRY START, 0
        CLRL R2                 ;parity will go here
        MOVB @#DATA, R1         ;get byte
        BEQL DONE               ;if 0, it has even parity
    ;else, check bit 7
        BLSS BIT7SET            ;bit #7 set, so increment bit counter
    ;else, bit 7 clear, so check bit 6
        BRB DOBIT6
BIT7SET:INCL R2                 ;one more bit set
        SUBB2 @#BIT7, R1        ;and clear bit 7 for next check
DOBIT6: SUBB2 @#BIT6, R1        ;check bit 6
        BGEQU BIT6SET
    ;else, bit 6 wasn't set, so restore and check bit 5
        ADDB2 @#BIT6, R1        ;restore bit 6
        BRB DOBIT5             ;and check bit 5
BIT6SET:INCL R2                 ;one more bit set
DOBIT13:SUBB2 @#BIT13, R1       ;check bit 5
        BGEQU BIT5SET
    ;else, done
        BRB DONE
BIT5SET:INCL R2                 ;one more bit set
DONE:   CMPL R2, #2             ;see if even number of bits set
        BNEQ EXIT               ;if not, leave R2 as it is
    ;else, clear R2 to indicate even parity
        CLRL R2                 ;0 for even parity
EXIT:   $EXIT_S
BIT7:   .BYTE ^X80             ;bit #7 only
BIT6:   .BYTE ^X40             ;bit #6 only
BIT5:   .BYTE ^X20             ;bit #5 only
DATA:   .BYTE ????
        .END START
```

3. If we have access to an assembler or compiler on another computer, it is possible to write a *cross assembler* (see chapter 17), and use the cross assembler to write an assembler. If we have only a bare machine, however, then we can write a machine language program that understands instruction mnemonics, symbolic labels, a few directives and a few addressing modes. Then, we can use this simple assembler to assemble an assembler that is more complex because it understands more of the features we'd like the assembler to understand. We continue this iterative process until we have an assembler that provides all the features we want in our assembler.

4. *

5. *

6. *

7.

a.   Result is: A87DDD3B.

b.   Result is correct if the addends are unsigned numbers.

c.   Result is incorrect if the addends are signed numbers.

d. $N = 1; Z = 0; V = 1, C = 0$.

8. *

9.

a.   16

b.   −64

c.   −1

10. *

11.

```
A:      .LONG 1, 2, 3           ;A
B:      .LONG 4, 5, 6           ;B
C:      .BLKL 3                 ;C (result)
        MOVL @#B, @#C
        MOVL @#B+4, @#C+4
        MOVL @#B+8, @#C+8
        ADDL2 @#A, @#C          ;add low order parts
        ADWC @#A+4, @#C+4       ;add middle parts
        ADWC @#A+8, @#C+8       ;add high order parts
```

It requires 7 memory references to fetch and execute each MOVL instruction (5 to fetch the instructions and 2 more to fetch and store the operands), and it requires 8 memory references to fetch and execute each ADD instruction (5 to fetch the instructions, and 3 more to fetch the operands and store the results). Thus, the six instructions require 45 memory references, which takes 22.5 microseconds.

12. *

13. *

14. *

15.

   a. F; b. F; c. F; d. F; e. F; f. T; g. F; h. F

16. *

17. Unsigned branch instructions should always be used with address comparisons, because addresses are unsigned numbers.

18. A jump table:

```
LIST:    .ADDRESS ZER0, FOUR, EIGHT, TWELVE, SIXTEEN
               .
               .
               .

CASES:   MOVL DATA(R0), R0
         JMP  (R0)
```

19. *

20. An arbitrary hexadecimal number can represent (1) a signed integer, (2) an unsigned integer; (3) an address; (4) an ASCII character code; (5) an opcode; and (6) an operand specifier.

21. *

22. The .BYTE 0, 0, 0 directive generates three bytes of 0; the .ASCII "000" directive generates three bytes of 30_{16}, and the .BLKB 3 directive allocates three uninitialized bytes.

23. *

24.

   a. N; b. C; c. V; d. Z; e. V; f. V; g. C; h. C

25. *

26. *

27. *

28.

	00001	10000	11110	11110	11111	10101	11111	01000	11001
	11111	10000	11101	11110	11111	01010	00000	11000	01101
answer:	00000	00000	11011	11100	11110	11111	11111	00000	00110
CC(NZVC):	5	7	9	9	9	8	8	5	1

29. *

30.

   a. 2; b. 5; c. 1; d. 4; e. 100345A6E; f. sum is correct as a signed or unsigned number

31. *

Selected Solutions for Chapter 8

1.

a.   FC B0 90 C0

b.   50 3F B0

c.   0C AA 77 68 44 C1

2. *

3. *

4. Four memory references are made in fetching and executing the instruction MOVB #7, (R0)+: one each to fetch the opcode, first operand specifier (which is short literal, and so also the first operand), and second operand specifier, and a fourth one to store the 7 in the location whose address is in R0.

5. 1000_{16}.

6. True or false:

   a. T; b. F; c. T; d. F; e. F; f. T; g. T; h. F.

7. *

8. *

9. *

10. A program that replaces blanks with minus signs can be written as follows:

```
        .ENTRY START, 0
        MOVAL STRING, R1        ;string address
LOOP:   MOVB (R1)+, R0          ;get next character
        BEQL DONE               ;null-terminated string
        CMPB R0, BLANK          ;is it a blank?
        BNEQ COPY               ;if not, put it back
     ;else, it's a blank, so replace with a minus sign
        MOVB MINUS, R0
COPY:   MOVB R0, -1(R1)         ;place character in string
        BRB LOOP                ;and do again
DONE:   $EXIT_S
BLANK:  .ASCII         / /
MINUS:  .ASCII         /-/
STRING: .BLKB          ?
        .END START
```

11. If LOOP is assigned address 0, then A will be assigned address 9. The following machine language will be generated by the assembler:

```
50   00000009 EF   D0   0000   LOOP:   MOVL A, R0
              F7   11   0007           BRB LOOP
         FFFFFFFF      0009   A:      .LONG -1
```

12. *

13. To fetch CMPB ABC(R3), @X requires five memory references: one for the opcode, one for the first operand specifier, one for the displacement, one for the second operand specifier, and one for the displacement (@X is assembled as displacement mode on the PC). Then, to fetch the first operand (whose address is ABC plus the contents of R3) requires an additional memory reference, and to fetch the second operand (whose address is the contents of the location whose address is X) requires two additional memory references.

14. *

15. True or false:

a. F; b. F; c. F; d. T; e. F.

16. *

Selected Solutions for Chapter 9

1. *

2. *

3.

```
        ;This subroutine has the address of its source string in R0.  It
        ;returns the same string, in the same place, but the string will
        ;have no contiguous occurrences of the same letter more than once.
SQUASH:    PUSHR #^M<R1, R2, R3>
           MOVL R0, R1              ;copy string address
           MOVB (R0)+, R2           ;get a character
           MOVB R2, (R1)+           ;copy it to the string
           BEQL DONE                ;null terminated string
      ;else, get next character, and see if it's the same as last one
LOOP:      MOVB (R0)+, R3           ;next character
           BEQL DONE1               ;null terminated string
           CMPB R3, R2              ;is it the same?
           BEQL LOOP                ;if so, don't copy it
      ;else it's different, so put it back in the string
           MOVB R3, R2              ;new "last" character
           MOVB R3, (R1)+           ;put it in string
           BRB LOOP                 ;and continue
DONE1:     MOVB R3, (R1)+           ;copy null character
DONE:      POPR #^M<R1, R2, R3>
           RSB
```

4. To examine the stack at run time, we can copy items from the stack (using displacement mode rather than autoincrement mode!) to memory, and then use the DUMP system service to examine the contents of memory.

5.

	DATA1	DATA2	ARG1	ARG2	WHO	FIRST	R5	SECOND
A:	17	20	0	4	?	?	8	?
B:	17	20	4	0	0	16	16	20
C:	17	20	0	4	?	16	16	20
D:	17	20	4	4	0	16	16	20

6. *

7.

	D1	D2	ARG1	ARG2	S11	S12	S13
A:	4	0	0	4	10	14	?
B:	4	0	0	4	10	4	0

8. *

Selected Solutions for Chapter 10

1. *

2. *

3.

a.   False: in the general case, the product of two **n** bit numbers is **2n** bits long.

b.   True: the EMUL instruction treats its operands as signed numbers, so the largest and smallest operands it can have are $2^{31}-1$ and -2^{31}, and the largest and smallest products it can have are $2^{63}-1$ and -2^{63}. If we multiply -2^{31} times -2^{31}, we get 2^{62}, which is much less than $2^{63}-1$.

c.   False: the remainder has the same sign as the dividend.

d.   False: when the amount of computing to be done is minimal, the overhead of converting to binary (and, presumably, back to ASCII coded decimal digit strings) outweighs the advantages of binary arithmetic over ASCII coded decimal arithmetic.

e.   True.

4. The subroutine call might be as follows:

```
MOVB TEST, R1
JSB PARITY
```

The subroutine itself can be written as follows:

```
;
;"Parity" computes the parity of the byte in R1, and returns with the
;N bit of the CC set if the parity is odd, and the N bit clear if the
;parity is even.  The subroutine places a 1 in R0, checks each bit of
;the byte in R1, and negates R0 each time that bit is 1.  Thus, if R0
;is negated an odd number of times (if R1 has an odd number of 1s),
;then R0 will be negative, and the N bit will be set.
```

```
;
PARITY: PUSHR ^M<R0, R2>            ;save R0 and R2
        MOVL #8, R2                 ;loop count
        MOVB #1, R0                 ;negate for each 1
LOOP:   BITB #^X80, R1              ;check high order bit
        BGEQ ZERO                   ;if N = 0, then it was 0
    ;else, high order bit was 1
        MNEGB R0, R0                ;negate
ZERO:   ROTL #1, R1, R1             ;get next highest bit
        SOBGTR R2, LOOP             ;do 8 times
        POPR ^M<R0, R2>             ;restore registers
        TSTB R0                     ;set N bit if parity is odd
        RSB                         ;done
```

5.

a. The code places numbers in R1 and R2, and the address of a counter (initialized to zero) in R3. If the number in R1 is not less than the number in R2, it swaps them. At Z, it checks to see if the smaller number (in R1) is zero; if so, the program quits (by branching to Y). Otherwise (if neither number is zero), we add the number in R2 to the counter, if the least significant bit of the number in R1 is set. Then we double the number in R2, halve the number in R1, and repeat from Z.

This code multiplies the contents of A times the contents of B (the numbers in R1 and R2). It performs the multiplication by adding successive powers of the number in R2, according to the number in R1.

b. Nothing would change: the purpose of lines 4 through 8 is to make sure that the larger number is in R2.

c. We would get the wrong answer.

d. 7FFFFFFF.

e. $56_{10} * 2 = 112_{10} = 70_{16}$

f. It will be much slower (in most cases) to add the number in R2 to itself, R1 times. It will be much faster (in most cases) to use the MUL or EMUL instruction.

6. *

7. *

8. This is a straightforward assignment; there is a large number of ways to do it correctly. Some things to check for are

1. Boundary conditions, such as 0, ^X80000000, etc.
2. Error checking: overflow, non-digits in the string, etc.
3. Empty string.
4. Etc.

9. *

10. In both cases, we convert to packed decimal as an intermediate step. From numeric strings to integers:

1. CVTSP (or CVTTP) (numeric to packed)
2. CVTPL (packed to longword)

From integers to numeric strings:

1. CVTLP (longword to packed decimal)
2. CVTPS (or CVTPT)

11. Without string instructions, the program can be written as follows:

```
            CR = ^X0D
            .LIBRARY /[PB]IOMAC.MLB/
            .ENTRY START, 0
            IOINIT
            MOVAB INSTRING, R0              ;input string
            MOVAB OUTSTRING, R1             ;output string
  CHECK:    CMPB (R0), #^A/Z/              ;largest upper case
            BGTRU SKIP                     ;ignore punctuation
        ;else, copy to output string
            MOVB (R0), (R1)+               ;copy
  SKIP:     INCL R0
            TSTB (R0)                      ;done?
            BNEQ CHECK
        ;else, done
            MOVB #CR, (R1)+                ;new line
            CLRB (R1)                      ;null terminate
            PUTS OUTSTRING
            $EXIT_S
INSTRING:
            .ASCIZ "This Is A String"
OUTSTRING:
            .BLKB OUTSTRING-INSTRING
            .END START
```

The program does not check for punctuation, or even spaces, so the output string will actually contain more than just the upper case letters in the input string.

With string instructions, the following program can be written:

```
TABLE:    .BYTE 0, 0, 0, 0, 0, 0, 0, 0, 0, 0, 0, 0, 0, 0, 0, 0
          .BYTE 0, 0, 0, 0, 0, 0, 0, 0, 0, 0, 0, 0, 0, 0, 0, 0
          .BYTE 0, 0, 0, 0, 0, 0, 0, 0, 0, 0, 0, 0, 0, 0, 0, 0
          .BYTE 0, 0, 0, 0, 0, 0, 0, 0, 0, 0, 0, 0, 0, 0, 0, 0
          .BYTE 0
UPPERS:   .ASCII /ABCDEFGHIJKLMNOPQRSTUVWXYZ/
          .BYTE 0, 0, 0, 0, 0, 0
LOWERS:   .BYTE 0, 0, 0, 0, 0, 0, 0, 0, 0, 0, 0, 0, 0, 0, 0, 0
          .BYTE 0, 0, 0, 0, 0, 0, 0, 0, 0, 0, 0, 0, 0, 0, 0, 0
INSTRING:
          .ASCIZ /ThisIsAString/
OUTSTRING:
          .BLKB outstring-instring
EXTRA:    .BYTE ^X0A, ^X0D               ;CR and LF
          .LIBRARY /[PB]IOMAC.MLB/
          LENGTH = OUTSTRING-INSTRING    ;length of input string
          .ENTRY START,0
          IOINIT                         ;initialize channels
          MOVTC #LENGTH, INSTRING, #0, TABLE, #LENGTH, OUTSTRING
          MOVAB OUTSTRING, R6            ;address for printing
          MOVL #LENGTH+2, R7            ;string, and CR, LF
LOOP:     PUTC (r6)+                     ;print characters
          SOBGTR R7, LOOP                ;until done
          $EXIT_S                        ;done
          .END START
```

This version of the program takes advantage of the fact that the ASCII NUL character is non-printing, so when lower case characters are mapped to NULs, no harm is done. The two programs are not equivalent, strictly speaking, however, because the first one creates OUT-STRING with consecutive upper case letters, while the second one creates OUTSTRING with upper case letters and NULs.

The second program (using MOVTC) used only that single instruction (not counting the loop for printing), while the first program used eight instructions. On the other hand, the first program required only enough data to store the INSTRING and OUTSTRING, while the second one required a table with at least as many entries as there are ASCII codes between the first upper case letter and the last lower case one.

12. *

Selected Solutions for Chapter 11

1.

a.   CTRL-G rings the bell

b.   CTRL-H backspaces the cursor

c.   CTRL-I is horizontal tab

d.   CTRL-J is line feed (new line)

e.   CTRL-K is vertical tab

f.   CTRL-M is carriage return

2. This is particular to the operating system/terminal combination you happen to be using.

3.

a., b. For UNIX, the **stty** command is used to examine, and/or change terminal parameters. For VMS, the SHOW TERMINAL command is used to examine terminal parameters, and the SET TERMINAL command is used to change them.

d.   If you tell the operating system that your terminal is in half duplex mode, it assumes your terminal will use local echo and so it does not echo what you type. If you set the switches so that your terminal is in full duplex mode, it assumes that the operating system will provide remote echo and so it does not echo what you type either. The result is no echo at all.

e.   If you tell the operating system that your terminal is operating in full duplex mode, it provides remote echo of each character you type. If you set your terminal's switches to half duplex, it provides local echo of each character you type. The result is that each character is echoed twice.

4. The following code can be used to convert Morse codes to ASCII codes, using two bytes for each Morse code: a bit count, and a code, with 0 representing "." and 1 representing "-":

```
;
;Morse code table, using 0 for "." and 1 for "-".  Entries in binary.
;
TABLE:
A:      .BYTE ^B10, ^B01        ;bit count, and code, for A
B:      .BYTE ^B100, ^B1000     ;bit count and code for B
C:      .BYTE ^B100, ^B1010     ;bit count and code for C
        .
        .
        .
```

```
Y:        .BYTE ^B100, ^B1011    ;bit count and code for Y
Z:        .BYTE ^B100, ^B1100    ;bit count and code for Z
TABLEND:
;
;calling sequence for Morse-to-ASCII subroutine
;
          .LIBRARY   /[PB]IOMAC.MLB/
          .ENTRY START, 0
          IOINIT
          MOVZWL B, R0               ;bit count and code in R0
          JSB MTOA                   ;convert
          SNAP
          PUTC   R1                  ;returns ASCII code in R1
          $EXIT_S
          .END START
;
;This is subroutine MTOA.  It converts Morse code to ASCII character
;codes.  The input parameter is in R0, and consists of a pair of bytes,
;the first containing a bit count, and the second containing the
;specified number of bits, with 0 representing "." and 1 representing
;"-".  The conversion algorithm is more or less brute force: compare
;compares every entry in the table with the desired entry.  This is
;done because there is no obvious relationship between the Morse and
;ASCII codes for a given letter.  R2 gets the number of bytes in the
;table (which is the number of characters times 2); this value is
;used as an index into the table.  The index is decremented by 2 each
;time through the table, until a match is found (if no match is found,
;0 is returned in R0).  When a match is found, R2 contains the offset
;from the beginning of the table, which is twice the number of the
;entry.  So, the value in R2 is divided by 2, and the ASCII code for A
;is added to it (the first number--A--has ASCII code 41, the 2nd has
;ASCII code 42, etc.).
;
MTOA:    MOVL   #TABLEND-TABLE, R1  ;length of table
         MOVL   R1, R2
LOOP:    CMPW   TABLE-2(R2), R0     ;check for code (use TABLE-2 as
                                    ;base because 1st element has
                                    ;offset 0, 2nd has offset 2...
         BEQL   HIT                 ;found it!
     ;else, check next table entry
         SUBL2  #2, R2              ;next entry address 2 less
         BGEQ   LOOP                ;go back and try again
     ;else, no match in table, so error
         CLRL   R0                  ;error code
         BRB    RETURN
HIT:     ASHL   #-1, R2, R2         ;offset into table/2
         DECL   R2                  ;off by one, otherwise
         ADDB2  #^A/A/, R2          ;ASCII code for A
         MOVZBL R2, R1              ;return ASCII code in R1
RETURN:  RSB
         .END START
```

5. *

6. Mapping a poor character set (Morse code) into a rich one (ASCII) is straightforward; it requires use of a subset of the rich character set's characters. Mapping a rich character subset into a poor one is more difficult, but can be accomplished by defining an ***escape character*** (or a shift character): one that means that whatever character follows it has an alternate meaning (like the shift key on a typewriter). This is the same idea that was mentioned in exercise 1.4.

7. EBCDIC:

a. 90.

b. 53.

c. Logical not (L rotated); plus-or-minus; cent sign.

d. Punch on; punch off; three customer-use codes; upper case; lower case; cursor control. Many codes are unassigned; of the 256 codes, 143 are used.

e. There are gaps between the codes for the alphabetic characters.

f. No: lower case codes are numerically smaller than upper case codes.

ASCII:

a. 95.

b. 33.

c. Square brackets; up-arrow; left-arrow; back slash.

d. No.

e. Yes.

f. Yes.

8. *

9. Two flags and four positions have more than eight combinations: each flag is independent of the other, so their are four *times* (not *plus*) four, or sixteen combinations. Thus, it requires four bits to encode a particular flag in a particular position.

a. The baud rate is the number of signal events per second. In this case, it is one-half, since it takes two seconds per flag setting.

b. Each signal event is equivalent to four bits of information, and we can send one-half signal event per second. Thus, the information transfer rate is four divided by 2, or 2 bits per second.

10. *

11. *

12. *

Selected Solutions for Chapter 12

1.

a. The undefined labels could be defined as follows:

```
        OCSR = ????            ;output device's CSR
        OUTBUF = OCSR + 2      ;output device's DBR
        OIV = ????            ;output device's Interrupt Vector
        ;
```

```
CCSR = ????            ;clock CSR
CIV = ????             ;clock's Interrupt Vector
```

b. The main program places the interrupt handler addresses in the interrupt vectors (with two MOVAL instructions), and then enables the clock for interrupts (with the MOVW instruction). Whenever a clock interrupt request is granted, the interrupt handler at CLOCK is executed. The handler increments R1 until it reaches 59 (which will occur every second for a 60 Hz clock). When the next interrupt occurs, R1 is cleared, MBOX is incremented, and the output device is enabled for interrupts.

The output device will (presumably) request an interrupt, and the handler at OUTPUT will execute. If MBOX is less than $3A_{16}$, then the character in the output device's DBR is output. If MBOX contains $3A_{16}$, however, then it is reset to $2F_{16}$.

c. Each minute (assuming a 60 Hz clock), the output device will display one of the characters in the list: /, 0, 1, 2, . . ., 9, :. After the ":" is displayed, it will start over again, and the next character to be displayed will be "/".

2. *

3.

a. Interrupts are particularly useful for I/O because I/O devices typically operate asynchronously with respect to the CPU, so the CPU has no way of predicting stipulating when an I/O device will need service. If devices couldn't signal the CPU (via an interrupt), the CPU would have to "signal" the device—with a busy-wait loop, for example.

b. An interrupt handler can call subroutines just as any other program can. Of course, any registers or other "global variables" must be used with care.

4. *

Selected Solutions for Chapter 13

1.   For the following decimal numbers, write the corresponding F_format VAX floating point number in hexadecimal.

a. −1/2: 0000C000

b. 36.75: 00004313

c. −127: 0000C3FE

d. .1: CCCD3ECC

2. *

3. The three fields contain the sign bit, the biased exponent, and the normalized fraction. Normalization ensures a unique representation for each number, and it allows one additional bit of precision (the leading 1, which isn't stored).

4. *

5.

a. largest unsigned integer: 4,294,967,295

b. largest signed integer: 2,147,483,647

c. largest F_format floating point number: $1.7 * 10^{38}$

d.   largest D_format floating point number: $1.7 * 10^{38}$

e.   largest signed 64 bit integer: 9,223,372,036,854,775,807

6. *

7. This code is a simple extension of the code written for the preceding exercise. If the D_format floating point numbers are in locations A and A+4, and B and B+4, then we can use the code above if they differ in their first 4 bytes. We need only add code to compare the long-words at A+4 and B+4 (the least significant 32 bits of the fraction) as unsigned numbers, which can be done with a single CMPL instruction and the appropriate branches. This code will be executed only if the longwords at A and B are identical.

8. *

9. An algorithm for converting binary fractions into decimal fractions is as follows:

1.   Multiply the binary fraction by 1010_2 (10_{10}).

2.   Save the part of the product to the left of the binary point as the next higher order decimal digit of the fraction, and the part of the product to the right of the binary point as the next number to multiply by 1010.

3.   If the part of the product to the right of the binary point is 0, we're done; if it's not, repeat from step 1.

For example, consider $.011_2$ ($.375_{10}$):

```
      1010
   *  .011
      ----
      1010
    1010
    ------
   11.110
```

The part of the product to the left of the binary point is 11_2, so the first decimal digit of the fraction is 3 (11_2). Now, we multiply the 110 from the right of the binary point by 1010:

```
      1010
   *  .110
      ----
     10100
    1010
    ------
  111.100
```

The part of the product to the left of the binary point is 111_2, so the second decimal digit of the fraction is 7, and we multiply the 100 from the right of the binary point by 1010:

```
      1010
   *  .100
      ----
   101.000
```

The part of the product to the left of the binary point is 101_2, so the third decimal digit of the fraction is 5. The part of the product to the right of the binary point is 0, so we are done: $.011_2 = .375_{10}$

10. When scaling two floating point numbers with different exponents, the binary point of the fraction must be moved over one place for each number by which the exponents differ. When the binary point is moved, the fraction may lose precision, and it is preferable for the smaller number (the one with the smaller exponent) to lose precision than for the larger one (the one with the larger exponent), since the smaller one contributes less to the sum than does the larger one.

Selected Solutions for Chapter 14

1. *

2. The address of element X[i,j,k] of a 3 by 4 by 5 array of 4 byte integers is:

4 * ((i-1)*4*5 + (j-1)*5 + (k-1))

stored by row.

3. Array access with a dope vector provides considerable flexibility: it is easy to change the size of any dimension of the array, or even the array's starting address in memory, at run-time. Array access with in-line code is faster than array access with a dope vector, but the increased speed is at the expense of flexibility.

4. The code for accessing item [i,j] of a 32 by 16 array is similar to that for accessing item [i,j] of a 3 by 4 array, which is shown for Exercise 1. Only three modifications must be made to the code written for exercise 1:

1. On the line with label A, the first operand of the ASHL instruction must be changed from 2 to 4, since we must multiply by 16 rather than by 4.
2. After the line with label B we must multiply the offset by 4; this may be done with a MUL instruction, an ASHL instruction, or a pair of ADD instructions.
3. The MOVB instruction mush be changed to MOVL.

5. *

6. In-line code for placing element [i,j] of a two dimensional array of bytes in R0 could be written as follows:

```
;ARRAY: address of the array
;NCOL: number of columns in the array
;I: row number
;J: column number
;
PUSHR #^M<R1>              ;save register
MOVL I, R1
DECL R1                   ;assume 0-origin
MULL2 #NCOLS, R1          ;(I-1) * no. of columns
ADDL2 J, R1
DECL R1                   ;(I-1) * no. of columns + (J-1)
MOVB ARRAY(R1), R0        ;return element in R0
POPR #^M<R1>              ;restore register
```

7. A simple program to sum all of the elements in a 100 by 100 array of longwords could be written in a high level language as follows:

```
sum := 0;
for outerindex := 1 to 100 do
    for innerindex := 1 to 100 do
```

sum := array[outerindex, innerindex];

This could be translated into assembly language as follows:

```
            CLRL R2                 ;running sum
            MOVL #100, R3           ;row limit
            MOVL #100, R4           ;column limit
            CLRL R0                 ;row number
    10$:    MULL3 #100, R0, R5      ;number of 1st column of next row
            CLRL R1                 ;column number
    20$:    ADDL3 R0, R1, R5        ;number of next element
            ADDL2 ARRAY[R5], R2     ;add next element
            AOBLSS R4, R1, 20$      ;next column
        ;else, calculate next row, and add its columns
            AOBLSS R3, R0, 10$
```

a. In this case, the first four instructions are executed once each, the next two instructions are executed 100 times each, then next three instructions are executed 10,000 times each, and the last instruction is executed 100 times. The total number of instructions executed is, thus, 30,304.

b. To sum a one-dimensional array of integers, with 10,000 elements, we could write the following code:

```
            MOVAL ARRAY, R0
            CLRL R3
            MOVL #10000, R1
    10$:    ADDL2 (R0)+, R3
            SOBGTR R1, 10$
```

In this case, the first three instructions are executed once each and the last two instructions are executed 10,000 times each. The total number of instructions executed is 20,003.

c. The ratio of instructions executed in part (a) to instructions executed in part (b) is 30,304:20,003; slightly more than one and one-half times as many instructions are executed in part (a) than in part (b). The ratio of instructions *written* in part (a) to instructions *written* in part (b) is 10:5, or 2:1. (We can do better. If we write an in-line program, we can add the 10,000 elements of a one-dimensional array with 10,002 instructions: a single MOVAL instruction, a single CLRL instruction, and 10,000 ADDL2 instructions.)

Selected Solutions for Chapter 15

1. I/O macros differ from installation to installation. Common input macros provide for input of a line or of a character, and for storing it in the locations named, by address, as arguments of the macro.

2. *

3. The program interchanges M3 and M4 twice—returning them to their original values—so M3 is left with 26 and M4 with 28. T1 also contains 28 when the program terminates. In one sentence, the program defines a macro to call a subroutine that interchanges its arguments. It is not clear why we would ever want to define a macro "in the middle" of a main program (as was done with M1), but if we do it, the assembler will not object.

4. Use of macros has no influence, in general, on program execution speed. Anything that can be written as a macro can also be written without using macros.

5. Use of macros *should* speed up program development, because macros can be used as a way of breaking large problems into small ones. Unfortunately, it is also possible to use macros in ways that contribute nothing positive to program development.

6. *

7. *

8. The MOVC3 instruction has the following format, MOVC LEN, SRC, DEST. We could write the following macro to "create" it:

```
          .MACRO MOVCHAR L,  S,  D,  ?LABEL
          PUSHR #^M<R6, R7, R8>
          MOVL L,  R6
          MOVAB S,  R7
          MOVAB D,  R8
   LABEL:  MOVB (R7)+,  (R8)+
          SOBGTR R6,  LABEL
          POPR #^M<R6,  R7,  R8>
          .ENDM MOVCHAR
```

9. *

10. A macro that will act just like the .BLKW directive, but will not use that directive, may be written as follows:

```
.MACRO BLOCK N      ;N is the word count
. = . + N + N       ;double N, because 2 bytes/word
.ENDM BLOCK
```

It is, in general, dangerous to use "." to refer to the location counter.

Selected Solutions for Chapter 16

1. Twenty records of 100 characters each is a total of 2,000 records. With the capability of reading 1,000 characters per second, it will take two seconds to read the characters. It will take one second to process twenty records at 50 msec per record.

a. If busy-wait I/O is used, there is no overlapping of I/O and processing, so the time to read and process twenty records is the sum of the read and process times, or $2 + 1 = 3$ seconds.

b. With interrupts and DMA I/O, the cpu can process a record while the DMA controller is reading the next record, so the time to read and process twenty records is, basically, the larger of the two times, or two seconds.

2. *

3. If interrupt handlers are well written, then their occurrence is be transparent to a program. However, non-I/O interrupts are caused by events caused by the program's execution—either by requesting them, or by generating overflow, divide by zero, etc. (these last are called *exceptions*, by the designers of the VAX). Thus, for a program to produce exactly the same results, all non-I/O interrupts must occur at exactly the same points in the program, but I/O interrupts need not.

4. Restoring the PC and PSL requires three memory references: one to restore each, and one to fetch the REI instruction. Saving the PC and PSL requires only two memory references (one for the PC and one for the PSL) because they are stored when an interrupt request is granted, and that does not involve an instruction fetch.

5. *

6. *

7. Rather than writing a backup program to copy the disk beginning with track 0, sector 0, and continuing to the last sector of the last track, we could write a backup program that reads the disk's directory, and copies the disk by *file* rather than by sector. This would take more time because there would probably be many more seeks than the one per cylinder required when backing up a disk by tracks. However, it can be used to check the file system for consistency, and if a user subsequently requests restoration of a file, it may be much easier to find the file when the disk is backed up this way.

8.

a. With a blocking factor of one, each logical record is stored in a disk sector. So, for 10,000 records we will need 10,000 sectors, and for 4,000 print lines we will need 4,000 sectors, for a total of 14,000 disk sectors.

b. If we use 1 KB (1,024 byte) physical records, the 10,000 logical records of 80 characters each require 800,000 bytes, and 800,000 ÷ 1024 = 782 records of 1 KB each, which require 1,564 disk sectors. Similarly, 4,000 print lines of 132 characters each constitute 528,000 characters, which require 516 physical records and 1,032 disk sectors. The blocking factor is the ratio of physical record length to logical record length. For the 80 character records, a 1 KB physical record is a blocking factor of 12.8; for the 132 character print lines, the blocking factor is about 7.76.

Selected Solutions for Chapter 17

1. *

2.

a. The macro definition is as follows:

```
            .MACRO EXTREMES LIST, MAX, MIN
            MOVL #^X80000000, MAX        ;smallest number
            MOVL #^X7FFFFFFF, MIN        ;largest number
            .IRP X, <LIST>
            M1 X
            .ENDR
            .ENDM EXTREMES
    ;
            .MACRO M1 X, MAX, MIN, ?A, ?B
            CMPL X, MAX
            BLEQ A
        ;else, new max
            MOVL X, MAX
    A:      CMPL X, MIN
            BGEQ B
        ;else, new min
            MOVL X, MIN
    B:
            .ENDM M1
```

b. The expansion of EXTREMES, invoked with the arguments

```
        EXTREMES <A, B, (SP), 16(R7)>, R8, R9
```

looks as follows:

```
            EXTREMES <A, B, (SP), 16(R7)>, R8, R9
            MOVL #^X80000000, R8      ;smallest number
            MOVL #^X7FFFFFFF, R9      ;largest number
            .IRP X, <A, B, (SP), 16(R7)>
            M1 X, R8, R9
            .ENDR
            M1 A, R8, R9
            CMPL A, R8
            BLEQ 30000$
        ;else, new R8
            MOVL A, R8
30000$: CMPL A, R9
            BGEQ 30001$
        ;else, new R9
            MOVL A, R9
30001$:


            M1 B, R8, R9
            CMPL B, R8
            BLEQ 30002$
        ;else, new R8
            MOVL B, R8
30002$: CMPL B, R9
            BGEQ 30003$
        ;else, new R9
            MOVL B, R9
30003$:


            M1 (SP), R8, R9
            CMPL (SP), R8
            BLEQ 30004$
        ;else, new R8
            MOVL (SP), R8
30004$: CMPL (SP), R9
            BGEQ 30005$
        ;else, new R9
            MOVL (SP), R9
30005$:


            M1 16(R7), R8, R9
            CMPL 16(R7), R8
            BLEQ 30006$
            ;else, new R8
            MOVL 16(R7), R8
30006$: CMPL 16(R7), R9
            BGEQ 30007$
        ;else, new R9
            MOVL 16(R7), R9
30007$:
```

3. *

4. The binary tree built is as follows:

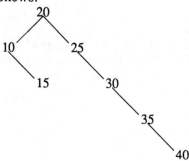

It *is* possible to build a more balanced tree, as follows:

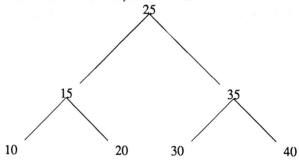

This tree would be built by the following sequence of numbers: 25, 35, 30, 40, 15, 10, 20. There are other sequences of the same numbers that will result in the same tree.

5. *

6. *

7.

a.   We can use a longword to store the part number, but the part name may vary greatly in length, so rather than storing it in the node, we can store it "somewhere else", and store only a pointer to it in the node. Thus, a typical node could be organized as follows:

   (PN, PD address, L, R)

   L refers to the address of the left subtree, and R refers to the address of the right subtree.

b.   The first way to reduce node size is to store the part number as a word rather than as a longword. A more complex method, which results in greater reduction in node size, is to store offsets (in units of numbers of nodes past the present one) in the L and R fields. If we limit the number of nodes in our tree to 256, then we can use only one byte for each of the L and R fields, and reduce node size from 16 bytes (or 14, if we use a word rather than a longword for PN) to 8 bytes. If 256 nodes is too few, we can limit the tree to 65,536 nodes and store 16 bit offsets (in units of numbers of nodes), and reduce node size from 16 (or 14) to 10 bytes.

c.   A recursive tree traversal subroutine traverses the root node's left subtree (recursively), then prints the root node, and then traverses the root node's right subtree. If the tree contains R nodes, and is composed entirely of left subtrees, then the stack will contain R return addresses (for the subroutine's recursive calls) and R root nodes (of the tree and all its—left—subtrees). This tree would look just like a singly linked list.

d. The minimum stack depth is when the tree contains only *right* subtrees, because when a right subtree is printed, its root need not be returned to, for both it and its left subtree have already been printed. Thus, the stack will contain only a single return address and the root of a single (sub)tree at a time.

8. *

9. For the invocation SAM ABC, the expansion would be:

```
MOVL ABC, R0
JSB JOAN
```

For the invocation SAM #PQ, ED, the expansion would be:

```
        MOVL #PQ, R0
        JSB JOAN
        BCC 30000$
        JMP ED
30000$:
```

10.

a. False. Inserting into the middle of an ordered array requires moving everything after the new item and then inserting the item. Inserting into a linked list requires only rearranging one (or two) pointers to insert the new node.

b. False. Arrays usually require only enough memory for the items to be stored, while linked lists require memory for the items as for the pointers.

c. True, usually.

d. False. The priority at which an interrupt handler executes is the same as the priority at which the device requested an interrupt.

e. False. Reentrant code must allocate work areas in memory that can be written, for the work areas are used for writing data that are unique to each sharer of the reentrant code.

11. In exercise 8 of chapter 15, we "created" the MOVC3 instruction, which moved L bytes from S to D. It is more efficient to move L bytes in units of 4 (longwords), so we can increase the efficiency of our macro as follows:

```
        .MACRO MOVCHAR L, S, D, ?LABEL1, LABEL2, ?X, ?XX
        X  = L/4                ;number of longwords
        XX = L - <4*X>          ;number of bytes left over
        PUSHR #^M<R6, R7, R8>
        MOVL #X, R6
        MOVAB S, R7
        MOVAB D, R8
LABEL1: MOVL (R7)+, (R8)+       ;copy longwords
        SOBGTR R6, LABEL1
        .IF NOT_EQUAL XX        ;some bytes left over
        MOVL #XX, R6
LABEL2: MOVB (R7)+, (R8)+       ;copy bytes
        SOBGTR R6, LABEL2
        .ENDC
        POPR #^M<R6, R7, R8>
        .ENDM MOVCHAR
```

Note that the macro includes MOVB instructions only if necessary. Note also, however, that this macro is not likely to be useful, because it requires knowledge of the length of the string at assemble time: it performs assemble time arithmetic on L, so L must be specified as an immediate operand, and not as the symbolic label of the location in which the length will be placed. This was not a requirement for the macro in chapter 15, and can be avoided in this case, as well, if we are willing to use the EMUL instruction, at run time.

12. *

13. *

14. Recursive programs can be made to run correctly on *any* computer. In the case under consideration, we'd have to make sure that the previous contents of REG were saved on a stack (that we may have implemented ourselves) before the JSB is executed, and that they are restored from the stack to REG after the RSB is executed.

15. If we use DB with no arguments, the SNAP system service request will be generated. If we use DB with two arguments (A and B, for example), the DUMP A, B system service request will be generated. If we use DB with one argument, an incorrect DUMP system service request will be generated.

16. *

17. A macro is an assemble time text-substitution device. It is provided only for the programmer's *typing* convenience, and you could not tell, by examining the machine language, whether or not macros had been used in the source module. A subroutine, on the other hand, is a control structure that is executed at run time. The machine language of a program looks different if it has subroutines in it (there are opcodes for subroutine calls), and it executes differently if it has subroutines (at subroutine call, the value of the PC is saved on the stack, and the PC changes according to the operand of the subroutine call).

18. An invocation of the macro with no arguments produces the following expansion:

```
        BRB 30000$
        SNAP
30000$:
```

An invocation with a single argument, such as GUESS, generates the following expansion:

```
        JSB GUESSIT
        BRB 30000$
        SNAP
30000$:
```

This macro seems to allow you to either use the SNAP system service, or to call your own subroutine. However, as it is written, the SNAP will never be executed. It can be rewritten to conditionally execute the SNAP, as follows:

```
.MACRO SOLVE PROB
.IIF NOT_BLANK <PROB>, JSB PROB'IT
.IIF BLANK <PROB>, SNAP
.ENDM SOLVE
```

19. *

20. a. False; .b. True; .c. True; .d. False; .e. True.

f.   False, but it is getting truer: as fewer and fewer people use assembly language, and as high level languages more universally adopt the notion of *scope*, parameters are more and more likely to be passed on the stack.

g.   False.

h.   This is false when stated in the simple manner of the question, but if the subroutine and its caller are separately assembled, then the same symbolic labels may be used in both source modules (but not the entry point or any other GLOBAL labels).

i.   False, in a language that supports recursion; true otherwise.

j.   False, but we must (of course) be careful to avoid non-terminating recursive expansion.

21. *

22.

a.   We don't usually think of overflow in conjucntion with an array, since an array has a fixed size.

b.   A linked list and queue are variable size data structures; they can overflow if we try to put more elements into them than the amount of memory we have reserved for their nodes.

d.   Stack overflow, of course, occurs when the stack pointer exceeds the limit we have assigned it, because we have pushed more things onto the stack than we reserved space for.

e.   Integer overflow can occur when we add two numbers with the same msb and the msb of the result differs from those of the addends, or when we subtract two numbers with different msbs and the msb of the result is the same as the msb of the subtrahend. When integer overflow occurs, the V bit of the CC is set.

f.   Floating point overflow occurs when we calculate a result whose exponent cannot be stored in the number of bits allocated to it (8 bits, 11 bits or 15 bits).

23.

a.   In the general case, using subroutines makes programs shorter, because only one copy of the instructions is stored in memory. It is jumped to (and returned from) during execution.

b.   If the absence of subroutines is accomplished by using in-line code, then the program using macros will execute more quickly, because there will be no instructions for subroutine linkage.

24. We can run out of memory at assemble time if the assembler (which is a program, and is running during assemble time) needs too much memory. Why might it need too much memory? One case is if we have a recursively defined macro that (accidentally) has no stopping condition: the assembler will expand it (recursively) indefinitely, until it runs out of memory to store its symbol table and other data structures.

25. *

26.

a.   A reentrant program is often slower than a non-reentrant one because the reentrant program must use indirection in finding each user's work area, rather than having its address stored directly in the program.

b.   Users of a system that uses reentrant code may find their jobs completing more rapidly than users of a system that uses non-reentrant code because when non-reentrant code is used, there may not be sufficient memory for multiple copies of compilers, editors, mail programs, etc. to be in memory at the same time, so some users will have to wait until memory is available. With reentrant code, the program may execute somewhat more slowly, but there need be only a single copy of it in memory.

27. Instead of ending each subroutine with the instruction JMP @(R0)+, we would end it with the following three instructions:

```
MOVL @(R0)+, R1
BNEQ SUB+4
JMP @(R0)+
```

This assumes that the subroutine's entry point is SUB, so SUB+4 is the address of the instruction which accesses the second argument. Thus, if the next argument is zero, exit occurs with the JMP instruction, but if it is non-zero, then the subroutine is re-executed, with R0 pointing to the first of another set of arguments.

28. *

29. *

Selected Solutions for Chapter 18

1.   In the VAX, if we wish to add corresponding elements of two one-dimensional arrays, and store the results as corresponding elements in a third one-dimensional array, we can initialize three registers to contain the addresses of the two source and one destination addresses, and then use the ADDL3 (R0)+, (R1)+, (R2)+ instruction, for example, in a SOBGTR loop. We only *write* two instructions, but of course we fetch and execute as many instructions as there are elements to be added in the arrays. We can use the MOVC3 and MOVC5 instructions as examples, however, and design instructions that specify two source addresses, a destination address, and number of elements, and a size for each element. Then, only a single instruction need be fetched (and executed) to add some large number of array elements. Supercomputers usually call such instructions *vector instructions*. A thorough comparison of the performance of vector instruction versus the VAX's *scalar instructions* is beyond the scope of this simple discussion.

2. Program size on a VAX is 2^{32} bytes (actually, it is limited to 2^{30} bytes of data and 2^{30} bytes of instructions). Many popular personal computers have program size restrictions of between 2^{16} and 2^{22} bytes. File space is often similarly restricted on personal computers compared with a VAX—especially personal computers that have only floppy disk drives. On such a computer, the maximum file size is less than the size amount of storage available on a floppy disk, which may range from 160K bytes to 1.4M bytes. On a VAX, on the other hand, large fixed disks may have files many tens of megabytes long. The maximum on-line disk storage is subject to similar considerations: a personal computer is often limited to the amount of space on one or two floppy drives, or perhaps one floppy drive and a relatively small hard drive (10 or 20M bytes). On a VAX, the maximum on-line disk storage is in the multi-gigabyte range. In terms of performance, also, a multiuser VAX will usually be faster than most personal computers. However, availability must also be considered: if each user is sharing a VAX's resources with 10 or 20 or 50 other users, then it is not necessarily true that the VAX will provide better performance than the personal computer.

3. *

Selected Solutions for Chapter 19

1. *

2. We saw the truth table for exclusive or in chapter 7, and it is reproduced here:

a	b	a xor b
0	0	0
0	1	1
1	0	1
1	1	0

We can create a gate from relays that implements the XOR function by combining OR, AND and NOT gates, according to the following:

a	b	a and b	a ¬and b	a or b	a xor b
0	0	0	1	0	0
0	1	0	1	1	1
1	0	0	1	1	1
1	1	1	0	1	0

The ¬**and** function is simply the inverse (**not**) of the **and** function. If we **and** the outputs of the ¬**and** gate and the **or** gate, as shown in the last column of the above table, we get the XOR function.

3. *

4. Some of the steps in executing a 2 operand ADD instruction would include the following:

1) fetch the first operand specifier
2) update the PC
3) fetch the first operand
4) fetch the second operand specifier
5) update the PC
6) fetch the second operand
7) compute the sum of the two operands
8) store the sum

For a 3 operand add instruction, the third operand specifier would have to be fetched, and the PC would have to be updated a third time.

5. *

6. Microprogramming is a way to simplify the design of design complex hardware. Since RISCs have only simple instructions, it is possible to implement them with "random logic". The reason RISC designers claim that microprogramming makes a computer run slower is partly a hardware issue that is beyond the scope of this book. However, part of the reason a microprogrammed computer runs more slowly than one that is not microprogrammed is that microprogramming adds another instruction fetch-execute cycle: instructions are fetched from memory, and the opcode is used as an address of the first of a series of microinstructions, each of which must be fetched from microstore. (It is the execution of these microinstructions which constitutes execution of the machine language instruction.)

Selected Solutions for Chapter 20

1. *

2. *

3. If a user is disconnected, the telephone line into the CPU becomes available to another user. If someone else calls in, they may be reconnected to the same line, and to the account of the user who was disconnected without logging out. Thus, someone other than the owner of the account of the user who was disconnected will have access to the user's files, etc. It is possible for the CPU to log a disconnected user out, because when the user is disconnected, the modem will detect loss of carrier, and report it to the modem controller, which can interrupt the CPU. However, before logging the user out, the CPU should try to save any work that is in progress.

4. Given the small number of bytes (maximum 30) that must be transmitted per transaction, it is cheaper to use a 300 baud modem than a 2400 baud modem. Consider the 300 baud modem: it can transmit 30 bytes in one second, and even with a 20 second delay for the response, the total transaction will take less than 30 seconds, which is the minimum telephone charge. If it were possible to "batch" transactions and transmit them together, then the 2400 baud modem might turn out to be cheaper, because it is possible to transmit 240 bytes per second with a 2400 baud modem. Thus, the 2400 baud modem transmits eight times as much information per second, but costs only three times as much to rent.

Selected Solutions for Chapter 21

1.   This is an open ended question. For the example shown in the question, a compiler would note that the code does not differentiate between an integer and an address. Some other constructs that are acceptable to an assembler but are considered errors in (some) high level programming languages include:

> using uninitialized variables
> adding ASCII character codes
> jumping into the middle of a subroutine
> jumping into the middle of a loop
> executing data
> using signed conditional branches for unsigned data
> not saving (or not restoring) register values
> using the wrong step size in accessing array elements
> calling a subroutine with too many (or too few) parameters
> using the wrong radix
> referencing a non-existent array element

2. There are no obvious situations in which an assembler would detect an error that a compiler would not. However, MACRO requires that all symbolic labels must be defined, while FORTRAN allows implicit definition of variables.

3. In principle, if you know the entry point of a load module, it is not overly difficult to write a disassembler.

4. Decompilation is more difficult than disassembly for the same reason that compilation is more difficult than assembly: there is not necessarily a one-to-one correspondence between machine language instructions and high level language program statements. However, if you are familiar with the compiler whose output you are trying to decompile, it may possible to write a decompiler that produces a correct high level language program—although it may be possible to decompile to more than one high level language program.

559

Spooling, 373
Square matrix, 336
Stack, 67, 188, 191
Stack history for nested subroutines, 210
Stack instructions, 196
Stack overflow, 215
Stack pointer (SP), 192, 193
Stack underflow, 216
Stage in a pipeline, 419
Start bit, 273
Static memory allocation, 194
Stealing memory cycles, 378
Stop bit, 273
Storage device, 459
Stored program computers, 19
Storing 1 bit, 458
Straight-line programs, 29
String instructions, 238
Subprograms, 189
Subroutine as a black box, 200
Subroutine call and return instructions, 197
Subroutine design, 204
Subroutine library, 204
Subroutine linkage, 197
Subroutine nesting, 207
Subroutines and stacks, 197
Subroutines, 189
Subtract instructions, 53
Subtract with carry instruction (SBWC), 149
Subtracting signed numbers, 144
Subtracting unsigned numbers, 145
Subtraction, 144, 151
Subtrahend, 145
Subtree, 400
Supercomputers, 449
Swapped out, 372
Swapping device, 372
Switched network interface, 470
Symbol table, 83
Symbolic label, 78
Symbolic representation of a program, 74
Symmetric (array), 336
Synchronous bus, 378
Synchronous communication, 472
System Control Block (SCB), 288, 289, 294
System device, 451
System service request, 85, 283
System stack, 193, 194, 195
System stack after procedure call, 215
System Stack and SP, 193

t

T (trace enable) bit, 428
Table look-up and character strings, 247
Tables, 394, 395
Tail (of a list), 395
Tape capacity, 361
Tape compatibility, 362
Tape data transfer speeds, 360
Tape devices, 364
Tape labels, 363
Tape mark, 361
Tape record-gap format, 359
Tape recording density, 357
Tape-drive, 357
Target computer, 4, 406
Telephone, 469
Telephone-computer hookups, 470
Teleprocessing, 469
Teletypewriters (TTY), 13, 264, 473
Terminal configuration mode, 269
Terminal driver, 405

Terminal emulation, 270
Thrashing, 448
Threaded code, 411
Three operand instructions, 66, 67
Throughput, 374
Timesharing, 373
Timing chart, 464
Timing disk, 464
Top-down problem solving, 189
Top-of-form, 267
TP (trace pending) bit, 428
Trace, 6
Trace fault, 428
Trace handler, 428
Trace of keystrokes, 7
Trace of instructions, 28
Trace table, 28
Tracing a Calculation, 7
Track on a disk, 357, 366
Track addresses, 368, 369
Trailer tape, 360
Trailing numeric strings, 239
Transaction, 473
Transducer, 379
Transistor, 455, 466
Transparency (of a subroutine), 199
Transparent subroutine, 207
Trap, 322, 428
Traps and program debugging, 428
Trees, 394
Truncation, 303
Truth table for AND, 223
Truth table for exclusive OR, 151, 226
Truth table for inclusive OR, 153, 224
Truth table for NOT, 223
TTY, 13, 264, 473
Tubes, 465
Turn-key system, 450
Turnaround time, 374
Twisted pair, 272
Two dimensional linked lists, 400
Two operand instructions, 66
Twos complement arithmetic, 136, 139
Twos complement representation, 133
Two-dimensional arrays, 329
Two-dimensional linked list, 400
Two-way linked list, 398

u

Unary function, 223
Unconditional branches, 104
Unconditional transfer, 29
Underflow, 216, 310, 322
Uniform access memory, 35
Unique representation, 303
Unsigned arithmetic, 141
Unsigned conditional branches, 152
Unsigned integers, 129
Unsigned numbers, 129, 141
Update in place, 359
Upward compatible, 264

v

V bit (of CC), 140
Vacuum tube simulating a relay, 466
Valid field (in a cache), 416
Values, passing, 200
Variable initialization, 59
Variable length macros, 383
Variable-length bit-field instructions, 228, 231
VAX family tree, 446
VAX instruction subset, 53